CONFESSIONS
of a God Seeker

A JOURNEY TO HIGHER CONSCIOUSNESS

Ford Johnson

Published by

"ONE" Publishing, Inc.
8720 Georgia Avenue
Suite 206
Silver Spring, MD 20910

www.onepublishinginc.com

"ONE" Publishing books and products are available through most bookstores and on-line through Amazon.com and Barnes&Nobles.com. To contact "ONE" Publishing directly, call (301) 562-2858, fax to (301) 562-9377, or visit our website at www.onepublishing-inc.com.

Substantial discounts on bulk quantities of "ONE" Publishing books are available to corporations, professional associations, and other organizations. For details and discount information, contact the sales department at "ONE" Publishing.

Typeset by Adam Sharif of "ONE" Publishing, Inc., Silver Spring, MD
Principal editor: Brian Downing, Ph.D.
Design concept: Ford Johnson
Original art: Michael Omoighe
Graphic art adaption and design: April Gratrix
Printed and bound in the USA by Edward Brothers, Inc., Ann Arbor, Michigan

9 8 7 6 5 4 3 2 1

"ONE" Publishing, Inc. strives to use the most environmentally sensitive paper stocks available. Our publications are printed on acid-free recycled stock, whenever possible, and our paper always meets or exceeds minimum GPO and EPA requirements.

"ONE" Publishing also publishes its books in a variety of electronic formats. Some content that appears in print may be available in electronic books or in audio formats.

Library of Congress Cataloging-in-Publication Data

Johnson, Ford, 1942-
    Confessions of a God-Seeker: a journey to higher consciousness / Ford Johnson.
        p. cm.
    Includes bibliographical references and index.
    ISBN 0-9728835-8-4 (alk. paper)
    1. Spiritual life. 2. Eckankar (Organization)--Controversial literature. I. Title.
    BP605.E3 J645 2003
    299'.93--dc21

                                                                    2003006774

This book is dedicated to the
Truth Seeker
and
ALL THAT IS

Contents

Acknowledgements

The author gratefully acknowledges the assistance and support of the staff of "ONE" Publishing in the completion of this book, including: Albert Bejo, Adam Sharif, Amanda Hollander, Lauren Johnson, Bianca Redhead, William Idoniboye, Jun Tang, April Gratrix and principal editor, Dr. Brian Downing.

Thanks also to early reviewers Darrell Johnson, Dr. Ewa Unoke, Alaya Johnson, Lisa Kyle, Mary Vorden, and Elizabeth Rice.

Special thanks to Graham Forsyth, whose inspired journal was the catalyst for writing this book.

And finally, to my beloved wife, Mary, goes my eternal gratitude for her support, protection, and counsel in climbing this mountain.

Ford Johnson

Introduction

The writing of this book has in every respect been a journey to higher consciousness. The events of November and December of 2001 were the turning point in a search for God-awareness that has been the center of my life. These events were the catalyst that led me to challenge and ultimately change my paradigm of the God-experience. As a result, my consciousness expanded from a modest house into what felt like a coliseum. This is what happens when old paradigms are shattered and new perspectives based in truth come into view.

This book chronicles that expansion of consciousness. It began in earnest more than thirty years ago. As the title suggests, *Confessions* reflects the journey of a God-seeker to discover truth. Truth, of course, takes many forms and exists at many levels. In the final analysis, it is what each person chooses to believe and act upon. Yet, there is the conception of eternal truth that does not bend to the whim of individual predilections. This has always intrigued me. I longed for something eternal, not a childhood construct like Santa Claus that was designed to be shattered or the dubious mythical foundations of most religious dogma. Indeed, it was this longing that propelled my initial search for spiritual truth.

Over many years and numerous spiritual teachings, paths, and religions my journey has taken me to what I have come to view as the heart of truth, the eternal bedrock that is unchanging and *just is*. In this book, I describe this journey and the often astounding discoveries and captivating revelations along the way. As you might imagine, it is a roller coaster ride at times. But that is the nature of spiritual growth, especially for the God-seeker.

This book addresses several audiences simultaneously. First, it is directed to anyone who seeks the God-reality that lies beyond religion, philosophy, or science. Thus, it speaks to those who treasure truth above all else. Second, it is directed to anyone associated with Eckankar its progeny or any similar teaching of the light and sound of God. These include the Radhasoami Satsang Beas, Ruhani Satsang, and Sant Mat teachings in general. All of these groups share common threads that help and hinder the God-seeker on his journey to the heart of truth. Third, it is directed to those who have ever wondered — as did I — about the origins and reality of Christianity, especially in light of evidence concerning sixteen other crucified saviors who predated Christ. Regardless, all paths and religions are important way stations on our journey to God, but they are *only* way stations.

This is the quandary I searched long and hard to resolve. When the facts about any religion or path are made known, it is easy to dispel the belief paradigms that hinder the seekers spiritual growth. But with what does one replace them? The adults in our lives were ready to dispel the Santa Claus myth with a sobering, albeit less exhilarating truth. Yet, the feelings and memories lingered as proof of the residual power of myth, even when overwhelmed by truth. Dispelling a spiritual paradigm can have a disquieting impact if not replaced with a more spiritually enlightened construct built on truth. After struggling with this dilemma, I proceeded with *Confessions* because I believe this requirement is fulfilled. Therefore, after presenting facts that will undoubtedly challenge cherished ideas and well-established spiritual paradigms, Part IV of the book presents an empowering exemplar that fills the void. It shows the nexus between science and spirituality and how both are saying the same thing; exploring the same truth. Using insights from both, keys to the movement of consciousness to ever higher levels are presented. They are coupled with practical steps to integrate spiritual wisdom into the mastery of life.

My orientation to studying and teaching spiritual and esoteric subjects has always been practicable — real world. I have had to apply these principles to running a business, raising children, married life and the realities of living in a modern world. I know from these experiences and the responses of those who have attended my workshops that what is outlined in this portion of the book actually works. More importantly, it provides a framework to evaluate the experiences of life from a spiritual perspective. Happiness, success, and accomplishment take on a different and broadened meaning when *every* experience is seen as a gift that is always present but often overlooked.

As one who is notorious for reading a book from the middle or the end, I am probably not in the best position to give this suggestion, but I will. *Confessions* reveals, and possibly astonishes as it lays bare false religious constructs with facts, history, and documentation that are powerful and verifiable. Then it builds and expands consciousness as it progresses from one set of concepts to the next. It is like rebuilding a house requiring fortification of its foundation before it can bear the load of new heights. Skipping too far ahead might confuse and raise questions that would have been answered at earlier points in the book. Likewise, it would be wise to reserve drawing conclusions too early; there are many twists and turns in this real-life spiritual journey. In the end, I believe the experience *will* lead to an expansion of consciousness, for this was certainly my reward as well as the response of those who participated in reviewing the book. Also, you may reach a point where the facts are enough and you are ready to move on to the next stage. If you reach this point, I suggest moving to Part IV of the book. Then you can return to Parts II and III from a more spiritually fortified position.

As you might imagine, I felt considerable inner trepidation in writing some of the chapters. I wondered if I should simply discontinue the writing and move on. But something within — my higher self — kept urging me on, forcing me beyond my outer fears to complete what I believe to be of great importance. One event that helped to reinforce this decision was a movie I watched while taking a break from writing. *Quiz Show,* an acclaimed drama, tells the true story behind the infamous television show scandal of 1959. Herbert Stempel, a disgruntled former champion, prompted a Congressional investigation into the popular game show *Twenty-One* with charges that the current champion, Charles Van Doren, a popular Columbia University lecturer, had been provided with answers by the producers. The investigator (and author of the book that inspired the film) became the trustee of truth, and it was his unpleasant task to see that it not be suppressed. The investigator was confronted with the same questions I had posed to myself. Why disturb people's happiness with the ugly truth? I know how he felt and also how he had no choice. Once the mantle of truth seeker is assumed, a road is traveled that leads in only one direction, though there are many curves and bumps along the way.

As the truth struggled to come out, I observed how delicate yet inexorable its power was. It could be suppressed, hidden, and falsely profiled, but it was unrelenting. Everyone has a deep and abiding love and need for truth, even if they are temporarily engaged in holding it back or benefiting from a deception. There is a divine spark that forces us to truth. That is why people confess to their crimes and feel relief in having done so. They cannot deal with its unrelenting pressure and pain. That is also why it is the infallible road to God, for *Truth is GOD of ITSELF*. Once we see truth for what it really is, we will also see ourselves and know that we are a part of the ONE. This cannot be achieved as long as we allow temporary expediencies and comforts to guide our lives.

A good friend had once argued:

> [T]his is a world of duality and nothing here is perfect. My yardstick is, "is it good enough." In our culture at a certain point in life we seem to loose the capacity to innocently idealize anything or anybody.

He was right in a way, but is "good enough" really good enough? I suppose "good enough" is alright when speaking of Caesar salad or bean soup, but what about spiritual unfoldment? Doesn't good enough imply stagnation, acceptance of the status quo, quitting, deceiving ourselves into thinking that we are there when clearly we are not? Without new insights and truth, we are apt to say it is "good enough." But when we see the truth in something, it leads us to new levels of awareness where the old is no longer good enough, because part of divine discontent is the driving force to want more and to want the best. Who willingly accepts something less when better is known and available as an equal choice? At first, we feel this drive as a desire for things and stuff. In time, it is sublimated to a desire for higher consciousness, to know who and what we really are. This is where truth leads.

But truth also can cause discomfort, for it is the catalyst of change. Change produces distress only when we reject where it is taking us. We always prefer the comfort of the known and reject, as long as we can, the mystery and uncertainty of the unknown. This entire discussion could be a metaphor for the underlying theme of this book: *good enough is not good enough if it means avoiding truth.*

However, even growth and change are not uniformly continuous. There are rest points in eternity. Points where we can sit back and absorb what we have learned and benefit from our advancement. When we tarry too long and are not challenged to advance to a new level of awareness, we are stuck in "good enough." To my friend and to others who read this book, I can only say that I hope it will be good enough for a while — but only for a while.

Ford Johnson
2003

PART I

THE JOURNEY BEGINS

Chapter 1 — The God Seeker

Who is a God Seeker?

Maybe you are. In truth, we are all God-seekers, only some of us are more aware of it than others. The proof is everywhere. The lover of music searches for celestial motifs once heard during a dream excursion that continues to beckon. The architect looks within, sees a finished version of his masterpiece, and is humbled by the knowledge that he has touched some higher force. The poet tries to translate inner ecstasy into words but is exasperated because he has experienced something words cannot express. The dancer moves with flowing lines to express a balance, a feeling that connects with something much deeper. The minister faithfully preaches the church's doctrine but wonders, questions, and inwardly explores the ageless conundrum: Is this all there is?

In time, these disguised longings for God initiate a search for truth that leads a person to become a conscious seeker. Eventually, all seekers reach a point where they realize that there is a force greater than them. They may even suspect that it permeates all things and is both powerful and intelligent.

Questions and doubts can remain for years. Some seekers will always question or doubt what they inwardly sense. Even with an intellectual or inner awareness of this force, their inability to trust it and surrender to it can persist. We experience the God force in many different ways. Our God may be personal, sensed within, and sustained by private and personal communication. Others, affiliated with a religion, may experience this force through the teachings, rituals, holy books, and inspired words of a spiritual leader or savior.

In spite of doubts, the God-seeker persists in believing because he has experienced miracles in his life. He has been rescued from too many scrapes, brought back from too many mistakes, and shown enlightenment in too many dark moments to remain a non-believer. Through these encounters, he has sensed a connection between his life experiences and his spiritual development. Yet, he may have erroneously attributed his many blessings to something or someone outside of himself. He does not understand, at least not yet, that the power lies within. He does not see that it is spirit coupled with the power of his belief, rather than the object of that belief, that is the true source of the power. But the God-seeker pushes on, looking for a bedrock upon which he can build an edifice of greater control over his life.

All searches for greater knowledge or truth are aspects of the search for God. But most of us get lost in the petty details of life. With so many complex layers of illusion dominating our lives, we remain estranged from the truth of our origin and our existence. Sadly, most of us define ourselves by marital status, number of children, nationality, location, job, sex, race, religion, musical tastes, sports preferences, and other predilections. But these details miss the point of life and delay the expansion of our spiritual awareness. Even if we are clever enough to realize that these social descriptors are only layers of illusion that do not truly define us, we are still apt to get lost in our physical bodies. We delude ourselves into thinking that we are what they are, identifying with our physical accoutrements, medical problems, aches, pains, and physical desires. But this too is an illusion separating the God-seeker from truth.

We may even identify with our emotions and feelings, but this is yet another illusion. They are merely aspects of ourselves that enable us to function in the physical dimension of reality. Through these layers of illusion, the self must navigate its journey to discover the truth about itself and its connection to the creator. This is the journey of the God-seeker. Like Odysseus's return home, the journey is long, complex, and fraught with perils. Thankfully, however, the journey can be completed.

Steps Along the Way

My journey as a God-seeker began at an early age. My late grandfather, an Episcopal priest, instructed me in the teachings of Christianity. As soon as I was able to put together a full sentence, I was asking questions, challenging his assumptions, and generally making life more difficult for this stern but loving man. I was a complete flop as an altar boy; I never became adept at my ceremonial duties. Whether to stand or to kneel, or what words to recite after a particular invocation by the priest, was always a mystery to me. I simply did not see the connection between the detail of church rituals and spiritual development.

Nor could I accept the notion that I was a sinner. I questioned how a creation of the Supreme Being could be inherently sinful. Why would God create such a wretched being? Being born in sin and spending the remainder of my life atoning for it made little sense to me. It was like a weight on my back that could never be removed. I wanted no part of it!

Up to this point, my religious exposure was limited to Christianity. If it had the best explanation of my relationship to the divine, then I preferred to believe in nothing. Little did I realize that this period of questioning was a fortunate and portentous cleansing, in which the dogmas of sin, guilt, hell, the devil, and similar concepts were expunged. No longer hindered by controlling rules and moral strictures that leave feelings of guilt and shame, I moved into a state of spiritual freedom. Fortunately, this sense of freedom did not lead to reckless behavior, as it does for many. I avoided this pitfall because, as I was later to learn, *I had lived before*. Expunging these constrictive beliefs was merely the continuation of a process of spiritual education that had started lifetimes ago. The lessons from each of these lives were ingrained into the core of my being. They were there to serve as stop signs, warning me when I tried to use that freedom irresponsibly.

Through my early education, college entry at age fifteen, service as a Peace Corps volunteer in Africa, and the "paper chase" at Harvard Law School, I made my way into life and full adult responsibility. Through successes and setbacks, I learned life's lessons. Questions were sometimes answered, sometimes raised, but a deep spiritual hunger remained. Despite a flurry of social events, continuous travel, and other forms of outer excitement, the feeling persisted. I discovered what all truth seekers must realize: that my life was focused primarily on my outer or physical existence. My senses of self-worth, satisfaction, and happiness depended on the approval of others, my achievements, and my possessions. I was searching outside myself for confirmation of who and what I was. Nothing could fill the void I felt when I sought only pleasure and outer fulfillment. This was one of the first clues that the life I had constructed in the outer world was not the final answer.

In moments of inner silence, I would cry out to be shown the way. This was a critical point in my life, as it is in the life of any God-seeker. When the God-seeker realizes that there is more, and that help is needed to discover it, it is as if all the forces in the universe converge to show the next step in the quest for truth.

Though the seeker is unclear about what is sought, there is comfort in words like "love" and "truth." Somehow, the God-seeker instinctively knows that truth is pure and powerful. Even in college, while others enjoyed sports and socializing, I found greater joy in engaging in debate — over virtually anything. I learned that as long as I stayed with truth and never allowed my ego to be trapped, I would never lose an argument. Invariably, as if in a Socratic dialogue, I would identify some error in fact or argument in which an opponent had become invested, shift the discussion to that vulnerability, and show the point to be untrue. I learned a great secret about the power of truth. Thus, I came to understand the sacred responsibility entrusted to one who seeks truth as a life goal and finds some measure of it.

During this time, a friend handed me some books on esoteric knowledge. At first, because I regarded mysticism and the occult as insubstantial, even flaky, I ignored them. These books, with their unusual titles and topics, had an increasingly strange allure, enough to keep them out of the trash can. Eventually, I picked them up. Their contents exploded with insights and perspectives on existence that I had never imagined. Here were the answers to questions with which I had annoyed and frustrated my grandfather. Once I picked them up, I could not put them down. My life as a God-seeker shifted into high gear.

A Higher Consciousness Primer

For many readers, it will be necessary to establish certain basic concepts in spiritual development. The expansion of awareness is a continuous process. In the early stages of my spiritual education, I was exposed to basic concepts of higher consciousness. In time, I became grounded in broader and deeper concepts of life and living. Years of spiritual study and contemplation would enlarge and expand these basic concepts. They will be explored in later chapters. However, to fully grasp the content and meaning of this book, especially if your background is in traditional religion or you are new to concepts of higher consciousness, this section will serve as a primer.

Know Thyself

Wisdom begins and, as we shall see, ends with an understanding of self. "Know thyself" has been the imperative voiced by philosophers, the spiritually enlightened, and sages from the beginning of recorded history. Yet, as much as we think we know ourselves, most of us have only a clue about who or what we really are. We are unaware of ourselves as spiritual, immortal beings living temporarily in human consciousness. We do not understand the extraordinary power and potential that we possess as soul because we identify so completely with our physical bodies, emotions, memories, and minds. We do not realize that they are only tools that we use to function in the physical and other dimensions of existence.

By the standard of time that we generally understand, the journey of soul is long and arduous. Our life as humans, in the physical dimension, is but a small part of that education. The purpose of this education is for soul to expand its awareness to encompass all of its God-like powers. With this knowledge, it can eventually take its place in running the universe.

Many of us have endured difficult and even harsh experiences during childhood. We accept these experiences as a necessary part of personal growth. In the same manner, soul must grow from the experiences encountered during its many lifetimes. Without these experiences, soul, in the human state, cannot pierce the illusion of life and experience divine reality. Even as humankind struggles to accept the concept of a sequence of lifetimes, the truth is even more remarkable. We live in the eternal now, and all experiences, reality, and lifetimes exist simultaneously. The illusion of a three-dimensional, holographic universe sustains the illusion of time as a sequential phenomenon and of space as possessing separateness, distance, and dimension.

These concepts seemed fantastic when I first encountered them. They seemed possible, but little was happening in my outer life to warrant an immediate change in my paradigm of life. As I began to embrace them, however, events of the past began to make more sense. I saw in these events a pattern that was inexorably moving me to a higher level of spiritual awareness. The idea of life consisting of layers of illusion was a helpful concept. It enabled me to rise above numerous social and ethnic labels and function from a neutral and detached perspective.

Even though I intellectually understood the power of soul, I found it no easier to manifest the things that I wanted in my life. In time, I would learn more about this power and how to harness it for my benefit and for the benefit of others.

The Classroom of Life: How Souls Evolve

Another concept that had an enormous impact on my early understanding of life was the idea that every individual is at a different level of spiritual development and awareness. Some individuals are highly evolved and manifest remarkable abilities and insights from an early age. Attempts to explain the phenomenon of the child prodigy from a genetic, cultural, psychological, or psychiatric perspective fail to account for her advanced level of development. Yet, when life is viewed as a continuum, and death a mere transition from one form of existence to another in an ever-evolving life cycle, this phenomenon is easier to understand. This perspective was vital to me in gaining an appreciation and respect for the spiritual beings that were to become my children. It enabled me to understand my sacred responsibility to guide them to discover the thread that united their many lives, pointing the way to their spiritual expansion in this lifetime. While I have always dearly loved my children, I have never felt a sense of possession that so often fouls the parent-child relationship.

Other souls may just be starting their cycle of incarnations in human form. Not understanding who or what they are as spiritual beings, they are likely to cause disruptions for those who are more spiritually evolved. We look at the actions of our fellow humans and sometimes shake our heads, wondering how people can do such things. From our present more enlightened perspective, the answer is difficult to fathom, for we have forgotten the actions, experiences and lessons from our own earlier incarnations. Yet, it has always been the case that more advanced souls must interact with less evolved ones in order to teach and guide them. That is why the accelerated interaction of nations and peoples that is occurring today will result in the greatest expansion of spiritual consciousness in recorded history. While this will lead to greater levels of upheaval, it is the price that must be paid for the movement of all souls to higher states of consciousness. It is not difficult to see the patterns of human migration around the world and the resulting growth of awareness spreading along with it.

Sin versus Learning

Sin, especially original sin, was a concept I always found repugnant. This was not because I wanted to avoid accountability, but because the concept and ideas surrounding it seemed geared to create guilt and entrapment rather than learning and emancipation. As my spiritual education progressed, I was gratified to learn that sin is not "sin," as my grandfather had taught me. Rather, it is a consequence-producing action that leads to an awareness-expanding lesson. Soul must have the experience, good or bad, in order to internalize the lesson. We see this everyday in raising our children. We can tell them what we want them to do, but only when they have personally experienced an event and its consequences do they understand for themselves. As much as we would want to spare our children many painful experiences in life, there are some lessons that are only learned this way. No amount of fear-evoking declarations of sin can teach a lesson that only life's experiences can convey. Of course, this is not the only way to learn. While experience is most often the best teacher, the old adage that a wise person learns from the experiences of others is certainly true. Once the God-seeker understands that there is wisdom in a teacher's words, the process of spiritual growth accelerates.

A danger that soul faces in its expansion of awareness is the limits imposed upon it by many religions. That is why the idea of sin is not only mistaken but also harmful. It focuses more on the act than on the positive lesson that can be learned. The system of sin even results in the individual looking to something and someone outside of himself for forgiveness. In this manner, it becomes a form of control, for it vests the power of absolution in an outside agent rather than empowering the individual with the knowledge that sin is simply a "control-by-guilt" mechanism. Thus, though the act of confession may serve as a temporary relief, in the end it misleads the individual and distorts her spiritual understanding. It fosters the illusion that the power for such absolution lies with the priest and the religion that established this indulgence. In actuality, the power lies within her consciousness. Here is where all power to change, forgive, and create ultimately derives.

Birth, Death and Reincarnation

My early upbringing in the Episcopal Church saddled me with ideas of heaven or hell in the afterlife, intended to shape my actions in this life. Not only were the notions of heaven and hell, reward and punishment, wrong, but they also had a crippling, fear-producing effect during their reign over me. Religious dogma has had its greatest impact in misleading people about the phenomena of birth and death. Religions have, since their inceptions, used the ideas of heaven and hell to keep followers in line. This simplification of life, death, and the afterlife is largely erroneous, and continues to lead people away from truth. Instead, it places them in a constant state of guilt and fear.

These myths of heaven, hell, and sin are shattered the instant the God-seeker comes to recognize that soul is eternal. Its very existence is evidence of a divine being, because soul is a spark, a part of a divine reality. Just as a drop of water from the ocean contains all of the characteristics of the ocean, so does soul, a part of God, contain all of ITS characteristics. This is the origin of the idea that we are made in God's image, which has mistakenly come to mean resemblance to our physical form.

Conventional notions of heaven and hell, salvation and damnation, are off the mark. Indeed, no less a personage than Pope John Paul II has gone on record as retreating from the literal interpretations of heaven and hell to a more enlightened, albeit limited, view of these two putative destinations. Of heaven the pope has said:

> In the context of Revelation, we know that the "heaven" or "happiness" in which we will find ourselves is neither an abstraction nor a physical place in the clouds, but a living, personal relationship with the Holy Trinity.[1]

On the more sensitive subject of hell, he explained:

> The images of hell that Sacred Scripture presents to us must be correctly interpreted. They show the complete frustration and emptiness of life without God.... More than a place, hell indicates the state of those who freely and definitively separate themselves from God. Hell is not punishment imposed externally by God, but the condition resulting from attitudes and actions which people adopt in this life.... So eternal damnation is not God's work but is actually our own doing.[2]

However, much more is known about the journey of soul at the transition commonly known as death. Once the life of the physical vehicle has ended, soul moves out of its shell into one of its other garments that permit it to have experiences in other dimensions of reality. Though we are seldom aware of it, this is precisely what happens each time we have inner experiences during our dreams. We are actually experiencing another dimension of reality using one of the outer garments suited for the matter that predominates on that inner plane. The vehicle used by soul in the second dimension of reality, commonly called the "astral plane," is the corresponding astral body. Indeed, the existence of parallel universes has been postulated by leading quantum physicists.

At the point of "death," soul expands its awareness to encompass this dimension of reality. Here, more advanced souls, functioning from a higher level of consciousness, review the events of its physical life. For more spiritually evolved souls, because they are eager to understand the past life's meaning and proceed to the next lifetime, this encounter occurs soon after death. In this meeting, soul learns how well it used its opportunities for spiritual advancement and what potential experiences lie in the next life. I have studied this phenomenon over the years and will enlarge on its implications later. For now, I think it is fair to say that death is not the dreaded experience most people perceive it to be. It is merely a transition and is nothing to fear. Indeed, so wondrous and sublime are many pre-death encounters that some do not want to return to ordinary physical life.

For less-developed souls, and especially those in religions that do not teach the reality of inner worlds, the death experience is quite different. Upon leaving the body, soul's journey can take a number of different forms. One of the more common encounters is the movement through what is often described as a tunnel at the end of which the individual may see a glorious flood of light. When soul moves towards the light, friends, relatives, or others with whom it would feel comfortable, meet it. More highly evolved entities serve as support in this dimension, and can manifest in forms recognizable and comforting to the individual. These images can take on the form of Jesus for the Christian, Muhammad for the Moslem, Buddha for the Buddhist, and so on. The death experience is not unlike that described by those who have had "near-death experiences" in the operating room or after terrible accidents. But, and this is crucial, it is also common to those who have developed the skill of consciously shifting awareness into these inner dimensions of reality.

The Law of Cause and Effect (Karma)

Reincarnation cannot be fully understood without considering a complementary law, the Law of Cause and Effect, commonly known as karma. Newton's laws of motion are a material articulation of a broader esoteric principle: for every thought, word, and action there is an equal and opposite reaction. Everything we do is a cause that has a corresponding effect. This cause-and-effect cycle explains all of existence and is the basis on which spiritual development is founded. In earlier stages of soul's existence (e.g., in plants and animals), laws of nature govern life, with little if any conscious decision making. As soul progresses into higher states of existence, consciousness expands, as does soul's responsibility for its actions. In the human state, the Law of Responsibility (a corollary to the Law of Cause and Effect) operates. Regardless of our knowledge or acceptance of universal law, we are responsible for everything we decide, and everything we think, say, and do. Spiritual growth is the product of the lessons learned from making these choices. Consequences can be experienced in this lifetime or in succeeding lifetimes — either way, they will be experienced.

Those whose lives reflect a string of tragedies are most likely experiencing early stages of spiritual growth. They have not yet drawn the connection between action and reaction. The early tendency is to blame other people and other situations. When soul comes to the realization that it is responsible for its own existence, it is then on the path to true spiritual freedom, taking control of its thoughts, words, and actions.

Until then, soul is the puppet of people and circumstances that it believes are responsible for its current state of affairs. While this explanation reduces the burden of accountability imposed by taking responsibility for all outcomes, in the end, it reduces the individual to a condition of powerlessness. While taking responsibility for everything that happens in our lives is often a bitter pill, it is the only remedy that emancipates us from the control of outside forces. Once we acknowledge that we have created our own circumstances, we empower ourselves to change them and make them whatever we choose. When soul actively takes control of its thoughts, words, and actions, it attains true spiritual freedom and control over life.

Another corollary to the Law of Cause and Effect (Karma) is the Law of Equilibrium. It holds that everything in the universe seeks balance, including all human expressions of energy — words, thoughts, and actions. All actions are balanced in conformity with this principle. In the process, our actions and their effects create opportunities for learning. When we take a particular action that produces a unique response, it either engenders pain or pleasure. The physical vehicle responds in a fundamental way. By its programming, it seeks pleasure and avoids pain. When an experience evokes a positive or pleasurable response (positive karma), we tend to pursue it. When an effect is construed as negative or unpleasant (negative karma), we tend to avoid it. It is through this simple mechanism that the Law of Karma and spiritual growth work. This principle has been long recognized in scientific research and has formed the basis of much of behavioral science. However, it also has deep spiritual implications.

Because the universe works in accordance with the Law of Equilibrium, it is not always possible to balance all energy flows in a single lifetime, that is, to receive the positive or negative effects of all of our thoughts, words and actions. Thus, unbalanced energy (karma) is stored and follows us from lifetime to lifetime. This is why life cannot be understood from the perspective of a single lifetime. When we grasp the concept of stored unbalanced energy, we begin to understand the shape of life. A person who has inflicted pain, injury, or death on others, for example, learns under the spiritual law by having to endure a similar fate or by balancing this energy in some other way, in a subsequent lifetime. One who has enslaved learns by being enslaved or perhaps by devoting his life to setting others free. Another who has given much in worldly possessions or other tokens of generosity, returns to receive the bounty of these actions. Thus, in this meeting of Eastern and Western religious thought, one reaps what one sows, either in this lifetime or the next.

The great secret to avoiding the effects of positive or negative karma lies in the attitude of neutrality, that is, in detached actions for the good of the whole. One is absolved of individual responsibility once this attitude is adopted. An example of this is in the behavior of those who use power entrusted to them by society. A policeman, when acting for the good of society (i.e., consistent with the laws agreed to by society), is absolved of individual responsibility for actions that may have resulted in harm to another. However, when found to be acting outside the scope of that authority (i.e., outside of societal parameters), then the protection is removed, and the policeman must receive the consequences for his actions.

Those who genuinely act in the name of a higher good such as God live by this principle. This is the highest state of consciousness one can exhibit while in human form. This is the state of consciousness of those who have unfolded to the highest level. This is the level to which the Law of Cause and Effect, through the exacting application of "tough love," inexorably leads all souls. The number of lifetimes it takes for one to reach this level varies from individual to individual. Death does not serve as an evasion of this path, and thinking that suicide ends it all is the worst of illusions. The essential point, however, is that no one, regardless of his position of power, can escape the consequences of his actions. How long it takes the individual to learn this lesson is a matter of choice.

As I progressed in my journey to higher consciousness, my understanding of these and other concepts of existence continued to expand and deepen. The journey to the heart of truth eventually took me to a point of understanding that will be expounded in later chapters. But before reaching this point in the journey, it is instructive to follow the stages of spiritual evolution that are presented in the confessions of this God-seeker.

Chapter 2 — The Path of the Light and Sound of God

When the Seeker is Ready....

In late 1969, my life as a God-seeker was progressing full force. My favorite haunt was an esoteric bookstore in Washington, D.C. that had an adjoining health food cafeteria. I remember smelling the sweet condiments that wafted over to my table while I was buried in my latest spiritual tome. Each insight brought a deeper awareness of my inner self and its capacity for omniscience. In the human form, I marveled at the illusions of life and how they masqueraded as ultimate reality.

Searching the bottom shelves of the outlying book racks, I encountered a small blue booklet, no more than fifty-pages long, written by Paul Twitchell, entitled *The Key to Eckankar*. I quickly flipped through the manuscript and discovered that it contained some very unusual words and concepts, but it was its description of an Eck Master called Rebazar Tarzs and his discourse on reality that I found utterly captivating. Tarzs spoke of the "I AM" principle, the concept of God (whom he called "SUGMAD") as the "self-definition of the Absolute."[1] He spoke of the responsibility everyone has for forming the life he lives each day. Every aspect of our lives is the result of our individual and collective thought forms.

His description of planes of reality beyond the astral plane really piqued my interest. It was the first time I had encountered any book that spoke of the existence of dimensions beyond the relatively common-place astral plane, which many religions call heaven. Yet, everyone experiences this dimension of existence in the dream state. When I returned home with my new acquisition, I underwent an explosion of consciousness that exceeded anything I had experienced.

After digesting the information contained in my first Eckankar book, I went on a spending spree acquiring an entire library of Eck-related materials. The insights they contained and the many related classes and seminars I attended had a profound impact. The Eckankar teaching was extremely comprehensive and provided answers to virtually every question I had ever raised. Indeed, by its own definition, Eckankar appeared to be all encompassing, the final step in soul's journey to the heart of truth. *The Eckankar Dictionary* defined Eckankar as:

> Religion of the Light and Sound of God; the path of TOTAL AWARE-NESS; the way of all things; means "CO-WORKER with God;" a teaching which gives knowledge of both the LIGHT and the SOUND which contains the total sum of all teaching emanating from God; the very foundation of all systems of science, and the key to success in unfolding all spiritual powers; the Ancient Science of SOUL TRAVEL. Projection of the inner CONSCIOUSNESS, which travels through the lower states until it ascends into the ecstatic states where the subject feels he possesses an AWARENESS of the religious experience of BEING; achieved through a series of spiritual exercises known only to the followers of this science.[2]

The Inner Worlds of God

After many years of studying Eckankar, I became quite proficient in traveling into the inner worlds. These trips had become as real to me as my everyday surroundings. In addition to the astral plane, the teachings of Eckankar encompassed the "causal plane," in which memories of past lives are stored. These records can be retrieved through the intriguing technique Paul Twitchell called "soul travel." The works of Eckankar also described higher planes of reality at ever-higher levels of awareness. The next highest plane, called the "mental plane" (corresponding with a mental body), is the one in which the heavens of many other earthly religions could be found. Twitchell's writings described a "soul plane:" a level at which the true self, or "soul," experiences spiritual liberation from the constraints of lower existence.

Like suits of clothes, these lower bodies are necessary for soul to function in the lower dimensions of reality. Paul talked about a spiritual hierarchy responsible for operating the inner worlds of God. Paul described a series of deities in each of these planes, whose names in Sanskrit reflected the experiences of those beings first capable of reaching these levels. Inasmuch as Eastern teachings laid the groundwork for exploration of the inner worlds, much of the language used to describe these regions comes from Sanskrit, Hindi, or other Eastern languages.

Paul described the journey of soul as encompassing more than mere travel to the soul plane. He set forth five additional planes of reality including the Agam Lok, the Hukikat Lok, the Alaya Lok, the Aluk Lok, and the Anami Lok. Each represents a higher plane of reality in which only the Law of Love prevails. Below this "Second Grand division" at the soul plane are the worlds of duality, where the forces of positive and negative are at play.

At the highest of these planes, the Anami Lok, there resides a being called Sugmad, who is the source of all creation. This being is believed to exist at a level of awareness and vibration from which it created Jehovah and all other spiritual being worshipped as God in other religions, as part of a spiritual hierarchy. Eckankar would maintain that Judaism is correct in its assertion of one God, but incorrect in its understanding of the level at which that God functions. The one God, Sugmad, utilizes subordinate manifestations of itself to carry out the operation of the several universes.

The Tibetan monk, Rebazar Tarzs, whom Paul recognized as his teacher and master, is said to be more than 400 years old, still living in his physical body in the Hindu Kush mountain range in Tibet. An advanced spiritual being, Tarzs is described as having the ability to travel in his soul-body and manifest himself in the presence of anyone, creating a body for himself as he moves through time and space. Paul described his encounters with Rebazar Tarzs in much the same way as Paramahansa Yogananda had described the appearance of his master, Sri Yukteswar.[3] Both masters were purportedly able to manifest a "body" that could be seen and touched, and through which they could communicate and teach.

Paul indicated that Tarzs works with a group of advanced beings called the Masters of the Vairagi Order. Eckankar teaches that these masters work in temples of golden wisdom scattered throughout the inner worlds. There, they function as guardians of a holy tome known as the *Shariyat-Ki-Sugmad*. According to Eck teachings, the *Shariyat-Ki-Sugmad* exists on each inner plane of reality, where these guardians watch over it. These books are said to contain the divine seeds of wisdom to enlighten mankind.

Paul took on the mantle of the "Mahanta," which, according to Eckankar teachings, is the highest state of consciousness known to humankind. The mission of this being is to gather all souls that are ready to return to the Godhead and to lead them through inner and outer instruction. The goal of each soul, supported by the Mahanta, is to achieve Self-Realization, God-Realization, and ultimately to become a co-worker with God. Paul was the most recent in a long line of masters, stretching back into ancient times, who worked in the inner worlds as the Mahanta and in the outer world as the Living Eck Master. As a physical being, the Mahanta uses a physical shell and has to deal with the same realities as all other men. But as the inner master, his powers are unlimited, for he is seen as the totality of divine spirit.

Altering A Spiritual Paradigm

Prior to finding Eckankar, I had read through more than two-thirds of the bookstore, including works on astrology, Egyptology, the occult, Rosicrucianism, Hinduism, Buddhism, theosophy, Islam, Sufism, Christianity, and every other "ism" I could find. All of these paled in comparison to the extraordinary insights contained in the myriad of books that Paul had written. But a God-seeker does not have his spiritual frame shattered without some signs of disorientation. Consequently, during the early period of my exposure to Eckankar, I was somewhat out of balance for weeks. My mind struggled to grasp the enormousness of the concepts I had encountered. What Paul was writing about made sense, and was highly appealing, but there was so much that I had to accept on face value. After putting his books down for a period — I had overdosed on spiritual books — I eventually resumed my study, more convinced than ever that I was on the right track and had encountered a gold mine of truth.

There was much that I did not accept from the teachings of Eckankar, even from the beginning, but I adopted an attitude of neutrality about the things I did not understand or accept. I tried to demonstrate and live the principles I understood, proving, one way or the other, whether they were true and worked for me or not. Having acquired most of Paul's books, I still wanted nothing more than to lose myself in the immense wisdom to which I had been exposed.

Despite embarking on a business career, my spiritual quest continued. Having completed law school and worked for several years with a private company, I decided to start my own firm. In a short time, we won several contracts and grew to a modest size. Even with business demanding more of my time, my greatest desire was to take time off to explore these materials. I would literally lock myself in a room and spend days reading Paul's works and practicing soul travel.

I knew I had found something I had been searching for all of my life. I knew instinctively that there was a deeper truth. For years I had been waiting for something to happen but was unsure of what it might be. Finally, I learned that our physical existence is not all that there is. Substantially more existed, and its discovery created a level of excitement and wonder that I could never have imagined before my exposure to Paul's writings.

In spite of my infatuation with its leader's writings, I approached Eckankar with a high level of skepticism, bringing the analytic rigor I had absorbed during my many years of legal study. But as much as I tried to deal with the issues intellectually, because so much of it involved an inner process akin to surrender, I could not approach these works with the same level of scrutiny. I had to learn to move beyond intellect and logic to something more basic — intuitive experience. On the surface, Paul challenged his readers not to believe anything he said. He merely asked them to keep an open mind and try the spiritual exercises he prescribed. In time, he maintained, the student would be able to prove the truth of his assertions to himself. I thought this fair, so I maintained neutrality on many of his pronouncements, even though some seemed like boasts, too grandiose and unsupported for my taste. Then too, there were inconsistencies and contradictions that were somewhat troubling but not fatally so. I attributed most of them to problems stemming from the sheer volume of material he produced in a short span of time.

A Spiritual Traveler is Born

The spiritual exercises of Eckankar were intriguing. They were an essential part of the teaching, for it was their regular practice that was the key to exploring the inner worlds of God. With them, I was supposed to be able to travel beyond my own physical body and experience the worlds that Paul described. If such travel were possible, then I would stick with them until I had experienced these inner worlds for myself. What could be more thrilling and challenging? I wanted to take the next step to understanding who I was and what was my mission in life.

At first, I used a spiritual exercise that Paul called the "Easy Way" technique. This exercise requires the practitioner to sit in a chair with back straight, yet relaxed. Her hands are interlaced and placed on the lap. The feet are comfortably planted flat on the floor or placed over each other while also resting on the floor. An important part of the technique (not unlike those of meditation) is to relax and clear the mind. After taking a few deep breaths to aid relaxation, attention is focused on a point between the eyebrows and approximately an inch or so inward. This point is called, in most Eastern religions and in Eckankar, the "spiritual eye." She then begins to sing the word "HU" in an elongated way, drawing the breath out with the intonation of "Huuuuu." She continues to breathe deeply while relaxing and keeping the focus of attention on the spiritual eye.

Eventually, a light or other object will appear on the screen of the mind. The seeker allows attention to be drawn into whatever she sees, observing and taking note of the details. It is precisely this shift of attention from the physical world to the images she sees on the inner screen that draws her consciousness from the physical into the inner worlds. The shift from body consciousness to the inner worlds is usually not recognized, just as the transition from wake state to dream state is not recognized. Yet, once consciousness has made the shift, the meditator may experience the sensation of flying or floating in space, among others. When this first happens, the seeker may become startled by the awareness that she has left the body, fully conscious, and traveled to another dimension. But if practiced over a continuous period, anxiety disappears and she is actually able to control the movement of consciousness. We need not be afraid of this exercise; there are always spiritual beings around to protect those just beginning to explore these inner dimensions.

After some fits and starts, I found myself moving regularly out of the physical body and into the inner worlds. One of my first encounters in the inner regions was seeing a group of enormous lights moving toward me. At first, it was somewhat frightening, but later I sensed the warmth and feelings of love and protection emanating from them. As they surrounded me, I could make out beings. Their outer appearances were much like normal people, except that they projected a brilliant light. I looked down at myself and discovered that I was also a globe of radiant light, floating in the center of this circle. I sensed their communication, not by words but by impressions. They greeted me with a joy like that of welcoming home a long-lost friend. I could not believe their excitement was directed at me! We communicated for some time, but the exact content I cannot recall. I only remember that I felt I had taken a new step and that I had been accepted as a part of a circle whose importance I could only surmise. This was only the first of countless experiences that I recall while traveling into these inner dimensions. Each experience left me with a feeling of oneness with a larger whole and of being protected in a way that made me feel very special.

I recall awakening many mornings with a glow, a feeling of warmth and love that lasted for many days. It must have appeared to my staff that something was wrong with me. Imagine the president of a company walking around all day with a giddy smile and a distant stare. They must have wondered what my drug of choice was! They never would have guessed that it was the radiance of the light and the love experienced in these inner regions of God. The source was no external object, it was inside me. In fact, it is inside all of us.

Following these early experiences, I journeyed almost daily into the inner worlds. I saw cities, visited places of learning, and talked with denizens of the inner worlds, all in full consciousness. Each experience was as real and as complete as the experiences I had everyday in the physical world. There was no question in my mind that it was real, for if it were not, then my life as the president of a corporation, a husband, and a father was also an illusion. I visited the capital of the astral world, which I had come to know as Sahasra Dal Kanwal. I relived past lives that confirmed the reality of reincarnation. I traveled into the mental world and visited the city of Arhirit, a city described in the Bible:

And the city lieth foursquare, and the length is as large as the breadth....
And the foundations of the wall of the city were garnished with all manner of precious stones.[4]

By the test that Paul had spelled out, I had apparently traveled to even higher regions, though I do not have as much memory of any forms observed on these planes. My only sensations on these planes were of sound and light. One of the tenets of Eckankar — derived from Shabd Yoga — is that God can be known as light and sound. The sound is the motion of the atoms of God as they descend into the lower worlds, giving life and sustenance to everything. As this wave of sound moves into different planes, it takes on different tones and different forms. In the inner worlds, we can hear these sounds as the buzzing of bees, the running of a brook, the tinkling of a bell, the celestial orchestra, the wind, the flute of God, and other wondrous sounds.

According to Eckankar, the sound of the buzzing of bees can be heard on the etheric plane. The celestial orchestras and the winds of God can be heard in the yet higher worlds of God. I have heard all these sounds. I have seen the radiance of the inner light, difficult to describe, but brighter, larger, and more magnificent than any view of the sun I have ever experienced. They are truly magnificent. Once we hear these celestial strains and see these inner sights, there is simply nothing in the physical world that can compare. All that is required is that we abandon fear and learn the techniques that enable consciousness to move beyond the body and into the inner worlds.

My first encounter with the inner sounds of God took place when I was living on a boat in Washington, D.C. Early in the morning, I went into the forward cabin to perform my spiritual exercises. On one occasion, I awoke suddenly when I heard the sound of bees seeming to come from another part of the boat. How strange that there would be bees on my boat at five o'clock in the morning. I went back into contemplation and the sound was even louder. I got up, walked through the boat, and looked at the pier to see if a swarm of bees had descended. There was none. Though I had read and heard about this sound, I had no idea that it could be so loud, so ferocious, and so real. I went back into contemplation and again the sound of the bees came, this time even louder, with hundreds and hundreds of buzzing bees swarming in my inner world. I eventually settled down, realizing that I was experiencing quite a blessing. I allowed my consciousness to flow with the sound and to become part of it. It was an illuminating experience that brought an awareness of experiencing the true inner realities of God.

This was the most exciting part of my study of Eckankar. No longer was I dealing with a religion that told me about the spiritual experiences of others and denied my capacity to have my own. Instead, I was able to experience the very things I had read about. Each morning, I could not wait to see what new adventure I would have and what new sounds I would hear.

One morning, the strangest of all sounds seemed to come from the docks. It was the sound of bagpipes, often compared to the cries of a cat in pain. Of all the sounds that I would have imagined to be heavenly, bagpipes were quite low on the list. As before, I thought it was simply an earthly sound. I wondered who could be playing bagpipes at five o'clock in the morning. So I came out of my contemplation, went outside, and stood alone in the silence. Of course, there were no bagpipes. As it turns out, bagpipes are commonly heard in the inner worlds. I smiled, returned to my contemplation, and was transfigured by the extraordinary sounds of bagpipes, with which I have subsequently fallen in love.

These are some of the experiences that anyone, if they take the time to try, can experience for himself. Having ventured this far with Paul's writings and instructions, I was perfectly ready to move deeper into the study and to learn more about what this extraordinary man had to teach. I became an Eckist and dedicated my life to becoming a spiritual master, the goal of all Eckists. Nothing was more exciting than the expansion of awareness in the inner worlds of God. Nothing could be!

A Life of Service

Eckankar teaches that God-Realization is not the ultimate objective. Beyond the realization of God lies the recognition that enlightened souls operate the universes of God. All beings on all planes (angels, guardians, and deities) are souls. But they differ from you and me in that they have unfolded to a higher level of spiritual awareness and have chosen to serve as conscious co-workers with God. Every spiritual being eventually learns that practice in this ultimate role of co-worker is an essential part of spiritual development. To simply sit back, receive wisdom, and not share it with the rest of humanity is not only selfish but also counterproductive. If an individual hoards the spiritual insights he has gained, his own spiritual growth will be delayed.

After several years in Eckankar, my life of service in spreading the divine message began to expand. My early years in Eckankar seemed very easy. Much of the material was self-evident. In less than the usual two years, and at the request of local leaders, I was initiated into the teachings of Eckankar, which enabled me to become an "Arahata," or instructor. This allowed me to speak at public gatherings and to teach those who wanted to learn more about the path. I began speaking at more and more events. I was at my third initiation for a relatively short period, when the Eckankar spiritual leader at that time, Darwin Gross, invited me to skip a level and receive the Fifth Initiation. This initiation is considered a very important stage in the spiritual development of a seeker, for at this stage the seeker is said to have attained self-awareness. Soul then has the opportunity to assist others in their exploration of the worlds of God as a part of their continuing spiritual service and development.

I became a fixture at Eckankar seminars, enthusiastically working with seminar directors to manage the larger convocations of Eckists that took place several times a year. Often, I was called upon to speak or conduct workshops on these occasions. These activities took me to many parts of the United States, Europe, Canada, and Africa. During these seminars, I worked directly with the seminar staff at the Eckankar International Office and also spoke at numerous seminars at the invitation of Eckists from around the world. The span of my involvement in this teaching, at this writing, is approximately thirty years. In the last five years, my role had become that of a major presenter of the Eckankar works at regional seminars worldwide.

As a guest speaker, I have met and spoken with thousands of God-seekers in various parts of the world. At major seminars in Africa alone, attendance has ranged from four to ten thousand. All of this was done in the name of service and to share the principles that I had learned and practiced. Sharing the truth of God is what I have chosen to do in life. As a married man with children, I have had to earn a living and provide for my family. This has given me an opportunity to put the spiritual principles I have learned into practice. I have done this in the creation and management of several companies. In many talks I have tried to show others how to use the God principles to bring abundance and happiness into their lives. This is a goal that is achievable by anyone willing to learn and apply the principles of spirit.

In my last five years with Eckankar, requests to speak and to meet with seekers at statewide and international events increased substantially. I began to develop and explore new dimensions of the spiritual truths that were spelled out in Eckankar works only superficially. Rather than simply relating stories of my experiences with divine spirit, I preferred to talk about the spiritual principles and the laws of the universe that empower people to discover and prove these principles for themselves. There is nothing wrong with stories, but, in my experience, they often leave the listener enamored or even moved by its contents, but fail to convey the underlying spiritual principles that can be applied generically. The audiences before whom I spoke, evinced a hunger to learn and understand these spiritual principles, which were seldom the focus amidst the flood of stories.

My role in Eckankar seemed to be one of bridging the gap between the profound but sometimes incomprehensible works of Paul Twitchell and the pleasant anecdotes and stories preferred by the present Living Eck Master, Harold Klemp. I have always thought that souls are different and require a variety of approaches before they can be reached. Paul thought this too, and so wrote poetry, prose, and fiction to get his message across. In my presentations, I attempted to bring a balance between the spiritual principles seekers needed to know and examples of how they worked.

Journey of the God-seeker

While this book deals with the experiences of one God-seeker as he journeyed through Eckankar and other paths to reach God-Realization, in a broader sense, it is the story of all God-seekers. Everyone hears this call, though some resist and others ignore it entirely. In the end, all will hear the call again and eventually respond. My journey through Eckankar is particularly important because Eckankar purports to be the highest spiritual teaching on the planet today. Indeed, it is a teaching that is profound in content, approach, and promise. On reading some of the Eckankar books, one is apt to think that they have found the final spiritual answer. In time, one learns, as did I, that when soul comes to understand its origin and returns in consciousness to the point of unity from which all derives, it has reached the "I AM" state, for all is here and now.

My public service in Eckankar continued until January 2002, when I made my last Eckankar presentation before a group of Eckists in Chicago, Illinois. It became clear at that time that my talks had been influenced by a string of events that altered my spiritual journey forever. Indeed, the events of November and December 2001 were extraordinary. They expanded my capacity to peer deeply into a teaching I loved dearly and to help the people in it whom I loved even more. It is because of my love for them, and the connection that I have with all souls seeking higher states of awareness, that I have written this book.

Chapter 3 — How the Journey Started

First Contact

It all began innocently enough. My staff and I were in the final stages of preparing for an upcoming speaking tour in England. The six-day, seven-workshop tour was taking shape, and I was looking forward to a reunion with friends I had made during speaking visits to England in prior years. About a month before my departure, a member of my staff brought me a communication that had been received through my company's e-mail. The message was unusual, in part because it came from a High Initiate (HI) in Eckankar who lived in England. It received my immediate attention. Here is the message:

From: Lisa Kyle
Sent: Friday, October 05, 2001 10:37 AM
To: Ford Johnson
Subject: Requesting Your Advice!

London, England
October 05, 2001

Dear Ford,

I am greatly in need of your wisdom and advice. I am presuming on my contact with you over the years at various seminars and on stage in the UK to ask for your trust and help in light of a rather extraordinary situation.

Myself and a fellow H.I., Mary Voaden, are in contact with an individual who is having the most profound inner experiences and initiations seemingly on the same levels and also beyond those of Paul and Harold.

Whilst I know that we do come across these individuals in Eckankar who make certain claims, the very nature and quality of what is occurring with Graham seems to be in a completely different league from anything that has come my way previously. As to Graham himself, rarely have I talked with someone so full of caring, integrity, love, and humility.

I would really appreciate, depending on how you feel after having read this, if I could email you some of Graham's journals and then perhaps arrange for us to have a meet-up when you are over in the UK in a few weeks time so you could meet Graham and also so he could talk with you.

The nature of the experiences detailed in Graham's journals and from what he is sharing with us are not only profound with new slants and information on certain aspects of the Eck teachings but are also utterly extraordinary on a spiritual wisdom level and could have wide reaching ramifications for Eckankar.

Graham's early journals tell of his experiences as he unfolds from Second to Thirteenth Initiate and detail his meetings and contact with all the elements of the hierarchy through all the planes and into the heart of God. In his latest writings, he shares his preparations for the Fourteenth Initiation and the Mahantaship and the subject matter widens citing such things as the site of the Oracle of Tirmer being replaced by the Cave of Tomsk on the inner planes due to the worsening effects of the conditions in Tibet and in the world; (Rebazar has now said that this is a fascia fronting a Temple above the Pyrenees where the ceremony will take place); information for the next phase for the movement of Eckankar; detailed descriptions of the Nine Silent Ones and a number of incredibly profound wisdom teachings from their named spokesperson (far from being cold and aloof these Beings are love itself); mention of an ancient Eck Master of the Sixteenth Initiation, who is rarely in embodiment and who works mostly within the Eck itself. This Master is preparing Graham for his next step spiritually under the protection of the Nine Silent Ones. The latest writings contain information most delicate/sensitive in nature.

Graham has been told that his journal has to be placed in front of Sri Harold sooner rather than later. Depending on what happens then, the next step will be made clear.

With love and blessings

Lisa Kyle

The contents immediately piqued my interest, and I instructed my assistant to ask Lisa to send me a copy of the journal so that I could review it firsthand. Upon review of the document, it was clear that it lived up to the billing that Lisa had given it. It contained more than sixty detailed accounts of the spiritual experiences of a devoted student of Eckankar. Over a period of about seven years (1994-2001), Graham meticulously wrote of a series of inner spiritual experiences, more profound and far reaching than any I had read in the Eckankar writings, with the exception of Paul Twitchell's *The Tiger's Fang*.[1] What was even more impressive was that all of the experiences occurred during Graham's reading of the discourses and while he was practicing the spiritual exercises that the spiritual leader of Eckankar had outlined for each chela.[2] (With Graham's permission, I have included portions of this journal in the following chapter.)

It was striking that Graham had consistently used his secret word[3] and other techniques taught by the Living Eck Master to test the validity of his spiritual experiences. So much was happening to Graham that he wanted to make certain he was not deceiving himself and that his experiences were valid. During most of these journeys into the inner worlds, Harold Klemp (Wah Z[4]) — or an image thereof — accompanied Graham. These inner travels also included experiences with many other masters, some familiar and others unfamiliar in Eckankar writings.

I had been contacted because the HIs assisting Graham felt that I might be able to present these materials directly to the leader of Eckankar, Sri Harold Klemp, the Mahanta, the Living Eck Master. The writings appeared to be those of a very responsible and dedicated God-seeker of the highest integrity. Whether true or not, they certainly were the works of someone who believed, with all his heart, that his experiences were pure and true. From his journal, Graham appears to have been compelled to agree to have his materials presented to Sri Harold.

After speaking several times by phone with Mary (a close friend of Graham and Lisa), and learning more about Graham, I requested that she contact him and set up a telephone conversation between the two of us. Mary told me that she had known Graham for a number of years and became aware that he was having experiences in the inner worlds that far exceeded anything about which she had encountered or read. They became friends and she encouraged him on numerous occasions to continue with his work, sensing its potential importance. It was on the strength of her personal knowledge of Graham and her certainty of his integrity that she and Lisa felt comfortable asking for my assistance in presenting the journal to Sri Harold Klemp. She then set the time for a telephone conversation.

Mary sent Graham's journal to me in two parts. The first consisted of spiritual experiences from 1994 through 2000. These were extraordinary enough, but not as sensitive in regard to Eckankar as the content of later materials from 2001. Mary sent me the first part of Graham's materials as a test to see if I could handle the more sensitive material. When I spoke with Mary, I told her that I found the materials to be consistent with other Eckankar's writings. Certainly, if the writings of Paul Twitchell, the experiences of Harold Klemp, and the books of Phil Morimitsu[5] and James Davis[6] were valid, then Graham's journeys must also be considered valid. In each instance, the experiences of the writer could never be proven objectively. They were accepted on the strength of the integrity of the individual writing them and on the assumption that no one would lie about experiences with God.

Later, Mary sent me the second part of Graham's journal. These were of a highly delicate nature because, if accepted by the Spiritual Leader of Eckankar, they would change the entire course and direction of the teaching. It was precisely because of the extraordinary and portentous nature of these writings that as a High Initiate, "chief channels for the Eck power,"[7] I considered it my duty and my obligation to bring these materials to the attention of Sri Harold Klemp.

Several days after reviewing the material, I phoned Graham to tell him that I considered his experiences extraordinary and his insights illuminating. My words evoked a palpable sigh of relief felt across an entire ocean. I cautioned Graham that it was not my place to judge the truth of his materials but assured him that I sensed his sincerity, honesty, and integrity — the only basis for judging spiritual experiences. I concluded by saying that I would do everything in my power to ensure that these materials were placed in front of Sri Harold Klemp.

As a follow-up, I sent him this letter:

November 2, 2001

Graham Forsyth
West Yorkshire, England

Dear Graham,

I have read your experiences several times and I am quite comfortable with what I have read in terms of presenting them to HK.

What you have brought forth, in the experiences you have shared, is extremely profound. Your writings convey a truth, power and light that I have not encountered except in some of Paul's writings.

The Master was entirely correct when he told you that the truth and sincerity of your writings would not be difficult for the truth seeker to see and accept. There are so many who have reached the level of the fifth initiation and who seem dead in their active service to Eckankar. They would be enlivened by much of what you have to say.

One of my concerns is what materials would you be presenting to HK? The entire record is too much to expect him to review in the short time that we will be there. Then too, there are some parts of the writings that I do not think should be transmitted. We can put the package together when we are in Washington but give careful thought to this. The human factor is still at play and you don't want to dig yourself a hole unnecessarily.

If HK rejects the appeal directly or refuses to meet or respond, then the next course of action is unclear. I would like to know what your thinking is about your next step if this is the outcome.

It is possible that HK might accept your experiences and invite you to Minnesota to work for Eckankar for a while as a type of apprenticeship. Working there for a while without the immediate responsibilities of taking over might be perceived as being in the best interest of the whole. I am only saying here that you might want to consider that this is one possible outcome. HK followed this approach himself before he took over as the LEM studying under Darwin Gross for several years.

Have you started a book or given consideration to one? Obviously this will be needed as soon as possible regardless of the outcome of the visit to MN. Your writings are very profound and form an excellent basis for your book.

What is your timetable on this or will you take it a step at a time as spirit unfolds it to you?

What direction are you getting on the inner on these questions?

I have many questions and issues to discuss and I am truly looking forward to meeting and talking with you!

May the Blessings Be,

Ford Johnson

P.S. Enclosed is a copy of the letter I sent to HK announcing our visit.

Sensing the importance of these materials and the possibility that Harold might need to meet and speak with Graham confidentially, I wrote to Harold Klemp, informing him of the events that had transpired and also telling him that Mary, Lisa, Graham, and I would be traveling to Minnesota following my speaking tour in England.

This is the letter that I sent to Sri Harold Klemp:

November 7, 2001

Ford Johnson
Sri Harold Klemp
The Mahanta, The Living Eck Master
PO Box 27300
Minneapolis, MN 55427

Dear Harold,

During the week of Nov. 2-7th I will be engaged in a Vahana tour in England set up by the English Chelas. This will consist of a series of 6 workshops in 6 cities in five days. It will be quite exciting and will prepare the way for the Regional Seminar in or near London the following weekend when A*B* will speak.

On October 5, 2001, I received a rather extraordinary letter from an HI in England asking for advice and assistance on a matter she regarded as needing to be brought to your attention as soon as possible. I encounter many of these situations during various speaking engagements for Eckankar during the year. But this one was truly different and was of such a nature that I felt it had to be brought to your attention.

The issue involves an English Chela named Graham who over a period of seven years has recorded a series of inner experiences that, in their content and detail, are on the order of Paul's writings in *The Tiger's*

Fang and your writings. Many of these descriptions involve meetings with many of the ECK Masters and contain messages from these masters that deal with Eckankar that Graham has been instructed to communicate to you.

In this situation, I believe it is my responsibility as a Mahdis to bring this to your attention for your disposition. The Chela in question and the two HIs from England that brought this matter to my attention both regard these communications as highly credible, having known this person for several years. Indeed, they have decided to accompany me back to the US along with Graham and travel to Minnesota to personally deliver these materials. I have read them also and do agree with the English HIs that the materials should be presented directly to you.

Accordingly, we will be arriving in Minnesota on Thursday, November 15, at which time I will contact SK* to give her a package containing these materials that, I trust, she will deliver to you personally. After that, Graham will be available to meet with you if you should choose to meet. The group will remain until Sunday morning, November 18 in hopes that you might wish to speak with one or more of them before they leave.

I realize that this action is somewhat unusual, but I can assure you that I would not even consider it if I did not think that it was of the utmost importance.

May the Blessings Be,

Ford Johnson
ESA

Having taken steps to bring these materials to the Living Eck Master, I continued with final arrangements for my speaking tour. I also went over Graham's journal again. The implications for Eckankar were staggering. I had no idea how things would play out.

Arrival in London: The English Tour

I arrived in England on the morning of Monday, November 5th, 2001. I was greeted by my old friend Albert, a dedicated Eckist with whom I had previously worked in spreading the message of Eck. An extraordinary amount of work had gone into preparing for the trip. The workshop posters, circulated in large quantities, laid the groundwork for what was to be an exciting and highly successful speaking tour.

Workshops were presented in Leicester, Edinburgh, Durham, Newcastle upon Tyne, East Sussex, Reading, Somerset and London.

Prior to coming to England, I had tried to arrange a meeting with Mary, Lisa, and Graham to discuss the content of his journal and our upcoming trip to Minnesota. The original plan was for just Graham and I to meet with Sri Harold Klemp. But because of Mary's and Lisa's support of him over the years and perhaps also because of the novelty of flying (he had never even left Britain), Graham asked if they would accompany him, and they accepted. Aside from the scheduling problems associated with my speaking engagements, Graham's circumstances also posed difficulties in arranging a visit with him.

Although one of the workshops took place about thirty miles from Graham's home, my schedule and the confidentiality of our communications did not permit a visit. Albert, who organized the tour and accompanied me to each site, knew nothing about my communication with Graham. The earliest opportunity to meet would be the day of our flight back to the United States. We planned to get together at Heathrow Airport prior to our flight to Washington, D.C., and later to Chanhassen, Minnesota, the site of the Temple of Eck. That was the best we could do. So, the idea of meeting, discussing, and planning was put in abeyance until our departure.

My attention was now focused on completing the tour and sharing what I hoped would be an empowering message on the workshop theme: "Making the Most of Life through Reincarnation, Dreams and Soul Travel." After the fourth workshop (Newcastle upon Tyne), we returned to London for a short rest before going back on the road for the final phase of the tour. During the London visit, I received a call from the Temple of Eck. It was from Sri Harold Klemp's assistant, who informed me that, because of his busy schedule, Sri Harold preferred that we not bring Graham's journal to Minnesota. Instead, he requested that I simply send the journal. The Living Eck Master would review it in due course. I sensed that something was up, but what?

Chapter 4 — The Spiritual Journal of Graham Forsyth

Preparing Graham's Journal for the Master

At times, the enormousness of the course on which we had embarked seemed overwhelming. Because of the sheer power, scope, and depth of Graham's journal, it simply had to be brought to the attention of the Living Eck Master. No one could guess what Harold's response would be, but it had to be sent. Like Jonah, Graham was reluctantly and almost defiantly resisting the implications of his inner experiences. Indeed, I think it would be fair to say that presenting his journal to the Living Eck Master was the last thing Graham wanted. Yet, for the God-seeker, there is little latitude in carrying out God's will. The inner push to answer the call is powerful and overwhelming. The inner assurances needed to bolster the God-seeker's compulsion to serve come when needed. This is what Graham was told during one of his inner journeys in September of 2001:

> Those few whom you have met and talked with will surprise you by their readiness to accept you. Remember, nothing is by accident, all is for a reason. You have been led, placed, kept, and unfolded very precisely. You've often wondered and asked why others accept your experiences very easily, in fact, more easily than you've accepted them yourself. Well, now you have the answer to this question that you've asked repeatedly; they have always been aware of you, according to design.[1]

The flight back to the U.S. was lonely but productive. When one's attention has been completely spiritual for more than a week, it is difficult to revert to the role of corporate president. The very next day, I was immersed in the latest details of home and office. After attending meetings and being briefed on the events of the previous week, I was pleased to find that nothing had blown up and that my excellent staff had done a superb job of moving things forward.

I immediately began work on the journal to give it more structure so that it would be easier for the Living Eck Master to review. I was sensitive to how busy he is. I remembered in the past I had written him long letters for which I had been good-naturedly chided. Revamping the journal involved giving each experience a title and developing a table of contents. After about two days, it was finally ready to be sent.

Some of the material in Graham's journal was so sensitive that I was concerned it might not receive a positive response. We wanted to avoid the all-too-human reaction of anger. Sri Harold Klemp, like anyone else, is subject to anger, ego, and all other human responses. Many who follow spiritual leaders often ascribe to them almost superhuman emotional control. Because of my past experiences with Harold, I thought it wiser to omit potentially inflammatory materials. However, I have included them in this book. (The full text of this journal is contained in a book authored by Graham.[2])

Perhaps some background on Graham would be of interest here. Graham was born, raised, and has lived his entire life in the small town of Keighley, in West Yorkshire, England. As he describes it, his life was nothing out of the ordinary for a person from a working-class background. His early years were largely influenced by his father, whom Graham describes as "a man of very narrow vision, short on understanding, devoid of patience and a Communist through and through." As testament to the power of soul to transcend any situation and environment, Graham made it through his early years with an interest in debate and a thousand questions with which he terrorized his middle-and secondary-school teachers. He took a keen interest in religion while in Senior School under the instruction of a Catholic teacher, who, according to Graham, was the most influential person in his life. Long after he left school, he remembered the words of his religion teacher: "There will come a time when you will believe in God."

After completing school, Graham became a blacksmith and welder and soon began having experiences of an unusual nature. Late one night, Graham awoke to find a young man, about nineteen years of age, with ginger-colored hair and a pale complexion, kneeling beside his bed. Thinking that he was being robbed, he lunged at him. When his hands and arms passed right through the young man, he realized that he was an apparition of some sort. He could see the door through his visitor's body! He was convinced he had just seen a ghost. When the entity disappeared, Graham made a mad dash for the safety of his brother's room. Receiving little sympathy from his incredulous brother, he reluctantly returned to his room, hopeful that the odd experience was over. The experience had a profound effect on his life. The initial incident was followed in short order by visits in his astral form to his parent's house (later acknowledged by his mother) and by participation in various forms of spiritualism.

After joining the Mother Church of Spiritualism, Graham participated in a development circle where he soon demonstrated the ability to make contact with entities in the astral dimension and to channel their input. One such being that worked through him was a Masai warrior chief named Wongoola. Speaking through Graham, this tall, twenty-five year-old being with an infectious sense of humor introduced himself to the group. The communication with Wongoola strengthened over the following weeks and months, until a struggle within the circle resulted in Graham leaving the group and eventually the church.

After marriage and the birth of his first child, Graham studied the path of Krishna, but soon was swayed by the writings of Julian Johnson, a member of the Radhasoami Satsang Beas and author of *The Path of the Masters*. Johnson's book exposed Graham to the Sant Mat teachings, an aspect of Shabd Yoga, the Yoga of the Audible Life Stream. Graham would later learn that this book and the wisdom it contained were primary sources for the Religion of Eckankar.

Before that, his inquires into Sant Mat led him to Maharaj Charan Singh Ji. Committed to higher consciousness, Graham practiced two and a half hours of daily meditation and observed a vegetarian diet, a regimen he still follows. The study of Sant Mat exposed Graham to the teachings of many great masters. When he finally found the path of Eckankar, he was completely familiar with the teaching, its terminology, and the role of the Living Master, because it was virtually identical to the Sant Mat teaching he had studied under Maharaj Charan Singh Ji.

The Sant Mat teaching encompassed the teachings of Kabir, Guru Nanak, Saint Paltu, Saint Dadu, Shamaz-i-Tabriz, Rumi, and many others. When his master, Charan Singh, died, Graham sought a new master. Eventually, through the inner influence of Param Sant Kirpal Singh Ji, the former spiritual master of Paul Twitchell, Graham was directed to Sant Ajaib Singh Ji (Sant Ji), the successor to Kirpal Singh. Graham's inner journeys with Sant Ji were filled with experiences on all the inner planes, and eventually led to the God-Realization experience itself.

Graham came to Eckankar in 1994. He did so because of an inner experience that he had with his then master, Sant Ji, who introduced him to Sri Harold Klemp, and, in a gesture, handed him over. It was not Graham's intention or desire to join Eckankar, but his inner communications from Sant Ji clearly indicated that it should be his next spiritual step. Graham remained a chela under the guidance of Harold Klemp for more than seven years. During this time, he compiled the most extensive journal of inner experiences I have ever read. This body of work compares in every respect to Paul's experiences in *The Tiger's Fang*.

Graham's journal was transmitted to Sri Harold Klemp on November 18, 2001. In addition to a brief letter of transmittal from me, the following letter to the Living Eck Master from Graham was included:

18th November 01

Sri Harold Klemp,
The Mahanta, The Living Eck Master

Dear Harji,

I have been asked by The SUGMAD to place before you this journal containing the experiences I have received while a member of Eckankar. I have also been informed on the inner that you have been made aware, and know the reason for it being asked of me. I have not undertaken this lightly, and it does not sit easily on my shoulders. It is not something that I myself have sought-it has sought me.

All that is contained within the journal has withstood the test of the secret words that are required to be used to prove their validity and all that you are about to read, I stand by as true.

To help place all this in front of you, I have been most fortunate in receiving the guidance of two high initiates, Mary Voaden and Lisa

Kyle. Without their support, I would have found it very difficult to achieve. It is very hard to have things placed in front of you by an ordinary Eckist, therefore we had that hurdle to overcome. Very kindly Ford Johnson offered to help bring this to your attention when we approached him.

I alone take full responsibility for all that has been written. It is as given, I have added nothing more. I realise that some of the experiences are of a sensitive nature, and what has been revealed through them. Your comment to Ford that you are aware of this, and that there was no need for me to come out to America has made the approach to you easier. Please feel free to ask anything you like of me. I will always do my best to answer your questions as openly and honestly as I can.

I remain yours in Spirit,

Graham Forsyth

Subsequent to sending Graham's journal to Harold, the manuscript was entitled, "In the Many Hands of God." Below are excerpts from it.

In the Many Hands of God
(Excerpts[3])
by Graham Forsyth

July 29, 1994 - Being Enveloped by the Light

While singing HU, an experience took place, where I saw myself standing on my own with a very bright beam of white light coming down from above and entering my body through the top of my head. The light then shone out of my body, as smaller beams through my eyes, ears, nose, mouth, and the two lower openings. Then, suddenly, my body was enveloped completely in this white light and its form could not be seen. It was as if each pore of my skin was emitting a ray of white light in the same way that a porcupine is covered with quills. I had a similar experience with my former Master, Sant Ajaib Singh Ji.

August 7, 1994 - Meeting Wah Z and the History of ECK Masters

While meditating, repeating the Master's spiritual name, Wah Z, within, I saw myself with the Master (Sri Harold Klemp) inside an office. It felt as though I was in America. He was talking to me as we both looked out of a large office window onto what appeared [to be] either a large garden or a country scene. The subject was life and the works of ECK. Suddenly the whole room was filled with a very bright white light and I saw what appeared to be like a shaft of chromed steel about three inches in diameter emerging from the light and impaling the Master in the solar plexus region. It entered the Master at an angle of about forty degrees from the horizontal. The Master stood facing the light with His arms open. He was smiling and showed no signs of pain.

Earlier that morning, I had read about Sri Darwin Gross leaving ECK-ANKAR. I had been greatly puzzled as to why someone would leave after such spiritual attainment. This experience was to show me that the silver cord, i.e., the chrome bar, was unbreakable, for the connection between the SUGMAD and the Mahanta is the strongest bond of all, and is never broken. This bonding is much, much stronger than that of the ordinary Chela. This put my mind at rest as to how I could have had an experience with Sri Paul Twitchell and Sri Darwin Gross before I came to ECKANKAR, and after Sri Darwin Gross had left the organisation.

October 3, 1994 - Further Meetings with Gopal Das and Studying the Shariyat

While contemplating, I was given the feeling to ask that I might be taken to a Temple of Golden Wisdom to study the *Shariyat-Ki-SUG-MAD* with Sri Gopal Das. So, going with this impression, I asked if it would be possible for me to do so. I quickly found myself in a large open square, surrounded by buildings of a Roman type design (the same as in the earlier experience of September 20,1994). Sri Gopal Das was there to greet me and then he left me alone to make my own way to the Temple (which I had also seen before). When Sri Gopal Das greeted me, He gave me a look as much to say "Are you here again?" but it was a beautiful and welcoming way in which he did it. I entered the Temple and approached the *Shariat-Ki-SUGMAD*, which was placed on a ped-estal a little in front of what I felt was an altar of some kind.

I stood at this pedestal and opened the book. A tremendously bright light came out of the book, yet I had no trouble with seeing. As I looked into the light, it seemed to go on forever, as though the depth of it could not be measured. At the same time, single letters as from the alphabet were also coming out of the book within the light and were passing into me, I could just feel a slight sensation as they entered. Then the letters changed into notes that are used in the writing of music. This went on for five to ten minutes. I have had this experience before but could not make out what the objects in the light were, so I never recorded it.

October 8, 1994 - My Encounter with SUGMAD and ITS Communication to Me

This experience took place on October 5, 1994, but I was reluctant to write it down, because of what it implied. Now I feel I have no choice but to put it down, as I've felt uncomfortable for not doing so. During contemplation, a voice spoke to me, it was not a voice as spoken in the physical world, but an impression which came across as someone speaking. I cannot remember all that was said and in what order it came, as I tried not to take much notice of it because I was afraid to accept it, let alone write it down. So in the name of the SUGMAD, I now will put it down in writing. The voice started talking about creation and how spirit plays its part in the order of things. Then it spoke to me in this way:

IN THIS WORLD YOU HAVE A PURPOSE TO PLAY, FOR YOU IT IS A MISSION. IN THIS WORLD THE MASTERS COME TO HELP SOUL BACK TO GOD. THEY ARE MY DEAREST SONS. FEW THERE ARE IN THIS WORLD AND OF THESE FEW YOU ARE ONE OF MY DEAREST SONS. YOU CAN NEVER KNOW OF MY DEEPEST LOVE FOR YOU. FOR YOU, THERE IS NO NEED TO FEAR OR WORRY. ALL YOUR NEEDS I MYSELF WILL TAKE CARE OF FOR YOU. ALL YOUR NEEDS, BOTH PHYSICAL AND FINAN-CIAL, AND YOUR HEALTH, I WILL LOOK AFTER THEM FOR YOU. FOR YOU, THERE IS NO NEED TO FEAR. KNOW THOU THAT I THE SUGMAD HAVE SPOKEN.

This is the truth of what I can remember being told. I did not want to put it down, but I have had no choice. Not to do so, I now feel would be a lack of faith. With my former Master, Sant Ajaib Singh Ji, I had the same experience as Sri Paul Twitchell when He was taken to see the SUGMAD by Sri Rebazar Tarzs. In this experience, I was allowed to speak to the giant form that had manifested (as described by Paulji) on different occasions. I do not want to make the claim that the SUGMAD speaks to me directly (for I know that GOD rarely if ever communicates with anybody in the physical form), but in *ECKANKAR the Key to Secret Worlds*, Sri Paul Twitchell has written on page 74 (I quote), "Here we can communicate with the spiritual travelers or we can have direct contact with GOD and, when we return to the earth, we will remember just as much of our communication as can be brought within the compass of brain activity."

I must admit I did not have the feeling of any raised consciousness when this took place, and so I cannot know at what level it occurred. That is why I was reluctant to write it down. After I had finished writing this down, I was about to put it away and asked again that, if I had written anything that was wrong or untrue, the SUGMAD would forgive me, as I did not want to make any false claim. As I asked this, the last sentence from what was spoken to me was repeated, and I remembered it again clearly from the experience. I had put it down wrong, so this is the cor-rected version. I now make this statement in the name of the SUGMAD and the Mahanta, the Living Eck Master, Sri Harold Klemp, that all that is written here is the truth to the best of my knowledge, and nothing has been put down that I know to be false. May GOD judge all that is written here.

October 25,1994 - Removing the Ball of Fear

While starting to try and do the ECK exercise of opening the heart centre to help remove fear the following experience took place: Repeating Master's spiritual name, Wah Z, I tried to imagine the picture of the exercise as given in the book, but with no success. I had tried this over the last few days, yet I found it hard to visualise the picture given. Trying again on this particular day, within moments the Master came, appearing in a setting alone with me. He stood facing me and then dropped onto his right knee right in front of where I was sitting.

Reaching out with his right hand, he pushed it into my body at the solar plexus centre and then pulled it out holding a black ball about the size of a grapefruit. Standing up, he then tossed it away while saying, "That's got rid of the ball of fear." It happened so fast, I just thought to myself, "This cannot be true" (although I was testing the experience and the Master's form by using His spiritual name). The Master just smiled and said, "OK, we will do it again," and repeated what he had just done. As this was different from the spiritual exercise I had been trying to do, I then asked the Master how I could continue the exercise to allow the light to enter into me. He just smiled and, again dropping down onto his right knee, said, "As we have removed the ball of fear, let us replace it with balls of light," and with this he placed his right hand, which was holding a ball of white light, into my body at the solar plexus centre. He did this four times, each time placing a ball of white light within me, and then the experience ended.

November 13, 1994 - Stepping into the Light (Accepting the ECK)

Using HU as my mantra, I started to do the spiritual exercise where Wah Z removes a black ball of fear from within me and replaces it with four coloured balls of light. As I visualised this within, Master appeared and knelt down in front of me (as was usual), but this time he had no head. I was singing HU mentally, yet the figure still stayed in my presence. As the figure reached out to touch me, I pushed away its hands and changed my mantra to the Master's name, Wah Z. Still the figure stayed, so I tried using the name of the SUGMAD and at the same time visualised the Master coming and removing the headless figure, which He did. Then, as this new figure of the Master knelt down in front of me, its head also disappeared. At this I stood up and walked away from the figure to where the tube of white light was shining (I've mentioned this before) and stepped into the light. The feeling of peace was overwhelming.

Within seconds of stepping into the light, Wah Z appeared with Sri Rebazar Tarzs at his right side. A faint smile was on their faces as they looked at each other and then at me standing in the light. After a moment or two, Sri Fubbi Quantz appeared at the left side of Wah Z. He had a knowing smile on his face, and while looking at me he said to Wah Z, "Hah! I see he has placed himself into the light. It is good, for now he has surrendered to the ECK of his own free will." A few moments later the experience ended, and it became clear to me what it was all about. During all my experiences within, I have been led by Wah Z or one of the other ECK Masters. They have shown and told me what to do. But Master came this time without a head to test me and see if I would reject the experience altogether or whether I would, of my own free will, trust in the light of ECK and go forward on my own with faith.

November 25, 1994 - A Visit To The Sun Worlds With Rebazar Tarzs

While singing HU, Sri Rebazar Tarzs appeared within with a pair of modern-day flip-flops in His hands, which he offered to me. I did not take them at first, because I wanted to keep on singing HU a little while longer (as I usually sing HU for at least twenty to thirty minutes). So Master Tarzs sat down and waited for me to finish. He had his wooden staff with him, which is the first time I've seen him with it. After singing HU, I changed over to my secret words that Wah Z had given me the day before, so that I could always test the experience. I accepted the sandals and put them on. Then, taking Master's left hand, we started to climb a very jagged, steep, rocky slope. I now understood why Master Tarzs had brought his staff and the sandals for me. When we reached the top, the walking became more difficult, as we had to walk upon rocks that were sharp and pointed, using them as stepping stones and having to keep our balance. The stones that we were walking on seemed to be about six feet above ground level.

Then, Master Tarzs stopped, and there before us, lying in a deep valley, was a city of golden light. High up in the sky was a brilliant yellow sun. As we watched, the sun started to get lower in the sky until it had covered the golden city in the valley and nothing of it could be seen. Then a few moments later, it rose up into the sky again and I could see the city once more, and now I could also see more of these golden cities; each in its own valley and each producing its own light. They had no need of the sun's light. Then, Master Tarzs pointed to the cities with his left hand and told me these were the sun worlds.

It was now clear to see that what I thought were just some pointed rocks we were standing on, were in fact high mountain peaks and they were like the hub of a wheel, with lower mountain ranges radiating out from them like spokes, and between these mountain ranges were the golden cities in the valleys. What Master Tarzs was showing me was the creative centre of the Sun Worlds. This was the point at which we stood and all the worlds of that region were shown as the golden cities in the valleys.

He put His arm around my shoulder, and I put mine around his waist (I looked about fourteen years old standing at his side), and he said to me, "Because of your speed of progress, you've been brought here to be tuned into the vibrations of this plane, and this will be so for all the other planes as well. Do not worry about the short stay in these planes, for you are not to be held up here. You are to progress on. Also do not forget the time difference that there is in the spiritual worlds; a few moments here can be the equivalent of a long period of time in the earth world."

The feeling of oneness and being completely loved and accepted by Master Tarzs is one that always overwhelms me. It is unlike anything I have ever felt before and it's the same with all the ECK Masters I have had the good fortune to meet.

December 12, 1994 - On Being Tested by Peddar Zaskq and Receiving the Golden Crown

While sitting listening to the sound current, the ECK Master, Sri Paul Twitchell (Peddar Zaskq), came to me within and asked me if I wanted to go with Him on a spiritual journey. I was eager to go, for the last twelve days had been quiet within for me, and I would have loved to have gone with Him. Yet within me, I had the feeling that this was not all that it seemed to be, although I have a great respect for Master Zaskq, for it was He who brought me to ECKANKAR in the first place. I told Master Zaskq I would go with him, but first I must have the permission of my Master Wah Z. If he did not give me permission, I would not go, for I had put myself completely in his hands. Master Zaskq was very persuasive in his offer, but still I would not go with him until I was told to by Wah Z.

After many attempts to get me to follow him, Master Zaskq broke out into a large grin and at the same time Wah Z appeared at his side, both looked very pleased with me, then they disappeared. A few moments later, Wah Z reappeared and placed on my head a simple golden crown. Then all was made clear to me. It had been a test to see if I would follow another Master, because I had been feeling that something was amiss with not having had any experiences for the last twelve days. During these twelve days, I had the feeling that Master wanted me to rest from the experiences that were taking place within, and that is why I felt, when Master Zaskq came for me, that all was not what it seemed. Therefore, Master Zaskq had come to tempt me to see if I would go with him. Because I would not until my Master Wah Z gave me permission, I had passed, and both Masters were very happy.

There was a lesson also learnt here and that is "When the experiences slow down or stop, there is a reason why the Master does this, and it's always better for the Chela to accept than to go elsewhere trying to force progress."

January 6, 1995 - Discussions with Wah Z about ECKANKAR and My Mission

While using my secret words in contemplation, I asked Wah Z to clarify a dream I had had the night before, since I was not sure whether the dream was showing me that I was going to move materially or spiritually. Wah Z told me I was going to move in both aspects, for as I was unfolding spiritually, the material environment I was in was now unsuitable for my needs, because of the spiritual role I had to do.

I then went into meditation still using my secret words and soon found myself in an office setting with Wah Z. We were talking about the spiritual work that had to be done in ECKANKAR, and he said the part I had to play in this work was unique, even for ECKANKAR. Then I saw myself with Wah Z in a cottage garden. All around the garden was a thick privet hedge, with just a tiny overgrown gate that was the entrance into the garden in which stood a little white cottage. Wah Z and I had a spade each and some cutters for cutting the hedge. Together, we started to remove the gate and also part of the hedge, until we had made an opening large enough for three cars to pass through side by side at the same time. I knew Wah Z was showing me symbolically how I was being opened up for the ECK to work through me; I was being made into a bigger channel for the work I have to do.

Then the scene changed again, the hedge had become a stonewall with two white marble pillars on which swung two wrought-iron gates painted black. The opening was as large as the hole Wah Z and I had made in the hedge, but the garden and cottage had disappeared. All there was to see was a light white mist on one side of the gate and a golden light on the other side. Then, Wah Z said this was showing me that, in the part I had to play in ECK, I would be a gateway to heaven for some people. I asked him how this could be so, for I was nothing special. Wah Z then reminded me of an earlier experience where I was given the name of Phoo Lin, The Light Giver, and that Wah Z himself had placed the light within me so that I could help those souls who come to me, in the service of ECK and the Mahanta, to find the path.

January 16, 1995 - Being Accepted Into the Vairagi Order

While sitting in meditation (using my secret words) I recalled the experience I had the other day, where a figure of what I now understand to be the SUGMAD came from out of a large sun and spoke to me in the presence of Wah Z. As I sat looking at the sun again today, from each side of it, and at a level below its centre, a line of figures holding hands came towards me. They looked like the paper-chain men we used to cut out of paper when young. They had no visible features other than their human shape and all were of the colour of the sun. They started to form a circle around me, and when it was completed, another one was formed around the first one. This went on until there were six circles surrounding me, each one encompassing the other, with me alone in the middle. I was looking around for Wah Z, when he appeared outside of the circle on the left hand side of the sun. He was gigantic. The sun looked like a ball of about three feet in diameter at a level with his head. Master was wearing black socks and trousers with a white shirt rolled up at the sleeves to his elbows and a thin black tie. He was dressed like this in the previous experience, and he was sitting in a crossed-leg position. I felt at ease now. I could see Master and just watched what was taking place around me.

When the circles had been formed, a voice, which was more of a strong impression than a spoken word, said, "THE VAIRAGI WELCOME YOU INTO THEIR MIDST." As I started to understand what it was all meaning, another impression of a voice came from the sun, it said "ONE MORE SON HAS RETURNED. I AM WELL PLEASED." I looked towards Wah Z, who was smiling, not at me in particular, but at all that was taking place. And this is a hard thing to describe now. From the sun I could feel waves of love that were washing over Wah Z. I can now understand the meaning of bathing in GOD's love.

July 21, 1995 - Beginning the Work of Spreading the Light of GOD

While doing the spiritual exercise of looking for the light, as given in the ECK Discourse No. 11, the Master Wah Z appeared within holding out his cupped hands in front of him. He walked towards me and, at the same time, opened his hands. The light that came from his hands was tremendously bright, and, as he stopped directly in front of me, he said:

TAKE THIS LIGHT THAT I OFFER YOU. I NOW COMMIS-SION YOU TO START YOUR WORK. SPREAD THIS LIGHT WHEREVER YOU NOW GO IN MY NAME.

After saying this, he showed me what looked like a huge oval diamond in his hand; it was what was giving out the light. He then placed the diamond to my forehead and, as he did so, I felt a powerful surge of light and energy flowing through my body. It made me feel as though I had been super-charged with an electric current and, at the same time, I was blinded by the light. The experience ended after this, and because it was so quick and subtle, I took it into contemplation, asking the Master if it was correct and that I had not made a mistake. Master assured me that all was proper and correct, and he added these words, "SERVICE IS A PRECIOUS JEWEL AND THROUGH THE JEWEL OF SERVICE THE LIGHT OF GOD SHINES."

March 28, 1996 - On Meeting the Spiritual Counsel (Nine Silent Ones) and Being Tested

While in contemplation, using my secret words (Master is making me experiment with words very frequently), I soon found myself with Wah Z, standing in a very bright light. Master led me to an ordinary looking chair and let me sit down. As soon as I sat, Master walked a few steps away from me, and then from within the light, nine shapes of a human form appeared. These forms were of the same bright light, they had no features. They were all behind a long crescent-shaped desk to which I was facing. The Master and I appeared as we do in the physical body. I thought of the Nine Silent Ones as they appeared in front of me and, as I thought this, I was told that it was the Spiritual Council.

I knew I was being asked questions, but I cannot recall what was asked or what I said. I did have the impression that it was to do with serving ECKANKAR. After the questions, the nine forms made a circle around me, at this point, I could not see Master anymore and my point of view changed to where I was looking down on myself in the circle of light. I could experience being in the circle and watching myself at the same time. The light then closed in on me, growing tighter and tighter around me. I was being squeezed by a great force. As the force grew stronger, I was then shot upwards at a great speed, like a bar of soap when squeezed out of wet hands. Then the experience ended. It was very subtle; therefore, I'm going to try it again in my afternoon sitting to see if I can have it made clearer.

Sitting again this afternoon, I went into contemplation, using my secret words, and soon saw a repeat of what I had experienced this morning. It was like watching a film within. This time Wah Z gave me an explanation: "As the Council of Nine are responsible for controlling the flow of ECK, they also play a part in helping to choose those who are going to be used as a channel for the ECK. At different stages you have been tested, this was just one more for you which you've come through. The Nine surrounding you in the light, which then shot you upwards, is the ECK being channeled to give you a boost upwards towards your goal of GOD realization and Mastership. Have no worries, all is well with you."

September 19, 1996 - Accepting My Experiences and Role as a Master in the Bourchakoum.[4]

With this new experience of being in the Bourchakoun, I asked Master while in contemplation why my spiritual progress had gone further than I was first told it would. He answered me this way:

> When your former Master told you that the path you were on was one of Mastership, it made sense to you, because of all that you were going through spiritually. As you progressed, he told you that in this lifetime you would be at the level of a Master. This made it

easier for you to accept the high experiences in Anami with your Master without becoming too unbalanced.

When you came to ECKANKAR, expecting your experiences to slow down, your progress continued without any let up. Again you were able to cope with all this and still keep a presence of normality. These experiences in ECK opened you up to the point where you could be told of your position in the Bourchakoun without any shock to you or your system. Remember, you have always been very discriminating on the paths you've walked, and this had to be taken into account. Discrimination is needed, of this there is no doubt, but you have the tendency to hold yourself back, because you find it hard to accept that this can happen to you.

You were given an experience only a short while ago, where you saw yourself in the centre of a circle of ECK Masters, and the light was coming from you to them. It was clearly showing you what your position was, but you were still reluctant to accept it, to the point where you telephoned the ECK RESA and asked for her guidance. She explained its true meaning for you, then you accepted it, for it confirmed what you had thought but found hard to accept.

If from the start you had been told the full truth, you would not have been able to accept and believe in it or yourself, so you were taken a step at a time through these stages, as are all who walk the spiritual path. I did give you a hint that something was going to happen when I told you that things were going to take place this year which would be beyond your imagination. Your son's surprise decision to join the army was not the only one of these, as you now know. It has not been easy for you, but you have done well and we are all pleased with you. May the blessings be.

October 22, 1996 - On The Prospect of Receiving the Rod Of ECK Power (Meeting with Masters)

For the last week, I have had experiences concerning the Rod of ECK Power. In these, I am always made to feel that I am going to receive it, but I have never really accepted any of this, and am always asking for clarification. Today, while in contemplation using my secret words, I found myself staying at the home of Wah Z and His wife. Because I had not brought many clothes with me, Wah Z gave me a maroon-coloured robe to wear, and then led me to some patio doors that faced onto a garden.

He indicated for me to step through, and, as I did, the scene changed to where I was following Master Rebazar, who was leading me along a very rocky path towards a white monastery-type of building with red-tiled roofs. It was constructed at the base of some huge, vertical rock faces and was on different levels with at least four round turrets, whose roofs were tapering to form a point like a sharpened pencil, though, where it joined the turret, there was an overhang. A zigzag slope led up to the front of the building, and there to meet us was Sri Fubbi Quantz, Sri Lai Tsi, Sri Yaubl Sacabi, Sri Gopal Das, and a few more whom I did not recognise.

As I came to each one in turn, they smiled and gave a nod with their heads to point me in the direction of a door. Coming to the door, I passed through, and the Masters followed. Inside, the room was empty except in its centre, coming down through the ceiling and disappearing into the floor, was a beam of brilliant white light of about four inches in diameter. I was told to take hold of this, for this was the Rod of ECK Power, and that this was a privilege being given to me by GOD. I took hold of the Rod, though I felt nothing, and was told these words: "You now hold GOD's heart in your hands." The experience then ended after lasting for twenty minutes.

Now I understood the meaning of the experiences of the last week, and that I was being given the Rod of ECK Power, but only as a gift from GOD, not as one who is going to accept it as the Mahanta. I looked in the ECKANKAR Dictionary and read the following words: "Rod of ECK Power: The power of the WORD of GOD, which is given to that being who has been chosen by the SUGMAD, as It descends and enters into the new Living Eck Master. The power makes Him the actual MANIFESTATION of GOD at the rites or the initiation of accepting the Rod of ECK Power; The power of the Mahanta Consciousness." This would also explain why I never felt anything as I held the Rod of ECK Power. It was Master's way of showing me it was a gift, not that I was going to receive it.

November 4, 1996 - Meeting With Master Yaubl Sacabi on Being a Living Temple Of Truth

Continuing with the same spiritual exercise, I now put my attention on the spiritual city of Agam Des and Master Yaubl Sacabi. It was a few moments though before I had any movement from within. As always, I used my secret words to test everything and I now found myself standing in front of Wah Z and Master Sacabi. As Master Sacabi took my hands in His, we were both instantly standing on the surface of a barren moon, looking like the physical moon that we see at night. All around us in a dark sky were worlds upon worlds — as far as I could see. Master Sacabi then said:

All places that you go to become sanctified by your presence. Wherever true devotion is, that place becomes holy. Even this barren moon has now life just by your presence alone. For as a channel for the ECK, IT will flow through you, going out to all and everything, for the ECK is the life force of all GOD's creations. You are now the living Temple of Truth, and it's your mission to take this truth to others.

Each ECK Temple of Golden Wisdom is a step up on the path towards GOD-realization. You are now a Temple for all truth, and, as that living Temple of Truth, you must go to those who are as yet unable to gain access to these Temples of learning and help them understand. Not everyone will accept what you say, nor will they want the help that you can offer, but never forget this, by your presence alone the ECK will radiate from you as ITS channel, and all will be given spiritual upliftment, though they may remain ignorant of it. In your last two visits to the other Temples, you've been shown how, as a channel, the ECK will work through you. Please do not doubt yourself and what is taking place. Accept what is being given to you, and that you are a living Temple of Truth, as are all, but you have now come to the stage of realisation of your true self. May the Blessings Be.

August 14, 1998 - On First Meeting the Nine Silent Ones

On the 12th and 13th, while sitting in contemplation, a group of strange-looking people came to me within. They stood about seven to eight feet tall, lean in build, with heads that were normal in width but about eighteen inches in length, tapering to a rather sharp point at the crown. They had no ears that I could see, their eyes were round and large, brown in colour, and they had a gaunt appearance about them. The eyes, nose, and mouth were positioned relatively the same as ours, but most of the head mass was above the eyebrows. They had no bodily hair, and a single white gown covered their body, yet at the same time it appeared to be their body, as though both were one and the same. Nothing was said to me on both occasions, yet I had a strong impression I was in the presence of the Nine Silent Ones.

Today, while trying to find a possible description of them to help confirm this experience, I found a passage in the *Shariyat-Ki-SUGMAD* (Book One, page 14) that said, "If he who seeks is a Chela of a Vi-Guru, he cannot be deceived by the Kal Niranjan. If he has not the armour of Spirit he can be misled." This could be Master giving me the answer through the Golden Tongued Wisdom; all the same I shall take this within to see if it can be explained further. I have been in front of these Nine before. Then their appearance was of a human form but with no features....

September 4, 1998 - Seeing the Cosmic Breath of GOD

While contemplating on the gaze of the Master and using my secret words to test everything, I soon found myself looking down on a large range of mountains. Then my position changed to where I was standing on these mountains, which, by now, were as small as pebbles under my feet. At the same time I was also able to watch myself from above. I was wearing a simple white, full-length gown, and my size was growing rapidly yet smoothly. Soon I was sitting crossed-leg in a black, star-filled sky.

Each time I breathed in, all the stars and planets in the sky were drawn into me by my breath, then as I breathed out they were expelled back into the black sky, giving the appearance of being in space. The moment I thought of what was happening, I was told this:

> This is what you are developing into, you are becoming without limit as soul, and soul is as GOD in likeness. What you are seeing is the cosmic breath of GOD. Each breath in destroys creation, each one out recreates it. These are the cosmic days and nights of the worlds of GOD, known better to you as the Yugas. This again is to help you understand better and accept that which you are becoming.

September 15, 1999 - The Role I Am to Play in ECK

Doing the same exercise as yesterday, as I concentrated on the star, a large golden figure emerged from it and sped across the sky. I recognised the figure immediately as Mercury, the winged messenger of the GODS, and once more the impression that it was the role that I am to play in ECKANKAR was given to me.

November 20, 1999 - On Traveling With Wah Z To A Temple and Resolving Inner Doubts

Doing this month's exercise, today, as yesterday, it started out differently. Once more, I was taken by Wah Z to where a large Temple, made from crystal, standing at the end of a narrow valley. Leading to the Temple, the valley bottom was covered in a fine mud tilth, which we had to walk through. As we neared the Temple, the light coming from it grew brighter and brighter. I had the impression that the mud I was walking through was symbolic of my karma, which was being reduced to a finer condition, and the light from the Temple was the light of Spirit of which I was now nearing. Before reaching the Temple, I stopped and told Wah Z that I would not go any further until both aspects of the path balanced out, i.e., the material and the spiritual. Wah Z tried to urge me on, but I would not take another step forward. I said that unless I started to see both sides of the path working in my life, then I would go no further, that, unless I had the belief in what I was doing, I could no longer go along with it. Wah Z once more tried to urge me on, and at the same time Rebazar Tarzs and the other ECK Masters came and watched to see if I would carry on, but I refused, saying at the same time, "If I myself have doubts about what I am to teach, I am no more than a hypocrite and hypocrisy is false."

After further urging from Wah Z, I once more said, "'Tis better to stumble in the darkness of truth than to see clearly in the light of falsehood."

I then walked away and sat down in contemplation. Here I was soon joined by Paul Twitchell, who came and sat with me. I am not sure if all this is a test, but as things are, I am not going any further till I feel right about them.

July 12, 2001 - On Traveling to the Temple of ECK with Rebazar Tarzs

While in contemplation, I saw myself in a rocky mountain setting. My physical size was huge, a hundred feet or more. Below me, I could see minute figures of Sri Rebazar Tarzs and Sri Yaubl Sacabi, with a few more figures that I did not recognise. I knelt down to touch them, I was feeling very embarrassed at seeing myself so large and towering above these great Masters. At this point, Rebazar appeared at my side, being the same size now as myself, and touching me on the shoulder. He said, "Rise up." Then He said, "Do not feel embarrassed with yourself, it is only the negative power trying to upset you. Because you, yourself, are finding it hard to accept what you are becoming, you are leaving yourself open to doubt, this the negative power is using against you. Ignore it; accept what has happened to you and where it is going to lead. By doing so, the negative's power will be weakened, and its effects on you will be reduced."

Then I found myself with Rebazar, both of us huge in size again. We were crouched over the ruins of a Cistercian Abbey, one I'd been to see only a few days earlier. Rebazar was brushing his hand over the ruin. Beneath his hand, it looked like a model. While doing this, he said, "It is not the temples that we need to build, but the devotion that filled them."

Once more the scene changed, and I found myself at the ECK Temple in America. Here I was being shown around the grounds by a group of people I knew to be responsible for the running of the Temple. A woman came up to me and said, "Do you not think that we have created a beautiful temple for GOD, and that HE would be pleased with it?" At this point, I saw an ant crawling in the grass. Picking it up, I showed it to her and said, "This tiny ant is a greater temple to GOD than one any man can build. Within this tiny physical temple is GOD HIMSELF. Within the stone temple, there is only the atmosphere of practised devotion. One contains the essence of devotion the other contains the REAL thing. To lose sight of this truth is to be lost in the illusion. When we have lost sight of this truth, the temples we build are only adding to the illusion, and, though we are building them in our devotion to GOD, they are becoming a stumbling block on our path to GOD. They become self-defeating."

August 8, 2001 (Afternoon sitting) - Why the Journal Must be Sent to Sri Harold Klemp

Asking again for answers to my questions from this morning in regards to the Cave of Tomsk, and its purpose that now replaces the site of the Oracle of Tirmer at the handing over of the Rod of ECK Power, Sri Yaubl Sacabi came through and said, "Due to the worsening effects of the conditions in Tibet and the world in general, this ceremony will now take place in the inner planes at the Cave of Tomsk." He then went on to explain the fourteenth initiation, and why it is to be given, despite Sri Harold saying that he will be followed by five or seven ECK Masters of the twelfth initiation. Sri Yaubl Sacabi said, "This has been decided to be given because of the falling level of power under Sri Harold. It is the boost that the movement needs to raise the level up again and enable it to go forward into the new phase of development. The difference that you are aware of between the inner and outer Master is caused by this, the two are no longer in tune with each other. The sending of your journal to Sri Harold will be his wake-up call to let him know to prepare to stand down. He has been informed that notification will be coming to him over this matter. Have no fears; all is well with you."

After writing this down, I was given the impression of "the Council of The Nine."

August 11, 2001

Taking the question to the SUGMAD in contemplation of whether ECKANKAR should remain calling itself a religion or not, I was given the following answer: "MY path is that of truth, the illuminated way as spoken of by Paul. ECKANKAR is not, was not, and never will be a religion. It is ever changing to meet the needs of humanity's evolving consciousness, it is the way of the eternal, the SHARIYAT-KI-SUG-MAD." I then asked by what name it could be called in the new phase to come, I was given: "ECKANKAR is a Spiritual philosophy in the way of the Eternal Light and Sound of GOD."

September 17, 2001 (Second morning sitting) - On Transference of the Rod of ECK Power

9:00 A.M.: Since the experience of September 15, 2001, when told the outer ceremony of the transference of the Rod of ECK Power may not take place on the outer, I have been asking why this may be so, though for a while, I've had the feeling of knowing the answer. Still asking for an answer, I was told:

> The outer ceremony will depend on whether Sri Harold accepts what is in front of him. . . . Whether or not he will now recognise you as the rightful successor remains to be seen. Irrespective of his actions, the inner ceremony will go ahead when the time is right.

This is one more reason why the ceremony has been changed. Whichever way it goes, you are going to have a hard time. . . .

You will know what to do after the ceremony has taken place, for with this will come even greater awareness. I know of your fears, I feel them MYSELF; I know of your tears, I weep with you; and yet I know of your strength, for what you hold to be true. Others before you have feared when called to this work. Yet, by writing this down, you have taken a great step forward in its acceptance, you have brought into being the truth that you hold inside. To doubt yourself is to doubt ME, please never do that, for I am always as YOU.

12:00 Noon: Sitting once more in contemplation, I soon saw myself within standing alone. Then the Nine Silent Ones came and formed a circle around me, facing me. Then they turned their backs on me and joined hands, still forming a circle, with me in the middle. As they did this, I was given this impression, "They are looking out for you." After this, the experience ended. In this experience, the Nine Silent Ones appeared in the form that I've seen them in before.

October 3, 2001 - On Meeting Chungchok, Spokesperson for Nine Silent Ones

8:30 A.M. Second morning sitting: Over eighteen months ago, I was told the name of Chungchok while in contemplation. It was not a name for me to use, that I understood inwardly. Though I tried many times to get an understanding of this name, nothing came through, so I wrote it down on a small piece of paper to keep. After talking with a friend yesterday, I mentioned having this name, though at the time I could not recall it properly. Having found the name I'd written down, today I used it in contemplation to see if I could find anything about it.

Going into a sitting using the name Chungchok as my mantra, this experience started: Very soon, on the inner, I found myself with the Nine Silent Ones. One of them came forward and placed a light blue cloak upon me. As He did so, I received the impression that he was Chungchok, the spokesman for the Nine. Two of the others also came up and helped settle the cloak upon me. These Nine were as I've described them before; seven to eight feet tall, large almond-shaped heads, long thin arms and fingers. The feeling of love and tenderness was overwhelming; their touch was the most gentle to experience. Far from being cold and aloof, these Beings were love itself.

Through this experience I was moved deeply to tears. While in the experience, I asked (by thought) why this was, for I had read that these Silent Ones are aloof and distant. Here I was told:

The nearer to GOD one is, the more one reflects love.

After this, the experience ended. I called my friend to tell her of this experience. She's been a tower of strength for me through all this, and she asked if this Chungchok was the same being as the one called Tom in a book she has which talks of the Council of the Nine. After a cup of tea and collecting myself, I took this question back into contemplation and found myself once more with the Silent Ones. I addressed the One I knew as Chungchok, though they all looked alike, and asked him if he was Tom from the book that Mary has which mentions this Council of Nine. Master Chungchok just bent over to bring his face closer to mine and said:

> I am Chungchok, I am Tom, and I am also Graham. I am all that there is, and so, dear one, are you, for all is ONE. The use of words, by their nature of terminology, causes differentiation. Are not words used to describe different things? As soon as words are used descriptively, they bring separateness to those who listen without the experience of Being and Knowing. You yourself know how words fail to convey the Being and Knowing of your own experiences. That which you put into words is not the greater part of the experience, it is only the manifestation of the experience. The Being and Knowing that comes from them cannot be described. Therefore, to answer your question I must know from which viewpoint you are asking it. If you are asking from the viewpoint of Being and Knowing, then, yes, I am Tom. But if you are asking from the viewpoint of NOT Being and Knowing, then no, I am not that Tom. The answer to this question, as to all questions, lies in the understanding of the questioner. With Being and Knowing, there is only the ONE; without understanding there is separateness.
>
> Now I'll ask you a question: what answer would you have me give you that would not cause separateness and yet all could understand? Each plane to some degree reflects the truth of the plane above it. Passing through each plane, one eventually comes to the Reality of the Reflected Image. You, my dear one, see the True and Real Image; others see only the reflection. But the reflection can only exist because of the Real Image. And to the degree of its reflection it exists. Now does this answer your question without causing separateness?

After saying these words, the experience ended.

October 6, 2001 - The Nine Silent Ones on Temples and other Concepts

Trying to find an answer to the question about the Nine Silent Ones, the host of Silent Travellers spoken of in ECKANKAR, and also the Council of Nine mentioned in books outside the teachings of ECKANKAR, I found myself unable to sleep. Going downstairs to sit in contemplation, still nothing came through. At about 8:15 A.M., I started to sit again, this time asking Master Chungchok for his help. The Master came through and said:

> Within this host of Silent Travellers, as spoken of in ECKANKAR, this Council of Nine exists, they are the Nine Silent Ones. There has been a mystical connotation put into all this that has damaged the simple truth concerning us. The Council of Nine and the Nine Silent Ones are the same. There is nothing mysterious about this Council and it is not separate from all the other Silent Travellers. Let us remove the mystery and see the truth for what it is. Like any large organisation, there are managing directors, managers, assistant managers, foremen, and charge hands, to name but a few of your word titles, that help in the over all running of a company. On the same principle, we Silent Ones carry out our role. This Council of Nine, or the Nine Silent Ones, depending on your understanding, is not an elite body selected for their superior ability above the rest. We voluntarily take on the role of being a part of this Council purely to help in the running of things. At any time, any one of us can withdraw from this Council and his place is filled by another Silent Traveller who, as of his own free will, offered to help in this way. As in the structure of a large company, there are those at the top and those at the bottom.
>
> The decisions taken at the top are passed down through the different levels of managerial staff until they are received at the lowest level. Hence, the decisions at the top are reflected at the bottom to a certain degree, and in varying degrees as it passes through each level of management. This is what I meant when I explained to you that each plane reflects to some degree the truth of the plane above it and, in its reflection, there is a reality. Where we differ in our structure to that of a human one is that we see each other as equals, no matter what role or position each one of us may hold. We take on these roles of our own free will. There is no top manager or bottom labourer, we know we are all ONE, and treat each other accordingly. We are open to all of creation, and whatever understanding and belief. We serve GOD by serving HIS creation that creation may know its CREATOR. There is no need for any mystery to surround us; we are here to serve and to serve lovingly all that is.

Master Chungchok then said:

> May I also take this opportunity to dispel another wrongly veiled mystery? There are no Temples of Golden Wisdom as written in some teachings. These so-called Temples are only schools of learning open to all who can enter them according to their ability. These schools are not hidden or secret in the mystical sense of the word. It is simply that until one is able to enter a school, one cannot attend it. You have the same principle in your world. In the inner worlds, these schools (FOR ALL) have their own vibratory field which pre-

vents them from being seen by those not of the same vibratory level.

The schools you visited as caves in the lower worlds until Rebazar showed you the true reality behind this fascia; it was an easy way to show you how until one is tuned into the same vibratory field of these schools one cannot see them. But this is not a mystery; it is the natural law that works throughout all of creation. Temple or school, pick the name for them that suits you, but do not wrap them in mystery to help endorse a teaching. Rather, unwrap them in the light of understanding that all may know of them and, by whatever path, teaching or way they choose to come, let them come and learn of their CREATOR and their oneness with all.

At this point, it finished, and I went to answer nature's call. While tending to nature, Master Chungchok came back and said:

Let us call these Temples and schools "Centres of Learning for All." This way, no teaching can limit access to them through their own practises. A teaching, as also the teacher, is there to remove limitations not impose them, though certain practises have to be followed to enable one to go beyond limits.
Chungchok

This now raised another question, so sitting in the afternoon I asked this: "If the inner teacher is Xanxangme and not Sri Harold, why then was I not shown these things in the light of what is now being explained?" I was answered:

It kept things within the idiom of the teaching of ECKANKAR and helped to spin the mystical intrigue. Being within the teachings as they are, and now seeing them in a truer light, you are in a better position to understand the confusion that many in this teaching will find themselves in.

October 8, 2001 – The Rod of ECK Power and Mahanta (Explained)

Given while in contemplation. I had not asked any questions to start this off.

Paul Twitchell's sudden death was not untimely from the point of view of spirit. It was brought about on purpose to end the falsity of what he had started. Twitchell had the ability to lead, but he let himself get in the way. . . . Becoming unbalanced is a sign of not being able to cope with what is coming through, and that too much is coming through shows a lack of inner guidance and control from whoever is supposed to be the guide.

Anyone can open up to spirit but to do this in a proper way and unfold according to one's ability is best done under a true teacher.

> He himself knows what to give the seeker the exposure to and in what quantity so that a balance is always maintained. The truth that could have been behind ECKANKAR is ebbing away, many are aware of this already. One more myth can now go, there is no such thing as the Rod of ECK Power. As you have rightly said, all true Masters are ONE. This so-called Mahanta consciousness is just one more write up, woven into the ECKANKAR teachings by Twitchell.
>
> Before you ask me, I know what your next question is going to be, and I have my answer here for you: you were given the experiences with the so-called Rod of ECK Power because it was written into the teachings. If we had laid all this on you from the start, your balance would have gone, hence, as true to spirituality under a true teacher, it was given a step at a time to unfold your ability to accept it all, for there is a lot to have to accept.

After this experience, I asked who it was that was speaking to me, for I had no impression of any personality or name. Asking this, I was answered:

> You need names and personalities after all this? Where is your oneness with all? That which is speaking to you is nothing more than your own true inner self, the ONE in ALL. Call it that still, inner voice of GOD, or a known Master, or one unknown, it is THE ALL in THE ONE, therefore all the same. Call this inner voice Xanxangme if you like, or Rebazar Tarzs, or Chungchok. Whatever name you give to it, it is still YOU when understood from the highest view. But I understand the need to explain this to others, so tell them:
>
> I am the voice of the GOD that you are and the voice of the GOD all others shall be. Remember, whatever names or personalities used in teaching others to help them understand more easily the ways of spirit, the names and personalities should be understood to be THE ONE in ALL.

Reflections on the Journal

While we waited for a response from the Living Eck Master, I had many discussions with Graham about his journal. I considered him to be sincere and was convinced of his belief in these experiences. As I had expressed in my first letter to Harold, in which I introduced the journal and explained my decision to send it to him, its contents deserved review by the Living Eck Master. There were many questions, however, that I intended to place before Graham.

Inner Experiences Geared to the Individual's Needs

In some respects, the records of Graham's inner experiences sounded self-serving, with innumerable platitudes about his position in the spiritual worlds and the role he was to play in Eckankar. But it was not the self-serving passages that were troubling. Every person's inner experiences are woven out of the fabric of present and past life experiences and consist of what is needed to move them along the path to God. Graham's apparent lack of confidence in some of his experiences and in the role that he was to play obviously called for the kind of embellishment and platitudes that he received. Rather, it was the conflict between these statements and his earlier inner guidance regarding the equal nature and oneness of all souls that was disturbing.

Each person is a spark of God and possesses all of the attributes of the divine. However, when one begins to see or be seen in a comparative way, a hierarchy is constructed that is contrary to the idea of placing no one above or below another soul. Ultimately, Graham faithfully recorded what he heard and observed. He was aware that others would be highly skeptical of his work and was diligent in testing and recording everything as accurately as he could.

Graham would sometimes have two or three multi-hour meditation sessions per day. Having been injured on the job some years earlier, he received government support for his medical condition, allowing him to pursue his spiritual path. So, as we have seen, every negative has its corresponding positive: Graham's injury gave him the time to devote to his spiritual study and meditation. I knew firsthand of the impact that devoting concentrated amounts of time on meditation could have on inner experiences.

As discussed earlier, I was enthralled by Paul's stories in *The Tiger's Fang*. I purchased every book I could find on the subject and followed their instructions. I was eventually drawn out of my body and propelled into the inner worlds for hours on end. The experiences I had and the lessons I learned laid the foundation for my understanding of the inner truths and the role I was to play as one of the major speakers in the teaching of Eckankar. It is therefore not surprising that Graham would have these experiences — and in the frequency and degree he described. Few have the opportunity to dedicate the amount of time and concentration to spiritual development that Graham was able to devote. This was not an accident; Graham's writings have been the catalyst behind this book as well as for a sequence of events that will result in another channel for spiritual truth in the world.

On Achieving God-Realization

Another question posed to Graham dealt with an important aspect of Eckankar doctrine, which holds that no one could have the God-Realization experience except through the Mahanta, the Living Eck Master. I asked Graham that if this were true, how could he have had the God-Realization experience with his former Master that his journal describes? The answer to this question was to be revealed more clearly in the weeks and months following the transmittal of his journal to the Living Eck Master.

Eckankar books offer contradictory positions on this issue. While it is clearly Eckankar doctrine, as expressed in the *Shariyat-Ki-Sugmad*, that God-Realization can be achieved only through the Mahanta, the Living Eck Master, Paul's earlier writings express a contrary view:

> No ECK Master will retain his former relationship with a neophyte after the latter has become skilled in Soul Travel and has been established on the Fifth Plane, the plane of pure Soul.[5]

Supporting this view, Paul explicitly states that the role of the Master is to aid the individual to the level of the fifth plane, from which they will negotiate the remainder of the journey by themselves. Paul later points out that when consciousness has been expanded to the point where the individual can perceive the inner worlds of God and transcend time and space:

> [W]e will no longer need the Spiritual Traveler as a constant companion. He is then able to release us to our own responsibility and help others who are struggling to gain a foothold in the spiritual worlds. We are then on our own. . . . We are in the state of Self-Realization, and nothing is able to stop us from reaching the highest realm, which is God-Realization.[6]

Therefore, contrary to some parts of Eckankar doctrine but consistent with others, an individual *can* reach God-Realization without the intercession of the Mahanta, the Living Eck Master. This is apparently how Graham, even under Eckankar doctrine, was able to have had this experience prior to coming to Eckankar. It is also important to bear in mind that Darwin Gross was only a second initiate before becoming the second Living Eck Master.

Why did Graham Join Eckankar?

One of the tougher questions I posed to Graham was, if he had the God-Realization experience, why did he join Eckankar in the first place? After all, Eckankar was created as a path to lead soul to Self Realization, God-Realization, and to becoming a co-worker with God. Since Graham believed that he had already achieved God-Realization, why join? Equally, why would his spiritual master turn him over to the Living Eck Master?

His response to these questions was not immediately clear. He later revealed that, as his experiences in Eckankar grew, it became increasingly evident to him that he had been led to Eckankar because of a mission he chose or had been chosen to perform. This mission was revealed to him more clearly in the latter part of 2001. The first step in that process was to transmit his journal to the Living Eck Master. That is when our paths crossed.

Graham acknowledged that the fulfillment of his mission in Eckankar would only be possible if the Living Eck Master accepted the content of his journal. If not, then he believed his mission would take a different direction.

One of the more curious parts in Graham's journal (not included in this book) was a letter of resignation from Eckankar written in November of 1999. How, I would ask, could he consider, and in fact initiate, a resignation from Eckankar in light of the mission he believed he was being prepared to complete? Further, why would he, no longer a member of Eckankar, ask me to present these materials to the Mahanta, the Living Eck Master?

Graham determined to resign because he felt that the teaching was too restrictive. Yet, after a brief hiatus in his inner journeys, he soon had experiences that challenged him to accept the mission. As his journal subsequently reveals, he changed his mind on leaving Eckankar altogether and continued his training and preparation for what he believed to be his mission.

Having made the change on the inner, Graham overlooked the need to reverse his action in the outer. I suggested that he immediately apply for reinstatement so that he would be an active member. After considering the suggestion, he reapplied, and again became an active member of Eckankar.

I asked Graham what accounted for several gaps in the recording of his spiritual experiences, which sometimes lasted for months. He revealed that, after periods of receiving great insight and new spiritual energy, he often went through hiatuses, which allowed the lessons and the energies to be absorbed. In this discussion, however, he revealed an interesting additional point: that these experiences tended to come to him, rather than him creating them or projecting into them — the opposite of the inner journey as we normally understand it. I asked Graham whether or not he had received the inner training preparing him to work directly and consciously with chelas in the inner worlds and take them on journeys into spirit. He indicated that he had not, and that he did not at that moment feel capable of consciously projecting into the inner worlds of others at their invitation.

Implications of Contact with the Nine Silent Ones

Perhaps the most striking and important parts of Graham's journal are his encounters with the Nine Silent Ones. Without this phase in his spiritual unfolding, the inner worlds and the masters of Paul's universe would not have been revealed so dramatically. Chungchok's revelations about Paul's demise, the fabrication of the Rod of Eck Power, and Paul's invention of the concept of the Mahanta, strike at the very heart of Eckankar doctrine.

Equally remarkable in his account of the Nine Silent Ones is the dramatic elevation in content and tone. I was curious as to whether the revelations about Eckankar, its diminished power, its mistaken focus on temple building, and its movement towards a doctrinal religious organization, reflected what Graham felt about Eckankar or whether they were independent observations of a highly evolved soul in the personage of Chungchok. I asked Graham if he had heard about these issues before and also if he shared these opinions at the time he transcribed Chungchok's observations. The issue was whether these inner experiences merely reflected information and opinions that he already held, albeit from an ostensibly unimpeachable source.

He responded that he did in fact have questions and doubts. He had perceived a vast difference between the inner master and the outer master. This was evidenced most strikingly in the thin content of Harold's writings, in contrast to the wisdom expressed by Wah Z in the inner. Yet, Graham stressed that what came through from Chungchok was new and for the most part outside his knowledge of Eckankar. He was of the view that Harold would recognize what was being said by the Nine Silent Ones. Graham had been told that Harold was informed, on the inner, of the contents of his journal, and that it would be forthcoming.

The revelations of Chungchok, transcribed by Graham, were monumental in their implications for Eckankar. For this reason alone, his journal had to be brought to the Master's attention. As a High Initiate in Eckankar who had been contacted for assistance to deliver this journal to Harold, it was my responsibility to see that the Mahanta received it.

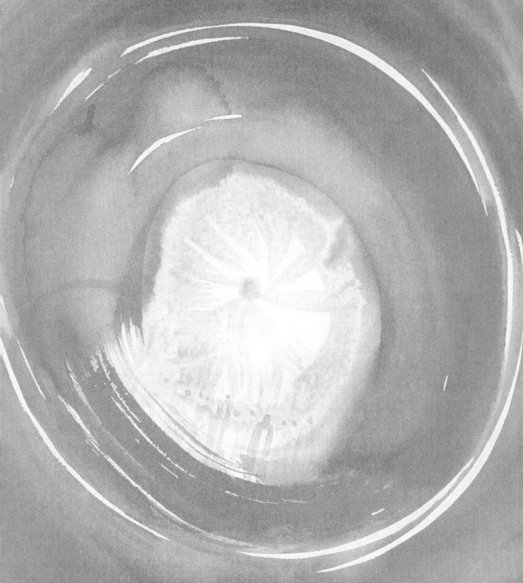

PART II

THE DISCOVERY

Chapter 5 — The Master Replies

Harold Klemp's Response to Me

Having sent the materials from the U.S. directly to the Living Eck Master at Eckankar headquarters in Minnesota, I was the first to receive a response. Here is Harold's letter to me.

ECKANKAR • P.O. Box 27300 • Minneapolis, Minnesota 55427
(952) 380-2200 • Fax (952) 380-2295 • www.eckankar.org

November 21, 2001

Ford T. Johnson

Dear Ford,

It causes me pain to see a higher initiate of ECK fall for such an old trick of Kal. The Mahanta, the Living ECK Master arranges for the announcement of his successor. No one else.

You are to stand aside from all ECK duties for six months. This includes service as an ECK Arahata, Initiator, ESA, and all other ECK offices.

In the meantime, to regain a solid footing in the teachings of ECK, you would do well to make a study of *The Shariyat-Ki-Sugmad*, Books One and Two. At the end of this six-month period of spiritual discipline, your future duties in ECK will receive a careful review.

You will remain a higher initiate if you undertake this discipline.

With love and spiritual blessings,

Harold

 Religion of the Light and Sound of God

After reading the letter carefully, I phoned Graham at midnight, England time. His son answered the phone, and soon Graham, drowsy but eager, got on to hear the verdict.

His first reaction was one of pain and hurt, not for the rejection of his work, but because of the action Harold had taken against me, for which he felt responsible. He certainly did not want to see anything harmful come to me for transmitting his journal. The following morning, at a more reasonable hour, I contacted Mary and eventually Lisa to let them know Harold's response and to find out if they had received anything themselves. They had not, probably due to delays in the mail. Because they had been mentioned in Graham's letter to Harold, they expected to hear something, either directly or through Graham.

Harold's response didn't shock me, nor did the discipline he imposed. I had been in a similar situation before and received a comparable discipline. But the brevity of his letter and his silence on the content of the journal surprised me. There was little explanation for my discipline, at least none that would help me, a chela, to understand the spiritual lesson I was expected to learn.

In a way, I think that Graham was relieved. He had followed his inner direction to present the journal to Harold, and that was all he felt "compelled" to do. He had already been told (through his inner experiences) that, either way, he would have a hard time. If Harold had relinquished his position, it would have been Graham's responsibility to reform Eckankar by correcting its falsities and distortions, a job Harold had actually started but, for whatever reasons, did not complete. But that is a subject for later chapters.

Prior to sending Graham's journal to Harold, I thought that, as a spiritual master who had traveled with Graham on the inner, he was aware of his spiritual encounters with Graham. Certainly, I thought, if Harold focused on them, he would recall them, see the truth in Graham's journal, and defer to the inner direction it contained. The possibility was not far-fetched. Darwin Gross, the previous Living Eck Master, had apparently stepped aside upon receiving inner nudges and a letter from Harold, which he read on stage before introducing him as the new Living Eck Master. I am sure that Darwin had other motives (after all, he retained the Mahantaship), but he nonetheless gave way to the new Living Eck Master.

Not so in Harold's case. No journal, not even one with admonitions from the Nine Silent Ones, would get him to give it serious thought. The mystery of why Harold did not recall his presence in Graham's inner experiences and rejected them as the Kal (in spite of the protection from such deceptions that is his avowed mission to provide), would, as events unfolded, become clear.

A Closer Look at the Letter

The first thing that struck me about Harold's letter was its focus on his position in Eckankar. Despite being the Mahanta, the Living Eck Master, responsible for the spiritual welfare of Eckists, he expressed no concern, spiritual or otherwise, for those who brought the journal to his attention in good faith. Second, there was no mention of the extensive spiritual experiences that ordinarily suggests remarkable development in a chela. The letter was solely about himself, strictly speaking, about his position in the organization.

The letter was highly accusatory and expressed disappointment for my failure to recognize an apparently obvious Kal (negative) trick. But what was the Kal trick? The only clue Harold provided was that only "the Living ECK Master arranges for the announcement of his successor." Was Harold saying that, because I had sent the journal, I had somehow announced a successor? Or was he saying that, because the journal referred to the possibility of someone else becoming the Mahanta, this constituted an announcement? Was the Kal trick the fact that someone presumed to raise the question of a successor? Or was it my decision that Graham's journal had sufficient merit to send it to Harold in the first place?

As to succession, the founder of Eckankar, Paul Twitchell, had written in the *Shariyat-Ki-Sugmad* that only the Living Eck Master named his successor. This was apparently the reference that Harold used as the basis of his decision that the journal was a Kal trick. Yet, succession after Paul did not follow this rule. Paul died suddenly, without naming a successor. Several months later, his wife, apparently in the dream state, was told the identity of the new Living Eck Master. Thus, by the standard Harold was applying, Gail Twitchell's dream must have been a Kal trick also, since it was an announcement made by someone other than the Living Eck Master.

As to the rejection of the deeper and more profound content of the journal, Harold's response was also confusing and his intentions unclear. Graham and I discussed it at length and ended with the opinion that the letter rejected the content of his journal and made a smooth transition of power impossible.

Because I was genuinely confused about the scope and intent of Harold's letter, I immediately began writing a response. As I did, I considered taking his statement at face value rather than risk reading something into it. He often gave very short and vague answers to questions. I never knew if he felt the answer was complete or if he meant to leave the person with something to ponder. But soon, another interpretation occurred to me. What if Harold was only concerned with the *manner* the information was brought to him, namely, that *I* presented it to him rather than Graham himself? If I had not been involved, it would have given Harold the opportunity to announce a succession himself, without third-party interference. Given the terseness of Harold's reply, it was possible to interpret it as focusing on the manner of presentation rather than the substance of Graham's work. I called Graham, Mary, and Lisa to offer my interpretation and to encourage everyone to be patient and not to react in anger or haste. I thought it was altogether possible that the Living Eck Master wanted to establish an independent line of communication with Graham. Although we thought this a possibility, no one thought it realistic. Nonetheless, everyone agreed to give it more time, to be neutral, and to wait and see what events transpired.

I proceeded to write my letter to Harold, as there were pressing issues on a range of responsibilities and obligations I had undertaken on behalf of Eckankar that required resolution. They were likely to change in light of my discipline. I communicated these and other concerns to the Living Eck Master in November 2001.

Because timing was so sensitive, I contacted one of Harold's assistants to ask if I could fax the letter. I had been invited to speak and already had scheduled a trip to Africa for a Regional Seminar in Port Harcourt, Nigeria in early December 2001 — there simply wasn't enough time to use the mail. I requested that she contact the Living Eck

Master to see if I should complete this obligation in light of the discipline. Here is my letter:

November 30, 2001

Dear Sri Harold,

Thank you for your letter of November 21. I will of course step aside from outer activities in ECKANKAR as you have directed. I feel nothing but love for you and for the ECK and ECKANKAR and never wish to do anything to cause harm or distress to anyone.

While I respect any decision that you make or discipline that you may direct, I request that you bear with me for a moment while I communicate my confusion about your decision. Almost 20 years ago, when Darwin had taken ECKANKAR materials to Oregon and I traveled there to ask him to return them and to end the discord that was tearing the organization apart, I wrote you a letter that expressed my conviction that Darwin, at least at that moment, seemed to want to work things out. I believe that subsequent to that, he did return the materials. The point of my bringing this up now is that my communication to you about that trip resulted in your imposing a similar discipline when you asked me at that time to step aside from the outer works. I believe that you felt that he had duped me and that I was somehow under his domination. This conclusion was totally incorrect, as I saw Darwin for what he was: someone who would draw the attention of the chelas away from their search for God to a selfish focus on himself and all the "wrongs" that he thought were being perpetuated against him.

Your sense that I was under his influence was incorrect, though at the time I understand [sic] your caution. However, the experience and the discipline were very useful as it taught me that the Mahanta the Living ECK Master is the heart and soul of ECKANKAR and not the outer organization, which was my misplaced motivation for going in the first place.

You assume here that I have "fallen" for this Kal trick. I have fallen for nothing except my sense of duty that you needed to see these materials and make your own judgment. This chela (Graham) followed the discourses that you sent him; practiced the spiritual exercises that you recommended; had numerous spiritual experiences (that you want us to have) and faithfully recording [sic] them. His experiences with Wah Z and the other ECK Masters are those that most chelas long to have. So when you say that it "pains you" that I would fall for this Kal trick, I am puzzled. Are you saying that the totality of his experiences, as recorded in these writings, are of the Kal — even though he tested them with the very words that you gave him to test them with? Or are you saying that only that part of his experiences that deal with statements about his possible role as the Mahanta are the Kal trick because only "The Living ECK Master arranges for the announcement of his successor?" Or is any communication to the Mahanta about succession, from any "outside" source, the trick of the Kal about which you are speaking? Certainly my sending the materials to you was not intended as an announcement. Indeed it was precisely because of the sensitivity of the materials that I undertook to bring them to your attention in the first place. I had scrupulously not discussed or shown these materials to anyone, not even my wife, Mary.

Graham did not know how to get these materials to you and that is why I was asked to do so. Aside from the two HIs in England that he initially contacted to seek assistance in getting these materials to you, no one else has seen them. Thus, no announcement of any kind has been made. As you rightly point out, that is not my role and I do not seek it nor have I attempted to undertake it.

I don't know if Graham considered the recording of his experiences as an announcement either. I think he felt, rightly or wrongly, that he had been directed to place them in front of you and that you would make any announce [sic] that you saw fit. If you did not, then you would reject them, as apparently you have. And that is fine; you are in the best position to judge the validity of his experiences as they relate to ECKANKAR. It is not my place to assess the truth or validity of these writings, especially as they pertain to the Mahantaship, which is why they were presented to you. Is there some fixed law about the manner in which such information should come to the Living ECK Master? I had always thought that the Living Word was dynamic and certainly not subject to any fixed limitations as might be stated or implied in Paul Twitchell's rendering of the *Shariyat Ki Sugmad*.

Sometimes it is the fate of the messenger to get shot. And I accept that fate if that is what you choose. But please do not confuse my sense of obligation to bring these materials to your attention, and keep them confidential, with my unquestioned acceptance of them. As soul, searching for truth, I do not close the door to any source but question and explore all input until I arrive at what is truth for me. Whatever is the succession of Mastership in ECKANKAR is a matter between you and the other ECK Masters. Keeping these materials confidential and bringing them to your attention, as I was asked to do, is precisely what I thought you would have wanted me to do.

On a more practical note, I am slated to go to Nigeria on Tuesday Dec. 4th to speak at the Regional Seminar. Needless to say, much preparation has gone into this and tickets and all arrangements are in place. There is also a Seminar in Chicago in January that has involved much publicity and effort on the part of the chelas in Ill. I am solid with the ECK and the ECK teachings. I read the Shariyat constantly and have been teaching a class on the Shariyat. I know that you are the Mahanta the Living

ECK Master, and I will continue to love and serve in any way that I can when I am allowed to. For now, I accept your discipline if you feel that this is best. I would like to be advised, however, on how best to handle this situation and what to say in canceling the many speaking engagement to which I have already agreed. Telling them that I have been asked to step aside does not trouble me. But to do so would raise many questions and create some confusion. It is not my intention or need to draw attention to myself.

There are many other Regionals and workshops that were planned latter [*sic*] in 2002. I can complete them and make no more commitments or I can cancel them. The Africa and Chicago trips are so close that they would create some real problems for the areas. I will call S to tell her of this verbally on Friday, as I need an answer rather quickly.

Finally, all that is important is one's love and commitment to serve Sugmad. I have no interest in titles or public acclaim. They are the most gross of illusions. I am comfortable with whatever you decide, because I control my love and my dedication to Sugmad and the ECK, and nothing from outside of me can or will affect that.

Yours in ECK,

Ford Johnson

Further Communications with the Mahanta

Harold's assistant called me the same day and indicated that I should proceed to the Nigerian Seminar and also complete the one in Chicago. After that, I should consider the discipline in effect. We discussed the impact of my pulling out of local activities in light of the fact I had conducted worship services twice monthly for many years. I was also concerned about keeping my word regarding future commitments. She suggested I say I was stepping aside "for personal reasons." I reluctantly agreed but felt uncomfortable about disingenuous language to explain my absence. The more I thought about it, the more uncomfortable I felt. Saying I had stepped aside for personal reasons, aside from being untrue, would misrepresent events. My departure from local activities would raise questions that I wanted to address honestly.

I wrote another letter to the Living Eck Master about these concerns but held off mailing it until I reflected more on the matter. There remained the possibility that Harold would establish independent communication with Graham. If my discipline was the price for this, then no letter would have been necessary. I was prepared to fall on my sword if my discipline was a way of getting me out of the picture. These factors suggested that I should wait before saying or doing anything more. After all, I would be out of the country for a week or more, and there was no rush to communicate all of this to local chelas. I still had to complete the African Seminar and the one in Chicago. I put the matter on hold and prepared for my trip.

During the seminar in Africa, I had time to consider the events of the preceding weeks and my possible response, but I was still troubled by Harold's reaction and its implications. While I saw benefits from the discipline — finally, I would have time to finish the books I had started — I did not understand Harold's reasoning. His actions were contrary to a key pronouncement in Eckankar taken from Paul's *Dialogues with the Master*:

> The true teachings do not discipline in anyway [*sic*]; do not set up duties or difficulties or tasks for teaching their disciples lessons or developing traits or good character.... They only ask that their word be heard and obeyed. Their mission on earth is to gather up Souls to be taken home again.[1]

When, at the Second Initiation, the chela is fully accepted into the teaching, the master promises he will never leave her, no matter what she may say or do. Indeed, the master proclaims that he is as close as her heartbeat, as near as her own breath. Yet Harold was pulling away. Or was he pushing me out the door?

I had seen Harold use his power before, especially when he felt his position was threatened. Darwin Gross, the previous Living Eck Master, once openly challenged Harold's position as leader of Eckankar, even after having given up the position and naming Harold the new Living Eck Master. For this act (and others, as we shall see), he was summarily excommunicated from the teaching and from the venerable order of Vairagi Masters. If this is what Harold did to a former Living Eck Master and Mahanta, clearly he was not afraid to use his power against anyone. I was not taking odds on my chances of withstanding his wrath if I did not get in line.

In spite of misgivings, I decided to make another attempt at honest, respectful communication with Harold. Perhaps he would help me to understand what I was to learn from these events. Up to that point, it made little sense, except as an act of control. Discipline is an act of love, intended to teach the student lessons that will enable him to learn, grow, and expand spiritual awareness. But for a discipline to be effective, its basis must be understood. The explanation that only the Living Eck Master can name his successor was not only superficial, but also suspiciously vague. Nonetheless, I chose to ask again.

I was not optimistic about receiving a response. In my experience, it was Harold's policy not to answer questions. Rather, he would "leave it up to spirit" to teach the needed lesson. Here is my second letter to Harold:

Sri Harold Klemp
The Mahanta the Living Eck Master

Ford Johnson
December 17, 2001

Dear Harold,

This letter is a follow up to my discussion with S on Friday, Nov. 31. Since then I have completed the Nigerian Regional at which F took over from J. There were some rough spots, but over all everything was smoothed out, and each person has assumed their new roles. My understanding is that I am to proceed to complete Chicago, which is in January, and then step aside from other speaking engagements.

Accordingly, I am writing a letter to the RESA, K that will be delivered shortly. I will formally resign from all outer positions as you have directed, which include the positions of Spiritual Services Coordinator in Washington, DC., Clergy for the second and fourth Sunday services each month, the *Shariyat Ki Sugmad* class that has been ongoing for more than one year, in addition to the numerous speaking engagements that had been planned for the coming year.

While I believe that I am as grounded in the ECK works as anyone in ECKANKAR, I shall never the less respect your request, and I will in fact study the *Shariyat Ki Sugmad* in even more detail and more closely than before. I must admit that I am still as confused about your decision today as the day I received your letter. I have raised the questions that your decision gave rise to in my last letter to you (attached). I suspect that I will be left to ponder the answers to these questions on my own (though a little help would be much appreciated).

The only aspect of the situation that I feel most uncomfortable about is S's suggestion to me to simply say, when asked why I am stepping aside, that it is for "personal reasons." Such an answer would be disingenuous if not simply untrue. I find it hard to believe that this suggestion came from you as opposed to S's attempt to be helpful in answering a question that I had posed in my last letter to you. Such an answer would imply that I am stepping aside voluntarily for reasons that I have determined out of my own free will. This would simply not be the truth and I would feel dishonest saying it. I have no problem with the discipline, but I do have a problem with not telling the truth. This answer might even give the impression that I am angry or upset with Eckankar or even that I have stepped off of the path. None of this would be the truth, and that is why I do not believe that this is the best way to explain the situation.

On the other hand, I have no intent to make a big thing of this. I simply want to be honest while protecting the sensitive content of what is at the heart of this matter. Accordingly, I would prefer to indicate, if asked or if required to give a reason (in the case of speaking engagements that I will have to break) that I was asked by the Living ECK Master to:

> "Stand aside from all ECK duties for six months. This includes service as an ECK Arahata, Initiator, ESA and all other ECK offices."

To the extent that it should become necessary to answer the question, why did this happened? I will only explain that:

> "in delivering some written materials from a chela about his spiritual experiences, the Master felt that I had fallen for 'an old trick of Kal' and that such discipline was in order."

This is the truth, and while confusing, it is the reality of the situation and the truth about what happened. I sincerely hope that this approach meets with your approval. If I have misread your intent or would be violating some other principle not known to me, I sincerely ask that you let me know.

I have preliminarily discussed this matter with my RESA who is concerned about the impact on chelas in the area, since I have never, in more than 25 years, voluntarily been inactive for any reason. Also, I have always lived by the principle, you have stressed, "Do what you say you are going to do." The discipline that you have instituted will not permit me to do this, with regards to the many ECK speaking engagements world wide that I had accepted. I have not yet informed them but will do so upon the completion of this round of communications.

As I was trying to learn more about discipline, from an ECK perspective, I ran across this passage in *Dialogues with the Master* page 172. I think that it bears directly on this situation:

> The true teachings do not discipline in anyway; do not set up duties or difficulties or tasks for teaching their disciples lessons or developing traits or good character, are not bothered with good or evil, neither will they care to [*sic*] much about the love of their disciple. They only ask that their word be heard and obeyed. Their mission on earth is to gather up Souls to be taken home again.

I am trying to hear, learn and obey the lesson but I simply do [not] understand what it is. I have spelled out the questions in my last letter (attached), the answers to which I have not been able to discern. Obviously, you know the answers, since it was your decision and reaction to the materials that I sent that prompted the discipline.

Harold, you have complete power with respect to Eckankar and the course of a chela's spiritual life in Eckankar. When you take the kind of action that you have taken, without explanation, it only promotes fear; fear of losing love; fear of losing ones standing with the person who matters most; and fear of the consequences of being honest with that person about everything. I can take the discipline, which is easy. But, at least help me to understand.

I am asking that you reconsider your decision. I do not believe that it serves my interest or the interest of the whole for me to sit in the corner for six months. Quite the contrary, I believe that it will confuse and hurt many more people than me, especially because confusion leads to fear. However, if on reflection you still think that this is in order, then I shall certainly comply and will do so willingly.

If I do not hear further from you or S, then I will continue forward with breaking my engagements and informing the appropriate people that I am stepping aside, as you have directed.

Love in ECK,

Ford Johnson

The Master's Response to Graham

Upon returning from Africa, I was eager to talk to Graham. I arrived into Dulles Airport late, so I waited until the next morning to call. Upon talking with him, I was surprised and disappointed at the Master's response to him. It speaks for itself:

ECKANKAR • P.O. Box 27300 • Minneapolis, Minnesota 55427
(952) 380-2200 • Fax (952) 380-2295 • www.eckankar.org

November 21, 2001

Graham Forsyth

Dear Graham,

In response to your letter and journal of inner experiences which led you to think you have received the Rod of ECK Power. You have not.

Your instincts were right not to believe this. The Kal misled you.

This happens more often than one would care to believe. People who fall for this trick and mislead others off the Path of ECK become responsible for the karma.

As a spiritual discipline you are put back to the First Circle of initiation and are to stand aside from all ECK duties for the present.

The experience you describe is a common test faced by Soul on Its journey back to God.

With blessings in ECK,

 Religion of the Light and Sound of God

This was quite an array of consequences for a chela who had followed the Master's instructions to the letter, but was perhaps too successful in the process. Harold's response raised a number of troubling issues, each of which must be taken up here. One of them involved a misstatement of fact:

> [Your] journal of inner experiences . . . led you to think that you have received the Rod of ECK Power. You have not.

Having read and reread Graham's journal, I am sure that he never claimed to have received the Rod of Eck Power. There is one reference to a passing of the Rod, but Graham is very careful to point out that it was purely symbolic and did not represent ascendancy to the leadership of Eckankar. Though receiving the Rod of Eck Power is held out as a future possibility, at no point in the journal does Graham say it occurred. Harold's statement reflects, at the very least, a faulty reading of the journal.

Harold continues with a statement that Graham's instincts to "disbelieve his experiences" were valid. But the experience to which Harold refers is Graham's belief that he had already received the Rod of Eck Power. This was never true. Therefore, Harold's conclusion that the Kal misled Graham into believing he had already received it, makes no sense: Graham never held this belief in the first place!

Harold then states:

> People who fall for this trick and mislead others off the Path of ECK become responsible for the Karma.

The reasoning here, which places responsibility on the chela, is dubious at best. To request assistance in placing a journal in front of the Living Eck Master, which is all Graham did, is certainly not intended to lead anyone off the path of Eck. If High Initiates are so fragile or gullible as to be drawn off the path of Eckankar by reading a chela's journal and placing it in front of the Master, then the position of High Initiate leaves much to be desired. Graham is not responsible for my karma — I am. I suspect other HIs feel the same. So why place this burden on the back of a second initiate, when the HIs are only doing their job by assisting? Certainly, this assertion by the Living Eck Master raises more questions than it answers.

Mary and Lisa did not fare any better than I did. Their discipline was similar to mine; their letters were virtually identical to mine. It seemed that if we wanted to stay in Eckankar, we would have to strengthen our indoctrination by studying the *Shariyat*, go into semi-seclusion and, perhaps most importantly, say nothing more of the matter. The next-to-last sentence of Harold's letter was ominous, even threatening: we could lose our initiations if we did not submit — quite a consequence for being duped by the Kal. Undoubtedly, imposing this discipline would send a message, far and wide, to chelas and High Initiates alike. The message was not one of spiritual love and concern. Rather, the message was that any direct or indirect action threatening or challenging the authority of the Living Eck Master, even if inner directed, would be dealt with harshly. But, as we shall see, this is precisely what the *Shariyat-Ki-Sugmad* calls for, despite its avowed purpose as a book about spiritual freedom and openness.

The Importance of Inner Experiences in Eckankar

Harold's rejection of Graham's spiritual journal and also the inner experiences Graham had with him brings into question one of Eckankar's tenets. Anyone who has studied Eckankar or talked to Eckists knows that it is the individual's grounding in his inner spiritual experiences with the Mahanta, the Living Eck Master that is the heart of the teaching. On this rock, the structure of Eckankar stands. From this rock, Eckankar has been able to withstand accusations and questions about its authenticity and veracity. Eckists believe that critics of Paul Twitchell and Eckankar simply do not understand them because they have not had the spiritual experiences that ground Eckist's beliefs. They have not seen the Living Eck Master in the inner worlds. They have not talked to spiritual masters, traveled to temples of golden wisdom, seen the light of God in the inner worlds, or heard the sounds of God on the inner planes. If they had, they would know the truth and the inner reality of this teaching.

It is a foundation of Eckankar that its founder, Paul Twitchell, gave the world an unassailable body of truth and wisdom. Eckists believe in the intrinsic truth of his teachings, regardless of their origins. This conviction makes up the second cornerstone of the Eckankar belief system.

As to the first cornerstone, the validity of inner spiritual experiences has always been authenticated by assurances from the Master, that if the charged words[2] are used, then the chela can rely on his experiences. This has also enabled Eckists to remain true to the path in spite of continuing challenges to its authenticity. But something goes amiss when these standards are applied to Graham's body of spiritual experiences, which are extraordinary to say the least. His body of work is at once:

- Copious
- Filled with light and sound

- Involves extensive inner contact with the Living Eck Master
- Describes spiritual encounters with most of the Eck Masters
- Depicts travels to the highest spiritual planes
- Is filled with new insights and wisdom
- Expands the Eck teachings by its portrayal of the Nine Silent Ones in great detail

Yet the Living Eck Master says that this journal is of the Kal! But, if these experiences are of the Kal, then what do we make of our own experiences? I have been blessed with numerous experiences in the inner worlds, with many spiritual masters. I have seen the light of God and heard the sounds of God on many inner planes. I *know* they are real. I have met with Harold (or his image) in the inner worlds of God. What am I to make of these experiences? Graham's experiences, in their recorded variety and depth, equal or exceed anything currently in Eckankar writings. If they are deceptions of the Kal, then what of Paul Twitchell's *The Tiger's Fang*, which contains a vivid and compelling account of his experiences in the inner worlds of God? What of everything that this teaching has used as the rationale for its existence and continuity throughout the years, namely, the validity of inner experiences? And what about the books written by other Eckists presenting their inner experiences, which were sanctioned by the Living Eck Master and published under Eckankar's auspices? And what of Harold's own experiences?

How can the Living Eck Master discount experiences involving himself, in the inner worlds in his radiant body, as experiences of the Kal? Is it because accepting them would compel him to accept the possibility that he is to relinquish his position? Is it because there is something fundamentally different in Graham's experiences that would enable the Living Eck Master to say that his experiences are of the negative, but that the experiences of other Eckists are not? These questions have been posed to the Living Eck Master. They simply cannot be ignored and must not be silenced.

Perhaps my own assessment of the journal's author is in order. Graham is one of the most genuine, sincere, and truthful individuals I have ever known. Furthermore, the two High Initiates in England who brought his works to my attention have known him throughout his time in Eckankar and also attest to his integrity and honesty. He is by all accounts filled with love and light. By sharing his journal, Graham has enabled each reader to peer deeply into his heart, enabling the reader to judge his honesty and integrity. Initially, he did not want to bring these writings forward. But like Jonah, he did so knowing he had a spiritual mission to fulfill.

And so Eckankar and the Living Eck Master face a fundamental dilemma they cannot brush aside. Experiences with the Living Eck Master in the inner worlds are the essence of the Eckankar teaching. They are the goal that every Eckist strives for, the goal of most of the spiritual exercises taught by the Living Eck Master and contained in Eckankar discourses and books. Yet, the Living Eck Master has rejected Graham's journal, the spiritual experiences of a seven-year period. He has done so in spite of the facts that:

- Graham's experiences occurred while reading *The ECK Discourses* written by the Living Eck Master

- He practiced the exercises set forth in those discourses

- He succeeded in his spiritual quest by having the very experiences that the Living Eck Master desired for each chela studying Eckankar.

Most of these experiences were with the Living Eck Master himself. Graham carefully checked his experiences with the tests and spiritual words recommended by the Master to ensure their validity. The teachings of Eckankar on this crucial matter make it clear that one should:

Be on guard, lest he who seeks without the Vi-Guru, the Supreme Guru, find those who only appear as the Holy One, claiming to be angels, or saints. Let none deceive the chela. If he who seeks is a chela of the Vi-Guru, he cannot be deceived by the Kal Niranjan.[3]

Without the clear vision of the Vi-Guru — he who is the Master — and the tests given by him, one cannot be assured of what he sees or hears.

Every Spiritual Traveler, or Vi-Guru, will give the Word to the chela to call upon the Master. If the vision fails to reply then it is false.[4]

The Conundrum

So, we have a conundrum. We cannot in good faith dismiss Graham's experiences: they happened, and they are proxies for our own experiences. What we learn about Eckankar and how the Living Eck Master deals with Graham and his experiences apply equally to us. How could it be otherwise?

As we ponder the puzzle of the Living Eck Master's rejection of Graham's experiences, we are left with several explanations. Bear in mind that solving this puzzle requires reconciliation with principles set forth in the Eckankar teachings, in addition to those quoted above. Chief among these are the following:

He takes them under his wing in loving care and is thereafter with them wherever they may be, whether it is on this plane or any of those in the heavenly worlds.[5]

Whenever the chela experiences any difficulty with himself such as falling into the negative trap, or even with Soul Travel, he should call upon the Master to assist him, or conduct him as the soul traveler to the spiritual worlds. *For the Living Master is bound by his mission to answer each and every call of this nature.*[6]

An even more disturbing question surfaces. Graham is one of the few chelas I know who has meticulously followed all the instructions Harold laid down in his discourses, particularly those involving the use of charged words to test the validity of inner experiences. Graham dutifully used these test words (the HU, Sugmad, Mahanta), as well as his own secret test words, yet the Living Eck Master claims that Graham's experiences are of the Kal. What are we to make of this?

How can any chela expect to be protected? What value are charged words to challenge inner experiences? Understanding why Harold, in an unexplained statement, nullifies all the guidance, instructions, and bedrock of this teaching with the flippant assertion that certain experiences are the works of the Kal, takes a better mind than mine, or at least one more in awe of organizational authority.

Again, we must examine the two rationales that have held Eckankar together and enabled it to withstand challenges. First are the spiritual experiences of each chela. Second is the intrinsic truth contained in the writings of Paul Twitchell. The Living Eck Master has challenged the first of these tenets. He has rejected the most complete set of extant written spiritual experiences in Eckankar. By rejecting Graham's journal, the Living Eck Master has undermined the validity of charged words and the inner experiences of chelas. He has done so without any reason as to how and why these experiences were rejected, without establishing anything to take their place.

These puzzling events forced me to focus on the second foundation of my belief structure within the teaching: the veracity of Paul Twitchell's writings. The materials contained in his *Shariyat-Ki-Sugmad* were brought under particular scrutiny, because they form the basis of the doctrine that has become the modern-day religion of Eckankar.

Subsequent chapters of this book will address whether or not trust in Paul's works is well-founded I can say at this point that spirit does indeed work in extraordinary ways. Nothing happens by accident. Spirit always works to light the way and end the darkness. In the short term, the negative polarity may have the upper hand. But, in the end, all attempts to stiffle the truth eventually fail. When it does, those suppressing the truth must answer. It is ironic that Harold's rejection of the spiritual experiences of a chela under his charge and the imposition on me of a discipline of required study, has set in motion the very cosmic direction that could bring light to the darker parts of Eckankar.

I have no questions concerning the reality of the sound and light of God. Nor do I question the power of spirit and its manifold ways of working with us in the physical realm. These beliefs have been the core of all the talks I have given in my years in Eckankar. But first and foremost, I am a seeker of truth. I have never spoken profusely about Eck doctrine or history, because the absence of historical evidence to support its claims has always bothered me. For years I remained neutral on the subject, but no longer. As a God-seeker, I will not rest until I have overturned every rock, read every page, and looked at everything I can find to reach the truth about this teaching, which events suggested lay hidden within Eckankar.

Chapter 6 — Eckankar: Revealed by Truth

Why I Looked Deeper into Eckankar

In my more than thirty years in Eckankar, I spoke before thousands of aspirants and Eckists in numerous talks, workshops, and presentations. Many told me that they joined or remained because of something that spirit had communicated through me. If they were influenced by these contributions, I feel a deep commitment to them. My work was in earnest, with the belief that I was communicating truth. After my long research into Eckankar, I am happy to say that, in large part, what I learned and communicated still stands the test of truth. However, as the real story behind the books, doctrines, and beliefs of Eckankar are revealed for all to see, some of it must be corrected.

The incongruities in Harold's rejection of Graham's journal prompted me to examine carefully the second assumption underlying Eckankar: that the concepts and principles in Paul's books are true. David Lane's exposé of Eckankar[1] did not irrevocably taint its fundamental precepts. When I first encountered Lane's work, I was willing to overlook Paul's plagiarism (though I had not fully grasped its extent) as long as the content of the materials was true. But Graham's journal raised many issues about Paul and Harold that placed the veracity of Paul's writings in question.

In his August 8, 2001 journal entry, Graham describes a ceremony where he was to receive the Fourteenth Initiation. Yaubl Sacabi advised him:

> This has been decided to be given because of the falling level of power under Sri Harold. . . . The difference that you are aware of between the inner and outer Master is caused by this, the two are no longer in tune with each other. [2]

Sacabi explained further that Sri Harold would be informed that the time had come for him to step down. He then instructed Graham to send his journal, with all its revelatory content, to Harold, who had already been informed on the inner that the materials were coming. When Graham inquired about Eckankar as a religion, he was told:

> ECKANKAR is not, was not, and never will be a religion. ECKAN-KAR is a Spiritual philosophy in the way of the Eternal Light and Sound of GOD.[3]

Yaubl Sacabi's statement is consistent with but falls short of the even more restrictive standards that Paul had proposed for Eckankar, which was to be run as a for-profit business.[4] Indeed, Paul was quite insistent that Eckankar should not be a religion or even a tax-exempt group.[5] Yet, he later established Eckankar's legal status as a non-profit, tax-exempt church. This status has been continued by Darwin and Harold, in spite of Paul's earlier warnings about the dangers of organizing spiritual works as churches, orders, or institutions.

In the afternoon of September 15, 2001 Graham was told:

> Because of the falling power of Sri Harold, He cannot hand over the Rod of ECK Power to you, it has been taken from Him. [6]

Later, Graham was informed that the ceremonial transfer of the Rod of Eck Power might not take place on the outer. Seeking additional insight on this point, Graham was told that the Rod of Eck Power had been removed from Harold and that, in response, Harold turned Eckankar into a full-fledged religious institution to ensure its survival and his own. Graham also learned that, if the succession of the new Mahanta were acknowledged, Eckankar could be returned to its original purpose, that of a spiritual path not a doctrinaire religion.

In addition to these significant revelations, Graham had many spiritual encounters with Chungchok, the spokesman for the Nine Silent Ones. Paul wrote extensively on these beings and their spiritual roles:

> These strange beings are responsible for the running of the planes of God on a mechanical basis.... They come and go like the wind to carry out the will and wishes of the Lord of the universes.... The Silent Ones are in command of the great Sound wave, in the worlds of the universes.... They have immense powers and great wisdom to carry out the assignments of the SUGMAD and, of course, unlimited freedom.... Out-

side the SUGMAD, these Silent Ones are the most powerful beings in all the worlds....[7]

Given the importance of the Nine Silent Ones in Eckankar's hierarchy, Chungchok's statements take on immense importance. Indeed, they go to the very validity of Eckankar. Chungchok explained to Graham that both the Temples of Golden Wisdom and the Rod of Eck Power existed only in Paul's writings. Graham was deeply troubled by this. How did it fit with his other experiences? Sensing this, Chungchok elaborated:

> Before you ask me, I know what your next question is going to be, and I have my answer here for you: you were given the experiences with the so-called Rod of ECK Power, because it was written into the teachings. If we had laid all this on you from the start, your balance would have gone, hence, as true to spirituality under a true teacher, it was given a step at a time to unfold your ability to accept it all, for there is a lot to have to accept.[8]

These revelations and Harold's reaction to the journal led to my investigation into Eckankar. Were there untruths and deceptions that somehow I had failed to see? If so, had I unwittingly become part of an ongoing deception that had mixed the seeker's sincere quest for spiritual enlightenment with a competing, though unrevealed, plan for spiritual control and power? I had to know for myself and for the many Eckists whom I have known. I owed it to them to uncover the truth about the path to God that we had chosen and faithfully served with both love and steadfastness.

I began with in-depth research. I read the books that were the basis for Paul's many writings. I examined the texts discovered by David Lane to have been plagiarized by Paul. I explored the Ruhani Satsang, founded by Kirpal Singh, which Paul had followed for almost ten years before founding Eckankar. I researched the works of his spiritual master during these years and those of the Radhasoami Beas line of masters. I searched other spiritual paths that claimed to be a direct path to God. I hunted down every resource possible to learn the true sources of the Eckankar teaching.

My research also led me to investigate the legal framework of Eckankar and the litigation in which it had been involved. I puzzled over the comments of Paul's wife, Gail, to understand why she rejected Eckankar and wanted no more association with it. Reading an explosive correspondence between Harold and Darwin, I tried to understand how one Living Eck Master could legally, financially, and spiritually destroy his predecessor. I talked to High Initiates, some who had reached the Seventh and Eighth Initiations, to understand why they left the teaching. I visited Paul's hometown (Paducah, Kentucky) and pored over the Twitchell Collection, which Paul had aided in establishing by assiduously sending news clipping, pictures, and other papers to his hometown library. I interviewed friends and acquaintances who had known Paul prior to his creation of Eckankar. I even sought Paul's military record and requested other official documents to determine the truth of his background.

At times, the research was painful. I often felt deceived, even gullible. If you are a member of Eckankar, you might also feel that way. If you are not an Eckist, I hope these revelations will cause you to look into whatever path or religion you are following, for what this research has found in Eckankar was also found to exist in other religions and spiritual teachings. The only difference was that the dust of history had covered the latter's origins and evolution more completely than the mere decades that protected Eckankar from its historical record.

Exploration of this more recent trail leading to the truth behind Eckankar will be challenging at times. This is how we grow spiritually. This is the only way that a loving, vulnerable, and beautiful soul can see and know Eckankar for what it really is. Only then, can the God-seeker decide how he may wish to continue his journey to God-Realization.

Standards of Religious and Spiritual Scrutiny

While writing this book, several friends asked me why I would risk my standing as a well-known speaker and Seventh Initiate in Eckankar. The answer was quite simple. Standing is unimportant if it is not of truth. The God-seeker looks to truth as the infallible guide to higher states of spiritual awareness. But truth is often difficult to discern above the cacophony of prattle posing as true spiritual teachings.

In examining the words and actions of Eckankar leaders, we are apt to judge them by ordinary standards. In Eckankar, the spiritual leader considers his position to represent the highest state of spiritual consciousness that can be expressed in the physical world. Indeed, Paul said:

> Each Living ECK Master has served as the Mahanta, which is God made flesh on earth. Therefore, we look to the Mahanta, for he is the representative of SUGMAD [God] in our midst today.[9]

This description is the official definition for the spiritual leader of Eckankar. It is reinforced throughout the Eck works, especially the *Shariyat-Ki-Sugmad*, the Bible of the Eckists. It has never been modified or reduced by Paul Twitchell, Darwin Gross, or Harold Klemp — Eckankar's line of spiritual masters.

A spiritual master of this stature should be held to standards that transcend those of average people. For if he were allowed their foibles, then what would there be to recommend the higher spiritual life to a God-seeker? What would be the point, if the "representative of God on earth" could not overcome the simple temptations and faults that mortals grapple with and often conquer? Certainly honesty, morality, and ethics are to be expected of such a spiritual master. As a parent, corporate president, and teacher of spiritual subjects, ethical standards for the good of the whole are essential to me. Lying and distortion are simply unacceptable when a seeker is looking to you for truth. Thus, every Eckist is justified in expecting the Mahanta, the Living Eck Master, "the representative of Sugmad [God] in our midst today," to live by these simple standards, if not substantially higher ones.

When a person comes to a spiritual teaching, listens to the words of its spiritual leader, and reads its sacred texts, he is in a vulnerable state: he might well be too trusting. Many who come to Eckankar do not question it. They believe that they are being told the truth and that a highly developed spiritual leader would not deceive them. All teachers carry great responsibility. A relationship of trust exists akin to that of parent to child. How much more sacrosanct, then, is the relationship between a spiritual leader and a student, especially if the former purports to be the manifestation of God? The student is apt to believe what he is told, especially if facile answers are readily available to assuage his concerns.

The Four Zoas of Eckankar

The Zoas are laws that govern our actions while in this world. Paul set forth four such laws by which the Mahdis,[10] those who serve as the right-hand of the Mahanta, are to live their lives. Unless the Mahanta, the Living Eck Master, is above these laws, then we would assume that the Zoas should apply equally, if not more so, to the Mahanta, for he is, presumably, the living embodiment of all that we seek to become. The Zoas are:

> (1) The Mahdis shall not use alcohol, tobacco, drugs; he must not gamble or be gluttonous in any way. No Mahdis shall be existent on the animal level. He is a leader, and he must fix his attention above the psychology of the brute.

> (2) The Mahdis shall not speak with tongue of vanity or deceit or unhappiness, criticize the actions of others, blame others for wrong-doings, quarrel, fight, or inflict injury. He shall at all times be respectful and courteous to his fellowman and show great compassion and happiness.

> (3) The Mahdis shall have humility, love, and freedom from all bonds of creeds. He shall be free from the laws of karma which snare him with boastfulness and vanity. He shall have love for all people and all creatures of the SUGMAD.

> (4) The Mahdis must preach the message of ECK at all times, and prove to the world that he is an example of purity and happiness.[11]

These are beautiful and noble sentiments — a worthy set of precepts for any God-seeker. Certainly, they are standards to which those who claim the mantle of Mahanta, the Living Eck Master, must adhere and demonstrate in all aspects of their lives.

The Standard of Truth

Paul set other important standards in Eckankar. They compose its foundation and are what attracted me to the teaching. This is how he put it:

> Man is able to tell what comfortable lies he likes to others but he must beware of telling them to himself — not because it is immoral but because, unfortunately, he will not be able to deceive himself. One cannot live happily with a person he knows is a liar.[12]

Having warned us about the liar, Paul then identifies the standard, indeed the imperative, for truth in our lives. He writes:

> Before you can give Truth to others, Truth must be known as the absolute need in your life. We must see Truth and know Truth and think Truth always.[13]

> This is the time for Truth, "the Truth, the whole Truth and nothing but the Truth." This is no time for half-Truths, for bewilderment and lack of understanding. These constitute the soil in which grief grows. In Truth alone is there comfort, understanding and courage.[14]

He even spoke of the untoward circumstances that befall anyone who fails to heed this admonition:

> Refuse to see Truth, pretend that it is impossible to know what is true and what is not, distort Truth, seek to mix it with Untruth, attempt to deceive both ourselves and others, give Truth in an unattractive manner, then chaos will reign in our lives.[15]

These are the principles by which the history of Eckankar and its leadership will be examined. Looking at this history will not be easy. It may even be painful. We all struggle to defend our beliefs and those in whom we have placed our trust. Indeed, we should not abandon these loyalties quickly. However, the God-seeker must choose between holding on to the familiar and moving on toward truth. Some will choose the familiar, at least until the call of soul shepherds them beyond their comfort zone into the unfamiliar, the unknown, where the next step in spiritual growth lies. Let us remember what Paul said:

> We must have Truth in order to have power. Be truthful in your thoughts. *Never shy away from a critical thought from a sense of mistaken kindness to yourself. Never make a deliberate effort to forget something unpleasant.* It is our responsibility to face the things we have created.[16]

Paul Twitchell and the Real History of Eckankar

Paul Twitchell faced a great dilemma. He had studied under his spiritual master for about ten years and had numerous inner experiences that spoke of a great spiritual role for him. Eager to tell his master, Kirpal Singh, of the experiences they had shared in the inner worlds of God, he sent a manuscript (later published as *The Tiger's Fang*), seeking his approval. But Kirpal Singh rebuffed him, saying his experiences were incomplete or inaccurate. (In this respect, Paul's experiences with Kirpal Singh were similar to Graham's with Harold.) Upset, he asked Kirpal Singh to return the manuscript and terminated his study with him.

In 1971, Paul completely disavowed his former Master in the harshest terms:

> I have never recognized you as a master, or that you give initiations, and that your work is not in the best interest of spirituality. Your teachings are orthodox, and as a preacher you are not capable of assisting anyone spiritually.[17]

Rather strong words for a master who earlier had evoked admiration and praise:

> My Saints are Kabir...Rumi, Hafiz, Shamusi-Tabriz and Kirpal Singh of India.[18]

> I have studied under many teacher [*sic*]. . . . I have so far had seven, some outstanding ones, including Sri Kirpal Singh, of Delhi, India.[19]

Paul eventually denied that Kirpal Singh had initiated him. Eckankar officially confirmed this in 1977 when Darwin Gross, the Living Eck Master of the time, through his secretary, stated:

> Kirpal Singh and the Radha Swoami [*sic*] group tried to "claim" Paul Twitchell and use him for their own purposes, as have other groups from the East and the West. Paul . . . wrote a letter to Kirpal Singh and . . . stating that he, Paul, would take Singh . . . to court if necessary. Due to the threats and harassment and material Kirpal Singh . . . tried to use against Paul Twitchell by faking Paul's signature on many papers. . . . Sri Darwin Gross, the MAHANTA, the Living ECK Master of ECKAN-KAR has stated that he knows for a fact that Paul Twitchell only had two ECK Masters during his earthly stay here: the Tibetan Rebazar Tarzs, and Sudar Singh, and no one else.[20]

Darwin was of course mistaken in his assertion that Paul only had two masters. He was also mistaken about letters from Paul to his then master presumably forged by Kirpal Singh's group. This was part of the official story line of Eckankar until Harold had to admit that Paul had studied under Kirpal Singh — so clear and incontrovertible was the evidence.

How Paul, and subsequently Eckankar, believed for so long that he could hide the truth is baffling. It is an ironic aside to this whole affair that Paul died of a heart attack around the time Kirpal Singh received his letter. His death occurred five, if not fifteen, years before he predicted that he would die, vitiating his own proclamation that a master dies only when ready and in a natural and predictable manner. This added to speculation about whether Paul was actually a master or something else entirely.

Paul Twitchell After the Break: The Idea is Born

Singh's rejection was a turning point in Paul's life. His reaction to this rebuff set him on a course that would forever be the bane of his newly formed religion, Eckankar. It started as a philosophy of what Paul called "the Cliff-Hanger," a person facing imminent death who suddenly sees life in a new way. Rather than being an ancient religion, it began as a philosophy drawn from his experiences:

> ECKANKAR, which I formed out of my own experience, is the term used for the philosophy I have developed for the Cliff-Hanger. It is based on Shabd-Yoga, a way out form of yoga. The word is Hindu locution for the cosmic sound current which is known in our vernacular as the cosmic river of God.[21]

In an article he wrote entitled "The Square Peg," Paul commented on the Cliff-Hanger and Eckankar that he had just started to formulate:

> This zany character is called the vanguard of a new religion, entitled "Eckankar," a Hindu word meaning Union with God.[22]

And in an advertisement for a talk on bilocation[23] in San Diego, Paul wrote that his philosophy

> . . . brings new techniques to those interested in Bilocation. Taking the old and putting together new ideas he has codified a system called ECKANKAR, for those concerned with out-of-the-body experiences.[24]

In connection with his biography, *In My Soul I Am Free*, written by Brad Steiger, Paul was asked when he started to formulate the message of Eckankar. He responded, "Probably when my sister, Kay-Dee, died in 1959."[25] When asked when he changed from being a Cliff-Hanger to a spiritual adept, he replied:

> The switchover from the Cliff-Hanger to ECK began taking place after I met my present wife, Gail. She insisted that I do something with my knowledge and abilities.[26]

The Creation Begins

This simple story behind the creation of Eckankar would probably have been quite acceptable to the millions who learned about and studied Paul's new religion. Initially, he readily admitted what he was doing

and why he was doing it. Then something changed. Paul was not satisfied with creating just another eclectic path for those seeking new
expressions of spirituality in 1960s California. Instead, with Gail's urging, he developed a westernized version of a teaching he had studied
for almost ten years and imbued it with a storyline that made it unique.
Paul claimed Eckankar to be the precursor and progenitor of every religion known to man. This statement might sound like an exaggeration
of Paul's words, but it is not. His grandiloquence coupled with his
desire to "one up" all other religions led him to write:

> ECKANKAR created and comprises all the religious ideas of the lower
> worlds. Art, writing, music, and sculpture are only developments of the
> higher ideals of ECKANKAR.... The major religions of the world have
> sprung out of ECKANKAR.[27]

Quite an accomplishment for a religion that had existed less than
ten years! Paul knew that the best way to build up Eckankar was to
make fabulous and gigantic claims that could neither be proved nor dis-
proved. Paul was no amateur when it came to the art of the "big lie."
Not content to claim credit for the formation of all world religions, Paul
expanded the history of Eckankar to encompass the lives of everyone
and anyone of any historical significance:

> The famous line of prophets in the Israelite tribes were trained in the
> teachings of ECKANKAR, as their prophecies well show. The Greek
> Masters Apollonius, Dionysius, Pythagoras, Socrates, Aristotle, and
> Plato were taught the art of ECKANKAR by the ancient Adepts. Practi-
> cally every man who has contributed to civilization has spiritually been
> a chela, or student, of the hidden teachings of ECK.[28]

The Historical Rewrite Continues

Paul's account of the founding of Eckankar, "the Ancient Science
of Soul Travel,"[29] laid the foundation for the extraordinary position he
was to create for himself. From the lone Cliff-Hanger who was the ava-
tar of a new religion, Paul ascended to the 971st Living Eck Master in a
long line of masters that he asserted had guided mankind from its genesis.[30]

Having disavowed his association with Kirpal Singh, Paul changed
the historical record by substituting the names of invented masters such
as Rebazar Tarzs. Similarly, he never disclosed his association with
Scientology and its founder, L. Ron Hubbard, who had been a mentor

of sorts and whose start-up likely provided a blueprint for Eckankar. This association foreshadows his use of many tactics and techniques that would be employed in the creation and promulgation of the new religion of Eckankar.

He also dissociated himself from the spiritual path and the lineage of masters comprising the Radhasoami Satsang Beas, out of which the Ruhani Satsang, founded by Kirpal Singh, had emerged. In their place, as we shall see, he created his own line of masters, complete with dubious histories and lineages. This fabrication was necessary to round out a history that started as an admitted creation of Paul and became the "Ancient Science of Soul Travel," the "only path to God."

Once Paul embarked on this dissembling course, he was forced to weave a web of stories whose persuasiveness was rooted in their magnitude and audacity. Weaving such a fiction took a type of unprincipled genius with which he had been abundantly blessed. It took a mindset that could abandon the fundamental principles of truth that he had propounded so eloquently. This is the paradox of Paul Twitchell: to convey spiritual truth, he created an elaborate lie.

I am not an analyst and do not pretend to understand fully the psychological motivations that prompted him to do what he did. However, an analysis of his actions and pronouncements suggests a psychological explanation that will be explored once we better see his amoral genius at work. To understand what Paul did requires a deeper look into the devices he used to make up the spiritual history, cosmology, and spiritual hierarchy, which form the basis of the religion of Eckankar today.

Chapter 7 — Twitchellian Techniques of Spiritual Creativity: The Ten Devices

Paul Twitchell systematically used ten devices to weave the history of Eckankar. Some are easily discernible; others are subtle, if not diabolical. Together, they create an elaborate fiction that will be laid bare using the facts and the paper trail he left behind. When the truth is revealed, Eckankar will be seen for the magical, mystical creation that it is. A creation that is reinforced by the inner and outer experiences of its members, which transform its myth into reality.

We will view Paul's actions by the standard he himself espoused, and return to this standard from time to time to underscore his pattern of deception:

> Refuse to see Truth, pretend that it is impossible to know what is true and what is not, distort Truth, seek to mix it with Untruth, attempt to deceive both ourselves and others, give Truth in an unattractive manner, then chaos will reign in our lives.[1]

Device One: Factual and Historical Inaccuracies

When Was Paul Born?

Discourse and controversy about something as simple as Paul's date of birth have filled gigabytes of space on the Internet and reams of paper. Paul has claimed or been ascribed no fewer than four different dates of birth. Arguments over his birth date would be irrelevant if not for important aspects of the history of Eckankar tied to it. Aside from the glaring disparities in the ages that Paul created or allowed to circulate, the validity of many of his claims is anchored by that date. It constitutes a "time line" from which the veracity of other claims can be judged.

The date of birth on Paul's death certificate[2], provided by his second wife, Gail, was October 22, 1922. It would be hard to imagine any reason for Gail to provide the medical examiner with anything other than what she believed to be the truth. Whatever the reason, it does appear that the 1922 date was no typo, as some have argued, since other parts of the death certificate show that Gail recorded his age at the time of his death as forty-eight years old, consistent with the 1922 date. Beyond this, the marriage certificate[3] *signed* by J. Paul Twitchell and Gail A. Atkinson clearly shows that Paul gave his date of birth as October 22, 1922, consistent with the date Gail had recorded on his death certificate. There was no typo and no mistake. This is what Paul wanted Gail to believe and this is what she believed. Why Paul told his much younger wife that he was a decade younger than he actually was, is open to easy speculation.

On his marriage certificate to his first wife, Paul entered his date of birth as October 22, 1912.[4] The weight of the evidence and the findings of Harold would place his birth date on or about October 22, between 1908 and 1910.[5] But the best evidence is a copy of a census form completed by a census taker in 1910 on which Paul's age was listed as six months.[6] It can be presumed that the parents of a six-month-old child would have truthfully responded to an official U.S. Government census taker visiting the home of a U.S. citizen, especially in 1910. Further, the U.S. Census Bureau confirms that the 1910 census was begun on April 15, 1910 and was concluded on May 15, 1910. Six months prior to this period would place Paul's birth date in October of 1909.

However, discrepancies in Paul Twitchell's age would not be significant except that similar incongruities recur, in ways small and large, throughout his life. The date of Paul's birth is the first major thread that begins to unravel the carefully woven stories Paul used to fashion the fabulous and intriguing history of Eckankar. Paul fabricated a myth about himself that would dovetail nicely with the dissolution of his relationship with Sri Kirpal Singh. He told the story of his early contact with Sudar Singh — first in Paris, France and later in Allahabad, India — when he was fifteen or sixteen. He explained his return to America right before World War II as due to his mother's illness.[7]

This story worked well in explaining where and from whom he had received his early spiritual training. It also established an early marker for the existence of and his association with the Vairagi Eck Masters. But there are substantial problems here. Once again, Paul seemed oblivious to the fact that his life left a paper trail. Of course, Paul could not have foreseen the information revolution of the Internet and the rising skepticism of a "duped-too-often" public. Unfortunately, for Paul and his many ardent followers (I certainly once counted myself among them), the facts do not support his story. Here is what we know:

- Paul was born in 1909.[8]
- He graduated from Tilghman High School in Paducah, Kentucky, in May 1931.[9]
- He entered Murray State College (Murray, Kentucky) in September 1931, remaining a full-time student until March 1933. He concentrated in General Education but did not earn a degree.[10]
- He attended Western Kentucky University from 1933-1935 but received no degree.[11]
- His mother died on April 26, 1940.[12]
- His father died on March 24, 1961.[13]
- His sister died on March 11, 1959.[14]
- His brother died on October 20, 1964.[15]

If Paul's mother died in 1940 and Paul was born in 1909, Paul was around *thirty* at her death. Paul's account, as written by his official biographer, Brad Steiger, has him *fifteen* at the time of his first visit to France and therefore on his return to America at the time of his mother's death. Paul and his sister, according to the Steiger account, returned to France where they met Sudar Singh and decided to accompany him to his Ashram in India. However, this recitation of the facts represents a fifteen or sixteen year discrepancy in age between Paul's story as told to Steiger and the facts of his life.

In fact, Paul did not finish high school at age fifteen, as he told Steiger. Records from his school reveal that he graduated in 1931. Thus, Paul was twenty-one years of age at graduation.[16] Paul's education proceeded without interruption, laying fallow his claim that he had journeyed to Paris with his sister, and later to India to meet the Eck

Master Sudar Singh. His attempt to lay an early marker for the existence of the Vairagi Masters and his involvement with them is just one of many Twitchellian inventions. As to Steiger's, (read Paul's) assertion that Paul graduated at age fifteen, Harold writes:

> But in those days high school was the way college is today — you could quit for a while and then go back. So Paul probably graduated from high school between age 18 and age 23.[17]

I commend Harold for his efforts to set *some* of the record straight. In this regard, he certainly did more than his predecessor, Darwin Gross, who appears to have fallen for all of Paul's claims. Harold tried to fill the time warp created by Paul's invention by asserting it was common back then for high school students to take time off for various reasons. Though Harold concedes that Paul graduated at a later age (thereby disputing Paul's account), he attempted to create a scenario that leaves room for and suggests the possibility of Paul's trip to France and India. In keeping with Steiger's account, Harold allows for the all-important meeting with Sri Sudar Singh.

When I heard this explanation, my first reaction was that Steiger could have made a simple mistake in recording what Paul said. As I was anxious to believe Paul, Harold's "added insight" was a straw that, at the time, I was happy to accept. I was thankful to Harold for restoring credibility to Paul's story and for dealing with the accusations of that David Lane fellow, who had so impolitely averred that Eckankar was riddled with lies. However, it was not to be so simple. The facts, as I learned, did not support Harold's spin, leaving the unpleasant conclusion that Paul did not "tell it like it was."

Steiger wrote that Paul and his sister, Kay Dee, went to France after his graduation from high school and then to India — staying for about one year — after his mother's death. Yet the registrar from Paul's high school indicated that there was no break in his education, and that he was a student at Murray State from the end of high school in 1931 until he left Murray in 1933. There appears to be no period when Paul was out of the country, much less in France or India. Paul Iverlet, the husband of Kay Dee, attests:

> [H]is wife never left the United States in her entire life. Also he claims that... Paul never left North America until the Second World War.[18]

Conversations with Paul Twitchell's first wife, Camille Ballowe, whom he married in 1942, are insightful. Her knowledge of Paul's travels from 1933 to 1942 was not unqualified, though she herself was a native of Paducah and knew him for some time before they were married. Ballowe insists that Paul took no trips abroad.[19]

Paul's official biography has him meeting Sudar Singh in India at age sixteen, after his mother's death in 1940. But according to Paul's account in *Difficulties of Becoming an ECK Master,* Sudar Singh died between 1935 and 1939.[20] Obviously, this doesn't add up. By this reckoning, Sudar Singh was *dead* before Paul *ever went to India* to study with him. In a clever attempt to provide cover, Harold asserts — with no backing, not even an imaginary death certificate for an imaginary master — that Sudar Singh "died in the 1940s."[21] This conveniently gives Paul the time to have studied under Sudar Singh before his death and then returned home. To stretch the cover a bit more and create a clear window of opportunity for Paul to have accomplished these meetings, Harold changed his own cover story. In his later writings, he asserted:

> Paul mentioned that he [Sudar Singh] died around the 1940s [Paul had actually said 1935-1939], but it seems to have been around 1955.[22]

Harold's stretching of his cover story by another fifteen years provided an even wider margin for error and was quite helpful, since Paul purportedly went to France and then to India to study under Singh after his mother's death. It corrects Paul's mistake of "killing off" Sudar Singh by 1939. Harold's attempts at obfuscation appear throughout his writings. But even Harold does not attempt to explain the discrepancy in Paul's alleged age of sixteen in 1940, when he was supposed to have met Sudar Singh, and the census record that demonstrates Paul was about thirty years old in 1940.

A final note about Harold's revision of the date of Sudar Singh's death to 1955 versus the — at the latest — 1939 date Paul had asserted.[23] It is hard to imagine how even Paul could have gotten the death of Sudar Singh wrong by fifteen years. But since Paul did not begin his study under Kirpal Singh (his real master) until 1955, the new date given by Harold for the death of Sudar Singh (also 1955) is a bit too convenient. Harold seems to be constructing a story that would support an unbroken chain of study under *some* master — even if not an Eck Master.

Even if Harold is correct, this convenient new date for the demise of Sudar Singh and the *known* commencement of Paul's study with Kirpal Singh in 1955, raises another question. Why didn't Paul begin his 1955 study under Eck Master Rebazar Tarzs rather than non-Eck Master Kirpal Singh? Inasmuch as Tarzs was supposedly on the scene and functioning as the Living Eck Master he would have been the obvious choice as Paul's master. Harold had pointed out that Rebazar Tarzs, who as we shall see was one of Paul's created Eck Masters, had taken over from Sudar Singh (another of Paul's created Eck Masters) after his death — either in 1939, the 1940s or 1955:

> If a Living ECK Master translated before his successor was ready, as with Sudar Singh, Rebazar took the Rod of ECK Power in the meantime.[24]

Harold specifically points out that Tarzs was giving initiations prior to 1965.[25] However, Paul Twitchell, the future Mahanta, the Living Eck Master was actually *initiated* by Kirpal Singh — the non-Eck Master — in 1955, rather than by the Living Eck Master holding the Rod of Eck Power, Rebazar Tarzs, who was presumably also giving initiations in 1955. It should be abundantly clear that some ferocious storytelling and revisionism is going on. None of it is ultimately successful and all of it simply adds velocity to this crumbling house of cards.

Where Was Paul Born?

Paul describes the line of succession of Eck Masters preceding him (the last being Rebazar Tarzs) when he writes:

> Following him is Peddar Zaskq, who was born on a packetboat in the midst of the Mississippi River, a few minutes after a great earthquake shook the mid-South and formed a great lake in this region.[26]

Since Paul had assumed "Peddar Zaskq" as his spiritual name, he was clearly talking about himself, in his present life, in this passage. However, this conflicts with previous statements about his birth, written in his biography. Paul said in his biography that he was born in China Point (no state given), not on a Mississippi packet boat. Darwin and his staff tried to fix the problem by claiming that he was actually born (in this lifetime) around 1812. Records indicate there was an earthquake in 1812 that resulted in the formation of a lake, but of course the rest of the story has no corroboration.[27]

Darwin went further to assert that Paul had been born, not in China Point, as Paul's biography had claimed, but on the Mississippi River on a packet boat as alleged in the *Spiritual Notebook*.[28] However, Darwin's version of this birth tale would result in a claim that Paul was a hundred years older than he actually was. Such a claim was a little hard to sell, even in Eckankar.

Recognizing the quagmire into which Darwin had walked, and attempting to reconcile Paul's various accounts of his birthplace, Harold created yet another scenario that he thought better fit the facts.[29] Harold attempts to salvage the Mississippi River account of Paul's birth by averring that it actually describes his birth *in a previous life*. Harold reaches this conclusion by combining a statement from *The Spiritual Notebook*[30] with parts of Paul's historical novel, *The Drums of Eck*.[31] By identifying an earthquake that occurred in 1812 and a lake that formed from it in northern Tennessee, Harold endeavors to breathe life into Paul's Mississippi packet boat story. A problem remains: the *Spiritual Notebook* speaks of Peddar Zaskq in *this* lifetime, not a person in a previous one. For there is no indication, as Harold would suggest, that a Peddar Zaskq was born in a prior lifetime (in 1812) who was an Eck Master in training during that life. Harold deftly bridges lifetimes in an effort to tie an earthquake in one century to a living master (with the same spiritual name) in the next. However, everything, including Eck writings, points to this 1812 person as a pure fiction, certainly not one of Paul's Vairagi Masters or a master in training. This is nothing more than an effort by Harold to keep the fabric from unraveling by stitching it with a yarn that might hold it together, at least for a while.

Paul himself contradicts Harold's story. In a little-read book published by Eckankar's Illuminated Way Publishing Company in 1980, based on transcribed interviews with Paul, he describes his past life:

> Now there are many things that I had to do, and it can go all the way back into the lifetime before this, in which I was born in the Caucasian [*sic*] Mountains and had to go through a series of trainings there, even to the extent of keeping myself inside. . . . Then I was trained in order to eventually come into this position as Living ECK Master.[32]

To call this unbelievable would be an understatement. The Caucasus Mountains (we can only assume he meant the Caucasus Mountains, as the "Caucasian Mountains" do not exist) are a great mountain range in Russia, Georgia, and Azerbaijan between the Black Sea and the Caspian Sea, quite a way from any packet boat on the Mississippi. Since Harold asserts that *The Spiritual Notebook* account of a birth on the Mississippi and the *Drums of ECK* version describe the same prior lifetime of Paul Twitchell, Harold must reconcile these two conflicting versions of where Paul was born in that lifetime.

While blindsided by Paul's account of his birth in a prior lifetime, Harold was convinced of the authenticity of Paul's account in *The Drums of ECK,* mainly because of statements such as this:

> The narrative which is laid down in this book, *The Drums of ECK*, may appear to the reader to be fiction but it is a true story. It is taken from my personal memories of what happened during the stirring times of the American-Mexican War [*sic*] which was fought in the years 1846-1848. . . . The characters who appear in this story, including myself as Peddar Zaskq, which is my real name, were actual people living in those times.[33]

From accounts such as this, we can understand the confusion that Darwin and Harold must have felt in trying to interpret what Paul meant by "characters who appear in this story, including myself as Peddar Zaskq . . . were actual people living in those times." Darwin, of course, interpreted this passage literally and maintained that this described Paul in this life, making him over 140 years old.[34] Harold interpreted it to mean Paul's immediate past life, in which he used the name Peddar Zaskq. Both were wrong!

Holding this issue in abeyance, we learn other fascinating things about the history and origins of Eckankar in this "true story . . . taken from my personal memories." According to this account, Eckankar was on the scene much sooner than Paul's earlier pronouncements on the matter:

> He thought of what Peddar Zaskq, that strange man who was acting as a scout for Blake's patrol, said about ECKANKAR, the Ancient Science of Soul Travel.[35]

These events supposedly took place on March 26, 1846. Contrary to the facts of Eckankar's creation in 1965, we appear to have a mid-nineteenth-century account of Eckankar in its present-day form, that is, the Ancient Science of Soul Travel. Apparently unaware of this 1846 reference to today's Eckankar, not to mention Paul's alleged study under Sudar Singh in the 1940s, and his assertion that it is the precursor of all known religions, Harold describes a Paul Twitchell in training, who may have been oblivious to the existence of Eckankar when he writes:

> Someday he would have a chance to take this teaching called ECKAN-KAR — *maybe he didn't even know the name then* — and put it in front of people.[36]

Why would Harold even suggest that Paul might not have known the name Eckankar when he has Paul's written historical record that, if true, would make this supposition impossible? How could Paul not have known, unless, of course, this history was not true and Paul actually hadn't heard of the name Eckankar before? Harold is trying, with subtlety and stealth, to lay a foundation of truth without destroying the fiction that is indispensable to the survival of Eckankar as a religion and the "Ancient Science of Soul Travel." Paul did not make his task easy; he left a trail that, despite heroic efforts, Harold could not cover up. For Paul clearly asserts that he knew about Eckankar and that it was an ancient path as early as 1846. As if this were not enough trouble, Paul contributes yet more confusion. In this account of Peddar Zaskq from *The Drums of Eck,* which Harold asserts placed his birth date at 1812, Paul is again less than helpful:

> He [Peddar Zaskq] was in some way associated with the strange religion called ECKANKAR. Somehow, Blake had heard that he was an American *over one hundred years old.*[37]

One hundred years old in 1846 would place the birth of *this* Peddar Zaskq at 1746, a full sixty-five years before Harold claims he was born in the "previous life" account. So much for the earthquake and the lake. Had Paul simply called *The Drums of Eck* an historical fiction, which it was, rather than to declare it true, his accounts would not be held to a different standard. However, his decision, and Harold's acceptance of this decision, to treat the book as a true story subjects both their statements to the much different and higher standard of truth. It shows how difficult, if not absurd, it is to attempt to turn fiction into truth and to weave conflicting fictional tales into a rational narrative.

In his inimitable way, Paul doesn't stop here with his *Drums of Eck* "true story." He lays even more land mines for Harold and his successors to defuse or step on:

> With the exception of a few, all had left their homes for gold, liquor and lust in this exotic land where the SUGMAD [God], the deity of that strange religion called ECKANKAR, would await ITS retribution for being aroused from a deep slumber over the centuries.[38]

The Sugmad asleep? The Sugmad awaiting ITS retribution? What are we to do with these assertions? And these gems go on and on. Harold accepts this account as true, since Paul has declared as much. Yet, our investigation reveals that it is simply an enormous fiction. In this and numerous other instances, Paul has created reams of fabrications that Harold must explicate to prevent this tightly woven fabric of fact and falsehood called Eckankar from completely unraveling.

Let us return to Paul's account of his place of birth in the "Caucasian Mountains" in his last lifetime. If Harold asserts that Paul was born on a Mississippi packet boat, he must now explain this second place of birth in his prior lifetime in order to salvage the cover that he attempted but was vitiated by Paul's own words.

The Spiritual Notebook account of the birth of Peddar Zaskq has another problem. The history and genealogy of the Twitchell family demonstrate that he was born neither on a packet boat nor on the Mississippi; nor did a lake form following an earthquake at the time of his birth. Instead, Paul was born on the Westside of Paducah, Kentucky to Jacob and Effie Twitchell.[39] Paul adds to the confusion by allowing Brad Steiger to write that he was born and lived his early years in China Point. This, too, was not true. As Harold points out:

> There is no such town as China Point in Kentucky. He [Paul] constructed the story to protect his family, so that later on, when people sought him out to learn about ECKANKAR, his family wouldn't be pestered by well-meaning people intruding in their lives.[40]

While well-intended, Harold's attempt to explain this yarn is dubious. At the time of the publication of *In My Soul I Am Free* (1968), Paul's immediate family (all of them) was dead, and so a case for family protection cannot reasonably be made. An alternative is that Paul preferred to add to his legend or to put people on a false trail so that they would not discover the truth.

The Real Paul Twitchell Revealed

Harold admits to Paul's self-promotional puffery in his attempts to get himself written about in *Ripley's Believe It or Not*. It seems that Paul took on a pseudonym "Carl Snyder" and wrote *Ripley's* spinning an impressive yarn about his life. On this episode, Harold writes:

> In this particular letter to *Ripley's*, Carl Snyder spoke about the things this Paul Twitchell had accomplished. Paul had a punchy style of writing. It was alive; it just glowed with life. He was drawing on his *creativity to survive*, so he wrote this promotional stuff. Snyder expanded on all of this talent: "College athletic trainer, swimming coach, track team" and *embellished it even more* by adding things like, "prizefighter" and "promoter of fights." He worked every angle on every job he ever held, giving each position all different titles. In addition, he said, "Paul Twitchell reads all the time. He reads a book a night, and sometimes doesn't even get a wink of sleep."[41]

Harold notes a few other examples of Paul's penchant for embellishment that will become important in later chapters. Paul also used the pseudonym, "Charles Daniel." Harold notes that if one finds any Eckankar-related materials by this author, or by other names along with the word "wink," then it's a pretty good bet that Paul was behind the pen.[42]

In another account of Paul's early exploits, Harold describes a young Paul Twitchell interested in making a name for himself while still in Kentucky. To accomplish this, Paul selected *Who's Who in Kentucky* as a vehicle for self-promotion. Harold writes:

> At 27 years of age, the most Paul had ever done was to teach physical education. But by the time *he wrote it all up, exaggerating and twisting the facts*, he had worked up a nice little paragraph about all the grand achievements of one Paul Twitchell. He *made it sound quite impressive*.[43]

Another charming story to be sure, but Harold seems to miss the point in his attempt to soften acts that we would never counsel our children, acts that could cost a person his job. This is lying, and it is universally detested. And especially in a twenty-seven year old "God-man to be," it cannot be condoned. Yet Harold justifies Paul's promotional prevarications in Machiavellian terms:

> I saw an article in the obituary column in one of the West Coast newspapers a few weeks ago about a seventy-seven-year-old lady who had founded a certain church many years ago. But who ever heard of it? This talent of self-promotion was necessary for Paul's mission.[44]

I did a double-take when I first read this, and I continue to be shocked with every rereading. Harold is not only excusing Paul's lying but actually declares it as "necessary for Paul's mission." I have to wonder just what was Paul's mission. Is the art of lying and gross exaggeration a necessary talent and training for a true God-man or for a true con-man? Surely, no one can begrudge a young and ambitious writer certain excesses in representing himself and his accomplishments. But Paul's exaggerations went far beyond this and approached the territory of misrepresentation. Thus, while the episode depicting Paul's early years in some ways describes the actions of "quite a rascal," as Harold had described him,[45] it is also deeply disturbing. Indeed, these would remain just charming stories if it were not for what Harold euphemizes as Paul's "creativity to survive."

It is likely that this finely-honed talent led to Paul's creation of Eckankar in the first place. The need for finance was cited by those who knew Paul as one of his key motivations for starting Eckankar:

> Problems between him and his wife Gail led him to believe she was going to leave him and he desperately wanted to keep her. So when she demanded more money and better living, he started to write things and copy from other books.[46]

This creativity to survive also reveals itself in his writing of the Eckankar works. He created a teaching that maintained a loyal following and revenue base for him and his successors. During the period of my research for this book, I traveled to Lakemont, Georgia to meet with Roy Eugene Davis, the director of Center for Spiritual Awareness and a disciple of Paramahansa Yogananda. He provided additional insight into Paul's early motivations in creating Eckankar and about Paul's "creativity to survive."

Davis is an internationally respected teacher and lecturer of the spiritual growth processes in the Kriya Yoga tradition and the author of numerous books on the subject. A contemporary of Paul Twitchell, he wrote of his association:

> I met Paul Twitchell during the early 1960's in Washington, D.C. At that time Paul lived in an apartment owned by, and on the grounds of the Self-Revelation Church of Absolute Monism of which the late Swami Premananda, one of my brother disciples, was the founder and minister. Paul contacted me after seeing a notice of my public lectures and after our initial conversation we continued to meet at his apartment from time to time.

> Unmarried at that time, Paul lived alone. . . . He told me that he had been initiated by Kirpal Singh but was no longer affiliated with him. During one of my visits Paul pointed to some notebooks and binders on a shelf by his writing desk and said, "One day those are going to make me rich." At a later meeting he said, "To be successful in a big way, you have to have your own movement. Paramahansa Yogananda had his Self-Realization Fellowship; L. Ron Hubbard has his Scientology; Eckankar is my thing."

> Paul moved from Washington, D.C. and later wrote me from Seattle, Washington. . . . After his move to San Diego, I began to see his articles . . . about Eckankar. . . . Some . . . featured testimonials from his students who claimed that Paul had appeared to them in dreams and visions. When I next visited San Diego, Paul and I had lunch. . . . I asked him about the claims of various people that he visited them in dreams and by astral projection. He chuckled, and said, "You know, if you tell people something long enough they'll start to believe it!"

> Since we were casual friends, Paul shared with me the progress of Eckankar and his plans for the future. Although some of the material he wrote is valid, he borrowed heavily from the writings of Kirpal Singh and from other sources. In the late 1960s a series of Paul's articles appeared in Orion Magazine, published by Christian Spiritual Alliance, based in Lakemont, Georgia. My articles were also published in Orion Magazine and I knew the editors very well. On one occasion they informed me that they had rejected Paul's then most recent article because he had used entire paragraphs from a book on Mental Science by Judge Thomas Troward. After that incident his articles were no longer accepted by the editors of Orion Magazine. I knew about this situation long before David Lane wrote about [it] in his book, which was published years later.

> Paul's claim that he was representative of a line of enlightened spiritual masters was fiction. My impression of him was that he had a deep psychological need for recognition and to accomplish something that would impress others. During our private conversations he was friendly, likable and somewhat shy.[47]

Harold looked at Paul's history and his acts of exaggeration, fact twisting, cover-up, and distortion and did what he could to rationalize them. He wrote about these questionable tendencies:

> But without realizing it, he was just practicing. Someday he would have a chance to take this teaching called Eckankar — *maybe he didn't even know the name then* — and put it in front of people. . .[48]

As discussed earlier, Harold's assertion that Paul perhaps didn't even know the name of Eckankar during these early years flies in the face of Paul's account of his history and Harold's confirmation of it. Paul had written that he studied under Eck Master Sudar Singh from age sixteen in India. If so, and if Eckankar existed — as it had to, since Sudar Singh was allegedly a real Eck Master — how could Paul *not* have heard of it? Why would Harold suggest this scenario unless he too was calling into question the veracity of the very history of Eckankar that Paul had so assiduously created? In fact, Harold not only questions this history but also virtually admits that it is not as Paul had represented. Harold wrote:

> The ECK [spirit] teachings have been here from the earliest times, *but they haven't carried the name of ECKANKAR.* They have been brought out under different names at different times. . . .[49]

Yet, Paul, without qualification, had written definitively about Eckankar's history. He left no room for doubt that he was speaking about Eckankar as a teaching that has existed from the dawn of time, not in the pale and placid terms by which Harold was prepared to acknowledge its history. Further, Paul made no reference to any other teaching by any other name that had been used as a channel to transmit the Eck teachings, as Harold had suggested when he wrote, "They have been brought out under different names at different times."[50] Thus, without any such reference, Paul wrote:

> ECKANKAR, which *is* the mainstream for all religions, philosophies and doctrines, *was the first* to show the people of the earth, through appointed saviors, that. . . .[51]

> ECKANKAR *created* and *comprises* all the religious ideas of the lower worlds. Art, writing, music, and sculpture are only developments of the higher ideals of ECKANKAR.[52]

There are no qualifications here! Harold's spin of Paul's version of history runs into problem after problem. This is what happens when attempts are made to reconcile fiction and fantasy with fact and verity: the pieces do not fit. The apologist is left to create one implausible story after another or to subtly admit exaggeration and fabrication. In essence, this is what Harold was forced to do. In so doing, he was admitting that the founder of Eckankar had not told the truth.

As we shall see, Paul's tendency to "embellish it even more" seems to have found its way into the writings that make up the bulk of early Eckankar manuscripts. Paul's skill as he "worked every angle on every job" is especially evident in his role as the creator and originator of the Ancient Science of Soul Travel. It cannot escape the reader that Harold's exquisite use of euphemism only clumsily obscures what would otherwise simply be called untruth.

The Mysterious Paul Twitchell

Paul had a special ability to create small historical falsehoods to chronicle his own life and add a note of mystery into the saga of the Vairagi Masters. Why would Paul spin such a yarn about himself? The answer seems to flow from his own description of his lineage. In describing the origins of one of his Eck Masters, Paul writes that he was born

> . . . in the usual manner of the ECK Masters — very mysteriously. Few know how they are born, but some family often adopts them during their infancy and while raising them, one member of the family, who is adept at Soul Travel, teaches them at an early age. Most ECK Masters are born either in the high mountains or on some body of water.[53]

Paul's lineage of Eck Masters was indeed mysterious. He was forced to construct a history for himself worthy of the standard he had set. Paul's great misfortune was that he wrote his numerous books at the dawn of the computer age. How could he have known the ease with which information could be checked and challenged, and the truth disseminated to millions at the push of a button? Most religions, as we will see in Chapter 12, have hundreds if not thousands of years to create and bury the truth of their origins. In time, myth circulates as truth, and there is little opportunity to challenge it. This is not the case for Paul Twitchell and Eckankar.

To some, these revelations are just a picaresque tale of a creative individual who wanted to add interest and mystery to his writings. They would argue that Paul should not be taken too seriously. Harold, in his defense of Paul, simply called him a "rascal," a quaint term that glosses over behavior that would more rightly be described with a harsher word. The yarn that Paul spun was far more extensive than Harold was prepared to reveal to the faithful. However, before we euphemize Paul's writings as sales puffery, we must return to the standard by which Paul Twitchell and the works of Eckankar are to be viewed:

> Refuse to see Truth, pretend that it is impossible to know what is true and what is not, distort Truth, seek to mix it with Untruth, attempt to deceive both ourselves and others, give Truth in an unattractive manner, then chaos will reign in our lives.[54]

The chaos that will follow the revelations in this book will not be of my making. Instead, it will follow the pattern that Paul so accurately predicts in his pronouncement on truth. Unfortunately, Paul did not heed his own advice. His reckless disregard for truth created an unstable foundation that will prevent Eckankar from reaching the heights he envisioned. The result will instead be ongoing chaos and tension in the ranks, which can only be ended by seeing the truth and moving on.

As the real Paul Twitchell is revealed, a foundation will be constructed that will enable Eckists and non-Eckists alike to fathom the extent of what he did. Without this foundation, it will be virtually impossible to even conceive, much less comprehend, the extent of Paul's deception and fabrication.

Device Two: A Failure of Attribution

> Plagiarize: *To steal and pass off [the ideas or words of another] as one's own: use [a created production] without crediting the source: to commit literary theft: present as new and original an idea or product derived from an existing source.*
>
> Plagiarist: *One who engages in an act of plagiarizing.*[55]

Plagiarism has both legal and moral aspects. The legal part involves the protection of a person's creative work so that another cannot take credit for and or financially benefit from it under false pretenses without violating the law. This is the purpose of copyright laws.

There is an exception called "reasonable use," which permits an individual, under specified circumstances, to quote an author without requesting or receiving his or her permission. Even in this exception, the writer must acknowledge the source and give credit to the author.

Apart from the legal component of plagiarism, there is also a moral one. Such acts are dishonest, for they seek to mislead the reader into believing that the plagiarist is responsible for something that he is not. Acts of plagiarism can range from the purely accidental to the blatant lifting of paragraphs and pages, which cannot be construed as accidental.

In the case of Paul Twitchell, plagiarism reaches such a level as to legitimately get him into *Ripley's Believe It or Not*. Indeed, I would venture that his plagiarisms are among the most widespread and systematic in the history of literature. In referring to Paul's book, *The Far Country*, David Lane writes:

> The work, amazingly, contains well over four-hundred paragraphs from Johnson's two books, *The Path of the Masters* and *With a Great Master in India*, without so much as a single reference note to them. It is likely that almost one-half of *The Far Country* is *not* of Twitchell's pen.[56]

Thomas Mallon in his book *Stolen Words* summed up my own reaction to the plagiarist:

> I was, through my research, eventually, and much more than I expected to be, appalled: by the victims I learned of, by the audacity of their predators, by the excuses made for the latter.[57]

Mallon relates a particularly interesting story of one Charles Reade who:

> Like the thundering evangelist who dallies with the devil, he managed in one pugilistic lifetime to be both a loud champion of international copyright and a shameless smuggler of work penned on the other side of the English Channel.[58]

Charles Reade was part of a tradition among English playwrights in the 1850s, who anglicized popular French plays and staged them in English theaters. This was made possible by a loophole in the 1851 copyright agreement between England and France. Not content with being a mere anglicizer, Reade desired to make a name for himself by borrowing copiously from the works of others and presenting them as originals. Ironically, he condemned literary piracy and was one of the leading advocates of his time for the enforcement of tighter copyright laws. Those who studied him marveled at the contradiction he embodied and the sheer audacity with which he engaged in plagiarism. Reade even went so far as to call this a type of kleptomania.[59]

Venturing a final hypothesis on the case of Reade, Mallon asks:

> Was he one of those people who just can't get it? Was he like the schoolchild who submits a published poem to a contest as her own and when caught is baffled, since she thought her discovery of it in a book *made* it her own? Reade was capable of making such bizarre statements about plagiarism — "A book-pirate may often escape by re-wording the matter, because in many books an essential feature is the language" — that one sometimes wonders whether parts of his mind were quite right. . . . The truth is that he can be explained in the algebra of most compulsions. He stole because he hated stealing and he hated stealing because he stole.[60]

Twitchell and Reade are remarkably similar. For example, Paul castigated the "fakers" who would enhance their standing by "thieving" the works of others:

> All philosophers, preachers and sages who have the odor of philosophy, religion and knowledge are not any of these. They are pretenders, those who have pretended to have undergone the profound experiences of God; the faker drawing on experiences of real mystics, and the thieving of turns of speech and materials in hope of conveying a conviction of genuineness.[61]

To label these words ironic is an understatement. The extent of Paul's plagiarism is so great that a web site called the Center for Twitchellian Plagiarism is devoted to finding new instances of his literary piracy.[62] Early members of Eckankar had an idea, from their own studies or their direct work with Paul, that the writings of others appeared, without attribution, in some of Paul's manuscripts. Dr. Louis Bluth, the first President of Eckankar, says that he specifically pointed this out to Paul, who gave a glib response and moved right along doing the same thing:

> He borrowed my books of Radha Soami and copied a large share from them. I helped him write the Herb book. . . . I confronted him with what he had done and his answer was "since the author of the book said it better than I could, I copied it." The trouble is that he never gave anyone credit as to where he got it.[63]

Public revelations of plagiarism in Paul's writings started more than twenty years ago, when the then student David Lane, in a college term paper, first levelled the charge. That document evoked a threatening letter from Eckankar's attorneys, promising a lawsuit if Lane published his work.[64] Sensing that the threat meant he was on to something, Lane redoubled his efforts.

In time, Lane wrote a second paper that bears the name of his eventual book, *The Making of a Spiritual Movement: The Untold Story of Paul Twitchell and Eckankar.*[65] His book and a similar work (based on Lane's book) by a Christian organization called the Spiritual Counterfeits Project created a storm throughout the Eckankar movement. I remember students of Eckankar from all over the world seeking my opinion about these books and their significance to Eckankar. Both works were and are taboo subjects in Eckankar. The unwritten motto is: "Don't ask, don't tell, don't read."

When I first read Lane's book, I was upset to say the least. Though many of his conclusions and inferences were questionable, his evidence seemed unimpeachable. The valiant efforts of Eckists over the Internet to defend the faith were feeble and sometimes embarrassing. However, as Lane was an outsider, I knew that he could not know the whole story. After a long, tortuous, and silent struggle with Lane's revelations, I emerged with a renewed sense of dedication. In spite of the facts presented, Lane's work never undermined the core truths and principles that Paul had espoused, even if they were plagiarized.

At that time, I had not made the connection between the standards of truth to which I personally adhered and those to which my "hero," Paul Twitchell, seemed oblivious. In addition, I had no idea of the extent of Paul's deception. It was beyond my comprehension that anyone could do such things. At the time, I reasoned that Paul was dealing at such a high level of spirituality that he did not have time to adhere to, or was even above, the standards of truth by which we mortals had to live. Indeed, all truth is from spirit, I reasoned, and Paul probably tapped into the same source as the original author — perhaps even from the same inner location. This would be a simple feat for one who claimed to be "God made flesh on earth."[66] All manner of explication is marshaled to preserve the sanctity of cherished heroes and dreams.

Besides, my inner spiritual experiences confirmed the validity of the spiritual works; nothing, not even the writings of a detractor like Lane, could take these away from me.

The events of November of 2001, when I brought Graham Forsyth's journal to the attention of Harold, set all this on its head. They also reopened suspicions that had first appeared when I initially read Lane's exposé. I reread his extensive account of Paul's deceptions, but this time without the blinders of a true believer.

Lane's work greatly aided my examination of plagiarism in the writings of Paul Twitchell. So too was the laborious research of Eckists and former Eckists, displayed all over the Internet. They obviously felt a commitment, as did I, to find the truth, and make it available to those still trapped by the doctrines of deception throughout Eckankar. I thank each of them for his or her extraordinary work without which my efforts would have been far more difficult.

Examples, taken from a variety of Eckankar books show Paul's remarkable talents as a plagiarist. Plagiarized segments abound in practically every Eckankar book published under the Paul Twitchell name. Comparisons of Paul's *The Far Country*, which appears to be the most extensively plagiarized of all of his works, with passages from earlier writings by Julian Johnson demonstrate systematic theft. Let us compare passages from the two writers:

Johnson: We ought to remember the words of Vivekananda about churches, and religions in general. We could not say it better, so let us quote him: ". . . A man may believe in all the churches in the world; he may carry in his head all the sacred books ever written; he may baptize himself in all the rivers of the earth — still if he has no perception of God, I would class him with the rankest atheist. And a man may have never entered a church or a mosque, nor performed any ceremony; but if he realizes God within himself, and is thereby lifted above the vanities of the world, that man is a holy man, a saint, call him what you will..."[67]

Twitchell: "Now a study of the Divine SUGMAD is in order" said Rebazar Tarzs, dropping upon the floor and putting his legs one over the other in a lotus position. . . . "A man may believe in all the churches in the world; he may carry in his head all the sacred books ever written; he may baptize himself in all the rivers of the earth, — still if he has no perception of the SUGMAD, I would class him with the rankest atheist. And a man may never enter a church or a mosque, nor perform any ceremony; but if he realizes the SUGMAD within himself, and is thereby lifted above the vanities of the world, that man is a holy man, a saint; call him what you will."[68]

This is a remarkable example of plagiarism — though a careless one, for several reasons. First, note that Julian Johnson is quoting (appropriately) the words of Vivekananda. Yet Paul, recreating the scene as another drop-in by Rebazar Tarzs, pretends that Tarzs is uttering Vivekananda's words. This is a common device used by Paul to take the words of others and attribute them to one or more of his created line of Eck Masters. This clever example of plagiarism is particularly revealing because, on the very next page of Johnson's book, Johnson continues with words of his own composition, having ended his quote from Vivekananda. Yet, Paul continues to attribute the words to Rebazar Tarzs, as if he is giving an uninterrupted discourse. Paul has thus combined the words and ideas of two people and placed them in the mouth of his presumed master without regard for who is uttering them. Here is another example:

> **Johnson**: First of all, it is not a *feeling*. Secondly it is not a metaphysical speculation nor a logical syllogism. It is neither a conclusion based upon reasoning nor upon the evidence of books or persons. The basic idea is that God must become real to the individual, not a mental concept, but a living reality. And that can never be so *until the individual sees Him.* Personal sight and hearing are necessary before anything or anybody becomes *real* to us.[69]

> **Twitchell**: First of all, it is not a feeling. Secondly, it is not a metaphysical speculation, nor a logical syllogism. It is not a conclusion based upon reasoning, nor upon the evidence of books or persons. The basic idea is that the SUGMAD must become real to the individual. Not a mental concept of IT, but a living reality. This can never be until the individual sees IT. Personal sight and hearing are necessary, before anything or anybody becomes real to us.[70]

This example puts to the lie Eckankar's continuing claim that Paul "got it on the inner," where such wisdom is available to everyone and, presumably, in the same words. Even if one is gullible enough to buy this argument — supported by Harold's "astral library theory" (discussed below) — it stretches mystical credulity. To suggest that the same quotes from Vivekananda would be on the same pages as the writings of Johnson, in an astral library copy, virtually word for word, is simply

beyond belief. Of course, there is the additional matter of Paul's assertion that he was told this — quotes and all — by Rebazar Tarzs.

The King James Version Lives!

Another classic example of Twitchellian plagiarism is this much
quoted passage in the *Shariyat-Ki-Sugmad* attributed to Eck Master Lai
Tsi. Paul writes (Lai Tsi speaking):

> Here is a short contemplation seed which I found in myself upon return-
> ing from the heavenly worlds:
>
> "Show me thy ways, O SUGMAD;
> Teach me thy path.
> Lead me in thy truth, and teach me;
> On thee do I wait all day.
> Remember, O Beloved, thy guiding light
> And thy loving care.
> For it has been ever thy will,
> To lead the least of thy servants to Thee!"[71]

The origins of this contemplation seed are from a source familiar to
most. It seems that Paul was not above plagiarizing from the Bible
either. The King James Version reads:

> Shew me thy ways, O Lord; teach me thy paths. Lead me in thy truth,
> and teach me: for thou art the GOD of my salvation; on thee do I wait all
> the day. Remember, O Lord, thy tender mercies and thy loving kind-
> nesses; for they have been ever of old.[72]

Paul had to work harder on this one, but the flow and tenor of the
two passages are virtually the same. In the search for plagiarisms, this
constitutes a find.

The Toothless Tiger

One of the most revered books in Eckankar is Paul's *The Tiger's
Fang,* an account of his spiritual travels into the inner worlds and his
eventual ascension to the God-Realization experience. It is regarded as
a road map of the inner journey that all souls will take to reach the highest plane in the region of Sugmad (God). Aside from changing the
name of the master, Kirpal Singh (whom he acknowledged actually
accompaned him on these inner journeys), to his averred master, Rebazar Tarzs, Paul plagiarized extensively from the spiritual works of others. Here are examples of critical passages that he lifted from Walter

Russell's, *The Secret of Light*.[73] These passages are integrated into a description of Paul's excursion into the "world of Soul, that of pure light and so brilliant. . . . The king of this mystical world lives in a temple . . . overlooking his worlds."[74] Having set this magical scene, Paul falsely attributes the words of Russell to the "God" of this plane, whom he called Omkar or Parabrahm.

Russell: God is consciousness. Consciousness is static.[75]

Twitchell: Know this that God is consciousness and consciousness is static. . . .[76]

Russell: Consciousness is the spiritual awareness of Being, of all-knowing, all-power and all-presence. . . . Thinking is the motionless principle in light which creates the illusion of motion.[77]

Twitchell: Consciousness is the spiritual awareness of Being, of all-knowing, all-power, and all-presence. Thinking is the motionless principle in light and sound which creates the illusion of motion. . . .[78]

Russell: The Self of man belongs to the static, invisible, conscious, unconditioned universe of KNOWING. We express knowing in the dynamic, visible, electrically conditioned universe of sensation.[79]

Twitchell: The Soul of man belongs to the static, invisible, conscious, unconditioned world of knowing. You express knowing in the dynamic, visible, electrically conditioned universe of perception.[80]

Russell: Sensation is the electrical awareness of motion simulating the spiritual QUALITIES of the One Idea by creating imaged QUANTITIES of separate forms which seem to have substance.[81]

Twitchell: Perception is the electrical awareness of motion simulating the spiritual qualities of God, who creates imaged qualities of separate forms which seem to have material substance.[82]

Russell: Consciousness is real. Sensation simulates reality through motion of interchanging lights, but the mirage of a city is not the city it reflects. . . . Man is the only unit in Creation who has *conscious awareness* of the spirit within him and electrical awareness of dually conditioned light acting upon his senses. All other units of Creation have *electrical awareness* only.[83]

Twitchell: Consciousness is real and perception simulates reality through motion of interchanging lights, but the mirage of a city is not the city it reflects. So man is the only unit in creation which has conscious awareness of spirit within him and electrical awareness of dually conditioned light acting upon his physical senses. All other units of creation has [*sic*] electrical awareness only.[84]

Other parts of *The Tiger's Fang* abound with stolen sections he attributes to Rebazar Tarzs or the ruler of some higher plane. While this book is both lyrical and profound in many respects, it is nonetheless a deception, for it portrays Paul and his encounters with higher beings in a manner that is not true. However lofty, inspiring, and enlightening this work may be, once the truth is known, it leaves the reader with a sense of betrayal, because Paul has mixed spiritual ideals with lies and deceit.

The Source of Eckankar Writings on the HU

From Paul's writings and the emphasis placed on it by Harold, most Eckists believe that the HU originated with Eckankar and the Masters of the Vairagi Order. This is not so. The HU features prominently in Sant Mat and is believed to have derived from Sufi teachings. Paul's source was Hazrat Inayat Khan's book, *The Mysticism of Sound and Music*. Here is a comparison:

Hazrat Khan: The Supreme Being has been called by various names in different languages, but the mystics have known him as *Hu* . . . the only name of the nameless. . . . The word *Hu* is the spirit of all sounds and of all words, and is hidden under them all, as the spirit in the body. It does not belong to any language, but no language can help belonging to it. This alone is the true name of God, a name that no people and no religion can claim as their own.[85]

Twitchell: The Supreme has been called various names in different languages, but it is known to those who recognize the real wisdom as HU, the name of the nameless one. The word HU is the Spirit of all sounds and of all words, and is hidden under them all as the Spirit of Soul. It does not belong to any language; no language can help belonging to it. This alone is the true name of God, a name that no people and no religion can claim as their own.[86]

Paul chose a powerful concept to incorporate into Eckankar. No one can criticize him for that. All who have used this word and chanted it regularly will attest to the impact that it has had in their lives. Some Eckists distribute small cards containing the word HU with instructions on how to use it. Paul's decision to incorporate the HU into Eckankar was an important one. However, Eckankar, contrary to the admonition "no religion can claim (Hu) as its own," has virtually kidnapped the word, making all who hear it think that its origin is in Eckankar and that it is Eckankar's gift to the world.

With such good intentions for the whole, why does Eckankar keep the origins of the HU a secret? Why kidnap the word and pretend that the Eckankar Masters originated it and passed it down to Paul Twitchell? What is wrong with telling the truth and honestly attributing the source of this insight? The answer is simple. The HU is one of the lock stitches in the fabric that Eckankar has woven about its origins and history. If Eckankar acknowledges that the HU came from somewhere else, the primacy of Eckankar as the source of all religions on earth begins to fall apart. However, as we shall see when tracing the origins of the HU itself, it is not as Hazrat Inayat Khan proclaimed it. Rather, he took this Islamic word, which actually translates as the male pronoun "he," and embellished it far beyond anything in Islamic scholarship. This, of course, does not make it effective or ineffective, but simply begins to place it in its proper historic perspective. However, the real origin of the word HU appears to be in ancient Egypt, not in Islam.[87]

Paul and Harold perpetuated Kahn's embellishment and then usurped it by not revealing the origins of the HU (and countless other aspects of the Eckankar teaching). The dilemma Harold faces is that if he makes a concession to truth, a bit of the Eckankar dogma unravels. If he were to reveal the distortions, the truths would still remain to contribute to the spiritual consciousness of humankind. The difficulty in untangling Eckankar is that truth and distortion are so tightly interwoven that separating them is nearly impossible. Paul has created such a mythical, mystical mix (espoused most prominently in the *Shariyat-Ki-Sugmad*) that, even forewarned of fabrications, the reader is still drawn ever so seductively into his mythology and mysticism.

I struggled with this problem as the truth about Eckankar revealed itself to me. In time, I was able to distinguish between myth and core beliefs still helpful in spiritual unfolding. I will share some of these insights in later chapters in the hope that they might be helpful to those who will face the same struggles I faced.

"In My Father's House There Are Many Mansions"

Eckankar's cosmology, or structure, of the inner worlds is also heavily plagiarized. Comparisons are again called for:

> **Johnson**: Next above Anda lies Brahmanda, the third grand division. This term means 'the egg of Brahm.' It is egg-shaped, like Anda, but is much vaster in extent. It is also more refined and full of light, markedly more than the physical universe. . . . In fact, spirit predominates in Brahmanda just as matter predominates in Pinda, while Anda is rather on the dividing line between the two.[88]

> **Twitchell**: Above the Anda world lies that which we call the *Brahmanda*, the third grand division, the "Egg of Brahm." It is like the Anda world, but greater in scope and immensity of space. It is also more refined and more full of light than any of the worlds below it. In fact, Spirit predominates the Brahmanda Plane, just as matter dominates the Pinda, while the Anda is in between.[89]

Comparing the sources of these two quotes, we learn that they share considerably more in common than this one selection. I was struck by how much Paul took from Johnson's book: changing some paragraphs enough that they appear dissimilar at first glance, yet express the same thoughts with many of the same words, though often in a different order. It amazes me how Eckankar can claim, in spite of extensive evidence to the contrary, that Paul did not plagiarize. It is like a jury that is shown the smoking gun, the bullet from the victim, a videotape of the shooting, the victim's death proclamation naming the accused, and a motive of jealousy, and yet is still not convinced of the defendant's guilt.

The cosmology in Eckankar's *God Worlds Chart*,[90] is taken from the cosmologies of Sant Mat and Theosophy. A reading of Johnson's *Path of The Masters* demonstrates this conclusively.

In examples such as this, Paul generally places his Eck Masters in a plausible historical context. Yet, he makes them, especially Rebazar Tarzs, the original thinkers, the "pioneers,"[91] of various spiritual ideas, and the authentic masters become mere epigones of his fanciful creations.[92] This is a good illustration of Paul's art of weaving known spiritual history with his mythical history of the Eck Masters in a manner that deceives the unwary.

In acknowledging some connection with the cosmology of the Theosophical Society, Paul writes:

> What the Theosophical Society calls their planes, or what we know of them through the Vedanta group, never particularly bothered me, for they are all the same and we are not troubled with making comparisons. All we wish to do is to keep straight in our minds those various planes and the governments on each. I have used the names given by the *Shariyat-Ki-Sugmad* which is the holy book of the ECK Masters of the ancient Vairagi Order.[93]

Paul concedes that there are other paths with names similar to those found in Eckankar. Yet, he claims that none of them is his source, and that he got the names of the planes from the holy book of Eckankar, not from these other paths. However, a reading of Johnson's *Path of the Masters* alongside Twitchell's *Eckankar: Key to Secret Worlds* reveals that the former is the real source of the names of planes and much of the text of the *Shariyat-Ki-Sugmad.*

Paul contradicts or at least greatly revises without explanation Eckankar's cosmology by arbitrarily changing it from one with eight planes to one with twelve. Somehow, over a short period, coinciding with the publication of the 1970 edition of the *God Worlds Chart,* heaven added four planes, four gods, and four sounds. In addition to changing the names of the planes, Paul added the Alaya Lok, the Hukikat Lok, and two others.

The differences in Paul's two cosmologies are very significant. First, it shows that Paul originally copied the Sant Mat cosmology plane for plane, building the heavenly structure that he credited the Vairagi Masters with pioneering. However, around 1970, Eckankar's vision of the inner worlds changed. What happened? Did heaven go through remodeling? Did someone sneak in and edit the *Shariyat-Ki-Sugmad* that Paul claimed was his actual source? We also have another problem: the sounds.

The 1970 edition of the *God Worlds Chart* drastically altered the landscape Paul had previously outlined. The sound of thunder was a sign to Eckists that they were on the Brahm Lok (Trikuti), but the sound seems to have shifted to the physical plane (Elam). Bells formerly alerted the traveler that she was on the astral plane (Sahasra dal Kanwal), but now she finds herself on the causal plane. Moreover, the note of the flute, that glorious sound that alerted spiritual travelers of their arrival at Bhanwar Gupha (Mental Plane), now heralds their entry into Sat Nam (Soul Plane). With the rearranging of planes and sounds, it's easy to see how hard Harold's job is. He must straighten out the pretzel course of truth Paul left for him to untangle.

One final note on Paul's dishonesty is in order. His deceptions were not limited to his published books but extended also to correspondence with his wife, Gail. In a series of letters written to her before their marriage, Paul expounded on various esoteric matters in order to instruct and educate her. She obviously believed that this insight was coming from Paul and was apparently quite impressed. Everyone who read these letters was equally impressed. They were eventually published in several volumes called *Letters To Gail*. Unknown to Gail and the original publishers, Paul had copied a large portion of the content from a variety of published sources.[94] He apparently never told her the real source, since they were later published with Gail's permission. (One of the volumes of *Letters to Gail* was eventually discontinued.) This is part of the pattern of the plagiarist. Deception became a habit until it is quite possible that Paul no longer considered that he was involved in it. He made it his by copying and transmitting it, and apparently for him that was enough. Eventually, word came to the Eckankar office that the books contained copyrighted materials, many taken from the works of Paul's early mentor, L. Ron Hubbard, of Scientology fame.[95]

The last irony in the saga is Paul's reaction when a former Eckankar student, John-Roger Hinkins, decided to start his own equally dubious path (the Church of the Movement of Spiritual Inner Awareness, MSIA) and "borrowed" heavily from Paul's "writings." Paul hit the roof and threatened Hinkins with a lawsuit.[96] From all accounts, Hinkins and MSIA have followed in the tradition of Paul Twitchell and Eckankar and have even added to the scandal associated with some of Eckankar's progeny. [97]

There are hundreds of examples of Paul's plagiarism that could be cited. Various web sites and Lane's book will lead to a treasure trove of additional evidence for those who may need more convincing.[98]

In Defense of Plagiarism: the Apologists Speak

Sensing the damage that the publication of David Lane's research would have on Eckankar, its lawyer, Alan Nichols, attempted to refute the charge that Paul had plagiarized the works of Julian Johnson. He wrote in a letter to Lane in 1977:

> With a wide background of study you will find many similarities both approximate and exact in many religious statements, history and mythology. . . . How did you know Johnson didn't obtain his information from Twitchell or Rebazar Tarzs [*sic*] or some other common source? Don't be surprised that many people find the same truths and even in the same words, commandments, etc., whether they are concepts, stories of events, or levels of God Worlds or consciousness.[99]

The argument is a stretch to say the least. As an attorney, he would surely not make such an argument in a court of law. At that time, it represented Eckankar's official position and remains so today. If Eckankar's argument were accepted, it would stand the entire moral-ethical-legal foundation of creativity on its head. Moreover, the argument fails for one basic reason. Granted, ideas are ubiquitous and are received and expressed by different individuals as original expressions. However, each person's expression of an idea is unique. No two things in the universe are exactly alike. No cell in our body, no fingerprint, no voice-print is exactly the same. The proposition that two people would express hundreds of paragraphs in an identical manner is to stretch credulity to the breaking point. And to suggest that Julian Johnson may have copied his book from Paul, who arrived on the scene twenty-four years later, is to extend the argument to the ridiculous. No, there is no plausible explanation but that Paul was one of the most prolific plagiarists of his time.

The Master Compiler Theory

As the principal defender of the faith, Harold attempted to explain away some of Paul's idiosyncrasies without referring to the accusations of plagiarism. Harold employed the euphemism of "master compiler:"

> Paul gathered up the whole teaching and took the best. Though it may be a strange thing to say, in this sense I see him as a master compiler.[100]

It is true that there is much chaff and little wheat in the vast fields of spiritual writing during both Paul's day and our own. Yet Paul's "compiling" seemed to be limited to a single row in a very small field. Paul was fortunate to have hit the jackpot early in his Eckankar book-writing days. Most of his compiling was taken from the books of Julian Johnson, Ruhani Satsang (Kirpal Singh's path), Hazrat Inayat Khan, H. P. Blavatsky, L. Ron Hubbard, Walter Russell, the Bible, Lama Govinda, and Neville. Visions of Paul, with thousands of books gathered from all over the world and picked through to find the gems that he included in his many books, is what I once imagined. This is the vision that Eckankar would still have its followers believe.

If one takes a trip to the Center for Twitchellian Plagiarism[101] on the Internet, a distinctly different view is advanced. It is not as altruistic as Harold makes it sound and certainly not the feat of creative culling and benign interpolation that Eckists believe. Instead, one finds evidence of a clever and accomplished plagiarist, who assiduously pilfered the works of a select group of authors. He claims their ideas as his and, through the clever insertion of his own mythology, converts their words into the doctrine and substance of Eckankar. Even books like *The Tiger's Fang,* which I had always assumed to be Paul's actual journey into the God worlds, is so rife with plagiarism that one wonders if or to what extent Paul ever had inner journeys. This is not "compiling" and these "high teachings of ECK" were not "scattered to the four corners of the world."[102] Instead, they were contained in a library 1/100 the size of even my modest library and culled for the nuggets of truth that Paul claimed as his own.

The Astral Library Theory

Harold's creativity was at its best when he gave life to the idea of an "astral library." In this esoteric locale, presumably, the original versions of spiritual books are there to be copied. In Harold's view, Paul's plagiarism becomes merely a visit to an inner library. He wrote:

> I'd like to conclude by mentioning how the libraries on the inner planes work. On these planes there are main libraries connected to the wisdom temples. But there are also many branch libraries. . . . Most of the writers from earth go to the branch libraries, so they don't get to use the best sources. But the good researchers—such as Paul, Julian Johnson, Paul Brunton, and others — can come in here and select the paragraphs that suit their audience.. . . In the margin next to the different paragraphs on the manuscript I was reading were notes written in Paul's hand: *"Far*

Country," "*Shariyat-Ki-Sugmad* . . . and so on. Under his notes a librarian researcher had placed the specific page reference where these ideas could be found in current manuscripts.[103]

It is hard to imagine a dream more ably orchestrated to meet the chorus of accusations about plagiarism that plagued Eckankar before and during the spring of 1984, when this talk was given. But, it is just a little too convenient. A room accessible only to the "good writers" like Paul and those from whom he plagiarized? *Please!*

This explanation is so nonsensical that it betrays desperation. I believe that Harold had a dream. I believe that it may have been exactly as he describes it. But, to write about it as though it is a true and factual description of an actual "astral library" from which all ideas come, is something else. By failing to label it a dream or even an inner experience, subject to the same subjectivity and personal tailoring of all dreams, is to be disingenuous. Harold rejected seven years of spiritual experiences of a chela as, essentially, the work of the Kal. Yet, he puts this experience forward as a true and factual explanation of how Paul's writings seem to be identical to those of so many other writers.

It is certainly true that everyone receives inspiration and ideas in the dream state, in flashes of insight in the waking state, and in numerous other ways. However, to imply that writers simply go inside with a note pad and copy whatever they need for their next paragraph or book is to trivialize the laborious, iterative process that all writers know. Even if two writers have the same idea at the same time, which is certainly possible, each writer will express that idea in a manner that is his own. The probability of literally thousands of sentences and paragraphs being identical, including quotes and mistakes, is so low as to be impossible.

From Sow's Ear to Silk Purse

In spite of the pall that revelations about Paul's plagiarism cast on the teachings of Eckankar, it is important not to lose sight of a great spiritual principle implicit in the Law of Opposites. This Law postulates that everything contains within it the seeds of its opposite. From this principle, we see good emerging from evil, and evil emerging from good. All things contain their opposites and have both negative and positive aspects existing coterminously. Paul's plagiarism nevertheless conveyed spiritual truth, for he purloined passages from truly great spiritual works. For that, I remain grateful. This is the reason Eckankar has survived in spite of Paul's dishonesty.

After first learning about Paul's literary piracy, I was more concerned about the truth contained in his pilfered selections than the fact that they weren't his. My daughter put it succinctly. She described a hand with fingers curled and index finger pointing, noting the importance of focusing on where the finger was pointing (truth) rather than the shape of the curled fingers (the source of the truth). Her analogy captured the essence of my approach to Paul's writings. I had learned a great deal from his books — plagiarisms and all. They greatly contributed to my understanding of higher consciousness.

However, this does not excuse or exonerate him. Paul's struggles with truth, from his early years through his last days, bring into question the validity of his mastership and his level of spiritual awareness. But we cannot question his brilliance. However, genius is not spirituality or mastership. The most ironic aspect of this probe into his plagiarism is the sense that he might have been capable of these insights on his own — a curious disposition of many plagiarists. In either misguided haste or covetous thievery, they commit acts that are unnecessary yet, for them, unavoidable.

The simple person who speaks "the truth, the whole truth, and nothing but the truth" is the true master. Truth is the quintessential expression of God-love and God-reality. Only a person who can speak the truth is capable of expressing the nature of the divine. Anything less brings chaos, for as Paul instructed:

> Refuse to see Truth, pretend that it is impossible to know what is true and what is not, distort Truth, seek to mix it with Untruth, attempt to deceive both ourselves and others, give Truth in an unattractive manner, then chaos will reign in our lives.[104]

Device Three: Substitution and Association

The device of substitution and association involves replacing names found in an original published work with new names or words in another published work. This device enabled Paul to create new ideas, words, and persons necessary in the formation of his new world religion.

The creation of myth and its transmutation into historical fact is difficult and time-consuming work. Like the magician who performs his legerdemain with everyone watching, Paul constructed a religion, a line of masters, and a revered position for himself, in full view of the world. He almost got away with it but for the paper trail that he left and the Internet that blossomed in the nineties. Paul started spinning the tale of his life with its mysterious and mystical components from an early age. Details of his date of birth, place of birth, and parentage were shrouded in such distorted and divergent accounts that confusion if not mystery was the result.

In the early sixties, Paul's writing prowess could barely feed and house him. With a new wife and a new life, he was pressed for time and money. He wrote discourses and gave lectures to supplement Gail's income and make ends meet, but it wasn't enough. This work and her influence were the foundation and the motivation for starting Eckankar as a for-profit business. As his start-up venture caught fire and his stature grew from cliff hanger to teacher to guru, Paul's vision of Eckankar began to take shape.

As much as anything, this motivated him to take shortcuts in publishing his books. Paul was aware that, if it were to have any legitimacy in a world filled with competitors, Eckankar had to have an impressive history and teaching. The simplest way to solve this problem was to make them up. Paul was quite aware that religious histories were filled with distortions, myths, tales, and dogma based on a few historical facts. While other religions had thousands of years to evolve, Paul did not have the time to wait. Besides, with his ingenuity and imagination, a perfectly plausible history and teaching could be crafted. To this end, Paul employed the devices of substitution and association to construct Eckankar.

This is how the first of Paul's Eck Masters, Sudar Singh, made his appearance in print. Paul inserted Sudar Singh's name in an article he wrote for *Orion Magazine,* in which he leads Paul to Kirpal Singh, his actual teacher. Establishing an association between a real master and the spurious Sudar Singh in a 1964 article for public consumption provided a measure of authenticity. Two years later, Rebazar Tarzs was born in a republication of the same article, this time in the booklet,

Introduction to Eckankar. Whereas the original *Orion* article refers to bilocation and Shabd Yoga, Paul replaces these terms with "Eckankar" in the new publication,[105] cleverly interweaving myth and fact. What followed was a systematic revision of his writings by substituting newly created Masters of the Vairagi for real spiritual teachers and masters with whom he had studied or been affiliated.

An example of Paul's skill is seen in the serialized version of *The Flute of God*, published by *Orion* in 1966. Paul writes:

> I remember very well when *Swami Premananda* of India . . . said "When someone asked Bertrand Russell what his philosophy of life was, he wrote several volumes of books on the subject."[106]

When Illuminated Way Press published *The Flute of God* in 1970, Paul altered the text:

> I remember very well when *Sudar Singh, the great ECK Master* said, "When someone asked Bertrand Russell what his philosophy of life was, he wrote several volumes of books on the subject."[107]

Paul combines substitution and authenticity by association in this next example. In the earlier serialized version of *The Flute of God*, He wrote:

> When *Jesus looked upon His People* and said, "I cannot tell you more because you cannot hear the whole of Truth," He was saying that they were so far down the spiral of life they could not grasp His meaning. To tell them all would bring disorder into their lives, for once exposed to Truth, those not understanding develop hostility.[108]

When this passage was republished by Illuminated Way Press in 1970, the text was changed to read:

> When the *ECK Master, Gopal Das*, looked upon his people and said, "I cannot tell you more because you cannot hear the whole of ECK," he was saying that. . . . To tell them all would bring disorder . . . those not understanding develop hostility. . . . [Gopal Das] was wise in his ways, as was [*sic*] Buddha, Zoroaster and many other Masters who have come to this earth. . . .[109]

Paul not only substituted his newly created master Gopal Das for Jesus, but also associated him with Buddha and Zoroaster in a declaration of their wisdom that lends credibility to his phantom master.

In another example, Paul again substitutes the name of one of his Eck Masters for the name of Jesus, used in the original published manuscript, and associates the new Eck Master's name with another actual spiritual notable, Jalaluddin Rumi. Here is how Paul did it. In the text of the original manuscript of *The Flute of God* published in *Orion,* he writes:

> Therefore, the principal [*sic*] involved here is: "We live and have our being in the Supreme Being," *Jesus said it in another way* as "we move and have our being in God." Other savants e.g., Jalaluddin Maulanana [*sic*] Rumi put it in another way. . . .[110]

In the book form of *Flute of God,* he changed the text to read:

> Therefore, the principle involved here is, "We live and have our being in the Supreme Being." *Lai Tsi, the Chinese ECK Master, said it this way,* "we live and move and have our being in the SUGMAD." Other savants state it in a slightly different vein. For instance, Jalaluddin Maulana Rumi said. . . .[111]

Aside from taking a statement attributed to Jesus and appropriating it for a new Eck Master, Paul adds to the credibility of his Eck Master by juxtaposing his name with that of Rumi, making his Lai Tsi (almost certainly a deliberate corruption of Lao-tse[112]) seem real. Other examples of this technique of substitution and association are too numerous for inclusion here.[113]

Another note of interest about Paul's art of substitution is a statement by a former editor of the *ECK World News,* an earlier Eckankar publication in newspaper format. In a personal interview with David Lane, he recalled his experiences with Eckankar's unique form of editing.

> I have personally seen the name "Kirpal Singh" crossed out in the manuscript form of *Letters to Gail.* The name "Sudar Singh" was written above it. I believe that Gail did the editing.[114]

We also see Paul reinforce his new name for God, Sugmad, which he introduced for the first time in his writings. Nothing is wrong with this in itself. We are all free to call God whatever we wish. But Paul created an expression for God and made it appear as an ancient name passed down from master to master. Eckists accept this name as an authentic expression of the Vairagi tradition handed down from the hoary past. Paul's failure to acknowledge that Sugmad is a creation or adaptation brings deception into the highest expression of human long-ing, the search for God. For in no literature other than in Eckankar, can the word Sugmad be found.[115]

If the term Sugmad did exist, it existed exclusively on the inner planes, for it had no known expression in the outer world before Paul's use of it. And this despite the 970 former Eck Masters that supposedly walked this earth prior to him. It does seem odd that none of them was influential enough to have this presumably ancient name for God ever recorded in the physical world. Such is the suspension of rational thought that is required to accept Paul's explanation for this and numer-ous other concepts and doctrines in Eckankar.

The device of authenticity by substitution and association is not by accident. On the contrary, Paul knew exactly what he was doing and did it repeatedly. The craft and skill that he employed would be the envy of any charlatan. Here are more examples:

> I am aware that there are many approaches to God. . . . What Mary Baker Eddy used as an avenue to Truth would be completely awry with that used by the Master Saint, Ramakrishna . . . in the Vedanta religion . . . or . . . Moses or Shankcharaya . . . and even with that of the greatest Sufi Saint, Shamus Tabiz. . . .[116]

A few paragraphs later, Paul writes:

> Here is an example of how it was explained to me in its elementary form. The great ECK Master, Fubbi Quantz, gave me this clue by the use of only two words. . . .[117]

In this example, Paul reels off a list of names known to most readers as having made substantial contributions to spiritual thought, then inserts the name of his Eck Master Fubbi Quantz, which, by association and close juxtaposition, confers credibility upon his creation. Several para-graphs later he writes:

> Development of the science of thought has brought man to the realiza-tion that prayer is *not* as Jesus was said to have taught, but is a fact of knowing, without reservation, that we live in the eternal NOW. Yaubl Sacabi, residing in Agam Des, the spiritual city in the Himalayas, states that "all is here now!"[118]

Here, Paul creates a disagreement between Jesus and a created master, Yaubl Sacabi, and even gives his address for an added touch of authen-ticity.

When I first read these passages, I felt quite at home with these masters; they joined the pantheon of other masters about whom I had read and studied. As an unsuspecting Eckist, my critical faculties were not focused on the masters themselves. I focused on the reasonableness of the truth conveyed. I had no way of knowing, and no reason to suspect, that Paul was stealthily planting the names and reality of these Eck "Masters" in my consciousness.

The Vairagi Masters are one of the most fascinating aspects of Paul's creation. This part of the fabric of Eckankar is woven so tightly that it takes close examination to find the threads that eventually cause it to unravel. We start with Paul's clear admission, "ECKANKAR, *which I formed out of my own experience...*"[119] and:

> The switchover from the Cliff-Hanger to ECK began taking place after I met my present wife, Gail. She insisted that I do something with my knowledge and abilities. [120]

An ancient teaching with a line of 970 former masters does not just get formed out of one's own experience or because one's wife insists on doing something with one's knowledge and abilities. The next in a line of leadership is quick to acknowledge his lineage and to pay tribute to those who came before him. Paul eventually does this, but only after he has had adequate time to construct the marvelous array of names, places, and events that make up the history of Eckankar and its masters.

Paul was even late in acknowledging Eckankar itself, despite his avowed earlier training in this teaching and his later assertion in the "true account" of his life in *The Drums of Eck,* in which he describes the existence of Eckankar in the middle of the nineteenth century.[121] One of the first articles that portrays the emerging popular writer who was soon to become the Living Eck Master, appears in a 1963 article in the *Seattle Post Intelligencer* entitled, "Paul Twitchell, Man of Parts."[122] Yet, Paul claims to have been guided and taught, since he was a boy of sixteen, by Sudar Singh and Rebazar Tarzs. Presumably, he was being prepared to assume the "Rod of ECK Power,"[123] also a piece of Twitchellian fiction.

Paul borrowed and modified an ancient word to create the name Eckankar. The term Eckankar appears to be derived from a term *Ekan-*

kar that means "One oneness, the body of oneness."[124] Eckankar was not officially founded until October 22, 1965, when Paul claims to have received the Rod of Eck Power from Rebazar Tarzs. In response to questions from Brad Steiger in his biography, Paul indicates that,

> . . . Rebazar Tarzs began to appear and give me intensive instructions. He had been appearing regularly in the later fifties, but he said that those sessions had only been designed to prepare me for the exhaustive drills which now faced me.[125]

Paul created a fifteen-year gap between the death of Sudar Singh and the resumption of his instruction in the late fifties[126] — a strange hiatus for one that would be the next Living Eck Master. However, as we have noted, Harold attempted to cover for this short coming by his assertion that Sudar Singh actually died in 1955. As we shall see, the only basis for this assertion appears to be a vague rumor gleaned by Eckist on an investigative trip to India. In spite of his claims of earlier knowledge of Rebazar Tarzs, Paul first acknowledges Tarzs' existence in a 1964 publication. This seems a belated way (about ten years late) to acknowledge the torchbearer of the ancient teaching he would some-day lead. In his earlier writings, Paul mentions not one of the names of the ancient brotherhood of Vairagi Masters until Sudar Singh appears for the first time in the January, 1964 issue of *Orion*, where Paul says:

> I began my study of bilocation under the tutelage of Satguru Sudar Singh, in Allahabad, India. Later, I switched to Sri Kirpal Singh of Old Delhi. Both were teaching the Shabda Yoga. . . .[127]

Prior to this, there had been no mention of Sudar Singh, even though Paul later wrote that he first met him while in his teens, and claimed to have visited Singh's ashram in India. There is no evidence that any such visit to India to see Sudar Singh, or anyone else for that matter, ever occurred. Further, no Sudar Singh was ever found to have existed, even though Harold made a number of intimations and insinuations that he did.[128] It is speculated that the name Sudar Singh was a corruption of Sudarshan Singh, a real master who resided in Allahabad, India for a period. This name is discussed in one of the primary books that Paul plagiarized, and probably was his source as well as the source of Harold's attempt to establish the authenticity of Sudar Singh.[129]

It is particularly strange that Paul did not mention this great master even once prior to 1964. If Paul was born in 1909, as official documents attest, even by Paul's timetable, he kept the name of this master a secret from the world for more than forty years. During that time, Paul wrote extensively about the many other masters with whom he had studied and who had influenced his work. The principal spiritual master mentioned throughout the period prior to the appearance of Sudar Singh was Kirpal Singh, Paul's actual master and teacher. Sudar Singh's name surfaced only when it became necessary for Paul to explain with whom he had been studying during the time he was actually with Kirpal Singh. Since he had already burned his bridge with his former master, someone had to be substituted, and another cover-up began.

Equally strange is Paul's description of Sudar Singh as a teacher of Shabd Yoga. Why would Paul not describe him as an Eckankar Master? After all, by Paul's historical reckoning, Eckankar was also the precursor of Shabd Yoga, and Sudar Singh was his first Eck Master. Why slight this most venerated of all religions along with his first master by claiming that he (Singh) was associated with a teaching other than the purported source of all spiritual teachings, Eckankar? The reason is rather clear. At this stage in the creation of Eckankar, Paul had not formulated the history and preeminence Eckankar was to assume, by Paul's hand, as the source of all known religions. At this stage he quite openly admitted to the authentic roots of Eckankar and its created masters, namely, Shabd Yoga.

Finally, given how meticulous Paul was about saving and sharing every shred of information about his life (remember his relentless self-promotion), it is difficult to imagine that, if the Eck Masters were real, he would not have written something, somewhere, about at least one of them before 1965. We know that he wrote extensively about his master Kirpal Singh, because copies of his correspondence with him are on file at Singh's ashram in India. It is also known that Gail transferred all of Paul's letters (he apparently made copies of everything he wrote) and other records to Eckankar (for a tidy sum) during the reign of Darwin Gross. If there were any proof of the existence of these masters in Paul's writings or letters, then Harold would almost surely have brought it forward in defense. During the years that he attempted to clean up the Eckankar house by selectively revealing enough truth to neutralize Paul's critics, he made many startling admissions about Paul and his colorful history. But not once did he bring forth any evidence that supported Paul's claim of early association with Sudar Singh, any other Eck Master, or anything resembling Eckankar — except for the teachings of Kirpal Singh that Paul would eventually use.

Device Four: Name Reversal, Letter Transposition, and Adoption — The Creation of the Vairagi Masters

We have just seen how Paul used association and substitution to create the illusion of historical validity for the Vairagi Masters. We shall now reveal the clever and resourceful techniques he used to create the names of the Eck Masters.

The technique of name reversal was used quite frequently to come up with an original and mystical name for a Vairagi Master. An interesting example of this is his creation of a fictional master living during the time of Emperor Vespasian in Rome (69 to 79 C.E.). History records the life of *Hevidius Priscus*, a Roman senator and part of a coterie of oppositional senators, who were thorns in the side of the Emperor. (Priscus was eventually exiled and later executed.) According to Paul's account, an Eck Master also lived in the same period as this Roman senator and, went by the name of *Priscus Hevidius*. But history records no trace of him. In this example, Paul did not bother to disguise the real person by changing dates or historical references (Paul's Eck Master was also a Roman senator). He simply reversed the names of the real senator to create his new member of the Vairagi Adepts.

Another example of this technique is seen in the creation of the Eck Master *Habu Medinet*, who, according to Paul, lived in Persia around 490 B.C. This name for Paul's Eck Master was taken from the name of an historical site called *Medinet Habu,* ("City of Habu" in Arabic), which is the site of the mortuary temple of Rameses III. The monuments in Medinet Habu, which was both a single temple and a complex of temples, were constructed between 1500 and 1100 B.C.E.

In Paul's methodology, a name reversal, along with, in some instances, the transposition of a few letters, was all that was needed to take an historical name or place and transform it into the name of an ancient Eck Master. A similar technique is name combination. Here Paul takes two words, usually with some independent spiritual connotation, and combines them to form the name of an Eck Master. The Eck Master *Asanga Kaya* appears to derive from an historical figure from India and a word associated with enlightenment. Paul describes this Eck Master as the Adept of the Hukikat Lok (also invented by Paul in his restatement of the Eckankar cosmology) and guardian of the *Shariyat-Ki-Sugmad* at the Temple of Golden Wisdom of Jertz Chong.

The real *Asanga* lived in India around the fourth and fifth centuries C.E., and was noted for his selection and elaboration of spiritual and esoteric concepts into a full yoga system. Asanga was noted for founding, along with his brother Vasubandu, the Yogacara school of Buddhism.[130] *Kaya* means "enlightenment body." Together they make up the name of Paul's Eck Master.

Another example of this art of creation is the Eck Master *Gopal Das*. *Gopal* is another name for Krishna (God). *Dasa* means "slave" or "disciple." Gopal Das was Eckankar's purported Living Eck Master in ancient Egypt.

The second technique Paul used in his invention of the Vairagi Masters, letter transposition, was, judging by its frequency, his favorite. Paul would add, omit, or reverse letters in names of real historical figures in order to create a new identity and a new Eck Master. Here are a few examples:

Lai Tsi was allegedly an Eck Master serving as guardian of the *Shariyat* in Arhirit. He is almost certainly adapted from the actual spiritual master, *Lao-tzu* (sometimes spelled *Lao Tse*), referred to in a number of Paul's writings.[131] Lao-tzu is considered the father of Taoism. To achieve this magic, Paul simply dropped the last letter of each name and substituted an "i" in each space.

Eck Master *Appolonius of Tyano* was, according to Paul, "a student of the Neo-Pythagorean pyramid." Paul started with a real historical figure, *Apollonius of Tyana*, and then performed minor surgery. By simply adding a "p" he constructed the first name. The second name was even easier. Drop the "a" at the end and add an "o" and presto: a new Eck Master! The real Apollonius of Tyana was also a neo-Pythagorean from Greece, who was reputed to have magical powers and died in the second century C.E. Paul's Appolonius lived over the astonishing time period of 4,000 years (3000 B.C.E. to C.E. 1000)[132] and was considered a contemporary or parallel figure of Jesus.

Descates, the Living Eck Master on the continent of Atlantis, was another invention. This name is a variation of the famous mathematician and philosopher, ***René Descartes*** (1596-1650), often considered the father of modern philosophy. Paul easily achieved this invention by simply removing an "r."

The third technique can be called adoption. In order to lend credibility to his ever-increasing line of Eck Masters, it was important that some of them be historical figures recognizable to the public. But in adopting the name of a known historical figure, it was important for Paul to select names whose detailed histories were lost to time. In this way, his claims could avoid rigorous scrutiny. Here are some of the names that Paul adopted into the Ancient Order of Vairagi Masters:

- ***Plato***: Paul claims the famous Greek philosopher as an Eck Master. Plato was of course one of the greatest philosophers of all time. He lived ca. 427–347 B.C.E. and founded a famous school in Athens known as the Academy, where Aristotle studied.
- ***St. Francis of Assisi***: Considered by Paul to be an "ECK Master who gave up personal attachments to give all to the cause of ECK." Actually, St. Francis was founder of the Franciscan order of Christianity and lived from 1181 to 1226. There is no evidence he had any religious beliefs outside Christianity.
- ***Chuang Tzu***: A follower of Lao-tzu and the first to fully develop the Taoistic thesis of the rhythm of life, a feat that put him on Paul's list. He lived more than 2200 years ago, apparently innocent of any knowledge of the Vairagi Order.
- ***Quetzalcoatl***: Ancient deity and legendary ruler of the Toltec in Mexico. It is unclear whether the ruler took his name from the god or was revered as a great ruler and later deified. Paul says he was the Mexican god who was a spiritual teacher of Peddar Zaskq.

In all, Paul gave names to about 125 of the 970 ECK Masters that he claimed preceded him. The popular explanation for why the remainder of these Eck Masters was not named is that their tenure was not of particular historical note. It seems there were about 750 mediocrities who rose to become Living Eck Masters.

Paul put an extraordinary amount of effort into creating his line of Eckankar Masters. I admit to a begrudging admiration for what Paul accomplished. He devoted the time and effort to come up with stories for 125 masters, a number high enough to suggest the plausibility of many hundreds more. After all, Paul had said that the lineage stretched back for as long as recorded time. Thus, he created enough stories to support the enormity of his fiction.

The authenticity of the line of Eck Masters is the doctrine underpinning the validity of the Mahanta, the Living Eck Master. For if the Eck Masters are not real, if there is no line except the one that Paul created, then the Mahanta, the Living Eck Master, is an empty title. We are left with a position whose powers and responsibilities, relationship to the divine, and capacity to lead all souls back to God, is fabricated. The unpleasant truth is that, like the Wizard of Oz, the holy man of Eck must stand with his created history and his religion based on deceit, and answer the question of the faithful, Why?

Has Harold bothered to explore the facts? Is he consciously leading the cover-up? Or, is he so convinced by and committed to Paul's fiction that he believes it has mysteriously and magically been transformed into what Paul claimed it to be? Actually, the latter explanation is quite likely. When a leader receives hundreds if not thousands of letters every month[133] attesting to the wonders of the Mahanta, it is very easy for him to believe in his own myth.

But this is not what causes it to work. A trip to any prayer tent or healing session will attest to the power of belief. It is never the leader, the priest, or the Mahanta, the Living Eck Master doing the work. It is always spirit in tandem with soul that is the true power. The student activates this power by belief in the teacher and the vortex of love that is established by him. When the teacher or master claims credit for this phenomenon, he usurps this power. It is a form of spiritual deception that, in the end, slows an individual's growth to higher consciousness.

An apple tree cannot grow from an ear of corn, nor can a path built on deceit lead to God.

A related device that Paul employs, which makes the presence of the Vairagi Masters and the magic of Eckankar palpable, is the idea that these masters are everywhere and that we can meet them at any time. He says:

> Yet, for your information, they are still with us today to give the Truth to all mankind. Yes, there are many here, though some do not show themselves to man. There are many who teach openly, and others who stay hidden in the deep recesses of the mountains, or those who walk among people in huge cities, not telling who they might be, but helping man in a way that is unknown to him!

> Did you ever meet a beggar on the street who made you wonder at his strange eyes, or his peculiar mannerisms? Care is needed in the examination of the ones who fit such a description for they could be ECK Masters in disguise, designed this particular way to bring a blessing to any they encounter.[134]

Adding mystery to life and seeing our fellow humans in a positive light is undoubtedly a good thing. I believe that there are persons who walk the streets doing good for other people. I believe it because I have done it myself, as undoubtedly have many others. But to attribute these actions to Eck Masters Paul invented in the sixties is to perpetuate a hoax. This particular hoax was useful in reinforcing the validity of the Vairagi Masters to Paul's followers. This idea so permeates the thinking of many Eckists that, to this day, I still find myself looking behind the faces of beggars for an Eck Master. At least, Eckists have been a boon to the economy of beggars.

Myths and illusions are part of the inner experiences of all humankind. The higher self, working with spirit to teach and guide, uses them because they are the visions we accept and in which we have faith. Therefore, the images of these created masters serve as useful voices of inner truth of God communicated to that soul. Having cut his ties to the line of Radhasoami masters following his disaffection with Kirpal Singh, Paul could no longer claim lineage from this tradition. The masters who made up this line of Sant Mat masters all lived and left footprints in the sand. Not one of the masters in Paul's Vairagi Order left a single footprint, except those, like Plato, who were posthumously impressed into service of the Vairagi Order.

But even in those cases where Paul claims known figures from history, such as Milarapa, the recorded history of their lives shows no trace of association with a path known as Eckankar or a line of masters known as the Vairagi. Indeed, Milarapa was a Buddhist whose every recorded action and word is consistent with the Buddhist tradition. Unless Milarapa, for example, chose to keep his association with Eckankar and the Vairagi Masters a secret, there is no credible explanation for Paul's claim of affiliation with Eckankar or the Vairagi Order of Adepts.

Device Five: Absorption of a Teaching — The Source of Structure, Terminology, and Practices in Eckankar

Most Eckists are convinced of the ancient nature of Eckankar. They believe that its terminology, structure, and concepts originated with and are exclusive to this teaching. But, of course, this is not true. Eckankar is an offspring of Shabd Yoga (the teaching of the audible life stream), and more specifically, the Radhasoami Satsang tradition of India. Shabd Yoga is the true precursor of all teachings of the light and sound of God. Recall what Paul said in article for *Orion*:

> ECKANKAR, which I formed out of my own experience, is the term used for the philosophy I have developed for the Cliff hanger. *It is based on Shabda-Yoga, a way out form of yoga.* The word is Hindu locution for the cosmic sound current which is known in our vernacular as the cosmic river of God.[135]

Eckankar was not only based on Shabd Yoga and the tradition of the Radhasoami Satsang and its progeny the Ruhani Satsang, but it also took their vocabulary, initiations, concept of a Vi-guru, cosmology, and many other elements. There is nothing wrong with borrowing from other religions or spiritual paths. Every major religion owes parts of its ritual, tradition, and teaching to precursors. Christianity, for example, is built upon Jewish written works, as to a certain degree is Islam. Many of the rituals and important celebrations in Christianity are derived from pagan celebrations and practices. Celebration of Jesus' birth was moved to December to coincide with the pagan winter solstice celebrations. Converts to Christianity, it seems, refused to wholly abandon their rituals, so pagan celebrations were simply incorporated into the Christian Church mythology.[136]

Syncretism, the selection and combination of different forms of belief, is the basis of all religions. Nothing starts from scratch or comes out of thin air. But Paul saw it differently. Even after having acknowledged that Eckankar was based on Shabd Yoga, he decided that his new religion should have a more illustrious place in history than that of an offshoot of some other teaching. It seems he concluded that if he wanted to create a new religion, why not link it to divine spirit and assert that it is the original teaching of God? Why not make all religions offshoots of his? In this way, it would not only be historically irrefutable but also plausible, since everything comes from God (Sugmad) through spirit. Clearly, this is exactly what he did. Once committed to this course, Paul declared that Eckankar was the source of all religions in the world today and not derived from any other teaching.[137]

But a religion that is the progenitor of all world religions must have a tradition that is ancient and original in every respect. How was Paul to pull this off? He had studied under another master for more than eight years and been exposed to the tradition of Sant Mat and Shabd Yoga. In that teaching, he had learned about the light and sound of God and had practiced a variety of spiritual exercises using the word HU (pronounced "Hooo" in Shabd Yoga) and other mantras to move into the inner worlds. He had been successful in traveling into these inner regions with his master and had written a book about their journeys.

Paul felt that the Radhasoami teaching had the content, traditions, and approach that could be the basis for the teaching he was developing. However, if he were to acknowledge his roots, he would not be able to make his claim that Eckankar is an ancient teaching and in fact the *source* of Sant Mat, Shabd Yoga, and all other spiritual paths. To accomplish this, he had to disavow his association with the teachings and Kirpal Singh. He did this by threatening to sue his former master if he dared reveal his past affiliation. An ocean and a culture away from India, Paul dared to appropriate aspects of the Radhasoami and Yoga teachings, make a few changes, and proclaim his creation, "Eckankar, the Ancient Science of Soul Travel."

An interesting side-note to Paul's intention to proclaim Eckankar the source of all teachings is Harold's subtle attempt to tie Eckankar and Paul Twitchell to the Ruhani Satsang line of masters that Paul had earlier disavowed. In a particularly disingenuous passage, Harold implies that Paul was the fulfillment of a prediction allegedly made by Kirpal Singh to his followers in India:

> Kirpal Singh told several of his close followers that his line of mastership would end with him [it did not], and that the mastership would then be picked up in one of the Western countries. But I sincerely wonder if he recognized Paul, a former chela, as being the carrier of this Light and Sound of ECK.[138]

This statement is quite remarkable. In spite of the fact that Paul had ended his relationship with Kirpal Singh on rather acrimonious terms, Harold tries to tie Paul's mastership to Kirpal Singh and the Ruhani Satsang teaching by implying that Paul was the person that Kirpal Singh was referring to, even though Singh had no idea it would be Paul. Harold provides no evidence that Kirpal Singh made any such prediction. Harold's statement appears to be an attempt to establish some legitimacy for Paul and his ascension to mastership by connecting Paul, by inference, to the Ruhani Satsang and the light and sound of Eck. This technique of inserting a new point of information, as if it were established fact, to bridge a gap in Paul's actual or fabricated history, is frequently used by Harold with great effectiveness.

Harold accuses Kirpal Singh of trying to "possess truth" because he wrote a letter to a California organization telling them that Paul had borrowed Singh's work.[139] Yet, Harold allows the *Shariyat-Ki-Sugmad* and *The Spiritual Notebook* to go considerably further than merely "possessing the truth." Indeed, these writings assert that all truth comes from Eckankar, and that all historical events, inventions, creations — everything and anything that is of any value to humanity — has also come from Eckankar.[140]

Device Six: Truth by Detail

To spin a good yarn, especially one as complex and diverse as Paul's, it is important to provide detail. Paul was not only good at his craft but also prolific. It came naturally. In his private talks with chelas and friends, his inimitable talents at filling in the details of a story to make it more believable were never at rest. In this passage, transcribed from a series of conversations with chelas, Paul fleshes out the life and times of Sudar Singh, the first Eck Master he created in a well-constructed story of his fictional excursions to France and India:

> We met with Sudar Singh who was the leading advocate at that time of Soul Travel. From Paris we decided that we would go back to his little ashram, which was five miles above Allahabad, on what they call the Old Canteen Road, near the army barracks where the native troops were bivouacked in at the time. It was a small place; I think he had about fifty maybe one hundred people that were there around him, and we found that life was pleasant. . . .

> [W]e were hoping to stay there for the Kumba Mehla, a meeting every twelfth year, where at the forks of the river there in Allahabad, they have a meeting of the holy men. . . . He was rather a tall, lean man. He had a very lean face at the time, and he had started out as a Sikh in his life and changed later because he was in his early twenties when he came back to ECKANKAR.[141]

Impressive detail, I admit. But we have seen he made no such trip to India. Harold attempted to prove the unprovable when he sent investigators to India to establish the existence of Sudar Singh. They returned virtually empty-handed. Even with leads from Paul's tale such as "his little ashram," "five miles above Allahabad," "the Old Canteen Road," and "near the army barracks where the native troops were bivouacked in at the time," they were still unable to confirm any of the facts in Paul's description or any other independent evidence. Harold wrote:

> We have begun a search for records that will document the life of Sudar Singh, the ECK Master who served before Paul Twitchell. *He was an elusive Master, and it's not easy to follow his trail.* A few months ago I sent two individuals to India to see what they could find out. These ECKists found two businessmen who knew something about Sudar Singh. One of them remembered him as a very old man giving sermons in the marketplace. *It was rumored* that when Sudar Singh began his sermons, even the birds would stop singing. He had an eloquent manner of speaking, and his audiences were always attentive. Another person who had been a student of Sudar Singh said the *ECK Master later left India and fled to Canada* because of a political uprising similar to the one that took place after Indira Gandhi was killed.

> Some would like to believe Sudar Singh didn't exist, because then it would be easier to claim that there is no ECK history. *So I'm looking for*

physical records, but I'm letting the initiates find the information for themselves. There are initiates looking all over, trying to establish a physical history for the linage of ECK Masters. Each time we find a record of one, we get a lead back to the one before him, thereby constructing the history back as far as we can.[142]

This statement was published in 1990. In spite of the efforts of "initiates looking all over," no evidence has been uncovered (or at least reported) to support the existence of any of Paul's masters. Given the ubiquitous names Sudar and Singh in India (much like John and Johnson in America) it is not surprising that Harold's representatives would encounter "someone" who remembers "someone else" with the name Sudar or Singh who may have been a master. David Lane has set forth a far more plausible explanation for the existence of Sudar Singh:

Further suspicion about the actual existence of "Sudar Singh" arises when we learn that Twitchell's account of his master is based upon the life story of Baba Jaimal Singh, the founder of the Radha Soami Satsang at Beas. . . . Although it is only conjecture, it would appear that Twitchell coined the name "Sudar" from the longer name "Sudarshan," who was the nephew of Shiv Dayal Singh, the originator of the Radhasoami path. This same "Sudarshan Singh" also resided for a time in Allahabad, India. . . . An interesting sidebar here . . . Sudarshan Singh died in 1936 [about the same time Twitchell says that his Sudar Singh died]. [143]

Harold is left with nothing more than the rumors of two businessmen and his ability — in the finest tradition of the three Eckankar masters — to weave yet another embellishment. This time, he invokes the magical spirituality of the man to explain why no one took notes: "when Sudar Singh began his sermons, even the birds would stop singing." But this has not deterred Eckankar from perpetuating and reinforcing the mythology of the Vairagi Masters with picture drawings of their images and Paul's stories of their triumphs and good works. Indeed they are so real in the minds of Eckists that their images and inner reality resulted in Graham's unparalleled journal of inner experiences with them. Eckankar has normally — and selectively — used these recorded accounts as evidence of their existence, except, as in the case of Graham, if the inner experiences threaten the position of the Living Eck Master or the teaching itself.

Elsewhere, Paul goes into detail about his adventures aboard ship during World War II:

> [T]his was among the incidents which happened during the service . . . but finally when I did go out to sea, they put me on an old flat boat that ran between San Pedro and Nome, Alaska. Then I got tired of that and I asked for another ship which would take me off of what they call the milk-run. That took me way out into the Pacific. For almost a year, between the Central American countries, the California ports, the Oregon ports, the Washington ports, Alaska, Canada, all the way up to Nome, Alaska, and then out to the Hawaiians and return. I decided that I would like to have a better ship. A ship that would take me far out into the war zone. So I applied for and got a ship that took us out to the Okinawas [*sic*], to the Philippines, to all the central Pacific islands, down in to the south Pacific islands, and into Surabaya.... Now, we were never in actual battle; we skirted the battles and only one time did we have any problems, and that is we were once attacked by the Japanese fighter pilots, and then we were stalked by submarines.[144]

"Join the Navy and See the World" seems to have been lived to the fullest in Paul's imaginary tour of duty. Some could listen to his captivating tale for hours on end. Such was the spell that Paul could cast. But even Harold, in his writings, has downplayed these stories; he concedes that none of this is true and that Paul was a member of the public relations staff at the Navy Department. This mere detail did not stop Paul from creating tall tale after tall tale that chelas would retell in the years and decades to follow.

Throughout the works of Eckankar and particularly in *The Tiger's Fang, The Spiritual Notebook,* and certainly in the *Shariyat-Ki-Sugmad,* we can see the extraordinary talents of this weaver of detail, creating the illusions that live in the unwary reader's imagination as truth and become the fabric of Eckankar today.

Device Seven: The Techniques of Fear and Deception

In a particularly revealing passage from a letter sent to his chelas, Paul provides sound advice on avoiding the tricks of fear that *other* masters use to trap their followers. Yet, even this advice is part of another device. When someone warns you of tricks others may play, he builds your trust and perhaps even lessens your suspicion that he is a trickster himself. Here is how Paul uses this device:

The oldest technique of keeping the loyalty of the chela by many teachers is with fear. This is true in the methods of those teachers on the
lower plane levels. Because they grow afraid of losing their chelas to a
Master on the higher level, the old fear tactics will be drummed into
those who desire to move away from the psychic plane elements into the
God planes. These threats are very common. They usually go like this:
"If you leave me, you will get caught in the astral and won't get out."[145]

After warning the chela of what to look for and why some teachers
indulge in fear tactics, Paul invokes the very same tactic:

The wrath of the ECK crashes down upon anyone who is still a slave to
the ego and deserts the Master. Not once will he see the connection
between his betrayal of the ECK and the horrendous troubles that strike
him down like a plague on every hand. And thus he goes downward on
the spiral of awareness until he leaves this body in hopeless despair, still
wondering why the fates have treated him so cruelly.[146]

A threat of violence is added:

Whosoever . . . shall divulge the secrets of his initiation . . . shall be
deprived of his sight and tongue in order to never again be able to say
anything about the degrees of initiation in ECKANKAR.[147]

And:

To ridicule, to scorn, to speak mockingly of the words of the Mahanta,
and not to have faith in him and the cause of ECK is to bring woes on
the advocator of doubt. It brings his karmic progress to a halt, increases
his incarnations in this world, and causes him to suffer untold hardships.

The ignorant and the naive will never understand, nor shall they learn
except by experiencing the slow death brought about by their own overt
acts against the Mahanta and the ECK. This is actually creating overt
acts against the SUGMAD.[148]

And finally:

But once the chela has become a member of the inner circle, he cannot
resign. . . . Those few have found that spiritual decay sets in immediately, affecting the health, material life, and spiritual life and brings
death more swiftly.[149]

And for those who have the temerity to see Paul's deception and revolt
in an effort to free themselves from it, he has planted a final land mine:

When the Living ECK Master's position is attacked by revolt, or by dis-
satisfaction by the followers of ECK, he will defend himself. Not in the
way many would expect, but in ways that few can recognize. The

defense will come from the inner planes, and by means of the ECK. Those who revolt or become dissatisfied cannot bring about any attack upon the Living ECK Master or his position in life. If they do, there is always the swiftest of retribution, which is not always recognized by the receiver nor [*sic*] those who might have observed the occasion.[150]

Many years ago, as a Peace Corps volunteer in Africa, our housekeeper refused to come to work because the local witch doctor had placed a curse that made her fear for her life. None of our confidence boosters could persuade her to return to work. Finally, she went to another juju man, who cast a powerful spell that she believed overpowered the first one. She then returned, much relieved that the power of the first curse had been dissipated.

What Paul has working here is the same technique employed by the witch doctor. It is a technique used by those in power to keep people in check and frighten them into staying. Paul was not above this. But the more important point for those who desire to break this spell is to know that no master, or any other person, has control or power over us, unless we believe in his power and doubt the control we have over our own lives. There are countless stories circulating among Eckists about those who have left the teaching and fallen into harm's way. But these experiences, if true, are of their own making. They were infected by the curses that Paul had created and this infection (belief) caused the curses to manifest in their lives.

Paul expounded other warnings to his chelas so they would be on guard for unscrupulous teachers who would practice other dark arts of control. He warns in the same letter: "Another cliché is: 'I've got the only path and if you leave it, you're in deep trouble.'"[151] Trusting Paul and knowing that he would *never* indulge in such a practice (after all, he just warned us), we find that he is no tyro in its use:

> Again and again I have pointed out that there is no other path than ECK. It is the original source from which all things spring, and anyone who tries another path is trying to start on a lower rung. It seems so foolish for anyone to use his human judgment in trying to select a spiritual path for himself, when it is laid out for him to move on to the original and only path to God.[152]

In a series of passages taken from Eckankar's Holy Book, Paul reinforces his second technique of entrapment:

> The teachings of ECK are the pure doctrine in this world. There are no others which can reach the same level as ECK.[153]

> Any initiate who violates the tenets of ECKANKAR will automatically be dropped out of ECK. This means that he will be put back in his spiritual unfoldment and will not have any opportunity for growth until the Mahanta, the Living ECK Master has reinstated him.[154]

And:

> Anyone who breaks away from ECK after receiving the initiation into ECK, will have to go through many future lives until he meets the ECK Master again and accepts him to be the Living ECK Master and surrenders to him completely.[155]

It is not difficult to see why there is so much fear in Eckankar, and why chelas do not speak openly or ask some of the questions that trouble them. Throughout the Eckankar works, there are references to dire consequences that will befall anyone who speaks against the Mahanta, the Living Eck Master, the teachings of Eckankar, or who utters negative statements regarding either. This curtain of fear is used, to some degree, in all religions to keep the faithful in line. But, surprisingly, it rises to a new level in the teaching of Eckankar. This is an interesting paradox. Most Eckists will tell you (as did I) that Eckankar is a teaching of love and that everyone is free to come and go without consequences. The fostering of this image is a case in point of the use of the old device of speaking with a forked tongue. When both sides of an issue are presented as the true position of a teaching or a person, one is apt to hear only what is most appropriate in a particular situation. This message is usually delivered with such strength and conviction that the listener is inclined to accept it as "the position" of the teaching or teacher.

We all have a tendency to hear what we want and ignore the rest. With all of the warnings scattered throughout Paul's writings, which have never been removed by his successors, the message that I heard was one of freedom. Finally, I thought, I had found a teaching that was not filled with threats of hell and damnation. But I was wrong! How did I ever expect to have attained spiritual freedom in the face of such overwhelming negativity? And, after reading these "curses," though in concentrated form, I wondered how I could have missed them?

Here is the answer. Paul could not have been more cynical or duplicitous. In the same letter in which he warns us to be on the lookout for *other* teachers who would practice these dark arts, he lulls us into a sense of trust:

> Within my love is the framework by which you are free to do as you choose. Whatever you choose to do is entirely within yourself, but it does not lessen my loyalty of heart to you and your family. If you choose to leave ECK for another path, it does not mean that we have parted in the way of separateness, but your freedom of choice is your self-determination. This is what I am trying to develop in people — their self-determination and responsibility by standing on their own spiritual feet.[156]

Comforting words indeed but clearly designed to lure the unsuspecting seeker into a sense of trust that leads to surrender and ultimate entrapment. The seeker also learns very quickly that some things are strictly taboo. Certain statements or questions are simply too negative. This conspiracy of silence has been perpetuated so long that most Eckists are afraid to ask questions that might reveal that they are having problems with soul travel or some other aspect of the teaching. Not wanting to reveal their ignorance or lack of progress (as Eckankar or their masters define it), they remain silent.

Those that hold the rank of High Initiate (HI) are caught in an even greater trap. They earned their station by virtue of continuous tenure in and service to Eckankar, not by spiritual advancement. They are regarded as experts in soul travel and purportedly possess many psychic and other spiritual powers. Yet, I have been to countless HI meetings where many had never had an inner spiritual experience, much less mastered soul travel. They felt like impostors, pretending to be more than they were but accepting their high status. I hasten to point out that this is not universally the case. Many in Eckankar — and this has nothing to do with initiation level — have had extensive inner spiritual experiences and are quite advanced in their spiritual unfolding. Graham is a perfect example of this. It has little to do with Eckankar and everything to do with soul, its openness, and level of spiritual development in past lives.

Paul provides one final warning to his chelas in which he warns of the negative practices of entrapment used by some masters:

> Another one is: "I'm the true Master, and having initiated you, will be with you until the end of eternity. I'm your Master always."[157]

Having warned us of how other masters make promises that entrap their students, Paul and his successors employ the very same devise of control when they promise, "I am always with you." This planting of a guardian in the chela's consciousness is what Paul has just warned us to look out for as a sign of a controlling master. Such pronouncements are designed to draw the chela closer and establish a mental and psychic link that can trap the chelas for many lifetimes. Having accepted his advice, we are less on guard and unsuspecting that such a tactic would be employed in Eckankar or by the Living Eck Master. A few examples found in the Eckankar writings illustrate this point:

> It makes little difference whether the person who is interested in ECK has read only one book, has just become an initiate, or has passed through all the initiations. *The Living ECK master is with him constantly.*[158]

And:

> The chela is never thrown upon his own while traveling the path, though it seems to many that he might be. This is by no means so, *for the Living ECK Master is always standing at his side, gently guiding him and taking him over the obstacles to the Godhead.* The path is long and so many times the chela becomes impatient, but he must feel that the Master is always guiding every step of his way into the heavenly worlds.[159]

And:

> The rejection of the Mahanta is sad indeed, for it means that the seeker must go on looking, reaching and trying to find the heavenly path of ECK and the ECK Master who will take him into the kingdom of the SUGMAD. But he seeks in vain for there will never be anyone but the Mahanta to give him life, to give him the way to the eternal source of All things.[160]

Such is the magic and power of the master's promise always to be with the chela. The seeker often comes to a new spiritual path with a feeling of loneliness and a need to connect with something that is everlasting. So strong is this desire and so seductive is this promise that, even when the seeker knows that she is being lured into a potentially pernicious attachment, she is nonetheless drawn as the moth is to a flame. For who wants to walk alone in the wilderness when the master's comfort and succor have been promised and are available for the asking?

When anyone begins a search for spiritual truth, confusion and lack of self-confidence may make it difficult to accept her own power. This is why teachers, saviors, and masters initially serve a useful role. It also, unfortunately, provides the opening through which an unethical teacher or religion can trap her. The true role of any teacher is to teach and then let go. Paul even acknowledges this as part of a two-sided approach that mixed words of empowerment and freedom with words of attachment and entrapment. Here are his words of empowerment and freedom:

> No ECK master will retain his former relationship with a neophyte after the latter has become skilled in Soul Travel and has been established on the Fifth Plane, the plane of pure Soul.

> You will find that I seldom use the word student, or chela, for once it is accepted by the reader he identifies himself as such. This is one of the lower aspects of all metaphysical teachings, for it raises one and puts another in an underclass. Since we are all spiritually equal, no ECK Master is going to stress the fact that he is on a higher level than another....[161]

And:

> Many Oriental teachers will tell you that it takes years to reach Self-Realization or God-Realization, and that they, the masters, are the only channels by which it can be gained. Nothing can be further from truth; and though you learn much from the ECK Masters, you will eventually give up all masters in a natural way. This is because the higher Soul travels into the spiritual realm, the more It becomes purified.[162]

Yet, just a few pages later, Paul displays the Eckankar of attachment and entrapment:

> Think only of the Living ECK Master and the experiences that come while traveling with him. He is the only vehicle through which one can reach the higher worlds, so take care and practice this technique correctly.[163]

And:

> The Spiritual Traveler is not the giver of life. He is, in a sense, the greater consciousness through which the power flows into the outer world, touching all those with whom he comes in contact. The essence of God in ITS true nature is often seen in the Spiritual Traveler . . . all life flows from God, through me, and vice versa. . . . It is a fact, then, that God, on occasion, descends to the human level to perform the duty of directing Souls back toward ITS realm again.[164]

The student is left to believe whichever version she feels comfortable with, for, earlier Paul declared:

> Therefore, we come to the understanding that God is unconcerned about what goes on in this world, for the world continues to function as does a machine after the switch is thrown to make it run. All God must do is watch over the world and its mechanical functioning.[165]

Obviously, these passages are contradictory and cannot both be true, except in the strange calculus of the Eck Masters where contradictions are paradoxes to be solved by the God-seeker. Here, by elevating the Spiritual Traveler (the Living Eck Master) to the status of God on earth, not limited by the restrictions of mere masters, Paul makes it easy to resolve the paradox. Paul is indeed masterful in weaving the myth of Eckankar around statements of wisdom and transcendent truth. He is also adept at inserting a convenient elevation in status to the Living Eck Master to overcome what would otherwise be seen as a blatant contradiction.

This is another way Paul traps the unwary. Even as the passages and the techniques that they embody are pointed out, there is a part of us that continues to hear the siren call of the Eck Master. They lead with a startling if not profound truth followed closely and ever so stealthily with another fiction intended to build the house of cards ever higher and seemingly stronger.

Paul concludes in his warning to chelas with these words of wisdom:

> These are a few of the techniques of fear used by most teachers of the psychic worlds. We can easily recognize them. *The very fact they use such methods to hold their students shows they are afraid of losing out to a true Master.* The real Master never drops any hints of reprisal to anyone who shows freedom of will and the capability of thinking for himself.[166]

Despite these words, it is clear that Paul knowingly placed words of fear and "hints of reprisal" throughout the Eckankar works. Because Harold has never seen fit to remove them, they continue as a part of the teaching under his leadership.

Spirit does work in mysterious ways to perform its many wonders. For a careful review of Paul's works has revealed a clear inconsistency between the loving and helping image of the master and the power-oriented reality aimed at self-protection through the controlling devices of fear and attachment.

Device Eight: Verbal Slight of Hand

One of Paul's most clever and effective devices to legitimize Eckankar is a technique that I call "verbal slight of hand." As the descriptor implies, there is a certain amount of trickery involved, but it is often difficult to detect. Even when it is detected, there is an easy acceptance of it as something unintended. It is so common in the works of Eckankar that it is often unrecognizable. It sounds insidious and deceptive, and it is, but it is also brilliant and effective. This device uses standard logic where, for example, the letter "A" is used to represent the word "Eckankar" and A1 through A5 represent different definitions of the same word. Paul uses this strategy by employing five different definitions and subtly establishing an equivalency for each definition. Thus, A (Eckankar) = A1 = A2 = A3 = A4 = A5. Similarly, Paul employs several different definitions for the word "Eck," an Eckankar word for divine spirit. We will use, for purposes of illustration, "B" to represent the word Eck, and B1 through B4 to represent separate definitions of the word. Each definition is used in an equivalent way, so that B or (Eck) = B1 = B2 = B3 = B4. Paul then equates all "As" with all "Bs." We then end up with a "A1 = A2 = A3 = A4 = A5 = B1 = B2 = B3 = B4" as an inescapable conclusion, thereby making Eckankar concepts fluid, interchangeable, and impossible to pin down.

Here is what this means. Paul formulated four distinct definitions for Eckankar (Harold added a fifth), all used interchangeably without contextual differentiation. Together, they merge into a single meaning in the mind of the reader. Similarly, Paul formulated four different and distinct definitions for Eck that also merge into one. Finally, he equates Eck and Eckankar so that all definitions become one. He then uses each term in different ways at different times to mean different things, without acknowledging to the reader that verbal slight of hand is taking place. To see how Paul uses this device, we must first examine the different definitions that he uses for Eckankar and Eck.

A1 = Eckankar — (As the mythical ancient spiritual path)

ECKANKAR: The Ancient Science of Soul Travel. Movement of the inner consciousness, which travels through the lower states until it ascends into the ecstatic states.[167]

A2 = Eckankar — (As Divine spirit of itself)

So far, our definition of ECKANKAR reads: The all-embracing spiritual force of the Sugmad which composes life and makes up all elemental substances, including the component parts of Soul. It is the Audible Life Force that we can hear and see with the spiritual vision and objective sight of materialism."[168]

A3 = Eckankar — (The outer organization)

The tax-exempt religious organization created in 1965 by Paul Twitchell and modified in the 1980s by Harold Klemp as a Corporation Sole (one person with total legal — and spiritual — control and authority).

A4 = Eckankar — (Omnibus definition)

Religion of the Light and Sound of God; the Path of TOTAL AWARENESS; the way of all things; means "CO-WORKER with God;" a teaching which gives knowledge of both the LIGHT and the SOUND which contains the total sum of all teaching emanating from God; the very foundation of all systems of science, and the key to success in unfolding all spiritual powers; the Ancient Science of SOUL TRAVEL. Projection of the inner CONSCIOUSNESS, which travels through the lower states until it ascends into the ecstatic states where the subject feels he possesses an AWARENESS of the religious experience of BEING; achieved through a series of spiritual exercises known only to the followers of this science.[169]

A5 = Eckankar — (Harold's update)

The name used to identify and distinguish the sacred teachings of the SUGMAD as taught by the Living ECK Master, as well as the hierarchical organization which is headed by the Living ECK Master.[170]

This final definition is important because it represents Harold's buy-in of Paul's elevation of the Eckankar teaching to the status of the "sacred teachings of the SUGMAD [GOD]." Moreover, Harold never removes these variable definitions from Eckankar literature so, by default, he is responsible for the continued use of Paul's verbal slight of hand.

For the multiple definitions of Eck, Paul writes:

B1 = Eck — (As a science or teaching)

[T]he science of God-Realization. It grows out of the experiences of Soul Travel into the state of religious awareness, which the subject gains at his own volition via the spiritual exercises of ECKANKAR.[171]

B2 = Eck — (As Divine Spirit)

The Audible Life Current. The essence of God, Holy Spirit.[172]

ECK is thus the thread, so fine as to be invisible yet so strong as to be unbreakable, that binds together all beings in all planes, all universes, throughout all time and beyond all time into eternity.[173]

B3 = Eck — (As same as Eckankar)

ECK, which is the short label for Eckankar . . . is not a yoga, religion, or philosophy, nor a metaphysical or occult system. It is merely a way to God-realization via soul travel.[174]

B4 = Eck — (Omnibus definition)

The AUDIBLE LIFE CURRENT; all that is life; the eternal truth and eternal paradox within all; encompasses all the teachings of religions and philosophies; stream of LIFE FORCE; the science of TOTAL AWARENESS that grows out of the experiences of SOUL TRAVEL; the realization of GOD CONSCIOUSNESS; the thread that binds together all beings in all planes, all universes, throughout all time, and beyond all time into ETERNITY; Asu; Life Force, self consciousness; the HOLY SPIRIT; the source of all; the CREATOR of all things; the great forming force which works in a creative way; the constructive forming force; is everywhere; the ESSENCE of the SUGMAD; the LIVING WORLD; the science of GOD-REALIZATION.[175]

Most students of Eckankar are aware of the usage of Eck to denote spirit and Eckankar to denote the organization. Indeed, in the Eckankar introductory booklet given free to newcomers, only one definition is given for each word. Eck means, "the Divine, or Holy, Spirit; the Audible Life Stream; the essence of God which supports and sustains all life; the Life Force."[176] And Eckankar means, "Religion of the Light and Sound of God. Also means Co-worker with God."[177]

These definitions are simple and straightforward. The newcomer and those in Eckankar for some time are clear about these distinctions.

Most students of Eckankar define the term as a spiritual teaching, that is, a religion. This is its legal status and public image. Eck, on the other hand, is thought of as "spirit," the divine force that sustains all life. Eckists, following Paul's lead, also use the term Eck as shorthand for Eckankar. However, these multiple uses for Eck are understood by Eckists who can draw a clear distinction with each usage. When referring to spirit, most Eckists will say, "the Eck." When using Eck as shorthand for Eckankar, Eck is paired with another word (e.g., Eck chela or Eck Seminar). The term Eckist is almost uniformly understood to mean a follower of the teaching of Eckankar.

When the Eckist confronts Paul's writings, strange things happen. It is clear that Paul intends to have both words mean something different at times and to mean the same thing at other times. This allows him to make claims like, "The major religions of the world have sprung out of ECK....,"[178] even though it is clear that Eckankar made its first appearance on this planet in 1965! When considering the usual definition of Eckankar as the organization, this claim is clearly unfounded. But if we accept Eckankar as "divine spirit of itself" (A2) or as the fictional "ancient science of soul travel" (A1), such a claim is believable. Paul never says which definition he is using, and the reader is apt to accept the statement at face value, never suspecting any word trickery. After all, who would make up something about a subject as important as the spiritual history of humankind? If the reader does question the assertion, it is easy to answer that the statement does not pertain to the present incarnation of Eckankar (founded in 1965), but to the invented ancient version of the teaching that has existed for eons as the secret teaching of Eckankar. If this were to be challenged, the definition of Eckankar as a word for spirit can be evoked to establish authority for the statement.

No one doubts that all religions are derived from divine spirit. That is why the multiple definitions help the mind to accept a declaration of Eckankar's supremacy as a religion when it is defined as spirit or derived from spirit. Once this is established, the role of the Mahanta, the Living Eck Master as "God Incarnate" is not far behind. Each concept reinforces the other. Who would not expect "God incarnate on earth," the Living Eck Master, to be at the head of the highest, most original, most ancient, spiritual teaching in the universe?

As the meanings blur, Paul succeeds, temporarily, in elevating his for-profit company, begun as a way for the cliff hanger to support himself and his wife and to impart his syncretic wisdom, into the acme of all spiritual teachings. While there are even more variations of these definitions, all relate to those given above. Often the word will have two or more meanings at the same time, as in "Eck Master." The phrase could mean a master of the teaching of Eck (divine spirit), a master in the teaching of Eckankar (the current organization), or a master of the teaching of Eckankar. Either definition would be correct with Paul's slight of hand approach, because each could apply. We do not know Paul's true intentions, and that is by his design. To illustrate how these different definitions are used in a confusing, multiple, jumbled, but ultimately plausible way, I have chosen to focus on a single chapter from *The Spiritual Notebook*.[179]

A sample paragraph illustrates the point. The probable meaning(s) are listed beside each use as A1, A2, etc.:

> Death and resurrection are basic principles taught in almost every religion.... But ECKANKAR [A1, A3, A4, and A5], which is the mainstream of all religions.... Philosophical writers and religionists have proven the existence of ECK [A1, A2, A4, and A5] throughout history.... The famous line of prophets in the Israelite tribes were [*sic*] trained in the teachings of ECK [A1, A2, A5].... The Greek Masters ... Socrates, Aristotle, and Plato were taught the art of ECKANKAR [A1, A2, A5].... Practically every man who has contributed to civilization has spiritually been a ... student, of the hidden teachings of ECKANKAR [A1, A2, and A5].[180]

Once the many definitions of Eckankar are accepted, Paul's history and the preeminence of Eckankar become plausible. And once any definition of Eckankar is accepted as plausible, the mind makes the connection of A = B, and the fictional becomes believable. Add to this the fact that we are not expecting anyone to employ verbal slight of hand, and it is easy to see how the reader is duped. To find an example where both Eck and Eckankar are used in multiple ways, we need look no further than the introduction to *The Spiritual Notebook*:

> These spiritually developed Masters . . . have kept themselves well hidden. . . . It is their duty to work for individual Souls who take up the path of ECKANKAR [A1, A3, A4, A5]. . . . ECKANKAR [A1, A3, A4, A5] is the ancient gospel which does not teach there is original sin. . . . Paul

> Twitchell has set out to show that every prominent person in history . . .
> has been a chela of the hidden teachings of ECK [B1, B2, B3, B4]. He
> speaks with authority on the supreme message of ECK [B1, B2, B3 and
> B4].[181]

This passage and ensuing ones illustrate Paul's use of this technique.
This slight of hand is indeed confusing. The mind struggles to discern
what Paul intends. The reader eventually stops trying to resolve the
definitional conflicts that Paul's inconsistent usage causes. Finally, the
unwary reader goes with the flow, accepting what Paul says with only a
nod of surrender replacing doubt.

In the first fourteen pages of *The Spiritual Notebook*, Paul uses the
word Eckankar thirty-six times. He uses Eckankar to mean "spirit"
forty-seven percent of the time (seventeen times) and to refer to the
ancient teaching thirty-six percent of the time (thirteen times). While
Paul uses Eckankar in referring to the present-day organization only
seventeen percent of the time (six times), the reader likely intermingles
as many as thirty usages of Eckankar (eighty-three percent) with the
present-day religion. What does this mean? It means that eighty-six
percent of the time, Paul is talking about his invented version of Eckankar, which he uses to establish credibility for the present day teaching,
which he refers to a paltry six times. But, it is enough to make the connection and the reader connects them (after all, it is the same word),
ascribing to the modern-day Eckankar all of the power and spiritual
verve that the other two fictionalized meanings connote.

Did Paul practice this slight of hand with malice aforethought
whenever he employed it? Probably not, for over time he likely become
blinded to his own devices. Yet, one conclusion is inescapable: he
intended that the reader believe the history and lineage depicted in this
and other Eckankar books was true, and that the Eckankar organization
of today is directly linked to this history and lineage.

None of the books containing this verbal slight of hand has been
withdrawn or redacted. Therefore, the current leadership of Eckankar
bears responsibility for continued deception. Throughout *The Spiritual
Notebook* and his other books, Paul intersperses Eckankar dogma with
passages of genuine insight and spiritual wisdom. But this is the nature
of any effective deception. It works because it artfully blends truth and
untruth — an enticing dish for the true believer.

Device Nine: The Many Faces of Eckankar

By going on record as supporting both sides of an issue, a writer is able to seek shelter on whatever side of the issue is convenient at the time. With many faces and multiple expressions of Eckankar principles, each individual inevitably constructs her own version of the teaching. I am convinced that there are Eckists with entirely different views of what it really is. Some of these conflicting views we have already considered. As I delved into the substance of the teaching, I discovered many faces of Eckankar that I did not know. They certainly were not the Eckankar that I had taught audiences over the past twenty-five years.

I did not notice the threats rampant in written works. I naively thought that this was the one teaching that did not hold on to its followers. I also believed that the chela is always free to leave. When I tried to reconcile my understanding of Eckankar with recently noticed parts of the teaching, I did find a basis for the version I accepted and taught. How do we end up with so many versions of a single teaching? As indicated, Eckankar masterfully stakes out all sides of the issues; the reader sees and accepts what he feels comfortable with and discards the rest. This is particularly true of material presented to newcomers. This is the benign image of Eckankar that most Eckists continue to hold until they confront its controlling side or they are exposed to revelations of deception.

Let us compare some contradictory passages. Some are from the free introductory booklet, *Eckankar: Ancient Wisdom for Today,*[182] others from other Eckankar writings. Each passage responds to a question a newcomer might ask. The initial quote is commonly presented in introductory sessions conducted worldwide. The latter response reveals the dark side of the teaching contained in other Eckankar books.

Issue 1- How should the Chela view the Mahanta, the Living Eck Master?

The Benign Face of Eckankar:

> [T]he Living ECK Master is not idolized. He is given respect and love, but he is not worshiped. It is the Master's function, not his personality that is important.[183]

The Entrapping Face of Eckankar:

> Each Living ECK Master has served as the Mahanta, which is God made flesh on earth. Therefore, we look to the Mahanta, for he is the representative of the SUGMAD [God] in our midst today.[184]

> The Sat-Guru [Living ECK Master] is the Son of God. This same expression was used to describe Christ during his stay on earth.[185]

> We cannot, therefore, consider the ECK Master as an ordinary human person, like the rest of us, for upon his shoulders fall the problems of the whole world. He is the singular one who is responsible for all things that go on within the universes of God. This sounds very strange but it is true.[186]

After reading passages that exalt the Living Eck Master to the status of a "Living God," it is easy see how an individual coming from a Christian background, for example, would tend to deify him. This is especially true when phrases like "the Son of God," are invoked. This is not by accident: it is designed to tap into emotional wellsprings that are well known and fully anticipated.

Having started with the soft face of Eckankar the newcomer soon becomes absorbed into the teaching and, in time, comes to see the "God-like" nature of the Living Eck Master.

Issue 2- Does the Eck student have the freedom to leave should he or she choose?

The Benign Face of Eckankar:

> The Master always grants total spiritual freedom to his students. They are never controlled or manipulated, and they have complete freedom of choice in every aspect of life.[187]

> ECKANKAR's respect for the sanctity of the individual shows itself in how ECKANKAR is taught and honors the rights, privacy, and personal space of others.[188]

The Entrapping Face of Eckankar:

> Within the *Shariyat-Ki-Sugmad* is found the quotation, "He who leaves the path of ECK, or refuses to follow it, shall dwell in the astral hells until the Master takes mercy upon him and brings him upon the path again."[189]

> Woe be unto him if he does [resign], for it is known among those who have reached these lofty heights and witnessed the consequences of the few who have. Those few have found that spiritual decay sets in imme-

diately, affecting the health, material life and spiritual life, and brings death more swiftly.[190]

This doesn't exactly sound like "total spiritual freedom," or like a group whose members "are never controlled or manipulated" and have "complete freedom of choice in every aspect of life."[191] The double-talk could not be more apparent. The newcomer is lulled into a sense of total freedom until she asks too many questions, hints at dropping out, or otherwise acts in a manner that goes against something the Living Eck Master has said, done or written. For in addition to the more severe consequences for more serious acts of "betrayal," there are similar consequences for acts such as writing a book like this. Paul writes and Harold sanctions:

> Many simply do not know or understand the nature of the Living ECK Master and will take it upon themselves to be snide with him. . . . They likewise do not understand the troubles that befall them as a consequence of their overt and covert attempts to belittle or ridicule the teachings of the blessed ECK. . . . One does not realize what these small acts might be, but on closer scrutiny we find that they are such minor things as belittling the Master's words; arguing with him over some point; the posing of needless questions; smoking in his presence; being doubtful of any promise that he makes, whether it be of what is to come into a person's life or some point on ECK; turning against him and refusing to act in accordance with his desires, which are for the benefit of the chela and his spiritual unfoldment; and acting snide with the Master.[192]

Incorporating the guidance from this passage into ones consciousness clearly leads to obedience and likely, blind obedience. And herein lies the danger to the God-seeker. Reading this passage more closely, it is clear why, in Eckankar, there is little discussion about controversial issues that perplex or disturb its members. But, there are countless stories of the wonders of spirit at work in the lives of Eckists. These stories are quite real and truly inspiring. But they are not unlike those heard at revival services in a thousand churches on any given Sunday.

I am not disparaging stories or testimonials per-se; they have their place and are marvelous teaching tools. But stories often crowd out serious discussion leaving the listener hungry to learn the principles by which these "gifts" materialized. Of course, in Eckankar as in every religion, the point of the testimonials is to reinforce the power of a Mahanta, Jesus, Buddha, a Master, or some other intervening force that is thought to have bestowed the blessing in accordance with the devotee's obedience and surrender. As we shall see, it is precisely this misdirection that leads the God-seeker astray believing in something other than the real source of the power, which lies within them.

I remember one seminar at which a woman from the audience asked Harold what provisions had been made for Eck Masters who were no longer the spiritual head of Eckankar — an obvious reference to Darwin Gross, the former Living Eck Master recently expelled from the teaching. The issue was obviously very sensitive to Harold, who had survived several disquieting years of conflict with Darwin. From atop his stool on the stage of this gigantic room, Harold raised his voice and chastised her for her impertinence. He concluded by suggesting that her light was dim, if not out. The rebuke was so unexpected and stinging that it devastated the poor woman. A moan and then a hush came from the audience. Few questions were asked after this exchange; a lasting impression had been made on everyone. This seemingly meek and mild-mannered man revealed a side with which one would trifle only at great risk.

I hasten to point out that this is not the typical mood at Eckankar events. Indeed, there is a strong sense of love, devotion, and service, which is at the heart of Eckankar's attraction. Yet, this malevolent face of Eckankar does exist and lays in wait with threats, injunctions, and dire consequences for those who would venture into prohibited areas of thought, word, or action.

Fortunately, I had other experiences that prepared me to deal with this side of the teaching. As mentioned, my stay in an African village exposed me to the daily impact of black magic, spells, control tactics, and juju on the lives of my African friends. This experience equipped me to understand and deal with the spells, incantations, threats, and curses that Eckankar had in store. And this is true of the threats from any church or religion that are used to keep the faithful in line. Whether excommunication, hell and damnation, or their equivalents, they are all the same. No words or incantations can affect anyone's life unless he believes and accepts them.

As I write these words, having considered the extraordinary passages written by "masters" who claimed to be leading me to spiritual freedom, my energies double with the knowledge that I must disseminate this book as soon and as widely as possible. I have already met, talked to, and read about those who have left Eckankar and other paths, voluntarily or involuntarily. Their pain and discomfiture in leaving the teaching and beloved friends have left them with a spiritual void that many have been unable to fill. There is fear and anguish as they wonder if the Eckankar curse will befall them for having the temerity to leave.

Friends who remain in Eckankar sometimes ostracize those who leave. They fear that their continued association would bring wrath upon them. As we shall see, the angst of separation has been spewed all over the Internet. There are whole web sites devoted to providing support and comfort to former Eckists and those from other paths dealing with withdrawal[193] — the direct consequence of tactics designed to control, trap, and instill fear. But those who have demonstrated the courage to make, or those who will make, the decision to see a spiritual path such as Eckankar for what it is are not abandoned. They are never without spiritual direction in taking the next step. Spirit is always there, guiding, providing for, protecting, and teaching them. Indeed, this book is intended as a spiritual source of that instruction and guidance.

Device Ten: The Land of Contradictions

Eckankar, as we have seen, originated as a scheme in Paul's head around 1965. Consequently, it had no established doctrine, except his earlier writings. The positions in these writings changed dramatically after Paul decided to transform Eckankar into the world's preeminent religion. Together, these older and newer views present very different images of Eckankar doctrine. A seeker is likely to embrace one of these positions and overlook or ignore others. Some of these have been presented already.

In most of Paul's earlier writings (*The Flute of God, Illuminated Way Letters,* and *Letters to Gail),* he presents more traditional, albeit enlightened, views on a range of topics. In fact, the word "Mahanta" (a Twitchellism) is cited in the index to the *Flute of God* only once (even though he refers to the term "Mahanta consciousness" twice). In his one reference to Mahanta, it is used as a synonym for spirit, nothing more.[194]

The Flute of God shows what Paul believed before he decided to invent the world's greatest religion. He wrote these books between 1960 and 1966, before he created the concept of "the Mahanta, The Living Eck Master," the manifestation of "God on Earth." How else does one explain the virtual absence of any reference to Eckankar and the Masters of the Vairagi Order in earlier works? If he knew and was being prepared to become "the Mahanta, the Living Eck Master" since he was sixteen, why does he act and write as though he is completely unaware of this fact?

There are two positions voiced by Eckankar apologists that help to sustain belief in the Mahanta, the Living Eck Master as one who "speaks for God on every plane"[195] and is the "the trinity discussed in the New Testament,"[196] "God made flesh on earth,"[197] and even "the Son of God."[198] The first effort to explain the absence of anything in his early writings about Eckankar, the Mahanta, or the Vairagi Masters, holds that Paul took a pledge of silence from age sixteen. This is when he is supposed to have begun his study of Eckankar under the tutelage of the Living Eck Master of the time, Sri Sudar Singh of Allahabad, India. However, it has now been established that Paul neither went to India at sixteen nor studied under Sudar Singh, and that Sudar Singh did not even exist.

Another explanation ventured by Paul's apologists is that he was being prepared for his future mission even though he did not specifically know about it until 1965. This is when, presumably, like Saul on the road to Damascus, he was overcome by an inner reality that demonstrated the entirety of Eckankar. Under this version of Eckankar apologetics, the history of Eckankar was hidden from the world, and from Paul himself, until he became the Mahanta, the Living Eck Master. Paul's task was then to gather its history, lineage of masters, and everything else necessary to establish Eckankar as the precursor of all earthly religions.

The late appearance of Eckankar still leaves a problem. There is no independent evidence of any of it, except where Paul impressed actual personages into his stories. It is no wonder that his writings were so inconsistent on so many points. Here are a few examples.

Paths to God

In his early writings, Paul presents the view that there are many paths to God:

> I am aware that there are many approaches to the SUGMAD, for nobody has a monopoly on any path.[199]

> When anyone lays down the phrase that "My way to God is the only way," be careful for he is only trying to postulate us into submitting to him.[200]

This statement is so clear that one wonders how Paul could have reconciled it with later writings. Either Paul thought that he and Eckankar should be exempt from this exhortation, or he simply forgot that he had made it. But this was not just a fleeting thought, for Paul restated this position many times throughout his early writings:

> God never established a definite group for the liberation of man. IT has given the power to many for the particular way to ITS kingdom. There are certain paths that one must follow, some better than others, because the masters of these particular ways have developed resources for their chelas in seeking the way. This is because men are on various levels of consciousness and not all can follow one universal way.[201]

The declaration that there is no single path to God is an honest recognition by Paul, in his pre-Eckankar days, of a universally accepted truth. When I first read this, it rang true and continued as part of my belief structure throughout my years in Eckankar. However, I must admit that, in a number of my Eckankar talks over the years, I veered from this position in an effort to reconcile it with Eckankar's doctrine of the role of the Mahanta in soul's journey to God-Realization. Many others in this teaching started with this view but were similarly persuaded to a more doctrinaire position consistent with Paul's later writings and current Eckankar dogma.

From an effort to sell personal spiritual insights to a small group of devotees, Eckankar grew into an organization with an army of followers. The decision to move from a simple teaching to a precursor religion required that the teaching become more doctrinal and exclusive. At this point, a major shift occurred. Paul moved from a more ecumenical view of the world to one in which Eckankar was its center. His earlier position, that there were many paths to God, took a dramatic and irreversible turn. Having established and positioned his new religion, Paul's writings also changed. Now, Eckankar was the *only* path to God, a view that was definitively expressed in the *Spiritual Notebook* and the *Shariyat-Ki-Sugmad*:

> All these things can be learned through the medium of ECKANKAR, the only and universal path to God.[202]

> Again and again I have pointed out that *there is no other path than ECK.* It is the original source from which all things spring, and anyone who tries another path is trying to start on a lower rung. *It seems so foolish for anyone to use his human judgment in trying to select a spiritual path for himself, when it is laid out for him to move on to the original and only path to God.*[203]

Paul also writes, rather messianically, "It is not possible to enter into the Kingdom of Heaven except through the teachings of ECKAN-KAR."[204] This leaves little room for debate. Paul was talking about Eckankar the religion and, typically, drew no distinction between the fabricated ancient version of Eckankar and the one that exists today. Why Paul stated such conflicting views is open to speculation. Did he start with one position and gradually move to another as the strength of his movement increased? Did he present one position to attract followers only to surreptitiously move them into a more doctrinal and exclusive view of Eckankar? Or was there something else at work, explained only by Paul's psychological state? (The latter possibility will be explored in a later chapter.)

In a document prepared with the assent of Harold, the Living Eck Master, some attempt was made to clear up Paul's excesses. This statement clearly evidences that Harold was well aware of what Paul had done. Through his attorneys, Harold conceded that:

> The word "Eckankar" . . . was not used to describe any religious doctrines until the mid-1960's when the term was coined, adopted and first used by Paul Twitchell, Eckankar's modern day founder.[205]

In spite of these admissions during the litigation between Darwin Gross and Harold Klemp (following Darwin's firing from Eckankar), Harold has never modified any of the Eckankar writings that contain the fictionalized and distorted version of Eckankar's history.

Need For the Mahanta, the Living Eck Master

Another issue critical to the God-seeker is the need of a master, teacher, savior, or guide in spiritual unfoldment. On one hand, Paul speaks to the responsibility of the individual for his own spiritual unfolding. On the other, he emphasizes that no one can make substantial spiritual progress without the Mahanta, the Living Eck Master. Individual spirituality leads to the development of strength and independence in the journey to God; the other road produces dependency on the Mahanta and the master, without whom spiritual unfolding is limited. These positions obviously conflict. A seeker remains confused or simply accepts the position he likes or one that seems consistent with Eckankar doctrine. Chapter 8 has, in part, been devoted to the issue of the need for a master. The reader is referred to that chapter for a thorough treatment of the subject. Further, the subject of the Mahanta and the core doctrines of Eckankar are considered in that chapter.

Responsibility of the Individual for Spiritual Growth

Here are Paul's views on the independence and responsibility of the individual as soul for his own spiritual development, a view expressed in his earlier writings:

> The SUGMAD *is*, and of course, Soul *is*, since the latter is a part of God. When we understand this as Truth, then we learn that all a teacher can do is to put our feet upon a path and point the way. No teacher, living or past, can give us the actual understanding of Truth. It is wholly dependent upon the individual to make his way to Truth.[206]

> If we get the teachings directly from the Supreme Being, by our own individual efforts, through our simplification of personal techniques worked out by our own understanding, we enter the true path in our own way.[207]

The notion that I am responsible for my own spiritual growth rang true to me and formed the basis of my spiritual journey in Eckankar. This was the view expounded in Paul's earlier book, *The Flute of God,* which became my bible for most of my time in Eckankar. In many respects, I was fortunate in this choice because it focuses on the necessity for soul to lift itself up and change its own circumstances through an understanding of how to work directly with spirit to manifest whatever is desired. I found this book empowering. This message formed the basis of most of the talks and workshops I presented in more than twenty-five years of active participation in Eckankar.

As I look back and reread the more controlling and doctrinal parts of Eckankar, I recall my struggles to accept them. I rarely talked about them, because of the respect that I held for Paul. I regarded these other concepts with neutrality, assuming that I would embrace them as my own spiritual awareness increased. In any case, the empowering language in *The Flute of God* defines one group of Eckists that focuses on this aspect of the teaching and simply let the other parts go. This is why, on reflection, it is now clear that there are many Eckankars, even though its followers believe there is only one. Other examples of the empowering message of Eckankar include:

> [T]here is not much to say about any of this except that one must simply be himself! That and nothing more. The quicker this is accepted, the better developed spiritually one becomes. The individual grows into spiritual serenity by becoming more of one's own self.[208]

And:

> The Supreme Consciousness will appear to anyone provided the individual furnishes the state of consciousness through which it can appear. Therefore, whatever anyone is receiving or lacking in the outpicturing and expression of his consciousness is each one's own responsibility. It is the result of his own consciousness. Until you can understand this, you can never have true freedom and liberation from this world. Until you can understand that nothing can happen to you, nothing can ever come to you or be kept away from you except in accordance with the state of your consciousness, you do not have the key to life.[209]

This passage has always been my favorite. To this day, it is an expression of a reality that I have learned, experienced, and demonstrated in my life. Whether Paul wrote this himself or lifted it from someone, I keep it with me as one of the greatest gifts from my years in Eckankar. Again, Paul makes it clear that the role of a master is strictly limited and should not continue beyond the initial period when guidance is needed:

> Anyone who claims to be a teacher or a master and allows a *chela* to lean upon him is not being honest with himself or with the chela. The *chela* must always walk alone. At first he will depend upon a teacher to show him the way, but when he has reached his maturity in the teach-

ings he must go on alone, for the teacher can no longer do anything for him.[210]

Indeed, how could it be otherwise. However, as we shall see, this concept underwent a dramatic modification as the role and importance of the Mahanta, the Living Eck Master emerged in Eckankar doctrine and practice.

Dependence on the Master

As definitive as Paul once was on soul being responsible for its own destiny and finding its own way to God, he was later equally definitive on the necessity of strict obedience to the Mahanta, the Living Eck Master, throughout soul's journey to God. On this later view, he writes, "Only the Living ECK Master can offer the chela a definite method by which he can prove all things for himself,"[211] and "No man comes to the SUGMAD except through the Mahanta."[212] Also:

> Only the living ECK Master is capable enough to give truth as it is to the chela. Unless he is under the Living ECK Master, the chela's gathering of truth has little value. He is unable to establish any link with the Godhead and, more importantly, is unable to find a way to discover truth for himself. The Master is the link between the chela and the Godhead, for he is the Living Word Itself. And he does not work only on the lower planes and planets, but in every plane throughout the universes of God.[213]

And finally:

> The chela must be dedicated to the ECK. Dedication is his greatest asset. He must give this dedication to the Mahanta, the Living ECK Master because he is the only manifestation of God that can be recognized by those in the human state of consciousness. If the chela is not possessed of this quality of dedication and loyalty to the path of ECK, his incarnations are lengthened in this world, and he shall not be able to enter into the next worlds at the end of his present life.[214]

These are only a few examples of Paul's insistence on the importance of the Mahanta, the Living Eck Master in the spiritual develiopemnt of the chela. Paul began as a simple student. As a chela of the Radhasoami Master, Kirpal Singh, Paul learned first-hand the hypnotic power of devotion to and adoration of a master. Paul incorporated this device into his new religion with a subtlety and sophistication that would make Kirpal Singh envious. In addition to establishing the co-dependency relation of master and chela as a central part of his teaching, Paul went a step further by elevating the Masters of Eckankar to a status heretofore unknown. The chela's relationship with the master was *designed* to move from devotion to reverence:

> Each Living ECK Master has served as the Mahanta, which is God made flesh on earth. Therefore, we look to the Mahanta, for he is the representative of the SUGMAD in our midst today.[215]

> The Sat-Guru [Living ECK Master] is the Son of God. This same expression was used to describe Christ during his stay on earth.[216]

> [A]ll the power of God must reach these worlds through the perfect instrument of the Mahanta, the Living ECK Master. There is no other way, for he is the distributor of the power.[217]

> Hence, the Living ECK Master is omniscient, omnipotent, and omnipresent. Each who has served his respective time in the worlds of God, including the physical plane, is known as the Mahanta, the Vi-Guru, the highest of all spiritual Masters throughout the universes of the SUGMAD. None are higher than the Mahanta for he alone possesses the shining consciousness of the SUGMAD.[218]

It is hard to imagine how the average person, confronting such passages and coming out of a religious tradition of God worship, would react in any manner other than to worship the one who is "God made flesh." If one does not worship "God made Flesh," the "Son of God," and the "distributor of the power of God," whom should one worship? In spite of the obvious effect such passages have on the devoted followers of the Living Eck Master, Eckankar maintains that "the Living ECK Master is not idolized. He is given respect and love, but he is not worshipped. It is the Master's function, not his personality that is important."[219] Harold has taken this disclaimer even further in a series of fascinating passages:

> Paradoxical as it may seem, my point in bringing out all of this has been to strengthen your faith in the Mahanta — but not at the expense of making a god out of the Mahanta's vehicle, which is the Living ECK Master. It's a price we cannot afford to pay. As soon as we set someone above us, in potential or in fact, we have committed a crime against ourselves: We have limited the opportunity for our own unfoldment.[220]

And even more startling:

> And so we have, perhaps, the death of an ideal. This means that no longer can we make a god out of a man. It was never intended. Many of us haven't done this, but some of us have.[221]

The death of an ideal? By saying that such adoration and worship was never intended, the Living Eck Master disputes Paul's earlier pronouncements. But what is Harold really saying? Is he declaring that Paul's description of the Mahanta, the Living Eck Master as "God made Flesh" is false and should never have been described this way? Is he saying that it was true but is now untrue in the wake of the "Death of an Ideal?" Is the Living Eck Master no longer "omniscient, omnipotent and omnipresent"? And what of the Living Eck Master's status as the "Son of God?" Is this suddenly invalid?

Harold's declaration raises as many questions as it answers. It is hard to read his statements as anything short of a rejection of Paul's assertion of the divinity of the Living Eck Master. One can detect an attempt to draw yet another distinction that would preserve much of what Paul proclaimed while killing a more publicly troubling aspect of Eckankar doctrine. Harold separates the Mahanta from the "Mahanta's vehicle," implying that it is acceptable to continue to view the Mahanta as "God Made Flesh," but not the Mahanta's vehicle, which presumably means his physical body. As if this distinction were not murky enough, Harold draws an even finer distinction in his attempt to "clarify" that the Mahanta, the Living Eck Master should not be worshipped:

> An individual working toward God-Realization is careful never to make the personality of the Living ECK Master into an idol or a god. I write, give talks, and do the best I can to tell you ways to have contact with the Light and Sound of God. I only do it to try to inspire you to do the work yourself.[222]

When all of this is taken together, what has Harold actually said about the "Death of an Ideal?" First, he tells us not to worship the Mahanta's vehicle, which is the Living Eck Master. Yet it is presumably allowable to worship the Mahanta. So by separating the two, we are not told to cease worshiping altogether, but only to cease worship of the Living Eck Master. Then Harold separates the Living Eck Master into three parts: the personality, the function, and the physical body. We are told not to worship the personality of the Living Eck Master, while leaving the inference that it is permissible to worship whatever is left. So we have five concepts floating about here: the Mahanta, the Living Eck Master, the body of the Living Eck Master, the function of the Living Eck Master, and finally, the personality of the Living Eck Master. Of these five, Harold has only killed off the ideal of worshipping the last one, the personality of the Living Eck Master — a brilliant way to have his cake and eat it too.

Apart from the confusion that these hair-splitting distinctions create in the mind of the true believer, I was ready to acknowledge Harold's integrity for at least attempting to step back from some of Paul's excessive and often embarrassing pronouncements. However, two factors made me hesitate. First, even though these statements were made in 1984,[223] and further expanded in 1986, no effort has been made to remove, modify, or explain any of Paul's more grandiose expressions of the spiritual status of the Mahanta, the Living Eck Master. The "Death of an Ideal" should involve more than a one-time statement; it should include the removal of anything that fostered deification of the Living Eck Master. This has never been done. And so the books still sell, and students still read about the "God" status of the Mahanta, the Living Eck Master, which remains a central part of Eckankar doctrine.

Second, having reduced the Mahanta's status from being "God," Harold seems to have changed his mind several years later:

> I'd like to expand the concept of the Mahanta, the Living ECK Master, so that you can better understand how it works on the inner planes.
>
> I often speak of the Mahanta as the Inner Master, and we might think that the Living ECK Master only exists on the physical plane, while the Mahanta works exclusively in the inner worlds. *Actually they are one and the same.* The Mahanta, the Living Eck Master is the full complement of inner and outer, and he exists in this full complement on each plane.[224]

Having retreated from Paul's more excessive positions, Harold entwines the two concepts again with all the old platitudes. Inasmuch as Harold has nicely resurrected an idea whose death he had proclaimed just two years earlier, it appears that Christianity is not the only present-day religion to have a resurrection in its history.

As recently as June 2002, Harold reinforced the previous deified position of the Mahanta. In a recent Eckankar publication, he writes:

> Keep true to the faith. . . . There is but one way. Base your Vahana (missionary) words and messages on the *Shariyat-Ki-Sugmad*. The *Shariyat* is our holy book. It is a guide for all who desire to be true to the eternal teachings of ECK.[225]

The eternal teachings to which Harold refers include every reference that he had earlier proclaimed as the "Death of an Ideal." These include:

> The Living ECK Master is always higher on the spiritual scale of God than any saints of the worldly religions . . . each in his time was the direct manifestation of God; the divine channel which God uses as ITS voice to speak to the worlds with ITSELF.

> Hence, the Living ECK Master is omniscient, omnipotent, and omnipresent. Each . . . is known as the Mahanta . . . the highest of all spiritual Masters throughout the universes of the SUGMAD.[226]

Harold proclaims loudly about the "Death of an Ideal" while quietly letting the *Shariyat* proclaim his status as "the direct manifestation of God." Not once has Harold pointed to a passage in the *Shariyat* for reinterpretation. It is clear that he intends for the reader to take the passages in this book the way any follower would regard a "holy book" — as the truth, the word of God. The chela is encouraged to "keep true to the faith," which means to base his words on the *Shariyat*.

Harold was not always so sanguine about the *Shariyat*. During the period when he was retreating from Paul's "God made Flesh" interpretation of the Mahanta, Harold also retreated from the sacrosanct status of the *Shariyat-Ki-Sugmad*:

> Paul encouraged people to read the *Shariyat-Ki-Sugmad* and make their own study. He never said to take the words as holy, as the last word. You take the words and check out the teachings from within: Does this work for me or doesn't it? You have to know. And based upon what you know is how you conduct your life out here.[227]

This statement was reiterated in 1984 when Harold was apparently still going through a "true confessions" period in which he seemed to have a genuine desire to reform some of Paul's positions. Clearly, Harold struggled to find a way to be truthful without destroying the teaching. He finally decided to retreat gracefully from some of Paul's stances, demystify them, and, in the process, hopefully move away from Paul's self-serving history, doctrine, and dogma. Unfortunately, in his efforts to downplay the *Shariyat-Ki Sugmad*, Harold misspoke and directly contradicted Paul's position. Paul had specifically declared this bible to be exactly what Harold was now claiming it was not:

> The essence of God-knowledge is laid down in these writings. Those who follow ECK are involved in the SHARIYAT-KI-SUGMAD for it is their bible, their everlasting gospel. All worldly doctrines on religions, philosophies, and sacred writings are offspring of the SHARIYAT-KI-SUGMAD.[228]

> The ancient books of the SHARIYAT-KI-SUGMAD are indeed *the true Light and the Word of God*. . . . One will find within these pages an answer to every question man has ever devised to ask of any greater ones. All that which is truth is here now, within these pages. [229]

In light of these descriptions of the *Shariyat-Ki-Sugmad*, it would seem difficult for Harold to sustain his position that Paul "never said to take the words as holy, as the last word." Paul expressly intended that the words contained in these books be regarded as "holy." How else does one treat "the Word of God?"

Harold's statements on the subjects of the Mahanta, the Living Eck Master and the *Shariyat-Ki-Sugmad* have moved full-circle several times. After some commendable forays toward honesty, Harold has retreated to a position that once again embraces Paul's grandiose view of the Living Eck Master and the *Shariyat*. He has now become the totality of what Paul created through fiction and deception. This is Paul Twitchell's legacy just as it has now become Harold's.

Chapter 8 — The Origins of Eckankar Doctrine

Usurpation: To take possession of without legal claim; To seize and hold (as office, place, or powers) in possession by force or without right; to take or make use of without right (e.g. the rights to her life story) 2. To take the place of by or as if by force; to seize or exercise authority or possession wrongfully. . . .[1]

Usurpation may seem like a strange word to use in relation to the teachings of Eckankar, but this is precisely what happened. What was usurped? The answer is more astonishing than you might imagine. For what was usurped was nothing short of the spiritual center, the inner direction of the believer. How can this be? Let's start with the foundation of the doctrine of Eckankar: the Mahanta, the Living Eck Master.

The Mahanta, the Living Eck Master

After seeing how Paul constructed Eckankar, it should come as no surprise that he also created the concept of the Mahanta from the traditions of other spiritual paths. Nor should it come as any surprise that his rich imagination added a few flourishes. The concept of Mahanta appeared for the first time in 1965, when Paul gave himself the Rod of Eck Power and anointed himself a Mahanta. He took the word, "Mahanta," from a Hindi and Pali word that means "head of a monastic establishment" as well as "big" (Pali).[2] Paul expropriated the title and gave it an entirely new meaning. In Eckankar, Mahanta (Consciousness) is:

The spiritual leader, or Godman; the head of ECK; all those who come to him in the present age have been with him since their advent into the world; the body of the Mahanta is the ECK, which is the essence of God flowing out from the Ocean of Love and Mercy, sustaining all life and tying together all life forms; the Vi-Guru, the Light Giver; a state of God consciousness which is beyond the titles given in religions which designate states of consciousness; the highest of all states of consciousness.[3]

One of the more intriguing aspects of the title of Mahanta, the Living Eck Master is how Paul Twitchell, Darwin Gross and Harold Klemp convinced or deluded themselves into believing the myth. Given the spurious origins of Eckankar and the Mahanta concept, it is clear that this is what happened. Darwin had been indoctrinated into Paul's mythology and knew Paul personally. Therefore, it is understandable how Darwin would accept Paul's stories in their entirety. After all, at the time of his ascension to the Mahantaship, Darwin was probably unaware that the concept and title first appeared in Paul's writings around 1965. Darwin's ascension was accompanied by his close association with and eventual marriage to the founder's wife, Gail Twitchell. This relationship undoubtedly reinforced his deep devotion to Paul and his teachings.

Darwin's comments and later ones by Harold indicated that neither of them had any outer confirmation or validation of his station as the Mahanta and the extraordinary role the *Shariyat* said they were to play in the operation of the universe. To be told, "He [The Mahanta] speaks for God on every plane through all the universes, from the lowest negative to the highest spiritual one,"[4] is a bit much for a new, inexperienced master (in Eckankar for only two years) to absorb. And to recognize that everyone is thinking of you as the only one who "has the key to the secret kingdoms,"[5] when you are still discovering for yourself the nature of the secret kingdoms, can be overwhelming. The only way that these burdens can be reconciled with the limited awareness of someone catapulted to such an exalted position is to assume that spirit (the Eck) is doing the work. The three Eck Masters have acknowledged that they have little if any conscious awareness of how these extraordinary responsibilities are being carried out in the inner or outer physical planes. This belief in the Eck as the modus operandi of the Mahanta, the Living Eck Master is reinforced by the simple fact that the *Shariyat* and Paul proclaims it.

The strength of the Mahanta's claim of omnipotence, omniscience, and omnipresence is backed by no more proof than the declaration that the sun rises every morning because we have willed it. Every morning we would receive confirmation of our power. In time, we might come to believe it. If we were then to give ourselves a title befitting our newly proclaimed power, we would only have to attract a following — true believers are always available — to have a movement. Thus, the position of the Mahanta is not only a station created by Paul, it is one that grandiosely claims to control events over which it has no more control than anyone else. When we add the essential ingredient of thousands of Eckists who believe in the Mahanta's powers, we have a spiritual movement that is based on a fabrication, and a deceptive one at that.

After David Lane's book was published, Darwin reacted with outrage and disbelief; he simply could not understand why anyone would question the word of Paul Twitchell. Darwin's reaction was not based on an analysis of Lane's arguments, but was emotional in nature. He urged the chelas to destroy these vile materials (the "spiritual counterfeiter" version of Lane's work), claiming that they were written by people who had another agenda or did not know the truth about Eckankar. Harold's response was more enlightened but still protective of Paul's legacy and his own position upon which it rested. Harold's defense was perhaps more honest than prudence might have dictated. Revealing details of the records Paul assiduously kept, Harold offered a brief look into Paul's life that revealed disturbing psychological patterns that led to exaggeration, tall tales, grandiosity, and worse — especially when it came to the position of the Mahanta, the Living Eck Master.

The legitimacy of the Mahanta rests mainly on the story of the passing of the Rod of Eck Power down the long line of the Vairagi Masters, from antiquity to Harold Klemp. It should first be noted that Paul likely "borrowed" the concept of the Rod of Power from theosophy — although there also can be found Egyptian and Christian references to a Rod of Power — which asserts that the great "Rod of Power" of the Logos (God, or Sugmad) is hidden in the sun and consists of four subdivisions (functions) for which a Rod of Power exists for each.

However, the Rod of Power aside, a better understanding of the legitimacy of the Mahanta can be gleaned from looking at the less than orderly transition of power between the various Mahantas. According to Eckankar lore, Sudar Singh received the Rod of Eck Power from Rebazar Tarzs. It was Sudar Singh's responsibility to train a successor and pass the Rod of Eck Power to him. But having purportedly started with Paul as a mere sixteen-year-old, who was not ready for the position at the time of his death in the late thirties, Singh seems to have failed in this task. Another twenty-five years would pass before a candidate would be ready to assume the responsibilities of the Mahanta. Yet, the Eck works state that:

> [The Living Eck Master] is not allowed to retire from his field of action in this life until another is ready and trained to replace him...[6]

But the Rod of Eck Power could not be passed forward to a precocious but unprepared boy. Never lacking for inventiveness, Paul had the Rod of Eck Power pass *backward* to the prior master, Rebazar Tarzs, who dutifully passed it on to him when he had supposedly reached the proper level of consciousness. This is the first but not the last time that the Rod of Power was tossed back to a predecessor.

Following in the footsteps of his first teacher, Paul departed this world without carrying out his responsibilities of preparing and passing on the Rod of Eck Power to his successor, as described above and as set forth in the *Shariyat-Ki-Sugmad*.[7] Paul's untimely death necessitated another reprise of the stalwart Rebazar Tarzs to save the day. Ever equal to the task, he assumed the title and quickly handed off to Darwin, a relative newcomer to Eckankar. As the story proceeds to the transfer of the Rod of Power from Darwin Gross to Harold Klemp, it becomes, as we shall later see, increasingly farcical. When all the fiction is removed from descriptions of the sacred nature of the Mahantaship, what remains are self-motivated individuals who hide the position's lineage.

Neither Paul's nor any of his successor's origins have much in common with the mystical births and lives of his band of Vairagi Masters. Paul writes:

> The Mahanta is always born near or on a large body of water. His birth is always mysterious and men of ordinary birth do not know his origin. Nor does any man know who his sires might be, their true names or their true origin.[8]

Paul accounted for the mysterious origins of some of the 760 previous Eck Masters in his writings and set out to spin tales about his own. He told Brad Steiger, the author of his biography, that he was born out of wedlock on a riverboat that plied the waters of the Mississippi. Paul claimed that his stepmother was a "proud, stern, half-Chickasaw Indian beauty." In saying this, he disavowed his own mother and went on to hint that his father might not have been his real one. Paul claimed that his grandmother told him these things when he was only a teenager:

> . . . Grands believed that her high-stepping son had fathered the boy, who had been born out of wedlock. . . . Her son had to admit that it was entirely within the realm of possibility that he could, indeed, be the lad's father, so he acquiesced to the demands of his wealthy mother.[9]

When Paul's family learned what he had been saying about his family and parentage, there was understandable consternation in the Twitchell clan, which was quick to point out the lies in his tale.[10] Paul was not born near a body of water (as in countless heroic myths), nor was his parentage ever in question, except in his own mind, as he sought to live up to the myth he created for the birth of the Eck Masters. Neither Darwin nor Harold fared any better in this regard. They were born quite some distance from any substantial body of water, and were both of known parentage.

Paul laid out even more stringent requirements for the birth of the Mahanta, the Living Eck Master:

> The ECK enters into the womb of a virgin, the queen of heaven, who has submitted to the true spirit of the universe. The consciousness of the Mahanta state is planted as the seed, and carefully nurtured in the womb. When the embodiment of flesh is brought into this world, a man-child is born. It starts its unfoldment over a period of years until the state of perfection is reached, in adulthood. Then the chosen one learns that he is the Living ECK Master of his times.[11]

While this is a fine story that plays well with those steeped in the tradition of a better-known virgin birth, it has some immediate problems. Paul already attempted to establish, through Steiger, that his mother was of dubious morality, which conveniently suggested unknown parentage. Unfortunately, Paul did his job too well when he led Steiger to write, "it was entirely within the realm of possibility that he could, indeed, be the lad's father. . . ."[12] Paul then had to make a virgin-mother out of this individual with whom the father acknowledges a sexual liaison. It would probably surprise Mr. and Mrs. Gross as well as Mr. and

Mrs. Klemp that the births of their sons had been elevated to the status of virgin births, and that each of their offspring was "the son of God."

A curious episode in Paul's early experiences as the Mahanta, the Living Eck Master sheds light on his thinking during this formative period. Having received the Rod of Eck Power in 1965, Paul continued to write for various magazines, even though he was functioning as "God made Flesh," "the Son of God," and many other exalted titles he bestowed upon himself. Yet, Paul participated in and wrote a truly bizarre column in the *Candid Press*. Paul indulges in prophecy and ribald satire as he unwittingly reveals much about Eckankar's early days and his own understanding of the "sacred" nature of his new position of Mahanta:

> Dear Guru: Things are so bad for this country that I must ask you to talk to God about the political future. I am asking as a loyal reader of *Candid Press*.
>
> JAN B.

> Dear Jan: I didn't want to make any predictions on certain events, but you caught me on a technical point.... The war in Vietnam will increase until late in 1968 when the doves of both sides come to the negotiating table. In 1968, Johnson and Humphrey will run against Romney and Percy--and win again! I HAVE SPOKEN!
>
> Paul Twitchell

Paul missed it on several points, in spite the inside knowledge his position should have afforded him. Johnson decided not to run for reelection in 1968, and the war of course dragged on into the Nixon Administration. Given the nature of free will, perhaps even "God Made Flesh" should be given some latitude in his predictions.

In the same *Candid Press Column*, Paul engages in a disturbing form of communications, which pokes fun at spirituality, mastership, and even God:

> DEAR MR. TWITCHELL: My penis is too long. Can you ask god to shorten it for me?
>
> BIG PETER

DEAR PETER: Why? That's what god said when He heard you wanted a smaller sex organ. God says that we can all be happy with what He gives unto us and you shall be happy to. I HAVE SPOKEN!

Paul Twitchell

DEAR GURU: I have the strange desire to wear lace panties. As I am a normal man in every other way, I want to know if god thinks this is bad?

FRILLY FRED

DEAR FRILLY: He doesn't think it is good. We talked over your fetish —for that is what you have. We both feel that your fetish is due to lack of female companionship. You wish to secure a relationship with a woman whose initials are P. I. Do not ask how I know nor shall you question this advice which I now sayeth unto you: call her and ask her for a date. She will accept. Do not wear your panties on the date... and you shall never again have a desire to wear panties. I HAVE SPOKEN!

Paul Twitchell

DEAR LEARNED ONE: My penis is too small for a man of my age. Can you talk to God and make my penis grow?

TINY MAN

DEAR TINY: God and I talked about your penis — and God has good news for you. He says that your penis is of average size and that you only believe it is too small for you failed to satisfy one woman when you were 19. Because it is of the proper size, there is no need for God to make it grow. I HAVE SPOKEN!

Paul Twitchell[13]

As a column by the man Paul Twitchell, we can see the humor and satire here. But when we recognize that this is the Mahanta, the Living Eck Master speaking, we wonder, What is going on? Given his mission of gathering up all souls and leading them to God, why would the Mahanta indulge in such sexual banter? Make of it what you will, but it does raise somber questions about the seriousness with which he regarded his newly created position of Mahanta, the Living Eck Master. After his movement grew and he began publishing his works through Illuminated Way Publishing, he never again engaged in such frivolity. Once others started believing, he started believing himself, and the fiction grew until a witty California columnist had become the Mahanta, the Living Eck Master.

Paul's integration of fiction with higher truth kept the critical faculties of most students busy deciding what to accept, what to reject, and what to hold in reserve for later consideration. This is where the higher self, that part of us that guides our decisions, comes into play. We rely upon it constantly, though sometimes unknowingly, for right discrimination. It is this part of ourselves that Eckankar attempts to replace with the concept of the Mahanta, the Living Eck Master. It is no different from looking to any other savior, teacher, master, or savant. Their role should be to empower the individual by helping him discover the spiritual power that is at his command as soul. When the role shifts and devotion, surrender and dedication are encouraged or demanded, then their role becomes one of usurpers of the inner direction and control that only comes from within. Ironically, this is precisely what Paul himself once articulated:

> If we get the teachings directly from the Supreme Being, by our own individual efforts, through our simplification of personal techniques worked out by our own understanding, we enter the true path in our own way.[14]

And as noted in a previous section:

> The Supreme Consciousness will appear to anyone provided the individual furnishes the state of consciousness through which it can appear. Therefore, whatever anyone is receiving or lacking in the outpicturing [*sic*] and expression of his consciousness is each one's own responsibility.[15]

When we allow an outside agent or ideal to substitute for our own inner direction, a fundamental shift occurs. Our attention shifts to a dependency upon a person or concept who acts as a surrogate for the real force at work in our lives. Every inner experience, dream, and inner perception is constructed or selected and directed by soul, not the Mahanta, the Living Eck Master or any other pretender. After all, were we not having dreams before we heard about Eckankar, Paul Twitchell, or any of his successor masters? Initially, guidance and mentoring are needed by anyone seeking to move to a higher level of awareness; it is the way we begin to learn and progress in all aspects of our growth and development. However, when we reach the point where everything that we say, think, and do is done in tribute to or in the name of a master of some sort, we have crossed the line and denied the divine guidance and direction of our own inner selves. It is replaced by a usurper, who would place himself above the spark of God (soul) that is the essence of each individual.

The Blue Light

Eckists believe that whenever they close their eyes and see a blue light, from within or from without, it represents the appearance of the Mahanta, the Living Eck Master and is a sign that the master is close at hand, as he has promised.

The truth is that the blue light is a phenomenon experienced by all humans. Paul chose this natural phenomenon to enhance and reinforce the thrall of the Mahanta, the Living Eck Master. To the degree that the word Mahanta is used as a synonym for spirit, then Paul's assertion is accurate. But the slight of hand that Paul employed to create the union between the Living Eck Master, the Mahanta, Eckankar, Eck, and spirit always stands ready to complete the magical transformation of virtually any concept, including the blue light, into the Mahanta, the Living Eck Master. Paul successfully usurped this natural phenomenon to establish and reinforce his promise, "I am always with you."

It has long been a part of occult thought that color is a distinct part of the life of every individual. Color itself is a manifestation of sound, which changes depending upon the plane (level of vibration) on which one is functioning. Color can be simulated or evoked by the use of imagination and is the principal technique used in psychic healing through color. It is also observable during periods of rest and calm, love and well-being. Esoteric literature contains many references to a blue light body, which is thought to be part of the etheric blueprint of each person.[16]

Paul was not the only one to take on the blue light as his symbol. Within the Tibetan Buddhist Karma Kangyu Lineage, the Karmapa Meditation also employs the blue light:

> From the heart level in the centre of Karmapa's [leader of the Black Hat (Kangyu) order of Tibetan Buddhism] transparent body, an intense blue light shines out. It fills the middle of our chest. Everything harmful now leaves our mind. Disturbing feelings and stiff ideas dissolve and our mind becomes spontaneous joy. It is space and bliss inseparable. Together with the deep blue light vibrates the syllable HUNG.[17]

In any case, the inner blue light has been with us since the dawn of humankind and long before Paul usurped it as the inner symbol for the Mahanta.

The Dream Master

In addition to all the other claims made for the Mahanta, Eckankar claims that Harold Klemp, the Mahanta the Living Eck Master is the Dream Master; that is, he controls our dreams and our movement into the various levels of the inner worlds. Paul writes:

> The only way that sleep and dreams are handled is through the direction and guidance of the Living ECK Master. *No ECK chela is given freedom in the sleep state, for he must be led by the Living ECK Master* through the levels of dreams until reaching the higher worlds.[18]

This too is one of Paul's fabrications. It is another usurpation of our inner spiritual self (soul). In a somewhat contradictory but more truthful statement of soul's role and responsibility in its own inner dream life, Paul writes:

> The Atma [soul], living in the dream consciousness of the psychic states, enjoys the subtle things of life, as thought, emotional joy, intellect, and mind stuff. All this is essential for the bodies of the psychic worlds, the Astral, Causal, and Mental planes. When Soul takes mastery over these states through dreaming, It becomes the supreme ruler of Its own universe.[19]

The Mahanta, the Living Eck Master, in the physical form of Harold Klemp, has admitted (several times) that he is not aware of what happens in the inner lives of all those who look to him or even in their inner experiences where his form is present with them. Yet, Harold, as Mahanta, still claims credit for the inner lives of Eckists. He often speaks of his role as the inner master, using the pronoun "I" to reinforce the image that the person standing before the chela is the Mahanta, the Dream Master, as did his predecessors, Paul Twitchell and Darwin Gross. This doubletalk allows the Living Eck Master to claim that he is a man, while providing enough fodder to perpetuate the myth of the God-like nature of the Mahanta.

We have already seen how Harold has disavowed the inner experiences of one of his chelas with no apparent recall or awareness that they ever happened. As we learn more about the truth, we see that this is to be expected, for neither Harold nor other masters who perpetuate this myth have any consistent recall of these experiences, if they have any at all.

In a later chapter, we will explore the remarkable life of Baba Faqir Chand. Chand is one of the few spiritual masters who admits that he is unaware of what goes on in the inner space of his chelas. Although he receives letters claiming that he has performed countless miracles in the inner, and with his physical form in the outer, Chand unselfishly attributes these occurrences to the power of spirit working with soul. Harold has also intimated this position at times, but at other times has reinforced the illusion that he is consciously aware of what is happening. Chand's honesty and candid presentation of the true role of a spiritual master sheds light on the pretensions of the Living Eck Master and all such masters. Further, it reveals that claims of being the Dream Master are simply another attempt at usurpation. It also shows that soul working through spirit is the true instrument, which creates the dream images we experience. This mechanism communicates to the lower self (our physical identity) the insights and wisdom necessary to expand awareness. No intermediary or outside force is needed to direct the inner life of the individual. It is spirit in tandem with soul that creates our dreams and directs our inner lives.

When an individual has spent years looking admiringly at the picture of a master, it is easy to understand why this image is used as an inner vehicle for experiences and communication. But this has nothing to do with the master per se. It is acceptance of a trusted image that becomes an effective vehicle for soul to explore higher awareness. *Any* such image will work. The master has only allowed his image to be used in this way. However, the effectiveness of this image is enhanced or diminished, depending on how the chela relates to the personality of the master.

Harold asserts that the chela's relationship to the image and personality of the master is a crucial factor in determining his effectiveness with the chela. Yet many chelas have reported a sharp drop-off in inner experiences between the time of Darwin, who was charismatic and accessible to followers, and Harold, who has been described as somewhat insipid and inaccessible.

I have come to understand the phenomenon of appearing in the inner worlds of an individual. I receive, from Eckists around the world, numerous accounts of encounters they have had with *me* functioning in the role of a teacher. I am certain that I am not responsible for this. Rather, spirit has used my image, because that soul has accepted it as a trusted channel for communications.

There are not many people in our lives, perhaps our parents if we are fortunate, to whom we look with a high degree of respect, love, and admiration. We use their forms as inner channels to communicate spiritual truth and to lead us to the realization of God. Viewing a picture or visualizing an image of someone who can serve this purpose establishes the inner image of this person as a guide. Those who work as spiritual teachers or masters understand this principle. If they are honest, they withdraw from this role as soon as they can, leaving the seeker to her inner direction to visualize whatever form she may choose. When masters are exploitative, they try to develop dependence on themselves and their images to take credit for the individual's inner experiences, which are actually spirit working with soul.

Eckankar Initiations

An initiation is an outer ceremony, much like a baptism or confirmation in the Christian Church, where the individual makes a spiritual commitment and forms a bond with spirit and the Master at progressively higher levels. In the Sant Mat tradition, from which Eckankar was derived, it designates a union with the eternal light and sound of God, and the acceptance of a particular master as spiritual guide on this leg of the spiritual journey. There is a great deal of mythology surrounding this ceremony. Its true essence is the inner commitment that the individual makes by accepting the form of a master as a part of his inner reality. The acceptance of this form and its appearance within the inner space of the individual, as we have seen, provides an important channel for the spiritual instruction that the individual will receive during his time with that master.

The *Shariyat-Ki-Sugmad* (Book Two) describes the growth of consciousness and the changes in behavioral responses that an individual is likely to demonstrate as he moves from initiation to initiation.[20] These descriptions are harbingers of the spiritual progress that a person *can presumably* achieve, if they follow Eckankar tenets. In this way, they represent goals to which the individual can strive.

Initiations in Eckankar have created as much guilt and tension as they have exaltation and joy. When an Eckist receives a "pink slip,"[21] an invitation to receive a higher initiation, he is at first elated. Later, however, he may perceive a disconnect between the lofty standards he is expected to meet and demonstrate in his life and where he actually is in his attitudes and behavior. This is particularly true of those who have reached the level of Mahdis (Initiates of the Fifth Circle). The Mahdis's expectations of spiritual attainment are:

> The initiation of the Fifth Circle is sometimes known as the transfiguration . . . . From this time forth the Mahdis is an illuminated person. He knows and sees the spiritual realities and understands those around him, and his and their standards of achievements.

> He begins to use and control all the psychic faculties within himself for a greater cause . . . and systematically for the progress of the whole human race and those beings in every plane within the universes of God.[22]

Because many initiates of the Fifth Circle do not see these qualities in themselves, they are bewildered and plagued by doubt. This is not surprising, because Eckankar (unlike other Shabd Yoga teachings) gives initiations beyond the second level that are tied to the continuous maintenance of membership. This, in turn, requires the payment of an annual membership fee. While other factors are taken into account, fulfilling this requirement is a prerequisite to higher levels of initiation.

It is a common belief in Eckankar that spiritual initiations are based on a display of spiritual qualities observed by and known to the Living Eck Master. However, this is not the case. Initiations are mainly based on the number of years of continuous paid membership along with written recommendations from High Initiates (HIs) regarding participation, service (not a requirement but a plus), and overall character and balance in life. Indeed, the process of selection for initiations is far more a function of the computer than the inner or outer knowledge of the Mahanta about his chelas. Harold amply demonstrated this fact in a communication during his years of conflict with the former Mahanta, the Living Eck Master, Darwin Gross. In the transcript of a meeting between Harold and a group of High Initiates held on Saturday, October 22, 1983 (which was part of the public documentation revealed during the legal dispute between Darwin Gross and Eckankar), Harold said:

> [M]any of the initiation records we had were destroyed, were by Darwin's orders erased. We've reconstructed much of this. We don't have very good records right now about your initiation levels I'm afraid to say. Another thing that was done and I have to be honest, that people were given 5th initiations by date and this is not the way to do it. Darwin just did a whole bunch here by date and anybody that had 5 years, they were sent a pink slip. There are some 5th initiates who aren't 5th initiates. . . . And another issue that has to be faced . . . we're going to sit down, as we can get to all of these things and put out a program of a checking and rechecking before a person is recommended for initiation.[23]

While the cavalier manner in which initiations were granted has changed since Darwin's time, their nature and the procedures by which selection is made remain essentially the same. Certainly, the process has not become more spiritual, only more efficient and protracted. There is still no relationship between each initiation level and the spiritual characteristics outlined in the *Shariyat*. Only with HI recommendations and the individual's computer record of membership payments can a determination be made to elevate a members initiation level.

This is puzzling to those new to the teaching. They observe some HIs acting haughtily, mistreating those under their authority, and otherwise behaving inconsistently with their, presumed, high spiritual station. This has occurred with such frequency that Harold often makes statements that denigrate the spiritual attainment of HIs.

Basing advancement in Eckankar on years in service makes no spiritual sense. Each individual comes into this world having lived through many past life experiences. These define the state of a person's spiritual attainment at the start of each lifetime. Thus, each of us begins our spiritual journey at a different level of spiritual awareness. We progresses at varying rates as our spiritual lessons are learned (or not). If initiations represent levels of spiritual attainment, which as we have seen are variable, how can a group who has participated as members of Eckankar for the same number of years receive initiations at the same time and at the same level? Certainly everyone in the group could not be at the same level spiritually. We observe this everyday, in all walks of life. People are different, and they progress at different rates. What does this mean in regards to Eckankar and its system of initiations? Simply put, initiation is a form of reward and control.

Eckists below the level of Fifth Initiate are unaware of the mechanical process by which initiations are decided. No one wants to jeopardize his standing and opportunity to move up in Eckankar. Receiving a pink slip denoting eligibility for another initiation might thrill the recipient, but it has nothing to do with one's level of spiritual attainment. As Paul sometimes acknowledged, a master cannot give spiritual attainment to a chela; all he can do is plant the individual's feet on the path and the rest is up to him or her. However, by relinquishing this authority to the Mahanta, we have effectively surrendered our divine power to someone else and abdicated our responsibility as soul.

The corollary to this is that the admonitions scattered throughout the Eckankar teaching, holding that certain actions and practices can cause the individual to lose initiations or otherwise be required to incarnate over and over again, is equally fallacious. Remember the true advice Paul gave in *The Flute of God*: nothing can come to you or be taken away from you except in accordance with the state of your consciousness. This includes initiations or any other acknowledgement of spiritual attainment. The spiritual unfolding of an individual does not diminish by removal of an initiation any more than spiritual enlightenment comes from receiving one. After all, it is still up to the individual to chart his own spiritual course and never to surrender that responsibility in exchange for a pink slip.

The Mahanta, the Living Eck Master or any other spiritual master can only teach and guide. He cannot nor should he be allowed to determine the speed or depth of our spiritual growth. If outer initiations have any value, it occurs when the individual makes a study of the high standards expected at different levels of initiation. If then the individual embraces and embodies these characteristics, the initiation, like any promotion or other form of outer recognition, will have a positive effect on the individual's sense of self, supporting both inner and outer growth.

People often grow to fit the vessel in which they are placed, just as they grow to meet the expectations they or others set. Initiations above the second level are of this nature. If the individual embraces them and shapes his life accordingly, the initiation has a salutary effect. On the other hand, if this practice is not assiduously followed, then initiations become like the garments worn by actors on a stage, mere coverings for a reality that is only pretended.

It is entirely up to the individual. Consequently, there are many who may come to a spiritual teaching who are more spiritually advanced than those who have attained high initiations within that teaching. Graham, our English colleague, is a perfect example of this. He obviously brought from past lifetimes a degree of spiritual attainment which, when activated in this lifetime, propelled him to a high level of inner awareness and experience. In the outer, Graham was a Second Initiate in Eckankar — as was Darwin Gross when he became the Living Eck Master. But, having written his journal and sent it to the Mahanta, the Living Eck Master, he was summarily demoted to a First Initiate. Graham often joked that he was "staring at the door to excommunication" for having inner experiences with the Mahanta and having the temerity to apprise the Eckankar organization of them. Rather than help this chela understand these experiences, Harold simply dismissed them as the work of the Kal and removed an initiation without further explanation. But, does the removal of an initiation cause a person to lose his present state of spiritual awareness? Does removal impact his ability to soul travel? Will the forces that worked with him on the inner planes be less inclined to expose him to more spiritual wisdom? Of course, the answers to all of these questions is a resounding NO!

Reincarnation

One of the promises of many spiritual paths is that under the direction of a true spiritual master, she no longer has to incarnate into this physical universe. Paul took this idea from Radhasoami and Kirpal Singh. A true spiritual master is supposed to take on or manage the karma of the individual chela so that she bypasses that fateful meeting with the "lords of karma," and continues under the direction of the master on some other plane of reality. Paul wrote:

> The Angel of Death is the agent of Kal Niranjan, who is relentless, merciless, and administers absolute justice to each and all, regardless of their position in life. But he who is under the Mahanta's guiding hand

will be free of all this; he will be met at the time of death by the Living
ECK Master and be escorted to the place where he is to enjoy life in the
spiritual worlds. He will never have to return again to the physical
plane.[24]

This promise has held great appeal to spiritual students around the
world who relish the thought of finally being done with this plane of
existence. But the "promise of escape" is dubious. The physical plane
provides opportunities for growth not found in other worlds. Specifically, the action-reaction sequence of thought to manifestation is
slowed down to permit the individual, through trial and error, to learn
the importance of and how to control thought. Aside from the promise
of not returning to the physical plane being a false and unsupported
claim, no more benefit would be derived from such an escape than
would be achieved by a third-grade student being placed into college.
The lessons of the third-grade are precisely what the student needs at
that time. Elevation in academic level without the prerequisite demon-
stration of proficiency would be counterproductive. Baba Faqir Chand,
the Indian sage and practitioner of Surat Shabd Yoga, points to those
who claim mastership and hold out this promise but are nothing more
than fakers seeking to maintain control over their followers.

In spite of these obvious problems with the claim of avoiding physical incarnation, there remain those who assert that it is possible if only
the student finds a true master. A true master is thought to be one who
has been "anointed" through a process of succession involving a
bestowal of authority from ones predecessor. This is the claim made by
those in the Radhasoami Satsang tradition and their progeny. The
Radhasoami Satsang Beas is slightly more that one hundred years old,
and its progeny, the Ruhani Satsang started by Kirpal Singh (Paul's
master), is of an even more recent date. While ostensibly representing a
line of masters with uncluttered lines of succession, nothing could be
further from the truth, as we will see in Chapter 11. Indeed, by this definition of true mastership, the evidence is that none of the masters of
the Radhasoami Satsang Beas tradition is a true master.[25] Today, there
are hundreds if not thousands of Vi-Gurus peddling their teachings
throughout India, Europe, and America, holding out the promise of
final escape from the trials and tribulations of the physical world. But

they are simply inveterate claims that travel from century to century in desperate search of contemporary validation, but finding none.

Assuming for the moment that there is some validity to the claim that a "true master" can shield his chela from another incarnation, Paul's claim to mastership is even more dubious than that of his own master, Kirpal Singh.[26] Paul was never given the authority from him to give true initiations. So, he invented his own master, Rebazar Tarzs, from whom he received the fictional Rod of Eck Power. Having established himself as an exalted leader, Paul wasted no time in putting forth the historic promise of all Radhasoami masters. Paul asserted that all who receive the Second Initiation in Eckankar would have their karma worked off, and would no longer be required to incarnate in the physical world.

But as we have seen, no initiation by a master, especially under the dubious origins of the Radhasoami Beas tradition, and even more so of Eckankar, can relieve one of his karma. It is much like the Christian promise of relief from sin by the intercession of Jesus Christ. We have heard this claim before. Just as no one can take away the sins of the world, no one will or can take on all the karma of another individual — though we can help out at times. These so-called sins are experiences that are essential to spiritual growth. It is imperative that we learn from them for they are created by our own actions. Nothing can short circuit this process, except the accelerated learning of the individual followed by a change in behavior and attitude.

True to Paul's penchant for ascribing supremacy to anything related to Eckankar, he wrote about the preeminence of the Mahanta and Eckankar as they pertain to karma and reincarnation:

> The Mahanta is the distributor of karma in this world and what he says is the word of the SUGMAD. All the Lords of Karma are under his hand and must do as he directs. . . . He has been the spiritual head of the world since its creation. . . .[27]

Eckankar's claim to shelter its initiates from further incarnations in the physical are improbable if not disreputable. The God-seeker should follow the sounder advice that soul must look to itself for the responsibility of elevating spiritual consciousness. As soul is exposed to and embodies truth, it moves to a level of spiritual awareness where it serves no purpose to incarnate on this plane of existence: this is when physical incarnations cease.

To achieve this, the individual must sit in silence, contemplating the inner realities of God and how it relates to daily existence. With time, this practice results in subtle yet profound changes in the individual and a distinctly different mode of operation. There is no question of avoiding incarnations, for soul must exist somewhere in some dimension of reality/illusion until it is able to encompass and dwell eternally in the here and now. Until then, where soul will continue its experiences depends entirely on what it needs for spiritual unfoldment. Its destiny is determined by how it has lived its past life and how it has served the universal cause of love and spiritual growth.

A master wins no prize for relieving a student's karmic burden and need to reincarnate in this dimension. Experiences on any plane are absolutely essential for the spiritual growth of a God-seeker. Learning to read is more rapid with a teacher than by teaching oneself. However, if the student doesn't study, if he doesn't follow the teacher's guidance, he cannot expect to progress very rapidly. The same is true with study under a spiritual teacher. If the student does not apply the lessons of daily contemplation, recording inner experiences, and following other fundamental practices, he cannot expect his spiritual progress to be substantial.

There is no free ticket to spiritual growth, and this is how it must be. When the God-seeker knows that the responsibility is on his shoulders, he views things quite differently. He realizes that participation in a religion such as Eckankar, paying yearly membership fees and receiving a Second Initiation is not enough to escape the responsibilities of life on the physical plane. He then awakens to the truth that it is and always has been in his own hands. Instruction and guidance are always available just for the asking. We are never alone, for our higher self, working with spirit and other entities dedicated to our spiritual growth, are always there. They are ever providing for, protecting, tutoring, and directing us. It is not that we cannot surrender and must shoulder the burden of life by ourselves. The test and the lesson, however, are to learn to surrender to and rely upon our higher self working with divine spirit rather than some intercessor who only blocks our direct connection to the ONE. The God-seeker must never be deluded into thinking that a master will relieve him of the burden of life and growth, no matter how appealing it may sound.

The *Shariyat-Ki-Sugmad*

The current Living Eck Master emphasizes the *Shariyat-Ki-Sugmad* as the Bible of Eckankar, and urges his followers to read it often and to follow its tenets. When he does this, he is essentially accepting and propagating every exaggeration, deception, and misstatement Paul ever made about Eckankar and the Mahanta, the Living Eck Master. A continued reading of this text leads to an unprecedented level of indoctrination into all the threats, hyperbole, and distortions it contains. This is precisely what Harold continues to recommend to every chela in Eckankar by his endorsement of the *Shariyat-Ki-Sugmad*. Harold's prescription for my transgression of sending Graham's journal to him was precisely this, to read the *Shariyat* for six months.

On the one hand, Harold acknowledges that, "Paul got into his early efforts to present the teachings of ECK even before he called them ECK and ECKANKAR." Harold makes this point because he has read the evidence revealing the truth about Paul and the origins of Eckankar. He knows that Eck and Eckankar were entirely of Paul's creation. Despite being aware of these facts, Harold encourages the chela to continue to read and be indoctrinated into the false claim that Eckankar is the most ancient spiritual teaching known to mankind.

Harold as much as admits that Eckankar was built, brick by brick (or perhaps card by card), during these early years, and had no ancient history, except what Paul invented. Indeed, during these early years he didn't even call it Eckankar — that came later.[28] Yet Harold leaves the *Spiritual Notebook* and the *Shariyat* unchanged and in print, continuing to spread the false history and dogma of Eckankar with no warning or revision.

Even though Harold presents the benign face of Eckankar to an unsuspecting public, the longer one stays in the teaching, the deeper the indoctrination. Such is Harold's skill, a skill made inevitable by Paul's actions, and honed by Harold during his twenty years of protecting the pernicious legacy of Paul Twitchell and Eckankar. As recently as June 2002, Harold continued his emphasis on reading and studying the

Shariyat. Harold's new strategy is to promote the *Shariyat-Ki-Sugmad* as a kind of self-help book for change:

> The *Shariyat-Ki-Sugmad* means the Way of the Eternal. Its descriptive title could well be the "Book of Change." It's all about change. The spiritual benefit of the *Shariyat* is that it's a guide to better living. "To improve is to change," Winston Churchill, the British statesman, once observed. "To be perfect is to change often."[29]

In this clever recasting of the *Shariyat-Ki-Sugmad*, Harold ties its content to the powerful idea of movement toward perfection. Accordingly, he mandates regular reading of the *Shariyat*, which will lock the unwary deeper into Eckankar. To help to ensure this, Harold concluded his comments in a *Wisdom Notes* article:

> The *Shariyat* is our holy book. It is a guide for all who desire to be true to the eternal teachings of ECK. Base your talks and actions on the words in the *Shariyat*, and you will reach those who are ready for Eckankar.[30]

Harold knows that if he can turn the attention of chelas to the subtle influences incorporated into the *Shariyat*, then the doctrine of Eckankar is strengthened in their minds. While there are uplifting and valuable insights in these books, we must never lose sight of the fear tactics, falsehoods, exaggerations, and dependency factor that the *Shariyat* promotes.

As to the fear tactics, the *Shariyat* uses the age-old methods of fire and brimstone when, as we have seen earlier, this holy book and its derivatives warn of: dwelling in the astral hells,[31] spiritual decay and swift death,[32] horrendous troubles that strike like a plague,[33] and increased incarnations in this world.[34] Other exaggerations subordinate all other paths and religions to Eckankar for the *Shariyat* promotes the distortions that:

- Eckankar is the only and universal path to GOD.[35]
- [T]here is no other path than ECK...[it is] the original and only path to God.[36]
- It is not possible to enter . . . Heaven except through the teachings of ECKANKAR.[37]

Adding to the hyperbole, the *Shariyat* deifies the spiritual leader of Eckankar:

- [T]he Mahanta, which is God made flesh on Earth[38]
- The Sat Guru [the Living Eck Master] is the Son of God [39]
- [A]ll the power of God must reach these worlds through....the Mahanta, the Living ECK Master.[40]
- No man comes to the Sugmad (GOD) except through the Mahanta.[41]

This is just a sampling of the snares that await the devoted student of Eckankar. No wonder Harold wants the Eckist to make the *Shariat* her major source of reading and contemplation. Without altering or modifying its content or recommending passages that might promote the "change," "perfection," and "better living" that Harold advertises, he simply invites the chela inside. Harold knows the impact that such entry will have and the entrapment that lies in wait. The result is clear. Everyone who follows his entreaty will fall deeper into the indoctrination. By simply directing the chela to this book, Harold has insured the perpetuation of the doctrine and the future of the teaching, for this is the nature of indoctrination.

The Spiritual Exercises of Eck and the HU

Origins of the HU

Fortunately, there is one aspect of the teaching of Eckankar that is based on tradition and practice, and is as ageless as humankind's search for the direct experience of God. Paul's master, Kirpal Singh, who founded the Ruhani Satsang, taught him the techniques of meditation and contemplation. Singh taught his chelas the practice of going within to contact the light and sound of God. The Ruhani Satsang taught the HU as the most sacred of all sounds and the "word" that was behind all other sounds.

In Islam, from which the word HU is more recently derived, it is considered the divine pronoun[42] and is translated by some literally to mean "he."[43] Recognizing that God has no gender, many prefer, in remembrance of the divide creator, to sing the word loudly as "WHO" or "Hooooooo.[44] The Sufi tradition of Islamic mysticism teaches that sound manifests in different forms as it proceeds through "ten different tubes of the body."[45] These sounds take on the form of thunder, the roaring of the sea, the jingling of bells, running water, the buzzing of bees, the twittering of sparrows, the whistle, and others, until it merges into the HU. From this, it is concluded that all sounds are derived from the HU, making it the most sacred of all sounds, the sound behind all sounds, the Word.

This interpretation is disputed by other world religions that claim the sound "OM" or "AUM" is the Word. Indeed, all of the attributes of HU are ascribed to OM including that it is the sound behind all sounds:

> OM moves the prana [spirit] or the cosmic vital force. In man, OM expresses prana or the vital breath. . . . In every breath, man utters it, repeats it unintentionally and inevitably. Every vibration in the body and in the universe emerges from OM, sustains in OM, and returns to OM. Every humming emerges from OM, sustains in OM and returns to OM. A child cries, "OM, OM;" musicians hum, "OM, OM;" bees buzz, "OM, OM" the ocean roars, "OM, OM."[46]

I would venture that God has no preference and also that all sounds and words are part of ALL THAT IS, and serve equally well in garnering God's attention.

The True History of the HU

As we have seen, Paul's basic writings on the HU are derived, word for word, from the text of Hazrat Inayat Khan. But Paul not only took the words, he virtually kidnapped the HU and made it the sole property of Eckankar. Most Eckists today believe that this is one of Eckankar's principle contributions to the world, and that it emanated from the tradition of the Vairagi Eck Masters. This, of course, is not true. However, Eckankar must be given some credit for popularizing the HU sound and explaining its use to the public. But, Eckankar has never acknowledged HU's origins in the Islamic or Egyptian traditions:

> The Egyptian god HU was one of the minor gods in some respects, but he was one of the most important gods for those serious about Egyptian deities. HU is the power of the spoken word. He personifies the authority of utterance.[47]

Harold put forth an entirely different version for the origins of the HU:

> [T]he teachings of ECK predate even the Aryan civilization, which began shortly after Atlantis went into the ocean. *The Living ECK Master at that time was a man named Rama, who came from the dark forests of*

Germany and traveled to Tibet. On his way there, he left the message of ECK— the teaching of the Sound and Light of God and how to reach the Kingdom of Heaven in this lifetime — with the primitive people of northern Europe. Even today, there is a faint remembrance of HU, the secret name of God that he left with the people. . . . When Rama spoke of HU, he was referring to the divine Light and Sound. . . . The word HU was later used among the Druids, but they eventually lost the information about its true meaning. All that remained of Rama's teaching was a dim memory of the Light. . . . This is why historians today claim the Druids worshiped the Sun God HU.[48]

Harold's account of the origins of the Eck teaching and of the HU is as false as many of Paul's tales. It must be viewed in light of Paul's penchant for grandiose claims. Harold's account conspicuously avoids any mention of the origins of the HU from sources that are known to recorded history — Islamic and Egyptian — in favor of a parallel history whose provenance cannot be ascertained.

It is true that the word HU was known within Druid history, but as the name Hu Gadarn, the Joshua of the Old Testament, who purportedly came to Britain in the early fourteenth century B.C.E.[49] The Gaulish Druids called their Sun God by the name of HU or HU Hesus. The British Druid's knew HU as the name Hu (Hee) Gadarn — sometimes interpreted as Son of the Creator — or simply "Hu the Mighty."[50] An interesting side note to this account of Druid history is the hypothesis that because of Joshua's link to the British Isles and the Biblical sanction to Joshua that, "Every place that the sole of your foot will tread upon I have given you, as I said to Moses" (Joshua 1:3), some claim that Joshua's presence in Ireland and England makes their natives, "a chosen people."[51]

Harold's attempt to insert Eckankar into the history of pre-Aryan civilization and the Druids' use of the word HU is disingenuous at best. Harold published this passage in 1988 in his book, *How to Find God.* However, in moments of truthful reflection, Harold acknowledged that:

But without realizing it, he [Paul] was just practicing. Someday he would have a chance to take this teaching called Eckankar — *maybe he didn't even know the name then* — and put it in front of people. . . .[52]

The ECK [spirit] teachings have been here from the earliest times, *but they haven't carried the name of ECKANKAR* [or ECK]. They have been brought out under different names at different times. . .[53]

The word "Eckankar" [and ECK] . . . was *not* used to describe *any* religious doctrines [or ECK Masters] until the mid-1960's when the term was *coined, adopted* and *first used* by Paul Twitchell, Eckankar's modern day founder.[54]

Obviously, these declarations invalidate Harold's 1988 reiteration of Paul's redacted history. Indeed, Harold's statements constitute an admission that a Living Eck Master named Rama never existed — much less influenced pre-Aryan and Druid civilizations. Along with the invalidation of these historical fabrications goes Eckankar's claim that it was the first to impart the HU to early civilizations.

The origins of the HU are, ultimately, not important to the God-seeker. The important point is that all sounds or mantras can enable the individual to transcend the physical dimension and experience the ecstatic states and the inner planes. I have personally traveled into regions where I have heard the inner celestial sounds using the mantra of HU, AUM, and many others. They all work and can enable the individual to hear the remarkable and awe-inspiring sounds of the inner worlds. Ascribing greater magic to one sound or mantra over another is much like arguing whose God is greatest. It is a meaningless debate for everything is part of the ONE. Further, when the practitioner has had some experience with these mantras and the inner experiences that follow, she will come to the realization that these are not outside sounds; they are a part of her.

The Validity of Spiritual Exercises

The basic spiritual exercise of Eck, which Paul called "the easy way," is also the basic exercise of the Shabd Yoga tradition, and, as such, carries with it the intrinsic validity of this practice in the Yoga tradition. In these teachings, the HU is sung "Hooooooo," whereas in Eckankar, it is sung "Huuuuuuuu" or "hugh" — Paul's effort to make it unique. The difference is of no real significance. Each sound will work and should be continued if it works for you.

Paul outlined many techniques by which the individual could transcend the physical and experience the inner realities. These are discussed in one of his earlier books, *Eckankar – The Key to Secret Worlds*. For the most part, this book imparts techniques that have been tried and tested within Eastern teachings to great effect. Paul articulated them in a way the West could better understand them, and, in this regard, Paul made an important contribution.

The endless parade of unpronounceable Hindu, Pali, and Sanskrit words is quite off-putting to most in the West, and this is one of the main reasons these practices have gained so little ground here. If one removes the hype and fiction from *Eckankar – The Key to Secret Worlds*, there is still much to recommend it. Ultimately, however, Paul defiled this book, as he did all those that preceded and followed it, with an assortment of falsehoods mixed with smatterings of spiritual truth.

In later years, Harold created and presented many additional techniques, most of them based on the principles of Shabd Yoga.[55] They all work, and generally are useful techniques with which to have inner experiences. However, one must be cautious in practicing Eckankar's exercises, because they are filled with imagery and fantasy that can sink the practitioner deeper into illusions and lies, especially when involving the Eck Masters. Only by realizing this, can one escape Eckankar's traps and regain his true footing as soul and continue his journey to God.

The Principles and Precepts of Eckankar

The student of Eckankar is taught that there are four principles that should be imprinted upon his heart and mind. Having seen the truth about Eckankar, it is not difficult to see how a subtle brainwashing is at work as the student incorporates these principles into his very being.

> There is but one God and Its reality is the SUGMAD.

> The Mahanta, the Living ECK Master, is the messenger of the SUGMAD in all worlds, be they material, physic, or spiritual.

> The faithful, those who follow the works of ECK, shall have the blessings and riches of the heavenly kingdom given unto them.

> The *Shariyat-Ki-Sugmad* is the holy book of those who follow ECKANKAR, and there shall be none above it. Spiritually, therefore, cannot be taught, but it must be caught.[56]

Once accepted and absorbed, these four principles speak for themselves as final evidence of the entrapping nature of the dogma and doctrine of Eckankar.

PART III

THE FINAL UNVEILING

Chapter 9 — The Psychology of Paul Twitchell

Throughout this book, we have encountered the strange mix of Paul's sincerity, brilliance, and spiritual insight as well as his fabrication, plagiarism, and deceptions. The scope and frequency of Paul's prevarication leave little doubt of their being normal behavior or responses to life. Paul's actions cannot be glossed over with sanctimonious references to his spiritual mission. Having exclusive access to all of Paul's documents, Harold and possibly Darwin knew of or suspected Paul's character flaws. In fact, Harold's defense is highly revealing; it provides information for understanding the conundrum of Paul Twitchell. We shall now explore this conundrum and show it to be consistent with an abnormal state described in psychological literature.

The Nature of Dogma

First, let us consider the meaning of dogma. Given what we now know, a reasonable question might be, What enabled the fiction "Each Living Eck Master has served as the Mahanta, which is God made flesh on earth"[1] to persist? Why did no one question this presumptuous statement: "The Living ECK Master is the only manifestation of the SUGMAD [God] on earth?"[2] The answer lies in the power of dogma, which *Webster's* defines as:

> Something held as an established opinion: a definite authoritative tenet: a code of such tenets: a point of view or tenet put forth as authoritative without adequate grounds: a doctrine or body of doctrines concerning faith or morals formally stated and authoritatively proclaimed by a church.[3]

The remarkable thing about dogma and its attendant doctrines is that they do not have to be true or even make sense. The "proof" and power of dogma lie in the belief followers place in it, not in anything intrinsic to it. Dogma is given life and power by the believer's faith in its originator, his teachings, and successors. For Paul's successors, it didn't matter whether they had any personal validation of the mystical power that supposedly inhered in the Mahanta. Paul said it and wrote it, therefore, it had to be true. Such was the belief and confidence Eckists had in his integrity, honesty, and even the beings with whom he claimed to communicate.

Darwin's belief was based solely on the love and confidence he placed in Paul and his writings. Harold's belief, in turn, was built upon the confidence he had in his two predecessors, that is, until he excommunicated Darwin for acts detrimental to Eckankar and the Mahanta — an ironic but revealing turn of events. After being exposed to the frauds Paul's records reveal, Harold could only look to the dogma of Eckankar and faith in Paul as the foundation of his belief. Initially, Harold felt compelled to debunk the dogma that deified the Mahanta, the Living Eck Master, but ultimately, he returned to and fully embraced it.[4]

What we have, then, is Eckankar's powerful dogma, which is based on belief in its founder, whose record cried for scrutiny and could not stand up to it. Even as I discovered distortion after distortion in Paul's writing, I continued to believe in his sincerity and the truth in his works. But his sincerity and deceptiveness were incongruous to me. I could not understand a man who could write about such magnificent truths one moment, then put forth an immense lie the next. The ethics of this cliff hanger completely eluded me.

Then during a staff meeting, I described this remarkable conundrum. I mentioned how he could announce the founding of Eckankar in the sixties one moment, then proclaim it an ancient spiritual path the next. Someone jestingly observed, "Paul Twitchell had some issues!" We laughed and continued our discussion, but the comment stuck with me. I could find no explanation for his paradoxical behavior that made any sense by standards I knew or by those in his writings. The discussion on standards describes what he presumably believed about truth and the principles that should guide the life of a God-seeker. Then, as example after example of a life lived startlingly contrary to his principles became clear, I began to find a common thread, a reconciling concept to explain these troubling anomalies.

During my research, I used the expression "serial prevaricator" as a euphemism, not appreciating the truth that lay in the term. Every time I tried to move past the issue of Paul's psychological state to another part of this book, something kept pulling me back. After combing through books on psychology, articles in professional journals, and the vast data on the Internet, an answer began to emerge. I found a thread tying things together and explaining this enigmatic man. The answer lies in an analysis of his distortions, inconsistencies, and lies as well as the psychological state that permits an individual to exude sincerity, belief, and aplomb. Paul, I came to conclude, went beyond the "rascal" Harold described, and behaved consistently with what psychologists call a "pathological liar."

The Nature of Mythomania

The suspicion that the founder of Eckankar was a pathological liar was initially difficult to entertain. I had read, studied, and followed his teachings for almost thirty years. Being suddenly forced to acknowledge that much of my belief was based on the works of such a person was a difficult pill to swallow. But I knew that if I did not confront the truth, whatever it was, I would never be free of Paul's and Eckankar's insidious effects on me. Paul's life has to be examined against what is known about pathological lying.

The following definition is the most comprehensive in describing this phenomenon:

> Pathological lying is falsification entirely disproportionate to any discernible end in view, engaged in by a person who, at the time of observation, cannot definitely be declared insane, feebleminded, or epileptic. Such lying rarely, if ever, centers about a single event; although exhibited in very occasional cases for a short time, it manifests itself most frequently by far over a period of years, or even a lifetime. It represents a trait rather than an episode. Extensive, very complicated fabrications may be evolved. This has led to the synonyms: mythomania, pseudologia phantastica.[5]

William and Mary Healy offered this definition in their respected study on the subject. This book is significant for its recognition of the need to look at the pathological liar as a special category of psychological phenomenon. They wrote:

A clear terminology should be adopted. The pathological liar forms a species by himself and as such does not necessarily belong to any of these larger classes.[6]

A. Delbrück, a late nineteenth-century German psychiatrist, conducted the earliest studies of this condition. He coined the term "pseudologia phantastica," later adopted by other writers on the subject. Delbrück's work provided early warnings of the harm such liars cause to families and society in general by their falsifications and deceit. During this same period, another German psychiatrist, Koppen, contributed to the analysis of the pathological liar and the nature of the lies he told:

> The pathological lie is active in character, a whole sequence of experiences is fabricated and the products of fancy brought forward with a certainty that is astonishing. The possibility that the untruth may be at any minute demolished does not abash the liar in the least. Remonstrances against the lies make no impression. On closer inspection we find that the liar is no longer free, he has ceased to be master of his own lies, the lie has won power over him, it has the worth of a real experience. In the final stages of the pathological lie, it cannot be differentiated from delusion.[7]

In an excellent and comprehensive 1997 compilation on mythomania, its editor asserts:

> Deception and truth are polar opposites on a continuum with various degrees of departure from blatant dishonesty to unbending truth. A small dose of duplicity may interfere little with family and social duties. . . . It may either pass unnoticed or receive endorsement within a culturally stipulated range of conduct. By contrast, some flagrant falsities that violate cultural codes by their ineptitude, absurdity, or extravagance . . . have long attracted the attention of the medical profession.[8]

Another closely related condition is "megalomania:"

> A psychopathological condition in which delusional fantasies of wealth, power, or omnipotence predominate; an obsession with grandiose or extravagant things or actions.[9]

In an elaboration of pseudologia phantastica, Bernard Risch in 1908 noted several important characteristics of pathological liars. He observed that they typically had mental processes similar to those with literary gifts. The same passion and creativity found in novelists, poets, and playwrights are found in pathological liars. Both are able to forget who, what, and where they are, and create a new and often convincing reality. The difference, however, is that the artist is creating this reality within a socially acceptable context: we know it is his art to fabricate a reality of sorts for our entertainment. But the pathological liar is an artist without a socially-valued talent; his audiences are unaware of their roles in his works. He plies his art to whomever he meets or to whoever reads his creation. He does not distinguish art from reality and wants us to believe that they are one and the same.

Does the Shoe Fit?

The more I compared Paul with these definitions, the more things fell into place. Paul, I came to see, was a talented but frustrated poet and writer, whose work did not win him the recognition or monetary reward he had hoped for. Paul published some of his novels through Eckankar later in life, when followers were always eager to praise his genius and reward his erudition. He was quite accomplished in the novelist's skills of character development and plot construction. Yet he was not always willing to allow his novels to carry the label of fiction. Instead, Paul wanted his audience to believe that some of his fictional creations were factual accounts of his life.

Nowhere is this clearer than in *The Drums of Eck*. In the opening of this account of the life of Peddar Zaskq (which later caused much confusion about where and when Peddar Zaskq [Paul Twitchell] was actually born), Paul betrays concern his book might be received as a mere story:

> The narrative which is laid down in this book, *The Drums of ECK*, may appear to the reader to be fiction but it is a true story.[10]

This tendency to blend fiction and reality in Eckankar found fuller expression in the Vairagi Masters. He diligently and cunningly developed their personalities and histories with great attention to detail. Paul's efforts, as we have seen, resulted in names and brief histories for about 125 of the 971 masters who had supposedly served before him. He knew that if he did his job well, the imagination of the individual would kick in and bring these characters to life in the inner and often the outer realities of followers.

Risch also observed that the pathological liar is predisposed to play the role of the person(s) in his fiction. The line between fiction and reality is blurred, and he believes in and becomes what he has created. Though Paul had studied the traditions of the Radhasoami Satsang Beas teaching and observed the ways of one of its masters, he cut off his association with this spiritual line. But it later suited his purposes to become a master, which necessitated a new line of masters, whose invented tradition he would step into and carry forth. He artfully created a new line of Eck Masters and became the 971st Mahanta, the Living Eck Master.

It was not enough simply to create a line of masters; it had to be the oldest, greatest, and most powerful line of masters. Here, we see Paul's disposition not only to fictionalize, believe in, and become what he created, but also, consistent with the tendencies of megalomania, to exceed in his creation anything heretofore known to mankind. Paul understood how to tell the Big Lie. He not only played the role of the Mahanta, but also evinced such strong belief from followers that, in his mind, he actually became the Mahanta. There is an interesting story in Eckankar circles of an encounter between Paul and a famous Hollywood starlet. Desiring to have a spiritual consultation with him, she gave him her address and directions. Paul is reputed to have mused, "Who does she think she is, if I'm who I think I am?"

Risch describes the pathological liar as demonstrating strong egocentricity. True to this form, Paul declared that, as the Mahanta, he was "God made flesh, the Son of God, and the most developed human on the planet." These and numerous other references are about as egocentric if not megalomaniac as one can get, at least not without delving into outright insanity.

Another tendency discussed by Risch is reduction in powers of attention. The pathological liar is unable to remember and eliminate discrepancies in his story. Paul demonstrated remarkable abilities in this area. He knew when to be vague and how to thwart the likelihood of detection. But even he could not pay attention to all of the details in the elaborate fiction of his many lives. This accounts for the discrepancies in his life and the history of Eckankar we have seen in previous chapters. Paul liked to tell of his military exploits during the Second

World War. He relayed stories of his combat experience to his biographer, who dutifully wrote:

> Once in the Pacific when the fleet was under attack by Japanese fighter planes, Paul was serving as gunnery officer with a small crew of men on a twenty-millimeter gun in one of the forward tubs aboard ship.[11]

Harold couldn't abide by that one and, in *The Secret Teachings,* he admitted:

> For some reason he never got assigned to combat duty. When his Navy bosses discovered his gift with words, they put him into public relations.[12]

But he could not let on that it was part of a pattern.

Finally, the pathological liar demonstrates debility in judgment. While demonstrably sound in most respects, there is disjuncture between ethics and actions. His judgment is also lacking in the ability to discern whether or not others perceive his mendacity. Paul had the remarkable ability to believe in and act in accordance with the fiction of Mahanta and other myths. He was not troubled by the flood of memories and inner warnings that alert most people to inconsistency between present statements and actual past. His inability to presage the inevitable discovery of his distortions and fictions shows a failure in judgment.

Current psychological discourse about this pathology starts with the classic description of "antisocial personality disorder profile," of which pathological lying is a part.[13] While many characteristics of the antisocial personality were evinced in Paul's life, our discussion will deal with only one of them. This characteristic focuses on pathological lying and forms the basis of the pathology "mythomania." This pattern includes:

> Deceitfulness, as indicated by repeated lying, use of aliases, or conning others for personal profit and pleasure. . . .[14]

As will be shown in the summary below, Paul's pattern of behavior is festooned with lying, making his life a living billboard for this characteristic. Harold has admitted that Paul frequently used aliases.[15] Paul used them not only for pseudonyms for his stories and articles, which, after all, is a fairly common practice among writers; but also for self-promotion by submitting stories and write-ups about himself, in which he "exaggerated and twisted the facts."[16] He was quite successful in these efforts and had articles containing fictionalized accounts of his feats printed in *Who's Who in Kentucky*[17] and (ironically) *Ripley's Believe It or Not.*[18] He would even create a buzz at public gatherings by dishonest means:

> Paul was a born promoter. His wife told me that Paul would attend county fairs and pay to have himself paged so people would hear his name. She gave me a postcard Paul had made up in the early 1940s of a lavish mansion . . . printed on the front was "Home of Paul Twitchell American Author" of course, Paul had never lived there.

> Paul never traveled out of the USA except to go the Canadian side of Niagara Falls . . . so he never did go to India. She read *In My Soul* and just laughed . . . "that's Paul," she would say![19]

As we have seen, Paul engaged in numerous deceptions and flat-out falsities that are easy enough to disprove. The false and misleading statements about his life were so easily uncovered that one wonders why he engaged in such blatant prevarication to begin with. I believe Harold recognized what Paul had done, and, in an attempt to clear the record of many of his indiscretions, admitted that Paul had a proclivity to exaggeration and impishness:

> To say he had a checkered life is an understatement. In many ways he was quite a rascal.[20]

Paul's self-promotion knew no bounds. I had many questions when examining articles in the Paducah Library's material on Paul Twitchell. They struck me as just a bit too promotional and rarely gave a date or the newspaper from which they came. Apparently, he wrote articles about himself, had a friend print them professionally, and then sent them to the local library where they masqueraded as legitimate news stories to be kept for posterity.[21] Many of Paul's apologists point to these articles as proof of his accomplishments and legitimacy, but in reality they are more instances of his deceptiveness.

Some of Paul's claims are undoubtedly true and are validated by information in Harold's *The Secret Teaching*. Other claims, however, simply fill the ledger of probable fiction in the life and times of Paul Twitchell. His claims most likely *untrue* are in boldface. Those most likely *true* are in regular type:

- Star high school athlete[22]
- **Star college athlete[23]**
- College athletic trainer[24]
- **Member of two college faculties[25]**
- **Professional baseball scout[26]**
- **River traffic manager for an oil company[27]**
- Public relations officer[28]
- **Professional boxer[29]**
- **Cabin boy on a Mississippi riverboat[30]**
- **Pearl diver in South America[31]**
- **Gold hunter in New Guinea[32]**
- **Student of voodoo in the West Indies[33]**
- **Accomplished mountain climber, almost dying while scaling an Alaskan mountain in mid-winter[34]**
- **Student for one year in an Indian monastery[35]**
- **Member of an Indian religious cult in Maryland for five years[36]**
- Writer for a magazine published in Japan by an Indian religious group
- **"Ancestry traced back to 1085 when Alvered De Inspannic, a Spanish gentleman of adventure received twenty-six districts in which was the district of Turchet, from William the Conqueror, for his services in the conquest of England. In the year of 1461 John Turchet received from Henry VI, the barony of Audley and was held until the year 1631, having developed the name of Turchet to Twitchell"[37]**
- **"According to word received here Paul Twitchell . . . is rated one of the highest in the history of free lancing in selling and publishing during the first year of any writer. Twitchell [since] 1940 has sold published more than 100 articles, stories and poems.... His works have been received by such institutions as Harvard, Yale,**

University of Michigan, Dartmouth and many others....[38]

- **"In his best writing year, Twitchell says he sold 1,200 stories and articles."**[39]
- **"Of the five novels he's had published (four of them in England), one, a mystery, may be filmed in England soon."**[40]

Some acts of dishonesty and self-deception are part of almost every person's life. It is simply a matter of degree. When we tell ourselves we look fine, though in reality a loss of ten pounds is necessary, esthetically and medically, we are engaging in a form of self-deception and avoidance. There are times we refuse to see excess weight and deceive ourselves through strategic amnesia. This foible affects all of us in some respect. Whether by elaborating our past or modifying aspects of our personal life (age, weight, accomplishments), most everyone has at some point engaged in some puffery or omission. Paul's behavior goes beyond these venial examples of deception and fits the description of the states of pathological lying and mythomania. Paul's tales of masters, inner temples, and of his own life compose a body of fiction and myth that is phenomenal in scope and audacity.

The sincerity and conviction in Paul's writing also fits one of the key characteristics of the pathological liar. Paul had the capacity to believe in the stories he had created. Paul's conviction was so absolute that he could talk and write at length about Sudar Singh and Rebazar Tarzs, although the evidence establishes they were fictional characters substituted for Kirpal Singh and other real masters. Yet, the unwary reader senses and is moved by the strength of Paul's belief in his words. When the ability to believe in the moment is accompanied by a disregard for the truth, there is a monumental problem created for all who have trusted and believed. With Paul,

> . . . a whole sequence of experiences is fabricated and the products of fancy brought forward with a certainty that is astonishing.[41]

As shown in a previous chapter, he wove and obfuscated the facts to make Eckankar synonymous with spirit and therefore the source of all knowledge and life in the entire universe. He made proclamations so fantastic that they exceeded every example of mythomania, if not megalomania, that could be found in a comprehensive review of the literature.

Pathological lying manifests over a period of years or even a lifetime.[42] From what we know, Paul's life followed this pattern. When the characteristics of the pathological liar are compared with Paul's life story, the parallels are remarkable. Paul's own family and those who knew him in his youth speak with one voice on his life-long tendency to tell tall tales. The widow of Paul's brother states that much of Paul's early life, as contained in Brad Steiger's biography, is untrue:

> Almost all of what Steiger wrote was a fanciful yarn developed over the years by Paul himself.[43]

In a painfully candid letter, Paul's brother-in-law, Paul Iverlet, writes:

> In his book [*In My Soul I Am Free*] he states he was an illegitimate child and that his mother referred to him as "you bastard." This is a lie. His mother was a good Christina [*sic*] woman, a member of the Church of Christ and so was his father. He goes on to say that his Grandmother was an old lady who used tobacco and was quite a gay old blade, and who financed a trip for her granddaughter, my wife, to study in France. This is another atrocious lie. His book is full of lies. Most everyone who knew him considered him a crook. The entire family is now deceased. I am sorry to hear of anyone being hooked on any of his teachings.[44]

An interesting side bar is an article in the Twitchell Collection at the Paducah Library. One of the articles had the startling headline:

Friction in Twitchell Camp of Liar's League:
Charter members quibble on best qualified for presidency

Two weeks ago, the Paducah Press started something when it proposed to organize the Paducah Press Liars League. It started out of fun, but now the liars are quibbling as to whom [*sic*] is the biggest liar and deserves the presidency of the league. . . . Paul Twitchell, head of the city recreation department, was the leading candidate for the crown last week but as we go to press, there is friction in the Twitchell Camp. . . . So all of you will know what the trouble is, here's a little inside information. The league is being organized to create a closer feeling among local amateur liars with professionals being ineligible. *Now the amateur status of Mr. Twitchell is questioned. . . .*[45]

As Harold read the details of Paul's life, contained in his private papers and unpublished books that Gail Twitchell sold to Eckankar, he obviously knew something was amiss. Describing his thoughts after reading letters Paul had written over the years, Harold wrote:

> His correspondence was so diverse that there were times I couldn't quite figure out if this was the real Paul Twitchell or if it was one of his masks.[46]

The "masks" to which Harold referred were part of the deception Paul used to great effect. He did not see a pattern of consistent honesty that one would expect from a normal person. Not that there would be no difficulty in completely understanding Paul, but one could reasonably expect to find a single face, an openness about his past, and a plausible alignment of facts. But, as Harold had to admit, Paul started his pattern at an early age:

> Early in his youth he was involved in a variety of activities, but he made it a point to obscure any facts associated with this life. In so doing, he left a trail so clouded that it's going to take our historians years to piece it together.[47]

This account fits the pattern described by the Healys when they wrote:

> [I]t manifests itself most frequently by far over a period of years, or even a lifetime. It represents a trait rather than an episode.[48]

As Harold likes to say, it couldn't be clearer. Paul started at an early age, warping the facts of his life so that there would be conflicting and exasperating evidence.

This also recalls the first characteristic in the definition: proneness to "falsification entirely disproportionate to any discernible end in view." While the pattern of many of the lies in later stages of Paul's life has specific objectives and are quite calculated, these early distortions have no discernible end. At this point, "early in his youth," Paul's distortions are better described as part of a character fault, an inclination to mislead and create a reality different from the truth. Harold helps us to see the seeds of this behavioral pattern. They had been highly developed by the time he decided to create Eckankar. In reviewing the written records of Paul's life, Harold provides us with a glimpse of Paul's reasoning and his strategy in obscuring his record. He likens it to a tax protestor trying to hide from the responsibility of paying taxes:

[O]ne way to obscure your record is to provide the computers with such a mishmash or volume of information that no one could keep up with it.[49]

Only Harold has access to these records, and only he is in a position to characterize what he has seen. In any case, it is difficult to square Harold's description with Paul's admonition about the "truth, the whole truth, and nothing but the truth." Harold provides even more evidence of this pattern:

At 27 years of age, the most Paul had ever done was to teach physical education. But by the time he wrote it all up, exaggerating and twisting the facts, he had worked up a nice little paragraph about all the grand achievements of one Paul Twitchell.[50]

Obviously, Harold's description of Paul's actions as "exaggerating and twisting the facts" is a euphemism. Harold tried very hard to paint things in the best light possible and attributed most of his findings to the experiences that Paul had to go through to become the Mahanta, the Living Eck Master. How else could a true believer or someone whose position depends on true believers describe it?

Some of Paul's more egregious distortions and lies include:

- His date of birth and allowing such distortions to persist[51]
- His place of birth, in this lifetime and in a past lifetime[52]
- His birth mother and her background[53]
- His birth father[54]
- His spiritual master[55] and training in India[56]
- His experience and achievement to get into Kentucky's *Who's Who*[57]
- His background and experience to get published in *Ripley's Believe It or Not*[58]
- His military service[59]
- His association with Kirpal Singh[60]
- Lies about his experiences in *The Tiger's Fang* (claiming that Rebazar Tarzs not Kirpal Singh accompanied him)[61]

- Hundreds of instances of plagiarism over many years; and persistence in the practice of plagiarism even after it had been demonstrated[62]
- The line of 971 Vairagi Eck Masters with cunning and imagination, and fabrication of historical references and histories for more that 125 of them[63]
- A super-deity called "the Mahanta, the Living Eck Master," endowed with such mythological powers (e.g., "God made flesh," "Son of God," etc.) as to constitute megalomania[64]
- Attribution of writings and plagiarisms to fictional Eck Masters rather than revealing their true source[65]
- Origins of terminology, concepts, and principles in the Radhasoami Satsang teaching
- Sources of inner planes to distinguish Eckankar's cosmology from that of Radhasoami Satsang from whom he copied it.

Normal writers openly carry their pasts with them. It is what constrains excess and causes them to hold to the truth in their work. The conviction in their writing comes from an inner comfort that they have been true to their past. There is even a perceivable note of caution in their writing as they scan their memory for inconsistencies. But the pathological liar has no such constraint. He is able to dive into his work and create a personal and self-serving reality that is complete and self-contained within a particular story line. His chief concern is that the story be consistent with what has been said or written before.

Lest we think the pathological liar is without charm or amicability, we are reminded that:

> While the normal liar and swindler is forced to be on his guard lest he divulge something of the actual state of affairs, and is therefore either taciturn or presents an evil and watchful appearance or, if a novice at his trade, is hesitating in his replies, the pathological liar has a cheerful, open, free, enthusiastic, charming appearance, because he believes in his stories and wishes their reality.[66]

As one reads the various accounts of Paul's personal life, as told by Patti Simpson, Harold Klemp, Brad Steiger, and others, Paul comes across as a kind, considerate, totally serious advocate for the Eckankar teaching. His cheerfulness and enthusiasm were infectious and evoked great dedication from Eckists:

> The one thing every single person remembered the most was the great love that Paul had for others. . . . He showed kindness and consideration for even the smallest concerns of others.[67]

These characteristics as much as anything make it difficult to ascribe malevolent motives to Paul. But these positive traits are consistent with those of the pathological liar. They are part of the act. Such a kind, considerate, and loving person, one is prone to believe, would certainly not lie. In assuming that Paul would always speak the truth, the seeker would also feel that the master was someone who could be trusted, and in whose hands she could surrender her spiritual life. Paul evoked total devotion from his followers. His warm personality was so disarming that no one ever publicly suggested that something underhanded might be at work. Such a revelation would have helped many Eckists who struggled to understand how a spiritually gifted man could indulge in something so base as plagiarism and distortion. That virtually no one connected the dots to see the pattern to Paul's behavior helps to explain how Eckankar has survived so long.

Defenders of the Faith

This leads to a fascinating question. What awaits the person who defends the life and teachings of a pathological liar? What price does he pay for misleading and allowing others to be misled by a teaching he knows to be false? Harold's writings show the dangers of defending the indefensible. Devotion to truth is replaced with devotion to an individual, an organization, and its dogma.

This was apparent following my last talk to an Eckankar audience, when I spoke of "the ONE" (God) and said that the true inner guidance comes from within, from soul. I presented techniques for tapping the inner power each of us possesses. I discussed how everyone must look inside for answers and not to a master. I likened the master's role to that of a parent or teacher: it is initially important but must eventually come to an end. Interestingly, these ideas are found in Paul's writings (contradicted in his later writings, of course) but are no longer part of Eckankar doctrine. It is the imperious passages of the *Shariyat-Ki-Sugmad* to which the attention of the Eckist is now focused. It is the dogma about Eckankar expressed in these volumes that is now the core of the teachings of Eckankar.

For such heresy, I received a letter from Eckankar reprimanding me for pronouncements inconsistent with "Eckankar doctrine" — their very words. They directed that I should no longer speak in the name of Eckankar. They were right of course, for, by that time, I had uncovered much of the truth revealed in this book and could no longer teach their doctrine, as they wanted. As a God-seeker, I could only communicate the truth as I knew and understood it. I have stated that truth is the sacred connection that we have with the infinite. It is the infallible road to the awareness of ALL THAT IS, of which we are all a part. To abandon truth for the fool's gold of a self-appointed master, the lure of pious initiations, and the promise of never having to reincarnate is to delay or abandon the quest for God-Realization.

Instead of the noble path of helping others toward God-Realization, Harold has detoured souls into an illusory world from which spiritual liberation is necessary before the journey to God-Realization can resume. Having chosen this course, Harold must now stand guard to defend his organizational prize from pretenders and reformers who would wrest it from him. For now, he has locked himself in his headquarters and linked his fate with the defense of a lie. Harold's attempt to rationalize deception and dishonesty betrays the path he has chosen. Harold is now the apologist-in-chief for the mythomania in the life and teachings of Paul Twitchell.

This does not mean that Paul and his successors did not integrate a measure of truth in their writings and teachings. They have, as I have tried to make clear. Had this not been so, the hundreds of thousands who have read and been influenced by Paul's writings and also those of Darwin and Harold, would have abandoned Eckankar long ago. Even when the fiction of the Vairagi Masters, the manufactured history of Eckankar, and the deification of the Mahanta, the Living Eck Master, is removed, important truth remains amid the shambles.

The journey to awareness of our oneness with the infinite has only experienced a brief detour, but perhaps a salutary one. The God-seeker need only disengage from personalities, organizations, and dogma and reaffirm truth as the center of life. There is a great deal that can be retained as she moves on in her spiritual growth. We have all been at this juncture before. Once realigned, her course is righted and she emerges from the experience wiser and stronger. There should be no regrets, for this is how soul learns and grows. The test is whether soul knows when to let go and move on to the next step in the journey.

Chapter 10 — Eckankar Following the Twitchell Years

Earlier chapters have presented the true history of Eckankar from its origins in 1965 to Paul's death in 1971. Most Eckists know little about this subject and virtually nothing about what has happened since Paul's death. Harold has put forth a sanitized version of this history, but it captures little of the organizational tumult of those years.

Outsiders who have read David Lane's exposé of Paul and Eckankar,[1] or who have scoured the Internet to learn from former Eckists, have a dramatically different view from those still in the teaching. Those who have seen behind the façade assume that Eckists are aware of Lane. They do not understand how followers could stay in the teaching after such troubling if not devastating revelations. For the most part, Eckists do not know Eckankar's history or controversies. They are busy spreading the message and studying Eck works. There is virtually no discussion or awareness of the real history of this teaching and the often bitter experiences of those who have left. In spite of the information on the Internet, both pro and con, Eckists, particularly those who have been in the teaching a long time, remain unaware of it.

Eckists tend to leave the path when they discover aspects of the teaching that cannot be reconciled with their quest for spiritual truth. Those who remain attribute departures to failure of belief and see themselves as more dedicated. They feel good about their teaching and the love that is palpable at Eck gatherings. It is this feeling of joyful community that was an important and beautiful part of my experience in Eckankar. But this harmony and love come at a high price. The faithful live in the dark, unaware of the deception and upheaval. When members of any spiritual path practice the policy of "don't ask, don't tell," they jeopardize their spiritual growth by avoiding the truth. And Eckankar carefully cultivates avoiding the truth.

Since the publication of Lane's book more than twenty years ago, wildfires of doubt and controversy have sprung up in Eckankar communities. When a community comes across a copy of Lane's book or other similar publications on the Internet, it explodes in controversy. I have talked to Eckists from many of these areas during my recurrent bouts of introspection and have helped them to work through the questions and remain committed to Eckankar.

For this reason, I bear responsibility for not discovering the truth earlier. There are many Eckists who respected my commitment to truth and remained because they assumed others and I had reviewed Lane's book and had found no substantial merit to his allegations. My failure to discover and communicate the truth about Eckankar at an earlier point is a shortcoming that I address by this book.

The Death of Paul Twitchell

Nothing has been easy in the unfolding of Eckankar. Even Paul's death in 1971 occurred amid confusion and wonder. Interpreting his death as ordained from on high, one of the more respected members of Eckankar at that time, claimed that, owing to disobedience to the Vairagi Masters, Paul had been "removed for cause."[2] Given the fictional nature of the Vairagi Masters, this explanation for Paul's transition from this lifetime may have been wishful thinking or imaginative reconstruction by someone ill-disposed to Paul. However, in light of later events, it is interesting in at least one respect: Graham's journal records an account of a conversation with a representative of the Nine Silent Ones who states that Paul's "assisted early exit" occurred because of falsities and distortions he had injected into the teaching.
Paul was not able to fulfill many of the commitments he had made to his chelas. First, he had declared that his mission was a five-year one, starting in 1965. But in 1970, Paul did not want to give up his position. It was necessary for him to develop a plausible scenario to explain continuing as the Mahanta, the Living Eck Master. After all the stories he had already come up with, this was simple.

Paul used the slow development of the next Living Eck Master to justify staying on. The putatively all-knowing one realized this only when his term was about to end. Consequently, Paul indicated that he would be passed over for the next candidate when the time finally came to step down. This change in Paul's story was one of the first public clues to Paul's deception and resulted in many Eckists leaving the fold at that time. In an attempt to quell the storm, Paul wrote a letter to the chelas in 1971, but it had little effect. Finally, Paul's attorney, in a letter to the chelas, proclaimed, on Paul's authority, that the next Living Eck Master was a child in waiting and would not be ready for another fifteen years.[3] Of course, this was a fabrication, but it gave Paul another fifteen years of power. He had no idea in 1965 that his spiritual start-up would be so successful. No sense turning over the company to a perfect stranger when things were going so well! Unfortunately, Paul's body was not up to the wait. Once again, his prognostication was faulty and the succession of the Eck Masters did not occur according to plan. For anyone counting, that would be the third time in three tries that the "succession thing" fell through because no new Mahanta was ready.

For a master who professed omniscience, omnipotence, and omnipresence, Paul was remarkably wrong about every aspect of this prediction. In fact, he died shortly thereafter, failing to fulfill his prophecy of staying in power for many more years. This fact alone raised considerable questions in the Eck community. But the show had to go on. Enter Rebazar Tarzs, who, once again, had to be summoned to rescue Eckankar so that the story could continue. While Eckankar searched for a fill-in for the Mahanta, the Living Eck Master, the legend of Rebazar Tarzs would suffice to fill the void temporarily.[4] These were particularly challenging times within the Eckankar family. Who would be the next Living Eck Master? Who would appoint him? How would he be announced?

I was not there at the time and only have second-hand accounts of what transpired. But it is certain that this transition was extremely difficult for Gail. How could she find someone who would carry on the story line? What if a successor discovered the truth about Eckankar's founding? How could she continue to play a central role in the religion if it was built around a man other than her husband? Even with the creativity endemic to Eckankar leadership, there was no scenario that could move her into a position of leadership.

It is unclear how much Gail knew of Paul's fabrication of Eckankar. However, Gail knew Paul before he came up with the concept of Eckankar and its august Mahanta, the Living Eck Master. Yet, Paul appears to have convinced her of his authenticity. This is not surprising given his capacity to believe his own fiction. But Gail certainly knew that this teaching, whose creation she had witnessed, was far from the most ancient on the planet and the source of all other religions. Even Paul's charisma and her adoration of him could not have deluded her into believing that fantasy.

Enter Darwin Gross, a handsome single man in whom Paul had placed a great deal of trust. His devotion and personal attractiveness might fill the needs of the operation. Darwin ascended the mountaintop in one gigantic leap. After only two years in Eckankar, he became the Living Eck Master. Shortly thereafter, he married Gail. They had pulled it off in spite of Paul's failure to fulfill a prerequisite of the *Shariyat-Ki-Sugmad* — to prepare and announce the next Living Eck Master. But true to their partnership and the requirements of the *Shariyat*, Gail announced that she had a special dream in which Paul named Darwin the next Living Eck Master. Eckankar had produced yet another story to fill the gap between fiction and reality.

Darwin's ascension to the position of Living Eck Master did not go unchallenged by many Eckists. There was widespread incredulity that a newcomer could become the spiritual leader of the "oldest teaching on the planet." As could be expected, many were disillusioned by Darwin's ascendancy and unseemly marriage to Gail. It all seemed to fit together too conveniently. The suspicious left and the true believers remained. Despite scandal and disillusionment, the personable and charismatic Darwin Gross directed Eckankar to tremendous growth.

The Darwin Gross Years (1971-1981)

Darwin was prepared for and presented to Eckankar by Gail and others, apparently convinced that he was who they said he was. There was nothing at the time to suggest to Darwin that Paul's claim of antiquity for the Vairagi Masters was not true. When the time came for Darwin to become Mahanta, he had nothing to guide him, except what Paul had taught and what Gail had reinforced.

Darwin was, at least initially, an extremely humble, devoted, and sincere God-seeker. I came to Eckankar soon after he had become the Living Eck Master. Darwin's talks were not particularly inspiring, but they were straightforward and shorn of excess emotion. I was struck by his music in those days. He once recorded an album of songs that were delicate and filled with love. This was a very different Darwin Gross from the one that emerged years later imagining himself an accomplished jazz and blues musician.

I worked with Darwin on a number of projects during those years, as a sometime-roadie caring for his xylophones, designer of a series of workshops on "The Universal Laws of Life," and member of a training team for High Initiate training. Darwin rapidly grew into his position and appeared to believe in his new role. He was an engineer, not a scholar or writer. His principal strength was his skill with people. He was marvelous at walking the aisles during a seminar, allowing the faithful to catch a glimpse of the "God-man," who would graciously touch those fortunate enough to get close or look him in the eyes in a ritual known as "the Darshan."[5] All of this was quite effective and always inspiring to watch. The belief of the membership in Paul's creation was very high.

The power is always in belief. Like any faith-healing tent on a warm summer evening, miracles happen for those whose belief is powerful enough. When people believe their work is for the highest representative of God on earth, their actions and experiences are filled with the force of spirit. This is belief at work. No wonder that spiritual experiences are common among Eckists, for Paul wove an awe-inspiring fiction that "programmed" their experiences.

Given Darwin's effectiveness in his role, one might well ask, what's the harm? If it works, why not just use it and stick with it? But there is only one problem with this. It is a problem that Darwin ultimately encountered and that Eckankar, by this book, will now encounter. The problem is truth. Truth has a funny way of rearing its head at inconvenient times. It often appears when the forces of suppression feel that they have won a permanent victory. But victory in suppressing the truth is never final. It is always temporary and ultimately unsuccessful. And when the truth is finally revealed, dislocation occurs that, while initially painful, always results in spiritual growth. What is lost is the effort and energy expended in a direction that must be reversed. This is the prerequisite to moving ahead on the path to God-Realization.

After a few years, Darwin's focus changed. He pursued worldly ambitions more intently than his spiritual mission. The inappropriateness of many of his actions became evident. It undermined his accomplishments and eventually got him banned from the teaching that he, as much as anyone, built into a sizable movement. Darwin was not prepared to live up to the high standards of the Living Eck Master. He spoke, often quite convincingly, about the standards of truth and the behavior articulated in the *Shariyat-Ki-Sugmad*. Indeed, he even wrote:

> The leaders of ECKANKAR have the eyes and ears of the world upon them at all times and they should have the highest ethics and morals known to man and if they don't, they aren't really and truly ECKists.[6]

But Darwin soon abandoned this position for a more flexible one that allowed him peccadilloes and eccentricities. He justified it by thoughts put forth by Paul in *The Spiritual Notebook*:

> The Living ECK Master stands alone; he is a law unto himself. He does as he pleases, has what he wants, comes and goes absolutely at his own will, and asks no favor of any man. Neither does anyone hinder him in the execution of his will, for he has all things at his own command. . . . He does not work by time, nor is he bound by any rule or custom outside of himself.[7]

It is not difficult to see how an individual with a predilection for the jazz life and celebrity, who just happened to be the Mahanta, might get carried away with the personal freedom that this standard would permit. Darwin was, apparently, quite prepared to follow this more liberal standard and even to stretch it if needed.

Darwin argued vociferously for his personal freedom in spite of his high spiritual responsibilities. In the preface to one of Paul's books, Darwin, after asserting that Eck Masters have a greater knowledge of spirit than "the average man can conceive," went on to say:

> [I]t isn't stated in the teachings of ECK [actually it is!], nor am I saying that the Living ECK Master is unfolded spiritually greater than the next man. For on the outer it wouldn't show, due to the fact that what one does and what one says does [*sic*] not necessarily mean that one should judge one's spiritual unfoldment.[8]

In this somewhat obtuse passage, Darwin tried to create space for himself by telling followers that his high state of spirituality should not be judged by what he did or by what was seen in the outer man. Darwin's view of spirituality and how it manifested in his life was a necessary construct for him to believe that he was still the Mahanta, "God made flesh," and the "Son of God." How else could he reconcile an incongruous pattern of indulgences that left his followers wondering about their master? Darwin seized upon Paul's proclamation that a master answers to no one and does what he pleases. If reports of his drinking and womanizing are true, then he was in grave need of a cover. That is undoubtedly why he grasped at straws to reconcile his behavior with the high moral and ethical principles for which Eckankar stood.

Before Darwin's behavior reached its acme, he and Gail divorced. This was closely followed by her shocking disavowal of Eckankar. Gail was quoted in two separate reports acknowledging that Eckankar was a fraud, that Paul had simply created it. Both reports have been in book and Internet form for many years, without, to my knowledge, Gail ever repudiating them. After selling her rights to Paul's writings to Eckankar for $500,000, she has had nothing to do with the teachings since then.

The first account of Gail's repudiation of Eckankar comes from one of her acquaintances, who heard a taped account of Gail's conversation with a friend who had doubts about Eckankar's legitimacy.

> I was in his [Charlie Wallace's] kitchen when he telephoned Gail about 1981 or 1982. At the time he had a ranch in California. He and Gail had been friends in the past. Charlie was one of the few guests invited to she [sic] and Darwin's wedding in Sedona. I taped the conversation. . . . Gail was helping her friend Charlie, to come to terms with Eckankar. She told him Paul made up the whole Eckankar thing. I was there during the telephone conversation . . . find Charlie and ask for the tape and hear it yourself.[9]

David Lane, when speaking about the legitimacy of Eckankar, writes: "How can this be possible when Twitchell's own wife (and, I would suggest, co-founder), Gail, has privately admitted that Eckankar is a 'fraud.'"[10]

After divorcing Gail, Darwin remarried but quickly had his new marriage annulled. From that point, allegations of drinking and womanizing grew.[11] His path to excommunication was paved with fun and excitement. He enjoyed traveling with his band, playing the xylophone, singing, and spreading the message of Eckankar. Darwin even purchased a private executive jet (with Eckankar money) to fit his new image of a high-flying jazz and blues man. This was an extremely sensitive topic in Eckankar and a closely guarded secret. To accomplish this, Darwin set up an Oregon company, Dharma Aircraft, to purchase and own the plane, a legal device to avoid California sales taxes.[12] This ploy got Eckankar embroiled in a tax investigation by the State of California.[13] (I once toured the plane during a stopover in Washington, D.C. when Darwin was speaking and performing at an Eckankar seminar. It was quite impressive!)

Darwin was also having a number of physical problems that interfered with his duties as the Living Eck Master. For this reason as much as any, Darwin sensed that the timing was right to step down and turn over some of the travel and spiritual duties to someone else. He had become a businessman by then and took great pride in his ability to wheel and deal. Darwin's plan was to take over the business operations of Eckankar and leave the travel and other spiritual duties to a successor.

Harold Klemp Becomes the Living Eck Master

Harold's dizzying ascension from proofreader to Living Eck Master constitutes another intriguing story in the line of the three Eckankar masters. In 1981, the transfer of the Rod of Eck Power took place as Harold Klemp became the 973rd (more accurately, the third) Living Eck Master. Harold was not named the Mahanta at that time as it was Darwin's intention to retain the Mahanta portion of the title. Then too, Paul had messed this up with a story line that a Mahanta would not follow him for quite some time.[14] Both Darwin and eventually Harold disagreed with this and came up with their own story lines to demonstrate that they were "the real deal."

Darwin thought that, though he had relinquished the role of Living Eck Master, he would retain control of the organization and continue wearing the mantle of Mahanta. Harold, he judged, had good writing skills but was meek and malleable. Based on my conversations with Darwin, he, essentially, saw Harold as a "wimp." It is probably for this reason, not an inner spiritual revelation or a mission to carry out the will of God, that Darwin selected him as the next Living Eck Master.

Harold Klemp and God-Realization

Harold presents his God-Realization experience in his *Child in the Wilderness*. It is worth looking at here. Remembering an encounter with a stranger who operated a drawbridge in the town in which he worked, Harold told of a rebuke he received from this stranger, who spoke with the wisdom of a spiritual master. This set the stage for his God-Realization experience:

> God-Realization may span from a profoundly beautiful experience to the ruthless tearing away of one's final illusions.[15]

His own such experience started with a series of entreaties from a bartender, who, unaware that he was being used as a spiritual channel, told his future:

> [B]efore the night was out I would face a challenge so dreadful that nothing in my past could compare with it. No matter what was said for me to do, it must be done instantly, with complete faith in the Mahanta. Further, I would ride in an ambulance before the sun rose in the morning. "Go to another town," he warned. "Don't let them take you to our hospital. An engine will be switching freight cars and block the tracks. Just when you'll need help fast."[16]

Shaken by the warning, Harold again ventured to the bridge and the shack of the strange man, which seemed to him to be a "way station on the road to God."[17] Freezing but enlivened by the stranger's words, he remained for a period until challenged to "meet yourself."[18] Accepting the challenge, Harold describes what followed:

> The stranger broke in on my thoughts. "Look there!" he said. "The Light of God!" From out of the night, as if from a distant lighthouse, came a searing bolt of blue-white light that pierced my heart. He smiled. "The Light of God; It shines for thee."[19]

Harold's adventure on the bridge that night was the foundational experience from which he claimed God-Realization and mastership. Whether or not it occurred, only Harold knows, but many have questioned the validity of this experience. Perhaps most problematic is the utter earthliness of the encounter, where the ocean of love and mercy was supposedly brought to earth on a bridge. This is in sharp contrast to the almost uniform experience of others, who were required to raise their vibration to transcend the physical and experience the inner realities of God.

Harold's adventure in God-Realization, and his claim to mastership, are further compromised by his conception of what it meant to serve God:

> My vision of what it meant to serve God was like that of many others: wander at will, shun responsibility, and appear saintly.[20]

But a spiritual master does not live a vagabond life, shirk obligations, and "appear" spiritually advanced — he *is* spiritually advanced. Harold's story describes an individual not in control of himself, desperately searching for a connection with God reality.

Let us return to his narrative. The wise stranger suddenly and inexplicably changed into an indignant bridge tender, who exclaimed, in a decidedly unspiritual manner, "What's a matter with you. . . . You some kinda jerk? Get away!"[21] Harold's own account almost concedes he was unbalanced. He was grasping at straws to regain some sense of himself and to find the meaning of the frightening experience:

> Contradictions boiled within me: I was joyous, yet pathetic; light, but melancholy; free, yet not free.[22]

> The overwhelming experience on the bridge had left me in a state of imbalance, but not completely robbed of my senses.[23]

What followed challenges Harold's assertion of not being robbed of his senses. Interpreting an earlier discussion with the stranger about the Mountain of Yama (Mountain of the King of Death), Harold somehow divined that he should jump into the river in order to confront his fear of death. In a more reflective and perhaps more balanced moment, Harold wrote:

> It is easy to say, A [*sic*] clear-cut case of delusion; or madness, brought on by too much stress. That is an easy way out. Before this experience was over, I would realize firsthand why some people commit suicide: to please a tyrannical God.[24]

Harold's God-Realization experience and attendant imbalance raise reasonable questions about his sanity and hence the experience's validity. Certainly, a delusional state is one in which there is the possibility, if not the probability, of experiencing other dimensions of reality. Without the grounding of knowing where one is and how properly to interpret what is happening, one is apt to be a pawn of some astral entity. Whatever the true nature of Harold's experience, it certainly had a transcendent impact on him, but one for which he was to pay a heavy karmic price.

Having made the plunge, Harold was surprised that the stranger he had counted on to throw him a lifeline was nowhere around. He had to save himself. Finding a cable anchoring a light pole, he pulled himself to shore. Saved from himself, he made his way home where he pondered what he believed was God-Realization. Concerned with pneumonia, he called an ambulance and soon was in the care of professionals, who assessed his condition and, from his perspective, saved him from Yama, the Angel of Death. In a fevered and delirious state, he insisted on going to a hospital in a neighboring town, in accordance with the bartender's instructions. Shivering from his exposure to the frigid waters, Harold recovered. In time, the doctors pronounced him fit to return home.

Harold's encounter with the light and sound and claim to God-Realization are among the most bizarre encounters I have come across in all my readings on experiences of God-Realization. But this does not necessarily invalidate it. No one can say exactly what the experience is, and no one can offer any proof of experiencing it. It is always a claim made by one who believes, or at least professes to believe, he has had the God-Realization experience.

Harold's adventures did not end here, for his continued unbalanced actions ultimately put him in a mental institution. The next part of his story is equally bizarre, but perhaps recognizable to those who have felt the deep longing in their hearts to serve God in any manner directed. The Biblical account of Abraham's willingness to sacrifice his son, if that was God's will, is an example. The willingness to abide the inner direction of God, in spite of its outer absurdity, is a common element in those who reach total surrender. But this desire for service and sacrifice can be taken to extremes. The individual can lose all perspective as well as that most vital of tools, common sense. This might be amply demonstrated in Harold's continuing saga. While all of the evidence was to the contrary, he was not cognizant of his state of imbalance at the time: "[I]t really never dawned on me that I was very out of balance at that moment."[25]

Divining that he must immediately go to Paul to assist in his work, Harold took a cab to the airport. He startled the driver when he thrust a wad of cash to cover a minimal fare, making the cabbie suspect that the passenger was a little touched. Continuing his mission, he moved deeper into a state of imbalance — a "catatonic state."[26] What followed can best be conveyed in Harold's own words. Following several inner nudges to make certain pronouncements to others in the airport, he caused the crowds to scatter for fear that a madman might be in their midst. Harold probably left them with little doubt:

> Waiting for the next flight to board, I pondered what else I might do to achieve complete surrender. Then the thought came to disrobe. Sick at heart, I nonetheless got up to follow out the latest instructions. As I removed my coat and tie and began to unbutton my shirt, a big man barked, "Hey, Mac, you can't do that! Call the cops."[27]

Pondering his situation from the local jail, Harold knew he had to get his balance back. Whatever he concluded, the authorities committed him to a hospital for an indefinite stay, where he underwent a psychological examination. Harold somehow emerged from his stay with a sense of his own mastership. Prepared or not, he would, in a rather short time, assume the position of Living Eck Master. This strange story leads us to his encounters with his predecessor, Darwin Gross.

Darwin Retakes Control

During his first years as the Living Eck Master, Harold dutifully carried out the tasks to which he and Darwin had agreed. As President, he handled the spiritual duties of the Living Eck Master while Darwin looked after the business side of Eckankar. Darwin was eventually successful in talking Harold into relinquishing the presidency to him and focusing his attention exclusively on the spiritual side.[28] Problems were not long in coming. In early 1983, Harold saw indications that Darwin was no longer giving him full support.[29] Darwin's disregard and disrespect for Harold grew until the Living Eck Master carried little weight. Harold had no idea what was going on within the organization, as Darwin ran Eckankar as his own fiefdom. The Board of

Trustees was nothing more than a rubber stamp;[30] the staff did whatever Darwin directed.[31] There was only one king in the castle at that time, and it was not the Living Eck Master. It was Darwin.

Mundane matters brought things to a head. Preferring to work at home, Harold requested a computer from the office, and the managers naturally complied. Darwin got wind of it, hit the ceiling, and ordered a stop. His predecessor had refused the Living Eck Master a computer! This resulted in enormous consternation and upheaval at the Eckankar International Office.[32] Darwin began to tell staff to keep all business information from Harold.[33] Harold learned of instances of Darwin speaking disparagingly of him in staff meetings, showing little respect,[34] and belittling his positions.[35]

Another sore spot was the disparity in salaries between the Living Eck Master, who was then earning about $19,200 yearly,[36] and Darwin, who pulled in $65,000.[37] To Harold's credit, he was frugal and responsible with Eckankar money. Darwin's attitude was quite the opposite. He viewed Eckankar as his personal business. He built it up and was responsible for its flush coffers. He acted on his own, spending whatever he wanted, whenever he chose, without the consent or knowledge of anyone, except the staff who signed whatever he directed them to sign.[38]

The Break

The break between Harold and Darwin was not long in coming. It was discovered that Darwin had transferred large sums of money to Dharma Aircraft, the company that had owned his private jet. Inasmuch as the transfer involved a considerable sum, concern was understandable, and naturally litigation ensued. Legal documents in the case between Gross and Eckankar reveal:

> In June and July 1983, plaintiff [Darwin Gross] transferred more than $2,600,000 to a dormant Oregon corporation [Dharma Aircraft, later renamed Glen Eden Ltd.].... Gross, who was a trustee of the Oregon Corporation, then obtained the resignation of the other two trustees without telling them of the fund transfers, and replaced them with two of his own followers. Thus, these funds were placed outside the control of defendant's [Eckankar's] Board.[39]

Darwin had also announced to the staff (July 1983) that up to twenty-one members of the Eckankar staff would accompany him to Oregon, where he would undertake projects he claimed would promote Eckankar.[40]

Taking such actions, without Harold's knowledge or approval (or that of the Board), prompted Harold to take action to wrest control of the organization from Darwin. This was achieved during a Board of Trustees meeting held August 7, 1983 in Menlo Park, California, without the presence of Darwin or the Eckankar attorney, Alan Nichols. The Board, by resolution, agreed:

> WHEREAS, it is in the best interests of Eckankar to make certain changes regarding officers of the corporation, it is hereby:
>
> RESOLVED: That Darwin Gross is hereby removed as President of Eckankar and his services as an officer and employee of Eckankar are hereby terminated, both such removal and termination being effective immediately; and
>
> RESOLVED FURTHER: That Harold Klemp is hereby appointed as President of Eckankar, effective immediately, to serve the unexpired portion of the current term of President. . . .[41]

The minutes reveal a tense proceeding with many strange side notes. It was later revealed that there was little discussion and consideration of the reasons for ousting Darwin. In response to a series of questions from Darwin's attorney, who sought to understand why his client was ousted, the new Chairman of the Board, Peter Skelsky, answered:

> Mr. Axelrod, the only reason I voted for removing Darwin Gross was because the Living ECK Master said it's time to terminate him. He's the leader of our religion.[42]

Another interesting development in the August 7 meeting was the appointment, by resolution, of Patricia Simpson Rivinus,[43] Paul Twitchell's secretary, as the new Secretary of Eckankar. Only one day later, she was, by resolution, summarily removed from this position and told that

> . . . her services as an officer are hereby terminated, both such removal and termination being effective immediately. . . .

Joan Cross (later Harold's wife) was

> . . . appointed as Secretary of Eckankar, effective immediately, to serve the unexpired portion of the current term of Secretary. [44]

The reasons for this sudden shift are not apparent from the minutes. However, we now know the conflict that caused it. Darwin's supporters and sympathizers were removed from positions of authority. The coup was complete. It had taken Harold more than two years of being kicked around to reach the point of deciding to assert himself. It took some coaxing from the Eckankar Spiritual Council,[45] but he finally realized that he had to use his power or lose it. Harold demonstrated that he was much tougher and more cunning than Darwin had imagined. He proved not to be a wimp at all.

A short time before this meeting, Darwin backed a truck up to the Eckankar office and removed papers, books, and the entire collection of Paul's unpublished works and personal effects then in Eckankar's possession. This was the material that Gail Twitchell Gross sold to Eckankar, releasing all of her rights.[46] The sales contract had named Darwin as custodian and protector, which gave him some claim to the documents, even though Eckankar paid for them. The Board took immediate legal action to secure their return.[47] The materials were spirited to Oregon, but a court order resulted in their eventual return to Eckankar.

I was present in Menlo Park during this sad episode. (The minutes of the meeting held on August 9, 1983 reveal that the managers "as well as visitor Ford Johnson" were present.[48]) I had been working very closely with the International Office during the time, running seminars and planning High Initiate training. We were informed about what had transpired with Darwin and the efforts of the Board to recover properties and money that belonged to Eckankar.[49]

Following the meeting, I spoke with Harold and asked why he and Darwin hadn't worked things out without lawsuits and threats. Certainly two learned masters could come to an agreement on how to serve God. I expressed concern that the dispute was tearing the organization apart. Many chelas were being pulled into camps, depending on their personal allegiances. When I asked Harold about the possibility of a split in Eckankar, he replied that he understood my concern and was prepared for the possibility. He even thought that if Darwin started a new movement, it would likely contain a higher truth than most of the other teachings available.[50] Harold had set his course, locked his rudder, and was determined to see it through. His words were a great revelation to me. I developed a deeper insight into Harold as a person and saw his inner resolve and strength. But I also saw the beginnings of his willingness to wield organizational power, a characteristic that displayed itself in unpleasant ways in ensuing months and years. I found the whole mess quite disturbing.

Even though I was present at that meeting, I knew little of the details of the power struggle. Those who worked at the headquarters knew far more, but they adopted a protective silence. The staff was far more professional about the matter than the two masters. I later learned that staff members had made efforts to get the two masters to iron things out, but with no success. Harold told me he simply did not trust Darwin anymore. Darwin apparently broke several agreements they had made in the past, and things had gone too far to be resolved.

Two individuals, one a former Living Eck Master, the other the current Living Eck Master, were fighting and shockingly unable to resolve their power struggle. It was unfathomable, and clear evidence to many who worked daily with both of them, that something was wrong. Many concluded that men who bickered like children could not be spiritual masters and chose to walk away from Eckankar. But my eyes were not yet open.

Darwin Gross vs. Eckankar

Prior to the litigation, I met with Darwin in Oregon. My purpose was to plead for reconciliation between the two, both of whom I still regarded as spiritual masters, in spite of growing evidence of their true nature. I explained to Darwin that his disrespect for Harold was undermining the very notion of the Living Eck Master and the authority he possessed. I asked why he did not show the respect appropriate to the Living Eck Master, the head of the Vairagi Order. I encouraged him to voluntarily return the materials to Eckankar and to write a letter to the Living Eck Master showing deference and acting in a manner befitting the status of a predecessor.

Darwin was not entirely receptive, but he did listen. Clearly more concerned with himself than with spiritual matters, he replied, "What do they want me to do, beg in the streets? How am I to support myself?" This shocked me. From my naive perspective, I asked why he didn't just trust in spirit, as he had taught us, and simply manifest whatever he needed from spirit. He looked at me as if I was joking, and the conversation ended. The next morning, a group of fellow Eckists and I had breakfast with Darwin, where the topic of an apology came up again. This time, he spewed out several profanities and stormed out of the restaurant. That was my last contact with Darwin. After that, I was off for a speaking engagement in Africa.

Upon my return, I received a letter from Eckankar ordering me to stand down from all outer activities. This was the first of the major disciplines that I was to receive. Harold feared Darwin and his followers. He couldn't be sure of my loyalties, since I had direct contact with Darwin and might have fallen under his influence. By this time, Darwin had become, in Eckankar's eyes, a channel for the Kal — the negative force. How quickly masters fall!

Darwin eventually returned the money and all of Paul's materials to the care and custody of Eckankar — probably not because of my entreaties, but more likely because of legal action that Eckankar had initiated. Darwin was in a difficult position. He was eventually shut off from a pension or any other support from the organization he had built. Darwin eventually sued Eckankar for breach of contract. What followed was perhaps the most sordid period in all of Eckankar's history.

I remember talking to Harold while attending an Eckankar Seminar some time after Darwin's firing (I was out of the doghouse by then), but before the legal battle between Darwin and Eckankar erupted. Harold described a litany of Darwin's execrable behavior. Harold even feared for his safety, a fact that explained and continues to explain the intense security whenever he appears around Eckists. Suffice it to say that *if* these statements were true — and given what we now know, not everything can be taken at face value — I can understand why Darwin was ousted.

But remember, Darwin maintained that his spirituality should not be judged by his actions. Darwin insisted that there was no connection between the morality of one's behavior and spiritual unfolding. He even said as much in court! Here is Darwin's testimony in a deposition taken during the trial between Eckankar and him in 1984. In response to a question clarifying Harold's statements on moral behavior and spiritual development, he responded:

> **A:** I stated one cannot judge one's morals, or that one's morals have nothing to do with spiritual unfoldment, that is my understanding of the teachings of Eckankar — or Eck, rather.

> **Q:** [A]s I understand what you've said, a principle of Eckankar is that.... morals have nothing to do with spiritual unfoldment?
> **A:** That's the way I've been taught.[51]

On reflection, the most remarkable aspect of this entire drama was how so many in Eckankar completely missed the point. From quest for truth and desire to achieve God-Realization and become a co-worker with God, the membership had been distracted by personalities and organizational infighting. They had shifted their attention from spiritual goals to two men embroiled in a sordid, juvenile clash of wills. It is clear that Darwin bears the brunt of responsibility for this episode, but it is also clear that Harold and the Board of Trustees could have demonstrated more magnanimity, rather than the hardball tactics they adopted.

Everyone was wrapped up with concern for the fate of the masters and the schism that their disagreement had created. Eckists took sides and lost sight of the reasons they entered the teaching in the first place. The entire episode and the inability of these supposedly God-Realized beings to reach an agreement offered compelling evidence that the emperors had no clothes.

Darwin and Harold each made valiant efforts in their depositions to cover up the more unseemly parts of their dispute. They evoked religious protections, like the priest-penitent privilege, when they did not want to divulge the content of a conversation. They summoned the "spiritual secret" rationale when they could not describe the high spiritual nature of a decision or action. Harold even dug up the venerable concept of "heresy" to justify Darwin's expulsion. As I read through the depositions, I got a taste for what it must have been like for the Catholic Church after Martin Luther posted his famous theses, though the juvenility of both Darwin and Harold made the taste rather unpleasant. The whole thing was a farce.

The absurdity is seen in further testimony from Darwin taken from the same deposition cited above.

> **Q:** And that role [the Living ECK Master] was entrusted to you by God, wasn't it?
> **A:** Negative. Paul Twitchell.
>
> **Q:** Did Paul Twitchell make you the living Eck Master or did God make you the Living ECK master?
> **A:** Paul Twitchell did. God doesn't choose the Living ECK Master.
>
> **Q:** Who does?
> **A:** Paul chose me and I chose Harold.
>
> **Q:** Harold?
> **A:** Yes, sir.

Harold strongly disagreed with Darwin on this subject, declaring a far more divine and sublime process for his selection than the mere choice of Darwin Gross:

> The Living ECK Master is chosen by God. His selection to this position is evidenced by receipt of the "Rod of ECK Power," the spiritual symbol of his authority.[52]

While Harold's version is far more impressive and more in keeping with Paul's propaganda, Harold was simply following the tradition of his predecessors and supplying an explanation that fit the need. Even here, the Eck Masters could not agree on the same story line. In another exchange, attorneys for Eckankar asked Darwin:

> **Q:** Who is the Living Eck Master today?
> **A:** I cannot say.
>
> **Q:** Why not?
> **A:** That's left up to the individual to find that out for themselves [sic].
>
> **Q:** Is that part of the teachings of Eckankar?
> **A:** Sure it is. Yes. . . .

Q: You've said many times, have you not, that Harold Klemp is the Living Eck Master?

A: Yes.

Q: Then when I ask you the question today, who is the Living ECK Master, why isn't your answer the same as it has been many times in the past, Harold Klemp?

A: To the best of my knowledge, it changed in January of this year.

Q: In January of 1983, the living ECK Master changed, is that correct, is that... [what] you just said?

A: January of this year.

Q: Did Harold Klemp pass the Rod of Power to someone?

A: He was asked to step aside.

Q: Who asked him?

A: Rebazar Tarzs and Yaubl Sacabi.

This testimony was taken on May 31, 1984. Five months earlier, Harold had issued an open letter to Darwin and the Eckankar membership:

Dear Darwin:

The Order of the Vairagi ECK Masters no longer recognizes you as an ECK Master. As the agent of the ECK, I have removed all of your initiations in ECK as well as terminated your membership in Eckankar. You are not capable or authorized to act or speak for or about the Vairagi ECK Masters, Eckankar or the ECK teachings, nor are you to hold yourself out as an ECK Master or ECK member.[53]

In February 1984, Darwin Gross responded with a letter to the membership that paralleled the testimony he was to give at his deposition:

Dear One:

Many individuals who are spiritually awake are concerned about the misguided information coming out of Menlo Park. The Vairagi Masters do recognize me as a Vairagi Master. My initiations cannot be removed by Harold or anyone else. Harold Klemp does not have that authority. He was given a spiritual responsibility, which he has lost. He no longer holds the Rod of Eck Power. . . .

These excerpts [sic] from letters come from Eckists around the world: Very quietly, this was what was spoken from the Eck. "Harold has been removed." I asked by whom? "Yaubl Sacabi." Who is the replacement, I asked? "Darwin Gross."[54]

What an extraordinary turn of events! Harold had apparently beaten Darwin to the special branch of the astral library, where story lines are kept. Here we have two spurious masters, each claiming the other to be bogus, using a fictional group of masters as proof. The irony is that each master maintained an unspoken agreement that, however else he hurt the other, he would hold true to the myth that both were masters. Neither of them wanted to destroy the fiction by telling the truth that each was an imposter. Oddly, each of them had probably convinced himself that he was what Paul had made him out to be. Neither knew the full extent of the deception of the man who had started them down this bumpy, gully-filled road.

We might return to Paul's dictum, this time with the acknowledgement of a small measure of prophecy:

> Refuse to see Truth, pretend that it is impossible to know what is true and what is not, distort Truth, seek to mix it with Untruth, attempt to deceive both ourselves and others, give Truth in an unattractive manner, then chaos will reign in our lives.[55]

The chaos that resulted would be hilarious if it were not so pathetic. Thousands of Eckists didn't know what to think. They believed in the Vairagi Masters, the Mahanta, and the Rod of Eck Power. Many stayed with Darwin, but the bulk of the membership, enthralled by the Rod of Eck Power, stayed with Harold and Eckankar. But such is the fate of those who believe and follow a lie, as at that time did I. All are destined to wander in the abyss until truth finally lights the way out.

But the drama was not over. Darwin launched his lawsuit, which resulted in reams of depositions, but more importantly in the opening to the public of Eckankar's records.[56] Some of the information reveals more of what was behind Darwin's ouster. Harold and his attorneys argued that Darwin was a "renegade master" who engaged in spiritual "heresy:"

> Plaintiff, a former Living Eck Master, has embarked on the path of heresy. For example, he claims that Mr. Klemp is no longer the spiritual head of Eckankar . . . that one's moral behavior is irrelevant to one's spiritual development . . . and he is promoting his own initiation scheme which is radically different than that of Eckankar.[57]

The chaos continued for quite some time. Harold wrote an article describing the ways of black magicians, implying that Darwin was practicing their craft. He recommended burning all pictures, books, and paraphernalia of the dethroned one.[58] Darwin made similar implications about Harold in his edited version of *Letters to Gail 3*. Specifically, Darwin alleged that Harold had inserted descriptions of black magic techniques that could be used by anyone wishing to invoke dark powers. Having retained a copy of Paul's original manuscript of this book, Darwin felt able to support this allegation.

This resulted in another lawsuit brought by Eckankar against Darwin to recover the *Letters to Gail 3* manuscript, which belonged to Eckankar. Eckankar survived the legal entanglements and Darwin Gross's name was banned from all Eckankar books, discussions, and materials. Eckists coming into the teaching after 1986 had little or no knowledge that Darwin had ever been a master. I had problems with Eckankar's denial of the past: it was a cover-up conducted with the complicity of every Eckist that participated in the denial of the real history of Eckankar. It was disingenuous to say the least. Darwin Gross, whatever his faults, was a major figure in Eckankar, and history should not be rewritten for organizational expediency. The truth still counts!

There are other incidents in this period in the history of Eckankar. However, enough has been revealed to provide a sense of how Paul's deceptions continued at the highest levels of the organization. Eckankar found itself having to continuously reinvent its story line. It illustrates the fate of those who continue to build a house on a faulty foundation. In the end, it cannot stand. TheTruth-Seeker web site[59] houses documents from courts and other sources about Eckankar's past and inner workings. If more is needed to confirm the incredible events of this period, then this is the source.

The Harold Klemp Era

With Darwin out, Harold began to discover what he had inherited and what needed to be done. Several years went by during which little changed in Eckankar's outer teaching. Harold was obviously digesting the facts about the organization that Darwin and Paul had left him. I am sure that Harold was stunned. The greatest shock must have been seeing the private Paul Twitchell reflected in the copious records that he maintained of his activities. Paul had planned well for the fame that he hoped would be his. At some point in his life, he obviously decided to speed things up and continued his usual pattern of fabrication with greater intensity.

As indicated earlier, Harold attempted to reveal the truth about Paul and to debunk the myths and fiction he had created. His famous "Death of an Ideal" writing indicated an intent to step from behind the lie and go with truth. I believe that this was his original intent. He faced a narrow tightrope, and he made an impressive effort to walk it. But in the end, he found it impossible. His ambivalence is evinced in the vacillation of his writings. As we have seen, he declared that the Living Eck Master is not God and that one should not become attached to the vehicle, or personality, of the Mahanta. But later, Harold made a complete reversal:

> The Mahanta, the Living ECK Master [Harold Klemp] is SUGMAD [God] on earth and has unlimited power to carry out the will of the Supreme One in all ITS countless worlds. This is a vain boast to the ears of the profane, nevertheless the ECK initiate learns the truth for himself during the daily spiritual exercises.[60]

Harold was not only perpetuating the fiction that Paul had initially created, he was now adding to it. In addition to his offerings on the astral library, Harold added:

> The ECK Masters hold meetings in a number of different locations. Although their home on the Soul Plane is known to be Honardi, the immense order of Vairagi Masters is apt to send specialists from among them to gatherings on the order of business seminars. One such location is the spiritual site of Bcero Corsa, a meeting place hidden in a remote part of the southeastern United States. The approaches to it are protected by thousands of vipers that infest the swamplands. No intruder is welcome, nor is the secret path to it ever revealed to an outsider.[61]

Harold embraced the mythology of Eckankar, in effect saying, "If you can't gracefully quit it, you might as well join it." Harold has recently launched an effort to extend the teaching to every part of the world. His new book, *Wisdom From the Master on Spiritual Leadership: ECK Leaders Guide,* outlines the methods by which he intends to spread the message of Eckankar:

My overall mission is to tell people everywhere about the Light and Sound of God.... [T]he ECK arranged the task in three major steps. First on the agenda was to set up the RESA (Regional ECK Spiritual Aide) structure.... After the RESA structure was up and running in your home communities, it was time for step two... we saw the Temple of ECK manifest upon the rolling hills of Minnesota.... Now comes the really big step.... This third stage is one big project. It is an open-ended plan, without a limit to the initiative and spiritual growth that can occur among both Eckists and the people of the earth.[62]

These are certainly noble goals. When I first read this book in late 2001, I was excited by the challenge. But it is now clear that imparting the knowledge and techniques of contacting the light and sound of God is not the only goal. Harold also has the insidious mission of luring more souls into this trap. He has embarked on another major fund-raising effort, this one urging Eckists to make Eckankar a beneficiary in their wills and insurance policies. These efforts seek to ensure that the teaching goes on and continues to gather-up the unwary. Eckists must now determine whether supporting and proselytizing Eckankar will advance the spirituality of mankind or simply further Eckankar's organizational interests. Today, there is a massive building program at the Temple of Eck site, where the resources of Eckists pay for more monuments to Paul Twitchell, Harold Klemp, and Eckankar.

The Future of Eckankar and Its Membership

It is a wonder that Eckankar has survived all its scandals and abuses. While growth has slowed over the years, core membership has remained steady. In the past, the true believers in Eckankar regarded each exposure as a test of their faith from which they emerged victorious. As one who survived many of these tests by ignoring the truth, the victory was, in retrospect, simply an exercise in self-deception.

There are many Eckankar employees who, because their jobs are tied to the organization, may feel trapped. Others might be too embarrassed to admit they were deceived. Still others may not want to acknowledge that the teaching is only an interesting diversion, not a direct path to God. Then there is also fear of the loss of friends and the sense of community that participation in the teaching provides.

There are always reasons people remain trapped in a religion, a relationship, or anything else. But spiritual growth is the fruit of engaging truth and following its course, wherever it leads. Truth is our only and infallible guide to higher consciousness and God-Realization. Those who fail this test forget this principle of spiritual growth. They may doubt their capacity to see and know truth. But within our inner recesses lies a capacity to know truth. Some call it a gut-feeling; others call it going with the inner flow; still others refer to it as that still small voice within — conscience. Whatever name it is called, it is the inner call of soul directing us to act in our spiritual interest. Those who are deaf to this inner direction have deferred their dedication to truth for an allegiance to a religion and its leadership. The two are not the same. But the true believer confuses this point. He mistakes religious teachings and doctrine for truth. Religious teachings and doctrine can contain truth, but the ultimate source of truth for each person lies within each of us. The most that a religion or spiritual teaching can do is to lead us to the inner reservoir of truth and show us how to imbibe.

Eckankar has human nature on its side. No one wants to admit he has made a mistake. No one wants to appear gullible or admit being deceived. No one wants to lose self-reinforcing beliefs and feel terribly vulnerable. This is especially true because there is much love shared and expressed within Eckankar. But remember: positive events, people, and circumstances contain seeds of the negative, just as negative events, people, and circumstances contain seeds of the positive. They grow out of each other. There is nothing in the universe that is all bad or all good, all positive or all negative. Everything has both aspects of this duality. The reality that we perceive and experience is a function of whatever part of this duality we choose to focus on. Accordingly, what may initially seem negative may lead to important positive results.

In the teaching of Eckankar, many High Initiates are unaware of the deception and fiction underlying the teaching. They feel they have experienced positive spiritual growth and have traveled into the inner God worlds. Many have reached a point where they had to search outside the teaching of Eckankar (at least on the physical) for the wisdom that will take them to greater spiritual development. Many have taken this course because they found Harold's spiritual nourishment to be thin soup. The reason is now clear. The three Eck Masters reflect supreme consciousness no more than any other evolved soul. Paul, Darwin, and Harold were spurious masters of a spurious teaching based on a spurious history. Unaware of the facts surrounding Eckankar, High Initiates such as myself continued to believe in the dogma of the teaching. Some feared the curses with which Paul had threatened anyone who left Eckankar.

I now laugh when I read Paul's threats. I know that it is only belief in the curse that creates power to affect destiny. But I also feel disgust for the treachery in a potentially beautiful teaching. The practice continues with Paul's successors, who present spiritual truths, in spoken word and in print, while allowing these odious statements to remain in other Eckankar books. Harold often shows the positive face of love and caring, which I believe is a genuine part of him. Yet the sinister parts of the *Shariyat-Ki-Sugmad* remain, and Harold urges followers to read and make it the cornerstone of their lives.

In the end, soul must make a choice. If this book seeks to accomplish anything, it is to remove the shackles of a religion, teaching, or path that instills fear of separation. Curses can be found in all major religions and in many personal relationships. If it is not hell and damnation, excommunication, or the devil, it is something else. Curses seek to frighten the individual into staying in place and following directions. In a later chapter, we will look at techniques for freeing ourselves and minimizing the pain of separation attendant to moving on.

One of the paradoxes of Eckankar is that the leadership's manipulativeness is not found in most Eckists. Nor is it found in staff at the Temple of Eck, despite the legacy of Paul and his successors. Staff members are dedicated, highly spiritually-evolved beings who believe the exalted claims of the Mahanta, the Living Eck Master. I have seen firsthand the love, sincerity, and beauty in their lives. They may have questions and doubts, but they accept the core doctrine of the teaching and their own inner experiences, as formerly did I.

Many staff, past and present, lived through some of the bizarre events that transpired. Yet, as true believers, they were able to explain away or ignore obvious inconsistencies between the Eckankar teaching and the words and deeds of its leaders. There will always be those with greater loyalty to a leader and his organization than to truth and God-Realization. They will learn in time. But they owe it to themselves to decide whether it is time to move to a more enlightened spiritual paradigm, one based in truth not deception. If their belief in Paul Twitchell and Eckankar can stand this test, then undoubtedly they are in the right place.

Collaboration of Eckankar Leaders

Some in the top leadership of Eckankar, past and present, who worked directly with the Living Eck Masters, were aware of much of what was happening. In reviewing the record,[63] they were directly involved in hiding the truth from the membership. They built Eckankar's reputation, particularly in the early years, as a litigious if not vindictive organization. They sued or threatened to sue anyone who challenged the authenticity of the teachings. They knew the extent of Paul's plagiarism and other aspects of deception and cover-up by Paul, Darwin, and Harold. Yet, they did not and do not now tell the membership the truth — if indeed they know it themselves — nor do they make an effort to correct the written record. Instead, at the behest of the spiritual leader, they have used every available legal device to protect the written works of Eckankar, plagiarisms and all. They hold to Harold's disingenuous astral library theory to cover Paul's literary theft. Their sense of duty and immersion in the fiction of the Mahanta has likely blinded them to the truth. In fairness, however, the doctrine of the Mahanta causes them to subordinate their thinking to the judgement of the spiritual leader who, after all, purports to be "God made flesh." They are allowed to see only part of the picture, never enough to put all the pieces together. If I had not received the unintended blessing of a six-month discipline of intense study, I too would probably have continued as a staunch defender of the faith.

The Responsibility of a Spiritual Leader

We return to the point of trust and the responsibility that spiritual leaders have to impart truth to those who come to their doors seeking to learn about God. How can they place their petty interests and concerns for financial survival above the interests of vulnerable and sincere truth seekers? How dare they betray such devotion and spiritual innocence? Would they betray their children with whom they have an equal responsibility? How can they hide the truth from the faithful?

Eckankar leaders in the field have never had access to the evidence of deception and scandal, at least not until now. David Lane brought some of the facts to light, but few in Eckankar have bothered to read him — appalling but telling. This is a measure of how much everyone, including me, trusted the leadership. Because of this trust and my belief in the teaching, I played a role in leading others down this mistaken path. But I am meeting my responsibility by setting the record straight through this book and other efforts to follow. All who have been touched by Eckankar and who now see it in a different light, will doubtedly feel the need, as do I, to share their insight with others who have been influenced by their participation and devotion.

No one has a monopoly on truth, and I certainly do not claim to have one. But each of us has an obligation to communicate what we now know to be the truth, especially if formerly we allowed untruth to use us. Some in Eckankar's inner circle failed this test when they covered up information they should have made known to the faithful. In my case, telling the truth means cutting the cord with the teaching that, for over thirty years, I faithfully served with love and devotion. When an individual or group dedicated to the spiritual upliftment of others knowingly blocks or conspires to distort the truth, their fate is sealed. In a telling passage from *The Tiger's Fang*, Paul writes:

> Truth once released can never be suppressed; although it can be limited and misused. . . . I asked, "What happens if a man should see God and fail in his duty? He would never completely see God. He might get very high on the ladder of spiritual success and fail. This is the source for the legend of the fallen angels."[64]

Eventually the house of one who would distort, block, or suppress the truth of God will come tumbling down, as we have recently seen with the Catholic bishops guilty of this spiritual offense (as will be discussed in a later chapter). But it is never too late. Whether an individual chooses truth or personal and organizational loyalty is a decision each of us must make.

"Beware of Moloch"[65] and Other Warnings

Harold dribbled out some of the truth about Paul and the history of Eckankar only when he felt it was necessary. But even then, he spun the tale of Paul's life in a manner that turned the exploits of a prevaricator into essential experiences and training for the Mahanta, the Living Eck Master, who alone in the universe is "God made flesh." Even more tragic was each of the last two Eck Masters turning truth on its head and sabotaging the credibility of the other. Harold, in a not so subtle reference to Darwin during the turbulent days of their dispute, wrote and spoke about the worship of Moloch,[66] attempting to discredit and demonize him. Referring to the same passage as above (from *The Tiger's Fang,* where Fubbi Quantz was speaking), he quotes:

> He might become the leader of the enemies of light, and his lack of integrity excludes him from the society of Saints. It is really only his weight of guilt that holds him off.[67]

As it turned out, both putative masters became enemies of the light, though one was more effective in using the label than the other. Both masters used personal attacks and misdirected the attention of followers from a quest for God to a test of organizational and personal loyalty. Harold's response exemplifies the kind of defense that he has used over the years to protect Eckankar and his position in it. Harold used this approach in his letter to Graham accusing him of leading others off the path and exposing himself to a horrendous spiritual fate. Remember: he never answered Graham's questions; he only protected his position and left a sincere God-seeker to twist in the wind. Failure to answer questions can be seen as the mercurial and enigmatic ways of a spiritual master. However, it can also be seen as the way of a power holder looking out for his interests. They are also the actions of one who has no answer and chooses to hide behind the mantle of master, leaving it to the individual to divine the truth.

Defending the Faith

Anyone who questions Eckankar is accused of being a pawn of the Kal. When these attacks are made in response to this book, the evidence that spirit has placed in front of the reader will light the way. It is equally likely that Eckankar will offer little if any guidance to leadership in the field to handle the charges. Practically none was offered after Lane's accusations, only the partial admissions in Harold's *The Secret Teaching.* Harold exposed as much as he safely could; Eckists were simply told to go on the inner. The leadership realized that loyalty to Eckankar coupled with the protective nature of the dream state would shield them and support the status quo. It was a safe strategy.

It is no wonder that so many have been kept off balance and confused for so long. They have trusted their masters' statements, not realizing that they were either manipulating them or terribly deceived themselves. For if Harold truly believes the *Shariyat-Ki-Sugmad*, as he encourages his followers to, then the extent of his self-deception is so monumental that those who follow him do so at their own risk. It is the choice of soul.

All we have is our inner and outer faculties to discern truth. When those we have trusted deceive and trick us, spirit will still find a way to lead us to truth and to the most critical lesson of all, that each of us is his own pathway to God. We can reach this level of awareness only by seeking truth and trusting our common sense, our instincts, and our inner guidance. Past loyalties and resistance to change encourage running away. But all we then do is postpone the inevitable. Change is inevitable; it will constantly be with us. We will never "get there," for we are already "there" — we simply have not come to realize it. The struggle for God-Realization is the journey of discovering this fundamental reality. Even with this realization, we remain in a state of becoming, ever expanding. The secret is to learn to enjoy the journey and sense when soul is directing us to take the next step.

The Death of an Ideal

In his "Death of an Ideal" pronouncement,[68] discussed earlier, Harold ironically set forth a helpful framework for handling the death of Eckankar's fiction, which this book announces. Harold cited the work of Elisabeth Kubler-Ross, M.D., who studied the stages of dealing with death: denial, anger, bargaining, depression, acceptance, and hope. This stage analysis is also applicable to most situations of an individual experiencing serious loss. Since my suspicion of deception in Eckankar, I have undergone experiences that in many ways parallel these stages.

Denial

When I first read Lane's work, the pain and dislocation were traumatic. I struggled to reconcile his findings with my faith and trust in Paul's writings and the Living Eck Master. I searched for a way to justify denying the implications. I was successful and emerged with explanations that were at least plausible. It was a form of inoculation: a small exposure that prevents greater harm. I withdrew my allegiance to a person and focused on the unchanging nature of spirit itself. I found safe haven in concentrating on *The Flute of God*. Of all the Eckankar books, this one has the least Eckankar doctrine. Although it contains plagiarisms and employs the literary trick of an Eck Master as the source, it is, for the most part, a useful spiritual treatise.

Darwin's ouster reinforced my focus — I wanted no more identification with any personality. I sought connection with the transcendent, the eternal. This second crisis did not lead to denial but rather to amazement. However, those encountering these revelations for the first time will undoubtedly go into denial. Kubler-Ross describes this phase as: "No, not me, it cannot be true."[69] It is important to note she does not regard denial as bad or undesirable. In small doses, it enables an individual to cope. She saw it as

> a healthy way of dealing with the uncomfortable and painful situation with which some . . . have to live for a long time. Denial functions as a buffer after unexpected shocking news, allows the patient to collect himself and, with time, mobilize other, less radical defenses.[70]

So denial is only a temporary defense and must soon be replaced with a willingness to accept, which often requires radical readjustment. Eckists underwent great change when they joined the teaching. Most left religions and paths that were incapable of meeting their spiritual needs, unable to answer their questions, or were found to be false or deceptive. As evidence against Eckankar mounts, later stages in this process of coping with a harsh truth are experienced.

Anger

The second stage of this process is anger. I must admit to some degree of disgust. I was upset yet relieved that I had discovered Paul's deception. I understood what he did, even if I did not fully grasp why he did it. As the analysis of Paul and his life proceeded, these feelings subsided and were replaced by a measure of compassion. When I suspected Paul's actions stemmed from a pathological condition, understanding replaced ire.

If you feel anger after seeing the real history of Eckankar, know that gratitude from finally knowing the truth can restore your balance. From here, your course can be righted. Of course, there is the possibility that your anger is directed at the author of this book and not at those who created the issue. If this is the case, I accept the burden that comes with being the messenger. However, I am comforted by the realization that whatever anger you feel will, in time, be assuaged by truth, which ultimately produces beneficial results.

Bargaining

The third stage is bargaining. Here the person struggles for some way to head off the dire consequences of accepting the truth. In my case, I was initially able to bargain my way out of the conclusion that Eckankar was not true and that I should leave. My bargaining took the form of rationalization. I was prepared to accept Paul's plagiarism because I was grateful that he had revealed so much truth to me, regardless of where he found it or from whom it was plagiarized. But I reached this conclusion only by assuming that what he had written was true. When, during my second encounter with the truth of Eckankar, it was revealed that Paul had corrupted the teaching with myths, lies, threats, and deception, I was no longer able to bargain. I had to face the possibility that I would leave the path — the last thing I wanted to do.

Giving up thirty years of association with a teaching and the people in it you love and care for can never be easy. But this is when the God-seeker must face the reality of how much bargaining can be endured. I could always bargain my way out by replacing my devotion to truth with my loyalty to a man, a group, or a teaching. But this would compromise the most fundamental tenet of my life: follow truth, as I am able to see it, wherever it leads. There is no room for bargaining here.

Depression

Depression is the fourth stage. I experienced a certain amount of melancholy, but nothing that could be called depression. A certain amount of melancholy is involved in any major change in our lives. I was sad because I was leaving something behind that had been very dear to me. But I was far more excited by the extraordinary spiritual insight that came from breaking with Eckankar. Everything exploded. I felt a clear inner direction, strangely similar to Paul's vision of his mission and to his inner experiences with the light and sound of God. This vision gathered truths in a process of syncretism[71] and brought them together to support the God-seeker in me on my journey to higher consciousness. This time, it would be done without the self-interest and deception of Paul and Eckankar. My vision was clear: bring the combined enlightenment of souls dedicated to God-Realization to millions trapped by religions and pseudo-masters. The result would be a spiritual focus containing the collective wisdom of those who had devoted themselves to intense spiritual study and inner exploration. The highest teachings would bring spiritual truth to all who sought it. It would be a true teaching of Higher Consciousness. The vision was powerful and energizing. It easily overcame feelings of sadness.

Acceptance

This stage was easy for me. I not only could accept this "death of an ideal," but I was able to give thanks to Eckankar for showing me higher truths. This is the role that all paths play. They are of value only to the degree that they lead us to the most basic of all truths. No religion or path is ultimately necessary to reach God-Realization, because each of us is a spark of God. But we need guidance, teaching, and instruction until we can stand on our own and continue the journey. Any path that does not wean the individual from attachments and intermediaries is a trap. Ceremony, magnificent buildings, history, and millions of followers may glorify it. But, if it leaves the individual believing that a master, priest, savior, or messenger is closer to God, or necessary to communicate with God, it is still a trap.

Hope

Throughout this process, one positive theme has run parallel to the stages of emotional readjustment that Kubler-Ross describes. That theme is a hope for the future, which, for me, took the form of gratitude for the expansion of awareness. While there was a lingering sense of loss of a close friend, there was the accompanying knowledge that I had moved ever closer to the truth of truths. We are one with the reality of God, and we need not go anywhere or do anything to receive the full power of the gift within us.

Voices from the Past

As each individual contemplates her relationship to Eckankar, or to any path, it may be useful to consider the experiences of others who have been there. They came to see the truth behind Eckankar and made the decision to seek a different spiritual course. Many put questions to Harold about inconsistencies in the teaching and Lane's revelations, but heard no answer. One chela read Lane's material and wrote Harold for answers to troubling questions:

What choice do I have now? I am told there is only one way to the true God or SUGMAD. And I am told if I leave the path I will suffer and in the end have to return to the Mahanta. Doesn't this monopolize spirit and God? I have no problem with a path being the quickest or most direct route, but somehow the prospect of having only one way back to God doesn't sit well with me. It leaves me no choice, no freedom.

Sri Harold. . . . These accusations against Eckankar and the overtones of cult-like mind-control need to be addressed. I am surely not the only Chela with these deep concerns. And I know many members have left over these issues, and more will follow. Will you not address them and put an end to this controversy once and for all. I would appreciate an answer to this letter.[72]

The author never received a response from Harold, in spite of the poignant nature of the questions: business as usual at Eckankar. I too can attest to experiencing Harold's silence. Every letter I have written him asking fundamental questions has gone unanswered. Eckankar's approach seems to be, "If they find out, let them go. Others will come; the faithful will remain." Flawed but obdurate, the teaching goes on.

Many other former Eckists have shared their experiences on the Internet. Here are a few moving examples:

The feelings of terror, which we and some of our friends experienced when we began to closely examine the foundations of Eckankar, was proof enough that we had separated from a group which has at its base a very subtle yet powerful force of mind control. In fact, two people that we know considered suicide because they felt so deeply betrayed by Eckankar and its leaders. . . . We cannot help feeling as though the leaders of Eckankar, past and present, have been deliberately playing on our desires of earnest spiritual liberation. Mr. Klemp, how can you profess to take souls into the true regions of God, when you cannot even tell your "chelas" the truth? Do you honestly believe, you have the ability to do so?[73]

Here's the problem, the outer organization of Eckankar has been seriously and irrevocably polluted with, of course, plagiarism and flat out lies by the founder that are intended to keep students off balance forever.[74]

I can understand why many Eckists would be loath to even question Harold Klemp. They believe bad karma will ensue. . . . The organization is like a leaning stack of cards. The leader is dependent on the members for his livelihood. . . . Yes, the teachings of Eckankar bring results to the initiates because they were appropriated from a true spiritual source. I am grateful to Eckankar for my lessons. I have no prerogative on truth. I am simply a struggling soul like many others learning above [sic] love. I have only wanted to leave a few breadcrumbs behind me for those sympathetic souls who have also become ensnared in Eckankar's deceit... [75]

If God wants to communicate with us or guide us in our dreams to higher planes of consciousness, He would be able to do so without the assistance of an Eck "master." The troublesome thing about Eckankar, in my opinion, was that it incorporated a mixture of valuable spiritual wisdom, half-truths, and what I felt were outright lies. Parts of Eckankar's spiritual program worked well, while other parts of it caused immeasurable damage to my mind and to the minds of others I know. [76]

Note that the last testimonial is from a web site for Eckankar "survivors." *Survivors*! This shows the damage wreaked by an organization whose support and guidance ceases once the hard questions are posed. Silence, lawsuits, and personal attacks have been the only concession to openness that Eckankar has been willing to make in the face of challenges to its veracity.

In recent years, the Catholic Church has been more forthright about its failings than has Eckankar, the so-called highest teaching one the planet. Members of the Catholic laity wonder if their church is dying. [77] For many of them, the deception has gone on too long; the Church's last-minute scramble to truth has come too late. Their leaders have betrayed them, just as the leaders of Eckankar have their followers. Their pain is spread over the media, just as the pain of former Eckists is spread all over the Internet.

Telling one's story is cathartic and helpful to others in the same plight. A new web site has been set up specifically for Eckists and others to share experiences and feelings on learning the full story about Eckankar. [78] I invite everyone to participate in this process of sharing, healing, and helping. It is an important part of moving on. One former Eckist discovered that resigning from Eckankar was not enough to end the hold that this inspiring yet insidious teaching had on him:

I [was] in Eckankar for some 22 years. [W]hen I first joined it was a frontier teaching focusing on how to expand our awareness beyond the physical into the finer states of love, wisdom and creativity. . . . However, I noticed at the beginning of the nineties that the teaching seemed to be dumbed down to the extent that it was no longer exciting and this seemed to coincide with the path becoming a religion.

Eventually twenty-two years after joining, I was on the inner planes when the silent beings from the ocean [of] light and sound (love and mercy) lifted me up out of the teaching. I found myself going through Soul Realization. I was shown many truths about Eckankar. The next morning I was a bit bewildered, I knew that I had to leave Eckankar. It was suddenly like an empty shell.

The next night, Wah Z [Harold Klemp] offered me a higher initiation, but I could not accept, for I knew the teachings now to be too limiting for me.

 One night after formally leaving, I was on the inner planes when this gargantuan being in a blue suit came lumbering towards me. This being had the face of Harold and was really chunky and bulbous. I realized this was the body of Eckankar looking for me, to absorb me back into its body. . . . I looked more closely [and] saw this body was stuffed full of chelas, it was hideous. . . . They looked ghoulish, desperate for freedom, but I could not help them . . . and I was in danger too of being consumed back into this body. . . . Next I called upon my infinite Soul power and [sent] these gold and white shock waves that flowed out of my heart center like radio waves. Each pulse of energy from Soul made this bulbous body stumble. After a few moments it stopped and looked at me, I was its match in power and had no fear. But it would not go away. Like a malevolent being it monitored me looking for a weakness. . . . So I sent it several more pulses of Soul energy, it stumbled severely, the body was now hurt so I decided to break it open and sent it several more energy shocks, but the body of Eckankar was smart and it turned tail and started to lumber off. . . .

Six months after leaving, I was chatting to a friend who told me . . . she had seen me fronting [channeling] the Eck energy, that I was still corded into the Mahanta, even though I had left the teaching. With that I went into the inner planes to check and my God she was right. . . . [S]o I went back onto the inner to access the situation. These cords looked like the rope that anchors ships, they had been there for years and all sorts of growths were hanging off the cording. The Angels of the Violet flame[79] illuminated each cord, and together we severed each one.

Over the next few days I repeated the mantra "I sever all connections through all time and through all dimensions with Eckankar and its teachings." On the Friday I got a severe jaw ache. That night I experienced the deepest pain I had experienced in my life, nothing would kill the pain, I knew this was the remnants of the higher physical cording finally breaking. It takes a while to move down through the dimensions.

It felt like all the nerves in my jaw were being severed all at once. I was in so much pain I could not stay in my body, as I floated out of my anguished body, I heard Harold say "Call upon the Mahanta and the pain will stop." I knew that this meant that the cord breaking would stop. I refused, the pain got worse. . . . In the morning I knew I was free of this cult in every way through all dimensions and all time.

To resign one's membership is not sufficient, one has to actually un-cord oneself from the teaching. . . . When I left I unfolded at an unprecedented rate. I cut through so many illusions and falsehoods...[80]

Finally, the next letter expresses sentiments about Paul that are shared by many. A man who at a very young age had met him and been impressed by his kindness and wisdom wrote:

I went through what many of you are still going through. . . . I spent many years in anger. Not just for the lies but for the cover-up and anger from the Living Eck Master. . . .

Over the years the pain diminished and I was able to reclaim my life again for myself. I may not know your hurt . . . but I know MY Hurt . . . and I can use that to understand how those who left Eckankar for the lies feel.

[Paul] was very very kind to me. I loved being around him and I watched him and mirrored him as best I could. Paul Twitchell, god man, con man, liar, truth giver, author, thief, husband, adulterer etc. . . . impacted my life and the way I still see the world. I think of him often.[81]

There are many other examples conveying the grasp that Eckankar once had on those who finally saw and confronted its deceptions. I urge all Eckists and potential Eckists to read them and judge for themselves.[82]

Chapter 11 — Sant Mat, Radhasoami, and the Myth of the Master

When I accepted the truth about Eckankar, my first reaction was to search for another teaching to continue my spiritual study. My instinct was to go to Eckankar's source where I might find the pure, uncorrupted teachings of the light and sound. More than anything else, Eckankar came from the Radhasoami Satsang tradition in India, a derivative of Surat Shabd Yoga. Paul said as much in one of his earlier articles, in which he called it a form of "way out Yoga."

In my view, Surat Shabd Yoga is one of the higher expressions of the search for the God reality. The word "Yoga" derives from the Sanskrit word *yunakti,* which literally means yoke or union, in our context, the union of soul and spirit. Surat Shabd Yoga is the means of connecting the soul (*Surat*) with the holy sound (*Shabd*) of God. Through its inner-directed techniques, soul transcends physical limitations and directly experiences the light and sound of God. While appearing to have roots in the period of the Upanishads[1] in India (800 to 600 B.C.E.), it is most closely associated with a line of masters that goes back 500 years, when the practice developed into the form known today. The Sants (saints) were associated with the Nirguna School[2] of Hindu poetry, which claimed such exponents as Kabir, Guru Nanak, Daduji, and Paltu Sahab.[3] The modern-day version of Surat Shabd Yoga is most closely associated with the Indian Yogi, Huzur Swamiji Maharaj (called Seth Shiv Dayal Singh [1818-1878]). He drew on the teachings of Hinduism, Sufism, the Koran, Tantric Yoga, and the works of Tulsi Sahib of Hathras, Guru Nanak, Paltu, and Kabir, among others, to formulate his own spiritual path. This path is called Sant Mat (holy path, path of the masters, or teaching of the saints) or Radhasoami (sometimes Radha Soami, "Lord of Soul"). Shiv Dayal Singh lived and taught in the city of Agra, in the Uttar Pradesh District.[4] While Sant Mat has a centuries-old spiritual connection, the Radhasoami tradition, as it is known today, is of relatively recent vintage.

History of Sant Mat

As we read the texts and references to Sant Mat (Radhasoami), there is much to remind us of Eckankar. For instance, Sant Mat is said to go back to the dawn of recorded history, and references to it can be found in all scriptures and religious traditions of the world, even though it began in the latter half of the 1800s. References to this more ancient lineage of Sant Mat go back to the time of Kabir (ca. 1398-1518). Kabir taught the union of all and the necessity of linking the individual with the sound and light of God in order to make the journey back to the Godhead.

Kirpal Singh, Paul Twitchell's guru, proclaimed it to be the essential teaching of all saints and masters since the dawn of time. He is reputed to have said:

> This Science of Spirituality is definite and natural with sure results. It has been given many names throughout the past. All the past Masters gave the same teachings, as did Jesus Christ. It is a universal teaching in all the religions of the world and this is amply borne out by the sacred scriptures everywhere.[5]

Does this sound familiar? It should, because it resembles the mythology that Paul used to anchor Eckankar. It is no wonder that many who left Eckankar found their way to Paul's teacher or his successor. Kirpal Singh had established the Ruhani Satsang, which grew out of the Radhasoami Satsang tradition, which in turn, traces its lineage to Shiv Dayal Singh. All of the present-day teachings of the science of the sound and light, including Eckankar, derive from Shiv Dayal Singh.

But as is true in many spiritual paths, Radhasoami was marked with charges of fakery and spiritual illegitimacy. The number of Sat Gurus claiming to be the God-man in India alone is literally in the hundreds. Most claim lineage back to Shiv Dayal Singh and present themselves as able to give the true initiation that links the chela with the light and sound of God.

The more research I conducted, the clearer it became that running off to India would get me no closer to truth. Why run from one discredited path and master to one perhaps less sullied, but nevertheless of doubtful authenticity? The research of Mark Juergensmeyer and David Lane (yes, the same David Lane) was invaluable in seeing the truth in these paths.[6] While still a *satsangi* (a student of Radhasoami) Lane took an academic interest in this teaching. He writes:

> Truth, as such, is not the issue here; rather, the human process of defin-ing truth, approaching truth, explaining truth . . . particularly as it relates to the transmission of spiritual authority from one leader to another.[7]

My interest was quite different from Juergensmeyer's and Lane's academic focus. As a God-seeker, my interest was entirely about truth, the golden road to higher consciousness. But sociological studies of religion could be helpful in this pursuit. They provide methods to help the God-seeker judge the validity of teachings and masters. Their find-ings form the basis of analysis undergirding many of the conclusions of this book. Thus, the history of guru succession provides insight into the integrity of the professed masters, the validity of their claims, and the intrinsic truth of their teachings. After my experiences with Eckankar, I was simply looking for an honest master and teacher, and a method for determining honesty.

I assumed that no matter how troubled or frustrated Paul's life was, the master under whom he had studied (and later denied), Kirpal Singh, was not of his ilk. I was hopeful that Kirpal Singh and his successors showed honesty, integrity, and genuine concern for truth that chela Paul Twitchell had failed to demonstrate. But as I examined the life of Kir-pal Singh, his contemporaries, and successors, as well as Radhasoami itself, it became increasingly clear that the problem lay with the mas-ters themselves, if not with the whole concept of "master."

Sant Mat and the Tradition of Masters

The Radhasoami tradition has always posited a master as the sine qua non of spiritual development. Julian Johnson makes this point repeatedly in what many regard as the seminal work on Radhasoami in the West, *The Path of the Masters*.[8] Johnson's book is a virtual testa-ment to, if not advertisement for, the necessity of a master in the jour-ney of a God-seeker (a point this book vigorously challenges). Paul copied the Radhasoami teaching and more particularly Julian Johnson, when he articulated the "three great facts [that] stand out in letters of light at the very entrance to the Royal Highway of the Saints."[9] Johnson described them as:

> Sat Guru — Shabd Dhun — Jivan Mukti (1) Sat Guru, *the Master*, the Saint, (2) Shabd Dhun, *the Audible Life Stream*, the melodious Sound, the Sound primeval, (3) Jivan Mukti, *spiritual freedom here and now*, meaning perfect liberation during this lifetime.[10]

Paul repeated the importance of these three requirements, especially the need for a master, which also formed the basis of his first set of discourses and the heart of Eckankar. This need for a master is a vital part of the Radhasoami tradition. It helps to support a virtual guild of masters in India, which now proliferates in the West. Each master claims to be God-enlightened and a direct representative of God, if not the only such representative. This is not to say that many of these teachers are not sincere and well meaning. Many certainly are. They greatly assist students in gaining deep insights into the inner and outer realities of life.

But the need for spiritual guidance does not justify elevation of a master to a role beyond that of a teacher. Over and over, we find a master treated as an object of worship — hardly surprising when he calls himself a "God-man" or "Perfect Master." Such a master may realize he is a spark of God, an embodiment of God on earth. But he fails to teach his followers that they too are sparks of God, embodiments of the Divine. Thus, he fails in his most important if not only role: helping the God-seeker see, know, and experience this reality for himself.

Such masters keep their students dependent and overlook the necessity for weaning, as any good parent understands. Even today, there is the tendency of masters to set themselves far above those they teach. This attitude, clearly seen in Radhasoami, Eckankar and its progeny[11] calls into question the master-chela relationship itself.

Succession Within Radhasoami Satsang Beas

In a line of masters and a path that is as putatively distinguished as Radhasoami, one would expect harmonious order and mutual respect in succession of leadership. But succession in the Radhasoami tradition has been as disorderly and scandal ridden as in Eckankar. As we read of the storied line of Radhasoami masters, their claims of succession, and the questionable lives many lived, we may see where skepticism about masters as a prerequisite to spiritual liberation derives.

Let's start with the life and times of Shiv Dayal Singh, the founder of Radhasoami. He was born in 1818, fulfilling the prophecy of the family's Guru, Tulsi Sahib: Mahamaya, Singh's mother "will have a son. But do not look upon the child as a mere human being."[12] Singh's principal historian, Rai Salig Ram, by claiming that Singh did not have a guru and was never initiated, elevates him to born Sant (saint). Yet, Singh's family, including his mother, followed Tulsi Sahib when they lived in Hathras. There may be those who elevate Singh to a born Sant, never requiring any instruction, but a child, even a spiritually advanced one, is still a child. It is hard to believe his family would keep from him the instruction that would certainly be provided for a special child.

Others clearly assert that Tulsi Sahib initiated Shiv Dayal Singh, who later left to form his own path. Indeed, L. R. Puri in his *Radha Soami Teachings* writes:

> As Swami Ji [affectionate name for Shiv Dayal Singh] was much younger, Tulsi Sahib looked upon him like his own son and treated him with great love and affection.[13]

Whatever actually occurred, the work of a spin-doctor is apparent. Singh's principal historian sought to disclaim any connection with any predecessor or teacher. This enhanced the image of a new divinely-inspired master, who needed no guru to achieve his exalted state.

In the same manner, the founder of Eckankar sought to dissociate himself from his teacher and roots. He wanted to claim exclusive providence over a teaching he planned to build into a personal empire. But it is strange for the founder of Radhasoami to claim he had no master. One of its tenets is the absolute necessity of a master. But presumably, this all-important tenet only applied to lesser souls who followed Shiv Dayal Singh, whom his adherents claimed to be the first incarnation of the Supreme Being, Radhasoami. Even during the life of Shiv Dayal Singh, he made no mention of his study under any other master. But this is not surprising for one who seeks to dissociate himself from his past and stand alone as an exalted leader. Such a leader often wants to be credited with accomplishments without the drain of recognition from acknowledging roots.

We see that the history, myth making, and fiction of the Radhasoami tradition were seeded in much the same way as were other major religions. Founders surround themselves with, or are surrounded by, fantastic stories to establish and celebrate their divinity or near divinity. Jesus was purportedly of virgin birth and attended by three oriental kings. While the Islamic prophet Muhammad had an ordinary birth, his grandson, the first Imam, was born in particular grandeur when Muhammad's daughter, Fatima, walked through the stone Kaaba as it opened to her and emerged three days later bearing a newborn child, Ali. The tales and the myths in the dogma of all world religions create the stuff of inner experiences that followers believe and accept as truth. These stories have no intrinsic truth, but followers attach truth to them. That is why anchoring our beliefs in myths and stories only place us in an attractive inner landscape for a while. In time we learn that the scenery is only as real as our belief in it. We can then gain mastery over the scenery and our movement within it.

The Beas Line of Radhasoami Masters

Drama within the Radhasoami movement started as soon as its founder died. Finding a successor was paramount. By all accounts, Swamiji (the name used by devotées of Shiv Dayal Singh) named Hazur Rai Saligram as successor. Saligram assumed this role and directed the activity of Radhasoami in Agra from 1878 to 1898. The Agra lineage of Radhasoami was always considered to be the pure line of succession, but their accomplishments as a movement pale in comparison to the branch started by Baba Jaimal Singh.

The life of Jaimal Singh is important because his efforts led to the more prominent branch of Radhasoami, the Beas line. This line of masters includes, among others, Sawan Singh (Julian Johnson's master), Kirpal Singh (Paul Twitchell's master), and Charan Singh (David Lane's and Graham Forsyth's master). Accordingly, an examination of the stories surrounding their ascension to gurudom is in order.

The two followers, Jaimal Singh and Sawan Singh, were authorized to give initiatiations under Article 16 of the Agra Central Administrative Council (CAC), a body that oversaw Radhasoami activities in the area. Both worked under several gurus on the CAC.[14] There is no record that Swamiji instructed Jaimal to go to the Punjab to give initiations as he claimed. In fact, many argue there is little evidence he ever met Swamiji. He was seen as a self-proclaimed master. The CAC took him to task several times for posing as a guru. He admitted that he was not a guru but continued to give initiations anyway.

The controversy gave rise to a bitter court battle that reached the high court of India. In a deposition from the case, the president of the CAC stated:

> I am president of RS Central Administrative Council at Allahabad. The 28 names selected for the formation of the council (in 1902) included the name of Baba Jaimal Singh. The name of Jaimal Singh was included because he had agreed that *he would give up acting as a guru. . . .* He was given general power of initiation in the very first meeting of the Council. But, he did not stick to his undertaking and *the said general power of initiation was cancelled.*[15]

The relationship between the CAC and Jaimal Singh did not improve. In June of 1903, it passed a resolution stating:

> After inquiry, it transpired that Baba Jaimal Singh did not consider himself to be Sant and that he had no objection to the entry of his name in the register of Satsangis.[16]

While Jaimal's relation with the CAC was rather contentious, he maintained positive relations with Shiv Dayal Singh's family. This relationship, and one with a blind guru who was an initiate of Shiv Dayal Singh, helped to legitimize his work and lay the foundation for the line of Beas masters that followed. Jaimal Singh was never verifiably authorized to give initiations by Shiv Dayal Singh or his successor, Rai Salig Ram. However, Jaimal claimed that he received his authority directly from Shiv Dayal Singh in 1877, nine months before his death. In spite of this, Jaimal Singh apparently waited seven years before he began to give any initiations.[17] In 1891, Jaimal started the Beas group. He initiated Sawan Singh in October of 1894.

In 1903, just three days before Jaimal's death, after complaints that he was posing as a guru and not sending in names of initiates, the CAC passed another resolution:

> [A] strong warning should be administered to him [Jaimal] through Chachaji Saheb by means of registered, acknowledgment due, letter and that in case of failure to comply with it, necessary action may be taken.[18]

At Jaimal's death, no effort was made to dissuade followers in the Punjab that their initiations were fake or questionable. Jaimal never stated he was *not* a guru and so left his followers to infer what any true believer would: that Jaimal had been a guru and even a Sant. This was a source of friction between Jaimal and the CAC from the beginning. Sawan Singh also looked upon him in this manner and used his association with Jaimal as the basis for his eventual break with the CAC and the original Radhasoami group.

Based on Sawan's association with Jaimal, he asserted that he too was a guru. But the story of succession from Jaimal Singh is anything but clear. At his death in 1903, some reports assert that he considered Sawan inept and powerless, and instructed those initiated under him to go to someone else.[19] Others report that the succession was clear, and that Jaimal Singh informed his followers that Sawan Singh would take his place conducting satsangs and giving initiations.[20] Still others report that the successions went through several other gurus before being taken over by Sawan Singh in 1915.[21]

Sawan Singh's assertion came out of thin air; he had no legitimacy as far as the lineage of Radhasoami masters was concerned. This was especially true of the line deriving from Swamiji and his written and stated wishes regarding succession. Sawan's claims of succession from Jaimal Singh were also dubious, even if Jaimal Singh himself had a legitimate claim to successorship. Nevertheless, Sawan Singh broke from the CAC and started his own line of masters, claiming Jaimal Singh as a legitimizing link to Shiv Dayal Singh (or at least his family). Sawan Singh and the Beas line of masters have been the principal teachers of the Radhasoami tradition. They now claim the largest number of Radhasoami followers in India and abroad, especially in the West.

Throughout this murky history, several points should be clear. Mastership has little to do with spiritual attainment. It has far more to do with being selected by a master or deciding for yourself that you have the right stuff, and proclaiming your status to the world. Succession works more like taking over a family business than a sacred anointment. Second, the fact that the courts of India had to intervene to settle a spiritual matter (remember Darwin Gross vs. Eckankar?) is evidence of dubiousness. Succession woes went on. Kirpal Singh defended his claim of succession by creating this mystical account of the transfer of authority from Sawan Singh to him:

> Hazur steadily kept gazing for three or four minutes into my eyes, and my eyes, in silent wonderment, experienced an indescribable delight which infused intoxication down to the remotest core of my entire body.[22]

And later, in 1955, he wrote about the same incident:

> The authority of giving initiation into the beyond and contacting with the Word, which he vouchsafed to me verbally on October 12, 1947, was thus completely transferred while going. The intoxication of that glance is still the life of my soul.[23]

Sawan Singh had not received his authority to be guru from a personal transfer of authority from Jaimal Singh. Yet, Kirpal Singh regarded this intimate transfer to be essential. He even argued that such a succession could not take place through a written will. However, the founder of Radhasoami Bias, Jaimal Singh, and his self-proclaimed successor, Sawan Singh, had both attempted such a transfer by will, or at least in writing.

Harold invoked the ancient mystification that only a master can name his successor (written into the *Shariyat-Ki-Sugmad* by Paul) as rationale for my discipline. But such a formal transfer has never occurred in Eckankar, except in the transfer from Darwin to Harold, which Darwin later rescinded. There is no eternal spiritual principle regarding a necessity for succession, anointed or otherwise.

Rules of succession are a contrived set of guidelines designed to control the franchise and limit the number of people claiming authority. It was and is a ruse, abandoned at the convenience of those claiming legitimate ties to some lineage. Paul abandoned the only line of masters with whom he had association. Seeking legitimacy, he invented his own line of masters and gave himself the newly forged Rod of Eck Power. The ritualistic passing of the Rod would, it was hoped, eliminate pretenders claiming a secret whisper and holy gaze in the night.

Initiations too are more administratively sanctioned spectacles than spiritual rites with inner significance. They allow the organization to hold members and ensure a steady flow of resources. We have already seen this in Eckankar, but it was the source of many conflicts between Jaimal Singh and the CAC. Jaimal would not turn over the records of those he had initiated, depriving the CAC of revenue.

Various masters only perpetuate the myth that *they* are connecting the chela to the light and sound of God rather than teaching that the light and sound are already a part of each of us. It should be clear that the rigid rule of successorship, with its mystical connotations of the passing of some special power, is sheer nonsense. A successor's belief can make it a truth, at least for him, but that is all. If the dogma of Radhasoami were true, then those initiated by the line of Jaimal Singh are illegitimate and should not be able to see the light or hear the sounds of God. But, if through initiation, which is really the individual's own efforts, a seeker is able to see the light and hear the sound, then the dogma surrounding succession is false. It is false because contacting the light and sound of God has nothing to do with master succession, or for that matter with a master.

Like anyone with a new job, a master starts out with little confidence in his abilities but grows into the role. A statement by Charan Singh is testimony to the lack of any exceptional spiritual attainment or intrinsic power inherent in a new master. He confessed he had no special powers or attainment and frankly didn't know what he was doing.

> When I look upon myself and my shortcomings I feel very perplexed and find myself unable to decide whether I am really fit for these onerous duties. This struggle has prevented me so far from meeting the Sangat [True Association] for which I ask your forgiveness. I wish to tell the Sangat quite frankly, however, that I do not make any claims whatsoever to any spiritual attainments; perhaps I lack even those excellences which a good satsangi should possess...24

If new masters were wise, they would not accept the hype surrounding their exalted positions and instead understand their limitations and sacred trust. But this is not often the case. One such guru was aware of these limitations and of the inherent problems affecting gurudom in general:

> Disciple hunters are not wanting. They are as numerous as leaves on a tree. For most of them, gurudom is a very profitable job which can secure enormous income which they cannot otherwise earn. A simple threat of a curse upon one who happens to displease them, may bring thousands to abject submission. . . . Not only this, but in order to ensure

monopoly of their profession they declare that none but one belonging to the privileged class has the right of being a guru. The popularly believed principle that a disciple can never break off the sacred connection with his guru under any circumstance, is also a cunning device adopted by those false gurus to make their position safe and secure and is nothing but fraud.[25]

There is little question that many masters have learned to hear the inner sounds, see the light, and travel within the inner worlds. But many masters have not; they merely mimic predecessors who might or might not have had these experiences. Everyone has the capability to see the inner light and to hear the inner sounds. It does not require mastership or master. It only requires that one know and practice techniques to quiet the mind and go within, techniques that are easy to teach though difficult to master. The propaganda about the need for a master is a form of control over those who are unaware of their own divinity and their capacity for inner exploration.

That we need a teacher to explain the methods of inner travel and the nature of the light and sound of God is unquestioned. But to insist that this can only happen at the knee of a master is not only disingenuous but also untruthful. If those in Eckankar can, through practice and discipline, hear the sound, see the light, and travel to the highest realms of God, then anyone can, for Eckankar's claim to a legitimate line of masters is as illegitimate as they come! Yet, I can personally attest to the validity of such inner experiences and of the numerous people who attest to having had them. The truth is, masters have virtually nothing to do with inner experiences or even their own appearance within our inner universes.

Experiences with the Light and Sound of God

During a visit to Africa on behalf of Eckankar many years ago, my colleagues and I conducted an introductory talk on the light and sound of God before an audience that had never heard of the phenomenon. The group numbered well over three hundred, which in itself was startling, given that we had advertised by poster for only three days prior to the event. We introduced the audience to the HU, a mantra used extensively in Sufism, Radhasoami, and later Eckankar, and showed and described the techinque of going within. Without telling them anything more, we allowed the audience to chant this sound aloud and then in silence. The group was queried afterward about what, if anything, they had experienced. Several persons raised their hands and announced they had heard the tinkling of bells, the buzzing of bees, the sound of the wind, a flute, or thunder. They also described seeing a light so bright that, ironically, they had to open their eyes. I was astonished, and a myriad of thoughts, about innate spirituality and about the Eckankar organization, rushed through my mind. No master was around, no special "Simran"[26] was practiced, and no special efforts were made to connect anyone to the light and sound. All that was needed was an audience of God-seekers and information on the techniques of spiritual exercises. The rest was up to them, or better put, the rest was inside of them. But even here, the tendency of Eckankar lore to usurp anything and everything that happened in the lives of its followers and everyone else would explain it differently. Eckankar asserts that it is the Mahanta, the inner master working with these newcomers who is responsible for their immediate attainment of the light and sound. Such is the ubiquitous nature of Eckankar methodology, and those of other masters, that a God-seeker is under their wing whether they know it or like it or not.

Yet, this experience always stood out to me as evidence that all is within. We need no one to connect us to something that we already are and that is part of us. A master only instructs us in the ways of inner travel; anything else steals credit for an innate gift we all possess. But this is the way of the masters. They repeat the same jargon that their predecessor repeated and everyone ends up believing the mythology. The founder of Radhasoami claimed not to have needed a master, and neither does any soul, which is not to say that a teacher is not needed, for we are all endowed with these God-given capabilities.

The Life and Legacy of Baba Faqir Chand

With so much deception, mythmaking, and fiction in all spiritual paths, I was heartened to discover a master whose honesty and integrity were so startling as to be monumental. He made it his mission to smash the clichés of his peers and proclaim the truth as his unique and declared mission in life. It was so refreshing to read about this man that I have read his works many times. I am speaking about the extraordinary Baba Faqir Chand.

Born in 1886, Baba Faqir Chand had a profound impact on the spiritual life of his followers. He followed the line of masters originating with Shiv Dayal Singh. His master studied under Rai Salig Ram Sahib, who succeeded the founder of the Radhasoami tradition. Sawan Singh even recognized him as a legitimate master — not that he needed it.

From a Brahmin family in the Punjab, he was aware from age seven of a deep spiritual craving. Not understanding its nature, he would call on Rama, Krishna, or God. Educated only to middle school, he joined the communication service at age sixteen. After a rambunctious youth filled with the normal assortment of worldly experiences, he began meditating on the images of Rama and Krishna, who would be with him whether he was working or walking. His contact with Lord Krishna became strained when one day he directed him to eat cow dung. Faqir complied but was puzzled by the strange request, for in all his studies he had never read of Lord Krishna directing a disciple to eat cow dung. His faith in the image of Lord Krishna was shaken. Yet he wept continuously for twenty-four hours, hoping to see him in the form of a human being. This episode produced a call to a doctor, who proclaimed he had gone mad. But persistence paid off and, at four in the morning, he saw the image of his new master, Shiv Brat Lal.[27]

Baba Faqir Chand was instrumental in destroying myths I once believed about the master-chela relationship. Many of the conclusions I had reached as a result of my own experience with masters and my continued inner and outer exploration of truth were confirmed by the words of this insider. What Chand did that was so revolutionary was to debunk the mystique that most masters build around themselves. Most prominent among these myths are their so-called powers and their conscious involvement in the inner and outer lives of chelas. Chand stressed that the power did not lie with the master but instead lay within the God-seeker. He averred that even the inner contact between chela and master is not the result of any action on the part of the master, but instead is generated by the individual's higher self, using forms and images comfortable and acceptable to the chela.

This in no way diminishes or invalidates the inner experience, for all forms, physical or inner, are the result of imagination acting on spirit (matter, motion, and consciousness) to produce an inner or outer manifestation. What Chand is pointing out, however, is that the inner-self and the beliefs of each person control the appearance of a master. The higher self is always directing and guiding our lives to realize the end of expanded awareness.

Our power as soul is limitless and embodies all of the properties of the whole of which we are a part, just as a ray of light reflects the properties of its source. We are limited in our ability to project and demonstrate the full potential of this power while we occupy a physical shell, but tremendous power is within us nevertheless. As we expand our awareness to identify and communicate with this higher part of ourselves, we begin to see the God-like qualities within. This is precisely what those who have ventured within and discovered the secret of all secrets have found. Those who have had this realization and returned to serve as a master or teacher often fail to see that *everyone* has the same latent capabilities. We differ only in the recognition and acceptance of the God power that we all possess in limitless supply.

This was the essential message of Chand. He conveyed this message in the language of the master-chela relationship by confessing what few if any members of his guild wanted known. Chand openly stated that he was completely unaware of the miracles that devoted followers ascribed to him. He had received countless letters from initiates attesting to his physical presence at crucial junctures in their lives, some crediting him with saving them from an awful fate. They wrote him about his inner and outer appearances before them and of the marvelous inner journeys they had taken together. Unlike most masters, who would simply put on an inscrutable smile of knowingness, he freely admitted that he had played no part.

This phenomenon has been clear to me for many years. After extensive speaking engagements in Europe, America, Canada, and Africa, I routinely received letters thanking me for some insight I had shared in an inner classroom, while journeying with them on some inner trip, or appearing before them to warn of danger. Many would write of an inner marriage with me or some other incident of a personal nature. I never regarded this as anything other than the use of my form by their higher selves to teach, guard, or guide them through a difficult situation. I did nothing; their inner faculties merely used my inner form because they felt an inner connection with me. My form became a bridge they could use for inner communication. It also became evident to me that unscrupulous or deluded individuals could use this phenomenon to enhance their own position and status as masters.

Some masters proclaim they know the condition of chelas and can project to them. Elaboration on this matter is in order. It is possible to project one's consciousness into the space of another in a manner as real as a personal meeting. While this can occur in the waking state, it most frequently occurs in the dream state. This can also occur by projecting one's consciousness to a physical location and becoming aware of events there. In popular parlance, this is part of the phenomenon called "remote viewing." This form of projection is not as strange as it might sound. Most people have "daydreamed" and shifted their awareness to another place or to another person, completely oblivious to the location of their physical body.

Over the years, there have been many experiments by practitioners of the art of projection and remote viewing. In these experiments, one person projects her consciousness to another location. The object of the experiment is to determine if the projected body (consciousness) can become aware of and accurately report on events and appearances in the other location. Many of these experiments seem successful but are not overseen by rigorous research standards. They have established, at least for the experimenters, the validity of out-of-body projection and remote viewing. Everyone has this ability and can demonstrate it to herself. It is not uncommon for individuals to have the experience of floating above their bodies or passing through a wall in full consciousness. The experiences of patients on the operating table who observe their operations and remember all that is said and done while floating in their astral bodies is a well documented example of this. These are all projection experiences, not unlike the contact that humans make with entities that have dropped their physical bodies and operate from their astral shells, the same body that we use while in the dream state or when projecting to another place or time. All of these experiences occur within the time-space continuum in which we live and are part of this construct. We shall see in later chapters that this construct is not as real and concrete as we commonly assume.

I became adept at projecting and identifying occurrences at a distant location during a period of being bed-ridden and virtually blind. With no television or books to distract me, I began testing my abilities at projection, the subject of several books I had been reading.[28] In a relaxed state, I imagined my office but forced my awareness away from memory of it. I also separated remote images from what my mind wanted to establish, from memory and logic, about what *should* be happening there. It took some doing, but after many attempts, I became proficient at this form of projection, and I continue to use it when traveling abroad. Of course, this ability carries with it the spiritual and moral obligation not to invade the space of another, without their knowledge and consent. This is a violation of spiritual law, which carries karmic consequences, as all acts do.

The point here is that a master, adept at the art of projection or the equal art of perception, may know the condition of a chela without being there. But it requires the person in the physical to focus attention on that person or particular circumstance, before the images come to conscious awareness. It would take more than twenty-four hours a day for a master to support thousands of chelas around the globe this way. Thus, while it is possible, it is not practicable.

This is why Sawan Singh (an acquaintance of Faqir Chand) knew of no involvement in the lives of his chelas, though he did concede it was possible. Instead, Sawan Singh postulated the "astral double theory" to explain how a master could be with his chelas at all times. He suggested that, at initiation, the master creates an astral double within the inner space of the chela. This double, presumably, was the entity that looked over the chela and reported back as needed. My problem here is that the master is again taking credit for something entirely under the chela's control. It is the result of an inner connection that has been established by the student, in the same manner as described in my experiences with various correspondents.

When an initiation occurs, with all its ritualistic flare, the connection is even stronger, for it is a marriage of sorts. The individual opens his inner space and establishes a bond of trust and love with the master. Through this bond, the image of the master is given effect and presence in the life of the chela. But it is not the master creating the astral double.

Each individual controls his own inner world — the world of imagination and visualization. If we see it with our outer eyes and then imagine it, we are apt to experience it in our inner space. This can occur in the dream state or during controlled projection.

This is why masters encourage followers to keep their image close at hand. They are instructed to look at the image frequently and keep attention on the master. Masters know that the stronger the image planted by outer vision and inner thoughts, the stronger will be their influence in the life of the chela. This can have a positive effect. A master is held in high regard and his image evokes positive thoughts that bring love and joy to the lives of his followers. This is especially true for someone who lacks self-confidence or is having a particularly difficult time of it in life. Faqir Chand provides an important perspective on this point:

> He who gives . . . [love, affection, and belief] to others gains himself. So, it is the belief of the people that benefits them. I do not do anything. Their faith and belief in me brings their cherished fruit to them. It is not "I" who manifests myself to them.[29]

In Eckankar, the "greatest exercise" is sitting in silence, staring at the face of the master, while chanting the sacred name of God, HU.[30] This strengthens the image of the master within the inner space of the chela. This phenomenon occurs with anything that one focuses attention on for extended periods of time. It is enhanced when the object of that focus is held in high spiritual or personal regard. Even knowing the bogus claims of Eckankar masters, they function in the lives of their chelas in the same manner as the greatest Radhasoami, Christian, Buddhist, or Muslim saints. Why is this so? Faqir Chand explains it very clearly:

> Patanjali, the great sage, has written in his book on Yoga that if you cannot do any inward practice then at least contemplate on the holy form of a Perfect Man.
>
> Now the question is, where would you search for a Perfect Man? I say that wherever or in whomsoever you have faith, *think* that He is a Perfect Man and Omnipotent [and] your purpose shall be served. If my form [or any other] manifests itself and helps those who have faith in me, then the form of other gurus also manifests themselves to their disciples and helps them.

> Leave aside the Saints, *[if] you put a wicked and immoral person on the seat of a Guru, [and] develop faith in him, his form too shall manifest and help you like the manifested form of great Saints. You are not helped by any Saint or Guru, but by your own faith and belief.*[31]

The images of Jesus, Buddha, Muhammad or the Living Eck Master are all powerful and effective. No one symbol or picture is more powerful than another, because the power does not derive from the picture, person, or object. The power lies entirely in the belief that one image is more powerful than another.

Bilocation and other seemingly miraculous events occur everyday of our lives. Healings, instant manifestations, and other events are also part of the life of the true believer. But what seems to be constantly missed, even by those who manifest these miracles, is that the power lies within them and is activated by belief and acceptance. The low self-esteem and low self-belief evident in most people cause an almost uniform feeling that something or someone else makes their destiny. Belief in outer circumstances determining reality shapes most people's lives. They think that they are powerless to control or even influence these forces. The truth is just the opposite. Outer realities are shaped by what we accept and know as truth. By accepting the premise that our lives are the effect of outer circumstances, we plant this false paradigm in our consciousness and our lives out-picture accordingly.

No one denies the beneficial effect a master may have on a follower. What is objected to here is a master's use of the belief of their followers to enhance their own images, while remaining silent about the role the student is playing in the process. It is the spiritual energy and belief constructs of the faithful that always make things happen. Here are the words of Baba Faqir Chand:

> People say that my form manifests to them and helps them in solving their worldly as well as mental problems, but I do not go anywhere nor do I know anything about such miraculous instances.

> When I adopted this path of life, I had pledged that I would follow this path with Truth and shall speak to the world my realization of this path.

> His Holiness had directed me, "Faqir, change the mode of preaching before abandoning this mortal frame."

> Which teachings should I change? The change is, "O man, your real helper is your own Self and your own Faith, but you are badly mistaken

and believe that somebody from without comes to help you. . . . This entire game is that of your impressions and suggestions which are ingrained upon your mind through your eyes and ears and of your Faith and Belief." This is the change that I am ordained to bring about.

I fearlessly proclaim and appeal to the present gurus of the religious world that either they should contradict what I say, or they should speak out the truth that they too do not manifest themselves to their respective devotees. If they too are sailing in the same boat in which I sail, then why do they keep their poor devotees in the dark and exploit them?

Ignorant masses are advised to get initiated, for they shall be led to heavens by their guru after their death. Had many of the present gurus not confessed to me that they too remain unaware about their manifestation [inner and outer appearance before their chelas] I would have thought that I am in the wrong.[32]

Baba Faqir Chand exited this world in 1981, having left behind the confessions of a true God-seeker, who had discovered the truth and was honest enough to cast aside the sacred veils of mastership. He revealed truths that few if any masters would admit even to themselves. He stands alone among Radhasoami masters, if not masters in general, for his honesty and candor. With miracles exploding around him and followers proclaiming his divinity, he stepped back and dismissed the glorification. Instead, he told the truth of truths, that we alone perform the miracles. We do the work of the masters, while they take the credit.

At long last, we come to an understanding of the proper role of a master. First, we must abandon the term "master," except when we use it as self-mastery or mastery of our own inner and outer universe. But having acknowledged this, are people thereby empowered to take responsibility for their own spiritual development? Probably not, for most people are short on self-belief and even shorter on understanding their power. It is the need for guidance that is perverted into glorification or deification of masters. This is a large part of the mystique of Radhasoami, Yoga, and Julian Johnson's *Path of the Masters*. This book has done more in the western world to exalt, deify, and establish masters as the quintessential need of the God-seeker than any other book. It only leads the individual into a trap from which he must escape. It is in many ways a siren call leading to a place where caution is the better alternative.

The Power of Belief

People need guidance and want to believe more than anything else. This desire is one of the strongest and more profound needs that we have as humans. It immediately opens our inner floodgates to an expression of emotional, psychic, and love energy that can be both dynamic and frightening. We have but to remember our first experience of falling in love to recall the magic and vulnerability that we experienced. When that love went south, as young love invariably does, we are heartbroken and physically ill. In fact, our first encounter with betrayal probably occurred during a romance, and it likely left a lasting impression. We were slow to open our hearts again, fearing loss of control and ensuing pain. For many, it is precisely this fear that leads us to other forms of belief and surrender.

There is an intrinsic need to believe and surrender. We are made up this way. We experience the totality of life only by allowing ourselves to believe in and surrender to something. This has deep implications. We are God-souls in training. We occupy our physical shells only because we need to learn our awesome powers in an environment with room for error and time for correction. We move at the forgiving rhythms of the physical universe, learning to control these powers and keep them in check. Thought, imagination, belief, and emotion are the tools of God with which this and other universes have been formed. With them, we create our lives and, collectively, the world in which we live. With them, we create our heavens and our gods. We are the creators of all of this. We have these abilities but do not realize it.

Those who understand this truth adjust their belief systems to tap the infinite power within. When this is achieved, the individual comes to believe, or rather, to know, that she is not only part of the whole, but capable of being one with the whole. She can then speak for the whole, for she has surrendered to it and become one with it. Every savior and saint is able to say, "I and the father are one." Jesus is purported to have seen this reality and spoken from this state of consciousness.[33] I, too, have ventured into this level of belief and experienced its awesome power. If it sounds false to proclaim such an experience, then your doubt suggests the real barrier to your spiritual unfoldment. Even Jesus is reputed to have said, "deeds greater than these ye shall do." He would not have been deprecating himself by these words. Rather, he would have been announcing to the world that he was not the exclusive incarnation of this ideal. Deeds greater than these we shall do, if we have the courage to cross into this region of belief and knowingness and tap the potential in us. Tapping this potential becomes all the more important when we discover the fragile underpinnings of spiritual truth found in world religions. In many ways, they too have usurped the inherent responsibility of soul, the higher self, and shifted the focus to dogma, ritual, relics and monuments that keep followers searching the past for traces of the God-reality. Ultimately, soul can progress only so far under a religious regime, for religions by their very nature place an intercessor — Jesus, Buddha, Mahanta, etc. — between soul and the goal of the God-seeker; to know the ONE.

Chapter 12 — Holy Books and the Sixteen Crucified Saviors

In uncovering the devices used by Paul Twitchell to create Eckankar, I was struck by similarities to those used by the Church in creating its doctrine and dogma. A closer look at the origins of Christianity is useful to illustrate how tenuous is the undergirding of one of the most powerful religions in the world. It also illustrates the many techniques and devices that Paul Twitchell used, which paralleled those used by the Church Fathers. Whether Paul knew about this history and actively copied it in the formulation of Eckankar is not known. But as we will see, the similarities are striking.

This review is instructive because it is indicative of the origins of every religion that has at its center a mythical or historical figure whose life has taken on God-like proportions. The stories and myths that evolved have shaped their rituals and dogma. Indeed, most religions have become ritualistic recapitulations of their own history surrounded by pomp and circumstance. An emphasis on ceremony and ritual is designed to evoke emotions and reinforce the institution's belief structure. But these practices have little to do with transcendent truth and virtually nothing to do with the inner search that is indispensable to the quest of the God-seeker.

That religious practices are vital to the life of its followers is undeniable. But, as pointed out earlier, religions are classrooms in an eternal process of expanding awareness. Yet many religions purport to control access to heaven if not to God itself; otherwise excommunication or its equivalent would have no impact. Presenting the fragile foundations of truth that underlie these teachings is not intended to demean their importance in spiritual unfoldment. Nor is it intended to suggest that they do not carry positive principles and lessons. Rather, a closer look at the truth of these teachings is part of a process that leads to spiritual awakening, which, in turn, leads to spiritual growth. Everyone must at some point break through the "Santa Claus Effect," the deliberate withholding of truth by a religion or society in the belief, perhaps well intended, that the faithful are not ready for it, or are happier and prefer living under illusion. However, unlike the Santa Claus myth, silence about certain religious truths has gone on for millennia. Religions, then, have become resting points of safety and security on the road to spiritual unfoldment, which, unfortunately have also discouraged or even forbade departure. The seeker must use other means to ascertain the truth about himself as soul and his awe-inspiring heritage as a spark of God. The keepers of the secret will not tell him, if by now they even remember themselves.

Old Testament Controversies

Debate over the origins of the Bible has been on going for centuries. So vigorous was the criticism at times that the field of Christian Apologetics arose to counter numerous assaults on the integrity, authenticity, and veracity of the Bible. Discovery of the true origins of the Bible does not diminish the value of its insights, though it has dimmed the light shone on many Old and New Testament stories. Religious scholars working within a fixed paradigm undertook the search for historical truth. But religious paradigms have so many layers of orthodoxy, dogma, and ritual that even the acknowledgement of a truth leaves the seeker only somewhat closer to higher truth, if at all.

An example of this is seen in attempts to resolve the centuries-old debate of whether the first five books of the Bible (Genesis, Exodus, Leviticus, Numbers, and Deuteronomy, often referred to as the Pentateuch or the Torah) were actually written by Moses. Belief in his authorship was and is so strong that one would think that the entire faith hinged on its validity. In spite of obvious inconsistencies that suggest Moses did not write these books, the orthodoxy prevailed:

> People observed contradictions in the text [Bible]. . . . It would describe Moses as going to a Tabernacle in a chapter before Moses builds the Tabernacle. People also noticed that the Five Books of Moses included things that Moses could not have known or was not likely to have said. The text, after all, gave an account of Moses' death. It also said that Moses was the humblest man on earth; and normally one would not

expect the humblest man on earth to point out that he is the humblest man on earth.[1]

The debate raged for more than six hundred years, with few scholars brave enough to question the obvious. In more recent years, the weight of orthodoxy has lifted somewhat from the backs of scholars and truth seekers. The new and more widely held view is that the "Five Books of Moses had been composed by combining four different source documents into one continuous history."[2] Eureka! After centuries, the debate was resolved, at least for the open-minded investigator. But the movement to truth through the refinement of orthodoxy remained an exercise in pedantry. The truth seeker was still focused on events of past millennia. He searched in the shadows of history to discover the reality of God that was and is within, always here and now. Old Testament controversy continues at an unprecedented rate, with challenges to the authenticity and veracity of most other books of the Bible. Indeed, there is increasing evidence that many parts of the Old Testament have their origins in the stories and myths of Egyptian culture.[3]

New Testament Controversies

The idea of the Bible as the word of God has evolved among many Christians to a more enlightened and historically accurate view that recognizes the labors of the men who actually wrote it.[4] What is most remarkable about this late recognition is the extent to which early Church leaders and scholars labored to deny or suppress the truth about the origins of the Bible and the history of Jesus. As we will see, truth was not their concern. Defense of orthodoxy was the motivation, and anyone who questioned it was branded a heretic or worse. However, the accounts of Jesus contained in the Gospels of Matthew, Mark, Luke, and John were viewed with great skepticism if not incredulity from earliest times. In fact, the first three Gospels, often called the Synoptic Gospels,[5] were so similar in content as to likely have been drawn from each other. Indeed, some scholars have maintained that they are plagiarisms, so similar is each version.[6] But even as alleged plagiarisms, there are numerous contradictions in the portrayal of various stories of the life of Christ.[7] No less a personage than St. Augustine (354-430) expressed the view:

I would not believe the Gospels to be true, unless the authority of the Catholic Church constrained [forced] me.[8]

Well, it did! He was not alone in his incredulity. The Gospels contained so many inconsistencies and parallels to each other and to other religious martyrs that, as early as 160-200, Church leaders were questioning stories of the life of Jesus that were appearing, for the first time, more than 120 years[9] (some say forty to seventy years[10]) after the purported death of Jesus in 33. One such Church Father labored to defend the faith from "pagan" criticism that claimed his new religion to be a fabrication.

Understanding their criticism about religious fabrication, yet holding to his belief in the divinity of Jesus the Christ and the Gospels, Father Tertullian, an early Christian theologian and polemicist, in an oft-quoted passage, used a rather extraordinary form of reverse logic to defend his faith. In it, he also seemed to be acknowledging the obvious questions raised by the historical anomalies in the story of Jesus the Christ. His statement "Credo quia incredibilis est"[11] ("I believe because it is unbelievable") is interesting enough, but he amplified it:

[T]he Son of God was born; why am I not ashamed of maintaining such a thing? Why! but because it is itself a shameful thing. I maintain that the Son of God died: well, that is wholly credible because it is monstrously absurd. I maintain that after having been buried, he rose again: and that I take to be absolutely true, because it was manifestly impossible.[12]

The charge that the Church had fabricated the stories contained in the Gospels, indeed the Gospels themselves, was made during the early years of Christianity. The charge had considerable gravity because there existed no written historical record of the life of Jesus coterminous with the years he is said to have lived and taught. This situation prevailed in spite of Church efforts, with varying degrees of success, to create documents establishing such a record.[13] In spite of this known deficiency and more than 125 years later, there appeared, in a series of writings to be called the Gospels, a story so powerful and profound that, if it occurred, it would surely have been known and extensively recorded by historians and scribes of the period. But it was not!

Was this the reason for Father Tertullian's strange flight of reverse logic? Was this the basis for Augustine's declaration that he would not believe in the Gospels except if the Church forced him to? What did these early thinkers know or suspect that the religious leaders and followers of today are oblivious to, have forgotten, or actively suppress? Why was there such skepticism about early Church efforts to piece together the story of Jesus? The answers to these questions are as enlightening to the truth seeker as they are disturbing to the true believer. They tell of a period in Church history that goes to the very heart of the truth about its doctrine and dogma. Even as it demonstrates the dangers of constructing a belief system on the zealous writings of true believers who intentionally invented or borrowed stories from history, it also confirms the power of such a belief system to impact the lives of millions, irrespective of the provenance or veracity of the story behind it.

In many ways, the history of the Gospels and their acceptance parallels the creation of Eckankar doctrine derived from the stories put forth by its founder, who also saw himself as the "Son of God." Both teachings sustain themselves not on the genuineness of their founders or the authenticity of stories that grew around them, but on the unquestioning acceptance of these stories. It is faith and belief that bring the stories to life and provide the spiritual energy on which inner experiences and modern-day miracles abound.

As I delved deeper into the mystery of the Gospels, I wanted to know who actually wrote them. Why was nothing written about Jesus during his life? Why were the Gospels named after disciples (two of them anyway) if they didn't write them? These and other questions were of particular interest to me for I found many similarities between the early history of Christianity and of the one Paul Twitchell created for Eckankar. Had Paul and his successors had the benefit of even several hundred years between Eckankar's formation and the present, the stories relayed in earlier chapters of this book might have been lost to modern investigators. Instead, revelations about Eckankar came during its formative stages. We can see who Paul Twitchell really was and how he built defenses for the challenges that lay ahead.

In this respect, the Eckankar leadership of today is in an even more difficult position than the Church founders. They had to explain and defend stories about a person for whom there were no records, only an oral tradition. The appearance of Jesus in later Christian writings resembles that of Sudar Singh of Eckankar lore about fifty years after Paul alleges to have first encountered him. However, unlike the Church, Eckankar must defend a person about whom there does exist a traceable history and written record, albeit, one that does not stand up to scrutiny.

Parallels between the histories of both religions are fascinating and instructive. To those in the new religion of Eckankar still concerned with the truth, they show how important it is to reveal the unvarnished story to the world, so that the dust of history does not hide the truth. For the Christian believer (I was once one), it sheds light on the intrinsic truth of the teaching and the motivations and intentions of Church Fathers vis-à-vis their followers. For those who wish to know this truth, the broad outlines of what happened are presented here with enough references to permit a more in-depth study.

The Early Role of the Church in the Formulation of the Gospels and Christianity

It appears that the Church encouraged the creation of writings that set the story of Jesus in the desired historic and eschatological context. Perhaps the greatest confusion regarding the Gospels is over whether Mathew, Mark, Luke, and John wrote them. Assigning authorship to four of Jesus' followers was intended to convey to the faithful that they were written during the time Jesus walked the Holy Land. Ascribing false authorship to a particular writing was common practice in the early Church. It was known as *pseudepigraphy,* a practice we will consider in more detail. However, most modern scholars agree that the Gospels did not appear on the scene or have any mention in literature until forty to one hundred twenty-five years after the death of Jesus. Views about the authenticity of these early documents range from more strident and incredulous positions such as:

> Although they are held up by true believers to be the "inspired" works of the apostles, the canonical gospels were forged at the end of the 2nd century, all four of them probably between 170-180, a date that just happens to correspond with the establishment of the orthodoxy and supremacy of the Roman Church. Despite the claims of apostolic authorship, the gospels were not mere translations of manuscripts written in Hebrew

or Aramaic by Jewish apostles, because they were originally written in Greek.[14]

Other views on the matter reflect a more supportive though not inconsistent view of the origins. Paula Fredriksen[15] writes:

> What then must be borne in mind when reading the canonical gospels for historical information about Jesus of Nazareth? First, the impression of orderliness conveyed by their connected narratives should not deceive us about their true nature: these are *composite documents*, the final products of *long and creative traditions* in which *old material was reworked and new material interpolated*. As they now stand, they are witness first of all to the faith of their individual writers and their late first-century, largely Gentile communities. Only at a distance do they relate to the people and the period they purport to describe.... *[T]he gospels are theological proclamation, not historical biography*.... Second, we must remember that forty to seventy years stand between the public career and death of Jesus of Nazareth and the probable dates of composition of the gospels.[16]

Admitting the unreliability of the oral tradition of Jesus, Fredriksen acknowledges that Christian scholars must stick to the written record about Jesus. However, Fredriksen fails to address the issue of the reliability of these written documents in light of the Church's avowed program of creating a written record establishing the historical and spiritual continuity of Jesus. She uses euphemisms to convey a faint picture of the Church's involvement in the creation of the Gospels such as "composite documents," "long and creative traditions," and "old material . . . reworked and new material interpolated." But euphemisms obscure the extent of the Church's involvement in creating the Gospels.

To uncover this part of the story, we must go back to the time of the Gospel's creation and see the practices of Church Fathers in formulating the story. When the unvarnished picture of the Church's role in creating the history of Jesus is seen, the integrity of the New Testament and Church doctrine must be reconsidered. From this perspective, the inherent flaws in the writings of today's Christian scholars, who look to the Gospels as proof of the reality of Jesus, are exposed. These writings are almost exclusively based on accepting as wholly true the testimony of the Gospels, when it is the very truthfulness and credibility of the Gospels that is in question. A close examination of the Gospels and how they were created exposes a vulnerability that renders them impeachable. This is a weakness at which scholars such as Fredriksen will only hint.

Pseudepigraphy, Pious Fraud, and the Greatest Story Ever Told

This discussion portrays a general atmosphere and philosophy that permeated the thinking and actions of Church Fathers from the earliest periods when the different versions of the Gospels were first formulated to centuries thereafter. For once the Gospels were canonized, the efforts of later Church Fathers were directed at reinforcing this anointed version of the story. This called for additional tales and myths to stimulate and strengthen the belief of the faithful.

It was essential for the Church to create stories around the existence of a personage that many, by that time, had accepted as real. What difference did it make? He was no longer around, and, in any event, only the memory and stories of his existence survived. If real stories did not exist, then it was possible, indeed necessary, to create stories appropriate for one who would become the Christ. And what if Jesus the Christ was a myth? Were there not other religions whose deities were regarded as myths, yet were no less powerful and effective once followers believed? To this point, the famous lecturer and Christian scholar, M. M. Mangasarian argues:

> And to the question that if Jesus be mythical, we cannot account for the rise and progress of the Christian church, we answer that the Pagan gods who occupied Mount Olympus were all mythical beings — mere shadows, and yet Paganism was the religion of the most advanced and cultured nations of antiquity. . . . [I]f the worship of Adonis, of Attis, of Isis, and the legends of Heracles, Prometheus, Hercules, and the Hindu trinity, — Brahma, Shiva, Chrishna, — with their rock-hewn temples, can be explained without believing in the actual existence of these gods — why not Christianity?[17]

What is remarkable about this is that the Church actually encouraged the creation of myths around Jesus. It was necessary to elaborate on a story that was active but sparse on details. No one actually knew what Jesus said or did. It is this void into which "pious fraud"[18] rushed, a practice sanctioned by the Church during the first centuries of its existence. The Church encouraged or at least accepted "divinely inspired" accounts of the life of Jesus, which were falsely attributed to Biblical figures, a practice called pseudepigraphy.[19] Nevertheless, these were inspired writers who believed they were serving a holy end. Nor was the pious fraud limited to writings. It also encompassed the forgery, creation, and presentation of objects and artifacts supposedly associated with Jesus. The reason was simple. The more detail that could be created, the easier it would be to convince the faithful of the reality of the Savior. Aside from misdirecting the attention of the devoted to objects and artifacts for spiritual succor, these misleading objects, the fruits of pious fraud, continue to emerge in later millennia to challenge the authentication skills of science and to rejuvenate the leaf of the faithful.

To better understand this phenomenon, which would be scandalous if practiced today, we must understand the thinking of the early Church as it attempted to keep the faithful in thrall and counter the criticisms of pagan antagonists. Joseph Wheless notes:

> [S]uch frauds of the Church were not confined to the Middle Ages; they begin even with the beginning of the Church and infest every period of its history for fifteen hundred years and defile nearly every document, both of "Scriptures" and of Church aggrandizement. As truly said by Collins. . . :

> In short, these frauds are very common in all books which are published by priests or priestly men. . . . For it is certain they may plead the authority of the Fathers for Forgery, Corruption and mangling of Authors, with more reason than for any of their Articles of Faith"[20]

It is hard to imagine that the Church would engage in outright fraud, albeit based in piety, but it was not seen in this light, even though it would clearly be seen so today. Whatever was necessary to convince an audience or to keep the articles of faith alive could be done in the name of salvation. When stories didn't fit, they were blended to make them fit. Several statements of early Church leaders further illustrate this point. Bishop Eusebius of Caesarea, the great "Father of Church History" (ca. 324) was considered by many as one of the most ardent practitioners of pious fraud. Of his early participation in the establishment of Church doctrine, it is written:

> Bishop Eusebius, as we shall see, was one of the most prolific forgers and liars of his age of the Church . . . . To such an extent had the *"pious frauds of the theologians been thus early systematized and raised to the dignity of a regular doctrine,"* that Bishop Eusebius, "in one of the most learned and elaborate works that antiquity has left us, the Thirty-second

Chapter of the Twelfth Book of his *Evangelical Preparation*, bears for its title this scandalous proposition: '*How it may be Lawful and Fitting to use Falsehood as a Medicine, and for the Benefit of those who Want to be Deceived.*'"[21]

Sharing Eusebius's Machiavellian view was St. John Chrysostom, who, in his *On the Priesthood,* advised his fellow clergy:

> Great is the force of deceit! provided it is not excited by a treacherous intention.[22]

I did a triple-take when I encountered this passage. It sounds like the credo of someone who lies to us for our own good. But to be an active practitioner of deceit and to proclaim its power, even endorse its use, so long as intentions are good, is a startling statement coming from a Christian saint. Acknowledging the penchant of early Church leaders to stretch the truth in their zeal to make all things right in the name of God, Cardinal Newman, commenting on this rather extraordinary piece of advice from St. John Chrysostom, said:

> The Greek Fathers thought that, when there was a *justa causa, an untruth need not be a lie....* Now, as to the just cause,... the Greek Fathers make them such as these — self-defense, charity, *zeal for God's honour,* and the like.[23]

This is surely magic, for Cardinal Newman has miraculously transmuted "deceit without treachery" into an untruth that "need not be a lie." Another commentator on the practice, the Great Latin Father St. Jerome (c. 340-420), asserted:

> To confute the opposer, now this argument is adduced and not that. One argues as one pleases, *saying one thing while one means another....* Origen, Methodius, Eusebius, and Apollinaris write at great length.... Consider how subtle are the arguments, how insidious the engines with which they overthrow what the spirit of the devil has wrought. Sometimes, it is true, they are compelled *to say not what they think but what is needful....*[24]

In case the good saint's position isn't clear, he is arguing that it is acceptable to lie if necessary to overthrow the position of the devil, a justification that could be easily broadened to condone "overthrowing" anyone who disagrees with the Church. While explaining the rationale for pious fraud, Jerome implicates the greatest writers and religious historians of the day, Origen, Methodius, Eusebius, and Apollinaris, in this practice. Obviously, these musings were troubling, even to Church Fathers of the day, for, in reference to Eusebius and the others mentioned above, he observes that they:

> [P]resume at the price of their soul to assert dogmatically whatever first comes into their head.[25]

And in a final startling note of honesty, he appears to express contempt for the gullibility of early Christian communities:

> There is nothing so easy as by sheer volubility to deceive a common crowd or an uneducated congregation.[26]

The *Catholic Encyclopedia* acknowledges the prevalence of this attitude:

> Enterprising spirits responded to this natural craving *by pretended gospels* full of romantic fables, and fantastic and striking details; their fabrications were eagerly read and *accepted as true* by common folk who were *devoid of any critical faculty* and who *were predisposed to believe* what so luxuriously fed their pious curiosity. Both Catholics and Gnostics were concerned in writing these fictions. The *former* had no motive other than that of a pious fraud. [27]

This disdain for truth, unless it served the ends of the Church, was the rule of the day. It colored everything that was written, said, and done from the earliest days of the Church's founding and for centuries thereafter.

But the practice of pious fraud was particularly virulent during the first four centuries when the foundations of the Church were laid. Nothing was as important as filling the void left by the absence of a written history or records on the life of Jesus. Church Fathers were given a free hand to invent and embellish whatever stories were necessary to sustain the Church and its following. And invent they did! St. Jerome,[28] who played a significant role in the translation and revisions to the Gospels, was also notable in this regard and actively demonstrated his attitude about the credulity of his audiences when he propagated such divine pearls as:

- The River Ganges has its source in Paradise.

- In India, there are mountains of gold that men cannot approach because of the dragons and huge monsters that haunt them.

- And his grandest tale of all in which he recounts the story of the 113-year-old hermit, Paulus, who had lived in a hole in the ground in a remote part of the desert for sixty years. In an inner revelation, he was shown the neighboring hole (four days away) of another hermit, St. Anthony, who was only ninety years old. Paulus set about to visit his neighbor and encountered several strange animals, including a half-horse, half-man, and other strange beasts know as Fauns, Satyrs, and Incubi. They conversed about the salvation of the lord. The good Father Jerome admonished the congregation, "Let no one scruple to believe this incident.... [I]ts truth is supported by [the fact that] one of those creatures...was captured and brought alive to Alexandria and sent embalmed to the emperor at Antioch."[29]

The story was apparently told in such convincing detail and with such startling proof that communities became convinced. Such was the practice of pious "prevarication" to communities or to anyone else if it was necessary to strengthen belief in the Church and Jesus. On this matter, Mangasarian states:

> The church historian Mosheim, writes that, "The Christian Fathers deemed it a pious act to employ deception and fraud.". . . The greatest and most pious teachers were nearly all of them infected with this leprosy. Will not some believer tell us why forgery and fraud were necessary to prove the historicity of Jesus?. . . Another historian, Milman writes that, "Pious fraud was admitted and avowed by the early missionaries of Jesus." "It was an age of literary frauds," writes Bishop Ellicott, speaking of the times immediately following the alleged crucifixion of Jesus. Dr. Giles declares that, "There can be no doubt that great numbers of books were written with no other purpose than to deceive." And it is the opinion of Dr. Robertson Smith that, "There was an enormous floating mass of spurious literature created to suit party views."[30]

Pious fraud had gotten so out of hand, infecting everything in the name of Jesus and the Church, that Augustine wrote a treatise addressed to the clergy entitled *De Mendacio* (On Lying, ca. 395), followed twenty-five years later by a second treatise, *Contra Mendacium* (Against Lying) — it always sounds more holy in Latin. These treatises rebuked the clergy for its fraud, but their main point wasn't nearly so high-minded. His principal concern was the deleterious impact lying was having on the Church. In fact, Augustine's treatise was, according to Bishop Wordsworth:

> [A] protest against these "pious frauds" which have brought discredit and damage on the cause of the Gospel, and have created prejudice against it, from the days of Augustine to our times.[31]

Augustine was against lying, even if used to trap a heretic:

> It is more pernicious for Catholics to lie that they may catch heretics, than for heretics to lie that they may not be found out by Catholics.[32]

In an atmosphere permeated by pious fraud, such that Augustine found it necessary to issue his admonition against lying for a second time, it was notable that someone stood up against the practice of lying. However, Augustine does not come right out and declare a moratorium on lying. Instead, he declares that the priesthood should live by a higher standard than heretics. This was a step in the right direction, even though truth was still not a full partner in the religious practice of the day. This is evident in the position taken by Augustine on the Church policy of *suppressio veri*. He argued in support of this policy of suppressing or concealing the truth for the sake of Christian instruction. This practice of shielding the faithful from the truth in order to encourage belief in the doctrine and dogma of the Church is practiced to this day, as the Church has never disavowed it. On this point, Augustine wrote:

> It is lawful, then, either to him that discourses, disputes, and preaches of things eternal, or to him that narrates or speaks of things temporal pertaining to *edification* of religion or piety, to *conceal* at fitting times *whatever seems fit to be concealed*; but to tell a lie is never lawful, therefore neither to conceal by telling a lie.[33]

Augustine was sanctioning concealment of any information, at any time and in any situation, if deemed appropriate by the clergy. Such concealment was deemed acceptable provided no lie was told to effect concealment. There was obviously no consideration of the standard that to conceal the truth was to mislead, thus to knowingly foster a lie, that is, a belief in something other than the truth.

This practice of concealment, which is only today being exposed, constitutes and evinces what I have termed the Santa Claus Effect:

> A state of belief or practice created and/or fostered by the active ongoing propagation of that belief and the simultaneous denial of facts or information that might challenge or destroy it, directed to a believer in the conviction that they cannot handle the truth at that time; or to perpetuate the belief in the patronizing opinion that it is in their best interest; or because it is in the best interest of the propagator.

When adults create or foster a story for the fun and enjoyment of their children, or convey a truth with euphemisms (such as the birds and the bees), that is one thing. But parents function as surrogates for spirit in whose care we are all ultimately entrusted. Even with such noble intentions, the child still feels a sense of betrayal upon learning the truth. But to exercise such control over an adult and intentionally withhold the truth is a violation of trust and is reprehensible.

As it turns out, St. Augustine should have included himself in some of his admonishments about lying, for he too told extravagant tales to hold an audience and enhance the power of the Church. In one notable example, he apparently couldn't resist a good story, even if he had to invent it:

> I was already Bishop of Hippo,[34] when I went into Ethiopia with some servants of Christ there to preach the Gospel. In this country we saw many men and women *without heads*, who had two great eyes in their breasts; and in countries still more southly, we saw people who had but one eye in their foreheads.[35]

Why all this lying was so rampant in the Church is largely a mystery. Perhaps it was that there was such a dichotomy between the Church hierarchy and the masses, that the former saw the latter as children, who needed stories to guide them and keep them in check. Yet, even with the greed and societal assertiveness of today, such sanctioned lying and deception is hard to conceive. As I read these accounts, they would have been even more incredible if I had not uncovered similar acts of fraud perpetrated by Paul Twitchell and Eckankar. I had seen first-hand how it developed and how leaders would do whatever it took to uphold the image of their religion and their positions in it. Neither the Church nor Eckankar was concerned with the sea of truth on which the boat of their religious teachings floated. Their concern was to keep the boat floating and bring aboard more passengers. Those who boarded knew nothing of the port from which the ship had sailed or the course that had been set. In the eyes of the leaders, they were only the faithful; they didn't need to know.

Creation of the Gospels: The Books of Matthew, Mark, Luke, and John

Against the backdrop of creating a history in the name of God, we now examine the actual process by which the Gospels[36] came into being. Fredriksen provides some insight on the authenticity of the Gospels as well as the uniqueness of the events they narrate. She points out numerous competing and conflicting writings about the life of Jesus that were reviewed and considered for inclusion in the Gospels. Church leaders were well aware of the various writings that would compete to become the Gospels. They feared that different stories being told in different places by different clergy would lead to splintering and would undermine belief among the faithful. Something had to be done. Namely, one or at least a few accounts of "the greatest story ever told," had to be selected as the official position of the Church. So, notwithstanding the pious fraud and pseudepigraphy that had stimulated the creation and copying of the many and varied versions of the Gospels, there had to be a winner. Some account of the life of Christ had to be selected that would best represent the Church, upon which everything else would be built.

Councils convened to decide which versions would prevail. One scholar who examined this period noted:

> Half a hundred . . . false and forged Apostolic "Gospels of Jesus Christ," together with more numerous other "Scripture" forgeries, was the output, so far as known now, of the . . . first two centuries of the Christian "Age of Apocryphal Literature."[37]

The unenviable job of making the selection and establishing the canon fell to Church Father and Bishop of Lyons, Irenaeus (ca.120-200), who settled on four of these "creative" works. Fredriksen notes:

> [T]he canon . . . represents an attempt [by] one branch of the . . . church to produce order, to authorize only some of the growing quantity of Christian writings for its members. . . . The four gospels collectively stand as the survivors of a process whose principles of selection had *more to do with competition between different Christian groups than with a disinterested concern for history.* And once the choice was made,

it was perceived and defended in terms persuasive and meaningful to its ancient audience.[38]

Bishop Irenaeus first had to defend his decision on *why he chose only four books* out of almost fifty versions that were available, to make up the Canonical Gospels. The good Bishop provided this arcane explanation:

> The Gospels could not possibly be either more or less in number than they are. Since there are four zones of the world in which we live, and four principal winds, the church . . . fittingly has four pillars, everywhere breathing out incorruption and revivifying men. From this it is clear that the Logos, the artificer of all things, he who sits upon the cherubim and sustains all things . . . gave us the gospel in four-fold form, but held together by one Spirit. . . .[39]

Thus was the number of Gospels decided. The story of their origins is almost lost to today's Christian who generally believes that Matthew, Mark, Luke, and John faithfully and laboriously recorded the words and actions of Jesus so that the world could hear and know the good news. Certainly, there was a great deal of good news in these writings. They contained, as do most religious writings, a great deal of truth and wisdom drawn from many sources, albeit mixed with pious frauds that comprised its many stories. But this account of the writing of the Gospels is far different from what today's Christians — including the clergy — have been led to believe. Fredriksen's observations make it clear that historical accuracy about the life of Jesus was not of primary concern — or even possible — in the selection of the Gospels. Indeed, given the nature of the source documents how could it be? It was all created history, written by well-meaning clergy, but based on nothing but stories inflated over the years into the stuff of Gods. Fredriksen makes it clear that "competition between different Christian groups"[40] was the rationale for the selection of the chosen books rather than concern for truth.

But who *did* write the Gospels? One clue is found in the language in which they were written. The use of Greek as the original language of the Gospels is a sign that they were not written by any of Jesus' followers. Why would Jesus' apostles write about the activities of their lord and savior in a language that was not indigenous to their land or to them? If they were Jewish and spoke Aramaic, why and how could they possibly write in the high-Greek style of these works?

> [A] Galilean fisherman could not have written what Kummel calls such "cultivated Greek," with "many rhetorical devices," and with all the *Old Testament quotations and allusions deriving from the Greek version of these scriptures, not from the Hebrew original.*[41]

The noted Christian apologist Norman Geisler glosses over this point even as he praises the erudition of Luke for the "high quality of the Greek" that he uses in writing the Gospel attributed to him. Jesus and his disciples lived and worked in Palestine, yet the authors of the Gospels make obvious errors in describing the geography of Palestine.[42] Why explain to a supposed Jewish audience such details of Jewish life as "the Pharisees and the Jews in general never eat without washing the hands. . . . And there are many other points on which they have a traditional rule to maintain."[43] Obviously, such descriptions suggest a foreign writer catering to an audience that understood little about the Jews and Palestine. Christian apologists seem unable to answer these and many other questions — and for obvious reasons.

Non-Gospel Sources for Jesus

There is no corroborating evidence of Jesus' life and works in the histories of authentic, disinterested writers. A possible exception can be found in the writings of Josephus, which Christian Apologists claim contains references to Jesus. Yet these have been found to be forgeries, as have all of the early non-Christian historical works attempting to establish the existence of Jesus. They were part and parcel of the age of pious fraud, an age so tainted by the pious but unethical actions of Church Fathers that scholars of today must hide or ignore the practice in order to make even a plausible argument of historical validity. There is simply no authentic record of the life of Jesus against which the Church renditions can even be compared. And while desperately needing such verification to establish the validity of Church claims, it was precisely the absence of such documentation that allowed pious fraud to flourish without fear of written historic contradiction.

We see how priests and writers of the time were inspired and sustained on stories of the life of Jesus. These stories inspired countless inner and outer experiences with Jesus. In time, his reality became unassailable in the minds and hearts of the faithful, just as it is today. Truth has little to do with it. Belief alone created it and sustains it.

Thus, we have, in the case of Jesus and his followers, a person about whom there was no historical record yet around whom a mighty religion arose. He was reported to have performed public miracles. His birth so frightened Herod that he ordered the first-born male child of each family killed. He spoke to multitudes and shook up the entire region. Yet, somehow, he inspired not one word to be written by any historian of the time. And these were times with many chroniclers. One such historian, Livy (59 B.C.E.-17 C.E.) wrote more than 104 volumes on this period. While many of these volumes were destroyed (purposefully, some allege), no mention of Jesus can be found in them. One of the modern-day writers of this period wrote: "No literate person of his own time mentioned him in any known writing."[44]

A Jewish historian and philosopher, Philo (20 B.C.E.-50 C.E.), similarly wrote nothing about this man who seems to have silently passed through, leaving no mark on the written record in spite of the historic, even monumental, events that were supposed to have occurred during his lifetime. In fact, of the more than forty other historians and chroniclers of the period, including Plutarch, the Roman biographer (46-120), who lived in the same area where large numbers of Christians supposedly lived, no mention was ever made of them, their religion, or their founder. Perhaps the strongest commentary on the historical validity of Jesus is:

> The fact that no history, sacred or profane, — that not one of the three hundred histories of that age, — makes the slightest allusion to Christ, or any of the miraculous incidents ingrafted into his life, certainly proves, with a cogency that no logic can overthrow, no sophistry can contradict, and no honest skepticism can resist, that there never was such a miraculously endowed being as his many orthodox disciples claim him to have been.

> The fact that Christ finds no place in the history of the era in which he lived... settles the conclusion... that the godlike achievements ascribed to him are naught but fable or fiction.... It would be a historical anomaly without a precedent, that Christ should have performed any of the extraordinary acts attributed to him in the Gospels, and no Roman or Grecian historian... make the slightest mention of one of them.... Such a historical fact banishes the last shadow of faith in their reality.[45]

As indicated, even the most famous historian of the period, Jose-phus (37-95) appears to have overlooked the extraordinary exploits of Jesus:

> [I]n the entire works of Josephus, which constitute many volumes of great detail encompassing centuries of history, there is no mention of Paul or the Christians, and there are only two brief paragraphs that pur-port to refer to Jesus. Although much has been made of these "refer-ences," they have been dismissed by scholars and Christian apologists alike as forgeries, as have been those referring to John the Baptist and James, "brother of Jesus." No less an authority than Bishop Warburton of Gloucester (1698-1779) labeled the Josephus interpolation regarding Jesus "a rank forgery, and a very stupid one, too."[46]

Contemporary Support for the Gospels

Flaws in the arguments of Christian Apologist to prove the validity of the life of Jesus by reference to the Gospels are apparent. Failure to confront this fundamental problem is the reason why volumes of these tainted documents — products of pious fraud and pseudepigraphy — continue to be touted as proof of their validity. That these materials were produced at the urging or sanction of the church is the historical problem that no amount of erudition or evasion can overcome. Yet it is scholarship and erudition that are at the center of attempts to turn this mountain of pious fraud into faint memories or a bastion of insight and wisdom.

To achieve this metamorphosis, rules were developed to aid in determining what parts of the Gospels were more authentic than others. In other words, how does one distinguish between acceptable pious fraud and unreliable pious fraud? These rules of transmutation are applied with seeming disregard of the environment, practices, and intentions of the Church that have been outlined.

To ignore this history is to accept a continuing policy of conceal-ment rather than to finally confront the truth. But this is precisely what has happened. In its stead, scholars have developed a tool for assessing the relative reliability of this mountain of dubious data. Here is a com-mentary on the basic tenets of that methodology, as summarized by Lee Strobel in *The Case for Christ*,[47] shorn of the shelter of historical amnesia.

The Intention Test: This test tries to determine, by the language of the document, if the writer intends to accurately preserve history. If one is engaged in pious fraud for the purpose of convincing opponents and adherents of the Church of its validity, any Church Father so inclined would make his creation credible. He would record history accurately and precisely. Like any good fraud, it works because of a stealthy blend of truth and deception. As we have seen, there was a phalanx of priests devoted to this end, and they were immensely successful in dodging their most ardent opponent — truth.

The Ability Test: This test takes for granted that the recorder had good intentions and asks whether the writer displays the ability to remember the information. Given the forty to, more likely, 120-year lapse between the supposed death of Jesus and the writing of the Gospels, this would seem a strange test for apologists to recommend. In spite of the stretch of credulity required to advance even a plausible case for "ability to remember," some have tried a somewhat despairing and equally flawed argument. They have advanced the dubious proposition that Rabbis became famous for having commited to memory the entire Old Testament.[48] as support for the proposition that Gospel writers had the "ability" to accurately remember the stories in the Gospels. Aside from the thundering question why a writer waited so long to record such momentous events, there is an even larger problem. It is one thing to memorize a written work and quite another to memorize a memory without severe inaccuracies. Fredriksen makes this point quite explicitly.[49] Given the stronger evidence for a 120-year gap in the writing of the Gospels, this contention is even more untenable.

The Character Test: This test looks at the credibility of the person to whom the writing is attributed and asks whether there is any reason not to believe them. Augustine had to write *two* treatises on lying to encourage his colleagues to stop the practice that existed from the earliest periods of the Church's history. This early and continuing practice occurred alongside pseudepigraphy and pious fraud. Both were sanctioned, if not encouraged before, during, and after the period of the formulation of the Gospels. These particulars would make the character test a measure that adherents would be well advised not to employ.

The Consistency Test: Are there contradictions in the Gospels that make them less credible than they might otherwise be? The evidence here is overwhelming, with literally hundreds of examples of significant and not so significant differences. But the issue is not just the discrepancy between these four books of the Gospels and other books of the New Testament. The larger question is that only four of more than fifty versions of the Gospels were selected, and the latter possessed even more inconsistencies and contradictions. How does one reconcile these fifty versions and a selection process that by its very nature acknowledged that none was authentic, original, and exclusive?

The Bias Test: Did the Gospel writers have any biases that would have colored their work? Obviously, the entire history of pious fraud shows that bias was the modus operandi of the writers of the Gospel.

The Cover-Up Test: Did the writers cover up any detail that might be embarrassing or reveal things that were embarrassing as proof of the documents' veracity? Answered within the context of pious fraud, the entire body of material produced during the gestation period of the Church was a known fabrication, making the test itself moot. Undeniably, the entire process was a cover-up, that is to say, a distortion of the truth.

The Corroboration Test: Can places, people, and events be corroborated against known events in history? Once again, given what we know of the policies supporting made-up stories to enthrall the faithful, such corroboration was elementary, as writers labored to create the most authentic and believable accounts of the life of Jesus. This was possible since there was no written history of Jesus' life to serve as a check against excesses.

The Adverse Witness Test: Are there contemporary sources who contradict the facts within the Gospels? To use the Gospels to make this point is to use a fraudulent document to prove another of its kind. The historians of the period serve as credible adverse witnesses and produce the most thunderous evidence by their sheer silence. As we will see, there are no legitimate non-Church sources to corroborate events in the life of Jesus as depicted in the Gospels.

There we have it, a contemporary methodology that fails to deal with the most salient evidence bearing on the authenticity and veracity of the Gospels and other books of the Bible. The silence of scholars and the Church on this point is all the more disturbing in light of the known policy of *suppressio veri,* which would encourage concealment of this history. To confront it would impose a burden of overwhelming proportion. But that is the nature of truth. The burden of its weight increases in direct proportion to the degree of suppression. Just as in earlier versions of the now much vaunted new version of the *Catholic Encyclopedia,* there are no references to pious fraud, pseudepigraphy, *suppressio veri,* or any other marker of the practices that were the dubious foundations on which Christianity was built.

This is the problem with most current theological research and books such as *The Case for Christ*[50] and even the more scholarly *From Jesus to Christ.*[51] In the former, journalist Lee Strobel interviews many noted Christian scholars to get their take on the difficult questions posed by Christian critics and researchers regarding the life of Jesus. In interviews with distinguished scholars such as Dr. Craig L. Blomberg, Dr. Bruce Metzger, Dr. Edwin Yamauchi, Dr. John McRay, and Dr. Gregory Boyd among others, Strobel elicits testimony supportive of the conclusion that Jesus was real and that the account of him outlined in the Gospels is accurate. Yet, in interview after interview, the evidence supporting their assertions continues to be the early body of fraudulent writings of Church Fathers whose only objective was to serve God by providing whatever written support was necessary to further the Church's objectives. Again, we confront the essential weakness of all the testimony that Strobel elicits, namely, the avalanche of pious fraud that corrupted the work of the Church and continues to undermine its authenticity and veracity today.

Strobel's defense did not go without criticism. Earl Doherty countered with his, *Challenging the Verdict: A Cross-Examination of Lee Strobel's "The Case for Christ."*[52] Doherty does a fair job of arguing the available evidence that is susceptible to alternate conclusions, but misses the main argument, namely, the impeachability of the entire record of historic documents, most particularly the Gospels themselves, given the record of deception in which the Church acquiesced or actively participated.

The Story Behind the Epistles of Paul

The Epistles of Paul are an important link in the chain that makes up the story of Jesus, for the letters of Paul are said to be the living link with the life of Jesus. Paul is said to have lived during the time of Jesus and thus was the only historical figure able to authenticate his existence and achievements. But even his letters have dubious provenance. Despite their importance in Christian thought, there is, astonishingly enough, nothing in Paul's letters directly about the teachings or life of the savior. About Paul, the writer and lecturer M. M. Mangasarian[53] says:

> Is it conceivable that a preacher of Jesus could go throughout the world to convert people to the teachings of Jesus, as Paul did, *without ever quoting a single one of his sayings?* Had Paul known that Jesus had preached a sermon, or formulated a prayer, or said many inspired things about the here and the hereafter, *he could not have helped quoting, now and then, from the words of his master. . . .*
>
> If Paul knew of a miracle-working Jesus, one who could feed the multitude with a few loaves and fishes — who could command the grave to open . . . is it conceivable that either intentionally or inadvertently *he would have never once referred to them in all his preaching?*
>
> The conclusion is inevitable that the gospel [of] Jesus is later than Paul and his churches . . . . [T]here is absolutely not a single hint or suggestion in them of such a Jesus as is depicted in the gospels. The gospel Jesus was not yet put together or compiled, when Paul was preaching.[54]

Of course, we now know that there were no writings about Jesus, which Paul could use in spreading the word about him. Paul knew nothing about Jesus' birth, life, or death, because no story existed and nothing had been created or written yet. If accounts of the lives of the disciples were true, Paul could have spoken with some of them. Certainly, they would still have been spreading Jesus' message immediately after his death. But, surprisingly, there is no evidence of any such communication. Paul mentions none of the disciples, in spite of their mutual devotion to Jesus and the spreading of his message. Consequently, Mangasarian concludes that the story of Jesus was made up, a creation from the pen of authors living long after Jesus died. Nothing later found in the Gospels was ever mentioned in any of Paul's writings. So the Gospels, thought to be telling the story of Jesus as it was lived, observed and recorded by his disciples, are, to put it kindly, creative fabrications!

This essential flaw in the Church's story of Jesus has plagued it since its inception. Subtle attempts at pseudepigraphy to address the problem have been undertaken by later writers in an effort to backfill and attribute to Apostle Paul words about the life of Jesus that he did not write. But these efforts were transparent and largely futile, except to true believers. On this question, Mangasarian explained:

> That the authorities of the church realize how damaging to the reality of the gospel Jesus is the inexplicable silence of Paul concerning him, may be seen in their vain effort to find in a passage put in Paul's mouth by the unknown author of the book of Acts, evidence that Paul does quote the sayings of Jesus. The passage referred to is the following: "It is more blessed to give than to receive." Paul is made to state that this was a saying of Jesus. In the first place, this quotation is not in the epistles of Paul, but in the Acts, of which Paul was not the author; in the second place, there is no such quotation in the gospels. The position, then, that there is not a single saying of Jesus in the gospels which is quoted by Paul in his many epistles is unassailable, and certainly fatal to the historicity of the gospel Jesus.[55]

On the question of whether the statements attributed to Paul in Acts were ever voiced by him, Fredriksen is in agreement with Mangasarian:

> [T]he information that Acts relates about Paul — most specifically, on the event and circumstances of his call to be an apostle to Gentiles, and on his later negotiations with the Jerusalem community — contradicts Paul's own statements in crucial ways. Finally, Paul's speeches in Acts, according to the conventions of ancient historiography, are the free compositions of the author. . . . For all these reasons, then, Acts is not used here as a source for reconstructing Paul's reflections on the figure of Jesus.[56]

Others have argued that it was not Paul's mission or message to speak so much about the life and miracles of Jesus. Indeed, this is the apparent position taken by Fredriksen:

> The source of . . . [Paul's] Gospel (by which he means "message"), as distinct from theirs, was neither the earthly Jesus nor a human tradition passed from man to man, but the Risen Christ, who had been revealed to him through a special act of God (Gal 1:11-17; but Cf. 1 Cor 11:23; 15:3a).[57]

While Fredriksen does not proclaim Paul's focus on the "Risen Christ" as an explanation for an absence of any mention of the life of Christ in his teachings, other historians have made note of this emphasis to explain the absence of any discourse about the life of Christ in Paul's writings. To this argument Mangasarian contends:

> It has been hinted by certain professional defenders of Christianity that Paul's specific mission was to introduce Christianity among the Gentiles, and not to call attention to the miraculous element in the life of his Master. But this is a very lame defense. *What is Christianity, but the life and teachings of Jesus?* And how can it be introduced among the Gentiles without a knowledge of the doctrines and works of its founder? Paul gives no evidence of possessing any knowledge of the teachings of Jesus, how could he, then, be a missionary of Christianity to the heathen?[58]

As it turns out, it is widely recognized that Paul did not write some or all of the letters attributed to him. Fredriksen acknowledges:

> [T]hough the basis of our investigation is solely the letters of Paul, not all the letters attributed to him in the canon are his. Fourteen of the twenty-seven writings comprising the New Testament are ascribed to Paul. Modern scholarship accepts as definitely Pauline only half that number.[59]

Other writers are far more critical of the validity of the Pauline letters.

> [T]he entire "Pauline group" is the same forged class . . . says Encyclopedia Biblica. . . ."[60] With respect to the canonical Pauline Epistles, . . . there are *none of them by Paul*; neither fourteen, nor thirteen, nor nine or eight, nor yet even the four so long 'universally' regarded as unassailable. They *are all, without distinction, pseudographia* (false-writings, forgeries). . . ." They are thus all uninspired anonymous church forgeries for Christ's sweet sake![61]

The Jesus Story — The One and Only Savior?

The words and life of Jesus have remarkable parallels to the lives of numerous other saviors and messiahs. For most readers, this may sound startling. I assure you, it was startling to me as I expanded my search for truth. There is a funny thing about the quest for truth. Once the door is opened, it never seems to close. The truth seeker is carried down paths that could never have been imagined.

I was taught as a Christian youth, that Jesus was the Son of God and the Savior of the world — *the only one*. While I had questions about the rituals and dogma with which Christianity had surrounded the teachings of this pious man from Nazareth, I never had any question, during those days, that this was "the savior who died for our sins" — an exclusive designation if ever there was one. I never would have imagined that there had been other saviors — *many others saviors* — whose lives paralleled and *predated* that of Jesus. Even more, many also claimed to have been "crucified and died for our sins!" What was going on?

As we will see, the Christian claim of Jesus as *the* Son of God who died for the sins of the world, must be reexamined alongside the histories of more than twenty other messiahs, saviors, and Sons of God, all of whom predate Jesus and the claim made for him. Their stories are oddly familiar and parallel many critical facets of the life of Jesus found in the Gospels. For example, the histories of these saviors include:

- Descent from heaven,
- Taking on human form
- Performing miracles
- Crucifixion and ascension into heaven[62]

What is more, these saviors were recorded in the histories of their time, establishing that they lived and did some of the things, though likely less than generations of embellishers would have us believe. Also, just as Jesus' coming was ostensibly foretold by prophecies, including some in the Old Testament — a dubious and contested proposition[63] — so too were the saviors that came before him. However, no special significance is attributed to the existence of a prophecy in establishing the divinity of a potential savior. It is presented here because much weight is given to this fact in Christian writings as evidence that Jesus was who they claim him to be. So, while it is a bogus indicator with no spiritual significance, similar prophecies were associated with the lives of many other saviors. In other words, these other prophecies undermine any claim of exclusivity to the divinity of Jesus as *the* Redeemer — even as all such claims to exclusivity or being a redeemer are bogus, since in truth, we are all soul, Jesus included.

These precursors arrived on the scene after prophecies of a divine redeemer coming from Heaven to liberate the people. Hindu-Buddhist writings prophesied a divine child:

> He will relieve the earth of sin, and cause justice and truth to reign everywhere. And will bring the whole earth into the acceptance of the Hindoo religion.[64]

These prophecies presaged the arrival of the Buddha. Similar stories abound from China[65] and from Persia, where Zoroaster declared:

> A virgin should conceive and bear a son, and a star would appear blazing at midday to signalize the occurrence. When you behold the star...follow it whithersoever it leads you. Adore the mysterious child, offering him gifts with profound humility. He is indeed the Almighty Word which created the heavens. He is indeed your Lord and everlasting King.[66]

Zoroaster's prophecy was made more than six hundred years before the birth of Jesus.[67] He was not speaking of Jesus. Instead, his prophecies presaged the Persian and Chaldean God, Josa.

In his book, *The World's Sixteen Crucified Saviors,* Kersey Graves summarizes:

> We are compelled to omit, for want of room, the notice of numerous Messianic prophecies found in the sacred writings of Egypt, Greece, Rome, Mexico, Arabia, and other countries, all of which tend to show that the same prophetic spirit pervaded all religious countries.... And we find as much evidence that these pagan prophecies were inspired, and also fulfilled, as those found in the Jew[ish]-Christian bible....[68]

So then, messianic stories predating the birth of Jesus abound. To any truth seeker, these accounts raise fundamental questions about the validity of Christian claims regarding Jesus' uniqueness and exclusive divinity. And as to claims that Jesus alone died for the sins of the world, it is evident that he merely joins the pantheon of other saviors.

As for crucifixion, resurrection, and ascension into heaven, the accounts of Jesus are also derivative of the stories of at least fifteen other saviors, further eroding any claim to exclusivity that is the popularly accepted view of his state. Paul proclaimed the death and resurrection of Jesus as the watershed event, proving incontrovertibly the divinity of Jesus, who by this act became the Christ. Paul's single-minded devotion to this story was the basis for the Church's proclamation of Easter as the most holy and indeed the most important of Christian holy days. Yet Paul, and those who followed him in the Church, appeared oblivious to the fact that the crucifixion, resurrection, and ascension story was old, even when Paul first propounded it. Indeed, other saviors who allegedly experienced, crucifixion, resurrection, and ascension include:

- Wittoba of the Telingonesic (crucified 552 B.C.E.): He is represented with nail-holes in his hands and soles of his feet. He is celebrated in the region of Madura, India.
- Quexalcote of Mexico (crucified (587 B.C.E.): He was executed upon the cross as a propitiatory sacrifice for the sins of mankind. Evidence of this is tangible and indelibly engraved upon steel and metal plates. One plate represents him being crucified on a mountain and another in the heavens, just as St. Justin describes in the case of Jesus. In some depictions, he is crucified with two thieves.[69]

These accounts are written in the sacred books of their respective countries and are just a few of the numerous accounts of other saviors and messiahs that dispute any claim of exclusivity that grew to become one of the tenets of Church doctrine.

Where the Story of Jesus Originated

The stories about the life of Christ that make up the Gospels did not come out of the blue and certainly not out of any historical records of his life. For as we have seen, there were no historical accounts of his life recorded by any historian of his era. But compelling historical evidence does exist to show that the story of Jesus is suspiciously similar to the accounts of other saviors and messiahs for whom there are recorded histories. These accounts do not conclusively prove that any of them was *the* source of the story or history of Jesus as found in the New Testament. But the parallels in the story of Jesus match so precisely with the life and history of Krishna as to convince all but the true-believer, for whom facts are irrelevant. The story of Krishna predates the birth, life, and death of Jesus by centuries. Further, the authors of the Gospels were obviously familiar with other religious myths, especially the life of Krishna, that were circulating in the Mediterranean World during that time. Many likely got mixed in with the actual stories of Jesus that were circulating by word of mouth forty to a hundred and fifty years before they were finally written down. From these stories, the Church Fathers wrote an elaborate new myth eclectically drawn from the stories generously told and exchanged with locals, traders, soldiers, emissaries, wandering prophets, and others.[70]

The life of Krishna (literally meaning "black," or "dark as a cloud")[71] of India, as described in the Baghavat Gita, predated Jesus by 1200 years. Indeed, not just the story of his life, as we shall see, but many of the sayings attributed to Jesus were also uttered earlier by Krishna.[72] Here are a few of the more than one hundred parallels between the lives of these two saviors. Combined, they raise questions about the authenticity of the life story of Jesus, if not his very existence as other than myth. As to Krishna:

- He was born of a virgin.
- The mother and child were visited by shepherds, wise men, and an angelic host, who joyously sang, "In thy delivery, O favored among women, all nations shall have cause to exult."
- The edict of the tyrant ruler Cansa, ordered all first-born to be put to death.
- The mother and child miraculously escaped by parting the waves of the river Jumna (the putative source of another well-known story) to permit them to pass through on dry ground.
- The retirement of Krishna to a desert for contemplation.
- His baptism or ablution in the river Ganges, corresponding to Jesus' baptism in the Jordan.
- His transfiguration at Madura, where he assured his disciples that "present or absent, I will always be with you."
- He had a favorite disciple (Arjoon), who was his friend, as John was the friend of Christ.
- He was anointed with oil by women.
- And more than one hundred other similarities.[73]

As we have seen, inventing or borrowing stories to exalt a "savior" as the center of a new religion was regarded as essential to strengthen belief of the faithful and the institution of the Church. But then as now, the faithful knew little if anything about the deception and untruth at the center of the teaching. Any institution based on a fundamental deception always runs the risk of discovery with the attendant consequences. This is not to say that, even from such a dubious and devious base, good cannot arise. Certainly it can, and there is much to be said about the tremendous good that the Church continues to contribute to civilization. But like Eckankar, where the good is built on a base of deception actively hidden from the view of the faithful, there is something fundamentally wrong. And it is this: people do not like being lied to and deceived. It goes against the most basic instinct that we have as humans and certainly as soul. "Tell me the truth and let *me* decide," is the mantra that all would voice if given the chance. And this is precisely what is intended in this chapter. Anything less than the truth is to perpetuate a hoax, no matter how well-intentioned: it is disingenuous if not dishonorable.

The Basis of Contemporary Belief

Whatever the facts surrounding Christianity, it has grown and spread as few other religions in history. The rationales of Christian adherents can be put into four categories. The first comprises the true believers, who do not care about the facts, but are comforted by the stories in the Gospels and can see the fruits of this belief in their lives. These are the fundamentalists who, ignoring or unaware of the facts of history, believe that the Bible — and thus the story of Jesus — represents the literal and unassailable Word of God. It is not to be challenged or questioned, lest one reap the consequences that flow from defying the Word of God.

A second group of Christian believers, the Euhemerists,[74] anchor their faith in the assumption that there was, in fact, an historical Jesus. How else, they would argue, can one explain the strength of Christianity? I can understand this position. From the earliest days, I was presented with a picture of Jesus, which in time filled my inner space and became as real as anyone in my life. My assumption of his historical reality only strengthened my belief in his mission and miracles. But a similar thing happened when I assumed the reality of Eck Masters. The assumption of historic validity gives inner and outer life to any creation of imagination.

Of course the image of Jesus has been depicted with many faces, in many races. This is to be expected when dealing with a figure that no one has ever seen or known. To the extent that Jesus was a mortal man elevated to the status of god, his ascension paralleled the track of many historical figures whose accomplishments were so venerated as to be elevated to this status. This has come to be known as "euhemerism," a word that comes to us from Euhemerus (a fourth-century B.C.E. Greek mythographer), who held that the gods were simply deified mortals.[75] In this school of thought, Jesus is portrayed as a rebel, who so incited the Romans that they executed him. But the problem with this hypothesis continues to be the dearth of any verifiable historic record of his life from sources other than those composed decades after his death. And, as we have seen, these were written by Church Fathers whose intentions were guided by anything but a concern for historical accuracy.

Third, there are the mythicists: students and interpreters of myth who adhere to the view that some supernatural persons or events originate in human imagination, especially as revealed in myth. Given the growing body of evidence that points to Jesus being a mythological figure, this school of thought adopted a more realistic and plausible view. They maintain that because the myths about Jesus appeared before he did, they constitute the core of a spiritual truth around which the history of the man and the movement came together.

In recent years, an intriguing fourth group of believers has emerged, basing their faith, at least in part, in *The Urantia Book*. In the words of the Urantia Foundation:

> The Urantia Book was written in 1934-1935 and published in 1955. The book proclaims to be authored by numerous supermortal (angel-like) beings as a Revelation to our world. It is the first Epochal Revelation since Jesus and the fifth since the beginning of human life on Earth. No humans are associated with authoring The Urantia Book and the technique whereby the papers were transcribed is unknown. Like all other religious books, the contents should be evaluated by the fruits of the spirit which the teachings produce, not by any claim of authorship....[76]

Either this book is an astonishing example of extraterrestrial cooperation or it is another example of pious fraud that, in regard to its alleged origins and scope, leaves all other examples in its wake. This book contains minute details of Jesus' life, including an intricate description of the compound, neighborhood, and physical environment in which he walked as a boy. It similarly contains other details of the life of Christ spread over more than seven hundred remarkable pages. Whatever its source, the Urantia movement is growing. For many, its version of the life of Jesus is more credible than that of the Christian churches because it is more detailed — remember the device of truth by detail?

A Final Word

As God-soul, the point of all religion and all worship is to eventually outgrow it and realize that the lives of the masters, saints, saviors, and redeemers are a preview of our own life. Each of us is a spark of God with the inherent potential of all other souls. But the deeper we become entangled in ritual, doctrine, and religious debate, the more we move away from learning the essential spiritual lesson for which we have come into this world, *yet again*. The stories of Christianity, Eckankar, and Radhasoami are only examples of what happens in any religion that establishes itself or its central figure as the conduit through which one must pass in order to know the reality of God. In the end, they all must be shown for the transient nature of the lessons they can teach. For ultimately each person is his own path to God and can never experience the divine reality in a religion or anything else outside of himself.

PART IV

JOURNEY TO HIGHER CONSCIOUSNESS

Chapter 13 — The Spiritual and Scientific Foundations of Higher Consciousness

The Nature of the Journey

My life has been a journey to the heart of truth. The pathway of truth is the only means by which soul can realize and experience the source of its being and what it truly is. This journey has taken me through fallow fields and others filled with a rich and wondrous bounty of insights and wisdom. All have added to my understanding of the infinite, that which I now refer to as the "ONE" or "ALL THAT IS." When I went astray, I was pulled back to truth by events that could not have been predicted, yet whose meaning was clear when they occurred. My encounter with Graham and the reaction of the spiritual leader of Eckankar to his journal were the catalysts that set me on this part of my journey. I discovered flaws in my paradigm of the God principle, which helped me refine my understanding of myself as a spiritual being and my identity in the oneness of ALL THAT IS.

I regret no part of this journey, for never was there a time when I was not learning and growing. During my journey's most trying segments, I encountered spiritual deception and misleading insights into the infinite. My discovery of this deception served to give me guidance that would keep the next leg of my journey on course. I am grateful for these experiences and for the awareness they brought. Without them, I would not have the appreciation I now have of how souls can so easily be misled, and once misled, how they often fight to remain in comfortable spiritual terrain.

Since I cleared away the confusion and deception Eckankar put in my way, my growth to higher consciousness has been breathtaking.

Through intense inner and outer explorations, I have come to understand the nature of religions and the transcendent quality they all possess. By the same token, however, I have come to understand their limitations and how they can be spiritually debilitating. These insights are part of every person's journey to the heart of truth. At the center, it is simplicity itself. Mankind surrounds this simplicity with ritual, dogma, and endless ventures into logic, which have no outcome except an infinite cycle of questions and answers. Such is the nature of the pursuit of truth when limited to the devices of the mind.

The Journey to God-Realization and the Heart of Truth

The promise of God-Realization is not limited to incarnations of men and women. When the whole puzzle is put together, we see that all existence, from the lowest to the highest, is evolving to more advanced forms. Indeed, we are one of the channels by which it is evolving. How can one experience the love of a pet without intuiting that this beloved creature is preparing for a higher expression of itself? How can we not be aware of the conflicts that abound within our own bodies without sensing that there is something else going on quite independent of our wishes and self-interest? There is much more going on within our inner and outer bodies than we realize.

We can see in these structures a microcosm of the entire universe. Souls are embodied in each germ and cell of our outer shell, experiencing life and learning lessons that we, as the dominant soul of this collective, are struggling to control and direct. That is why it takes so many incarnations in the human form alone to "get it all together." Thus, our experience here is not ours alone. We live in the company of other beings that are evolving as we are evolving. The more we establish harmony with all that we are, the more everything that composes our being unfolds.

Just as our level of awareness aids in the expansion of consciousness of other beings struggling for spiritual growth, there are souls far more advanced than us working to assist in our spiritual development. How could it be otherwise, for the Great Work of every sentient being within all universes is to assist others in the expansion of awareness? Just as there are souls behind us in the unfolding of consciousness, there are also souls ahead of us, often far ahead — not better, not greater, simply more advanced. This is the universal love system in which we have our existence. Despite events that may appear to the contrary, all events lead to growth in awareness, which, in turn, lead to God-Realization and a greater self-defined role in the running of the universes.

It is an incredible universe *that we are* and in which we live. We cannot completely understand it through the prism of science with its limitations and, far too frequently, arrogant blindness (though this is rapidly changing). We can only understand the inner and outer universes through a more comprehensive process. This process involves not just scientific exploration of the outer world but also meditation and inner travel to investigate other dimensions of reality. The journey to higher consciousness requires a focus on the proper objective and an ability to look past form to the unity of everything. We learn in time that masters, like teachers, must be left behind. We learn that light and sound are but fireworks compared to the reality of the ONE.

We are all capable of seeing and knowing this reality; we must progress beyond the limitations of inner constructs that are misconstrued as the journey to God. The cosmogony and cosmology of the inner worlds propounded by various spiritual paths do have an objective reality of sorts. They exist to the same degree that "objective reality" in the physical world exists. But in the inner worlds, we have the capability to create instantaneous reality/illusion by the thought forms and beliefs that we hold. That is why the myths and promises of every religion are experienced by its adherents as they move into the inner regions.

These experiences occur either at the transition point known as death or through inner exploration encompassed in dreams, soul travel, astral travel or consciousness shifting. Thus, constructs of the inner worlds exist and are created by our imagination (and outside of our imagination through the imagination of others) but are brought within the reach of our experience through our beliefs and expectations. We can change these constructs and thus change the course of our inner journey by altering our beliefs and expanding our awareness. This places us on an entirely different track of inner experience and enlightenment.

There is no intrinsically valid inner journey, destination, or geography, *for we are already there, which is to say, here.* The outer and inner reality/illusions that we experience are only props that have been established by creative souls that have gone before us or by ourselves. These reality/illusions are no more inevitable, absolute, or final than our ability to imagine something different. As we shall see, moving beyond these inner and outer constructs to a higher and more lasting awareness of ourselves as God-soul is not as difficult as it may sound.

The journey to higher consciousness requires a careful balance of query, analysis, doubt, intuition, belief, inner awareness, and knowingness. In the end, falsehood is purged. Truth emerges with an immanent power that satisfies the most critical analysis. This truth pierces the varieties of forms that masquerade as religion, philosophy, and society itself. What is left is the center of all things, the only reality that exists. This reality is awareness, beingness, and "is-ness" — the qualities of God-soul, whose true home is formless and spaceless. In time, we come to know the secret of all secrets, that we are an expression of ALL THAT IS.

This chapter presents the foundation for understanding this conclusion. When coupled with the inner journey, we come to understand and know truth for itself. This journey to higher consciousness, indeed, to the heart of truth, passes through a doorway opened by a mastery of direct perception, dream travel, meditation, contemplation, awareness shifting, or whatever we wish to call the experience of transcending physical and other lower aspects of consciousness. It all leads to the stillness, the oneness that is the reality of here and now, the gift that we already have when we finally come to realize it. This is the end to which divine discontent propels each of us and the whole of humankind, the quest that is the reason for our very existence. It is the journey that takes us everywhere, only to learn that we are already here. It is the journey to higher consciousness, the journey to the heart of truth.

The Law of Unity

There are spiritual laws that define the manner in which the inner and outer universes operate and our relationship to them. Many of these laws have been discovered by physical science, in so far as their physical attributes can be discerned. Many others we have intuitively sensed in our life experience. Others remain hidden and elusive, understandable only when we transcend earthly consciousness. Together, these laws form the foundation on which all things operate, under which all natural and spiritual phenomena can be understood. The overarching law, from which all other laws derive, is the Law of Unity, or the Law of the ONE.

The Law of Unity embodies the concept that the universe was created and is guided by a single, conscious, intelligent force — the unity from which all creation has emerged. ITS purpose, as best IT can be described, is to achieve expansion by and through the expansion of awareness of all sentient beings. To better understand this Law, it is necessary to understand more about the nature of ALL THAT IS and how our lives reflect what IT is.

The Illusion of Life

It is often said that we live in an illusion created by individual and collective assumptions and conventions of civilization. However, for most of us, the illusion is far too real to be recognized as such. It demands our full attention to simply survive and hopefully to prosper. The illusion of daily life becomes our reality. Thus, we shall call it "reality/illusion." Every experience of life is designed to expand our understanding of who we are and to peel back the layers of reality/illusion so that we can see it for what it is. Dream creation (an aspect of imagination) as well as accepting and living so many roles in life exemplify the myriad levels of illusion we have created.

In a famous example of how quickly we accept illusion as reality, a group of young men was recruited and taken to a location in Stanford University's Psychology Department, which simulated a prison. None of the young men had been convicted of a criminal act; each had simply agreed to participate in an experiment. They were "prisoners" in an illusionary world in which they were watched over by another group of volunteers acting as "guards," though all were drawn from the Stanford's student population.

The prisoners were sprayed for lice, strip-searched, and put in leg-irons. The guards were given authority to create the rules under which the prison operated. The experiment went on around-the-clock, though each participant could leave at any time. With little more than these ground rules, the guards began to humiliate the prisoners in an apparent effort to break their wills. So completely did each group adopt their roles and live the illusion, that the experimenters thought it might become dangerous, and the experiment had to be halted after just a few days. The psychologists concluded that "circumstances can distort individual personalities — and how anyone, when given complete control over others, can act like a monster."[1] While the latter part might be a stretch, the experiment does illustrate the degree to which illusion can become reality, and how our actions, words, and thoughts can be influenced by illusion.

We encounter this same phenomenon everyday when we listen to the news and become emotionally engrossed in it. We see it when we identify with a movie character and feel what he feels. The roles we play in life (mother, father, priest, lawyer) and social groupings (race, sex, sexual preference, height, weight, religion, nationality) are all examples of the different levels of reality/illusion that we move in and out of throughout the day.

Another example of the power of reality/illusion can be seen in the competition to win, especially in team sports. Our games place the individual in an illusory matrix in which participants are often prepared to sacrifice their bodies to accomplish a result that an illusion presents as desirable. Once the prize is reached, however, the victor is often unable to explain what it all means. She must conjure up a meaning, for one is not intrinsic to the experience. It is only upon reflection that she perceives the growth of inner strength and awareness as the real meaning in the reality/illusion.

When we look at life in this manner, we see that it is similar to our dream experiences, except that the scenery changes more rapidly and the transitions are not as smooth and predictable. The significance of dreams has long been known to be a hidden, intrinsic meaning not necessarily related to the scenery or the characters, except symbolically. These are only a few of the many clues that parade before us daily that hint at the illusory nature of reality.

We learn and grow only when we are engrossed in something and react as if it is reality. When we watch a movie and focus on the cinematography, acting, scenery, script, and other technical components, we easily see it as a created illusion. From this perspective, we are little affected by the plight of the characters. We are above the illusion. We think of cleverer ways to manipulate the variables of the drama. We can then weave even more convincing illusions with ever-greater impact. On the other hand, if we become engrossed in the drama, sensing and feeling the experiences of the characters, we may learn the lessons they would learn. In like manner, the lessons we learn in the reality/illusion of life depend on the level at which we enter into and participate in the illusion.

At first, we are the effect of all of life, for we cannot see that we are in an illusion. We are less likely to perceive the lessons we must learn to move to the next stage in our emotional, intellectual, and spiritual development. In time, we learn to see the illusion for what it is and detach from it, even as we live through and confront the illusion. Experiencing life from a higher consciousness lessens the emotional pain in life's illusions, but it does not blunt our response to the point that we become disinterested observers. We simply learn at two or more levels of awareness simultaneously.

Illusion: A Scientific Perspective

A scientific perspective of the reality/illusion of life is useful in understanding the process of creation itself and the ways of ALL THAT IS. Recent scientific findings shed light on this phenomenon, at least in so far as it manifests in the physical realm. In 1982, a research team from the University of Paris, headed by physicist Alain Aspect, performed a series of experiments that suggested a holographic paradigm for the universe. Aspect later expanded the implications of his findings to an even more profound cosmology. To better understand the startling implications of this research and how it supports the idea of an illusory reality, it is useful to review earlier research.

The television series *Star Trek* and the movie *Star Wars* popularized the idea of a hologram. A holographic image is a three-dimensional representation of a real object that visually represents all aspects of it, but lacks physical substance. The present state of holography is not even remotely close to its depictions on the "Holodeck" of the *Starship Enterprise*. Yet, it has come far enough to propel our understanding of reality/illusion from where we were not too long ago. One scientist described the incredible potential of the holographic paradigm:

> [T]here is evidence to suggest that our world and everything in it — from snowflakes to maple trees to falling stars and spinning electrons — are also only ghostly images, projections from a level of reality so beyond our own it is literally beyond both space and time.[2]

Proponents of this view include the highly respected quantum physicist David Bohm[3] (a protégé of Albert Einstein) and Karl Pribram, a Stanford University neurophysiologist and author of *Languages of the Brain*.[4]

Let's look more closely at this phenomenon. Holography is a means for storing and displaying on photographic or other light-sensitive material, a three-dimensional image of a thing or person. The plate on which the image is exposed is a hologram. When a laser light is projected through this plate, a holographic image is produced. The production of this three-dimensional representation of a real object is a clue to a much deeper truth. Could this obvious illusion demonstrate a principle that has important parallels in understanding the true nature of the cosmos? This question intrigued Pribram, who found that the holographic paradigm was more useful than other theories in explaining memory. His observations suggested that memories were distributed throughout the brain rather than localized in a particular part, as earlier research had suggested. He came to this conclusion on observing the ability of subjects to recall particular memories, even though the part of the brain thought to hold that memory had not been stimulated.

Similarly, Bohm found the holographic paradigm explained previously puzzling phenomena in quantum physics. While Dennis Gabor (Nobel Prize winner in Physics in 1971) is credited with the discovery of holography, Pribram and Bohm are credited with expanding this discovery into a paradigm that explains many formerly inexplicable phenomena. This theory not only explained natural phenomena, but also paranormal phenomena such as precognition, dreams, telepathy, etc., subjects that science had assiduously avoided. In short order, the holographic paradigm was used to explain near-death experiences, the workings of the brain, the dream world, and synchronicity (unusual coincidences that are more than chance).[5]

Alain Aspect and his Paris team discovered that sub-atomic particles appear to instantaneously communicate with each other, whether the distance between them is ten feet or ten billion miles.[6] Aspect's findings carry implications that most scientist are unprepared to accept. Bohm, on the other hand, went far ahead of his colleague and put forth the interpretation that objective reality does not exist, that despite its apparent solidity, the universe is a phantasm, a gigantic and splendidly detailed hologram. In other words, the physical world is an illusion, the full nature of which we are only beginning to understand.

Seeing the universe as a gigantic hologram is a useful though incomplete bridge to seeing the greater miracle of creation and life encompassed in ALL THAT IS, the ONE, or GOD. It has long been a tenet of higher consciousness that each of us is a reflection, an image of that from which we derive. The properties of the hologram illustrate this to some degree. When a holographic plate containing the image of an apple is illuminated with a laser beam, the object appears as a perfect three-dimensional image of the original. If we were to cut the plate with the image of the apple in half, then project the light onto each half separately, we would reasonably expect to see only one half of the image. But this is not what happens! Even though we project the light onto only half the hologram, we see a three-dimensional image of the *whole* apple. The image is smaller (the plate is smaller by half) but it is as complete in all details as the original image. What if we were to cut the plate into fourths, eighths, sixteenths, and so on? Each time we project the laser onto a smaller fractional part of the hologram, we continue to see the image of the whole apple, though proportionately smaller.

The hologram is more than a metaphor for our relationship to and reflection of the ONE. It has profound implications. It demonstrates that everything is part of the whole, even though it appears as a subdivided part. Bohm embraced this expanded concept of the whole, as have others, for it offers a useful way to see and understand the universe and our relationship to it.

In his *General Theory of Relativity*, Einstein astounded the world by arguing that time and space are not separate but are smoothly linked and part of a larger whole he called the "space-time continuum." Bohm takes this idea a giant step further. He says that *everything* in the universe is part of a continuum. Despite the apparent separateness of things, everything is a seamless extension of everything else, and ultimately even the implicate and explicate orders blend into each other.[7]

Science has made us aware of other examples of this intriguing phenomenon. Every cell in our bodies contains a complete record of who we are (our genetic history) and reflects the whole of which it is a part. This is the basis of cloning. Each cell can be used to replicate a virtually identical specimen, just as the fractional hologram can produce an image of the whole. In like manner, we are not only a part of ALL THAT IS, *we are an infinitesimally small replica of IT.* And, just as the cell can produce a fully developed adult of the same size and capability, so are we capable of growing to become that from which we derive. This concept may appear blasphemous or inconceivable at first, but it is consistent with the spiritual law of expanding consciousness and that of the ONE. Like the acorn to the giant oak tree, we too are in the process expanding to the ONE.

We are limited in our reflection of ALL THAT IS only by limits we set on our acceptance of a deeper understanding, awareness and acceptance of ITS nature and ways. All religions place limits on the expansion of awareness by espousing static spiritual paradigms. It is as if they are saying, "GOD is no more than what we know HIM/HER/IT to be right now; we have the answer, and that's that."

Expanding or Changing Paradigms

Webster's defines paradigm as:

> Example, Pattern; *especially*: an outstandingly clear or typical example or archetype . . . a philosophical and theoretical framework of a scientific school or discipline within which theories, laws, and generalizations and the experiments performed in support of them are formulated.[8]

In other words, a paradigm is a way of looking at things. It represents the combination of our assumptions, beliefs, and accepted facts on a given subject, which influences the way we think and the decisions we make. Our ideas about dating, homemaking, and God are examples of paradigms. Throughout this section, we will refer to this concept to better understand how our thought patterns and archetypes influence our view of ourselves and the universe in which we live.

The lessons about spirit and ALL THAT IS apply to all dimensions of reality. Once we learn them, we also learn the ways of the universe itself. Far from a purely physical phenomenon understandable in scientific terms, the creation and operation of the universe is first and foremost an inner "spiritual" process. It employs the same methods that we are in this physical classroom to learn. I use the word spiritual because there is in fact no "scientific" process or "spiritual" process as such. They are actually one. However, these designations are used to separate that part of our knowledge discernible by certain methods of inquiry from another. They are, in fact, a continuum with the line of what is spiritual constantly moving as scientific discovery intrudes. Once we depended on spiritual myth, misguided doctrine, dogma, and reverence to breach the barrier that allowed us to accept and believe. As science brought forth more rational explanations, we abandoned doctrine and dogma and accepted what we came to regard as fact. Science has not yet breached the void between life and death, reality and dreams, imagination and manifestation. Consequently, we still view these areas as "spiritual", as distinct from "science," and continue to look to the former for guidance and explanation.

When we come to see that both are inextricably connected, a continuum only, we will see the fallacy and the futility of the fixed paradigms of religious dogma. Thus, the problem with the term "spiritual" is that it is surrounded with reverence and deference that eschew rational inquiry. It implies that blind trust, acceptance, and abandonment of critical faculties are prerequisites. But, as indicated, science and spirituality are merely different ways of describing the same body of knowledge. Each answers in its own manner, who we are, why we are here, and what we are to do.

Therefore, spiritual inquiry should be treated as a form of scientific inquiry. Then, we can abandon the entrapment of doctrine and dogma that masquerade as truth. But spiritual inquiry, as an extension of scientific inquiry (or vice versa), requires adoption of new and different assumptions and methods to expand the range of knowing truth. Scientific paradigms have been expanded in the popular mind by science-fiction writers, who often take what we know and add imaginative fancy in a manner that distorts the macro-paradigm of our existence: *I AM, GOD IS, WE ARE ONE.*

Horror movies, mysteries, and the like instill fear of anything outside of the norm. They limit growth, for fear limits growth. However, the universe is, or becomes, whatever we think it to be. So, there is truth in what these writers have imagined, but only because they allow these images to come into inner and outer existence. Science-fiction writers have positively expanded our concept of what is possible, but they have also left emotional scars and paradigm-distortions. In addition to "sci-fi" writers, perhaps it is time for a new genre of writers called science/spiritual, or "sci-spi."[9] They would combine what we know about the universe through science with what we know about spirituality.

Scientific inquiry demands that experiments be predictable and replicable. Scientific inquiry in the spiritual realm must adapt and adjust its basic rules in order to make the jump into other parts of the continuum of existence. It must come to grips with the subjective nature of dimensional existence,[10] which makes predictable and replicable results less likely. Indeed, this is precisely what science is now grappling with as it confronts the unpredictable and uncertain nature of quantum physics. Science must shift its paradigm in order to encompass transcendent processes such as belief and thought as creative vehicles. This lessens the expectation of predictable-replicable results, the bane of modern scientific research into the spiritual-psychic unknown. The change in approach that leads to this type of inquiry is already seen in holographic research and quantum physics, where the connection between thought and outer results is becoming more apparent.

Further, while the scientific method demands an open mind and willingness to consider all possibilities, the truth is that the scientific method itself works within a paradigm of belief that defines the limits of what is considered appropriate for inquiry. For example, the work of Dr. Ian Stevenson (University of Virginia School of Medicine[11]) provides compelling evidence of reincarnation. Certainly, it is sufficient to warrant more scientific inquiry but has met with indifference if not derision by many in the scientific community. The work of researchers into abduction phenomena[12] and evidence of genetic manipulation of the species have met with similar disdain. The latter research contains impressive evidence of advanced beings spreading science and culture, resulting in phenomenal advances of homo sapiens in an inexplicably short time.[13] Yet, such research is ignored as unworthy of the label of science. Consideration of this evidence would alter the comfortable evolution-paradigm or the genesis-paradigm that today forms the limits of scientific inquiry into the nature of existence.

However, a promising development in recent years has been the formation of the Society for Scientific Exploration,[14] a group of science professors from major American universities. They seek to promote the study of anomalous occurrences traditionally avoided by the scientific community. They publish a refereed journal, *Journal of Scientific Exploration,* which covers various fascinating phenomena.

In time — I believe sooner than later — religion and science will be forced to adjust, if not abandon, old paradigms and embrace broader more expansive ones that explain existence and cosmogony. This is essential because the paradigms that form the basis of our culture cannot address the challenges humankind will soon face.

In recent years, the idea of different dimensions of reality — different planes — has found support in scientific literature. The scientific idea of parallel universes embraces this idea and is now considered "so real that we can reach out and touch them, and even use them to change our world."[15] David Deutsch of the University of Oxford asserts, "our universe is part of a multiverse, a domain of parallel universes that comprises ultimate reality." According to *New Scientist,* Deutsch claims "For seventy years physicists have been hiding from it, but they can hide no longer." The significance of this development is the view expressed by Deutsch and other scientists that the fate of universes can be molded and exploited. From a scientific perspective, the multiverse construct explains the perplexing mystery of why atoms behave so differently from the expectations of Newtonian physics or quantum mechanics, which have led to the scientific advances we have experienced as a civilization.

Quantum theory postulates that atoms can be in more than one place at a time. The mystery is that the atoms that compose the things that we see and use everyday can be in only one place at once, for instance a table. Yet, as we move into finer and finer levels of matter, the constituents of matter behave quite differently and cannot be explained by conventional quantum physics. We have seen that the holographic paradigm offers some explanation of this phenomenon but is not wholly satisfactory. The multiverse paradigm is not only consistent with the understanding put forth by spiritual travelers of the existence of inner planes, but also explains phenomena that cannot be explained by reference to a single *universe* construct.

The multiverse paradigm postulates that there is no difference in the application of quantum mechanics in the table and the microscopic universe of sub-atomic particles. If this is true, then atoms should still be able to exist in more than one place at a time. Yet this is not what we observe. However, the multiverse paradigm suggests that there is another table existing in another universe but the instruments of this universe cannot observe it. The astral world, by this description, contains a parallel reality for everything that exists in the physical world, including ourselves. By logical extension, there also are universes and dimensions, where every possibility already exists.

The implications of the multiverse paradigm are staggering. Yet these ideas are not new. They have been tenets of higher consciousness thought for millennia, yet the scientific community claims to have discovered them in 1957. This it is another example of how the separation of these two worlds — science and spirituality — works to the detriment of both. The mere articulation of this theory by science adds credibility to the self-evident awareness of spiritual teachers who have known and taught these principles for eons. On the other hand, the scientific community would do well to consider the perspective of spiritual teachers whose insights into existence continue to be well beyond these encouraging scientific steps. An enlightened view of this confluence would have both relating to each other far more than is apparent today.

A notable exception to this tendency is the work of Stanford University professor, William A. Tiller, who has pioneered research involving the nexus of these two worlds of science and spirituality. His book, *Science and Human Transformation,* is a tour de force in its promulgation of scientific theory to explain psychic phenomena usually treated with a nod and a wink by most in the scientific community. He ventures to explain, scientifically, such subtle energy phenomena as remote viewing (projecting and seeing with the astral body), precognition, telepathy, mind reading, clairvoyance and clairaudience, psychokinesis, telekinesis, levitation, and other phenomena.[16] As to the multidimensional nature of the universe, Dr. Tiller readily acknowledges that there is a great deal going on about which we know virtually nothing. He has put forward the existence of other dimensions and joined the vanguard of those introducing this paradigm to the world.

However, most people, because of the inadequacy of existing religious and scientific paradigms, reject much of what we are discussing here. It is the same problem faced by primitive inhabitants of a rain forest if confronted with technological wonders of modern civilization. One can imagine an encounter with our civilization by a small group of these inhabitants and how unbelievable their accounts would be when told to village elders. Rejection and disbelief would result because their paradigm could not explain modern life. When this occurs, the protective nature of humankind rejects the information. The population of the village would follow the elders. They have been trained to; it is their way. Even if repeated encounters with civilization occurred, the elders would still control what was believed.

We face a similar situation with our conflicting scientific and religious paradigms. Further, the religious hierarchy is loath to accept scientific discoveries such as the one that asserted the earth revolved around the sun. Once constructs are enlarged, progress can occur at a rate that reflects more than mere advances in cell phones, computers, cloning, and genetics. Indeed even these discoveries will be limited until the current paradigms, bounded by moral stricture and religious doctrine, are reevaluated from a perspective that reflects a higher state of consciousness.

How We Create Our Reality/Illusion

The reality/illusion in which we live is like the props on a stage, a play that we are writing and in which we are acting. It is a gigantic dream, or hologram, that we, knowingly or unknowingly, project into life. We are responsible for its content and its outcome. The content of our lives is propelled by thought and belief through which we function as cause or effect. When we function as cause, we decide and create for ourselves; when as effect, we react and separate ourselves from the creative process. We believe we have no control over life; whatever happens is determined by outside forces. But we are not separate or different from the creator. We use the same process of creation that was the original method by which we were allowed to be.

The Dream of Creation

We have noted that the world we see as mountains, planets, star systems, cities, and the beauty of nature is illusory at its core, though real in perception. While a brilliant advance in science, the holographic paradigm is inadequate to explain the solid, interactive nature of the reality/illusion in which we live. The models of the dream and imagination/visualization are more accurate in describing the true nature of reality than any corollary of the holographic paradigm or theorem of quantum mechanics. When we consider the infinite scope of dreams and the limitless span of imagination, we are closer to understanding the true nature of creation and the ways of ALL THAT IS.

The best way to understand the creator is to understand the creation, for we reflect ALL THAT IS. In the Book of Genesis it is written, "So God created man in his own image, in the image of God created he him; male and female created he them" (Genesis 1:27). And so it is, except that this passage speaks of the male and female body forms rather than the more transcendent qualities of the ONE, which are formless. To understand the transcendent qualities, indeed the very nature of the ONE, those that are beyond form, we must look within to understand ourselves. Each of us reflects in every detail the characteristics of omniscience, omnipotence, and omnipresence that epitomize the ONE. However, we have not evolved to a level of consciousness in which we can fully understand, accept, and manifest these qualities. Likewise, there is much that we do not understand or accept about the connection between dreams, inner travel, and our higher selves — an idea we shall explore later. These capabilities are vital links to expanding our consciousness so as to encompass ALL THAT IS.

The accounts of creation in the Bible and other religions and myths are of course metaphorical. They had to be simple to fit the consciousness of the time. They depict a process humankind still regards as beyond its capability to even contemplate much less replicate. Indeed, it is difficult for us to imagine that we are more than props on a gigantic stage in which we have little or no control. However, a different view of creation, which requires a higher state of spiritual consciousness, reveals that we have much more in common with the process of creation and the creator than we imagine.

The Law of Unity starts from the ONE and describes everything as derived from and within the ONE. The process of creation involves imagination, visualization, and knowingness identical to our latent capabilities. Indeed, since we, like the hologram, are an infinitesimal yet complete replica of that from which we derive, how could it be otherwise? Similarly, our dreams are capable of expressing or enlarging upon any experience, idea, or vision in the same manner that the ONE dreamed, envisioned, and allowed our independent expression of the same powers of creation. When we imagine and visualize, we tap into the same creativity. However, we are able to control imagination and visualization to a greater degree than we are able to control the content of our dreams. Dreams, imagination, and visualization are all reflections of the same process by which everything has been created, in both the outer and inner worlds.

Most people imagine that their lives are controlled by forces and circumstances outside themselves. The truth is that everything that manifests in our outer lives is created by the assumptions and beliefs of our inner world. In most instances, individuals are caught in a loop in which they believe that external events and circumstances control their lives. They accept the premise mandated by outer circumstances and extend their existence. This action forms a seemingly endless cycle until broken by a more powerful belief. Powerfully held beliefs such as "my luck has to change" or "the rainbow follows the rain" may reverse a negative spiral in thought patterns and thereby in life. Likewise, fear of losing what one already has is a belief that may reverse a pattern of positive momentum. In either case, the individual believes in forces outside himself rather than in his inherent power to create. It is the belief structure that is in control, even though prior actions already in motion must play themselves out, even as a new chain of events is set in motion.

We are here to learn this process of creation. It is a microcosm of the process of creation, which brings everything into existence. It continues every second for every God-soul in the multiple dimensions of reality/illusion in which expansion of awareness occurs. When the lesson of our own creation is understood and we become conscious creators in our own right, we are then able to participate as co-creators in the ever-expanding dream of ALL THAT IS.

The Levels of Reality/Illusion Creation

The dream of creation proceeded through levels with aspects of ALL THAT IS manifesting itself through imaginative dreaming at each level of formation. These levels of reality/illusion we call planes, densities, or inner worlds. They are dimensions, or levels, of the all-encompassing dream of ALL THAT IS. At each level, the power of creation is embodied in the consciousness of God-souls that compose a part of the whole but reflect ITS properties and characteristics. Throughout this created universe, God-souls reflect the power of ALL THAT IS to the extent that they are aware of and identify with IT.

Every God-soul, at every level of creation, is responsible *to* and *for* the whole of creation. Every God-soul ultimately devotes its all toward the goal of expanding the consciousness of ALL THAT IS. This occurs through the experiences of those who live within a particular level of the DREAM. This is as it must be, for the only reality is ALL THAT IS, and everything else is a created manifestation within that reality/illusion. But what propels this dream? What is its source and purpose?

Some thinkers have spoken of a divine agony that propelled this UNITY into a desire for expression, for release.[17] This was the starting point for all creation and explains, in part, the why of the reality/illusion we experience. These levels of THE DREAM of creation are experienced during the dream state or during inner travel. As reflections of ALL THAT IS, we are moved by the same desires and expectancies of ALL THAT IS. Just as we are compelled to act to realize our dreams, desires, and expectations, so to is ALL THAT IS driven to express the inner compulsion within ITSELF.

I have felt this powerful motivation. Indeed, this book is a manifestation of it. It started in fits and starts many years ago and exploded into reality after the events of late 2001. To not respond would have been to deny a commitment that had struggled for expression. Expressing this commitment was part of a larger design latent in all God-souls. It is ITS desire to have every part of ITSELF achieve self-realization — the awareness that God-soul is part of the whole. This same need for expression was the motivating force behind the eventual release of these inner parts of ITSELF, these God-souls that clamored for expression. To realize ITSELF, IT had to release these dream components, these ideas that had been crying out for release. Accordingly, IT created the universe of inner and outer planes.

Succeeding levels of creation emanated from each preceding level. Through this process, the inner and outer universes were created. Each expression, that is, each God-soul, of ALL THAT IS manifests a different level of awareness requiring a mechanism to expand awareness. This is the sole purpose for the creation of the planes of the inner universe. It also defines the role of all sentient beings. Each God-soul is placed in a position within THE DREAM best suited for its spiritual growth. Those at higher states of consciousness are entrusted to serve and teach so that all parts of ITSELF can become aware of their source. And so, the process of spiritual unfolding for all souls within the DREAM proceeds.

While there is agreement in all religions and spiritual paths — and now from science — that there are inner worlds, or parallel dimensions, there is no agreement on their structure and composition. Both the Bible and the Koran depict the creation process and the structure of the inner worlds in simplistic terms, describing a single divide between heaven and earth. The Koran employs the plural, "heavens" and even refers to "seven heavens."[18] Both the Bible and the Koran were designed for the consciousness of the people of their times. They are allegorical in nature. They sought to establish spiritual paradigms by which social harmony could be maintained and a connection with a supreme being made.

However, the spiritual insights in them limit the evolution of spiritual consciousness by their static nature: "that's our story and we're sticking to it." This is fine, as far as it goes; but spiritual unfolding is stymied. Though seldom mentioned from the pulpit, there is a Christian tradition that taught methods of inner exploration. The major proponent of this tradition was St. John of the Cross, whose practices came to be called Christian mysticism. Revered as a saint by the Church, he held that contemplation through prayer could lead to the mysterious experience of God's presence. But Christian mysticism does not help the seeker understand the nature of inner experiences. Because it does not present a cosmology, or road map, to guide inner experiences, Christian mysticism leaves the seeker with a feeling of love and contact, but little is learned. In this respect, it is like Transcendental Meditation, which leads to little more than a sense of peacefulness. But there is so much more.

The teachings of the Koran are very practical in nature, focusing the adherent's attention on divine worship and servitude. However, a mystical sect of Islam, Sufism, speaks of direct experience of God and the reality of inner worlds. While the Sufi is loath to reveal the secrets that inner experiences reveal, there is much to the inner dimensions of reality in Sufism.

The same can be said of the Kabbalah sect of Judaism. The Kabbalah grew out of astrology, myth, magic, Zoroastrianism, and other early non Judeo-Christian sources.[19] The insights of the Kabbalah were pursued in spite of admonitions within Jewish scriptures:

> Ye shall not go after other gods, of the gods of the people which are round about you; lest the anger of the LORD thy God be kindled against thee, and destroy thee from off the face of the earth (Deuteronomy 6:14-15).

The Kabbalah provides an important perspective on cosmology, or the structure of the inner worlds. Indeed, it outlines a series of roots with predetermined cause and effect relationships. The follower of the Kabbalah seeks to achieve a deeper understanding of the reality of God and the immensity of His universes. An underlying theme is the notion that this sacred knowledge is not for everyone. There are only certain individuals — traditionally only men — who become enlightened ones. The Kabbalah describes two parallel orders, drawing downward from above and upward from below. The former involves receiving the wisdom and assistance from higher worlds as revealed only to the enlightened, who understand and follow the order's dictates. The upward movement is similar to the enlightenment of Eastern religions, except that "attainment," the revelation of Godliness, is achieved by following a precise pathway dictated by rules.

One of the strengths of the Kabbalah, which is also one of its limiting factors, is the notion of attainment itself. Indeed, the Hebrew word for attainment, *hasaga*, connotes more than mere comprehension. It necessitates a knowingness that requires direct experience, which can be defined and explained by name or word. And herein lies its limitation, for there are regions beyond *hasaga* that are simply *beyond* word or name. Indeed these inner worlds are often without form and are perceived only by light and sound and inner knowingness, whose reality can only be hinted at, but never expressed in words. I have traveled into many of these regions; they are indeed beyond description. I can only relate a feeling of expansiveness, of oneness, whose full description lies beyond the awkward limitations of vocabulary.

The Kabbalah recognizes the existence of four inner worlds: Atzilut, Briah, Yetzirah, and Asiah. The first and highest of these worlds is Atzilut, descending to the lowest, the physical world, Asiah. Each world is thought to be identical in every detail and event, except that they are different in discernment and substance of reality (level of vibration, in our words) in each world. It is a tremendous feat for the Kabbalah to have developed a lexicon to explain the nature of inner experiences. Certainly, few if any other spiritual paths that espouse inner travel for spiritual enlightenment have evolved such a vocabulary.

While different in name, the Kabbalah's descriptions of inner planes are similar to those described in Shabd Yoga (the yoga of the audible life stream) that admits of five main worlds, from the physical to Sat Lok — the abode of the One God. While different names are given to different regions within the inner worlds, they likely describe the same realm.

Even in Eckankar, which as we have seen was taken from the Radhasoami teachings, the planes are virtually identical, though Eckankar uses more conventional Western terminology to describe them. Again, these planes are the physical, astral, causal, mental, and soul planes, plus a second level of planes within the "higher worlds" (several of which were formulated and first described by Paul Twitchell).

Similar descriptions are used in other paths, such as theosophy, which is an admixture of Pythagorean Hylozoism, Sufism, Buddhism, and Taoism, among others.

Perhaps the most complex cosmology of the inner worlds is found in the work of Henry T. Laurency, which builds on the teachings of Pythagoras, later termed Hylozoics (spiritual materialism). In this school, all matter has spirit or consciousness, just as all worlds, both inner and outer, are spiritual in nature. This view is that all matter is alive, either in itself or by association with the ONE, and is undergoing some stage of spiritual unfolding, whether conscious or pre-conscious. Adherents claim it as the most logical and correct view of creation and existence. Proof of its correctness can be established, they claim, through logic, explanation, prediction, clairvoyance, and experimentation.[20] While complex, Pythagorean Hylozoics offers one of the most comprehensive, albeit controversial, explanations of the origin of the world (cosmogony) articulated by any spiritual path or scientific theory.

Hylozoics defines all existence as an aspect of a trinity of matter, motion, and consciousness. They are interdependent and coterminous. All existence, whether physical, astral (dream), causal (memories), mental (thought), or higher, consists of this trinity. What we perceive as formless and without matter (say, a dream) consists of its own form of matter, along with motion and consciousness. It functions at a level of vibration indiscernible by physical instrumentation. The entire concept of Hylozoics pertains not only to the ways of the manifestation of the reality/illusion, but, as we shall see, also with the nature of the source of that manifestation.

Pythagoras called the fundamental units of matter, "monads," the smallest units capable of possessing or developing consciousness. Defined this way, the idea of consciousness expands to include potential consciousness, passive consciousness, and active consciousness. Thus, the reality of every plane is "alive" to the possibility of expanding awareness to encompass the ONE.

The cosmological view of the Hylozoics is massive in scope. First, the cosmos, as we conceive of it, is but one of countless cosmoses at various stages of expression. Each cosmos can be seen as a "globe in primordial matter." It starts small and, as it grows, taps an unlimited supply of this primordial substance. Space is thus an inexhaustible supply of matter. The inner worlds, as well as the physical world, are part of a given cosmos and continue to expand until as systematically built as ours. Each higher plane supplies the primordial material for the construct of the plane below it and interpenetrates that plane. Thus, all planes occupy the same space in the universe.

And here is where the Hylozoic construct of the universe takes a complex and fantastic departure from the most advanced articulations of inner world formation and structure put forth by any religion, spiritual path, yoga, or scientific theory. Hylozoics postulates the existence of forty-nine separate and distinct planes, grouped in a series of seven levels, with each series consisting of seven planes — the physical being the lowest plane of the last series of seven levels. The implication then is that we have *forty-eight more levels to go* before we achieve the highest level of spiritual awareness! If Hylozoics is correct in its formulation, I guess we'll be seeing a lot of each other!

The Law of Soul and God-soul

The idea of soul is found in all religions. It is a concept that distinguishes that part of us that survives the mystery of death and enlivens flesh to constitute a living person. It may be helpful to deal with some terminology. Soul has been used to express different concepts about the real self. Some refer to this real self as "spirit" and confuse it with soul. Soul and spirit are similar but actually different. Soul is an individualized and aware unit of spirit, whereas spirit is the energy from which it evolved and which sustains it. Soul can also be thought of as the "I Factor," the real self, which is contrasted with the "i-Factor," the ego that we think we are.

Soul, the "I-Factor," is a concentrated, individualized expression of this energy or life force that has the capacity of awareness. In its simplest terms, that is what soul is, and that is what we are. Our true form is more accurately pictured as a globe of light, a force field of knowing, aware energy. Though individualized, we are clothed in and surrounded by this life force called spirit, *chi, prana,* and many other names. It sustains our existence and activates, energizes, and manifests, both in outer and inner reality, the impressions and thought images generated in the act of thinking. Thought, in turn, is an expression of the awareness that we are.

This awareness, which expresses our unique beingness as soul, fulfills its highest expression as knowingness (omniscience), oneness, or unity (omnipresence), and the capacity to tap, at will, the power of spirit (omnipotence). These we will call the "infinite capabilities." Every soul possesses these capabilities, but few are able to express them in daily life. (We will come to see that learning to express these capabilities in life is why we are here in the physical dimension of reality.) So vast are these powers that soul must endure rigorous training in the physical realm and other dimensions of reality/illusion before it can function in its pure state, exercising its infinite capabilities. To prepare soul for the conscious expression of itself, it takes on outer forms in dimensions of reality below the soul plane, its "base of operation" so to speak. At the level of the soul plane, it can express and experience these infinite capabilities without limitation.

It is important at this juncture to draw a distinction that I did not grasp during my early studies of esoteric wisdom. The concept of soul, as traditionally taught, represents only a small portion of the whole that makes up who we are spiritually. The greater, more substantial aspect of our being I have referred to as "God-soul." You have encountered this term several times, but it is now appropriate to delve into it more deeply. I have coined this term to represent this higher-self. Its reality is not unknown to us; we encounter it daily. Some call it the "still small voice" or conscience. Sigmund Freud referred to an aspect of it as "superego." He taught that superego is the source of negative guidance, in the form of prohibitions, criticisms, and inhibitions, and of positive direction in the form of aspirations and ethics. He gave it little spiritual significance, preferring instead to attribute this guidance simply to the internalization of parental and societal standards.

While these factors are undoubtedly powerful influences, especially during formative years, they do not explain everything. Our aspirations, impulses to achieve, and predilections arise from a deep, transcendent place, not simply from parents and society. Nor does this explain the guidance we receive, unrelated to conscious thoughts, to help us in day-to-day life and guide us in an emergency. Most of us have experienced the protective nature of the higher self in moments of distress. Something within directs us in ways that often astonish us. It is involved in the tiniest details of our life: how much salt to add to a soup, how many rolls of toilet paper to buy. It is the higher facet of who we are. We often fail to heed it. So persistent is this voice at times that we may resort to alcohol or drugs to quell its counsel. When we continuously ignore it, it recedes and waits for the moment when experience moves us to listen. These experiences are evidence of its existence, yet they are often misconstrued. We are apt to credit a savior, master, mahanta, spirit, guardian angel, or something else rather than our higher selves. This is because our present state of consciousness tells us we are not powerful beings. As we shall see, it is God-soul that is the true master, teacher, and guardian.

God-soul guides our outer life and also the lives of other parts of itself experiencing existence in other dimensions of reality simultaneously. Together, they make up the totality of who we are. This may be difficult to comprehend, but the many and varied experiences of our dreams are clues that something else is going on within our inner universes beside our experiences in the physical dimension. Indeed, almost everyone has returned from a dream, initially startled to find herself in a physical body. It takes a moment or two to become reacquainted with her host shell. Once the reality of our shell is acknowledged, we are again overwhelmed by reality/illusion and proceed with our lives as if nothing had happened in the dream worlds. Yet faint recollections of the dream linger and whisper who we really are and the role of our higher-selves. Soul then, represents a part of God-soul that expresses itself through this life but is not the totality of our spiritual being. But it is still who we are, not a stranger in our midst. (Throughout this book, I refer to soul and God-soul interchangeably, because distinction would be more pedantic than helpful.)

Another point needs to be addressed. There are many entities that are like us but more spiritually advanced, who act as teachers, guides, and protectors. They serve those who venture into the inner realms. They are there to aid and assist soul in its unfolding as their part of the Great Work. But the higher self is the primary tutor and screener of such assistance. Trust in its guidance strengthens the connection between our higher self and our conscious outer self. Fear and loneliness only play into the hands of entities that prey on those who manifest vulnerability. Such people do not know their power and bow to anything that may inwardly appear to them. This is how orthodox religions do a great disservice to their followers. They provide them with a weak inner paradigm, akin to a child and Santa Claus, as preparation for the inner experiences they will encounter. With no understanding of the distinctions in the roles of inner beings and their often dubious level of spiritual attainment, they are apt to follow any being that may appear, as if God spoke to them. In short, those who follow orthodox religions, and even those under the mystique of a guru or master, are in need of a paradigm overhaul to understand what is occurring in their inner worlds.

Our true power as God-soul is so vast that we cannot access it until we expand our awareness. We must encompass and become aware of that aspect of our physical shell that animates it (soul) and lives far beyond its demise. In time, consciousness expands to encompass God-soul. In stages, we become aware of God-soul, surrender to it, and then live through its consciousness. God-soul awareness is beyond what is commonly thought of as self-realization, which encompasses awareness of ourselves as soul but not our higher selves. Other expressions of our higher self manifest in other dimensions of time-space but are integrated with the whole and contribute to the expansion of awareness of the greater part of ourselves. The higher self can appear as something apart from and greater than who we are. Communication with our higher self can often be misconstrued as "conversations with God," which is accurate only to the extent that we are a spark of ALL THAT IS. Accordingly, this level of inner awareness is sometimes misconstrued as God-Realization.

The Nature of ALL THAT IS

It is the growth of awareness of soul that expands the awareness of ALL THAT IS, for IT is a collective of enlightened God-souls functioning as ONE state of consciousness. Once expanded to this level of awareness, God-souls can choose to enfold with ALL THAT IS or function as individual consciousness carrying out tasks within the whole, for the good of the whole.

Our bodies reflect this same reality. Each body cell is a separate unit of awareness functioning as part of a collective in which we, as the predominate God-soul, attempt to direct and control its course. Often this mass of cells is more intent on following its own course than on functioning as a part of the whole. The harmony we seek within our own universe is achieved only when we understand the state of consciousness that stimulates inner unity and cooperation, then strive to live within this state. This is the goal of self-mastery, a state that many claim to have achieved, but few actually have, for the essential ingredient that propels God-soul to the state of mastery is love.

The Law of Love

Aspects of this law are widely recognized in religious and modern literature. Love is the glue that unites and supports all that happens in the universe and in the lives of every living being. Thus, in that it defines the singularity of purpose and the ways for all life, the Law of Love is another expression of the Law of Unity. Most people conceive of love as an emotion, a feeling. In many respects, this identifies characteristics of this property of ALL THAT IS. But beyond what we experience as love from the human state of consciousness, love is a force, an energy field, a vibration, distinct from the emotion that human consciousness attaches to it. Thought of in this manner, love is a harmonic vibration. When we align ourselves with it, we contact, vibrate at the same level as, and connect with the highest qualities of ALL THAT IS. Any other state of consciousness separates us from the uniting force of the universe. We feel unconnected as we look for that elusive something. The problem is that we look somewhere else, rather than realize love is here and now — within us. We are the source of love and can tap its enormous power, the power of the universe, only when our conscious vibration, by choice of thought, is to love.

As we move higher up the ladder of consciousness, from mineral to plant to animal to human, we are given assistance. In lower levels, it is in the form of instincts and genetic predispositions. Later, we are given the ability to make conscious choices that have instructive consequences, leading to increasing levels of choice and more instructive consequences. In the end, we learn to choose love as the binding, transcendent force that liberates us from the pain of earthly existence. In the state of consciousness of love, we rise above distractions of money and things. Our motivations and goals change. Serving the ONE becomes the most important aspect of our lives.

This concept is initially difficult to grasp. How can everything be an expression of love when negativity and evil are rampant? How can the notion of a God of love be reconciled with occurrences that are hardly expressions of love? To better understand this, it is necessary further to explore the meaning of soul and spirit. As we have seen, soul is the animating principle in all-living things. It is composed of and is a vitalized unit of spirit. It expresses and is a spark of its divine creator. In its pure form, it is capable of expressing the characteristics of its creator: omniscience, omnipotence, and omnipresence. Spirit is the force that permeates the universe, sustains all life, and expresses itself through and comprises all living things.

The creation of the universe, all levels and aspects, is for the purpose of teaching soul its innate power and ultimately its role and responsibility in the operation of the universe. Without grasping this, it is impossible to understand life and soul's purpose in being here. The seen and unseen universes make up a series of classrooms in which soul is provided the necessary experiences that lead to recognition of what it is, its inherent powers, and its ultimate purpose.

That is why the notion of sin is so misguided. It may be comforting to believe that someone or something has taken away our sins, but it is a misleading palliative. For we have already seen how sin is the stuff from which lessons of spiritual growth emerge. Forgiveness becomes necessary only because of the fallacious idea that man is born in sin. Fortunately, saviors abound to grant the absolution that sinners need, forming a cycle of dependence for those with low self-esteem. The need for help in life is unquestionable, but not the variety peddled by most religions. Their help comes at a price, for we are kept from the truth that leads to spiritual empowerment, the recognition of ourselves as God-soul.

Before soul is allowed to exercise the awesome powers that are its birthright, it must demonstrate, by the exercise of free will, decision-making, and choice, that it is prepared for this responsibility. The training is difficult and cannot be mastered in a single lifetime. Indeed, it requires numerous lifetimes, in many life forms. The support soul needs for this training is embodied in spirit. Spirit, in turn, is an expression of pure love. In other words, soul exists not because of God's love for it so much as because soul's existence is what gives conscious expression to ALL THAT IS. Soul is what IT is. They are ONE.

Love is the fluid of life, the connection between the ONE and all souls that are but the children of ITS dreams. They are allowed to experience, to know, and to be, thus expanding the scope of ALL THAT IS. Without love, IT could not create. With love, all is explained, all is understood. This vast universe and all of the dimensions of reality, known and unknown are sustained by love. Thoughts and imagination are allowed existence through our love for, and spiritual energy directed at, their manifestation.

Love is not the simple expression of good we might imagine. It is pure force, energy directed equally into all thoughts, good and evil. Viewing love in simple, emotional terms is wrong. But it does have a salutary end. Using this power for ends that are essentially negative produces results in conflict with the creative, expanding nature of this force. IT allows negativity to exist to teach soul the consequences of using this energy in that way. Such experiences lead soul to choose the sustaining, caring aspect of this force. Thus, every negative choice and the lessons learned lead to soul's growth.

From this perspective, negativity takes on a completely different meaning. Evil is usually explained as the opposite of Good. But it is not opposite or even separate; it is a necessary part of growth and expansion of awareness, which is the true manifestation of love in our lives. As the universal design is more fully understood, it becomes clear that negativity is part of the divine force. It plays a vital role in the education of soul. The simplistic, anthropomorphic renditions of the devil, the Kal, and the like miss the point. They also, as often as not, provide a scapegoat for actions and consequences that their progenitors would rather disavow. A child cannot learn the vital lesson of avoiding fire until it experiences pain. This is where the Law of Duality comes into play. We can only learn and know something in relationship to its opposite. Soul can make the choice to move in a positive direction only if it has the freedom to choose and experience its opposite. This is why soul is given the gift of free will. This is why freedom is so vital to our spiritual development.

Soul seeks to return home. Its happiest moments are but a faint memory of a bliss for which it endlessly searches. Once this quest for spiritual happiness and joy begins, soul searches everywhere. At first, it reaches for "all the gusto it can find," thinking that it only "goes around once." Hedonistic pursuit is part of soul's journey and lesson. In time, it comes to see the futility in this and yearns for something lasting and fulfilling. In time, soul seeks a higher expression of consciousness and eventually yearns to realize the source of its creation. But soul must choose the quest for spiritual growth. That choice only comes through the exercise of free will. This involves a voluntary selection from available alternatives that include evil, negativity, and all other expressions of life.

Avoidance of negative experiences provides little understanding of the reality of life. It may even stimulate a temptation to try "everything I've missed." On the other hand, an individual might live in an ego-driven state of moral superiority masquerading as understanding. That is why morality and rules, while essential for society and as guidance in the early stages of spiritual growth, only go so far. In the end, they do little for individual spiritual development if they only keep us away from experiences against our will. No matter how far the individual may appear to drift, living life and having experiences are necessary parts of spiritual unfolding.

Therefore, excessive emphasis on morality and religious strictures as a substitute for inner spiritual guidance only delays spiritual development. A decision made in ignorance of the options or without free will is not helpful to spiritual growth. When soul freely experiences all aspects of life and their consequences, it eventually learns that there is only one path to the divine. It is then that the yearning to find the path increases and a God-seeker comes alive. The enlightened exercise of free will eventually leads to participation in the operation of the universes of ALL THAT IS, the Great Work. This is the destiny of all souls.

The full meaning of love cannot be understood within the span of a single lifetime. A problem of most religions is their inability to explain why a loving God would allow calamities to befall humankind: the birth of a crippled child, the poverty of a nation, the slavery of a people, and the death of thousands due to natural or human causes. When viewed from the perspective of a single lifetime, most of these phenomena do not make sense. People justifiably wonder what they have done to deserve such a result. It is precisely this logic that has been the basis for explanations of tragic events since the beginning of civilization, and they continue to be heard today. These calamities were and still are seen as the acts of a vengeful God, set to punish an individual or group for a transgression. This logic has supported the concept of a God to be feared. Only the concept of conditional love (if you are good, you are blessed; but if you are bad, you are punished) provides a spiritual rationale for events when viewed from the perspective of a single lifetime.

When one considers that soul lives many lifetimes and expands its awareness through countless experiences, the idea that all events are part of the system of love designed to teach and train begins to make sense. Exercising the gift of free will makes individuals responsible for their circumstances and creations, the foundation on which all spiritual growth occurs. To blame our situation on anything or anyone else is to miss the essential point of soul's freedom and the gift of free will.

The loving parent, while teaching and guiding, permits the child to have its own experiences and to learn from them. To shelter the child from consequences may seem an act of love in the short-term, but it hampers the child's development in the long-run. Tough love requires that parents sometime permit the child to experience painful consequences of their actions. This is the most difficult yet the highest and most beneficial expression of love. Divine love is the highest expression of this tough love. It permits soul the full range of expression and total responsibility for the consequences of its actions. This is how all living things progress and expand in awareness. At first, the lessons are simply about survival. The animal learns what it must do to survive. It is, in time, reborn in another life form to learn more lessons that lead to a greater capacity to survive. As brutal as the law of survival may appear, it is an expression of divine love, though shorn of the emotionality, morality, and judgment that clouds our ability to perceive love in its divine and pure state.

As this awareness expands, soul is given the experience of living in a higher form capable of providing it with a greater range of experiences and choices. Thus, divine love permits us to have our own experiences to learn the lessons of life and expand consciousness. The act of a loving God, just as that of a loving parent, is to guide and teach the child while allowing it to learn from its own experiences. This is precisely what happens to soul.

Soul may not have the opportunity to complete a full life-cycle and may end a particular lifetime at any point. But the lessons of soul do not end then. Soul retains a record of all that it is, has done and learned, over its many lifetimes, in various body forms: not the mundane facts and trivia of life, but the transcendent lessons that apply to any time period or culture. These experiences set up the conditions of its subsequent lifetime. This is what is commonly known as karma, or the Law of Cause and Effect. The individual who has inflicted pain on another could return and experience the same pain by living his life as a victim of some sort. Or, he may return to care for an afflicted person as part of the learning necessary for soul's evolution. Experience and ingrained recollections are designed to prevent him from repeating the same experiences. But if soul repeats the transgressions, it must repeat the consequences until it has learned and can move on. This is the system of love that allows soul the experiences it needs to liberate itself from the cycle of cause and effect. When we see life's continuity and recognize that soul learns best through its own experiences, we are able to grasp the concept that soul lives in a love system, which permits it to have countless experiences, from lifetime to lifetime, aimed at the single goal of expanding awareness.

Our visible universe is indeed nothing more than a classroom. It was never intended to be a place of "peace on earth, goodwill toward men." It was always intended as a place of learning, where souls in different states of consciousness experience life, express themselves, and receive the consequences of decisions and actions.

The Spiritual Hierarchy

The Law of Unity encompasses not only the fundamental system of love underlying everything, but also the structure by which this system is administered and the levels of creation that are part of soul's classroom. These planes constitute the worlds in which soul has its experiences, once it has mastered the lessons of the physical universe. These inner worlds are not as strange and unknown to us as we may think. We have all traveled into them during the dream state but have usually dismissed these travels as meaningless. These regions are far more than simply "the stuff of dreams." The inner worlds make up a vast cosmology, including the many universes that exist in completely different dimensions of reality. Few have explored them, but they are open to all who develop the consciousness to experience them.

The various dimensions of reality are vast, far greater in size, dimension, and wonder than the visible universe. The physical universe is the lowest of these dimensions. It is the beginning classroom, the first grade in soul's development. It is watched over by "administrators." They aid soul in its upward movement and expansion of consciousness, until, one day, it assumes its role in administering the universes of God.

These planes are given different names by different spiritual paths. The number of planes ranges from five to as many as forty-nine, depending on the path. Though there is debate on names and numbers, for now, it is sufficient to name and describe those planes for which there is fairly common agreement. We might also submit that soul may journey into worlds heretofore unknown. The planes are:

- The Physical Plane: Encompasses the entire physical universe, including the stars, planets, and all material phenoena.

- The Astral Plane: Encompasses the universes most commonly visited during dream experience, out-of-body travel, and the dimension first experienced by soul at the transition known as death. This vast region encompasses cities, regions, and other places appearing much as they do in the physical world.

- The Causal Plane: A dimension of reality that is the repository of past life experiences and of the future time track, which exists only as possibilities. This is the region that prognosticators such as Nostradamus were able to visit to foresee events. This is also the dimension that individuals visit in order to learn of and experience past lives.

- The Mental Plane: This region functions at a higher level of vibration and corresponds to a unique universe where the heavens of most major world religions are located. It is the plane where the city with streets paved with gold (referred to in the Bible) is reputed to exist. This is the highest level thought to exist in most world religions.

- The Etheric Plane: Another universe thought to be associated with the upper regions of the Mental World. It is most closely associated with intuition. It is an aspect of the mental region but represents a higher faculty than reason and therefore functions at a higher vibration level.

- Soul Plane: The level at which soul lives in its pure form, shorn of all lower bodies, and capable of moving into any part of any level of existence. It is the level at which soul experiences pure knowingness beyond the level of mental knowledge or intuition.

The Law of Duality: The Nature of Good and Evil

The Law of Duality expresses the idea that the full meaning of something is only known in relation to its opposite. Put another way, reality consists of two equally valid components. Our growth flows out of the experiences we have in one aspect or the other of a thing. We would not understand the meaning of "up" except in relation to the concept of "down." "Beauty" has meaning only in relation to "ugly." The Law of Duality provides a basis for our understanding of the experiences of life. It also offers, in every situation, a choice that permits the exercise of free will. A brief extrapolation from this Law leads to the realization that duality exists in every situation, experience, and aspect of life.

Another aspect of this Law is that all events, circumstances, objects, and things are inherently positive and negative simultaneously. It is the reality that we see within them, accept as truth, and act upon that defines a thing or situation as positive or negative. Most individuals do not recognize this or its implications. Our nature is to simplify, to see only one dimension of a thing at any time. We even go so far as to characterize "no news" as "good news." In this simple example, we find an important misinterpretation of the Law. "No news" is really "no news." And even when the result, the actual news, presents itself, we are still left with the decision of which aspect of the reality to focus on — a choice that determines our future.

We see the Law of Duality at work in the reaction of two people to the same event. The loss of a job is a tragedy for one who sees the event from the perspective of only its negative implications. Yet another individual, longing to break free of the constraints of that job, might view the same event from the perspective of its opposite and see opportunities in new freedom. "One person's trash is another person's treasure," is a common expression. Because we view only one side of the continuum of duality as correct for a particular situation, we constantly jump to one reality or the other, choosing to see only one side of duality. This mass consciousness can lead to ostracism, or worse, for speaking one's mind on a certain side of a matter. The term "politically correct" has emerged as a way of expressing societal constraint on voicing affirmation or negation. This is not to say that society cannot or should not impose restraints on the articulation of certain truths. Indeed, because of the action of universal law, it is a necessary constraint. Societies, however organized, have a tendency to protect themselves by praising or condemning certain ideas and thoughts. What is important is what ideas are controlled and who does the controlling.

The person who chooses the path of fame, wealth, and glory may discover, upon reaching these goals, that she is trapped, hounded, lonely, and unable to fully enjoy or appreciate her "good fortune." Ironically, some persons in this situation wish to experience life as average persons. Others are able to fully appreciate the set of positive options and freedoms that their position offers and focus on the joy and happiness it presents, while accepting its limitations.

Accordingly, no choice or situation is devoid of its opposite. Another way of expressing this is that every situation has possibilities and limitations. The homeless come and go as they choose, free of bills, mortgages, commitments, and obligations. In some ways, this is the ultimate expression of freedom, with possibilities and choices far greater than those of the celebrity who must disguise herself to experience a degree of freedom. But homelessness also entails great hardship, which calls for no elaboration.

We may consider ourselves blessed or cursed. Both realities exist; both realities are true. Thus, the exercise of free will is present in every situation, at all times. Life boils down to the choices we make every instant of our lives. Our inner and outer reality is always a reflection of the choices we make between these two realities. Both exist and both are equally logical and possible. It is all a matter of the exercise of free will, the exercise of choice. Let me give a personal illustration.

My company had long depended on a particular business relationship, which suddenly came to an end. Our initial reaction was fear and gloom: jobs would be lost and paychecks would not go out on time — concerns that nagged the staff. From one perspective, the future of the company was bleak, until, in a staff meeting, someone announced that this was good news. After the voices of "are you crazy?" ebbed, a positive view of the situation was presented. The comfort of the former business relationship had held the company back from seeking other clients. We had an opportunity to step free and use the energy created by this change to pursue options that had always existed but were never explored. This perspective won the day, and the company propelled itself to a new level. This new posture for the company may never have been reached without choosing to act upon the "good news" rather than brooding about the "bad news."

The Law of Polarity

Similar to the Law of Duality is the Law of Polarity. It focuses on another aspect of this reality. The Law of Duality focuses on the positive and negative possibilities in a situation. The Law of Polarity addresses the tendency of events to evolve into opposites, depending on the choices we make. Thus, from the adversity of early childhood, the adult developed great strength and confidence, which made him a leader. From the seeds of this apparently one-sided hardship came internal strength, dedication, and perseverance, which led to later success. Equally, from the seeds of wealth, opportunity, and privilege, as with the life of Howard Hughes, came isolation, loneliness, and paranoia. From negative traits arise the seeds for reversal, a reversal guaranteed by the painful reminder that the consequences of continuation will go on until changed.

The Law of Polarity can be seen in history. Some events appear on the surface to be wholly good or bad. Though it may be difficult to see the opposite reality in an event, greater distance, or greater levels of consciousness, are necessary to see the opposite reality and its potential emergence. The existence of Hitler, while grotesque in its impact, also served as a catalyst for positive consequences that might never have occurred — the creation of a Jewish homeland. But from this came the displacement of the Palestinians, leaving them without a homeland. And so it goes, on and on, each event in itself perceived as good or bad but also containing the seeds of its opposite.

In considering this aspect of spirit, we might ask, what is the purpose of it all? How can we ever win the game of life? It seems as if the entire deck is stacked. How can we understand events if things that appear positive have negative consequences? Toward what purpose is this design directed? The answer is not as difficult to comprehend as we might think. The generic nature of spirit is to respond to every thought form placed within it to expand awareness through experience to the full recognition of soul's unity with ALL THAT IS. Through this process, soul ultimately becomes a conscious partner with ALL THAT IS in the maintenance and operation of the universes.

The Law of Spirit

Understanding the nature of spirit is essential to comprehending the forces that shape our lives. Variously called spirit, *chi*, the force, *shabd*, *prana*, it is all the same. It expresses itself as intelligence, creativity, wisdom, protection, guidance, and is integrally involved with every aspect of our lives, small and large. It is the vehicle that sustains all life in all universes. It works in all life forms: through instinct in lower animals and through conscious choice in humans. It is ubiquitous. It functions as the source of all knowingness. It represents the database, the repository of all wisdom and knowledge. Such knowledge need not be retained by a single individual, but can be tapped, as needed, from the wellspring of all knowledge. Spirit, flowing from ALL THAT IS, is the source of consciousness and comprises consciousness itself. Soul itself is an aware, concentrated aspect of spirit consciousness. As soul, it coalesces and unfolds into an individualized unit capable of independent thought and awareness. It works in harmony and partnership with its origin, ALL THAT IS and the higher-self. Spirit responds whenever a thought form is put forth. Every thought form makes an impression on this unformed energy field. In turn, it responds creatively to produce an effect in the outer world. It manifests thought forms consistent with its generic nature, which is to serve the whole.

To understand the workings of this universal force is to understand life itself and also to participate in its process. Where do we start in trying to understand spirit? It is with energy. At one level, it is molecules and atoms and electrons and protons and quarks, and even smaller particles or waves. It also manifests as light and sound, though these are not its principal constituents. Instead, and more fundamental in nature, it is motion, matter, and consciousness. Light and sound — indeed, all wave and particle manifestations — are but aspects at different levels of motion, matter, and consciousness. What is perceived as wave, particle, or some other form of energy, is, at the next higher level of existence, perceived as a form of matter. But in each case, it combines the properties of motion and consciousness, which together create existence at all levels and dimensions of reality.

This concept is more fully developed in Pythagorean Hylozoics[21] (discussed earlier), which expresses a view of the fundamental nature of spirit, and therefore of life itself. Quantum theory and the holographic paradigm hint at the nature of spirit, that is, they present some of its complexity, yet miss much of its simplicity. At the most fundamental level, it is thought, it is feeling, it is love. It is everywhere and makes up everything. It transmutes into all forms and exists at all vibratory levels, in the physical dimension and every other plane within the inner and outer universe. The things that we observe in our dreams and conscious inner travels are also made of this stuff, though existing at a different and finer level of vibration and substance. That it has consciousness is axiomatic, for it flows from the reality of ALL THAT IS, which is all consciousness.

Spirit is in touch with all. It comprises thought forms and dimensions, which make up the substance of the illusion called life. There is a purpose for this illusion, a scheme behind creation. It is both explicable and purposeful. But more foundation is required before it can be fully understood. For now, it is sufficient to say that spirit is all that there is, because it is the way of ALL THAT IS. We are it; we live in it; we respond to it; and it responds to us.

When trying to grasp something as omnipresent, omnipotent, and omniscient as spirit, we are forced to describe it from many viewpoints. There is much that is known about this force and more that can be said about its nature. Apart from the responsive aspect of its way, spirit appears to have a plan or purpose — a nature — that is no less than to carry out the prime directive of ALL THAT IS. That purpose, as best can be discerned, is to work with each soul to enhance its survivability and promote the expansion of consciousness of that soul. The expansion of consciousness moves each soul to a point at which it becomes aware of itself as a part of spirit and ALL THAT IS. It comes to understand its innate power and its eternal role as a partner with the infinite. It then serves other souls by helping them to achieve an expansion of consciousness to an awareness of ALL THAT IS. I call this the Great Work. Spirit does this in a way that enhances the growth and learning of all souls, no matter their state of development.

Works for the Good of the Whole

Of all the concepts that describe spirit, the one that best conveys its nature is that it works for the good of the whole. The concept of serving the whole may appear strange in a society that stresses individualism. Life is a reflection of spirit's capacity to meet the needs of each and every life form. Yet the outcomes of life's experience often seem not to fulfill our specific wishes. This is particularly true when those wishes are of a selfish nature, devoid of concern for others. This is where spirit defines the outcome of our wishes to balance the selfishness of those still functioning in lower states of consciousness.

It is not the nature of spirit to assist only a part, that is, the concerns of one person or group. When selfish outcomes are attempted, the result is often short-lived or detrimental to the person. It is the nature of spirit to spread its blessings so that the totality of life benefits. In this statement lies a vital clue to the nature of true success. When goals are achieved that benefit more than just the individual, it is considered magnanimous, powerful, special. Society awards accolades to those who manifest such highly developed levels of awareness. They become our saviors, lords, masters, saints, Nobel Laureates, heroes, and philanthropists. Their uniting characteristic is that they are "givers," serving the good of the whole, serving spirit.

Another way of describing its nature is love — a love for all life. When we try to limit the blessings of spirit to our loved ones and ourselves, we are working against its nature and placing limits on its capacity to bless us. If we fail to understand this, we experience disappointments in life and perhaps even turn away from spirit in the belief that it does not exist, or is too perplexing for us to want it in our lives.

Everything in the universe is created from spirit and is spirit. Yet in its undifferentiated form, it is pure energy, unformed, undefined, waiting to be activated by thought. The pure energy of spirit is hardly a blind, dumb force. Indeed, it formulates plans and strategies and executes the impressions made upon it by thought. Operating beyond time and space, it is not limited in its capacity to receive our thoughts and respond by using the channel that is open and willing to respond. Such is spirit's genius in working out ITS plan, remaining consistent with its generic nature, even as it manifests our thoughts and dreams.

This is how the marooned sailor or the lost camper is found. As thought is sent into the infinite, unlimited, unmanifested center of pure consciousness, it responds. Willing entities (free will is always at work) receive thoughts and suggestions to take a different route, to act in a particular manner, all as part of a solution. It is stimulated and enhanced by the power of belief, knowing, and certainty. Thought and belief, which are of course within our control, determine the speed and certitude of success in our mutual endeavors with spirit. But, it is also our action in response to the opportunities that it presents, which is determinative. For, we are the vehicles that carry out the work of spirit and complete the formula of a mutually reciprocal relationship.

Responsiveness of Spirit

Responsiveness is one of the wonderful characteristics of spirit that explains its interaction with us to achieve our goals. We knowingly or unknowingly work with it every moment of our lives. Sometimes we are so presumptuous as to think we control it. But this reflects how little we know of spirit's ways. It leads to adverse outcomes that are an inexorable part of life. In this regard, we can see that most people do not realize that the cause of adverse consequences is themselves. Responsiveness is the quality of spirit that reflects back in life the thoughts, feelings, and images we place in it. We place a great deal of emphasis on action, as indeed we should, for we can see its consequences more clearly and more immediately. Yet, we seem to pay little attention to monitoring our thoughts, attitudes, and feelings, despite their importance in shaping our lives.

We can learn a great deal from sports, where there is an appreciation of monitoring what the athlete thinks. Successful athletes know that physical prowess is not the most important factor in victory. Success turns on the ability to control moods, feelings, and thoughts. We see this frequently in a contest when momentum has clearly swung to one side, which, in our terms, is the shift in thought and belief that manifests in the actions of players. Those with momentum on their side make Herculean efforts. Those who have lost it try hard, yet cannot do their best. Unless they change their thoughts and feelings, the game is over. A slip, a bobble, or great play is all it takes to change non-belief to belief. If these same athletes learn to better control thoughts, feelings, and beliefs, they will have the key to success.

This is precisely what great athletes have over others. They induce the desired state of consciousness when needed to maximize performance. This ability is not difficult to learn. It is not that we are born with it as much as we stumble into it. But it can be taught and will be presented in a later chapter.

If the true power of thought were understood, we would more vigorously control our exposure to gossip, negative persons, and distasteful media presentations. They would be avoided as we would any other unpleasantness. We are what we think, and our lives reflect the thoughts and beliefs we let predominate. "Reaping what you sow" is a popular expression that suggests our culture's partial understanding of spirit's responsive nature. This aphorism is usually associated with action, but action is preceded by thought. Hence, their importance must be realized too.

Every thought, word, and action, no matter how small, makes an impression on spirit. Spirit hears every expression from every life form. It can be likened to sand on a beach that receives an impression, depending on the force of the object placed on it. Fortunately, not every thought, word, or action makes a sufficient impression on spirit to result in an out-picturing, or manifestation, in the physical realm. This is the safety valve installed at this level of existence (the physical plane) to prevent us from wreaking havoc on ourselves while learning the principle of mental discipline. This aspect of the law of attitudes protects the person who shouts in anger, "I wish you were dead!" Within a matter of minutes, he may have completely different thoughts and feelings. The one who holds this idea longer, and attaches feeling and visualization to it, may cause it to manifest in physical form and harm others. However, the spiritual price for this is severe. Soul eventually learns through the balancing aspect of spirit, the Law of Cause and Effect (reaping what you sow), that such powers are not to be treated as toys.

The Nature of Prayer

Prayer is a means of calling upon the responsive nature of spirit. However, it often fails due to a misunderstanding of its nature. Most prayer proceeds from the assumption of a benevolent deity that responds to our entreaties or not, depending on our worthiness. This has some validity, at least in an oblique way. Yet, it misses the point that spirit's responsiveness to our prayers has nothing to do with morality, as we normally use the term, and everything to do with the Law of Spirit. This holds that spirit is responsive to any idea or thought placed in it. Once placed there, the duration and intensity of focus and belief determine the extent and speed of spirit's responsiveness. These subordinate laws will now be examined.

The Power of the Individual's Belief

"The faith of the mustard seed" is a metaphor describing the purity of belief in effecting change, even "moving mountains." The seed, as a living thing, is in spirit and communicates with it. It has total and complete belief, knowingness, and a certainty that it will become a mustard tree. A belief this total can achieve anything: walk on water, multiply loaves and fishes, and even create universes. Everything happens through the power of spirit, initiated by thought, exponentially expanded through belief, and brought into being by its inherent intelligence and formative power.

Associated Visualization or Feeling

"What you see is what you get" should more appropriately be "what you see and feel is what you get." Spirit responds not only to our thoughts, but also to our clear visual images with accompanying sensation and feeling. This combination makes the greatest impression and has an accelerating impact on the formative action of spirit. In many spiritual teachings, God's creation is performed in a dream, a metaphor with great relevance for us. It is an apt account of the creative method by which the creator and, in turn, soul works with spirit to create an effect in the outer world. In our lives, we must form an inner picture of the reality we wish to bring about, hold that image, and learn to dream it as well.

Duration of Focus

In the realm of spirit, where time is an illusion, we must consider the concept of duration, which can be thought of as a remembered sequence of present moments. It is the focus of attention that is all-important. As we hold our attention on a thought, the extended focus enhances the impact on spirit. This impact is in turn a measure of the flow of creativity, as spirit moves to fill the mold that our thoughts, inner pictures, and feelings create. The flow of spirit intensifies as more of our focused consciousness is brought into play. We feel excitement generated by the impending manifestation of our vision. As we feel and experience other aspects of this inner vision, spirit moves in corresponding measure to supply the life force necessary for final manifestation.

The Action Component

Action is an important aspect of the responsiveness of spirit. In its purest form, the action of visualization, which includes thought, vision, and feeling, is sufficient to produce any effect in the outer world. However, most people lack the faith of the mustard seed. Their thoughts are filled with doubt about the nature of spirit and whether it will work this time.

For most people, doubt enters the process, no matter how many times spirit has worked in the past. The greater the doubt, the more action is required. Action plays two roles. First, it enables spirit to have a greater and faster impact on elements of the physical world, for spirit can be slow, at least to human minds — look at the motion of glaciers. Second, by strengthening the individual's belief, action has a reinforcing and reciprocating effect. As we do more things and see more things happen, we are inclined to believe more. This enhances, speeds, and supports spirit as it works for us and through us.

The Reciprocal Nature of Spirit

Spirit not only responds to our thoughts, feelings, and actions, but also acts in a reciprocal manner. The more we trust and believe in its role in our lives, the more it responds to us and acts like a partner. During a busy day, with the demands of family and business, I sometimes forget my dear friend and ally. But when I remember, its presence is palpable, and I acknowledge it. In a world of change and impermanence, spirit is always there — steady, dependable, eternal. Spirit has never let me down. If you learn to trust it, it will never let you down either.

Trust is the measure of our relationship with spirit. The more we trust it, the more it responds to us. When we ignore it, and act as if it does not exist or is irrelevant in our lives, then it responds accordingly. Our lives lose the magic enjoyed by those filled with spirit and fully trusting in its wondrous capacity. The responsive nature of spirit has it behave exactly as we believe it will. It will become whatever we believe it to be.

Spirit's way is quiet and gentle, not loud and vituperative (though sometimes I wish it were!). We must become more silent in order to hear its message coming through our higher-self. That message comes in subtle nudges, flashes of insight, "good vibrations," waking dreams, and hundreds of other ways often unique to the person and her capacity to hear.

Spirit and You: Getting the Roles Straight

A goal is a finite picture, end point, or conclusion. Our job is to set the goal; spirit's job is to develop and guide the process. Any idea, vision, thought, or feeling that makes a sufficient impression on spirit becomes a goal or target to which its action is directed. This aspect of the Law of Spirit seems well applied, if not fully understood, in the action of our daily lives. We all know the importance of setting a goal. Countless books, tapes, and courses teach us how to do that.

Indeed, we have even learned to teach our machines how to do this. A car's Global Positioning Satellite system (GPS) is an example of how machines have been taught to emulate this spiritual principle. While showing our location at any time, its true capability is seen when we program a destination — a goal of sorts. The GPS system even provides options such as the fastest, shortest, or most scenic routes. Once locked in, it responds by showing and telling us each turn to take. When we miss a turn or stray from the route, the system recalculates the best route, from wherever we are. If we cancel our destination, ignore the directions, or change our destination, the GPS responds accordingly, and we continue in whatever direction we choose.

Spirit works in a similar way in our lives to achieve the goals we set. Once the destination has been programmed, the driver can sit back and relax. The driver can rely entirely upon the workings of the system to direct his course to the destination. In working with spirit, our actions should be the same. Instead, we all too often do not hear spirit, ignore it, fight it, or debate it. Ultimately, we reject the direction of our spiritual guidance system. Just as the GPS system contains a map of the city and gives us the desired route, so does our spiritual system have an overview of all circumstances, conditions, and options. Our inner guidance is far more capable of navigating the labyrinth of life than are we alone. It is our failure to hear or trust the guidance of spirit working with our higher self that explains why we do not achieve many of our goals.

Spirit responds to every thought, feeling, and action. When we fail to cooperate with it as a partner, the fault is our own. The process of navigating through life is, of course, far more complex than the task of the GPS system. Indeed, if we were to follow a simple city map without a GPS system, we could probably reach our destination. But life has no such map, and its complexity is greater than any road trip. All the more reason we need to understand our spiritual partner's ways, how to listen to it, follow its options, and make our way.

There is a spiritual axiom that goes, "As above, so below." This describes the source of all discovery, learning, and knowledge in the physical world. It is in this manner that we have obtained our knowledge about goal setting. We have applied this knowledge into the working principle of our machines. We must now put it to work in our lives. The close connection between humans in the physical dimension and spirit in others is little seen or understood. Yet it is the foundation of all life, progress, and spiritual development.

Impartiality of Spirit

Our notion of a benevolent, compassionate, and loving creator supports the idea that spirit is partial to certain types of people, ideas, or actions. This is where the mistaken and ethnocentric notion of a "chosen people" has arisen. The expression might make us look for a spin doctor in Antiquity. Spirit is impartial in responding to and manifesting the thoughts, words, or actions of anyone. This impartiality is an essential part of the nature of spirit. It fulfills the requirement of the prime directive that necessitates the exercise of free will by all souls. The exercise of free will calls for soul to learn from every decision and action by experiencing consequences. If spirit were partial to one set of decisions, one group of people, or one nation rather than another, it would exert an influence in a particular direction. This would be inconsistent with soul's need to experience all reality and to consciously choose a course of action leading to its expansion in consciousness.

Spirit is neutral and will manifest any idea, thought, or feeling placed in it, whether positive or negative, good or bad. But humankind's capacity to believe and control thought is not the same. Those who believe they are victims remain victims. Those who feel powerful and in control become and remain so. It has nothing to do with favoritism and certainly nothing to do with victimization. It only has to do with how the principles of spirit are understood and put into practice. Thus, the notion that spirit and things spiritual are about "good and evil" does not reflect an understanding of the impartial nature of spirit.

Spirit and Beauty

One day, while practicing a contemplation exercise, I had a vision of an amphitheater, much like the Roman Coliseum, with doors along the entire perimeter. There was a single word engraved on each door, such as "happiness," "joy," or "order." On the door I entered was written "beauty." As I entered the outer room, I could see into the amphitheater. It was filled with light and glorious music. I sensed the energy and love of spirit all around. All other doors entered into the same area and provided access to the magnificent light and music coming from the center.

I interpreted this dream to mean that each of the words on the doors represented states of consciousness. Once the seeker focuses on one of these states, she gains access to the heart of spirit itself. When she contemplates beauty, she is immediately confronted with the question, what is it? It is obviously not a single thing and cannot be defined in absolute terms. It varies depending on the state of consciousness of the person and in this regard truly is in the eyes of the beholder. But this is not the most important or most interesting question. Is there something transcendent in the nature of beauty that moves consciousness to a new or different level? The beauty of a flower opens our heart to the marvels of the creation. The beauty in the shape of a woman or the physique of a man evokes a somewhat different response. This also moves the energy of spirit within a person, but most often at a different level. Each of these forms of beauty evokes an internal response that taps into the heart of spirit at some level. Every creation carries with it a continuum of vibrations that represents the various ways it can be perceived. A particular perception vibrates at a certain level and strikes the viewer at that level. This accounts for differences in taste and different responses to the same expression of beauty. We are touching on the expression of spirit at different levels. But what are these levels? How can they be experienced? How can they be differentiated? Answers are considered in more depth in a later chapter. Here it is sufficient to say that spirit manifests its energy in different forms and at different levels, all of which can be evoked by a particular expression of beauty.

The creativity of an artist, of any genre, is a common way of tapping into and experiencing spirit. The outcome will be as different and as varied as there are individual expressions of creativity. But the level of spiritual connection from which creation emerges cannot foretell the nature or quality of the output. In other words, the final creative expression of beauty has nothing to do with the purity or level of the connection with spirit that the creator taps. Two people may see the same sunset and feel a deep spiritual connection with the sight. One painting may be seen as hideous, another as magnificent. Yet, who is to say which artist tapped spirit at a higher or more profound level?

Many people deny themselves the opportunity to experience a connection with spirit, because they are concerned with the quality of the painting, song, book, or dish they would prepare. Society has created a false standard that holds if we cannot perform a creative act that someone else might like, then we should not bother. By bowing to this standard, we lose the joy of creating for our own enjoyment and for the attendant connection with spirit. The reaction of others should not determine whether we use this form of expressing beauty or creativity or not. It is enough to do it because it makes us happy.

Intelligence (Creativity)

Spirit's intelligence, or creativity, allows it to know what you want and need before you do. As a partner in the experience of life, it is constantly directing situations and people to your path who appear at exactly the right time and place to meet your needs and satisfy your wants. This process occurs so naturally, that we usually do not recognize it. I recall a time when my company was in need of a capital infusion of several hundred thousand dollars. I had no idea where it might come from, because our bank was not willing to expand our line of credit. I contemplated the situation using all of the rational powers that I possessed, but to no avail. Whether it was from a dream or from an earlier realization, I do not recall, but I was certain that spirit would reveal some answer — it always did. I knew that spirit evolves solutions from conditions present in our lives. Answers are quite frequently right under our noses.

My family and I had recently bought a new house with several adjoining lots. We had not lived there very long, and our knowledge of property values stemmed only from our recent purchase. One day, I noticed a new house going up several lots from ours and inquired about the asking price. I was astounded to find out that the price was almost twice what we had paid only two years earlier — and the new house was smaller. I figured it was some mistake, because the estimate came from a worker at the site, a good fellow but no expert in property values. Out of curiosity, I contacted our real estate broker to ask if this was a mistake, and what were the current conditions in the marketplace. She said there was no mistake; property values had skyrocketed in the preceding two years. In fact, our extra lots had more than quadrupled in value and were worth several hundred thousand dollars more than our original purchase price! I was humbled and astounded. The solution was indeed right under my nose. I had been walking on it everyday, not realizing that spirit had already provided the solution long before I knew of the problem.

It would be easy to conclude that these developments had nothing to do with spirit or me. "Property values were just going up and you happened to be in the right place at the right time," some might argue. Maybe so, but I could have remained oblivious of the rising market conditions had I not had the inner impulse to ask the worker about the value of the nearby property. Then too, wouldn't it be presumptuous to assume that spirit would set these forces in motion to benefit me, even while blessing the whole? Maybe so, but when you see this situation present itself in your life over and over again, you realize there is a power working with you and for you. It blesses you, as it blesses all those similarly situated. Indeed, when I accepted this possibility as fact, I grew to expect spiritual intervention. My acceptance and expectance seemed to increase the frequency of similar occurrences. I could no longer dismiss them as mere coincidence.

But spirit's capacity is far greater than this. Spirit may be called the master planner, for it devises intricate plans in the most complex situations, which will ultimately help us accomplish our goals. Architectural designer, city planner, writer of constitutions, corporate merger expert, all these are small jobs to spirit. Responding to a dream or vision, it created planets, stars, the cosmos, the universes — all that we know, see, and cannot see. It is the workhorse of the universe, of ALL THAT IS, manifesting in different forms to satisfy the needs at various levels of existence.

Anyone who has ever been involved in a creative project can tell of the strange signals and impulses they have received as nudges, visions, dreams, or waking dreams. We are often blinded to the involvement of spirit by the insidious nature of ego, which constantly rears its head and takes credit for everything. Ego has its place, and an interesting one at that. For now, it is enough to become aware that we must look behind and beyond ego to discover the truth of spirit in our lives. Spirit never sleeps. It is always alert, always there, waiting to fulfill its next task.

Spirit is Order

Much like beauty, order is also in the eyes of the beholder. But whatever our perception of order, once the individual realizes it, a sense of harmony with spirit is achieved. As parents, my wife, Mary, and I deal with the continuing tragedy of disarray in our children's rooms. Venturing there is truly a walk on the wild side. Our children argue, "It looks perfectly fine." They are happy with it and are upset if items are organized. I could argue the practicality of our concept of order in that at least we could find their dirty clothes. With their sense of order, everything was mixed up, and often they couldn't find anything clean to wear. They still argued their concept of order was equal to ours, but our argument won the day. We were satisfied with this victory, but their argument lingered with me.

While in a park, I viewed a beautiful array of plants that landscapers had prepared for the public. As I walked to the edge of a planted area and into a wooded forest, I observed trees fallen at all angles and leaves scattered across the ground. In other words, the forest seemed like my children's room, and the landscaped area like my concept of order. As I looked further into nature's version of order, I observed that, in a way, everything was in perfect balance. Every fallen tree had stopped at a point where the downward force had been balanced by the upward force. Everything was in equilibrium. The same was true for every branch, every leaf, and every object I saw on the ground. Was this order? Was my vision of order superior to or simply different from the order that nature had created? After deeper reflection, it was quite clear to me that there were different forms of order.

First, there is man-made order. This is a combination of natural aspects of order combined with a more rigid and structured system that aligns itself with the illusion of a straight line. There is something about straight lines, squares, circles, and other "perfect" forms, which gives us a sense of comfort. Perhaps it is the simplicity of the design that creates a feeling that we have more control over things structured this way. This is the conventional concept of order. It is expressed in the objects we create, in the manner we organize our thoughts, and in other forms that embody color and form.

The second form might be called natural or spiritual order. This is what I observed in the forest. We see it in the order in the array of stars in the sky. In natural order, everything is different. Everything is unique. All things unfold in accordance with a higher set of laws, which are not always comprehended by human consciousness.

The third type of order might be called randomness or chaos. It may be strange to regard this as a form of order, yet it is. It was this form of order that my children, in a way, referred to. The order represented in chaos is unique to each agency creating it. In my company, I am often confronted with staff members who insist upon their own form of order. They argue that everything is in proper order, they know where everything is. They may be correct, but I hasten to remind them that others work in the company too. Everyone is required to pass the broken-leg test: can order be perceived and understood such that important items can be found if he is not at work?

While no form of order is spiritually superior to another, the world would not run very efficiently if there were not common acceptance of certain standards of order. Every facet of our lives is organized in this way. From highway and building design to language and information, there is a standard of order that defines society's accepted approach. When we align our consciousness with these standards, they form a definition of order within our own universe. When our actions and environment are aligned with this definition, we feel harmony and balance. This in turn establishes a link with spirit, which then flows more freely into our consciousness.

We experience this when we clean our car, keep it shiny and in good repair. The same alignment with spirit occurs when we straighten our desk or room. All of these situations align us with our internal sense of order, and that links us with spirit. Again, order can be found in man-made, natural, or random forms. Spirit will flow into and help manifest any form of order with which our consciousness has aligned. It will manifest all forms that in turn reflect what the individual perceives as inner and outer harmony.

As a seeker, I practiced an exercise that greatly assisted me in moving from one internal sense of order to another. When I started in business, the demands required me to align with the standards of order in that world — not the standard with which I was then aligned. Twice a day, I opened a box of toothpicks and threw them on the table. Slowly and methodically, I placed each toothpick back into the box. The visual image of moving from random order to structured order became impressed upon my mind.

As a result, my personal space was more conventionally neat and orderly, my desk was better organized, my logical processes were crisper, and other aspects of my life also reflected this order. As I embraced and felt attuned to it, I was careful not to fail to appreciate other forms of order. By shifting to other forms of order we tap creative, spontaneous, and innovative thinking, which random and chaotic patterns of order are capable of producing. In the end, it all comes down to choice. All aspects of universal order are available to us, and they all have validity — but our kids still had to clean up their rooms!

The Illusion of the Straight Line (The Law of Cycles)

Though all of our experiences are to the contrary, we often envision moving toward a goal without setbacks, delays, or disruptions. In fact, most people are busy trying to avoid responsibility for their setbacks, delays, mistakes, and difficulties. Many have become risk-averse. Setbacks are seen as failure or evidence of inability to control the forces in our life — a common mistake. While minimizing disruptions and setbacks certainly reflects an understanding of universal principles, their occurrence is part of the natural order. Yet the ideal of the straight line persists.

No significant achievement occurs without problems. The straight line is a creation of man. In nature, everything flows as an aspect of wave motion. This pattern can be seen in the simple shapes of objects in nature: from trees, clouds, and waves, to the most complex observations of astronomy. Translated into our lives, this means that nothing can move from goal to accomplishment without ups and downs. Furthermore, our ability to predict the precise movement of these ebbs and flows is at best minimal. All that we can say is that persistence in the movement toward the accomplishment of an objective, with adjustments made for events as they present themselves, leads inexorably to their realization.

The Source of Our Doubt and How to Trust Spirit

Maybe the doubt is not about spirit at all. Perhaps it is about whether we can count on ourselves to do our part. After all, we have blown it in the past. The old aphorism jingles in our ear: "Spirit cannot do for us what it can only do through us," and we are reminded of the importance of self-responsibility. Spirit needs us as a channel and as a distributing agent to bring into existence the things we are seeking. But can we trust spirit enough to get beyond these questions? Can we move from fear and doubt to faith, belief, knowingness, and certainty? In time, we will. It is a long journey on a hard road, but we can do it. This is the real key to life's journey. It is about the interaction of God-soul and spirit. Each of us, whether we realize it or not, is seeking to solve the great paradox. First, we must go through many tests, ask many questions, and find some answers. As the process unfolds, our confidence and willingness to trust spirit expands. It's much like our first contact with romance. At first, there is some reluctance — we don't want to get hurt. But in time, we let down our guard and open up to that person. This is the relationship we must have with spirit. It will be rocky at first, especially if we have always taken pride in being strong and self-reliant. Why should I trust this force that I cannot see? How do I know it even exists?

These questions have been the source of religious and philosophical speculation for centuries. I first encountered it in a college humanities class. We were discussing the rather heady topic of the "Teleological Suspension of the Ethical." The Danish religious philosopher, Soren Kierkegaard (1813-1855), put forth this idea in his seminal work *Fear and Trembling* (1846), in which he explores the suspension of moral law for the sake of a higher law. He raises this dilemma in the context of God commanding Abraham to kill his son. Abraham's devotion to God compels him to obey. Yet, to do so would be murder, a violation of the law and morals of his time. To commit this act, he would have to suspend his ethical standards for a higher belief.

As we encounter the power of spirit in our lives, we are continuously called upon to suspend our belief in our own capabilities and logic and surrender to a force we cannot see or directly know. We are faced with a similar dilemma, though probably one not as agonizing as Abraham's. Yet as we proceed in our relationship with spirit, we too are placed in situations that call for increasing levels of trust and belief. Sometimes our tests call for the suspension of societal principles for the sake of higher principles. In time, as we go through good and bad, we come to trust it more. We come to know its ways a little better. As we trust it, it comes to trusts us. The message of spirit and the way of surrender is, *Don't ask me how I am going to solve this problem for you, or what the exact result will be before it manifests, trust me,* and *Tell me what you want and believe.* But this is not easy, especially if we take pride in asking tough questions and being analytical. We have been to elementary school, high school, university, and beyond, read hundreds of books, and kept abreast of current events. Are we to put aside these skills?

The answer is, Yes! If we wish to know this universal force, we must learn *how* and *when* to turn off our analytic capability. Herein lies the key. The mind will never get us there. But how do we break down the hardness, the mental questioning, and the analytical tendencies of the critical faculty within the mind? How do we push it aside and allow ourselves to feel the flow of spirit? We have all felt it for short periods. We have all had glimpses of the promised land. We have all felt, if only for a moment, what trust in spirit means. But what is it like to really surrender to spirit and experience this for hours at a time, living in a state of joy, with no worries, no concern, all of the problems we drag around cut loose? The answer lies in just letting go and focusing our attention on trust and surrender.

That is why any religion steeped in an intellectual tradition can only take us so far. At the gate of heaven, the most learned person weeps at its doors, not understanding the coin that guarantees entry. The Catholic Church is a prime example of this. No religion has contributed more to the thinking of humankind about spiritual life. Treatise after treatise has been written about the most refined spiritual points. Such pursuits are useful at the beginning to quench our thirst for the divine. But after a point, it can take us no further.

How do we get to the point of trusting spirit so explicitly that we seek its guidance every moment of every day? This is where the great and profound "leap of faith" that leads to trust and surrender, comes into play. As we shall see, reaching this state involves controlling our thoughts, which, in turn, control our states of consciousness. In the end, trust and surrender are reached in the same manner by which we control all thoughts. The more we live in a state of trust and surrender, the more our problems solve themselves. Surprisingly, our intellectual and analytical capabilities actually expand by virtue of the partnership with spirit that develops. Indeed, the God-seeker develops an intimate partnership with spirit. He develops an absolute knowingness that it will provide for his every need. He comes to realize that this omnipresent force protects him, leads him in the correct path, meets his every need, and enlightens him through all of his experiences.

However, when we place our feet on the path to God, we know that we are going to be in for a struggle, because we have initiated a process of continuous change, which we generally fear and fight. The degree to which we struggle depends entirely on the degree to which we surrender and accept change. How many times must we butt our heads before a lesson is learned? If we don't like pain, then it's wise to accept change quickly and gracefully, with no judgment as to its nature, good or bad. For change is neither. It depends entirely on what we do with circumstances placed before us. If our attitude is to turn events to our advantage, then life can never defeat us. We will always listen to that still quiet voice inside pushing us ever forward toward our inevitable rendezvous with God.

Chapter 14 — The Spiritual Practice of Higher Consciousness

Towards a New Spiritual Paradigm

A paradigm is a model, a pattern, or an archetypal ideal of something in form, experience, or concept. In a spiritual context, it is a pattern of beliefs, images, and practices that form inner and outer thoughts, words, and actions. Almost by definition, a religious paradigm is limited, for it sets forth a standardized depiction of inner and outer experiences that conform to the framers' beliefs and accepted images.

But there are no absolutes within the unbounded scope of ALL THAT IS. Instead, there is infinite choice, for we are creative beings without limits. We are free to choose our beliefs, our paradigms. In turn, beliefs form our inner and outer spiritual constructs. That is why myths are so important to humankind. C. G. Jung and C. Kerenyi in *Essays on a Science of Mythology*[1] as well as Joseph Campbell in *The Power of Myth*[2] demonstrate the importance of myth in civilizations. Similarly, the ubiquitous nature of some myths (e.g., the flood, the child-god, the savior) suggests something transcendent at work. But what is conspicuously absent in these studies is the role myths play in structuring spiritual paradigms, which form the context for all inner experiences. Thus, life experiences, stories, beliefs, and myths are the substance from which dreams and inner experiences are made. As the mythology of a person differs, so do his inner experiences.

Graham's journal is a classic example of how myths shape inner experiences, even experiences of an astonishing variety. Paul Twitchell created his myths of the Eck Masters, temples, and inner experiences in 1965. Yet they became the inner and often the outer reality of trusting

Eckists. They visited temples and met masters of Paul's mythology. How can this be? Similarly, those believing in angels have inner experiences with angels. Children who believe in Santa Claus report dreams and inner experiences with the jolly one.

An interesting dialogue between Campbell and interviewer Bill Moyers touches on this:

> **Moyers:** How does one have a profound [inner] experience?
>
> **Campbell:** By having a profound sense of the mystery.
>
> **Moyers:** But if God is the god we have only imagined, how can we stand in awe of our own creation?
>
> **Campbell:** How can we be terrified of a dream? You have to break past your image of God to get through to the connoted illumination. The psychologist Jung has a relevant saying: "Religion is a defense against the experience of God."[3]

What Campbell is saying is that inner scenery and images of Jesus, the Buddha, Muhammad, the Living Eck Master, among others often block experiencing what is transcendent in the experience. Indeed, the scenery only provides a context in which spiritual awareness can be expanded. Thus, religion might more aptly be considered a barrier to experiencing God. Campbell continues his response:

> The mystery has been reduced to a set of concepts and ideas, and emphasizing these concepts and ideas can short-circuit the transcendent, connoted experience. An intense experience of mystery is what one has to regard as the ultimate religious experience.[4]

Campbell's perspective on the ultimate religious experience may be an accurate description of the nature of inner experience for those filled with the doctrines of heaven, hell, and god, in western paradigms. However, it is not an accurate description of the experience of the light and sound of God or the planes beyond form. Through Moyers's probing, Campbell goes on to articulate this point:

> **Moyers:** There are many Christians who believe that, to find out who Jesus is, you have to go past the Christian faith, past Christian doctrine, past the Christian Church.
>
> **Campbell:** You have to go past the imagined image of Jesus. Such an image of one's god becomes a final obstruction, one's ultimate barrier. You hold on to your own ideology, your own little manner of thinking, and when a larger experience of God approaches, an experience greater

than you are prepared to receive, you take flight from it by clinging to
the image in your mind. This is known as preserving your faith.[5]

Campbell is right of course. And herein lies the limitation of
mythology and religious doctrine in reaching transcendence. All religions have planted images and stories about the nature of the transcendent experience, or the master, or the savior, which block spiritual
growth and experience. But Moyers does not probe far enough. Even as
he implies the need for escape from the limitations of Christian doctrine, he holds on to Jesus as the end point in the search for God. He
seems unprepared or unwilling to seize on Campbell's broader point
and to let go of his paradigm.

Letting go is a frightening prospect. But how can a true God-seeker
be limited by an image, concept, or paradigm? How can any comfortable teaching or paradigm encompass the limitless scope of ALL
THAT IS? Truth as well as trust in spirit and in our higher self form the
only path to the ONE. Our responsibility is to create the goal; a spiritual
paradigm that is compatible with the universal nature of soul and spirit.
We see this principle of goal-setting at work in our lives everyday.
Indeed, it is the basis of the modern practice of project planning. While
we are able to anticipate the steps involved in a particular manifestation
on the physical plane, all planners and managers know that changes
occur that cannot be anticipated. We adjust to the changes and move
on, reaching our goal nonetheless. In many ways, this book is such a
planning document for achieving our highest spiritual goal. It is
detailed only as far as can now be described. But the process, always in
the control of spirit, will lead us to our ultimate spiritual goal because
that is the nature of spirit and the process. We will explore this principle
in considerable detail in Chapter 16. There, we shall look at the practical workings of spirit and how we can employ it to fulfill our dreams
and goals in life.

So, what is the process? It is that we set the forces of spirit in
motion by what we think and believe. When we hold an image or feeling in our minds, spirit, in concert with God-soul, leads us unerringly to
this goal. It will reach its object, no matter the deviations along the way.
Thus, we move in the direction of our beliefs, which form the substance
of our spiritual paradigm. Once locked in, spirit working with God-soul
leads us to know the ONE. It matters little that we do not have full com-

prehension of what the ONE is. It is sufficient that we know, sense, intuit, and believe in the ONE. This alone will lead us there.

A remarkable aspect of spiritual unfolding is that even though our higher-selves must use stories and myths to expand awareness, they will turn them into lessons for our liberation. We see this in Graham's journal. Even as he had experience after experience within the Eckankar paradigm, the fiction that underlay it was finally exposed and served as the pathway for his liberation.

Considering the thousand-year tradition of many religions, one is justified in asking: How can something so new as Higher Consciousness guide us to God-Realization? Having studied and participated in numerous paths and under many teachers, I have learned there are hundreds of different ways claiming to take us to this goal. Each path insists theirs is the one true way. I have observed two basic points in this search. First, thousands of years have elapsed since the founders of most religions (or those in whose names they were formed) had the defining God experiences on which those religions were based. Since that time, the transcendent truths that they tried to convey have been buried under mountains of ritual, debate, bureaucracy, hierarchy, and practices. The message that all enlightened beings come to this plane to convey is that each person is a spark of God. But in every religion, this message has been lost. To free an adherent from the clutter of this ritual and dogma could take lifetimes without much progress.

Second, in teachings like Hindu Yoga, Buddhism, and Sufism, the God-seeker is faced with an entirely new language and vocabulary, not to mention thousands of gods and innumerable inner planes with names unfamiliar to most. One is apt to conclude that the language of God is Sanskrit, and that if we don't use it to express spiritual concepts, we can't connect with the highest truth. Nothing could be further from the truth. The language of God is whatever you understand and with which you can communicate. The outer formality of language means nothing so long as inner sincerity, love, and a burning desire to follow truth and to know the God reality, is upper most in your thoughts and actions.

So, while a seeker can respect and learn from millennia of spiritual history, God is here and now. We need not search through dusty archives and study ancient rituals for the secrets to inner travel. God is not hiding from us. It is we who have covered our eyes from the light of God. No union of masters, pope, mahanta, or anyone else controls the experience of God. That is the stuff of control, egomania, and usurpation. This knowledge is not to be bargained or bartered for loyalty or coin. It is the gift of those who have traveled the road to God-Realization and returned to share their insights. There is much to learn and know about this mystery. One *does* need a teacher and the right information. But more than this is vanity, for who can place themselves above another without blaspheming?

This book presents the truth as I have come to understand it. There is no hidden agenda. The insights shared here can aid in brushing away the rubbish of ritual, doctrine, and dogma, a process which will allow the God-seeker to move on to the truth within. Once we experience the sublime realities of the inner Oneness of God and the unfathomable love there, we see the true path that lies within. Still, there is much to be learned. Hopefully, this book will help you on your journey to truth and enable you to tap the infinite knowledge within you. The teachers who carry this message, as part of the Great Work, will provide instruction and guidance. But they are not masters. Their role is to guide and teach, making way for the student to become the teacher.

The insights of the Higher Consciousness Movement, which embody the Great Work, draw from ancient traditions. Yet they cut through language, ritual, and excess baggage, leaving what is necessary for the inner experiences leading to God-Realization. I have experienced the sublime realities of light and sound and more in many levels of the inner worlds. Graham and many others with whom I have worked have also had these experiences. This was achieved through study, devotion, and the guidance of the higher self, using images cherished by that person.

Finally, we don't have to go to India, Tibet, or Minnesota to learn about God. It is a gift we already have; we simply have to open up and prepare ourselves for the transcendent experience of ITS reality. Let's look at the methods and principles by which we can open our gift and experience the inner realities of ALL THAT IS.

Soul Unbounded

The limitless nature of dreams and inner experiences is part of the limitless freedom bequeathed to every soul. Why is there such freedom? It is because soul learns, through proper discrimination, to make decisions that lead to expanded awareness and recognition of itself as God-soul. By making choices and experiencing their consequences, soul expands to an awareness of and partnership with ALL THAT IS.

As humans, we search for the purpose of life. We have traveled everywhere and experienced everything to learn who or what we are. In moments of reflection, we realize we have traveled nowhere and experienced only the offshoots of our minds and dreams. As souls, we are the builders of the heavens, the hells, the planes, and the inner worlds. They are constructs, just as the world around us is a construct of imagination, thought, knowingness, effort, and perseverance. As expounded earlier, the purpose of this is to teach soul its divinity and prepare it for the Great Work of spiritual liberation. The potential for reaching the goal of the God-seeker is omnipresent and ubiquitous. The goal we desire to reach is within us, here and now, yet it can be as far away as the peak of the highest mountain.

To grasp the here and now and understand how soul lives in it, we are placed within an earthly framework in which eternity is divided into segments, which we know as time. We see time as linear, but it is not. The illusion is fostered by events. Einstein and his contemporaries were close to expressing this spiritual principle in the language of science. Einstein had postulated gravity as equivalent to acceleration and as a geometrical phenomenon. Indeed, he saw gravity as a bending of time and space. David Bohm embraced this idea in his exploration of the holographic paradigm. The idea of linear time is created by a construct that separates "now" into segments that evidence "now's" passage. The sun rises every morning, and we call it another day. But what has changed except an event that divides duration and repeats itself? Even the aging of our physical bodies marked by a birthday and change of appearance is nothing more than a series of events that create the illusion of time. But at the transition called death, our true self emerges from the physical shell essentially the same as when we entered it, only wiser and more aware.

The circular movement of the hands of a clock is more than a metaphor for time. It is a symbol of eternity, for it moves endlessly in a circle, giving the illusion of the passage of time. But it has gone nowhere. The clock's hands have simply repeated a cycle. Understanding this provides another clue to the transcendence of now, for all that really changes is our awareness, our consciousness.

A final analogy might be helpful. The life of soul in eternity is like seeing a movie. The scenery, characters, and story change, but we remain the same. A projection of ourselves is involved in the drama of physical life, as in a movie, except in this production we are the character. In the drama of physical life, a part of us actually feels the blows and experiences the pain. Yet from the perspective of the observer, the coach, the guardian angel sitting in the chair, we have only changed our perspective, our perception of events, and have really moved nowhere. After countless movies, scene changes, and role switches, we are still sitting in the theater — soul living in the eternity of now. Through the experiences unfolding on the screen of life, we have definitely changed. We are more aware of our stillness and the illusory nature of the world swirling around us. The Biblical passage, "Be still and know that I am God" (Psalms 46:10) speaks of this stillness. In time, we grow tired of the illusion, for it is no longer needed. We are eager to live from our true nature as soul — pure conscious energy. We are now able to assist in the Great Work that is performed at higher levels of reality/illusion, ever aiding souls in their unfolding to truth.

Most religions and spiritual paradigms leave us with a story line that, like the Santa Claus myth, we eventually outgrow. When this happens, we often have feelings of betrayal and deception. This is because, like the illusion, we must believe and become engrossed in it for it to have maximum effect on our spiritual growth. Actually, this is an important psychological point for the God-seeker. For, as discussed, if she thought she had found something second best, how would she believe, how would she learn from the experience?

But we are always searching for a higher truth, something closer to the ultimate, something we will never have to abandon. We will never find it of course — the final step, that is. For there is always a "plus element" in spiritual expansion, something more to learn and experience.

But we can come closer. We can discover penultimate truth and it will serve us for the remainder of this lifetime and into eternity, for the Great Work does not end. This is the objective of the Higher Consciousness Movement. It will never have the final answer, but it will not create deceptions, fictions, myths, or personal deities. It will expand as consciousness expands, never lapsing into a fixed paradigm. But for now, the working paradigm that comes closest to the truth of all truths, which can be encompassed with the limited tool of mind is:

I AM,

GOD IS,

WE ARE ONE

Our journey to the heart of truth is the growth to full awareness of this tenet that underlies the journey to higher consciousness.

The Spiritual Practice of Higher Consciousness

The practice of higher consciousness embodies the highest ideals of our spiritual reality. It is not unlike the practices God-seekers have followed throughout history. Spiritual practices must be integrated into our lives to provide the guidance and support we need to deal with daily life and still lead us to the realization of ourselves as God-soul. Before laying out the spiritual practice of higher consciousness, perhaps it is important to define the spiritual goals so that we have a better idea of where we are going.

Soul-Actualization

In the preceding chapter, we described the properties of soul and the concept of God-soul. This is the aspect of ourselves with which we are least familiar. Most people identify with impulses, feelings, and energies emanating from their physical bodies. Within the human consciousness, there is little distinction between the ego (the "i") and God-soul (the "I"), which is the greater part of ourselves. This higher self directs our lives in ways, but we are quick to give credit to things other than our higher selves. This is our great mistake, for we relegate our self-conception to a position only slightly higher than the animal that our bodies represent. We even claim that our bodies have a soul, rather than that we as soul use a body in this dimension of reality. The difference is tremendous. It is the first step to understanding who we are as God-soul, but this is only intellectual recognition. The next step is to *live* from this state of consciousness.

Those great souls who walked the earth and came to this realization lived from this state of consciousness. They were able to say, "I am one with the creator." As soul, they recognized their oneness with ALL THAT IS and reflected this awareness in what they said and did. But civilization, from the most primitive to the most modern, could not comprehend their state of consciousness. They were declared gods, and religions were established in their names. This is how every religion and spiritual path has been created, and, for this very reason, each has missed the point. For the life of every great soul is a reflection of what we are destined to become. There is no other message, for this is the essence of the Great Work. If it were otherwise, they too would have missed the point and not reflected the high state of consciousness with which they were credited.

The capabilities of God-soul exhibited through the physical body, are remarkable indeed. Some have called them psychic powers manifested through the use of etheric energy or Sedi powers. Others simply regard them as the stuff of miracles. But these "powers" are merely reflections of the capabilities of God-soul manifested on the physical plane. Everyone has these abilities, but like any skill, they require recognition, belief, interest, and practice before they manifest in our life. Science is still trying to establish the reality of these powers with the limited instruments of the physical world. But progress is being made by pioneers who are asking tough questions and attempting to find scientifically-based answers.[6]

However, the source of these capabilities lies in regions undetectable by any known instrument. It is like measuring the amount of light or sound in a dream. These inner abilities include telepathy, remote viewing, psychokinesis, levitation, healing, bilocation, intuition, reading past and future events, and countless others we have already touched upon. They may frighten us or leave us with heightened skepticism, but they should be explored for this is the real "new frontier." It is key to answering the ageless imperative, "know thyself."

Many pretenders have claimed such powers and charmed thousands of unwary believers. Because of this legacy, many are skeptical of the existence of these capabilities. While skepticism is healthy, it is a barrier to manifesting these qualities in our own lives. Everything starts and ends with belief. Thought coupled with belief gives us the power to move mountains. The over development of the critical faculty in the West is the main reason that the East is ahead of it in spiritual understanding. Yet the East's strength has also resulted in a host of fraudulent masters exploiting the gullible. With the underdevelopment of the critical faculty, most cannot distinguish between a faker and a fakir.

While in many ways East has met West, the need for greater spiritual interaction between the two is important. The same is true of Africa and the West. Because spirituality is intrinsic to their belief systems, Africans are more open to understanding inner worlds and inner spiritual experiences. They also exhibit an extraordinary capacity for love, as most western visitors attest. But that is a story for another time.

As we understand more about our spiritual nature, we learn that it is always directing, protecting, providing for, and teaching us. We have to surrender to it and believe in it completely in order to experience life as it is intended. When we do this, we lose the fear that accompanies a focus on the "i." We live from the perspective of God-soul, which is who and what we really are.

God-Realization

We have seen how scientific discovery and spirituality are finally coming together. Indeed, they are the same search, only from different perspectives. The scientist asks "how?" and develops theories to unravel and control the mystery. The God-seeker asks "why?" and seeks to know the reason behind the mystery — a question that leads to knowledge of the ONE. The why is to teach us that we are IT of itself. The "how" takes us through endless combinations and permutations of a creative idea. This is the by-product of learning how a mechanism works and learning to control it. What we call reality and measure, probe, and discover is a complex creation of our making. Its purpose is to teach us about our creative capabilities so that we can know what we are and, in time, take our place in the Great Work. Until then, we wander in complexity, complimenting ourselves on our inventions and discoveries.

Of course, we must go to work, raise our children, fight our wars, and continue our search for that elusive something that brings us inner joy, peace, and happiness. As we live our lives, practicing the spiritual principles of higher consciousness, we can know that we have correctly set our course and that *this time* it will survive the test of truth.

The Higher Consciousness Contemplations of Life

Many years ago, while an active member of Eckankar, I developed a contemplation that embodied the essence of the teaching. It was widely reprinted and used as a daily confirmation of key beliefs by Eckists around the world. It filled a critical need to provide a summary of core beliefs. Not unlike a prayer or inspirational verse, the contemplation recalled an aspect of the particular spiritual paradigm whenever needed. The demands of life require constant recall and recitation of core beliefs to keep us on track.

Since that time, my understanding of the universal laws has enlarged to embrace a higher level of awareness. I have rewritten this contemplation in two forms, each containing the essence of the spiritual paradigm of higher consciousness. It is meant to guide the God-seeker in their outer and inner life to achieve fulfillment in both. The longer version is more poetic for those who can more easily put this format to memory. The shorter version covers most of the same concepts and may be preferred by others.

There are also two affirmations that can be recited before contemplation or used at any time. The first speaks to the preeminent truth taught in Higher Consciousness. It is the center of our reality. However, it is difficult for human consciousness to comprehend this simplicity and function from its center. It is the nature of human existence that we must go everywhere and experience everything before returning to this reality. By centering our attention here, we are guided on a direct path to ALL THAT IS by the inexorable action of spirit. The second affirmation confirms the same reality but speaks also of the nature of our union with the ONE. It too is a reminder of our central truth. When attention is similarly centered here, it clears away distractions and illusions, bringing us back to the heart of our being.

Whichever version of the contemplation or affirmation you choose, it is important to put them to memory or at least carry them with you. In this manner, the power behind the words and concepts is available at all times to inspire, direct, and restructure your inner and outer spiritual paradigm.

THE HIGHER CONSCIOUSNESS
CONTEMPLATION OF LIFE (I)

I am one with ALL THAT IS.
I surrender to my higher self,
God-soul that is me.
In the eternity of now,
I rise above time and space
Into infinite spirit.

In this creative center
Of pure consciousness,
Where all things exist,
I accept into my life
That which I choose
For my wellbeing and spiritual unfoldment.

I think neither good nor bad
Of events in my life,
For they are without form.
Neither good nor bad,
Either good or bad,
My choice
Makes it my own.

Outcomes flow from
What I think, and
What I deem is true.
For how I act,
And what I accept,
Steers the course
That will ensue.

I focus on my higher self,
God-soul that is free.
A spark of GOD, part of the whole
That watches over me.
It meets my needs,
And steers my course,
On my journey home, to THEE.

I center
On my love for GOD,
And GOD's boundless love for me,
A love that provides, protects
And guides my way,
To know the ONE
In me.

ALL THAT IS, is
All there is.
And I as part of THEE,
Claim freedom
Joy, success
As mine,
GOD's endless gift to me.

THE HIGHER CONSCIOUSNESS
CONTEMPLATION OF LIFE (II)

I am one with ALL THAT IS.
I surrender to my higher self
God-soul that is me.
In the eternity of **now**,
I rise above all problems, tensions,
And burdens of this day,
Into pure consciousness, into Spirit.
I keep my thoughts ever on my goals
Of Soul-actualization and God-Realization
For I know that Spirit is ever working
Towards their fulfillment.
I think neither good nor bad
Of events in my life.
I know that they are neutral
And become what I make of them.
I do my part, relax and trust in Spirit.
I surrender to its loving care and
Its perfect plan of unfoldment.
I know that this day, I must live a life of love
A life dedicated to ALL THAT IS.
I accept this perfect day in my life,
As wonders follow wonders,
And the gifts of spirit never cease.

HIGHER CONSCIOUSNESS
AFFIRMATION (I)

I AM
GOD IS
WE ARE ONE

HIGHER CONSCIOUSNESS
AFFIRMATION (II)

DIVINE ONE
I AM NOW WITH THEE.
FOR THOU ART ME,
AND I AM THEE
BOUND BY LOVE AS ONE.

The spiritual and philosophical foundation for these contemplations and affirmations has already been presented, but a brief discussion on the spiritual power behind them is in order. When I was a boy, attending church with my grandfather, I was always struck by how the congregation recited prayers together and issued rejoinders to various incantations. There was a great deal of pride attached to knowing what to say on cue, but it struck me as robotic. The practice is largely ineffectual because it does not focus attention, a requirement for unlocking the power inherent in the words. As we will see, such a focus coupled with emotion is necessary to tap the power of words.

The spoken or written word is only a symbol of the energy, power, and state of consciousness that lie behind it. It is a key that opens our inner awareness to a vast panorama of thoughts, feelings, and spiritual force. While we know the power of a harsh or kind word, we often gloss over the power of language in ordinary conversation. This power can be used, knowingly, to affect our state of consciousness at any time.

We tap this power most effectively with focused repetition of sacred words, a practice long known in most religions. The rosary, for example, is a religious exercise in which prayers are recited and counted on a string of beads or a knotted cord. Similar practices are found in other Christian faiths, Hinduism, Buddhism, and Islam. A similar practice is the *japa*, a Yoga practice involving the repetition of a mantra, verse, or name of a spiritual being. All of these practices are based on the idea that words, even letters of words, are energy, and their use — in thought or words — releases power that can be experienced. Every word is therefore connected with a thought form, a state of consciousness composed of feelings that have a primordial connection to our being. We often use them carelessly and, even more so, allow words, images, and thought forms to pass through our consciousness, oblivious of their impact. This is where the proactive control of images, words, and thoughts play an important role in the life of a God-seeker.

Just as the rosary reinforces an inner spiritual paradigm, other practices can replace a spiritual paradigm. The *Contemplations of Life* can do this. When compared to any spiritual teaching that employs repetition, these contemplations are quite different. Rather than focusing on a master, guru, or savior, which, intended or not, relegates the individual to an inferior position, it emphasizes our connection as soul with the infinite, with ALL THAT IS. This enables the individual to accept the power, freedom, and responsibility that accompanies spiritual growth. The journey to the heart of truth is not a group tour. Each person is his own path to GOD.

Read this section and use the contemplations and affirmation frequently. The affirmations and techniques presented have been carefully refined over more than thirty years of study. They reflect the practices of spiritual pioneers whose wisdom echoes from centuries removed. They are the insights of a God-seeker who has lived them and can affirm that they work, but you must make them work. The magic is always in consciousness, not simply in the words. As we have seen, words as sound carry vibrations that affect our consciousness and bodies at all levels. But the effect of a word or vibration alone is minor compared to its power when combined with consciousness. Thus, words and their vibrations carry energy, but we trigger, direct, and enhance their effect by the focused attention of soul.

Using the Affirmations and Contemplations

Throughout the day, I practice reciting the whole or parts of these contemplations as a means of controlling my thought flow. The affirmations are also repeated continuously instead of idle and undisciplined thoughts that can create havoc in my life. As we will see further in the next chapters, we create our inner and outer reality by our thoughts and beliefs every moment of our lives. We can take control of our thought patterns and create what we want, rather than accept what we are stuck with by our failure to exercise mental discipline. The principle of proactive thought selection coupled with focus is the key to unlocking the power.

When I started this practice, before I put them to memory, I found it helpful to copy or print the contemplations on a card and use them throughout the day — I still do. For example, I am able to counteract negative and destructive thoughts and feelings by inwardly reciting these lines:

> *I center on my love for GOD, And GOD's boundless love for me.*

This always fills me with inner joy, and my loneliness immediately disappears. When worried about some problem, I often focus on:

> *I think neither good nor bad of events as they unfold in my life.... I do my part, relax, and trust in spirit. I surrender to Its loving care and perfect plan of unfoldment.*

When I recite these lines a few times, slowly focusing on each idea and the feelings they evoke, my state of consciousness is transformed from worry to confidence. I am reconnected with my higher self and spirit. Consequently, it affects how goals and desires out-picture in my life. As you work with these contemplations and unlock the energy that they evoke, you will discover their power. This routine will keep you on track, living moment by moment with the joy of a spiritual being capable of positive experiences, no matter the situation.

You might tire of a particular line or word, so change as frequently as you need to, and select just the word or passage appropriate for the moment. A quick read-through of the entire short or long form contemplation will undoubtedly lead you to settle on the perfect idea or word for that moment.

Practice this often. Use the affirmations as a declaration before meals, before driving, or at anytime you feel disconnected from the source of your being. This is not hard to spot. If you are unhappy, you are disconnected. If you are worried, you are disconnected. But if you feel love and trust in spirit and your higher self, then you are connected. You are living as you were intended to live: as a spiritual being occupying a physical body. It requires discipline and a willingness to make this practice part of your life. I *know* this will make a major difference in your outer and inner existence. It has transformed my life and that of many others with whom I have shared these insights.

In the end, we cannot escape responsibility for our lives. We are creators whether we like it or not, whether we believe it or not. Ignorance and failure to consciously practice discipline of thought, word, and action provides no escape from their consequences. Because we are responsible, we might as well choose what we want. So try it, you will only gain happiness and success — quite a payoff for something that only requires a little effort and discipline!

Establishing Inner Communication — How I met *Me*

More than twenty years ago, I became aware of an inner something that was part of me, if not entirely me. I marveled at how it reminded me each morning of things I had forgotten. This inner guidance was with me long before I came to Eckankar, even though Eckankar tried to persuade me that its Mahanta was doing all this for me. This never sat well. Every religion that teaches followers to credit a savior or master usurps the power of God-soul. My grandfather, the Episcopal priest, always encouraged me to give thanks to the Jesus. Somehow, I was always left holding the bag when it came to the bad stuff. This never sat well either.

When I came to Eckankar, I had a problem with the master concept. It didn't feel right. I put aside the conflict by focusing on the power of spirit. After witnessing one of Eckankar's tumultuous successions, I felt vindicated. And with the results of my research for this book, it was clear that my higher self had protected me from the grave mistake of looking to another person as the symbol of the God-principle in my life. Besides, the inner direction I had received, long before coming to Eckankar, was the same "still small voice." It had not changed.

I realized I should establish inner communication with this something, rather than place my trust in a person or image whatever his title or appearance. I had to distinguish between my outer-self and this inner something. I needed a symbol, an identity, for this part of me. My earthly name was too closely identified with my outer life and personality. It evoked no identification with my higher self, which remained a stranger without a name.

Selecting a new name was like new parents naming a newborn. Unlike the parents search, mine took almost three years. At times, I thought it was stupid: Who was I to take on another name? Only masters had inner names, I thought. But the idea continued to intrigue me; it continued to make sense. I was always carrying on an inner dialogue, like an implacable tennis player chastising himself over his obdurate body. Anyway, "we" didn't always agree. In fact, we disagreed most of the time, at least at first. The pleasure side, represented by the demands of my body, usually won out. I would park myself in front of the TV or indulge in a special delicacy. One half of me was happy, while the other half was disappointed. There was always a war raging.

The physical side was clever to say the least, though its agenda was quite simple. It wanted pleasure and sought, at all cost, to avoid pain or anything that came close to it. Of course this simple formula was also the key to its management — a finding that Pavlov had amply demonstrated. I began to study its ways and how it would take over the apparatus of the mind. My inner self was always gentle, never screaming its wants, only suggesting, always gently. But my body was loud and demanding. It would flash pictures and feelings on the screen of my mind that would takeover whatever I was thinking or doing. If it wanted pizza, it *demanded* pizza.

Finally, I settled on a name for my inner self and held a small ceremony at which I introduced me to *me*. The inner name I received was TANJI. It was a strange meeting, but it held great personal significance. In fact, I found that using TANJI as a mantra worked quite well in moving me beyond the body consciousness. I had the feeling that someone was indeed "watching my back." I felt more at ease with surrender, which is an essential part of the unfolding to higher consciousness. I found it comforting to know that in all situations this higher self (I), was far more capable than my little self, ego (i), that is, the personality identified with my legal name.

In time, I was more successful in resolving disputes between my competing impulses. Through regular inner dialogue, peace broke out. It was clear that my physical self was not equipped to lead — and "it" knew it. It went along with the inner direction as long as it wasn't too harsh. Clearly, there were at least two different parts of me that had to be reconciled. This was essential if I was ever to realize what I came into this life to accomplish — though that was not yet clear. In due course, I developed a deeper understanding of this complex vehicle I had been given for this incarnation.

During my earliest years in Eckankar, when I first began speaking before audiences, I would write outlines for the talks. At that time, I didn't know about the higher self and felt the pangs of anxiety that most new speakers experience. I felt nervous and tense, depending on my notes — a characteristic of the little self. In time, I stopped preparing outwardly at all. I had read and reread the essential books. Certainly, some wisdom had seeped through during this lifetime. It was in there somewhere, I simply had to learn how to get at it — or was it letting the wisdom get to me? Besides, wasn't I suppose to be omniscient as soul? Why not let it do the work? These were the early hints that I could align myself with a higher force and rise above the trepidation associated with speaking.

I allowed the topic to move through my consciousness. I developed a feeling about what I would say and an inner picture of the result or feeling I wanted to have after a talk. When time for the presentation arrived, I often walked onto the stage completely blank! It was quite thrilling, much as I imagine jumping out of an airplane would be. I enjoyed the feeling because it was truly living on the razor's edge. It required complete trust and surrender. I knew that the moment I began to speak, this higher self, now known to me by name, would take over. I simply had to learn to let go and get the "i" out of the way.

The Physical and the Inner Bodies

I learned through study and inner experiences that I had several distinct bodies, which pertained to the inner worlds I had explored. It should be pointed out before describing these bodies, that the esoteric student confronts a welter of confusion, countless terminologies, and disputes at every turn. This is not surprising, because we each perceive our experiences in different ways, and construct and decorate our inner landscape as we grow. Those who wish a simple answer to the composition and structure of the inner worlds and our inner bodies will not find one. But don't be discouraged. There is sufficient agreement between various inner explorers and paths that we can still construct a useful road map.

The theosophical writings of Blavatsky,[7] Steiner,[8] Besant,[9] Leadbeater,[10] and the cosmology of Radhasoami, can teach us much, but they can also sidetrack us. Here, I provide an amalgam of these perspectives and what I have learned from both inner and outer exploration. It is not definitive, nor can it ever be. It is a useful road map, the details of which you must fill in as you explore on your own. In the future, a more expanded version of this cosmology will be presented, but this will suffice for now. It should also be noted that Paul Twitchell used some of these sources, especially theosophy and Radhasoami for structuring his own cosmology as well as other arcane information contained in the *Shariyat-Ki-Sugmad* — most notably his writings on the *yugas*,[11] the root races,[12] and the ancient civilizations.

The Physical Body

The physical plane and its corresponding body are well known. We must recognize them for what they are: an instrument for functioning in this dimension of reality. The physical body has an energizing aspect associated with the aura and centers of energy transformation commonly called *chankras*. They aid in transmuting spiritual energy into a form that sustains the human body.

The Etheric Body

The theosophist's description of this body is more accurate, in my view, than other teachings that attribute this function to the astral or emotional body. Theosophy considers it the link between the physical body and the inner dimensions containing an equivalent for all functions and parts exhibited by the physical machine. This etheric form also connects the physical to the higher bodies in an unbroken continuum from the physical body to soul itself. We often think of these bodies as distinct, but they merge into one another, like the colors of a rainbow. Its parallel functions are so completely replicated in the physical body that science has been able to formulate perfectly workable hypotheses for its operation without reference to this component. Only acupuncture and other eastern medical disciplines, which emphasize energy flows as a significant cause of illness, have paid meaningful attention to this unseen aspect of our physical bodies. The contributions of Barbara Brennan[13] and Professor William Tiller[14] are notable in their attempts to understand, measure or work with the effects of this energy on our physical bodies.

Emotional Body

Next is the emotional body, a separate but integrated part of each of us. It coincides with what is commonly termed the astral plane, the dimension where most of our dream experiences take place, and where we go at the transition called death. This "other" body is most commonly called the astral body but by many other names in various religions.[15] Most commonly referred to as a "ghost" — a misnomer — it is simply another instrument used by soul in this dimension of the inner worlds. We all have one and use it all of the time. However, we can see it when soul exits the physical shell. It has a higher vibratory rate than the physical body, which is why (like most gases) we cannot normally see it.

The astral body is quite different from our physical body. When the physical is dominant, as during eating or sex, the sensations and feelings are distinctly recognizable. When the emotional body is dominant, the feeling is quite different. We experience fear, anger, sadness, hurt, joy, happiness, love, and ecstasy, which overwhelm other feelings and impulses. If you have ever felt the pain of breaking up with someone, then you remember that bodily impulses didn't matter. Forces of the emotional body supplanted them. Similarly, anger can certainly spoil sexual urges of the physical body. Therefore, the emotional body can displace the impulses of the physical when attention is directed there. It can even overcome the instinct for physical survival, as when depression brings suicidal thoughts. People whose personalities reflect a strong emotional bent are most influenced by this body.

The Mental Body

The mental body predominates in those who spend most of their time in thought. Each of us is quite different when either of these bodies controls the actions of the physical shell through the control center in the mind. A famous person "loses it" in public and shocks his audience. What has happened? The person has allowed the emotional body in tandem with the physical body to predominate. His higher self was not in control.

Each inner body is progressively higher in vibration and state of consciousness. Beyond the mind, there is the level of intuition associated in some teachings with the intuitive body, considered a higher aspect of the mental body. This is a higher faculty, even though it is not held in such regard by a mind-oriented culture.

The Soul and the Causal Body

Beyond the level of mind and intuition, there is soul itself, which reflects omniscience, omnipresence, and omnipotence — the properties of ALL THAT IS. When we function from this level, the more appropriate term to describe ourselves is God-soul, for then soul has the capacity to reflect ITS characteristics. The full array of bodies encircles — but is coterminous with — soul and permits it to function in the lower worlds. There is one other body, variously portrayed in descriptions of the inner vehicles of soul. This is the causal body. In some cosmological systems it is thought of as the third body in succession of finer vibration. In others, it is considered an aspect of soul as distinct from a separate body having a corresponding plane. In either system, it is thought to maintain the record of all experiences, on all planes, in all lifetimes. This aspect of soul is essential because it is from this repository of experience that we draw guidance for everyday life. It is the only aspect that continues with soul from incarnation to incarnation. Thus, the terminology "aspect" — associated as a fine garment — is used to describe its connection to soul when it is thought of as other than a distinct body. Whether regarded as soul itself, an aspect of soul, or simply another body used by soul, its function is the same. It is dropped only when soul ventures into higher regions or levels of awareness where the need for bodies of lower vibration is no longer present.

When soul reincarnates into a physical body, all other inner bodies are discarded, just as the physical shell is discarded at death. In time, all discarded inner bodies dissipate and return to the substance of the plane on which they functioned. When soul reincarnates into a new physical body, it develops new inner bodies to accompany it in its inner and outer life experiences. But the causal aspect, functioning as the data-bank linking lifetimes, accompanies soul into each incarnation.

Expanding the paradigm of who we are is essential to spiritual growth. A paradigm based only on the physical body offers little chance for soul awareness, much less soul-actualization. However, when we expand our paradigm, we understand ourselves better. More importantly, we can exercise control and discipline over a physical machine that will totally dominate our lives unless placed in its proper position vis-à-vis soul.

Meditation and Contemplation

We have already touched on the importance of meditation and contemplation. Some teachings maintain a difference. Meditation is often regarded as a passive technique, while contemplation is thought of as more active. *Webster's* defines these terms as follows:

> **Meditation:** [T]he act of meditating: steady or close consecutive reflection: continued application of the mind . . . to keep the mind in a state of *contemplation*: dwell in thought: engage in studious reflection.

> **Contemplation:** a: *meditation* on spiritual things as a form of private devotion. b: a state of mystical awareness of God's being or presence: an ecstatic perception of God: a state of rapture . . . in which the soul is freed from its senses and organs and lost in pure *contemplation*. . . .

Obviously, these definitions are interrelated if not interchangeable. Both involve withdrawing attention from the physical shell to the ecstatic states or regions beyond the physical dimension. In practice, both techniques are essentially the same. Both contain an active and passive component. In the first stage, the practitioner remains passive, surrendering to an inner force or object of devotion. In the second stage, the practitioner shifts her awareness to an inner plane in full consciousness, and then decides, requests, or surrenders to whatever experience is next. If the practitioner goes no further than the first stage, conscious awareness is often not maintained; the individual returns with a feeling but no specific recollection of an inner experience. She has transcended the physical, though not much more. This describes Transcendental Meditation (TM), which, though beneficial, does not approach the level of experience achieved once we have learned to remain conscious and actively participate in the experience.

My first encounter with meditation was with TM, and it was beneficial. However, what I learned and practiced had nothing to do with the reverence I was asked to show to the picture of a bearded guru (Maharishi Mahesh Yogi), a gift of flowers, and a mantra that only they, supposedly, could give me. I was later to learn and eventually teach more effective methods of meditation/contemplation. They had nothing to do with the rituals of TM, the main purposes of which, aside from sharing a valuable insight into inner experiences, was recruitment and fundraising.

Active participation in meditation, contemplation or what some call spiritual exercises[16] requires surrendering the type and place of experience to our higher self, an inner force, or inner guide. However, it still requires an active choice — the proactive part of the process. The actual practice of meditation/contemplation is quite simple and requires no costly course or purchase of a mantra. I have practiced and taught its techniques for more than thirty years.

At times, I have been rewarded with brilliant transcendent experiences in worlds beyond description: oceans and beings of light coupled with the most glorious sounds imaginable. I have met beings from other dimensions of reality that talked to me, taught me, and otherwise interacted with the same clarity and realism I experience in waking life. If one was real, the other was as well — there was no difference. On the inner planes, we use a body that corresponds to the material substance of that plane. Hence, when we touch things, they feel as they do on the physical plane. Smell, color, and other sensations are considerably enhanced, especially on the astral plane. As we move higher, we seem to see and experience less, as form diminishes in importance. The experience of pure love and pure energy is more descriptive of the encounter, though awareness is not diminished.

At other times, nothing happens. I sit for my thirty minutes to one hour and arise refreshed, nonetheless having had a transcendent experience. The quality of my inner experience is related to the degree of my involvement in business or another outside activity. If I am engrossed in these pursuits and focus less on things spiritual, my inner experiences, both dream and meditation, reduce in intensity and frequency. This is not a necessary result, but if we allow problems or issues to stay with us during the evening and morning period, they will displace and drain the spiritual energy needed to transcend the physical. However, the moment I read something uplifting and allow my imagination and excitement to focus on inner experiences, I am transformed, and the inner experiences flow again. The number of techniques for meditating or performing these spiritual exercises runs in the hundreds, if not thousands. It is important, however, not to be a shopper, always looking for something bigger or better. Find those that work for you, but remember that what works may change over time. When this happens, you will know, because your higher self will direct you to new experiences and a new approach to continuing your inner journey. I will outline several basic techniques that will work if you are patient and persistent. First, let's look at the mantra.

The Mantra

The word mantra is composed of two Sanskrit words: *man* meaning mind or thinking, and *tra* meaning to release or free. Thus, by singing or chanting a mantra, we free the mind from the dross of material life and transcend the outer world and the cycle of birth and death. There are many who argue that the mantra is crucial and that there are certain sounds that are the basis of all other sounds. Let's look where human sounds come from.

The letters and words of language evolved from the grunts and noises of our prehistoric forbears. Within each primitive group, certain grunts and sounds came to mean certain things. As groups consolidated into tribes and eventually nations, the predominant group imposed its set of sounds on others. From grunts and noises, modern language grew to express virtually every concept and thought the human mind can conceive.

Eastern civilizations have developed a deeper and more profound understanding of higher consciousness concepts and practices than have western ones. Western societies are more concerned with the physical than the spiritual. The "spiritual" principles by which the West lives are articulated in the Ten Commandments, which deal with practical matters of physical existence. On the other hand, the Upanishads and the Vedas deal with contacting the infinite and realizing God potential. No wonder the language of the search for God is primarily eastern. To western ears, the sounds are strange, but when we remember they are noises that have come to represent thoughts and words, we demystify them. It is not the word, the letter, or the noise that is the quintessence of the mantra. Acceptance of what the sound means is equally important. Together, individual acceptance, the vibratory impact on the physical body, and the relaxing influence that repetition has on the mind, explain the full extent of the mantra's effect on us.

The Nature of the Mantra as Sound

When considering the mystique of the mantra, too much emphasis has been placed on the sound or word itself and too little on the inner process: the effect from focusing our attention on that sound. The HU as the source of all sounds is a concept that was initially articulated by Hazrat Inayat Khan in *The Mysticism of Sound*. This book has unfortunately taken on the quality of a sacred text, which it is not, but nonetheless has much to recommend it. In the end, it reflects the bias and single-mindedness of an explorer of the inner regions who felt his experience was the final word in spiritual growth. This "my mantra is the pinnacle of all sounds" view might be intrinsic to inner experience itself. If we did not believe that our experience was the ultimate, then our belief would be diminished. Once a great master has uttered what appears to be truth, others pick it up and repeat it. In time, it becomes locked in outer reality as Law, and is never questioned.

The proposition that the sound HU or AUM (OM) is the source of all sounds is absurd on its face because the advocates for each claim a position of preeminence that only one could hold. Each sound has a particular vibration and puts forth a particular sound wave pattern. Each sound emits a unique vibration, or frequency. In the physical realm, science has defined the physical characteristics of sound, how it is produced, and how it is perceived. Remembering that science represents the discovered laws by which the infinite works in a particular dimension of reality (in this case, the physical), the claims of transcendence for the HU or AUM/OM have dealt primarily with their physical manifestations. Thus, both the HU and the AUM/OM have been described as the sound behind all sounds and the Word made flesh. Aside from the competing boasts of both mantras, there are common-sense problems with either assertion. To suggest that a particular sound with a distinct frequency and wavelength contains all other frequencies and wavelengths in the universe is to postulate a principle that does not stand the test of common sense, much less that of science. Even if true, who is to say that *every* sound does not also contain all other sounds of the universe?

Sound, science tells us, is produced through vibration. Whether through vocal cords or a reed in a wind instrument, it is all a function of vibration. The movement of the resulting vibration to our ears is perceived as sound. Sound is defined by four measures: frequency (pitch), wavelength, intensity (loudness), and quality (timbre). Each aspect helps us to understand the nature of the HU and the AUM/OM, and how they are *not* unlike other sounds or mantras.

One of the elements that helps us to understand sound is frequency, which is the pitch or note, commonly measured by a unit called a *hertz*. The more an object vibrates (e.g., our vocal cords), the greater the frequency, or pitch. Thus, whether we are chanting the HU the AUM/OM or some other mantra, the frequency of the sound is a far more important measure of content than the choice of guttural utterance. Different pitches have a distinctly different impact on the physical and the inner bodies. The deep sound and bitonality of Tibetan monks illustrate a choice of one frequency (or set) over another. This is also illustrated in the use of various instruments to aid in experiencing inner sounds. The use by the Sufis and others of the double flute, bells and gongs, horns, conch shells, and other devices are all designed to carry the individual into the inner planes. Today, these traditional methods are being supplanted by the use of binaural brain entrainment recordings, which move the vibration of the brainwave patterns to levels that approximate those achieved in deep states of meditation. This is a study in itself, but suffice it to say, research on the impact of different frequencies on our outer and inner bodies is well worth the time. It can greatly enhance our potential to experience inner dimensions of reality.

Another quality of a mantra, related to frequency, is wavelength. Just as frequency is the number of waves that pass a given point per minute, the wavelength is the distance between any point on one of the waves and a corresponding point on the next wave. Thus, as the pitch/frequency gets higher, the number of waves passing a point increases, and the distance between each wave is shorter. As the note gets lower, the inverse is true.

In spite of our scientific advances, we perceive an infinitesimally small range of the sound all about us. This point can be easily illustrated if we consider the sounds we hear during the dream state or during an inner experience. I have heard great symphonic scores, unrecognizable sounds, lyrical songs, and countless others through the inner faculty of hearing we all possess but rarely develop or use. I perceive these experiences as sound and can return to the physical to write them down and hear them at a frequency that is audible to my physical senses.

But what was I hearing on these inner planes? If I had a tape recorder on during these inner experiences, why didn't the sounds get recorded? The range of sound perception of the tape recorder is at least as great as my ear, yet they cannot be heard on tape. The reason is that these sounds were heard at octave intervals that reached a different dimension of reality. What is fascinating about this phenomenon is that my inner perception of these sounds and melodies has outer equivalents. This suggests that inner sound is nothing more than the same note that we can hear occurring at a frequency or pitch well beyond the capability of any physical measuring devices. But these sounds do exist. Ask any musician that is inwardly attuned and she will humbly admit that many if not all of her compositions were first heard in these inner regions with inner faculties.

Loudness and timbre are two other components of sound in the physical dimension. These sound components impact the effectiveness of the mantras that we chant. Whatever sound we choose, its loudness and quality make up part of our "chanting strategy." For example, with respect to loudness, we might start out chanting a mantra loudly and progress to softness and then outer silence. At the same time, we might vary the timbre from the nasal to a deep diaphragm sound. These same qualities are perceived and exist at each succeeding dimension of reality. They exist at different frequencies and vibration levels, just as all that we perceive in the physical is itself distinguished by the different frequencies at which they exist.

Mantras that are unique and best suited to the individual increase the capacity for meditation. Often they link with the same sound in another dimension of reality that vibrates at a related, but substantially higher frequency (octave). When this occurs, the vibration of the note we control through the singing of our mantra causes the same note at a higher octave to vibrate (as do tuning forks affected by the vibration of a similar note). This process opens an inner doorway through which consciousness can move into a higher dimension of the inner reality. This is the essence of the mantra: the vibration of the note is far more important than the word.

So, to get back to our HU or the AUM/OM sounds, we see that frequency, wavelength, intensity, and timbre are the important components, not anything intrinsic to H-U or A-U-M/O-M. Beyond the sound selected, the most important factor in the use of these sounds/mantras is our capacity to focus attention on a single point, idea, or sound long enough for consciousness to shift from the physical universe to the inner realms.

Any mantra can contact the infinite and change the course of our lives. Those who make a fetish of secret words and mantras in their spiritual teachings mislead the seeker by implying, if not teaching as dogma, that a master or path has a secret only it can dispense. As we have seen, each of us has the ability to contact the infinite. We come into this life fully equipped to complete our journey home. Such teachers unscrupulously use their "special knowledge" of mantras to trap sincere souls seeking truth. They are lurking everywhere.

Technique One: Basic Meditation/Contemplation Technique

Let's turn now to basic meditation techniques. We need to find what works best for each of us. Start with these suggestions, then let your inner self make the adjustments. It is *your* journey. If you set your goal on leaving the body consciousness and traveling into the inner worlds, your inner self in tandem with spirit will unerringly lead you there. Learn to follow your higher self; it will always be with you — it is you.

Sit comfortably in a chair and position your hands interlaced or laying one in the other. Place your feet flat on the floor or crossed, whichever is more comfortable. Relaxation and comfort are important. Keep your back erect enough to prevent falling asleep but not enough to cause discomfort, which will only draw your attention back to your body. I have often tried sitting up in bed, under a blanket, but alert. This can be done, but it is more difficult because you might fall back to sleep, especially if attempted in the early morning. Take several deep breaths to relax. Imagine that you are inhaling pure spirit and exhaling all worries, anxieties, doubts, and fears. Negative thoughts during meditation/contemplation will only add energy to them. If there is a problem that you can't shake, you can rid yourself of it by displacement or replacement. Remember, you cannot rid yourself of a thought by negation: try to stop thinking about a green and purple elephant! Instead, think about love or happiness and repeat these words rapidly. In short order, you will replace negative feelings and prepare yourself for the adventure ahead.

Once ready for the inner adventure, focus your attention gently and lovingly at a point between the eyes, the same place where you see an object when imagining it. During my early experimentation, I did this as if I were following a recipe. I was never sure whether I was getting it right or not. Don't waste your time on minutiae! Ask your higher self if you have it right. Always rely on inner direction to fine-tune steps on your inner journey.

Let's take a second to explore this inner screen, the point where imagination and visualization take place. This will help you gain confidence that you are doing it correctly. Imagine, for a moment, your bedroom. Do this with your eyes *open*. You can probably see it quite easily. Take note of your viewpoint. It will likely be at an angle, usually up, from where your normal vision focuses. You will be looking through your eyes but not seeing anything: your attention will be on the picture in your imagination. This is your eye of imagination, your spiritual eye.

Try this same experiment with your eyes closed. Most people have greater difficulty. Strangely, we see through the eye of imagination better with our eyes open than closed. But if you practice, you will see just as well with your eyes closed. In any event, you no longer have to speculate about where your eye of imagination is, and you can go to the next step confidently. I may have just saved you two years of speculation, but then I was a slow learner!

At this point, you may want to chant a mantra to reduce the mind's tendency to jump from thought to thought. Let's look more closely at this. The effect of repeated sounds on the mind is similar to hypnosis.

Hypnosis works because the subject translates a suggestion into words that come from himself: "you will wake up" becomes "I will wake up." The same principle is at work in self-hypnosis, except that we give ourselves the suggestion.

Several things are at work here, especially in self-hypnosis, which parallels but is somewhat different from what occurs in meditation when using a mantra. First, in hypnosis our directions are verbal cues that the body follows. The practitioner tells himself he is becoming relaxed and his eyes are heavy and can no longer be held open. In meditation, the person consciously relaxes every part of the body. The essential point in meditation is to calm the jumping of the mind by suggestions to calm and relax which is often accompanied by taking several breaths that also help in the process.

A second facet of meditation is the repetition of a mantra that has the effect of further calming the mind or "boring" it into quiescence. The mind loves repetition and takes to it quickly. Play with children amply demonstrates this principle. If a game is played in which the child is patted on her head two times, spun three times, and says "wosh, wosh, wosh," she will remember the exact sequence of actions and words. If a pat or turn or "wosh" is missed the next time, she quickly tells us. The mind loves grooves and repetition. They keep it busy so that we can do more important things.

The mantra gives the mind something to focus on while we shift to the spiritual eye and observe what is taking place there. Many forms of meditation also employ the device of following a *pattern* of chanting, which may, for example, involve five chants followed by five breaths, then repeating the sequence perhaps five times. Our mind is then busy not only chanting but also auditing our performance to ensure we get it right. This activity distracts and occupies the mind until, in time, it settles down, or gets bored, and we can shift our attention into the inner dimensions.

A third facet of the mantra, which we have previously touched on, involves the word itself. In my experience, all words and sounds are equally effective, though some are more suitable to one person than another. The first two principles are much more important than the particular word or sound. Some religions and paths would have us believe that the magic and power lie in the word itself. We have seen that sound vibration can have a salutary effect on a person, and that vibration and sound are integral parts of what and who we are. Neither of these is as important as the individual's focus of attention. If it were otherwise, everyone would have his own magic word, and we would have far less work and worry to contend with in life. Alas, it is not so.

Still, the word or sound we choose can be helpful. Some of the sounds, mantras, or words that I have found to be very effective are:

HU — In Sufism, from which the word is derived in its current incarnation, Hu is considered the divine pronoun and literally means HE. The word is sung or chanted as "WHO" or "Hooooooo" by its originators. Chanting it as "Hugh" (an adaptation of Eckankar) works just as well if that is your preference.

AUM, OM — Om and Aum are variations of each other. The Om is considered by many eastern religions to be the WORD referred to in the Bible. It is used in Hinduism (Yoga), Sikhism, and Lamaism (Tibetan Buddhism).

Rrr — Thought to have masculine connotation signifying control, leadership, etc. There are "many different language renditions of father, pater, fater, pere, padre as well as ruler, rex, royal...."[17]

A or AH — Thought to be universally representative of the sound of energy. A mantra utilized in Tibetan Buddhism.

M or MM — Thought to be associated with the feminine nurturing principle as in mother, mutter, madre, maman, mater, etc.[18]

RA, MA, RAMA — Variations and combinations of the basic sounds outlined above and can be used as mantras evoking the masculine, feminine, and energy principles all together.

MEH — Part of the traditional chant for many spiritual paths. Makes up the traditional "Jewel in the Lotus" mantra used in Tibetan Buddhism (Om MAH-nee PEH-meh Hung). This mantra also contains other basic sounds, each of which can be used as a single sound mantra or in combination.

HUM — Mantra used in many religions sung as "HuuuuuuM."

Nam-myoho-renge-kyo ("salutation to the *Lotus Sutra*") — Chant used in Nichiren Daishonin Buddhism, or Japanese Buddhism. Those who use this mantra are saying that they will devote themselves to the ultimate truth of life (the law) and base themselves upon the wisdom (Buddha-hood) they thereby tap. The power of the chant is associated with the level of belief in the teaching and its associated doctrine. Otherwise, any part of the chant can be used individually as a mantra if desired.

UM — Mantra sung in many eastern teachings thought to combine energy of the U sound and nurturing vibrations of M sound. Sung "Uuu-uuuuMmmmmm."

LOVE — Works very effectively as a mantra when sung as a single word or spelled out as L-O-V-E. It taps both conscious and unconscious centers, uniting with the binding power of the universe.

GOD — Effective for obvious reasons. It unites the individual in conscious and inner levels with ALL THAT IS. When using as a mantra, combine chanting with deep sense of gratitude and a circle of outflow and inflow of love. Can be chanted or sung by spelling it out, as in LOVE.

ONE or ALL THAT IS — As the idea of the one becomes a part of your consciousness, this sound will have special inner and outer meaning. It is very effective in raising vibration level. Imagine the light or request to be shown the deeper meaning of the ONE, and it will be yours.

Virtually any word or sound with a high vibration or attached meaning can be a mantra. There are literally hundreds listed in books and on web sites. Using any of these mantras coupled with the insights and techniques presented here will enable you to travel into the inner dimensions, if you choose.

Many of the sounds and words used as mantras have been found to have a particularly beneficial effect on some part of the body. This is valid, for the mantra or sound therapy (use of instruments or other mechanical devices) can be efficacious. But when using a mantra for healing or another beneficial purpose, sound is still combined with focused attention and thought to bring about the desired effect. Thus, it is difficult to say that the results stem from the mantra or from the thought energy.

Technique Two: Self Selection of a Mantra

Over my more than thirty years as a God-seeker, I performed hundreds of initiations in which I selected or assisted the seeker to find her own mantra. I preferred to let her choose her own word following her inner direction. The "one size fits all" approach to selecting a mantra is not ideal. Just as our DNA code records our historical uniqueness, our causal sheath knows the potential impact of every sound. Because we carry our inner and outer histories, it is not surprising that we would respond to one sound over another.

Choosing a mantra involves working with vowels and consonants to find the most suitable combination. While sitting in the normal meditative position, chant each vowel inwardly (or aloud if you prefer), dwelling on each for at least thirty seconds. One or more vowels will resonate with you. Next, select a consonant. Proceed in the same manner, or in a random pattern. It might be faster and work just as well. Work with those that come to mind. Continue until you select one that feels right for you. Now, combine the vowel and consonant into a full sound. If the two don't work together, repeat the process and change one, the other, or both. What is important is that you select what feels right for you. It is also very important that you trust your inner guidance.

The final step is determining the number of syllables. At the beginning, it may be best to use one syllable. There is no rule, of course; you determine what is right. Simple is sometimes best. If you determine that two or more syllables are best, follow the same procedures to select the second syllable and combine them until it feels right. You may also receive a word or sound in the dream state or while driving down a highway. Spirit is always communicating to us through our higher self. If a word, picture, or sound makes a strong impression on you, then it might be a sign of what will work best for you. Never allow yourself to be the puppet of an external force or person. Remember, you are one with ALL THAT IS. You are growing through this process to a fuller realization of this truth.

Words and phrases that we use everyday can also make an effective mantra. I quite frequently use "love" as my mantra. At other times, I will use a short line, word, or thought from the *Contemplations*. The advantage here is that we don't depend on an effect stemming from a Neanderthal incarnation, but can tap the power of words that have a clear and present impact on our physical and inner bodies. Love is certainly such a word. This may feel like too much freedom all at once, but as Johnny, a brick-mason who once built an imperfect wall for me, said: "You'll get used to it."

Let the Chanting Begin

These guidelines will enable you to begin your own meditative experiences and make the necessary adjustments as needed. This section presents insights I have gathered that will help you succeed. The length of time for meditation is also something you must decide. I was initially accustomed to meditating thirty minutes a day, but after a while it became ineffective. I was approaching each morning's meditation with a sense that it was a chore I had to complete. I even experienced relief after completing my contemplation. As often as not, I never consciously went anywhere or experienced anything. I felt more relaxed and on top of things, but that wasn't why I contemplated. As a former student of TM, I knew I was transcending, but I came back with no recollection of anything — no inner experience.

Meditation did help me to stay up for extended periods writing business proposals. After only twenty or thirty minutes, I was able to continue my work for another two or three hours. But I longed for inner experiences. I once traveled everywhere in the inner worlds and enjoyed numerous varied experiences. In the intervening years, many things had changed in my life. My company had grown; I had gotten married, had children, and took on a mortgage and even a pet. I had quite a bit to keep me busy. My focus had shifted to many outside distractions and away from adventures in the inner worlds of God. And that was the problem.

One morning, after completing my thirty-minute meditation, I moved from my chair and lay flat on the floor. I'm not sure why I did this, but I did. I experienced an unfamiliar relaxation partly because I had fulfilled my "obligation." Because I was totally relaxed, everything was still — no worries. All of a sudden, I felt a "swoosh" in the area of my spiritual eye and immediately found myself peering into another world, as though I were looking through a window. It was as if a blindfold had been removed from my eyes, allowing me to see another dimension. I still had awareness of my body, but I was looking through into this completely different region.

My excitement thrust me immediately back into my body. I mused over the experience and determined to try it again. In an instant, as easily as before, I was not only peering into this strange land, but I was actually there! I found that shifting my focus to something in the scenery drew me deeper into the inner experience. Soon, I forgot my body, even though I was fully awake and aware. My senses were in high gear, except that I had capabilities far exceeding those of my body. My eyes were like binoculars. I could focus on objects and bring them closer to me. I could move to different parts of the scenery by simply thinking. At first, I tried to walk or move with a swimming motion, but it didn't work. I quickly learned that I moved by controlling my thoughts. The colors on this plane (the astral plane) were brilliant beyond measure, like the colors in a flower garden or a color cartoon.

This taught me several things about inner travel. First, a feeling of obligation to meditate is a bar to success. Far better to shift to eager expectancy for what is about to occur. Even when changing from obligation to excitement, I found that I had to take more time to become sufficiently relaxed to move into the inner worlds. I was to learn that periods of twenty to thirty minutes are fine for achieving balance and other benefits of meditation. But shorter periods are largely insufficient to achieve inner travel. After developing inner stamina, discipline, and a strong desire to travel in the inner worlds, you might consider extending these periods to one hour or more to achieve success. I certainly found this to be the case, but that is something you must determine for yourself.

Another interesting discovery was the ease with which I was able to achieve inner travel on the weekends, even after only thirty minutes. Every Saturday, I would wake later than usual, about nine in the morning, and remain in bed in a seated position, back erect. Sometimes, these journeys would last for two hours — so exciting and varied were they. I later reasoned that I was successful because I was habitually awake at this hour and I could resist going back to sleep. There were times when I experimented by going into various regions, asking question of denizens there, and returning quickly to write down or tape my encounters.

Many of these trips were on the future time track, where I saw images of America decades into the future. Some experiences were in the lower planes, as evidenced by the uninspiring conversations I had with dwellers of these planes. At other times, I was carried into the light, which would completely transform my body. I heard celestial music and felt ecstasy that was complete and final — an experience I never wanted to leave. I met and talked with many individuals whom I thought of as masters. Many bore the names and appearances of the Eck Masters that Paul had made up. (This does not validate the Eck Masters: I learned, of course, that God-soul uses earthly images such as Jesus and other spiritual symbols as guides to make the novice feel comfortable.)

The inner reality is akin to a visualization or dream. It has an aspect of reality, but it is far more transitory than the reality we experience in the physical. Physical manifestation takes more effort and energy before it finally comes into existence. The inner reality is more akin to the formation of a cloud than to anything containing the dense matter of the physical plane.

Once you have started having inner experiences of a high spiritual variety, you might ask, as I did, What's next? This is a fascinating question because many feel that once they have experienced the bliss of God and seen the ocean of inner light and love, that's it. Not so. It is only the beginning. Once we experience these inner realities, we feel a tremendous responsibility to do something with the experience. After all, why would these experiences be wasted on someone who just wants to sit around contemplating his navel? There is much work to be done; in the end, that is what this is all about.

No joy is greater than giving and sharing the love and insight each of us has been given. This is the Great Work: to spread the truth and free God-souls from entrapment that prevents them from understanding the true source of their inner guidance — themselves. The teachings of higher consciousness are intended as an outer vehicle in the Great Work. The goal of all who share this message is to insure that it continues to reflect truth.

Chapter 15 — Dreams: A Bridge to Higher Consciousness

Dreams are not simply random thoughts and symbols playing about in our minds as we sleep. They are vital clues to understanding ourselves and aiding in the journey of the God-seeker. A history of humankind's attempts to understand these inner experiences shows the central role dreams have always played in the our lives.

Dreams in Culture and History

As early as the Twelfth Egyptian Dynasty (1991-1786 B.C.E.), dreams were accorded great significance for daily life.[1] In fact, the Egyptians even initiated a process called "dream incubation," in which a person with difficulties in daily life visited a temple for a night's sleep. In the morning, the dream was recorded and interpreted by the priest.[2]

In some cultures, dreams have had the same status as outer reality. Indeed, among many peoples, this view results in traditions that may appear strange to westerners, who tend to regard the dream as simply "a dream." Among the Zulus in southern Africa, for example, friendships can be broken off if a dream portrays a friend to be an enemy or mean harm. A Macusi Indian of Guyana reportedly dreamed an expedition leader required him to haul a canoe up a dangerous cataract. Upon waking exhausted, he was infuriated at the leader and could not be convinced his dream did not have the same importance as outer reality to these strangers. In Borneo, if a man dreams his wife is an adulteress, her father must take her back. Among the Kurds, it was traditionally expected that if someone dreamed of something valuable, he could claim it as his own, taking it by force if necessary. Among the Kamchatka natives of far-eastern Russia, if a man dreams a woman has givenhimsexualfavors,sheisobligedtodosointhewakingstate.[3]

Dream Interpretation in Greece and Rome

The early Greeks believed dreams were the work of the gods. Heraclitus, the fifth-century B.C.E. philosopher made the heretical suggestion that dreams were created by each person's mind. Aristotle picked up this notion, and began a rational study of dreams and dreaming. Some of his observations carry the skepticism of the modern scientist and little of the wonder of the inner traveler. In his *De divinatione per somnum,* he states: "[M]ost so-called prophetic dreams are to be classed as mere coincidences, especially all such as are extravagant." As to interpreters of such dreams, he notes: "The most skillful interpreter of dreams is he who has the faculty of absorbing resemblances. I mean that dream presentations are analogous to the forms reflected in water."

Aristotle felt that dreams were not god-sent, but were in fact of purely bodily origin. As described in Freud's *Interpretation of Dreams,* Aristotle's view was that:

> Dreams . . . are not of a divine character, but . . . they are "daemonic," since nature is "daemonic" and not divine. Dreams . . . do not arise from supernatural manifestations but follow the laws of the human spirit, though the latter is . . . akin to the divine.[4]

Aristotle's view differed substantially from that of writers before him who considered dreams to be divinely inspired, rather than a product of the dreaming psyche. Aristotle and Hippocrates held that dreams told of a person's physical health and that proper interpretation of dreams could be the basis of a diagnosis, a view shared by many doctors today.

The Greek soothsayer, Artemidorus Daldianus (second century C.E.), in a massive five-volume work entitled, *Oneirocritica (The Interpretation of Dreams),* elaborated on Heraclitus's view that dreams were unique to each person. He proposed that the person's occupation, health, social status, and other factors of his life determined the symbols in his dreams. Macrobius,[5] in his *Commentary on the Dream of Scipio,* writes about Cicero's dream in which Scipio Africanus the younger is himself dreaming about his great-grandfather, whose name he bore (and who defeated Hannibal during the Punic Wars). Macrobius uses this work of Cicero to put forth a scheme for analyzing dreams.

His scheme is important because it formed the basis for dream interpretation that was accepted by medieval scientists, scholars, and theologians. Aspects of it can still be found today, though by other names. Macrobious's scheme was similar to that of Artemidorus. He classified dreams as significant or insignificant. The major group of dreams according to his schema is what would today be called "symbolic dreams." He considered these to be enigmatic, useful in foretelling future events, but requiring an interpreter. He further subdivided these dreams as personal, alien (about someone else), social (regarding a social setting), public (about the city, town, etc.), and universal (the world, cosmos, etc.).

Sigmund Freud and the Interpretation of Dreams

The works of Artemidorus and Macrobius were closely studied by generations of thinkers and formed part of the foundation for much of the work of Sigmund Freud (1856-1939) and many of his followers. Freud's *Interpretation of Dreams*[6] contains an excellent summary of the history of dream interpretation up to 1900. Freud's work revolutionized the study of dreams and made the connection between dreams and the deepest aspects of our lives. Freud disagreed with many of the theories of dream interpretation put forth up to the early twentieth century, with the exception of the work of Albert Scherner, who in 1861 put forth the idea that fantasy takes control during sleep and translates thoughts into pictures. These pictures in turn compose the drama of which dreams are made. Long before Freud, he wrote about sexual symbols and hypothesized, for example, that the penis might be represented by a clarinet, a cigar, fur, and so on. Scherner did not discern the function of dreams, but nevertheless laid the foundation for the work of Freud and others.[7]

Freud speaks of two methods of analysis in use at the beginning of his study. The first involved symbolic dream interpretation:

This is "symbolic" dream-interpreting; and it inevitably breaks down when faced by dreams which are not merely unintelligible but also confused. An example of this procedure is to be seen in the explanation of Pharaoh's dream propounded by Joseph in the Bible.[8]

Freud's view of this approach is that it "goes to pieces," that is, it simply does not have a rational basis with a potential for replication in its methodology. Indeed, it was his view that:

It is of course impossible to give instructions upon the *method* of arriving at a symbolic interpretation. Success must be a question of hitting on a clever idea, of direct intuition, and for that reason it was possible for dream-interpretation by means of symbolism to be exalted into an artistic activity dependent on the possession of peculiar gifts.[9]

The second method of dream interpretation discussed by Freud was one that he called a "cipher method," because it treats the dream as a kind of "secret code in which every sign is translated into another sign of known meaning, according to an established key." In this method, the interpreter uses a dictionary or dream-book in which symbols are translated into precise meanings and the code of the dream is thereby broken. This method is simplistic and was seen by Freud as a step backward from the insights of Artemidorus and Macrobius that interpretation should take into account the individual's social position and personality. Freud further criticized the symbolic method for dividing the dream into parts and attempting to discern meaning from fragments. He also criticized both approaches for their emphasis on the predictive or prophetic function of dreams. He felt that both approaches forced a predictive or oracular interpretation.

Freud credits Artemidorus with "the most complete and careful elaboration of dream-interpretation as it existed in the Graeco-Roman world." The principle in Artemidorus's method was association: the dream was interpreted by what it recalled to memory. But Artemidorus insisted that interpretation be based on associations in the mind of the *interpreter*. Freud introduced an approach, which in its simplicity seems obvious today, but at the time was novel, if not revolutionary. He focused on what the dream meant to the *dreamer*.

One of Freud's most quoted passages, "The interpretation of dreams is the royal road to a knowledge of the unconscious activities of the mind," speaks to one of his central themes, the unconscious mind. Freud believed that dreams reflected waking experience. He distinguished between *manifest* content of dreams, the objects seen in the dream, and *latent* content, the underlying meaning of the dream. Freud's use of the unconscious avoids anything dealing with the world of spirit, soul, or an infinite power expressed as God. Freud and most scientists do not recognize a spiritual dimension, but of course such bias limits their work. It is like describing the workings of an automobile while denying the existence of the engine.

Each dimension of our reality exists on virtually parallel, though interspersed and interactive, planes of existence. For every component of our physical body (and life) there is an equivalent within the etheric body or in the astral dimension, which can be perceived through the aura as well as by perception, and which supports all bodily parts and functions through imagination (visualization). This body is necessary to explain the totality of life, especially as it relates to the higher aspects of our being that connect with other dimensions of reality. This awareness aids us in understanding the purely physical functions of our body and psychology. Despite limited appreciation of our complexities, Freud's work makes him perhaps the most influential psychologists of the twentieth century.

Carl Jung and the Archetype

Carl Jung (1875-1961) studied under Freud, and was even groomed as his successor. However, he eventually disagreed with Freud's views on dream interpretation, a schism developed, and they parted company, far from amicably. Jung believed in the unconscious but did not view it as instinctive in the manner of an animal. He saw a spiritual dimension to the unconscious and its dreams.

Instead of seeing dreams, especially symbolic dreams, as attempting to hide something from us, he saw them as helping us to come into unity with ourselves. Freud saw dreams as expressions of repressed ideas and feelings; Jung saw them as compensatory, helping us to balance those aspects of ourselves that are not adequately expressed in daily life. The dream was part of a totality that extended throughout daily life, some of which presented itself during the dream state. Dreams did not reveal repressed material as much as they expressed elements of ourselves underrepresented during the wake state. On this view, dreams only required interpretation if a person was not living a well-balanced life, suffered from bad moods, or had other symptoms. Jung believed that dream analysis was useful, but his approach differed from Freud's. He did not focus on a single dream, dissecting it, using free association with the subject. Instead, he preferred to collect a series of dreams and analyze them as a whole to see patterns of an underlying problem.[10]

Jung also believed in "archetypes," or basic concepts impressed into the human mind. They are reflected in the myths of every culture. The archetypes of the Shadow (the unconscious dark-side of personality), and the Syzygy (Anima-female aspect of soul; Animus-male aspect of soul)[11] are examples of archetypes.[12] (In this respect, his research paralleled the later work of Joseph Campbell.) Jung saw a connection between dreams and the myths, art, and legends of a culture. He considered archetypes of the concept of god to be different from the idea of one God. The multifaceted idea of god as embodied in the Christian concept of the Father, Son, and Holy Ghost are such archetypes, for they respond to the mind's ability to imagine "numinous reality" — a natural object or phenomenon inhabited by or considered as a spirit or deity. These archetypes compose the objects of myths and are useful because their images appear in our inner worlds as spiritual guides.

The issue of intrinsic reality is not nearly as important as their function as a means of inner communication through dreams or conscious inner experiences. In this regard, we see in the Trinity, the 4000 facets of the Buddha, the Masters of the Vairagi order, Ascended Masters, or any other myths, that each has the capacity to become numinous reality by activation through conscious thought. But they are no more than this. Belief increases their effectiveness as inner communicators of transcendent wisdom, but by that fact they also limit spiritual growth, for we have a tendency to hold on to them and bestow credit upon them.

Nevertheless, they provide images people can relate to in their inner travels to self-realization. Jung believed that many of these archetypes were elemental forces that play a role in the creation of the world and the mind of all humankind.[13] Many archetypes, Jung argued, are so basic to our nature that even the savants who purport to have escaped such primitive thinking are still guided by them. Jung's idea of a Universal Unconscious has great currency among esoteric students. This concept is quite similar to the notion of ALL THAT IS, which is put forth here, except it is more impersonal and limited. Yet this concept certainly deserves careful consideration in grasping the development of the concept of the ONE. My difficulty with this is its denigration of the capacity of God-soul to create and change archetypical ideas that flow from the ONE.

Current Dream Research

Research into dreams moved into a new era with the discovery of rapid eye movement (REM) in 1953. Within an hour of sleep, most subjects exhibit a burst of rapid eye movement along with a change in brain-wave patterns, as measured by an electro-encephalograph (EEG). Dreamers have an experience, though there is not necessarily a physical response. When awakened during REM sleep, almost seventy-five percent report having vivid dreams. When subjects were awakened during non-REM sleep, only seventeen percent recalled their dreams. Interestingly, dreaming sleep, or "D-state," has been observed in many animals, including monkeys, dogs, cats, rats, elephants, and even some reptiles.[14]

Current research reveals that:

- The first stages of sleep are dream-free, with dreaming occurring about every ninety minutes, induced by external or internal stimuli.

- Almost all forms of inner experience are regarded as hallucinations or a form of self-hypnosis. The commonly reported experience of leaving the body and floating over it is called "autoscopic hallucination."[15]

- About twenty percent of sleep time is spent in a series of dreams, each taking about ten to fifteen minutes (as measured by EEG).

- Just before waking, there is a period of perceptual release experienced as dreams of increased intensity.

- Outside stimuli (e.g., water drops or spoken words) affect the content of a dream, but only to a limited degree.

- People recall about forty percent of their dreams.

- Non-recall reflects repression or denial of experiences, not their absence.

- Watching vivid movies before going to bed has some influence on the content of dreams, but only a limited amount.

- The dream content of individuals susceptible to influence can be affected by auto- or outside suggestion.

- The amount of D-state activity does not depend on daily activities, personality, or work differences.[16]

In a set of experiments during the 1960s and 1970s, Dr. Montague Ullman, founder of the Dream Laboratory at the Maimonides Medical Center in New York, recruited volunteers (with no known psychic abilities) to test the impact of ESP on dream content. As one subject slept in one room, another subject in a different room concentrated on a randomly selected painting. The subject looking at the painting tried to get the sleeping subject to dream about it. The experiment produced mixed results, but did establish enough similarity between the dreamer and the observer's transmitted picture to lend credibility to a causal relationship.[17]

Current research is fascinating, but it is oceans away from the reality of these inner planes. Unfortunately, the subjective nature of this experience may forever keep science on the outside looking in, unless an entirely new methodology is established (e.g., methodologies suggested in the works of Ken Wilber[18]) for assessing the validity and meaning of subjective experience. However, the flaw in any such methodology is that it is like measuring the number, decibel level, duration, and reasons for the cheers in a football game from the parking lot. We would never know what was really going on inside. We want to go inside and participate fully in the game, understand the plays, and control the outcome. Even when we do this, that is, have the inner experience, whether dream or otherwise, how can any external measure tell us what is real or true? Truth and reality are what we create in our own lives as well as in the inner worlds. Besides, any methodology places far too much emphasis on an analysis of the path on which we are walking rather than the destination to which the path is leading. The operation of our inner faculties is guided by the goal, the destination. When we focus excessively on the path itself, through analysis, it becomes the goal, the destination — for this is where we have placed our attention.

I hasten to add that there is value in developing an epistemology of inner experiences. William James put forth a conceptual framework, of sorts, in his seminal 1902 work, *The Varieties of Religious Experience.* Currently, Ken Wilber and others are bringing more insight to this much-neglected area under the rubric of "transpersonal experience." But earlier cautions are wise to remember. In the pursuit of spiritual insight — the quest of the God-seeker — intellect and ratiocination have their limitations. They are best used as reinforcing methodologies, too limited to serve as a principle modus operandi to reach the goal of the God-seeker.

Mathematical precision and scientific certainty are interesting but ultimately distracting. It is only because the physical plane is slowed down to provide the illusion of certainty that scientific confidence has supremacy in our minds. As we move further in states of awareness, as scientists are beginning to discover, the rules are not certain or ultimately determinable. This is the realm in which the inner-traveler learns to be comfortable, where transcendent lessons are drawn and limited attention is paid to dream scenery and personages — mere details that are forever changing. Interestingly, Bertrand Russell came close to seeing through this illusion of life:

> It is obviously possible that what we call waking life may be only an unusual and persistent nightmare. I do not believe that I am now dreaming but I cannot prove I am not.[19]

Toward a Workable Integrated Dream Paradigm

After considering the methodologies of Artemidorus, Macrobius, Freud, Jung, the postulates of Wilber and others, and working with these systems in interpreting my own dreams, I developed a related but somewhat different system for classifying and interpreting dream experiences. Over the many years that I have conducted workshops on dreams, this is the system I have taught and used. Many have found it helpful, as perhaps you will. There is no fixed system for everyone, and no road map that will assure success. Studying dreams is important for understanding yourself, your health, and your future. In the end, the debates over the millennia have attempted to proclaim a single function and purpose for dreams. I have found that they serve many. Dreams are a window to the past, present, and future. They become what you make of them, for we are never without the creative power to shape every facet of our lives.

I must admit to a certain sacrilege when it comes to dreams. I once felt that I could face the reality of life without the need for symbols and other indirect messages. I have also learned that this was at times only arrogance, for there was much in myself I was unwilling to see. Indeed, there were symbols that regularly recurred. In time, I understood and appreciated that my higher self was trying to help me perceive what I was ignoring in my outer life.

One such dream symbol involved a pack of dogs chasing me. I would run, usually in vain, attempting to escape. Unable to face the peril, I woke in a sweat. The dogs were a clue that something was bothering me in my outer life — some problem I was unaware of or didn't want to face. I learned to pay attention to the message as it recurred. I searched my outer life for what I was avoiding, the problem that was lurking just out of view. Invariably, the dream's warning was useful.

The dogs reappeared one night. This time, I did not run or try to escape by waking up. I stood my ground, determined to fight, and, if need be, to bite them as hard and as ferociously as they would bite me — or I would die in the attempt. This time, they stopped, became meek, then disappeared. I woke feeling that I had won a major victory. And it was, for many of the problems I had been struggling with immediately disappeared. I learned to confront them early and fearlessly, as I had faced the dogs. After that, every time I confronted a difficult situation, I remembered my courage against the dogs and smiled, concluding that this was nothing in comparison. The reality of dreams to our emotions and instincts is no different from those we face in our waking state. Growth through experience can occur in the dream state as in daily life. Even when we do not remember the entire dream, we are left with residues, or engrams, that fire in our brain, alerting us to solutions leading to success.

Another recurring dream was walking into one of my old law school classrooms at Harvard to take a test — totally unprepared. The feeling was terrifying! It always got my attention. This dream would appear when I had not done my part, procrastinated, or was not prepared for some task. I scurried to make a to-do list and complete everything on it. I didn't want to wake up with that feeling again. I usually knew what the dream referred to, but to be safe, I did everything on the list.

These are just two examples of dreams that came to mean a great deal to me in determining the course of my life. These and many other dreams that I personally experienced or discussed with workshop participants clearly demonstrated that they serve many purposes. Indeed, the disputes between Freud and Jung about whether dreams portray our pathologies and repressed ideas or reveal steps needed to develop our true potential seem useless and pedantic. For surely it must be that dreams are always fulfilling some life-balancing purpose. Given that we are unique as soul and are part of a larger whole, spirit and ALL THAT IS, how could it be otherwise? When the spiritual paradigm is embraced and then expanded to encompass the totality of existence, an entirely different view of dreams emerges.

The nature of the dream also depends on the needs of the individual at any time. They can: balance, inspire, instruct, inform, warn, scare into action, enlighten, or let in experiences of a transcendent spiritual nature. The individual knows the message of a dream experience when he arises with a sense of its purpose. Often these feelings or insights are fleeting, and, because drum rolls and the voice of Charlton Heston do not precede them, they are often dismissed. However, as we have noted, the voice of our higher selves does not shout. It comes floating on clouds, clear but faint, discernible but easily missed. From here, the higher consciousness methodology of dream interpretation proceeds by determining the type of dream. There are six types:

Symbolic Dreams

By far the largest grouping. It can be subdivided to aid interpreting the endless symbols in them. (Considered in more detail below.)

Balancing Dreams

A subset of the symbolic dream but having a clear and distinct purpose of balancing physical excesses (e.g., too much food) or psychological stress (e.g., an emotional, violent, or disturbing movie) that might have negative effects if not confronted.

Precognitive or Prophetic Dreams

Dream experiences involving awareness of future events. These dreams can involve the individual or the state, nation, or civilization (e.g., prophecies of Nostradamus, Sitting Bull, Revelations). They may involve symbols, but are usually direct representations of events or persons involved.

Reincarnation Dreams

Dreams that involve past lives or the histories of nations or civilizations.

Conscious Inner Experiences

These are deep, significant experiences in the inner worlds, for example, Graham's journal. They can occur or begin at the outset of dreams. When they do, they are of the same fabric and content, only begun in a different manner. The subject is completely alert and able to remember the content, as with experiences in the physical plane.

Spiritual/Ecstatic Dreams

These are dreams of the highest spiritual content. They involve the subject, usually as God-soul, with direct experiential contact with the light and sound as well as other aspects of the infinite reality. It is a mistake to consider the light and sound as the ultimate or principal expression of ALL THAT IS. For, as the name suggests, it is impossible to limit that which is ALL THAT IS. The nature of these experiences can be classified as ecstatic because the individual experiences feelings of indescribable love, protection, and bliss. These powerful dreams constitute the most frequent of inner spiritual dreams or experiences, for they manifest in different ways and in different dimensions of reality. Included within this group are dreams of spiritual instruction that can encompass elements of the above, but their main purpose is to provide spiritual instruction regarding the secrets of the universe itself.

With the exception of symbolic dreams (considered below), each category is what it is. They tend to follow a discernible, logical pattern and can be described easily. Their form and content are designed to put us at ease. They contain familiar elements from our lives. The inner worlds are as fluid as our thoughts, more malleable than clay. They become whatever we think or wish them to be. They make us comfortable so that we are receptive to what is imparted.

Interpreting Symbolic Dreams

We now turn to the symbolic dream, which, in its variety and complexity, requires considerable skill and "in-touchness" in order to understand. The first step in interpreting a symbolic dream is to determine what aspect of our lives it is addressing. To do this, we might consider our lives as divided into six distinct categories:

Spiritual: Daily focus on spiritual goals, God-Realization.

Physical: Our body, health, fitness, appearance.

Financial: Our money situation.

Social: Our family, friends, groups.

Personal: Our selves, personal interests (writing, art, music).

Professional: Our jobs, career preparation, school.

We take the dream segment as a whole and ask ourselves, which category of my life is this dream addressing? At first, the process will go slowly. But in just a few days, it will take only seconds to ask the questions and listen inwardly for the answer. It will come in the form of a feeling of comfort or assurance that this is what it is. At times, several interpretations will be revealed as potential meanings.

At this juncture, an important point needs to be made. Too often, we worry about the correct interpretation and whether we are getting it right. This should not concern us. Whatever clues we receive about actions we should take are worthy of consideration. If we get it wrong, that is, do not respond to the aspect of our lives the dream addresses, we will have another dream. In the meantime, by acting on whatever is suggested by the dream, we enhance our lives and move things forward. When the appropriate action has been taken to address the focus of the dream, we will experience a diminution of stress in our sleep patterns and outer life. Both will be easier and more comfortable. It all fits together and is in perfect balance. So don't worry whether you "got it right," for the dreams will speak to you until you do.

Recording and Using Dreams: Day and Night Journals

Many people keep a dream journal. It's a good idea, for there is a recurring pattern of symbols in dreams best discerned by systematic study. I have used many different techniques of recording dreams, including writing a journal, dictating into a tape recorder, and my current approach of waking up and quickly analyzing the dream. I tend to write down dreams only when they are non-symbolic in nature, for I believe I can decipher and understand my dreams without recording them. I have talked to many people who exercise great discipline in recording their dreams but spend little time in analyzing them for significance in their lives. The first step without the latter seems rather pointless, but to each his own — as long as it works.

The interpretation and use of dreams can be enhanced by keeping a day journal, something akin to a diary, used in conjunction with a dream journal. The day's events are recorded alongside the dream of the following night. When the pattern in our outer life is compared with our dream life, the symbols, meanings, warnings, advice, and instructions are more easily seen. In fact, one without the other is, in my view, like attempting to decipher Egyptian hieroglyphics without the Rosetta Stone.

There is a small class of dreams that disturb most of us but are nonetheless beneficial. These we may call "traumatic dreams." There are times when past actions and thoughts lead to consequences in our outer lives that would be best avoided. Whatever the consequences that we experience, whether in the outer or the inner, the purpose is to teach us. If the lesson can be learned on the inner through dreams, then its effect can be avoided in the outer, a result most of us would prefer. The key is paying attention to traumatic dreams and ascertaining what they are trying to teach us or what karmic cause it is resolving. If we learn the lesson and change our thoughts and actions accordingly, we can avoid further inner and outer trauma. But if we fail to heed the guidance from within, we destine ourselves to experiencing a shocking lesson in our outer lives. This is the nature of the aid and assistance we receive. Though it might seem harsh, it must be considered in light of our existence in a love system, where everything that happens to us is part of the fabric of love, albeit tough love at times.

Dreams, then, are part of the fabric of our existence as valid and as real as the waking state. It is for us to put together the puzzle and learn whenever and wherever we can. Dreams can be as exciting and antici-pated with as much glee as the child waiting for Christmas morning — that is, if we make it so.

Dreams of Harm

If acting on the dream's message would result in harm or danger, then avoid action, for it is a misreading or the consequence of a psycho-logical aberration that may require professional attention. The higher self seeks our advancement and growth, never our destruction or harm. It is who we are. Functioning in the normal manner, it will always pro-tect, provide for, teach, and steer our course.

Let me give an example. I once worked with an individual who was clearly out of balance. She called me to say her master had instructed her on the inner to place a hot iron on her body as a test of her love. On another occasion, an inner suggestion told her not to pay her bills. Such inner nudges often come from malevolent entities of the inner worlds. Advice and proclamations from "above" and from the inner worlds are not always from high spiritual entities. Inhabitants of the inner worlds are not necessarily elevated in smarts or consciousness. They are the same beings that plague us in physical manifestation when they inhab-ited a physical form. They can be as immature there as they are here. The astral world is structured very much like the physical world, with laws, rules, and police to keep the inner regions from chaos and protect its denizens, in much the same manner as occurs in the physical world.

A Dictionary of Dreams?

Much of the popular literature on dreams takes the approach that Freud described and discarded. This approach translates various sym-bols according to a dictionary. The approach makes two major mis-takes. First, dreams are unique to the individual, and so general definitions of symbols do not work. It is one thing to accept, as a practi-cal convention, a definition for a word, but quite another to accept a definition for a symbol emanating from the unique context of your life. The two processes are simply not the same, even though the logic of the one has influenced the use of the other: our comfort with a word dictio-nary has translated into comfort with a dream dictionary. They can be found all over the Internet and in bookstores. But ubiquity does not prove utility. There is one way that this approach can be helpful: as suggestions of *possible* meanings, to be accepted or rejected, depending on the inner response we have as we explore other possibilities.

The second fallacy in this approach is the tendency to treat dreams as a series of disjointed parts, rather than a whole picture-story. The dream story may take many turns, and characters within the dream may perform in many ways, not all related to the message the dream is trying to communicate. Taken together, there is a message and the *entire* story conveys it. Just as a movie has a central theme and message, even though it has many characters, plot twists, and props, so do our dreams, which are themselves inner movies that we ourselves direct but don't always understand fully.

Dreams beyond Time and Space

Most of the dreams we have are lucid; the dreamer feels wide awake, as in real life. A passive dream, in which we are lethargic and mere witnesses to events, is the hallmark of a symbolic dream. Symbolic dreams can also change objects, scenery, and characters in the blink of an eye. We tend to accept these transformations because we are not hampered by the logic of the wake state that requires "A" to precede "B." In dreams, time and space are not fixed constructs. The action moves as quickly as a movie changing times, places, and colors. In the dream, we rearrange everything easily and quickly. A car becomes a bicycle or a horse, and the scenery changes accordingly. These symbols are meant to convey the idea of transportation, moving or being moved. Events in the dream state might shake us if we experienced them while awake, but they don't trouble us as much if they remain in a dream. That is why movies are similar to dreams. Both have minimal effect on us because both suspend time and space. Both are creations that carry messages transcending the events in them.

Our view of dreams completely changes when we embrace the illusion of time and space within human consciousness. If we view reality as only that which we are conscious of and focused on at a given moment, we begin to understand the illusion of time and space. It goes back to the old philosophical question, did the tree fall in the forest, if we did not see or hear it fall? From the perspective of time as linear, and space as three-dimensional, we can safely say that it did. But when we consider time and space as only here and now, then the answer is a resounding No, for reality is only what we perceive at a given moment, and duration is merely the extension of this focus. We must shift this focus to be able to embrace the fallen tree and see it at least in our mind's eye. When we do, it becomes reality to us. Without this action, it is nothing; it does not exist, for there is no reality outside of what we are focused on at any given moment.

Every idea we have and every thought we project creates a future possibility in our lives. That is what being creative really means. What is more, we can experience these future realities in the dream state and even be warned about the direction that a careless thought is leading. In this way, we confront a future self that provides us with clues to where we should focus our attention "now" in order to continue our proper unfoldment.

This takes us, interestingly enough, to the idea of fate. There are those who believe that their destiny is set, that there are pathways that we are bound to follow, regardless of decisions and actions in the present. This perspective is only partially true. The overriding concept in life is free will, the capacity of all sentient beings to shape their future by conscious action. Fate, or something like it, does exist, but its origins are in our thoughts and conception of our future. Thus, we define our fate by the thoughts and beliefs we hold. If we believe, for example, that the stars or some other outside force determines our destinies, we are giving way to our past thoughts and visions, unaware that just as we created our fate, so too can we change it. Thus, fate is not the consequence of actions and decisions outside of us; it is that we have chosen not to change prior thoughts, decisions, and actions.

To the degree that there is fate or destiny, I have fulfilled something akin to this that I have felt since I was eight years old. I did not know what form it would take, but I knew it would have something to do with spiritual insight and helping others. My friends from youth might be surprised to learn this — given the other things they saw — but it was there all along. When I was diverted, I felt pangs of unhappiness — I was wasting my time. I now feel a sense of comfort and a benign lack of concern with the outcome of this book, though I realize that there is much work ahead. I know that I have fulfilled the agreement I made to myself about my life's work. The direction has been set, the choice made, and the action taken. But it did not have to be; I chose to make it so. And that is the way fate works if we choose to follow that inner direction that makes things "right" inside.

Chapter 16 — The Practical Side of Higher Consciousness

Measures of Success

No spiritual or philosophical concept, no matter how simple or profound, is of much value unless it is practiced in daily life. The closer a seeker comes to truth, the closer he comes to discovering the tools that bring success in life. Indeed, the "secrets" of outer success are not secrets at all. In sports, business, law, the arts, and sciences the spiritual principles of success, even if appearing fortuitous, are the same. Life as we know it is short, but its lessons transcend a single lifetime. If the eternal nature of existence is not fully understood and incorporated into our lives, we cannot comprehend the larger truth fundamental to higher consciousness.

But what is success? The question has been debated for centuries. Definitions vary, depending on the level of consciousness and what we perceive as our purpose in life. The hedonist proclaims: "You only go around once, so go for all the gusto you can!" The object of life here is obviously limited, even if fleetingly satisfying. A more commonly accepted definition of success is acquisition of wealth, possessions, and power. Interestingly, this definition often has a spiritual dimension, though not immediately apparent.

Frequently, such people engage in philanthropy and community service, which are certainly noble and help to reconcile spirituality with a life devoted primarily to acquisition and power. Worldly achievements, community service, and noble gestures often result in schools, bridges, and highways named after the benefactor. In a material and competitive society, these have become widely accepted as the epitome of success. And they are no small accomplishments. Anyone who has struggled with the challenges of everyday life rightfully admires such accomplishments. Nonetheless, these pursuits are spiritually hollow. Even with the best of intentions, such acts of generosity often result in ill will, contempt, or dependency on the giver.

However, our definition of success can be expanded to encompass more than the experiences of a single lifetime. It can include the entire breadth of existence, in all dimensions of reality/illusion, and our ultimate spiritual purpose in life. Defined in this manner, the more materialistic measures of success are not only shallow, but also counterproductive to spiritual growth. The path to material or socially defined success is fraught with peril for those seeking a higher spiritual purpose in life. Indeed, while the end may justify the means under a materialistic definition of success, to the enlightened person, the means are more important than the end. The person who lives an honest life, honoring truth and living by its call, respecting others and giving to life and those around him, may accomplish more, spiritually, than the most honored figure in history.

What emerges is a definition of life and success in which outward accomplishment, though important, is not the most important measure. The competitive standard of life, defined as winning and acquiring, is only one part of a larger unfolding drama. Recognizing and living both dimensions simultaneously are the keys to the practice of higher consciousness. This is the greatest challenge we face. The two have many parallels and divergences. An unsuccessful job is usually viewed, from a physical life perspective, as a failure, and it can lead to feelings of defeat. But from a spiritual perspective, the measure is how well the individual maintains inner and outer balance and spiritual awareness throughout the experience. The test is whether she focuses on the spiritual lessons offered by the experience or the traditional measures of outward success or failure. This illustration carries into every aspect of our lives. Frustration, disappointment, deadlock, and delay are all around us all of the time. Too often, our focus on outcomes rather than inner processes affects the actual outcome and, more importantly, our spiritual growth. Viewing life from only one perspective destines us to be the effect of life, forever wandering, never finding the levers of control.

The person who understands the spiritual side of life and believes that prayer, visualization, and other inward processes are all that is required has, surprisingly, also missed the mark. So too has the individual who places exclusive emphasis on intellect, work, and outer efforts, for he does not realize that inner processes are equally important. The enlightened person understands that both are necessary, and in appropriate balance, to achieve complete success. Such a person understands that material success is only the means to a greater spiritual end.

Producing an Effect in Life — The Art of Manifestation

Too Much Stuff

There is a spiritual dimension that relates to outcomes. Learning to work with spirit to produce an effect is an essential lesson in spiritual development. While outcomes are important measures of spiritual progress, a lack of understanding of how spirit works causes many to miss the spiritual lessons that manifestation is designed to teach. It also leads to frustration when we cannot understand why some things seem to work and others don't.

We have seen in a previous chapter how spirit and soul work together to achieve the goals we desire. Understanding this is a prerequisite to producing an effect in life, that is, learning how to manifest what we want or need. *Thus, the spiritual component of success is that every experience is an opportunity to learn the workings of spirit in producing an effect.* This lesson is but one step in a process that leads to the spiritual goal of the God-seeker.

As we achieve goals in life and discover our intrinsic power to manifest what we choose, a strange transformation takes place. God-seekers become bored with acquisition and manifestation. They want more, which in spiritual terms means wanting less "stuff." Indeed, saturation with stuff leads to a desire for less. The country singer, Delbert McClinton, said it best in his song, *Too Much Stuff*.[1]

It is spirit's nature to manifest our goals, dreams, and desires. Once we learn how to work with spirit and how it works with us, we will have discerned the secret to achieving our goals. The end of the journey is to apply our knowledge in the Great Work, that of liberating and uplifting souls. Excesses in acquisition, power, and pleasure lead to a transformation of worldly desire into a longing for service to the whole. Soul is left asking the old refrain popularized by Peggy Lee, *Is That All There Is?*[2] This question is continuously asked until soul realizes the endgame of our experiences in life is service to the whole. But there is no rush to the door. Everyone will know when they are ready to take the next step. This step also prepares soul for its spiritual journey and eternal mission in the inner worlds of the ONE.

I've had many bouts with acquisitiveness: speedboats, yachts, sports cars, multimillion-dollar homes, and other stuff. Been there, done that. I can honestly say that the greatest lesson I learned was that possessions are overrated. I was serving my possessions far more than they were serving me. If I was not getting them fixed, paying taxes on them, worrying about their condition, or what others would think of them, then it was something else. Indeed, as a yachtsman, I soon appreciated the adage: "The two happiest days in the boat owner's life are the day he buys it and the day he sells it." I couldn't wait for either. In the end, I am far happier without the stuff. But that was *my* experience, and everyone must have his own to reach the point where he too asks, Is that all there is?

Most people are a long way from asking this question. In fact, the American dream, and increasingly the world's dream, is based on acquisition and accumulation. Of course, there is a positive side to acquisition: it keeps the economies of the world running and people able to provide for themselves. Yet it is still a diversion from life's ultimate purpose of embracing its spiritual dimension.

While we are learning the ways of spirit, we must keep searching for the end game. Failure to do so can easily lead to a wrong turn of seeking endless pleasure, power, wealth, stuff, and the ways of the negative. In the short run, they are always attractive and seductive. But when out of balance, they are destructive, effete, and counterproductive.

The Ways of Spirit in Manifesting our Goals

Having set manifestation and acquisition in a spiritual perspective, let us now explore the ways of spirit so that we can experience its gifts firsthand. Most of our early education and socialization stress the virtues of hard work and perseverance. This is a key element in achieving success. In fact, at times, hard work seems like the only thing that is under our control. However, hard work is only part of the process.

An inner component is equally important in solving the mystery of how to work with spirit. But where do we learn these principles? They are not taught, except, to a limited degree, in religion and some spiritual paths. However, in the secular world, writers and lecturers such as Wayne Dyer and Deepak Chopra have imparted valuable insights for higher consciousness and achieving outer success.[3] I believe, however, they would be among the first to say, at least in private, that they have revealed only the tip of the iceberg. They have taught basic spiritual principles, though not by that name. The practices they teach do work and pay immediate dividends.

Without guidance, the individual is left to trial and error to discern how to optimize outer and inner processes. This is the object of the practice of higher consciousness: to unite the outer and inner processes so that they are seen and lived as a whole, with both components consciously present in all aspects.

The River: A Metaphor of the Workings of Spirit

For many years, the way of spirit was a great puzzle to me. I could not understand why spirit appeared to work erratically to manifest the things I initiated. I was not fighting spirit; I cooperated with it as best I could. Still, I could not understand something: if spirit responded to thought, as I had learned, why didn't it just produce the results I desired? After all, spirit is the essence of omnipotence, omnipresence, and omniscience. Why didn't it work more predictably? Why didn't it just "do it?" Frustration and anguish about the seemingly unfathomable tendencies of spirit are among the main reasons people lose faith in the spiritual process.

After much introspection, I concluded that spirit, though intelligent and responsive, *didn't know* how it was going to manifest a particular goal. That is why the process of manifestation always seemed unpredictable. How was I to reconcile the principle of an omniscient, omnipresent, and omnipotent force with the apparent uncertainty and randomness I observed?

The solution to this paradox lies in another universal principle, which works hand-in-hand with the power of spirit: the principle of "non-interference." Spirit does not know how it will manifest a particular thought-form, because it will not force a sentient being, or anything else for that matter, to act against its will, or against the laws established to maintain universal balance. The exercise of free will is a prerequisite of spiritual development; it is the underlying principle of soul's evolution. Soul evolves by making choices and learning from consequences. This is the basis on which the principle of cause and effect works. Without the exercise of free will, the process of soul's evolution could not occur. (That is why the American Constitution is an intrinsically spiritual document, for it embodies an appreciation of free will.)

The paradox of spirit's omniscience and unpredictability was resolved for me during an inner experience in which I was taken above a river. I could see its source, its many tributaries, and its path to the sea. I came to understand that the formation of a river is an example of the pure action of spirit without human intervention. Viewing its formation, I understood the principles by which spirit operates and discovered the parallels to how spirit works in our lives.

When water builds beyond its normal level, the law of balance requires that it move to a lower level and continue to flow until it reaches a balance point, the sea. As it makes its way, it seeks the path of least resistance (another expression of non-interference or balance), which causes the winding course of most rivers. It is never a straight line, a pathway we might expect from an omnipotent, omnipresent, and omniscient force. A forming river also receives and sends out "feeder" or "feeler" streams, which merge or form tributaries and forks that eventually come together as the river moves closer to its destination. The probing, initiating feature of spirit requires many options and possibilities. Many go nowhere. Others merge with the primary flow and move inexorably to the sea. A small stream may narrow, only to enlarge again, perhaps even becoming the main channel — an unlikely outcome from the view upstream.

If from this metaphorical experience you can discern parallels to how things unfold in your life, then you are beginning to discover the ways of spirit. The accumulation of water that starts the formation of the river is like the goal we set in our lives. One is initiated by physical forces of nature, the other by the power of thought, but the process is the same. As the river makes its way, it sends forth many feeler streams for it does not know what channel will offer the least resistance. As we begin to manifest our dreams, our higher self, working with spirit, generates many possibilities. We do not know which ones will be successful, so we must try them all. The resistance we encounter lets us know which ones to pursue and which ones to let go. We pursue each option knowing that spirit has no ordained solution, only possibilities in the process of becoming. Just as the river does not know which pathway offers the least resistance, spirit does not know what individual or organization is open and willing to assist in achieving our goals.

Nature is unrelenting. It simply will not stop. The force of the water knows only one goal, reaching the sea — if the force of the water is strong enough. If not, it will settle into a lake or pond or be absorbed into the soil. The same is true of the manifestation of our thoughts and goals. We must place enough energy into them. If a goal is not strongly felt or believed, then it will turn into something else. This happens all too often. We abandon our dreams, believing that they are unattainable or unrealistic. But how can we know this? We cannot see downstream as spirit can. Our job is to provide the force — thought, belief and action — to keep the dream alive. We must make the effort to evaluate each possibility and judge its promise. We must provide the arms and legs that spirit cannot provide. Spirit cannot act for us where our efforts are required to make things happen.

If everything comes together in perfect balance and harmony for the whole, then the goal is reached; the river reaches the sea, and a pathway for creation is established. For all the waters that follow, the way has been shown and the trip is smooth. It is this way in life as well. Once we discover the means by which an outcome can be manifested, we pursue it with the ease and joy of a pioneer who has blazed a new trail. When we follow the path to success that others have followed, our way is also made easier. This is the course most choose in life. The bold and the brave are the pathfinders, and, because they have created a way for others, an effort that supports the whole, their rewards are also greater. Thus, the ways of spirit follow the twin principles of non-interference and inevitability, if the vision or goal is held to, no matter what.

"Row, Row, Row Your Boat"

My first encounter with these principles occurred during a crisis in my life. I had just lost a business that had taken several years of effort. I was distraught and looking for a way to rebound. At the time, I only felt the sting of failure and could not see the positive lessons in it. I had just started exploring higher truth at the time and stumbled upon the principles by which all things in the physical world manifest. These principles were not only intriguing, but for someone who had just lost a company and several hundred thousand dollars, a Godsend. If they were true, I would be able to recoup my losses and regain the success I had enjoyed.

The principles of spirit I was learning challenged me to manifest something that, given my circumstances and resources, I did not believe possible. I needed to compare the effectiveness of these new principles in manifesting results with those I had formerly employed. With nothing to lose, I accepted the challenge and attempted to manifest something that I had dreamed of owning but, given my finances, never believed possible. Here are the steps in the process and how it worked in manifesting my experimental goal.

Decide What You Want

The first step is deciding what you want. As simple as this sounds, it is often the greatest obstacle to achieving happiness and success. Some people are like children at the beach who gather more and more buckets into which they place one or a few scoops of sand. This course is chosen rather than concentrating on a few buckets and filling them to the top. We are often filled with so many conflicting and competing dreams, wishes, and aspirations that we are constantly creating new dreams, like new buckets, within our imagination.

Then there is the individual so beaten by life that he feels incapable of manifesting anything. He is afraid to even place his bucket on the beach. Whatever the reasons for not taking this first step, it is the starting point for understanding and eventually mastering the laws of manifestation, on this plane and beyond.

For me, the first step was easy. I considered it merely an experiment, an important attitude I later learned. The object of my dream was a yacht. I had owned and even lived on smaller boats and longed to return to life on the water. I never ceased visiting boat shows in the Washington-Annapolis area and knew the image with which to fill my inner vision: a forty-seven foot motor yacht. I had just lost a business, was deeply in debt, and saw no way this dream could manifest. I was prepared to become an instant believer if these techniques could manifest a magnificent yacht under those inauspicious circumstances.

Skeptical but willing, I embarked on the experiment designed to produce a beautiful yacht, but more importantly, to learn the principles by which spirit worked and how I could work with it. If I could learn this, I could take control of my life in a way I had never imagined. So, step one in the process was accomplished.

Elevate the Goal to the Highest Level — Levels of Manifestation

This is not so much a step in the process as a point of information between steps one and two. It involves understanding the various levels from which a manifestation can originate and the differences in how they out-picture in our lives, depending on the level from which we start them. A physical manifestation carries a particular energy that determines its nature and how we react to it.

The demands and impulses of the physical shell are well known to be undisciplined and animal-like, with little thought for our greater welfare. They are concerned with the avoidance of pain and the pursuit of pleasure. Their counsel should not always be heeded, except on matters of survival. Pain says to avoid a particular action. Hunger (not desire) is a clear signal to feed the organism. Sexual urges are, of course, impulses to procreate and perpetuate the species. These impulses are well known and encountered everyday. However, as a civilization, we long ago solved the basic needs for survival and have moved into sheer indulgence where the body shouts "more of the pleasure, please!" Manifestations at this level are primitive and require great effort to discipline. In the physical, they can become excessive and easily get out of control. The vibration is low, basic, short-sighted, and short-lived.

The second level from which manifestations emanate is the astral or emotional level. Physical manifestations work with this level to create the sense of urgency to get us to respond and act, but the source of the impulse is the physical shell itself. Manifestations emanating from the astral level respond to emotional urges that do not originate from a desire to appease the physical body. They arise more from ego, which functions primarily from the emotional level. This is the awareness level of most of humankind and is at the base of most of civilization. Actions to enhance, protect, assuage, or glorify ego (and emotions) are behind most societal activities. These motivations stem from lower vibrations compared to those emanating from soul and use our higher capabilities (mental) to rationalize our actions. A fight in the school-yard or a war between nations can start from an insult to individual or national ego. In both instances, the faculties of mind are used to ratio-nalize and justify actions that might otherwise be seen as ego driven, which is to say, shortsighted and harmful.

Many manifestations of the emotional level are purely emotional in nature and have limited shelf lives. A simple example is seen in a trip to a shopping center, where — forgive a few stereotypes here — a man passes a hardware store and sees a tool that "he must have." He may already have five of the same tool, but this one is "essential." A woman passes a boutique and sees a dress that "she must have." The price is just right — too low to pass up! Both cases involve spur of the moment, emotional decisions supported by rationalizations. They emanate from the astral world of emotions and as such are unstable and short-lived. The indispensable tool ends up at the bottom of the tool chest, buried and forgotten. The woman puts the dress in the closet and never wears it. When we act from this level, the energy is short- lived and the action is often one that we later regret.

Causal manifestations flow from the dreams, images, and even fairy tales of our youth. We think we no longer want to realize them. Yet from the storehouse of our memories, they exert influence. The desire for a princess-like wedding complete with white gown and every sensible and nonsensical accoutrement imaginable lies dormant. Then that special moment arrives and a flood of images cascades forth, call-ing for actualization. Similarly, a young man's desire for conquests might be dormant but later lead to actions the adult neither wants nor enjoys, but nonetheless pursues to fulfill a vision in his memory. Some images carry over from lifetime to lifetime. They can be counteracted by conscious recognition of their influences and determination to stop them. Manifestations from this level often carry the feeling of going through the motions, even of being compelled to act, but lack the fulfillment and longevity of manifestations from higher levels.

Manifestations with a heavy mental component, whether or not the originating impulse is mental, tend to be more lasting, stronger in content, and also more usable. The higher vibrations of the mental level produce outcomes of a superior nature. Most manifestations of civilization are of this sort. Planning creates equivalents of the manifestation in the inner worlds, which work through various inner levels long before they finally out-picture in the physical. In recent years, "computer aided design" has greatly enhanced our minds' capacity to get machines to do our thinking. By replicating the mind's logical processes in computers, we teach it to think, which in turn has sharpened our own thinking.

Artificial intelligence has come a long way and, according to the forecasts of Ray Kurzweil,[4] it will go much further. Kurzweil sees a day when our memories will be transferred, or downloaded, into a computer, which raises fundamental questions about the nature of life itself. When computers are able to speak, think, and recall from memory banks, as we do, they might argue someday that they are as sentient as we. From a purely scientific point of view, the arguments might seem to have merit. However, from a spiritual perspective, the essence of what and who we are far exceeds mere memories (causal or otherwise) and logical thinking. Our physical shell is not what we are, no matter how complex and extraordinary it may appear or how well we are able to replicate its functions.

As God-soul, our destiny is to consciously function in a higher dimension of reality, the reality of the ONE. Until a computer can bridge the divide between the physical and the inner worlds — a highly unlikely occurrence — we will only have created machines that are smarter, more productive, and capable of replicating some of our higher functions. However, Kurzweil is probably correct that machines and artificial intelligence will someday exceed the thinking capacity of humans in the physical dimension.

The higher vibration level and the ability to consider and select from competing possibilities make creation from the mental level superior to the examples we've mentioned. Should our tool aficionado ask himself, "Do I really need this?" he would doubtless receive an inner nudge saying he already has enough, thwarting his emotional tool binge. The impulse shopper would likewise receive a nudge saying that another dress — regardless of the price — was not really needed. When we elevate our feelings to the mental level and ask a few questions, we receive superior advice. Remember: our body and emotions respond to our desires and wants. Our minds respond to our needs and practicability — higher concepts that help us with the often shrill demands of our bodies and emotions.

Finally, we can choose to start a manifestation or to question an impulse from the perspective of soul. At this level of awareness, we ask whether an action or creation is for our spiritual growth and the good of the whole. If we think about it, this is how to spiritualize our every thought, word, and action. We raise ourselves, actions, and lives to a higher level. What is more, we increase our chances of a successful and positive outcome. When we find a way to benefit others as well as ourselves, we merge with the impulses of the ONE and bring the vibration of this higher perspective into the physical, where it benefits all.

A moment's reflection tells us this is the formula on which all great success is based. A song, painting, book, product, or service are all manifestations whose success is optimized to the degree that they seek to benefit all. It certainly benefits the creator even more, but this is the natural by-product of understanding and working with this principle. It not only makes commercial sense, but is also in accord with the highest spiritual principles.

When I was experimenting with manifestation of the yacht, I was trying to understand the ways of spirit, how manifestation works. I determined to use the lessons by imparting the message of spirit to everyone who wished to hear it. In succeeding years, I told the story of the yacht and its ramifications to all. Hopefully, my retelling inspired others to make their own experiment with spirit to prove its reality for themselves. The retelling was for the good of the whole. Thus, I had elevated the exercise to the highest level, increasing its chances of success and expanding me spiritually at the same time.

Develop a Clear Image with Emotion and Detail

Once your goal has been aligned with a higher level and purpose, you are ready to proceed with the remaining steps in the manifestation process. The next step is to form a clear image, complete with sound, light, emotions, and scenery, of whatever you are creating. This is not particularly difficult, even though my inner picture of the yacht was at times blurred. I soon learned that perfect visualization of an image is not essential; the emotional element is far more important (assuming you have first elevated the creation to a higher level). This involved seeing the picture and experiencing the feelings that would result from acquiring the boat.

It was easy for me to close my eyes (or open them) and feel the wind on my face and the sea spray against my skin as I cruised the yacht to parts unknown. In time, this image became so real that I spent my free time deep in my inner picture. I could feel the experience as if I were there. This isn't very hard — any good daydreamer has done it many times. We have all felt our attention drifting to some other place and time, such that we forgot where we were or what we were supposed to be doing. By the conscious focus of attention on selected inner visions, we can turn daydreaming into productive and spiritual ends.

Visualization became an important part of my recovery from the emotional dislocation accompanying my business setback. Every time the sting of this setback came to my attention, I dealt with what I had created. But as soon as I had done all that I could responsibly do, I moved back into my vision, where I experienced great joy and happiness.

Getting Out of the Way: The Proper Attitude for Success

I once felt — wrongly, I was to learn — that worrying about a problem would help to solve it. When we worry, however, we give negative mental and emotional energy to the situation. This simply pollutes the soil in which our dream is growing. Practicing visualization took me completely away from this mode of thinking. Instead of worrying, I was happy and filled with energy and excitement over the vision — the new reality I was creating. When my staff asked how I remained so happy in the face of such a setback, I would smile inwardly and answer obliquely, for I had planted a seed that required silence to ensure its unfettered growth. Silence is an important part of the process. When we are in the delicate and precious process of creation, too much talk not only evokes negative thoughts and words from naysayers, but also drains us of vital energy needed for visualization and action.

Detachment is also important. When we are too attached to an action, we are anxious and block the flow of vital spiritual energy. This is called the "principle of reverse effect." Athletes know it well. They realize that trying too hard makes them tense, hurting their performance. The same is true of our efforts in manifestation, the more we want something, worry about it, and tense up, the more we block the flow of spirit. When we relax, even see the fun in the experience, we become detached and more able to do our best. We also become clearer channels for spirit, enhancing our chances for success. I always taught my children three magic words: *Simple, Easy, Fun*. These words open our creative centers and allow thoughts to flow with the vibration and state of consciousness associated with these words. My children would eagerly anticipate what they were trying to accomplish with an attitude of fun. This is a healthy and powerful attitude. It might seem the opposite of detachment, but eager anticipation — trusting in the power of spirit — engenders detachment from tension by an excited expectation of what spirit will bring. This is especially true if this attitude is linked with any of the three magic words. When we eagerly anticipate something, like a child on Christmas Eve, there is an acceptance, surrender, and, depending on your Santa Claus, a certainty about the outcome of the morning's haul. This attitude recognizes a partner, a second force that can be trusted to "deliver the goods."

An attitude of experimentation is similarly harmonious with the process of manifestation. Experimentation is an attitude associated with detachment from results along with a curiosity, if not a fascination, with what is taking place. In this case, it is a fascination with the process by which the miracle of spirit works. All of these attitudes support detachment, which is necessary to a successful manifestation.

Follow Through on All Leads and Ideas Presented by Spirit

It took about a week before things began to happen, things that I did nothing to initiate except for my assiduous practice of inner visualizations. The first sign was an unsolicited call from a yacht broker. It came from out of the blue. I had not heard from him since I attended a boat show in Annapolis years ago, when I boarded a forty-seven foot yacht. This boat quickly became my dream boat. Though the show had taken place years earlier, I only recently had made it the object of my experiment. The salesman, sensing my surprise at his call, offered that he had retained the cards of people expressing interest in the craft. Leaving my card was a small price to pay for the privilege of seeing and inspecting this beautiful vessel. I was very interested at the time but, sadly, very broke as well. He explained that the yacht I admired so much (and apparently so obviously) had recently been put up for sale. He then asked if I was interested! I blithely replied, "I might be," and made an appointment.

I was soon aboard the boat, which had been the object of my inner vision for the prior two weeks. It was magnificent! We navigated the boat down a small inlet and then into the Chesapeake Bay. I felt the wind and the spray, just as in my vision. The only difference was that I was simply a prospective buyer, not the owner. But I was satisfied. Not bad for two weeks of visualization, even if I was only a prospect, and one with no money.

Two weeks later, to my utter amazement, I received a call from a second broker offering another of these rare yachts. I traveled to Richmond, Virginia, where the second craft was located, and enjoyed yet another cruise. This second call was further confirmation that something was happening quite outside of my direct control. I was encouraged and persisted with renewed vigor. The second craft was quite tempting but having already built up a head of steam for the first one, it was ultimately my choice. The "only" obstacles to realizing my dream were the huge down payment and financing. But I was not about to stop. By this time, I was impressed with the experiment and determined to see it through. My confidence was growing by leaps and bounds, for I saw that something I did — my thoughts and visualizations — had had an impact on forces outside of me. My inner actions made a difference. I had the power to make inner pictures that had an impact on what was happening. When this connection is experienced for the first time, it is one of the most powerful and empowering experiences a person can have. It is the first taste of our vast creative abilities.

The experiment was progressing well, except for a small matter of a large down payment. Toward the end of the third week, an auditor for another company I operated inquired about the other business venture that had ended. He informed me that the losses might result in a sizable tax refund (because of a rule allowing losses to be used against tax payments in prior years). I invited him to look into the matter and, within a week, he returned with startling news: I was entitled to a substantial refund. Even more startling, it was the exact amount of the down payment!

I was surprised by my reaction. There was calm, a sense of inevitability, which grew out of realizing I had consciously and purposefully tapped into the power behind events. I reached a point I would return to quite often over the years, when I stopped trying to manipulate events. Instead, I understood that my role as creator of my universe started with the decision of what to create. Then, it shifted from initiator to implementer, where I would follow all leads and opportunities. As seen in this example, because of the principle of non-interference that underpins all spiritual growth, the final direction from which our dreams and visions will manifest cannot be known in advance. Manifestation depends entirely on what channels are open, that is, what people or institutions are willing to participate in the manifestation of a particular thought, dream, or vision.

After much vacillation about the use of my tax windfall, I decided to see the experiment through and signed a contract to purchase my dream boat. Confident but not certain, I proceeded to the next stage of acquiring financing. I suppose I thought I had the Midas touch and that this next stage would proceed as easily as the others. I was sadly mistaken. I was still several hundred thousand dollars in debt. Even spirit was not able to prevent a string of rejections from banks.

I was at a loss. I thought spirit would just breeze through the experiment and somehow persuade a dazed banker to sign off on the loan. That proved not to be the case. I was chastened. Then, I remembered that the rules dictated that, no matter what happens, do not focus on outside events as the measure of success. Do not allow outer factors to diminish belief in the power of spirit to manifest your dream. I continued to repeat this principle to myself and actually convinced myself of its merits by contemplating the creation of the planets, star systems, and life itself. Now that was first-class creation! What was my little boat (Noah had to build his!) compared with the marvel of these creations? I stuck with it, not knowing what or how this final hurdle would be overcome, but I believed it would be.

It happened, as no one should be surprised by now, in a most unusual way. While purchasing a car for my brother, I met the dealership owner and mentioned the pictures of beautiful boats in his office. After chatting about our common interest, I mentioned my anticipated purchase. He asked if I had selected a bank for the financing. I answered that I was "talking to several" — I hid the pain well. My response led him to volunteer that a friend ran the bank that handled his company's financing. He continued that he would be happy to arrange a meeting. Not wanting to trouble him — and with my desperation well hidden — I "reluctantly" accepted his offer. The very next day, I went to the bank and, after some preliminaries, got the loan.

It was now about six weeks from day one of the experiment. And, to my utter astonishment, I was proudly aboard my new yacht, sailing up the Potomac River to its new berth in Washington, D.C. The final picture of standing on the fly bridge of *my* boat, wind and spray in my face, was like a snapshot come to life, for the vision that I held for those many weeks was finally a reality. More importantly, a true believer was born.

I repeated this experiment numerous times over the years and with the same positive results. What is remarkable and also regrettable is that I still went through periods during which I forgot this lesson and returned to the old ways of worry and control. Worry didn't work before, and worry didn't work then. In fact, it hindered me even more. Fortunately, I would quickly remember my lesson and the joy of the process. Abandoning worry and returning to my partnership with spirit always felt like a rebirth, and indeed in many ways it was. Each time, I shed the illusion of separateness and of not controlling events of my life. As a partner working with spirit, I knew my role and remembered the lessons of my earlier success. Each time I returned, I reinforced the lessons until they became ingrained into my mental processes and thus a part of me.

This story illustrates the dual purpose of all worldly experiences. The manifestation of the boat was not remotely as important as understanding the process. The lessons transcend time and space; they remain with us into eternity. It is my duty in this lifetime, my part in the Great Work, to teach these principles to all who wish to learn. This story also illustrates how easy it is to miss the real lessons of life when our attention is focused on winning, acquiring, and having. The end does not justify the means. Instead, the means *give meaning* to the end. The goal is achieved when we understand the spiritual principles by which life operates and consciously incorporate these principles into our thoughts, words, and actions. To achieve this, I will start with the most basic of spiritual principles. It is called the Master Principle.

The Master Principle

The process by which all creation comes into being begins with the choice of our state of consciousness. Stated another way, our state of consciousness depends on our initial choice of thought, for a state of consciousness is nothing more than focused thought, which initiates attitudes, feelings, and actions. "I think, therefore I am" has long been the credo of those who revere the thought of René Descartes. But "I think and *that is what* I am" might be an even more profound insight.

The creative font of all things is thought. When coupled with our inner capacity to visualize and feel what we are thinking (imagination), we have touched the very modus of creation itself. This is the process of creation for everything we see around us, whether created by nature or humankind. While my examples reveal many steps in the process of manifestation, it all starts with the *choice* of thought. This takes us to what I call the Master Principle. Once we have mastered mental discipline, we have the key to working with spirit. This is not achieved at the macro-level. Rather, it is a process that begins at the micro-level and extends to every single thought.

The Master Principle
The greatest power that I possess is the power to decide what I will think next. From this decision my future is constructed.

This principle affects everything from our moment-by-moment thoughts to great decisions in our life. Most people live as the effect of what happens around them, allowing their thoughts to shift and move depending on outward stimuli. Whether television, the latest song, a phone-call from a friend, a problem at the office, or a casual comment heard in passing, we allow our thoughts to be controlled or directed by external forces, often without complaint. We relinquish control of our thoughts and feelings to world events or the slightest trivia that come our way. We do not see the impact this has on our lives. We do not understand the connection between thought and the manifestation of events and circumstances that unfold around us.

Our feelings and attitudes, moment by moment, are shaped by the thoughts we project into spirit. As we have seen, these thoughts make an impression, much as when we press our hands into sand. The force and extent of the thought makes a deeper impression on this spiritual sand and thus influences the speed and precision of what ultimately manifests. Fortunately, we are placed in the physical reality precisely because it is very forgiving and requires a certain focus of attention before it out-pictures. If it were not so, a careless thought would have done us in years ago!

I remember a vivid inner experience that dramatically illustrated this point to me. I was traveling at the astral level, where flight is quite easy. If you have ever had a dream of flying or falling, then you know what I mean. It is a glorious experience. I could actually feel the wind on my face (the astral body relates to astral substance in the same manner as the physical body relates to physical substance) and delight in the thrill of flight.

I noticed a woman some distance from me, walking along a street. I noticed she was somewhat portly and pondered my observation. Suddenly, I saw an object draped in a black sheet diving at the woman from above, attacking her. She shielded her face and braced for another attack from what were now several assailants. I flew past her and observed other strange attackers and their victims. In each case, the victim was someone about whom I had ventured a careless opinion, intruding into his or her space with an idle, pejorative thought. After a few encounters of this nature, it was clear that *I* was the source of these black marauders. They were reflections of my negative thought forms. This experience taught me the critical importance of monitoring my thoughts for careless gossip or idle speculation about people.

Negative thought forms reach out and touch people. They can enter a person's dreams and attack them. Idle space-invading thoughts can also initiate disturbing feelings in a person that cause unsuspecting mood swings. The thoughts we carelessly entertain are restrained to some extent by the very nature of the physical plane. After all, this is the "first grade" of spiritual instruction for all God-seekers.

Thought is the starting point, but focus is the incubator that gives thought "critical mass" for action and manifestation. When we set a goal and focus our thoughts on its accomplishment, we can see the working of the Master Principle in our lives. We choose a thought (our goal) and give it energy by continued thought and visualization. We act on the ideas that flow to us for implementation. But what happens when we are not consciously thinking about our goal? What about our thoughts as we listen to the news? What of our reactions to something said in the office that upset us? What happens if we dwell on it need-lessly and expend emotional energy imagining what we might have said or done? What about the fears that blight our dreams? These thoughts hinder realization of our goals. We must control these thoughts lest we become the effect of everything and everyone around us. When we learn to turn these idle, careless, and destructive thought patterns into productive, positive, and creative ones, we take control of our lives and the outcomes that manifest. Indeed, with a decision to take control of thought, we can even counteract the most insidious of all destructive thought patterns — what I have come to call "background noise."

Background noise is the flotsam and jetsam of thoughts and words that flow through our minds in daily life — at least when we do not consciously control or monitor them. It is the backwash of experiences and feelings, often worked out in the dream state, that have become part of our conscious stream of thought. Its influence in our lives is greater than we imagine, for it garners the same mental energy that we bestow upon our cherished life goals. This is the destructive baggage that lurks behind our positive thoughts, whispering words of discouragement, fear, and despair. It can produce debilitating states of panic, worry, or anger, leaving us puzzled about their origin. Background noise can be positive or negative, depending on our habits and experiences. Whatever its content, we must identify it as friend or foe, supportive or destructive of our hopes and dreams.

During a workshop on the art of manifestation, I assigned the class a take-home experiment. They were asked to keep a journal of thoughts occurring every thirty minutes. They were to record the tone and message (content) of these thoughts — positive or negative — to try to discern a pattern. The object was to discover the background noise that was unknowingly affecting their accomplishments and happiness. Many were startled by the results. One participant, who was thought of as one of the most positive people in the group, courageously volunteered that she heard a great deal of negative chatter in the form of anger. She was eager to learn to counteract it. Another participant learned that his background noise contained a great deal of fear, which he came to see as the cause of his timidity in facing new experiences. He saw it as the reason behind much that had *not* happened in his life.

I too discovered underlying messages in my background noise that I had to undo. But how to undo something that had been constructed over many years was the question of the day. Something so elusive, recognizable only in moments of introspection, is a formidable challenge to spot and replace. I found the solution in the application of the Master Technique — a means to implement the Master Principle.

The Master Technique

The Master Technique involves the application of the Master Principle outlined above into a moment-by-moment practice. The monitoring and selection of our thoughts is the key to controlling events in our lives. Using this technique assumes that you have accepted the premise that *you* are responsible for what happens in your life. Without this fundamental understanding, we are destined to be the effect of life. As painful as this may be to accept, it is liberating to realize that we also have the power to change anything in our lives. The workshop experiences show the workings of this principle. It is not just a theoretical supposition; it has immense practical value.

We have established that thought coupled with focus are the foundations for controlling what happens in our lives. I will deal with the choice of thought presently, but first let's consider focus and how to master this all-important skill. The focus of attention is the length of time we concentrate on a particular idea and bring, from all five senses, the totality of our thought power, emotion, and visualization. This makes an impression in spirit and fills it with the spiritual energy to effect change in the outer world. When I was focusing on the boat, I saw it on the screen of my mind and moved myself into this picture, eventually seeing the boat, walking its decks, sensing the weather, and feeling the pride of having it. This focus controls the direction, speed, and ease of the manifestation.

But most people cannot hold a thought. To illustrate this point, let's try something. You will need a timer of some sort. Close your eyes for a moment to reduce distractions then think about bread — any kind of bread. When you become aware that your attention has shifted to something else, stop and see how long you were able to hold your attention on this thought. For most people, it is thirty seconds or less. If you held your attention for longer, then you will be especially successful in using these techniques.

If this was difficult, then you must practice holding your attention. In time, you will be able to do this with ease and increase your power to focus. The method of extending focus is a mechanical one that combines an awareness of the mind's preference for order, structure, and repetition with a visualization aid that prolongs the focus of attention for whatever period we choose (the longer the better). The basic technique is the visual template we form within our mind in units of twenty-five. (You can develop your own template later, but try this first.) We do this by repeating a word or idea, such as "success," on which we wish to focus twenty-five times while completing a five-by-five template in our minds. Each time you say the word and think about it using emotions, visuals, and so on, make a mental mark or circle that indicates that you have completed one or more of the twenty-five repetitions. In your mind, the five-by-five template may look something like this:

X X X X X
X X X X X
X X X X X
X X X X X
X X X X X

Before providing a few tips to enhance your success with this practice, let me introduce another concept. It is called a focus-unit. It is the length of time that is spent thinking about (focusing on) a single word or thought as you move through the completion of your matrix. The number of focus-units placed on a word or thought impacts the length of time and the ease with which you will control manifestations and ultimately your life.

Some tips:

1) Vary the approach in completing the template, because the mind likes variety. For example, start filling in at each corner, then the middle of each side then, fill in the middle along the outside borders, then complete the outside borders, leaving a three-by-three matrix in the center of the template to complete. There are of course countless variations. You may find some more interesting than others.

2) Place only momentary attention on completing the template so that your energy, thought, and emotion is focused on the idea or word you have selected. Remember visually where you are on the template, so don't get off track — this is very easy to do!

3) Always complete a set of twenty-five. Make this a commitment and you will get in the habit of controlling large periods of focused thought on any idea or state of consciousness.

4) You might get bored with a particular word or state of consciousness. You can vary this by making each line of your matrix a different word while placing extended time on each word for each of the five focus-units.

5) Choose the number of sets you wish to complete. Holding a thought for periods of three, four, or even ten sets (count of 250 focus-units) is not unusual. You can even commit to focus on a particular idea for up to a count of a thousand in a day; dividing the number of times you complete a set(s) throughout the day. This is a marvelous way to

plan controlled focus. Remember, the longer you keep your focus on an idea, the more quickly and powerfully it will come into existence.

6) Add emotion and visual imagery. This can be done inwardly (if you don't want to scare the neighbors) or shouted out if in your car or another private place. Whatever it takes to gather excitement and passion in your focus and visualization process, the more effective.

7) Don't just focus on things. Remember that your overall state of consciousness is the soil in which your ideas and dreams grow. Anger, worry, fear and hate create poor soil. Indeed such soil is a killer of dreams except those that are decidedly negative. Happiness, joy, love, and ideas with a high vibration produce fertile soil in which any positive idea will flourish.

8) Use busy time such as driving, waiting, bathroom breaks, exercise, etc. to practice your disciplined-thought gardening. Just think: if I am not planting the seeds that I choose, what am I planting instead? What am I creating for which I do not want to be responsible? I am responsible for what out-pictures in my life, so I might as well choose what I want!

9) Consider the amount of time you devote to TV, radio, and magazines. How are these inputs affecting your life? Do you have them out of balance? Are you getting emotionally involved in them? We must all read and stay informed, and entertainment is fun and an essential part of a balanced life. The issue is balance, emotional commitment, and focus.

10) Always remember to respect the space of others especially in your inner visions. Without their permission, inclusion of their images in your vision is a violation of their space, for visions create reality.

Words as States of Consciousness

If thoughts are things, words are mountains. What we say, hear, or read reveals only a small part of the meaning, variation, related emotion, and the deep — even ancient — responses that those words can trigger. Everything we experience has a word or words that convey a picture, emotion, or a level of intensity of that experience. Words as thoughts combined with concentrated focus, visualization, feeling, and knowingness form the basis of power that we observe in the universe. It is the way of creation. It is the process that we are here to learn. As we master it, we learn greater universal wisdom until, in time, we achieve our goals of soul-actualization and awareness of the ONE. When we view life this way, we begin to understand that every incident presents an opportunity to learn and practice this principle. We see that life is indeed a spiritual experience, and that we are all God-seekers, though we may not appreciate the opportunities for spiritual growth that present themselves every moment of our lives.

Words, feelings, and attitudes compose what we commonly call a state of consciousness. Thus, every word shapes a state of consciousness. We can understand, even sense, what "is" is (sorry, I couldn't resist!). Consequently, we must choose the words, goals, and pictures on which we focus our attention, for they determine what we will see in our lives next week, next month, and next year. Another important dimension of word power is the effect that words have on enhancing the power of our thoughts, images, and feelings.

To illustrate this, consider the word "success." For most of us, it evokes a positive response, even an exciting one. When we think about this word for a period of time, it usually places us in a state of consciousness with considerable positive energy and power. Add a simple adjective "sweet" and we have "sweet success." This new phrase evokes the same positive feelings, but now they are enhanced, and a more powerful feeling is engendered. Such is the power of words. They also create more powerful inner images and stimulate the energy that flows from strongly held feelings.

The spiritual energy that is employed in the physical dimension (sometimes called "etheric energy") is the inner power that we bring to our aid by the use of imagination and focused attention. When we extend the period of focused attention through the Master Principle, we feel better not only because of the state of consciousness we have tapped, but also because of the length of time we have dwelled in this state. Other adjectives are equally effective in boosting the energy of this or any other word. Words like "powerful," "exciting," "immediate," "overwhelming," "dazzling" also work well in providing a more powerful image, thus evoking more spiritual power to a manifestation. Whether we use an adjective, adverb, interjection, or other part of speech, remember to use them in your verbalizations and inner images to expand the power of the technique.

The Breath of Life

Another technique I have used over the years is an old Yoga breathing exercise. I have found it very effective in increasing the store of spiritual (etheric) energy necessary to manifestation and in maintaining balance throughout the day. (As with any exercise, be mindful of your physical condition and consult professional medical advice if you are in doubt about starting any new regimen.) Sit in the meditative posture. Inhale deeply from the abdomen and through the nose to a count of seven. Hold this breath to another count of seven, then exhale through the mouth to a count of seven. Repeat the process seven times. Aside from being a comfortable number of repetitions, the number seven also has great spiritual and psychic significance for many people.[5]

This exercise will make you feel more positive, if not giddy, and you can use it to enhance the Master Technique. Use each count as a focus-unit, filling your image with the energy you are generating. Imagine this energy is flowing into your inner and outer body with each breath and that all negative thoughts are flowing out as you exhale. You might imagine you are standing in the light as it flows into your body. Alternatively, image that you have traveled to the sun and are absorbing its energy, which enhances everything in your life.

A companion exercise works in the opposite direction. We use this approach when we are "hyper," agitated, or generally need to "cool it." Sitting in the meditative position, exhale from the mouth to the count of seven. Hold your depleted breath to the count of seven. Don't faint; breathe if you have to! Inhale again through the nose to the count of seven and repeat the cycle seven times. The calming effects are astounding. Both practices also have health benefits by increasing or decreasing the spiritual energy available to help the inner and outer bodies to function properly.

If you are beginning to see the point of this, then you are recognizing that it is imagination coupled with words, images, feelings, and thoughts, enhanced through focus, that give power and effect. The power of thought cannot be overemphasized. Indeed, the Master Principle needs to be frequently stated or otherwise placed in front of our attention at all times:

> *The greatest power that I possess is the power to decide what I will think next. From this decision my future is constructed.*

We cannot avoid thinking and therefore creating. Even as you read this passage, if skepticism is high in your mind, you are adding energy to that thought form. You are at this moment actively creating this by your choice of thought. Ask yourself, Is this what I want to create? Do I want to control my life or be a cynic doubting everything until it is proven to me? The problem with this line of thinking, if you are a victim, is that *you must prove it to yourself.* Equally, in life, you must also *do it for yourself.*

We have already been given the gift through which we can have everything. But success goes to the believer or at least to the person willing to shed doubts and skepticism long enough to try. Only then, will you prove it to yourself. Remember the story of the boat. I was as skeptical as a well-trained, egocentric Harvard Law graduate could be. Yet I was willing — prompted, I admit, by the pain from business setbacks — to experiment. It was my willingness to shed intellectual snobbery and try something different that opened up a whole new world to me. I did not have to abandon my analytic propensity or my questioning nature to embrace this new world. Perhaps I digress too much regarding skepticism, but I know this state of consciousness well and realize the power it restrains. Skepticism is often built on fear: fear of looking dumb, stupid, or gullible. But, like falling in love, we never know what it is or can be until we take the leap of faith and risk pain to venture into this unknown land.

A Personal Treasure Trove: Words to Live By

We have considered the Master Principle, the Master Technique, and the power to affect our inner and outer world lying behind all words. We have also considered the importance of formulating goals and using states of consciousness to stimulate their growth to manifestation. The "magic" inherent in this process is the only true magic. We are often impatient with the ways of spirit. We want it to work on our time schedule, not in the perfect ways of spirit, reflecting concern for the whole of life. Remember the imagery of the river. It is exemplary of the pure action of spirit and tells us much about its formative ways. There is no greater power, for it is the only power that is.

I have had opportunities to experiment with words to find the most powerful ones for me. Before considering the actual words themselves, I recognized very early the importance of a system for remembering the words I selected. I sought a portable reminder device — a chaplet — which would always be with me. Whenever I saw or touched it, I would be reminded of the words of power that I had selected to monitor and direct my thoughts and thus my life. I chose the ten fingers of my hands as the device. Each finger was associated with a category of words. Each word represented a powerful state of consciousness sufficient to maintain balance, no matter the circumstance.

During the day, I gauged my thoughts. If sad or fearful, I selected a powerful state of consciousness and substituted it. Every morning and throughout the day, I repeated each word for at least five focus-units. I always found the perfect word to achieve the desired state. Remember the amphitheater with hundreds of doors? Each door represented a state of consciousness, such as love or beauty, which carried a high spiritual vibration capable of propelling the seeker into the center of the light of spirit. This is what a focus of attention on special words of power achieves: it propels us into the center of spiritual energy, into pure consciousness, where all creation begins.

Most people achieve a state of consciousness such as happiness by recollecting a scene or incident. Memories hold good and bad feelings. By recalling events, we are either helped or deterred in reaching our goals. However, there is another way to achieve this state of consciousness. It does not depend on memories, facsimiles, or recall. As we have seen, words are doorways to states of consciousness that represent far more than the words themselves. They exist apart from memories and events that evoked them. We can tap into this pure area of consciousness merely by contemplating the word and moving into this inner region, where states of consciousness exist in pure form.

Here is a short experiment. Repeat the word "happiness" or the phrase "I am happy." Do this at least twenty-five times. You will begin to feel happy long before you get to the twenty-fifth repetition. Say the word with energy and use your imagination to act out and feel the state of consciousness. Resist the temptation to recall a specific event. You are trying to learn how to create any state you desire merely by using the Master Technique of repetitive focus-units.

I have faced situations, especially in my business, when fear, if not panic, was the soup of the day. In fact, it was precisely during a period like this that I discovered the power behind the Master Technique. Try as I might, fear and worry persisted; I could not break their hold. I found that by repeating a word (rapidly at first, to prevent other thoughts from entering) I was able to maintain my focus long enough for the desired state to take hold. Once I began to feel it, I persisted to build more energy around the thought form. I shifted from fear and worry to courage and happiness. Always remember: the ability to change thoughts and inner states is the ability to control our lives.

I remember conducting a workshop in England several years ago during which a woman volunteered: "Sir, what can I do? I don't believe that I can do anything." I asked for clarification, for certainly she could not mean that literally. She related that her confidence was so low she did not believe she could do anything in her life. The audience let out a sigh of sympathy and looked with anticipation for my response. I asked her to say "God loves me," but she hesitated. I asked her to try, and after a few moments, to her seeming amazement, she succeeded. I prompted her to repeat the phrase five times. She balked again, expressing doubt about this more difficult task, but I persisted. With the audience's encouragement, she made the attempt and, to thunderous applause, she reached the fifth recitation of "God loves me." When I asked her how she felt, she offered that she indeed felt much better. I then encouraged her to repeat this phrase and add "I am powerful and capable." Gaining confidence and encouraged by the audience, she broached a smile and started her new assignment. Success brought a standing ovation, and she beamed with a newfound sense of empower-ment. I advised her to repeat the exercise every half-hour for the first several days, then every hour afterward, progressively increasing the space between "inoculations" until she was able to maintain this confi-dent and happy state.

I was later told that she became a new person. I was also told that others in attendance, not as willing to reveal their less acute but similar state, benefited as well. It does work — and immediately! It is the power to change our thoughts and, more importantly, to control our very next thought.

The Portable Chaplet

The diagram below depicts a set of words and practices that represent powerful states of consciousness that can be used to balance negative moods or enhance positive ones. Consistent practice, using them to fill the moments of idle, floating, destructive, background noise, will change your life. We have only to look to ourselves for what we have manifested. As we look at our lives, few are satisfied with everything they see. It is no simple machine, these bodies that we have been given. But the reward that comes from diligent practice of these words of discipline, happiness, and control, is indeed transforming.

LEFT HAND (facing you)

Spiritual	Harmony	Achievement	Discipline	Strength
Surrender Humility Gratitude Balance Truth Love	Happiness Joy Peace Bliss Calm Relax	Success Financial & Spiritual Abun- dance Achievement Passion Easy, Simple, Fun	Organization Order Discipline Self Control	Courage Toughness Fight Detachment Trust in Spirit
Thumb	Index	Middle	Ring	Pinky

RIGHT HAND (facing you)

Spiritual	Harmony	Achievement	Discipline	Strength
Higher Con-sciousness Affirmation (1)	Higher Con-sciousness Contempla-tion (1)	Personal Goals	Higher Con-sciousness Contempla-tion (2)	Meditation and the Higher Con-sciousness Affirmation (2)
Pinky	Ring	Middle	Index	Thumb

These techniques will not only enhance your life but can also be used to improve the performance of teams, companies, marriages, families, or any group. It is very difficult to develop group cohesion and focus when other members are not aware of these principles or are reluctant to practice them. We can counteract much of the negativity created by their undisciplined thought forms by utilizing these techniques for longer periods. We often see this in team sports when a plague of negativity infects a team spiraling downward. Of course, the opposite occurs for a winning team. Understanding and practicing these principles can help the team in a tailspin reverse the trend quickly, and the one enjoying a winning streak to sustain it.

When our family sets a new goal, my wife, Mary, and I agree on a picture to evidence it's accomplishment. We agree to allow the other to be pictured in the vision — a critically important step so as not to invade the free will of another. We hold this vision for extended focus-units until the goal is realized. Businesses in the West are only beginning to practice these principles. The popularity of teams, the recognition that management does not have all the answers, and the solicitation of genuine participation from everyone are examples of the recognition and adoption of these principles. Of course, business did not adopt them because they are spiritual, but rather because they have been found to work.

Exploring the underlying spiritual principles behind this success can have an equally transforming effect on more advanced methods. Some companies discuss the vision and the goal they wish to accomplish. Once agreement is reached, the organization proceeds smoothly. When detractors continually put forth negative energy, the harm they do cannot be adequately measured. Teams and organizations are aware of the negative impact that negative thinkers can have. But because we do not place as much emphasis on thought as we do on action, we permit far too much destructive energy to be released before anything is done.

Integration of the Contemplations

A great deal of emphasis has been placed on the tools, strategies, and tactics needed to deal with the demands of our increasingly fast-paced life. One of the great debilitations with which we must contend is the problem of "immersion," the distracting and engrossing nature of daily life that results in a loss of spiritual perspective, a temporary amnesia. However, if we remember, master, and practice the principles and stratagems in this book, we will flow through life, in control, successful and happy. Unfortunately, most of the time, daily life leads us to forget them. That is why it is so important to frequently reread this and other chapters. It will refocus your attention and strengthen your revamped spiritual paradigm. The alternative is to be the effect of life always reacting to its entreaties rather than directing its course.

Another debilitating habit of thought is one I have termed "telescoping." This is the tendency to view a current problem and see its impact into the future without the benefit of intervening counteractions. This is what my son did when he worried about his ability to meet the requirements of an adult and a father. He saw himself faced with these responsibilities without the benefit of intervening years of growth, maturity, and learning. Indeed, he had no way of knowing that any of these things would or could happen. He only knew where he was at that time and what he would face. He telescoped and increased his anxiety and worry. What is more, persistence with that form of thinking would in time produce some version of the very incompetence he dreaded. That is why it is so important to live in the "now" the present moment knowing that there are a thousand "nows"— opportunities for change — that can and will intervene to change our outlook and thereby the outcome.

Of all these, worry and fear are the two greatest debilitations. When we are locked in the mundane, we forget our higher self, why we are here, and the power we have to control our lives. Forgetting these principles leads to negative states and surrender to forces outside of ourselves. We believe more in what will *not happen* than in the possibility that with spirit we can *make things happen*. This underscores the importance of practicing and using the Master Technique. Remember, it is always at our disposal. Whatever device reminds us of it and its underlying principles must be employed. At the outset, we are trying to overcome years of bad habits of thought and worry — negative background noise. But the principles and techniques outlined here will accomplish the changes we desire, as long as we practice them diligently.

Finally, the contemplations presented earlier should become a daily routine. Integrate them as part of your finger chaplet, if you need to be reminded of them. The fingers of the left hand have been designated to remind you of this. As you view the right hand, the first finger reminds you of the affirmation in the previous chapter. The HC Contemplation (1) is the longer contemplation. The goals (center) finger is a reminder to go over your life goals everyday to remember what you are trying to accomplish.

Goal Setting

If you have not considered your life goals for some time, take a moment to consider the six aspects of your life we outlined earlier. I recommend writing them down and developing an inner image of your goal in each area. Remember, we are setting goals all of the time. But if we are not careful, the things we see on TV, the books we read, and a hundred other external inputs will program our inner computers and set our goals for us. It is time to think seriously about what we want and to accept responsibility for what we get. Don't let prior patterns of so-called failure stop you from trying again. What you may have perceived as failure was probably spirit's way of saying you need more information — so, go get it! Your perception of failure may have stemmed from looking to only one stream as the path to the ocean, rather than seeing there are many. You must be the hands and feet of spirit trying all of the options. Don't stop until you have tried them all.

The six areas again are:

- **Spiritual:** clearly the most important. Set this goal in the form of things you are going to actively read or practice. For example, go through the fingers at least once daily and review the spiritual goals articulated in the contemplations. Remember to reconcile all other goals with your spiritual goals.

- **Physical:** Goals can be physical exercise, weight targets, and the like. Reconcile your goals by relating them to your commitment to serve spirit in the Great Work, whatever you choose it to be. For example, I seek to remain healthy to serve spirit better.

- **Financial:** What are you trying to achieve? What do you need to live as you would like? Don't be afraid to ask for what you want. See yourself looking at your bank statement and feeling happy with the balance. Follow the other principles of word power and relate them to the spiritual. For example, a stronger financial picture will enable you to give more to spirit. Remember, relate to the generic nature of spirit. The more we see others benefiting in our picture, the more we too are blessed. Don't just seek to bless yourself!

- **Social:** See yourself with your family or group, and what you want to see for them. This includes your children, spouse, or other important personal association. Whatever you want, set it in motion and do what it takes to achieve it.

- **Personal:** Don't forget yourself and what you need to achieve personal fulfillment. Does singing, painting, writing, gardening, and the like fulfill an inner need for expression? If so, see yourself doing it and taking action

— immediately and every time an idea comes to you. Relate it to your spiritual goal.

- **Professional:** School, training: you name it, then do it. If you can't take big steps in this or any other direction, at least take small steps. Determine how it will relate to your spiritual goals.

Your goals are your life. Again, if you don't set them, external events will set them for you — and you may not like what you get! If you look at what has manifested in your life in each area, then you will know what your goals have been. If there is nothing, then you have asked for nothing. If it is not what you want, you have nonetheless believed that this is what you would get, and consequently you have manifested it.

Each day, as you contemplate, write down what ideas come to you in each area and take some action, no matter how small, on each one, each day. It is certain that some areas will occupy more of your time and attention during certain periods of your life. And that is as it should be. The word "balance" in the first set of words on the first finger (left hand) is there to remind you not to neglect other parts of your life, or else you will find things manifesting you don't want.

The fourth finger of the right hand is to remind you to go over the second contemplation, or shorter version. Read it and eventually set it to memory. It represents a paradigm that you will be able to stay with, for this lifetime and into other dimensions of your existence. It incorporates your relation with the ONE, the source of your existence. Simply remembering and living from this awareness puts you in a special place, for there are many, at all levels of awareness, who have forgotten.

The last finger on the right hand is a reminder to practice the meditation/contemplation exercises daily and to use and always remember the Higher Consciousness Axiom that defines its basic tenet:

I AM
GOD IS
WE ARE ONE.

Finally, don't follow what is written in this book, or any book, as though it is etched in stone. Nothing is. It is all ultimately up to you. I have spent decades in study, both inner and outer; to present what is contained here. In the finally analysis, they are only suggestions to help you find your way to the ONE. Accept some or all if you like, or throw them out if that is your inner direction. But keep seeking! We are God-souls helping each other to gain a deeper and wider understanding of the ONE.

The principles presented here are precious. If you see their value and perceive that learning and teaching them to others will be mutually beneficial, then you too have heard the call of soul.

Chapter 17 — The Call of Soul

The call of soul is the eternal voice that asks all who hear, to join in the Great Work. It is the call of soul to serve as a pure channel of truth to convey the message of spiritual liberation and empowerment. This call initially attracted me to Eckankar. In it, I heard wisdom, truth, and a promise of spiritual freedom I had never heard before. Like a siren call, it attracted me. It was strong and shook me from my spiritual lethargy. I was fully prepared to devote the remainder of my life to this path, for I saw it as part of the Great Work. Alas, it was not to be.

While Paul Twitchell undoubtedly heard the same siren call, character flaws prevented him from following through. He corrupted the truth and misled hundreds of thousands of honest, loving God-seekers. He was not alone in this. His successors and hundreds, if not thousands, of spiritual masters and leaders like him, as well as major world religions, continue to mislead. They hide, if indeed they even know, the essential truth that every person is soul, and soul is part of the ONE. The proper measure of the spiritual greatness of any leader is not the extent to which he sees this truth in himself and allows others to marvel in his light. It is the extent to which he helps others to see the light within themselves and rejoice in their collective unity in the ONE.

In the end, we take from Paul Twitchell and Eckankar what is valuable, thank them, and move on. The call of soul must be answered and the message carried forth by others. It falls to those who hear this call to contribute in the manner they are most capable. For we are all part of the whole and *we are equally responsible to and for the whole.* How could it be otherwise? The call from within propels us to give back to the whole, for this is the only way we grow in awareness and oneness with ALL THAT IS.

Law of Duality/Polarity Still At Work

It must be remembered that all efforts in the physical world, aimed at expressing the Great Work, must deal with the inherent Law of Duality/Polarity, including the Higher Consciousness Movement. As we have seen, this is the way the physical world is designed. Within everything that is positive there lie the seeds of its transformation to the negative. Then too, both the positive and the negative exist simultaneously in every situation and thing. To illustrate the point, in this context, the revelations contained in this book will, for many, cause temporary pain and inner dislocation. This might be perceived as a negative. Yet, from it also flows emancipation from constricted and restrictive ideas. This liberation leads to spiritual growth and empowerment. It is in this framework that the Great Work functions. This is also why there must be constant vigilance by enlightened souls that hear and respond to this call. The aims and objectives of the Great Work must not be subverted by base motives. A focus on spiritual goals, turning every situation to serving the Great Work, will insure it stays on course and remains true to ALL THAT IS.

Working Together with Purity of Purpose

In the Great Work, concerted effort is essential. United in purpose, a force, a movement in the Great Work, can be created to inspire seekers whose direction is uncertain. Here, they can find a haven of truth and spiritual guidance, to help themselves and every God-seeker find the ONE within. This is the goal of the Great Work — nothing more. The process, institution, and mechanism for reaching this goal must never become the goal itself. If so, by that very fact, it will be corrupted in truth and purity. History shows us too many cases of this.

The Catholic Church's pious fraud is such an example. These distant legacies echo from the past and mirror themselves in the revelations of betrayal of youth entrusted to the care of the Church. It likewise manifests in the concealment of these acts and their continuation. The Church has demonstrated that an institution can become, at least to its guardians, more important than the flock it claims to serve. But the interests of a spiritual or religious institution must always be secondary to the souls they are created to serve. Indeed, the purpose for which all spiritual organizations, churches, and paths were established, whether they remember it or not, is to assist in the Great Work. Unfortunately, most have forgotten this. Their spiritual founders were perhaps aware of it; their missions were pure. They would weep at the direction their messages have taken. Establishing their images and lives as objects of worship corrupts their mission and distorts the Great Work. Their true message was and is to assist soul to see the light within themselves and to manifest the properties of the ONE.

This is the call of soul. Those now or formerly in Eckankar or any other path or religion who have come to understand this call are carriers of higher consciousness. It is their responsibility to transmit the message of liberation to all who are ready to hear and live by its glorious truth. But it is not a mandate, for each soul has the freedom to do as it chooses. Those ignited with love and devotion to spirit and the ONE choose their own role in the Great Work. It is through the concerted efforts of these God-souls, many of whom have lived through spiritual deception and become stronger, that the light of this message will go forth.

Not everyone is ready for this message. Many are at early stages of spiritual unfoldment. And this is as it should be. That is why established religions are still needed, even if distorted and image-laden. Spiritual growth, like schooling, occurs in stages. As we have said, just because a college textbook contains more truth than a third-grade equivalent, doesn't mean a third-grader should study a college text. The third grade is just fine for the third-grader. However, if the teachers and the school, through ignorance or conspiracy, keep a student trapped in the third grade, then they have failed in their mission. Their job is to teach what they can and prepare the student for the next level of education. Our awareness grows, as must we.

But religions and spiritual paths place minefields on the boundaries of their teachings. They warn of the consequences of straying. Violators will be cast into hell, excommunicated, lose worldly possessions, or worse. Behind the face of love and freedom shown to newcomers, there are frightening and powerful warnings. They prevent or delay moving on. The stories of those who have ventured outside and negotiated the minefields are posted all over the Internet and the news.

"Let my people go, if they want to" is the eternal cry of ALL THAT IS and of the Great Work. All paths have a divine obligation to clear the minefields and prepare their followers for expansion of consciousness, whether they accept this obligation or not. They should know that in spite of efforts to control and limit, spiritual growth will occur, for the call of soul cannot be stopped, only delayed. And those who block its progress only trap themselves, just as a slave-owner is trapped by his slaves. We cannot liberate ourselves without allowing others to be liberated. Liberation means giving space, freedom to choose, and insight to see higher truths.

We saw in Chapter 1, the pope's statements admitting that conventional notions of heaven and hell might not be true. But the pope is also trapped. He knows more but cannot reveal it. The flock is not ready; or the Church is not ready to let them go. However, some are ready. The challenge of religion is to find a way to establish avenues for movement to higher consciousness rather than to bog down the faithful with dogma and doctrine. They must clear the minefields so the faithful can move on when ready. This is the redemptive step that would again align them with the Great Work.

It Happens in Due Course

The earlier story of my son, who when twelve-years old came to me practically in tears, demonstrates an important spiritual point. He said, "Daddy, I'm afraid that I will never be able to do what you do as a man and as a father. It seems so much to me." My job, of course, was to assure him that he didn't have to worry. I told him he was daunted by a role he was not yet prepared for, but that, as each year passed, he would learn to do these things, and more. This is the message that all in the Great Work must convey. Every seeker must understand that it is *inevitable* that she too will evolve to higher consciousness. While it is natural to look up to a teacher, reverence only delays the spiritual unfoldment of the student and the teacher. The seeker consigns herself to perpetual inferiority when she looks to a teacher, master, mahanta, mahatma, guru, pope, or savior as the source of salvation. She does not realize that she too will achieve this level of spiritual attainment, and more.

As we have seen, the mythology, dogma, and doctrine of religion are like the stories we tell our children about Santa Claus, the Tooth Fairy, and the busy stork delivering the next generation. These stories are easily understood by children and help adults avoid the sticky truth. We gradually reveal the truth to our children as they comprehend more and assume responsibility. We do not hold them to the original versions. But in ignorance or by design, this is what religions do.

History reveals that this is what the Catholic Church did when confronted with the cosmological theory of Copernicus. His findings disputed Church doctrine that the earth was the center of the universe, which established Earth and therefore humankind as holding a central position with God. After years of struggle, the Church finally admitted error. The sun is but one star in an immense universe, and the earth is merely one of many planets orbiting the sun. It is inevitable that dogma will be challenged as it tries to remain a fixed truth in a universe of change.

The Next Step

In the physical and other dimensions of reality/illusion, institutions are needed to carry out any objective, even one as transcendent as the Great Work. This book is the first step in a process of providing the conceptual framework allowing soul to move past intermediaries to a direct connection with the ONE. Other books will follow, written by enlightened souls that have other perspectives to share on the message of spiritual liberation and oneness with ALL THAT IS.

To carry out this objective, the Higher Consciousness Society has been created. It is designed to bring the message of spiritual liberation to those who are ready. There are literally millions of souls that have outgrown their teaching or feel deceived by one. Enlightened by their experiences, they can become the vanguard of the Higher Consciousness Movement, sharing their experiences and leading others to truth. Some will remain in their paths. They will eventually see their mission as leading souls out of the darkness and into the light. Many are comfortable in their teaching. One day they will recognize the sometimes painful truth that precedes higher consciousness.

The Higher Consciousness Society is establishing chapters and centers around the world to provide the bridge, for those who are ready, from existing teachings and religions to the level of higher consciousness that is the Great Work. The movement will be a pure channel and protector of this work with the Society functioning as the legal entity around which the outer organization will evolve. This movement will work closely with an affiliated structure responsible for revealing truth about religious and spiritual deception. This organization is the Friends of Truth, which will work primarily through its web site, www.thetruth-seeker.com.

Many seekers have already participated in a spiritual path. They have been prepared for a higher spiritual mission where their services can be directed toward fulfilling the promise of the Great Work. Its objective is to provide spiritual instruction and guidance to those seekers who are ready. It will also provide an environment in which more experienced seekers can assist each other to reach the next step in their spiritual unfoldment. For each person is a teacher and a student. This will always be the case, for there is always someone ahead of us and someone behind us in spiritual awareness.

In carrying out this mission, the link, www.higherconsciousnesssociety.com, will serve as the channel for information, classes, forums, chat rooms, music, interviews, children's activities, worldwide events, and much more. The wisdom and vision of the Great Work will be shared with the world through this site. The requirements for setting up a chapter of the HCS and volunteering service to the Great Work are presented on this web site. In addition, regional, national, and international gatherings will be organized at which the liberating and empowering message of the Great Work will be presented to the world. An ongoing dialogue on Eckankar and other paths or religions, challenged by this book, is also presented at www.thetruth-seeker.com to establish pathways for growth and liberation.

Finally, this call to soul is to join the mission of protecting and disseminating the eternal message of true spiritual liberation and empowerment, which is the essence of the Great Work. This will insure a clear, pure, and truthful channel to impart this message to those who are ready, both here and in regions beyond. The greatest support each of us can now give is to place this book in the hands of others or to tell them about it, so they too can begin the journey to higher consciousness — the journey to the heart of truth.

APPENDIX

Historical Bases of the Vairagi Eck Masters

Name	Eckankar Version	Likely Origin	Disguise Technique(s)*	Likely Historical Source	Source
Ahmad Qavani	"The Living Eck Master who was allegedly present at the signing of the Magna Carta in 1215." Source: *Eckankar Dictionary*, p. 4.	(Mirza) Ahmad of Qadiani	A, B	Mirza Ahmad of Qadiani was the founder of a movement within Islam called Qadianism. Followers are called either Qadiani or Ahmadi. He died in 1908.	http://www.hizmetbooks.org/Islam_And_Christianity/16.htm
Apollonius of Tyana	"An Eck Master in the third century B.C.E. who saved himself from death by transportation, or "teleportation:" direct projection of the physical body. He was a student of the Neo-Pythagorean pyramid and Egyptian wisdom schools." Source: *Eckankar Dictionary*, p. 8.	Apollonius of Tyana	B	Apollonius of Tyana was a neo-Pythagorean reputed to have magical powers. Born in Asia Minor about the time of Christ, he traveled to many Eastern lands and, according to legend, performed many miracles. His eminent power over evil spirits and demons made him, in the minds of pagans, a formidable rival to Jesus Christ.	http://www.themystica.com/mystica/articles/a/apollonius_of_tyana.html

*Disguise Codes:

A: Name Reversal	D: No Disguise
B: Spelling Change	E: Name/Word Combination
C: Word Deletion	

Historical Bases of the Vairagi Eck Masters

Name	Eckankar Version	Likely Origin	Disguise Technique(s)*	Likely Historical Source	Source
Decates	"The Living Eck Master of his time in the city of Sar-Kurteva on the continent of Atlantis." Source: *Eckankar Dictionary*, p. 32.	René Descartes	B	René Descartes (1596-1650) is one of the most important Western philosophers, although also famous as a physicist, physiologist, and mathematician. He restarted philosophy in a fresh direction to fully integrate philosophy with the new sciences. Descartes changed the relationship between philosophy and theology by subjecting belief in God to rational inquiry. He also tried to prove God's existence.	http://www.utm.edu/research/iep/d/descarte.htm
Gakko	A state of relative perfection within the Atma Lok (the world of Soul) where ECK Masters who are not doing duty in the other planes and worlds reside. Source: *Eckankar Dictionary*, p. 53.	Gekka-o	B	Gekka-o is the god of marriage in Japanese myth. He binds the feet of lovers with a thread made of red silk.	http://www.pantheon.org/articles/g/gekka-o.html

*Disguise Codes:

A: Name Reversal	D: No Disguise
B: Spelling Change	E: Name/Word Combination
C: Word Deletion	

*Disguise Technique(s)

Historical Bases of the Vairagi Eck Masters

Name	Eckankar Version	Likely Origin	Disguise Technique(s)*	Likely Historical Source	Source
Habu Medinet	"The Living Eck Master in Persia ca. 490 B.C.E." Source: *Eckankar Dictionary*, p. 59.	Medinet Habu	A	Medinet Habu was both a temple and a complex of temples dating from the New Kingdom in Egypt. The ancient Egyptian name for Medinet Habu (in Arabic the "City of Habu") was Djamet, meaning "males and mothers." Its holy ground was believed to be where the Ogdoad, the four pairs of first primeval gods, were buried. The monuments in Medinet Habu are thought to have been built between the 1500 and 1100 B.C.E.	http://www.touregypt.net/ram3tmp.htm; http://www.touregypt.net/featurestories/habu.htm

*Disguise Codes:

A: Name Reversal	D: No Disguise
B: Spelling Change	E: Name/Word Combination
C: Word Deletion	

Historical Bases of the Vairagi Eck Masters

Name	Eckankar Version	Likely Origin	Disguise Technique(s)*	Likely Historical Source	Source
Hermes	"A great prophet and powerful figure known to have been a student of the various mystery schools such as Essne, which are all offspring of the Ancient Order of the Vairagi Eck Masters. The Eck Vidya doctrine of cycles is based upon the "hermetic axiom" of correspondence. Possibly originated in Greece." Source: *The Spiritual Notebook*, p. 2.	Hermes	D	Hermes, the herald and messenger of the Olympian gods, is son of Zeus and the nymph Maia, daughter of Atlas and one of the Pleads. Known for his cunning and shrewdness, he is the god of shepherds, land travel, merchants, weights and measures, oration, literature, athletics, and thieves. His duties as a messenger also included taking the dead to the underworld and bringing dreams.	http://www.pantheon.org/articles/h/hermes.html
Jacquila or Juquila	"An ECK Master at the time of the Spanish-American War (1898). He introduced the wedding ceremony used in Eckankar." Source: *Drums of Eck*, pp. 210-18.	Juquila	D	The Virgin of Juquila is a two-feet tall statue brought over from Spain and eventually placed in a chapel near the town of Juquila. It was reported that the statue repeatedly moved out of a chapel near the town and instead ended up in the town itself. It thus became attributed with deep magical powers.	http://www.ralphmag.org/juquilaZL.html

*Disguise Codes:

A: Name Reversal	D: No Disguise
B: Spelling Change	E: Name/Word Combination
C: Word Deletion	

Historical Bases of the Vairagi Eck Masters

Name	Eckankar Version	Likely Origin	Disguise Technique(s)*	Likely Historical Source	Source
Malati	"The first ECK Master of record among the Polarians, who was sent by the SUGMAD to give man his first spiritual knowledge of God." Source: *Eckankar Dictionary*, p. 93.	Malati	D	Malati is a Sanskrit word for a white, late-afternoon blooming jasmine.	http:// www.behindthename.com/ nmc/ind.html
Milarepa	"Eck Master whose origins date back to Tibet in the eleventh century. He began life as a black magician but later became the spectacular saint of Tibet. His secret life was concerned with the teachings of Eck." Source: *The Spiritual Notebook*, pp. 218-19.	Milarepa	D	Milarepa is one of the most widely known Tibetan Saints. He took to a solitary life of meditation until he had achieved the pinnacle of the enlightened state, never to be born again into the Samsara (whirlpool of life and death) of worldly existence.	http:// www.cosmicharmony.com/ Av/Milarepa/Milarepa.htm

*Disguise Codes:

A: Name Reversal	D: No Disguise
B: Spelling Change	E: Name/Word Combination
C: Word Deletion	

Historical Bases of the Vairagi Eck Masters

Name	Eckankar Version	Likely Origin	Disguise Technique(s)*	Likely Historical Source	Source
Sudar Singh	"An Eck Master who lived in Allahabad, India and taught Peddar Zaskq, better known as Paul Twitchell, in this life." Source: *Eckankar Dictionary*, p. 136	Sudarshan Singh, Kirpal Singh	C, E	Sudarshan Singh, the nephew of Shiv Dayal, who created the Radhasoami path. Sudarshan Singh resided for a time in Allahadbad, India.　　　Singh Kirpal Singh, an Indian guru and founder of Ruhani Satsang, which acts as a center for "imparting purely spiritual teachings and training for mankind irrespective of class barriers." He died in 1974. Paul Twitchell was Singh's student for a brief period and credits him which much of his spiritual growth.	David C. Lane, *The Making of a Spiritual　Movement*, pp. 51-55; Julian Johnson, *With A Great Master*.

*Disguise Codes:

A: Name Reversal	D: No Disguise
B: Spelling Change	E: Name/Word Combination
C: Word Deletion	

Historical Bases of the Vairagi Eck Masters

Name	Eckankar Version	Likely Origin	Disguise Technique(s)*	Likely Historical Source	Source
Rebazar Tarzs	"The torchbearer of Eckankar in the lower worlds; the spiritual teacher of many ECK Masters including Peddar Zaskq, or Paul Twitchell, to whom he handed the Rod of ECK Power in 1965; said to be over five hundred years old, Rebazar Tarzs lives in a hut in the Hindu Kush mountains and appears to many as he helps the present Living ECK Master in the works of Eckankar. He served as the Mahanta, the Living ECK Master." Source: *Eckankar Dictionary*, p. 120.	Rebasar	B,D	"Rebasar" is a Spanish word meaning "to pass" or "to go beyond." It is commonly used in street signs in the area between San Diego and Tijuana, where Twitchell lived in the early to mid-sixties while he was creating Eckankar lore.	

*Disguise Codes:

A: Name Reversal	D: No Disguise
B: Spelling Change	E: Name/Word Combination
C: Word Deletion	

Historical Bases of the Vairagi Eck Masters

Name	Eckankar Version	Likely Origin	Disguise Technique(s)*	Likely Historical Source	Source
Zadok	"The Living ECK Master in Judea, north of Jerusalem, who founded a mystical organization which exists today in the Middle East and accepts the Mahanta. He taught a man named Jesus the basic funda-mentals of ECK. Out of this knowledge of ECK came what we know today as Christianity." Source: *Eckankar Dictionary*, p.159.	Zadok	D	Zadok was a priest who, according to 1 Kings: 1-2, supported Solomon in his struggle for succession to David's throne against his brother.	http://www.britannica.com

*Disguise Codes:

A: Name Reversal	D: No Disguise
B: Spelling Change	E: Name/Word Combination
C: Word Deletion	

Historical Bases of the Eck Temples

Name	Eckankar Version	Likely Origin	Disguise Technique(s)*	Likely Historical Source	Source
Temple of Akash	"The Temple of Akash is located in the Agam Lok, the Inaccessible Plane. The Shariyat-Ki-Sugmad contained within is guarded by Agnotti." Source: *Eckankar Dictionary*, p. 4.	Akash Bhairab Temple in Katmandu	C	The Temple of Akash Bhairav (the god of sky) is situated at the densely populated Indrachawk, close to the core bazaar of Ason, in the capital Kathmandu, Nepal. It has a unique architecture, somewhere between a three-stories house and a temple. The golden windows and a pair of lions on its first floor are the specialty of this temple.	http://www.nepalnews.com.np/contents/englishweekly/sundaypost/2002/jul21/2ndpage.htm http://www.nepalinfo.com/nepalguide/kathmandu.htm
Temple of Aluk or Temple of Jartz Chong	"The Temple of Golden Wisdom on the eighth Plane, or Hukikat Lok, also called Temple of Aluk." Source: *Eckankar Dictionary*, p. 6.	Aluk	D	"Aluk is the sacred word that the Vairagis, the adepts of India, use as their sacred chant. In the word Aluk are expressed two words, 'al' meaning 'he,' and 'Haq' 'truth,' both words together expressing God the source from which all comes." Hazrat Inayat Khan, *The Mysticism of Sound* (1923).	http://www.rosanna.com/message/ll/llp1.htm
Askleposis Temple	"The Temple of Golden Wisdom on the Astral Plane, where Gopal Das the great ECK Master is the guardian of the fourth section SHARIYAT-KI-SUGMAD." Source: *Eckankar Dictionary*, p. 10.	Asklepios	B	"The Sanctuary of Asklepios at Epidaurus was the most celebrated healing center of the ancient world. The cult is attested as early as the sixth century B.C.E. when the hill-top sanctuary of Apollo Maleatas was no longer spacious enough for the public worship of the Epidaurus city-state. The Asklepieion survived until the end of antiquity, having experienced a second heyday in the second century C.E."	http://www.culture.gr/2/21/211/21104a/e211da03.html

*Disguise Codes;
A:Name Reversal
B:Spelling Change
C:Word Deletion
D:No Disguise
E:Name/Word Combination

Historical Bases of the Eck Temples

Name	Eckankar Version	Likely Origin	Disguise Technique(s)*	Likely Historical Source	Source
Temple of Gare-Hira	"The Temple of Golden Wisdom located in the spiritual city of Agam Des, home of the Eshwar-khanewale, the God-eaters in the Hindu Kush on the earth plane. Yaubl Sacabi is the guardian of the second section of the SHARIYAT-KI-SUGMAD here." Source: *Eckankar Dictionary*, p. 55.	Cave at Gare-Hire	D	Gare-Hira was the cave where Muhammad perceived the "sound in ether."	http://www.chinghai.com/INTROquan.html http://www.davidicke.net/emagazine/vol12/articles/epi-justice3.html
Temple of Karakota or Temple of Dayaka	"Temple of Golden Wisdom in the city of Arhirit on the Etheric Plane or Saguna Lok. Lai Tsi is the guardian of the SHARIYAT-KI-SUGMAD there." Source: Eckankar's "List of Ancient Temples of Golden Wisdom," "The Golden Temples of Wisdom," and *Eckankar Dictionary*, p. 32.	Karakota Dayaka	D	"Karakota was a dynasty that dominated over a territory up to Bengal in the east, Konkan in the south, Turkistan in the north-west and Tibet in the north-east. Its king Lalitaditya (697-738 AD) built a majestic sun temple at a place called Matan. Its archaeological finds are still the most conspicuous objects of the antiquated architecture of Kashmir." Dayaka: a word that means, Giver, Patron, or a Supporter.	http://pib.nic.in/feature/feyr2001/fnov2001/f16112001l.html http://www.geocities.com/Athens/Academy/9280/go-g.htm
House of Moksha	"The Temple of Golden Wisdom in the Pinda Lok, or physical world, in the city of Retz, Venus." Source: *Eckankar Dictionary*, p. 64.	Houses of Moksha	D	"The Moksha houses, according to Eastern Astrology, relate to the three water signs: the fourth-Cancer, the eighth-Scorpio, and the twelfth-Pisces. These are the houses that liberate or free the soul of the chains of earthly karma, and they have to do with the past, fear based emotions, and the essence of the soul."	http://www.newageinfo.com/vedic/ http://www.newageinfo.com/vedic/#The Houses of Moksha

*Disguise Codes:
A:Name Reversal
B:Spelling Change
C:Word Deletion
D:No Disguise
E:Name/Word Combination

Historical Bases of the Eck Temples

Name	Eckankar Version	Likely Origin	Disguise Technique(s)*	Likely Historical Source	Source
Param Akshar Temple	"The Temple of Golden Wisdom, the House of Imperishable Knowledge on the Soul Plane, the Atma Lok; Supreme Lord; another name for God." Source: *Eckankar Dictionary*, p. 112.	Param Akshar: The First Akshar-Purushottam Temple in Bochasan	E	"Param: The Supreme Temple in Bochasan, India, where the true upasana (worship) of Akshar and Purushottam was idolised." "Akshar: Eternal abode of Lord Swaminarayan, and in its personal form, Akshar serves Purushottam in his abode and manifests as his choicest devotee on this earth."	http://www.swaminarayan.org/ pramukhswami/searchingquestions/ glossary.htm http://www.miraura.org/lit/skgl/skgl-15.html http://www.swaminarayan.org/ shastrijimaharaj/life/34.htm
Temple of Sakapori	"The Temple of Golden Wisdom on the Brahmanda Lok, the Third, or Causal Plane, in the city of Honu." Source: *Eckankar Dictionary*, p. 128.	Pori Temple and Temples at Har Ki Pori	E	"Pori Temple, the largest temple on Namsan, is run by Buddhist nuns, and a seated stone Buddha (Sakyamuni Buddha), thought to have been made in the 8th to 9th century, is found there. Also, Temples at Har Ki Pori, close to the Holy Waters of Ganga Mata, in India."	http://korea.insight.co.kr/english/ knamsan/tour7.html http://website.lineone.net/~sabharwal/

*Disguise Codes:
A:Name Reversal
B:Spelling Change
C:Word Deletion
D:No Disguise
E:Name/Word Combination

NOTES

Notes

Chapter 1 — The God Seeker

1   John Paul II, "Heaven is Fullness of Communication with God," *L'Osservatore Romano,* (July 28, 1999), referring to the Pope's speech in the general audience in Vescovo di Corumba, Brasil, on July 21, 1999. For full article see http://www.vatican.va/cgi-bin/w3-msql/news_services/bulletin/news/5306.html?index=5306&po_date=21.07.1999&lang=it.

2   John Paul II, "Hell is the State of Those Who Reject God," *L'Osservatore Romano,* (August 4, 1999), referring to the Pope's speech in general audience on July 28, 1999. For full article see http://www.vatican.va/cgi-bin/w3-msql/news_services/bulletin/news/5335.html?index=5335&po_date=28.07.1999&lang=en.

Chapter 2 — The Path of the Light and Sound of God

1   Paul Twitchell, *The Key to Eckankar* (Minneapolis: Eckankar, 1995), p. 5.

2   Harold Klemp, *A Cosmic Sea of Words: The Eckankar Lexicon* (Minneapolis: Eckankar, 1998), p. 56.

3   See Paramahansa Yogananda, *Autobiography of a Yogi* (Los Angeles: Self-Realization, 1977).

4   Revelation 21:16, 19.

Chapter 3 — How the Journey Started

1   See Paul Twitchell, *The Tiger's Fang* (Menlo Park: Illuminated Way Press, 1979).

2   "Chela — A student, disciple, or follower of the ECKANKAR spiritual teacher." Harold Klemp, *A Cosmic Sea of Words: The Eckankar Lexicon* (Minneapolis: Eckankar, 1998), p. 30.

3 "Secret Word — The holy ECK, or the word given to the CHELA at the time of INITIATION, which must be practiced in silence or vocally only when alone." Klemp, *The Eckankar Lexicon*, p. 185.

4 "Wah Z — The spiritual name of SRI HAROLD KLEMP...." Klemp, *The Eckankar Lexicon*, p. 229.

5 See Phil Morimitsu, *In the Company of ECK Masters* (Minneapolis: Eckankar, 1987).

6 See James Davis, *The Rosetta Stone of God* (Minneapolis: Eckankar, 2000).

7 Paul Twitchell, *Shariyat-Ki-Sugmad*, Book One (Minneapolis: Eckankar, 1987), p. 176.

Chapter 4 — The Spiritual Journey of Graham Forsyth

1 See Graham Forsyth, *In the Many Hands of God* (Silver Spring, MD: "ONE" Publishing, 2003).

2 Ibid.

3 This abridged version has been edited to aid the reader. Changes have in no way altered the content or meaning.

4 "Bourchakoum — Those known as the EAGLE-EYED ADEPTS; the LIVING ECK MASTER; the ADEPTS of the Ancient Order of the Vairagi." Harold Klemp, *A Cosmic Sea of Words: The Eckankar Lexicon* (Minneapolis: Eckankar, 1998), p. 23.

5 Paul Twitchell, *Eckankar: The Key to Secret Worlds* (Crystal, MN: Illuminated Way Publishing, 1987), p. 45.

6 Ibid., p. 72.

Chapter 5 — The Master Replies

1 Paul Twitchell, *Dialogues with the Master* (Menlo Park, CA: Illuminated Way Press, 1983), p. 172.

2 Charged Words (e.g., *Mahanta, Eck, Sugmad*) are considered to carry great spiritual energy because of the idea forms and states of consciousness they represent.

3 Paul Twitchell, *Shariyat-Ki-Sugmad,* Book One (Minneapolis: Eckankar, 1987), pp. 7-8.

4 Ibid., p. 8.

5 Ibid., p. 187.

6 Paul Twitchell, *Eckankar: Illuminated Way Letters 1966-1971* (San Diego: Illuminated Way Press, 1975), p. 130 (emphasis added).

Chapter 6 — Eckankar: Revealed by Truth

1   See David C. Lane, *The Making of a Spiritual Movement: The Untold Story of Paul Twitchell and Eckankar* (Del Mar: Del Mar Press, 1993).

2   Graham Forsyth, *In the Many Hands of God* (Silver Spring: "ONE" Publishing, 2003), journal entry, August 8, 2001.

3   Ibid., journal entry, August 11, 2001.

4   "I do not run Eckankar as a non-profit organization. Most people in this line of work do indeed use the religious non-profit organization provisions as an escape clause on their taxes. Eckankar is licensed in the state of Nevada as a business organization. I do this because I feel that it is only proper and fitting that I make my own way instead of trying to get under a tax shelter. It is hard, of course, but I manage to do it." Paul Twitchell quoted in Brad Steiger, *In My Soul I Am Free* (Menlo Park, CA: Illuminated Way Press, 1983), p. 69.

5   "There is too much dishonesty among those who try to get tax shelters because they claim to be religious groups. God didn't establish non-taxable foundations, so why should I try to get under such claims? If ECK cannot take care of itself, then it can be of little value to anyone else." Paul Twitchell quoted in ibid., p. 70.

6   Forsyth, *In the Many Hands of God,* journal entry, September 15, 2001.

7   Paul Twitchell, *Eckankar: The Key to Secret Worlds* (Crystal: Illuminated Way Publishing, 1987), pp. 104-106.

8   Forsyth, *In the Many Hands of God*, journal entry, October 8, 2001.

9   Paul Twitchell, *The Spiritual Notebook* (Golden Valley: Illuminated Way Publishing, 1990), p. 223.

10 "Mahdis – The INITIATE of the FIFTH CIRCLE (SOUL PLANE)...." Harold Klemp, *A Cosmic Sea of Words: The Eckankar Lexicon* (Minneapolis: Eckankar, 1998), p. 132. "The works of Eckankar depend mainly upon the Mahdis." Paul Twitchell, *The Shariyat-Ki-Sugmad,* Book Two (Menlo Park: Eckankar, 1986), p. 49.

11 Paul Twitchell, *Shariyat-Ki-Sugmad* II: 48.

12 Paul Twitchell, *Shariyat-Ki-Sugmad*, Book One (Minneapolis: Eckankar, 1987), p. 215.

13 Paul Twitchell, *The Flute of God* (Menlo Park: Illuminated Way Press, 1982), p. 127.

14 Ibid., p. 128.

15 Ibid., pp. 127-128.

16 Ibid., p. 127. (emphasis added).

17 Lane, *The Making of a Spiritual Movement*, p. 63. From an article by Dorothe Ross, "All That Glistens is Not Gold," *Leadership in ECK* (July-August-September, 1976).

18 Ibid., p. 63. Paul Twitchell, "The Cliff-Hanger," *Psychic Observer.*

19 Paul Twitchell, "The Flute of God," *Orion Magazine* (March-April 1966), p. 32.

20 Letter from Bernadine Burlin, Secretary to then Living Eck Master Darwin Gross, to David Lane, April 5, 1977. See http://vclass.mtsac.edu:940/dlane/doc2.htm.

21 Lane, *The Making of a Spiritual Movement*, p. 34. Twitchell, "The Cliff-Hanger."

22 See Dean McMakin, "The Life Of Paul Twitchell, Modern-Day Founder of Eckankar," (Documents from the McCracken County Public Library Special Collections, Paducah, Kentucky, 1992). See also http://www.thetruth-seeker.com.

23 Paul used the term "bilocation" to describe the ability of his body to be in one place as his soul body (awareness) was located elsewhere. He later calls this phenomenon "soul travel."

24 Paul Twitchell, "New Concepts on the Ancient Teachings of Bilocation," *SCP Journal 3* (1979): 51.

25 Steiger, *In My Soul I Am Free*, p. 63.

26 Ibid., p. 64.

27 Twitchell, *The Spiritual Notebook,* pp. 11-12.

28 Ibid., p. 1.

29 Ibid., p. 62.

30 Ibid., pp. vii-2.

Chapter 7 — Twitchellian Techniques of Spiritual Creativity: The Ten Devices

1 Paul Twitchell, *The Flute of God* (Menlo Park: IWP, 1982), pp. 127-28.

2 See David C. Lane, *The Making of a Spiritual Movement: The Untold Story of Paul Twitchell and Eckankar* (Del Mar, CA: Del Mar Press, 1993), pp. 11-13.

3   See Dean McMakin, "The Life Of Paul Twitchell, Modern-Day Founder of Eckankar," (Documents from the McCracken County Public Library Special Collections, Paducah, Kentucky, 1992). See also http://www.thetruth-seeker.com.

4   See http://vclass.mtsac.edu:940/dlane/doc11.htm.

5   Harold Klemp, *The Secret Teachings* (Minneapolis: Eckankar, 1989), p. 141.

6   See McMakin, "The Life Of Paul Twitchell Modern-Day Founder of Eckankar;" http://www.thetruth-seeker.com.

7   Brad Steiger, *In My Soul I Am Free* (Menlo Park: Illuminated Way Press, 1968), p. 47.

8   See McMakin, "The Life Of Paul Twitchell."

9   Letter from Paducah Public Schools to Friends of Truth, May 3, 2002, listing Paul Twitchell among students graduated on May 21, 1931. See http://www.thetruth-seeker.com.

10   Response from Murray State University to Friends of Truth, May 30, 2002, at http://www.thetruth-seeker.com.

11   Letter from Western Kentucky University to Friends of Truth, May 22, 2002, at http://www.thetruth-seeker.com.

12   See McMakin, "The Life Of Paul Twitchell."

13   Ibid.

14   Ibid.

15   Ibid.

16   Letter from Paducah Public Schools to Friends of Truth, May 3, 2002, at http://www.thetruth-seeker.com.

17   Klemp, *The Secret Teachings*, p. 142.

18   Lane, *The Making of a Spiritual Movement,* p. 15.

19   Letter of Camille Ballowe about her association with Paul Twitchell, at http://members.tripod.com/~dlane5/cam.html.

20   *Difficulties Of Becoming The Living ECK Master* (Menlo Park, CA: Iluminated Way Press, 1980), p. 45.

21   Harold Klemp, *How to Find God* (Minneapolis: Eckankar, 1988), p. 162.

22   Klemp, *The Secret Teachings*, p. 246.

23   Ibid.,

24 Harold Klemp, *Ask The Master*, Book One (Minneapolis: Eckankar, 1993), p. 189.

25 Klemp, *The Secret Teachings*, p. 170.

26 Paul Twitchell, *The Spiritual Notebook* (Golden Valley: Illuminated Way Publishing, 1990), p. 221.

27 Ibid. See also Lane, *The Making of a Spiritual Movement,* p. 19.

28 Darwin Gross's account of Paul's age assumed that the description in *The Spiritual Notebook* of Paul's birth was speaking of the Paul Twitchell in this lifetime, the one actually born in 1910.

29 Note the irony of two self-professed omniscient beings — Darwin Gross and Harold Klemp — unable to agree on a fundamental detail about the life of another omniscient being.

30 Twitchell, *The Spiritual Notebook*, p. 221.

31 See Paul Twitchell, *The Drums of ECK* (Menlo Park: Illuminated Way Press, 1978).

32 *Difficulties Of Becoming The Living ECK Master*, p. 12.

33 Twitchell, *The Drums of ECK,* p. 5.

34 Statement from the Eck staff during a meeting with David Lane, at http://members.tripod.com/~dlane5/typos.html.

35 Twitchell, *The Drums of ECK,* p. 8.

36 Klemp, *The Secret Teachings*, p. 143 (emphasis added).

37 Twitchell, *The Drums of ECK,* pp. 22-23 (emphasis added).

38 Ibid., p. 9.

39 McMakin, "The Life Of Paul Twitchell."

40 Klemp, *The Secret Teachings*, p. 142.

41 Ibid., pp. 195-196 (emphasis added).

42 Ibid.

43 Ibid., pp. 142-143 (emphasis added).

44 Ibid., p. 143.

45 Ibid., p. 139.

46 Letter by Dr. Louis Bluth, former President of Eckankar, one-time follower of Sawan Sing, and Paul Twitchell's personal doctor at the time of his death in 1971, at http://members.tripod.com/~dlane5/eck.html.

47 Affidavit of Eugene Davis, August 13, 2002, at www.thetruth-seeker.com.

48 Klemp, *The Secret Teachings*, p. 143 (emphasis added).

49 Ibid., p.144 (emphasis added).

50 Ibid..

51 Twitchell, *The Spiritual Notebook*, p. 1 (emphasis added).

52 Ibid., p. 11 (emphasis added).

53 Ibid., p. 220.

54 Twitchell, *The Flute of God*, pp. 127-28.

55 *Merriam-Webster's Collegiate Dictionary,* Tenth Edition (Springfield: Merriam-Webster, 1993), p. 888.

56 Lane, *The Making of a Spiritual Movement*, p. 77.

57 Thomas Mallon, *Stolen Words* (New York: Harcourt, 2001), p. xii.

58 Ibid., p. 42.

59 Ibid., p. 85.

60 Ibid., pp. 86-87.

61 Paul Twitchell, *The Tiger's Fang*, (Menlo Park: Illuminated Way Press, 1979), pp. 46-7.

62 See http://vclass.mtsac.edu:930/phil/center.htm.

63 Letter by Dr. Louis Bluth, at http://members.tripod.com/~dlane5/eck.html.

64 Lane, *The Making of a Spiritual Movement,* p. xv.

65 Ibid.

66 Twitchell, *The Spiritual Notebook*, p. 223.

67 Julian Johnson, *The Path of the Masters* (Punjab: R.S.S.B, 1985), p. 28.

68 Paul Twitchell, *The Far Country* (Menlo Park: Illuminated Way Press, 1981), pp. 127, 129.

69 Johnson, *The Path of the Masters*, p. 29.

70 Twitchell, *The Far Country*, pp. 129-130.

71 See Paul Twitchell, *Shariyat-Ki-Sugmad*, Book Two (Menlo Park: Eckankar, 1986), pp. 146.

72 Psalms 25: 4-6.

73 Walter Russell, *The Secret of Light* (Swannanoa: University of Science and Philosophy, 1974).

74 Twitchell, *The Tiger's Fang*, pp. 33-34.

75 Russell, *The Secret of Light,* p. 22.

76 Twitchell, *The Tiger's Fang*, p. 36.

77 Russell, *The Secret of Light,* p. 22.

78 Twitchell, *The Tiger's Fang*, p. 36.

79 Russell, *The Secret of Light,* p. 22.

80 Twitchell, *The Tiger's Fang*, p. 36.

81 Russell, *The Secret of Light,* p. 22.

82 Twitchell, *The Tiger's Fang*, p. 36.

83 Russell, *The Secret of Light,* p. 23.

84 Twitchell, *The Tiger's Fang*, p. 36.

85 Hazrat Inayat Khan, *The Mysticism of Sound and Music* (Boston: Shambhala, 1996), p. 172.

86 Twitchell, *The Flute of God*, p. 75.

87 "The Egyptian god *Hu* was one of the minor gods in some respects, but he was one of the most important gods for those serious about Egyptian deities. *Hu* is the power of the spoken word. He personifies the authority of utterance. *Hu* and Sia were partners. Sia was the personification of Divine Knowledge/Omniscience, the mind of the gods. *Hu* was the personification of Divine Utterance, the voice of authority. So far, we know *Hu* as the personification of Divine Utterance. However, some legends maintain that he was not just a part of creation, but that he was the creator. It is said that as *Hu* drew his first breath, there was in that sound the essence of his name. Hence, we have the name *Hu*, which sounds remarkably like the sound of an expelling breath." See http://www.touregypt.net/featurestories/hu.htm.

88 Johnson, *The Path of the Masters*, p. 203.

89 Paul Twitchell, *Eckankar: The Key to Secret Worlds* (Crystal: Illuminated Way Publishing, 1988), pp. 193-94.

90 Twitchell, *The Spiritual Notebook*, pp. 118-19.

91 Paul Twitchell, "The Bilocation Philosophy," *Orion Magazine* 10 (1964): 52.

92 Paul Twitchell, "The Flute of God," *Orion Magazine* 11 (1966): 32.

93 Twitchell, *Eckankar: The Key to Secret Worlds,* p. 190.

94 Lane, *The Making of a Spiritual Movement,* pp. 26-27.

95 Ibid. While still studying under Kirpal Singh, Paul joined Scientology in the late fifties where he became a "clear." He also helped with public relations and teaching out-of-body techniques.

96 For Paul's position on (articulated by his supporters) and the facts behind this assertion see http://members.tripod.com/~dlane5/doug4.html.

97 "What would you do if you learned one day that your spiritual teacher sexually harassed his male disciples and covered up his sexual affairs; a plagiarist who lifted his teachings from other traditions without due reference; a spendthrift who lived extravagantly, though he took a vow of poverty; a questionable business man who engaged in risky and possibly illegal activities; and a religious charlatan who consistently told untruths about a variety of issues?" See "A Critical Analysis of John-Roger Hinkins and M.S.I.A." at http://home.hetnet.nl/~ex-baba/engels/articles/johnroger.html.

98 These facts are found in several sources: The Center for Twitchellian Plagiarism, under "Eckankar plagiarizes the Bible," at http://vclass.mtsac.edu:930/phil/center.htm.; "Eastern Mysticism" at http://www.angelfire.lycos.com/doc/general/angelfire_popunder.html?search_string=twitchell+and+plagiarism; and http://www.eternalministries.org/archives/eastern_mystic2.html. See also Lane, *The Making of a Spiritual Movement*, pp. 169-179.

99 Ibid., p. 78.

100 Klemp, *The Secret Teachings*, pp. 159-160.

101 See http://vclass.mtsac.edu:930/phil/center.htm.

102 Klemp, *The Secret Teachings*, p. 159.

103 Ibid., pp. 164-65.

104 Twitchell, *The Flute of God*, pp. 127-28.

105 Lane, *The Making of a Spiritual Movement,* p. 54.

106 Twitchell, "The Flute of God," *Orion Magazine* 11 (1966):32 (emphasis added).

107 Twitchell, *The Flute of God*, p. 5 (emphasis added).

108 Twitchell, "The Flute of God," *Orion Magazine* 11 (1966):37 (emphasis added).

109 Twitchell, *The Flute of God*, p. 11 (emphasis added).

110 Twitchell, "The Flute of God," *Orion Magazine* 11 (1966):30 (emphasis added).

111 Twitchell, *The Flute of God*, p. 18 (emphasis added).

112 Johnson, *The Path of the Masters*, p. 32.

113 Lane, *The Making of a Spiritual Movement,* pp. 57-62.

114 Ibid., p. 66.

115 Of the 583 web sites on SUGMAD, every one is about ECKANKAR. Libraries and other compendia reveal the identical pattern.

116 Twitchell, *The Flute of God*, p. 14.

117 Ibid.

118 Ibid., p. 15 (emphasis added).

119 Twitchell, "The Bilocation Philosophy," p. 52.

120 Steiger, *In My Soul I Am Free*, p. 64.

121 *The Drums of Eck* was not published until 1970, when these historical assertions first appeared.

122 See Jack Jarvis, "Paul Twitchell, Man of Parts," *Seattle Post-Intelligencer,* July 9, 1963.

123 "Rod of ECK Power. The power of the WORD of God, which is given to that being who has been chosen by the SUGMAD, as It descends and enters into the new LIVING ECK MASTER; the power which makes him the actual MANIFESTATION of God at the rites, or the INITIATION, of accepting the Rod of ECK Power; the power of the MAHANTA Consciousness." See Klemp, *The Eckankar Lexicon,* p. 175.

124 Johnson, *The Path of the Masters*, pp. 221-22.

125 Steiger, *In My Soul I Am Free*, p. 64.

126 It is perhaps for this reason that Harold, having first asserted that perhaps Sudar Singh (Paul's alleged first teacher at age 16) actually died in the forties to cover Paul's assertion that he died sometime between 1935 and 1939 (a year before Paul went to India to study under him), was to change this story. He later indicated that perhaps Singh died in the fifties, thus providing a connection between Paul's work with one Eck Master, Sudar Singh, and his transfer to another, Rebazar Tarzs, who Paul asserts began his instruction of him in the fifties as well. All tolled, this makes three sets of dates for Sudar Singh's death.

127 Lane, *The Making of a Spiritual Movement,* p. 53.

128 Klemp, *The Secret Teachings*, p. 246.

129 Lane, *The Making of a Spiritual Movement*, p. 51.

130 See http://theosophy.org/tlodocs/teachers/Asanga.htm.

131 Twitchell, *Eckankar: The Key to Secret Worlds*, p. 21.

132 See http://www.magna.com.au/~prfbrown/atyana00.html.

133 Chelas are asked to write the Living Eck Master each month and to mail it to him at their option.

134 Twitchell, *The Flute of God*, pp 11-12.

135 Twitchell, "The Bilocation Philosophy," p. 52 (emphasis added).

136 "One widespread explanation of the origin of this date is that December 25 was the Christianizing of the *dies solis invicti nati* ("day of the birth of the unconquered sun"), a popular holiday in the Roman Empire that celebrated the winter [solstice] as a symbol of the resurgence of the sun, the casting away of winter and the heralding of the rebirth of spring and summer. Indeed, after December 25 had become widely accepted as the date of Jesus' birth, Christian writers frequently made the connection between the rebirth of the sun and the birth of the Son. One of the difficulties with this view is that it suggests a nonchalant willingness on part of the Christian church to appropriate a pagan festival when the early church was so intent on distinguishing itself categorically from pagan beliefs and practices." See http://www.britannica.com/eb/artcle?eu=84610&tocid=0&query=christmas.

137 Twitchell, *The Spiritual Notebook*, pp. 11-12.

138 Klemp, *The Secret Teachings*, p. 155.

139 Ibid., p.156.

140 Twitchell, *Shariyat-Ki-Sugmad*, Book One (Minneapolis: Eckankar, 1987), pp. 1-5.

141 *Difficulties Of Becoming The Living ECK Master*, p. 40.

142 Klemp, *The Golden Heart* (Minneapolis: Eckankar, 1990), p. 178-79 (emphasis added).

143 Lane, *The Making of a Spiritual Movement*, p. 69.

144 *Difficulties Of Becoming The Living ECK Master,* pp. 60-61.

145 Paul Twitchell, *Eckankar: Illuminated Way Letters 1966-1971* (San Diego: Illuminated Way Press, 1975), p. 94.

146 See Harold Klemp, *The ECK Satsang Discourses*, Third Series, Letter 8. See also http://www.geocities.com/Athens/Acropolis/1756/eck/txt.

147 Twitchell, *Shariyat-Ki-Sugmad*, II: 150.

148 Twitchell, *Shariyat-Ki-Sugmad*, I: 107.

149 Twitchell, *Shariyat-Ki-Sugmad*, II: 166.

150 Twitchell, *Shariyat-Ki-Sugmad*, I: 119.

151 Twitchell, *Eckankar: Illuminated Way Letters 1966-1971,* p. 94.

152 Twitchell, *The Spiritual Notebook*, p. 221.

153 Twitchell, *Shariyat-Ki-Sugmad*, II: 14.

154 Ibid., p. 17.

155 Paul Twitchell, *Letters to a Chela* (Menlo Park: Eckankar, 1980), p. 107.

156 Twitchell, *Eckankar: Illuminated Way Letters, 1966-1971,* p. 94.

157 Ibid.

158 Twitchell, *The Spiritual Notebook*, p. 229 (emphasis added).

159 Ibid., p. 142 (emphasis added).

160 Twitchell, *Shariyat-Ki-Sugmad*, II: 10.

161 Twitchell, *Eckankar: The Key to Secret Worlds,* p. 45.

162 Ibid., p. 46.

163 Ibid., p. 52.

164 Ibid., p. 69.

165 Ibid., p. 33.

166 Twitchell, *Eckankar: Illuminated Way Letters 1966-1971,* pp. 94-95 (emphasis added).

167 Twitchell, *The Spiritual Notebook*, p. 62.

168 Ibid, p. 11.

169 Klemp, *The Eckankar Lexicon*, p. 56.

170 Harold Klemp, *The Book of ECK Wisdom* (Minneapolis: Eckankar, 1986), p. ix.

171 Twitchell, *Eckankar: The Key to Secret Worlds,* p. 230.

172 Ibid.

173 Twitchell, *The Spiritual Notebook*, p. 76.

174 Steiger, *In My Soul I Am Free*, p. 18.

175 Klemp, *The Eckankar Lexicon*, p. 55.

176 Todd Cramer and Doug Munson, *ECKANKAR: Ancient Wisdom for Today* (Minneapolis: Eckankar, 1993), p. 9.

177 Ibid., p. 10.

178 Twitchell, *The Spiritual Notebook*, p. 12.

179 Ibid., p. vii.

180 Ibid., p. 1.

181 Ibid., pp. vii-viii.

182 See Cramer and Munson, *ECKANKAR*.

183 Ibid., pp. 108-109.

184 Twitchell, *The Spiritual Notebook*, p. 223.

185 Ibid., p. 18.

186 See http://www.angelfire.com/hi2/eckankarsurvivors/godman.html. The source of web-site reference is Twitchell, *The Spiritual Notebook*, 5th printing 1977, p. 38. (Quote removed from 1990 edition.)

187 Cramer and Munson, *ECKANKAR*, p. 106.

188 Ibid., p. 23.

189 Twitchell, *The Spiritual Notebook*, p. 221 (emphasis added).

190 Twitchell, *Shariyat-Ki-Sugmad*, II: 166.

191 Cramer and Munson, *ECKANKAR*, p. 106.

192 Twitchell, *The Spiritual Notebook*, p. 90.

193 See "Eckankar Survivors" web site at http://www.angelfire.com/hi2/eckankarsurvivors/.

194 Twitchell, *The Flute of God*, p. 46.

195 Twitchell, *The Spiritual Notebook*, p. 18.

196 Ibid., p. 21.

197 Ibid., p. 223.

198 Ibid., p. 18.

199 Twitchell, *Eckankar: The Key to Secret Worlds,* p. 49.

200 Twitchell, *Eckankar: Illuminated Way Letters 1966-1971,* p. 67.

201 Paul Twitchell, *The Key to Eckankar* (Minneapolis: Eckankar, 1995), p. 11.

202 Twitchell, *The Spiritual Notebook*, p. 15.

203 Ibid., p. 221 (emphasis added).

204 Twitchell, *Shariyat-Ki-Sugmad*, I: 96

205 See Answer, Affirmative Defenses, and Counterclaims, p. 2, filed by Michael J. Esler, attorney for Eckankar, on April 30, 1984, from the case Sri Darwin Gross vs. Eckankar, a California nonprofit religious corporation, Civil #84-228, in the United States District Court for the District of Oregon. See also at http://www.thetruth-seeker.com.

206 Twitchell, *Eckankar: The Key to Secret Worlds,* p. 49.

207 Twitchell, *The Flute of God*, p. 6.

208 Ibid., p. 8.

209 Ibid., p. 9.

210 Twitchell, *Eckankar: The Key to Secret Worlds,* p. 71 (emphasis added).

211 Twitchell, *Shariyat-Ki-Sugmad*, I: 96.

212 Ibid., p. 107.

213 Twitchell, *The Spiritual Notebook*, p. 141.

214 Twitchell, *Shariyat-Ki-Sugmad*, I: 109.

215 Twitchell, *The Spiritual Notebook*, p. 223.

216 Ibid., p. 18.

217 Twitchell, *Shariyat-Ki-Sugmad*, I: 118.

218 Ibid., p. 103.

219 Cramer and Munson, *ECKANKAR,* pp. 108-109.

220 Klemp, *The Secret Teachings*, pp. 160-161.

221 Ibid., p. 162.

222 Harold Klemp, *Cloak of Consciousness* (Minneapolis: Eckankar, 1991), p. 156.

223 ECKANKAR International Youth Conference, Las Vegas, Nevada, April 21, 1984. Klemp, *The Secret Teachings*, p. 166.

224 Klemp, *Cloak of Consciousness*, p. 218 (emphasis added).

225 Harold Klemp, "The Wisdom Notes," in *The Mystic World of Eckankar* 34 (2002): 8.

226 Twitchell, *Shariyat-Ki-Sugmad*, I: 103.

227 Klemp, *The Secret Teachings*, p. 161.

228 Twitchell, *Shariyat-Ki-Sugmad*, I: vii.

229 Ibid., pp. xiv-xv (emphasis added).

Chapter 8 — The Origins of Eckankar Doctrine

1   *Merriam-Webster's Collegiate Dictionary,* Tenth Edition (Springfield: Merriam-Webster, Inc., 1993), p. 1302.

2   See "Mahanta" at http://209.238.146.143/m.htm.

3   Paul Twitchell, *Eckankar Dictionary* (San Diego: Illuminated Way Press, 1973), p. 92.

4   Paul Twitchell, *The Spiritual Notebook* (Golden Valley: Illuminated Way Publishing, 1990), p. 18.

5   Ibid., p. 39.

6   Harold Klemp, *A Cosmic Sea of Words: The Eckankar Lexicon* (Minneapolis: Eckankar, 1998), p. 125.

7   Paul Twitchell, *Shariyat-Ki-Sugmad*, Book One (Minneapolis: Eckankar, 1987), p. 191.

8   Ibid., p.111.

9   Brad Steiger, *In My Soul I Am Free* (Menlo Park: Illuminated Way Press, 1968), pp. 33-34.

10 Letter from Paul Iverlet to Jim Anderson, March 31, 1975, at http://members.tripod.com/~dlane5/iverlet1.html. Substantiation comes from Mattie Twitchell, widow of Paul's brother, Howard Clyde, who knew Paul's place in the family. According to her account, almost all of what Steiger wrote was a fanciful yarn Paul developed over the years. Indeed Mattie's son warns: "It's a very good thing my daddy wasn't living; he would have beaten the hell out of [Paul] for telling lies about his early life." See Wilson, *Courier Journal Magazine,* (January 10, 1982), quoted in David C. Lane, *The Making of a Spiritual Movement: The Untold Story of Paul Twitchell and Eckankar* (Del Mar: Del Mar Press, 1993), p. 14.

11 Twitchell, *Shariyat-Ki-Sugmad*, I: 111-112.

12 Steiger, *In My Soul I Am Free*, p. 34.

13 Paul Twitchell, "Talk to God," *Candid Press* (December 10, 1967), quoted in Lane, *The Making of a Spiritual Movement,* p. 97 (emphasis added).

14 Paul Twitchell, *The Flute of God* (Minneapolis: Eckankar, 1987), p. 6.

15 Ibid., p. 9.

16 See Barbara A. Brennan, *Hands of Light: A Guide to Healing Through the Human Energy Field* (New York: Bantam Books, 1988).

17 See http://www.diamondway.org/3lights.html.

18 Paul Twitchell, *Shariyat-Ki-Sugmad*, Book Two (Minneapolis: Eckankar, 1988), p. 64 (emphasis added).

19 Twitchell, *Shariyat-Ki-Sugmad*, I: 23.

20 Twitchell, *Shariyat-Ki-Sugmad*, II: 193-208.

21 Initiations are announced to the Eckist by a pink slip contained in a blue-windowed envelope.

22 Twitchell, *Shariyat-Ki-Sugmad*, II: 200.

23 See Plaintiff's (Sri Darwin Gross's) Sur Reply, p. 9, Exhibit B, 13, filed by David W. Axelrod, attorney for David Gross, on October 9, 1985, from the case Sri Darwin Gross vs. Eckankar, a California nonprofit religious corporation, Civil #84-228RE, in the United States District Court for the District of Oregon. See also at http://www.thetruth-seeker.com.

24 Twitchell, *The Spiritual Notebook,* p. 133.

25 See David Lane, *The Radhasoami Tradition: A Critical History of Guru Successorship* (New York: Garland Publishers, 1992). See also http://radhasoamis.freeyellow.com.

26 Ibid.

27 Twitchell, *Shariyat-Ki-Sugmad*, I: 34.

28 Harold Klemp, *The Secret Teachings* (Minneapolis: Eckankar, 1989), p. 156-57.

29 Harold Klemp, "Another Look at *The Shariyat*," *The Mystic World of Eckankar* 34 (2002): 2 (emphasis added).

30 Harold Klemp, "The Wisdom Notes," *The Mystic World of Eckankar* 34 (2002): 8 (emphasis added).

31 Twitchell, *The Spiritual Notebook,* p. 221.

32 Twitchell, *Shariyat-Ki-Sugmad*, II: 197.

33 See Harold Klemp, *The ECK Satsang Discourses*, Third Series, Letter 8. See also http://www.stormpages.com/truthbeknown66/eckankar11.html.

34 Twitchell, *Shariyat-Ki-Sugmad*, I: 107.

35 Twitchell, *The Spiritual Notebook*, p.15.

36 Ibid., p. 221.

37 Twitchell, *Shariyat-Ki-Sugmad*, I: 96.

38 Twitchell, *The Spiritual Notebook*, p. 223.

39 Ibid., p. 18.

40 Twitchell, *Shariyat-Ki-Sugmad*, I: 118.

41 Ibid., p. 107.

42 "Allah! There is no god, but only HU, the Living, the Self-subsisting, Eternal. No slumber can seize HU nor sleep. HU's are all things in the heavens and on earth. Who is there to intercede in HU's presence except as HU permitteth? HU knoweth what (appeareth to HU's creatures as) before or after or behind them. Nor shall they compass aught of HU's knowledge except as HU willeth. HU's Throne doth extend over the heavens and the earth, and HU feeleth no fatigue in guarding and preserving them for HU is the Most High, the Supreme (in glory)" The Koran, Sura 2:255.

43 See http://www.angelfire.com/sys/popup_source.shtml?search_string=HU+chant+in+Islam.

44 Ibid.

45 See Hazrat Inayat Khan, *The Mysticism of Sound and Music* (Boston & London: Shambhala, 1996), p. 171.

46 See http://www.lightparty.com/Spirituality/OmAum.html and http://www.srichinmoy.org/pdf/questions_and_answers/aum.pdf.

47 On the Egyptian source of HU see http://www.touregypt.net/featurestories/hu.htm (by: Catherine C. Harris) and http://www.angelfire.lycos.com/doc/general/insite.html?search_string=The+HU+and+egypt&member_url=http://www.angelfire.com/sys/popup_source.shtml%3fsearch_string=The+HU+and+egypt.

48 Harold Klemp, *How to Find God* (Minneapolis: Eckankar, 1988), pp. 313-314 (emphasis added).

49 See http://www.cryaloud.com/joshua_hu_gadarn_druids.htm and Herman L. Hoeh, *Compendium of World History* Volume II, pp. 49-50.

50 "HU the Mighty." See http://www.geocities.com/area51/shire/3951/druid4.html; "Who was HU Gadarn? Gadarn is a Welsh word. It means 'the mighty.' HU was a short form of the Old Celtic name Hesus.... Hesus is the Celtic — and also the Spanish — pronunciation of Jesus.... Jesus was merely the Greek form of the Hebrew name Joshua. HU or Hesus the Mighty was Joshua the Mighty, the great general who led Israel into Palestine." See http://www.cryaloud.com/joshua_hu_gadarn_druids.htm.

51 For the early dwellers of the British Isles as "chosen people" see http://www.cryaloud.com/joshua_hu_gadarn_druids.htm.

52 Klemp, *The Secret Teachings*, p. 143 (emphasis added).

53 Ibid., p.144 (emphasis added).

54 See Answer, Affirmative Defenses, and Counterclaims, p. 2, filed by Michael J. Esler, attorney for Eckankar, on April 30, 1984, from the case Sri Darwin Gross vs. Eckankar, a California nonprofit religious corporation, Civil #84-228, in the United States District Court for the District of Oregon. See also at http://www.thetruth-seeker.com (emphasis added).

55 See Harold Klemp, *The Spiritual Exercises of Eck* (Minneapolis: Eckankar, 1993).

56 Twitchell, *Shariyat-Ki-Sugmad*, II: 53.

Chapter 9 — The Psychology of Paul Twitchell

1 Paul Twitchell, *The Spiritual Notebook* (Golden Valley: Illuminated Way Publishing, 1990), p. 223.

2 Ibid., p. 224.

3 *Merriam-Webster's Collegiate Dictionary,* Tenth Edition (Springfield: Merriam-Webster, 1993), p. 343.

4 Harold Klemp, "The Wisdom Notes," *The Mystic World of Eckankar* 34 (2002): 8.

5 See William Healy and Mary Tenney Healy, *Pathological Lying, Accusation and Swindling: A Study in Forensic Psychology,* Chapter 1, at http://ibiblio.org/gutenberg/etext96/pathl10.txt.

6 Ibid.

7 Ibid., Chapter 2, p. 4.

8 Michael S. Myslobodsky, *The Mythomanias: the Nature of Deception and Self-Deception* (Mahwah: Lawrence Erlbaum, 1997), p. 2.

9 *The American Heritage Dictionary of the English Language,* Fourth Edition, at http://www.bartleby.com/61/92/M0199200.html.

10 Paul Twitchell, *The Drums of ECK* (Las Vegas: Illuminated Way Press, 1970), p. 5.

11 Brad Steiger, *In My Soul I Am Free* (Menlo Park: Illuminated Way Press, 1968), pp. 54-55.

12 See Harold Klemp, *The Secret Teachings* (Minneapolis: Eckankar, 1989), p. 144.

13 See American Psychiatric Association (2000), *Diagnostic and Statistical Manual of Mental Disorders: DSM-IV.* 4th ed., at http://www.psych.org/clin_res/dsm/dsmintro81301.cfm.

14 See http://www.mentalhealth.com/dis1/p21-pe04.html.

15 See Chapter 7 of the present work.

16 Klemp, *The Secret Teachings*, p. 143.

17 Ibid.

18 Ibid., p. 195.

19 See Message 362 at http://www.angelfire.com/sys/popup_source.shtml?search_string=tuzahu.

20 Klemp, *The Secret Teachings*, p. 139.

21 "Another local Eckist also was very close to Paul, Mary Hald. She and I became such close friends. She used to own a printing company. On a number of occasions she would print up what would look like newspaper clippings of events about Paul. He would call or write her with a news brief and she would print it on her old printing press on newsprint so it looked like it was a clipping from a paper. She and I never considered the facts of the events weren't legitimate." See http://www.angelfire.com/hi2/eckankarsurvivors/tuzahu.html, Message 357.

22 See *The Courier-Journal, Roto Magazine,* Louisville, Kentucky, (November 7, 1943), from Dean McMakin, "The Life Of Paul Twitchell Modern-Day Founder of Eckankar," (Documents from the McCracken County Public Library Special Collections, Paducah, Kentucky, 1992). See also http://www.thetruth-seeker.com.

23 Ibid.

24 Ibid.

25 Ibid. Paul was a student at two colleges, never graduating from either and never a confirmed faculty member of either.

26 Ibid.

27 Ibid.

28 See Jack Jarvis, "Paul Twitchell, Man of Parts," *Seattle Post-Intelligencer,* July 9, 1963. See www.thetruth-seeker.com for photocopy of article.

29 Ibid.

30 Ibid.

31 Ibid.

32 Ibid.

33 Ibid.

34 Ibid.

35 Ibid.

36 Ibid.

37 See *Hardin County Independent,* Elizabethtown, Illinois (August 10, 1939), from Dean McMakin, "The Life Of Paul Twitchell Modern-Day Founder of Eckankar." See also http://www.thetruth-seeker.com.

38 See "Local Writer Attaining Wide Fame for Work" from Dean McMakin, "The Life of Paul Twitchell Modern-Day Founder of Eckankar" (Documents from the McCracken County Public Library Special Collections, Paducah, Kentucky, 1992). See also http://www.thetruth-seeker.com.

39 See Jarvis, "Paul Twitchell, Man of Parts."

40 Ibid.

41 William Healy and Mary Tenney Healy, *Pathological Lying, Accusation and Swindling: A Study in Forensic Psychology,* Chapter 2, p. 4, at http://ibiblio.org/gutenberg/etext96/pathl10.txt.

42 Ibid.

43 See accounts of Mattie Twitchell, in Wilson, "Courier Journal Magazine," (January 10, 1982), quoted in David C. Lane, *The Making of a Spiritual Movement: The Untold Story of Paul Twitchell and Eckankar* (Del Mar: Del Mar Press, 1993), p. 20.

44 Letter from Paul Iverlet to Jim Anderson, March 31, 1975, at http://members.tripod.com/~dlane5/iverlet1.html. Also quoted in Lane, *The Making of a Spiritual Movement,* p. 14.

45 See "Friction in Twitchell Camp of Liar's League," from Dean McMakin, "The Life of Paul Twitchell Modern-Day Founder of

Eckankar." See also http://www.thetruth-seeker.com (emphasis added).

46 Klemp, *The Secret Teachings*, p. 139.

47 Ibid., p. 141.

48 Healy and Healy, *Pathological Lying,* Chapter 2, p. 4, at http://ibiblio.org/gutenberg/etext96/pathl10.txt.

49 Klemp, *The Secret Teachings*, p. 141.

50 Ibid., pp. 142-43.

51 See Chapter 7 above, Device One.

52 Ibid.

53 Ibid.

54 Ibid.

55 Ibid.

56 Ibid.

57 Ibid.

58 Ibid.

59 Ibid.

60 Ibid., Device Three.

61 Ibid.

62 Ibid, Device Two.

63 Ibid, Device Four.

64 Ibid.

65 Ibid., Device Five.

66 Healy and Healy, *Pathological Lying,* Chapter 2, pp. 9-10.

67 Klemp, *The Secret Teachings*, pp. 152-153.

Chapter 10 — Eckankar Following the Twitchell Years

1 See David C. Lane, *The Making of a Spiritual Movement: The Untold Story of Paul Twitchell and Eckankar* (Del Mar: Del Mar Press, 1993).

2 "Dr. Louis Bluth, one-time President of Eckankar, reported seeing Twitchell's soul carried out in a celestial cloud of light. Yet, he later changed his story, claiming instead that Twitchell had disobeyed the

orders of the Vairagi Masters and was carried away in chains."Ibid, p.43.

3 Lane, *The Making of a Spiritual Movement,* pp. 43-44. See also http://www.geocities.com/eckcult/chapters/tmsm4.html.

4 "If a Living ECK Master translated before his successor was ready, as with Sudar Singh, Rebazar took the Rod of ECK Power in the meantime." Harold Klemp, *Ask the Master: The Living ECK Master Answers Your Questions,* Book One (Minneapolis: Eckankar, 1993), p.189.

5 "Darshan — There are two parts of the Darshan: meeting with the Master outwardly and being recognized by him, and meeting with him inwardly and traveling with him; seeing and being seen by him, and the ENLIGHTENMENT which comes with this act." Harold Klemp, *A Cosmic Sea of Words: The Eckankar* Lexicon (Minneapolis: Eckankar, 1998), p. 44.

6 Darwin Gross, *The Wisdom Notes,* Vol. II (Menlo Park: Eckankar, 1983), p. 85.

7 Paul Twitchell, *The Spiritual Notebook* (Golden Valley: Illuminated Way Publishing, 1990), p. 172.

8 *Difficulties Of Becoming The Living ECK Master* (Menlo Park: Illuminated Way Press, 1980), p. iii.

9 See Message 386 at http://www.angelfire.com/sys/popup_source.shtml?search_string=tuzahu.

10 Quoted in Lane, *The Making of a Spiritual Movement,* p. 133.

11 "There have been people who are in clergy, clergy of Eckankar, who have come up to me and have told me on occasions where he [Darwin Gross] has been out drinking with them." See Deposition of Peter Skelsky taken before Beverly Ciechanski, a Notary Public, C.S.R. #6421, on September 12, 1984, p. 70, from the case Sri Darwin Gross vs. Eckankar, a California nonprofit religious corporation, Civil #84-228, in the United States District Court for the District of Oregon. See also at http://www.thetruth-seeker.com.

12 See Deposition of Sri Darwin Gross taken from Steinbock Mundt Galisky & Capri, Court Reporters, in Oregon, on May 31, 1984, p. 197, Gross vs. Eckankar. See also at http://www.thetruth-seeker.com.

13 Ibid.

14 Letter from C. Lydon Harrell, Jr., lawyer of Paul Twitchell, to chelas, on May 1, 1971, quoted in SCP Publication. See also at http://www.thetruth-seeker.com.

15 Harold Klemp, *Child in the Wilderness* (Minneapolis: Eckankar, 1989), p. 126.

16 Ibid., pp. 127-28.

17 Ibid., p. 128.

18 Ibid., p.128.

19 Ibid., p.129.

20 Ibid., p. 135.

21 Ibid., p. 136.

22 Ibid., p. 141.

23 Ibid., pp. 138-139.

24 Ibid., p. 142.

25 Ibid., p. 167.

26 Ibid., p. 169.

27 Ibid., p. 172.

28 "I recall that much to everybody's surprise that was in on that meeting [Board Meeting 1982], Darwin had suggested the idea that Harold not be President and then in turn was basically harking out the idea of who would be President and the next thing you knew it was back in his lap." See Deposition of Don Ginn taken before Rita Arlene Howell, a Notary Public, on May 18, 1984, pp. 15-16, from Gross vs. Eckankar. See also at http://www.thetruth-seeker.com.

29 See Deposition of Harold Klemp taken before Gretia R. Capri, Court Reporter and Notary Public, in Portland, Oregon, on May 30, 1984, p. 130, Gross vs. Eckankar.

30 "The board was really being executed, after my viewing of it, as a rubber stamp of what Darwin Gross wanted to do and had been that way." See Deposition of Peter Skelsky taken before Beverly Ciechanski, a Notary Public, C.S.R. #6421, on September 12, 1984, p. 17, Gross vs. Eckankar.

31 "So I was trained that you do follow the guidance of the Living ECK Master and the ECK Master, too, and you don't question those things. I personally felt that that was one reason I was put in the role I was put in because I didn't question this with Darwin." See Deposition of Don Ginn taken before Rita Arlene Howell, Notary Public, on May 18, 1984, p. 23, Gross vs. Eckankar.

32 "I'll state that was the general attitude that he had adopted towards Sri Harold and a total lack of cooperation, and one good example is Sri

Harold had needed a computer terminal at his home and Darwin went out of his way to make sure nobody took a computer terminal to his home.... He [Darwin] went into an uproar at the idea somebody was going to do that and he demanded that they not do it...." See Deposition of Don Ginn, p. 27, Gross vs. Eckankar.

33 See Deposition of Harold Klemp taken before Gretia R. Capri, Court Reporter and Notary Public, in Portland, Oregon, on May 30, 1984, p. 151, Gross vs. Eckankar.

34 See Deposition of Don Ginn taken before Rita Arlene Howell, Notary Public, on May 18, 1984, p. 26, Gross vs. Eckankar.

35 See Deposition of Harold Klemp taken before Gretia R. Capri, Court Reporter and Notary Public, in Portland, Oregon, on May 30, 1984, p. 148, Gross vs. Eckankar.

36 See Agreement of October 1, 1982 between Eckankar, a non-profit corporation, and Harold Klemp, Exhibit 1, p. 2, Gross vs. Eckankar (text is not signed).

37 See Employment Agreement of October 1, 1981, between Eckankar, a non-profit corporation, and Darwin Gross, Exhibit A-2, p. 2, Gross vs. Eckankar.

38 "...I was trained that you do follow the guidance of the Living Eck Master and the Eck Master, too, and you don't question those things. I personally felt that...I was put in the role...because I didn't question this with Darwin [Gross]...." See Deposition of Don Ginn taken before Rita Arlene Howell, Notary Public, on May 18, 1984, p. 23, Gross vs. Eckankar.

39 See Defendant's (Eckankar's) Memorandum in Support of Motion for Partial Summary Judgment, filed by Attorneys Michael J. Esler and Alan L. Schneider, p. 10, Gross vs. Eckankar.

40 See Deposition of Sri Harold Klemp, taken from Steinbock Mundt Galisky & Capri, Court Reporters, in Oregon, on May 30, 1984, p. 141, Gross vs. Eckankar.

41 Minutes of a Meeting of the Board of Trustees of Eckankar, held on August 7, 1983, in Menlo Park, CA, Exhibit 3, pp. 1-2, Gross vs. Eckankar.

42 See Deposition of Peter Skelsky taken before Beverly Ciechanski, a Notary Public, C.S.R. #6421, on September 12, 1984, p. 28, Gross vs. Eckankar.

43 See Minutes of a Meeting of the Board of Trustees of Eckankar, held on August 7-8, 1983, in Menlo Park, CA, Exhibit 3, pp. 2, 5, Gross vs. Eckankar.

44 Ibid., p.5.

45 A group of initiates of the eighth circle that provides spiritual support to the Living Eck Master.

46 See Assignment, signed by assignor as "Gail Ande Andersen, formerly known as Gail T. Gross, also formerly known as Gail Twitchell," on July 15, 1982, recorded in the Copyright Office of the United States, The Library of Congress, on September 7, 1982, Volume 1930, pp. 267-271. See also the Agreement of Sale of the Works of Paul Twitchell, signed by Gail A. Andersen and Sri Darwin Gross for Eckankar on July 15, 1982, from the case Eckankar, a California nonprofit religious corporation vs. Darwin Gross, Civil No. 89-1150-JC, in the United States District Court for the District of Oregon, Complaint for Breach of Contract and Claim and Delivery, filed by Michael J. Esler on behalf of plaintiff Eckankar on October 26, 1989, p. 37, Exhibit E. See also at http://www.thetruth-seeker.com.

47 See Minutes of a Meeting of the Board of Trustees of Eckankar, held on August 7-8, 1983, in Menlo Park, CA, Exhibit 3, p. 6, Gross vs. Eckankar. See also at http://www.thetruth-seeker.com.

48 Ibid., p. 7.

49 Ibid.

50 Personal conversation between Harold Klemp and Ford T. Johnson, Jr., August 8, 1983.

51 See Deposition of Sri Darwin Gross taken from Steinbock Mundt Galisky & Capri, Court Reporters, in Oregon, on May 24, and 31, 1984, pp. 46-47, and 95-6 respectively, Gross vs. Eckankar. See also at http://www.thetruth-seeker.com.

52 See Answer, Affirmative Defenses, and Counterclaims, p. 3, filed by Michael J. Esler, attorney for defendant Eckankar, on April 30, 1984, Gross vs. Eckankar.

53 See Letter by Sri Harold Klemp to Darwin Gross, on January 4, 1984, in Reply Memorandum, Exhibit C, filed by Michael J. Esler, attorney for defendant Eckankar, on May 6, 1985, Gross vs. Eckankar.

54 Lane, *The Making of a Spiritual Movement,* pp. 113-114.

55 Paul Twitchell, *The Flute of God* (Minneapolis: Eckankar, 1987), pp. 127-28.

56 See http://www.thetruth-seeker.com.

57 See Defendant's Memorandum in Support of Motion for a Partial Summary Judgment, pp. 3-4, filed by Michael J. Esler, attorney for

Eckankar, from the case Sri Darwin Gross vs. Eckankar. See also at http://www.thetruth-seeker.com.

58 Harold Klemp, *The Living Word* (Minneapolis: Eckankar, 1989), pp. 131-32.

59 See http://www.thetruth-seeker.com.

60 Harold Klemp, *The Eck Satsang Discourses* Fourth Series, (1996), pp. 15-16, at http://members.tripod.com/~dlane5/sub.html.

61 Ibid., p. 23.

62 Harold Klemp, *Wisdom from the Master on Spiritual Leadership: Eck Leader's Guide* (Minneapolis: Eckankar, 2001), pp. 3-4.

63 See depositions, motions and court transcripts, Gross vs. Eckankar, at http://www.thetruth-seeker.com.

64 Paul Twitchell, *The Tiger's Fang* (Menlo Park: Illuminated Way Press, 1979), p.156.

65 "Moloch was a pagan God for one of the ancient races in the Middle East, long before Christ.... It was a dishonest practice of religion with the people — done by the priestcraft." Twitchell, *The Tiger's Fang,* pp. 150-51.

66 Klemp, *The Secret Teachings*, pp. 35-36.

67 Twitchell, *The Tiger's Fang,* p. 156.

68 Klemp, *The Secret Teachings*, p. 162.

69 Elisabeth Kubler-Ross, *On Death and Dying* (New York: Simon & Schuster, 1969), p. 51.

70 Ibid., p. 52.

71 "Syncretism — The combination of different forms of belief or practice." See *Merriam-Webster's Collegiate Dictionary,* Tenth Edition (Springfield: Merriam-Webster, 1993), p. 1196.

72 Letter from Pietro Valentyne to Harold Klemp, March 29, 1996, at http://www.caic.org.au/eastern/eck/valentyn.htm.

73 See http://members.tripod.com/~dlane5/eckresign3.html.

74 See http://members.tripod.com/~dlane5/ex-eck.html.

75 See http://www.caic.org.au/eastern/eck/valentyn.htm.

76 See http://www.angelfire.com/hi2/Eckankarsurvivors/albert1.html.

77 Andrew Sullivan, "Who Says the Church Can't Change," *Time Magazine* (June 17, 2002), p. 63.

78 See http://www.thetruth-seeker.com.

79 The Angels of the Violet Light are thought to be a healing order associated with Saint Germain, considered one of the Ascended Masters. The "energy of the violet flame" is said to work on whatever "issue has come up for healing" while you sleep at night.... See http://www.geocities.com/HotSprings/Resort/1239/Violet2.html.

80 See message from A. Nelson to L. Kyle on November 6, 2002, at http://www.thetruth-seeker.com.

81 Message 377 at http://www.angelfire.com/sys/popup_source.shtml?search_string=tuzahu.

82 Ibid.

Chapter 11 — Sant Mat, Radhasoami, and the Myth of the Master

1   "Upanishads — A group of writings that make up the last section of a collection of Hindu scriptures called the Vedas." The word literally means to sit close to. See http://sanatan.intnet.mu/.

2   For general information on Hindu literature see http://www.cs.colostate.edu/~malaiya/hindiint.html and http://www.culturopedia.com/Religions/hindudharma.html.

3   Mark Juergensmeyer, *Radhasoami Reality: The Logic of a Modern Faith* (Princeton: Princeton University Press, 1991), p. 21.

4   Uttar Pradesh District is located in the northern region near the border of Nepal and between Delhi and Rajasthan.

5   See http://www.santmat-diewahrheit.de/englisch/kirpal/elixir/21.htm

6   This is an interesting story in itself, and one deserving of some attention. It seems that after Lane completed his critical study of Eckankar, he began to view the Sant Mat, which he had followed for some time, very differently. From his early studies in religious history and phenomenology, Lane shifted to a study of the sociology of religion and knowledge. Lane studied under Professor Mark Juergensmeyer and others in this field, and assisted Juergensmeyer in the completion of *Radhasoami Reality*.

7   David C. Lane, *The Radhasoami Tradition: A Critical History of Guru Successorship* (New York: Garland Publishers, 1992), p. 2.

8   See Julian Johnson, *The Path of the Masters* (Punjab: R.S.S.B., 1985).

9   Ibid., p. 391.

10   Ibid., p. 392.

11   Most notably A.T.O.M. — Darwin Gross, M.S.I.A. — John-Roger Hinkins, Morningland — Sri Donato (possibly), The Divine Science of Light and Sound — Jerry Mulvin, MasterPath — Gary Olsen, The Sonic Spectrum — Michael Turner.

12   Lane, *The Radhasoami Tradition,* p. 8.

13   L. R. Puri, *Radha Soami Teachings* (Punjab: R.S.S.B., 1982) p.6.

14   Juergensmeyer, *Radhasoami Reality*, pp. 45-46.

15   See http://radhasoamis.freeyellow.com/page5.html (emphasis added).

16   See Lane, *Radhasoami Beas Secret History,* Chapter 4, p. 1, at http://radhasoamis.freeyellow.com.

17   Juergensmeyer, *Radhasoami Reality*, pp. 36-37.

18   Lane, *Radhasoami Beas Secret History,* Chapter 4, p. 1, at http://radhasoamis.freeyellow.com.

19   Ibid., Chapter 3, p. 1.

20   Lane, *The Radhasoami Tradition*, Chapter Three, p. 1.

21   Lane, *Radhasoami Beas Secret History,* at http://radhasoamis.freeyellow.com.

22   Ibid., Chapter 2, p. 4, at http://radhasoamis.freeyellow.com.

23   Ibid.

24   Radha Soami Satsang Bulletin No. XVI, p. 4 (1951) from Lane, *The Radhasoami Tradition*, Chapter Three, p. 7.

25   Ram Chandra, *Complete Works*, Vol. One, p. 362, at http://radhasoamis.freeyellow.com/page3.html.

26   "Simran. Repetition of the holy names of God." Harold Klemp, *A Cosmic Sea of Words: The Eckankar Lexicon* (Minneapolis: Eckankar, 1998), p. 191.

27   David C. Lane, *The Unknowing Sage: The Life and Work of Baba Faqir Chand* (Walnut: Mt. San Antonio College Press, 1993), Chapter 4, Part 1, p. 3, at http://www.hindunet.org/alt_hindu/1994/msg00860.html and http://www.angelfire.com/realm/bodhisattva/chand.html.

28   DragonStar and S. Panchadasi, *How to Travel to Other Dimensions*; Linda Strength, *Soul Travel: An Experience*; John Perkins, *Psychonavigation: Techniques for Travel Beyond Time.*

29   Lane, *The Unknowning Sage*, Chapter 3, Part 3, p. 3, at http://
www.angelfire.com/realm/bodhisattva/chand.html.

30   Paul Twitchell, *Shariyat-Ki-Sugmad*, Book One (Minneapolis:
Eckankar, 1987), p. 138.

31   Lane, *The Unknowning Sage*, Chapter 3, Part 4, p. 2, at http://
www.geocities.com/truthis_myname/faqir/chand-3d.html (emphasis
added).

32   Ibid., Chapter 3, Part 1, pp. 1-5, at http://www.angelfire.com/realm/
bodhisattva/chand.html.

33   John 10:30.

Chapter 12 — Holy Books and the Sixteen Crucified Saviors

1   Richard Elliott Friedman, *Who Wrote the Bible* (New York: Harper
Collins, 1997), pp. 17-18.

2   Ibid., p. 24.

3   Gerald Massey, *Ancient Egypt: The Light of the World,* Two Volumes
(Kila: Kessinger, 2002); *Book of the Beginnings,* Two Volumes (Kila:
Kessinger, 1992). On this issue, Doane offers more detailed evidence
to prove that parts of the Old Testament have their origins in Egyptian
culture: "There is indeed, hardly a great or fruitful idea in the Jewish
or Christian systems, which has not its analogy in the (ancient)
Egyptian faith. The development of the one God into a *trinity*; the
incarnation of the mediating deity in a Virgin, and without a father;
his conflict and his momentary defeat by the powers of darkness; his
partial victory (for the enemy is not destroyed); his resurrection and
reign over an eternal kingdom with his justified saints; his distinction
from, and yet identity with, the uncreate incomprehensible Father,
whose form is unknown, and who dwelleth not in temples made with
hands-*all these theological conceptions pervade the oldest religion of
Egypt....*" T. W. Doane, *Bible Myths and Their Parallel in Other
Religions* (Pomeroy: Health Research, 1985), p. 414.

4   See Friedman, *Who Wrote the Bible*; Paula Fredriksen, *From Jesus to
Christ: The Origins of the New Testament Images of Jesus* (New
Haven: Yale University Press, 1988).

5   "The Gospels of Matthew, Mark, and Luke. Since the 1780s, the first
three books of the New Testament have been called the Synoptic
Gospels because they are so similar in structure, content, and wording
that they can easily be set side by side to provide a synoptic
comparison of their content. The Gospel of John has a different
arrangement and offers a somewhat different perspective on Christ.
The striking similarities between the first three Gospels prompt
questions regarding the actual literary relationship that exists between

them. This question, called the Synoptic problem, has been elaborately studied in modern times." See *Encyclopædia Britannica*.

6 Joseph Wheless, *Forgery in Christianity: A Documented Record of the Foundations of the Christian Religion* (Kila: Kessinger, 1997), pp. 191-192.

7 Ibid., p. 192.

8 Ibid., p. xvii.

9 G. A. Wells, *Did Jesus Exist?* (London: Pemberton, 1986), p. 78.

10 See Fredriksen, *From Jesus to Christ.*

11 Wheless, *Forgery in Christianity,* p. 145.

12 T. W. Doane, *Bible Myths and Their Parallel in Other Religions* (Pomeroy: Health Research, 1985), p. 412.

13 See Acharya S., *The Christ Conspiracy: The Greatest Story Ever Sold* (Kempton: Adventures Unlimited Press, 1999).

14 Ibid., p. 34.

15 Paula Fredriksen is a Boston University Professor of the Appreciation of Scriptures in the Department of Religion, and consultant and featured speaker on the PBS *Frontline* series "From Jesus to Christ."

16 Fredriksen, *From Jesus to Christ,* pp. 4-5 (emphasis added).

17 See Mangasar M. Mangasarian, *The Truth About Jesus: Is He A Myth?* (Chicago: Independent Religious Society, 1909), chapter "Jesus of Paul," at http://www.infidels.org/library/historical/m_m_mangasarian/truth_about_jesus.html.

18 *Webster's Revised Unabridged Dictionary* defines pious fraud as "a fraud contrived and executed to benefit the church or accomplish some good end, upon the theory that the end justified the means."

19 "Spurious writings, especially writings falsely attributed to biblical characters or times. Also a body of texts written between 200 B.C.E. and C.E. 200 and spuriously ascribed to various prophets and kings of Hebrew Scriptures." See http://www.cometozarahemla.org/others/movocabulary.html.

20 Wheless, *Forgery in Christianity,* p. xxii.

21 Ibid., p. xxiii, (emphasis added).

22 Ibid.

23 Ibid., p. xxiv (emphasis added).

24 Ibid., (emphasis added).

25 Ibid.

26 Ibid., pp. xxiv-xxv.

27 See *Catholic Encyclopaedia*, under "III. Apocrypha of Christian Origin, (1) Apocryphal Gospels" at http://www.newadvent.org/cathen/01601a.htm (emphasis added).

28 See "St. Jerome" at http://www.newadvent.org/cathen/08341a.htm.

29 Wheless, *Forgery in Christianity*, p. xxv.

30 See Mangasarian, *The Truth About Jesus,* chapter entitled "Jesus of Paul," at http://www.infidels.org/library/historical/m_m_mangasarian/truth_about_jesus.html.

31 Wheless, *Forgery in Christianity*, p. xxvi.

32 Ibid.

33 Ibid.

34 Hippo is near what is now Constantine, Algeria.

35 Wheless, *Forgery in Christianity,* p. xxvi (emphasis added).

36 *Merriam-Webster's* defines the Gospels as "the story or record of Christ's life and teachings contained in the first four books of the New Testament...containing narratives of the life and death of Jesus Christ ascribed respectively to Matthew, Mark, Luke, and John. The good news concerning Christ, the Kingdom of God, and salvation... the teachings of Jesus and the apostles as a body or system."

37 Wheless, *Forgery in Christianity,* p. 101.

38 Fredriksen, *From Jesus to Christ,* p. 6 (emphasis added).

39 Ibid., pp. 6-7.

40 Ibid., p. 6.

41 Acharya S., *The Christ Conspiracy,* p. 35 (emphasis added).

42 Wells, *Did Jesus Exist?* p. 78.

43 Ibid.

44 Acharya S., *The Christ Conspiracy,* p. 49.

45 Kersey Graves, *The World's Sixteen Crucified Saviors* (Escondido, CA: Book Tree, 1999), pp. 322-3.

46 Acharya S., *The Christ Conspiracy,* p. 50.

47 See Lee Strobel, *The Case for Christ* (Grand Rapids: Zondervan, 1998).

48 Ibid.

49 See Fredriksen, *From Jesus to Christ*.

50 See Strobel, *The Case for Christ*.

51 See Fredriksen, *From Jesus to Christ*.

52 See Earl Doherty, *Challenging the Verdict: A Cross-Examination of Lee Strobel's "The Case for Christ"* (Ottawa: Age of Reason, 2002).

53 "Mangasar Magurditch Mangasarian was born in Mashger, Turkey, on December 29,1859. His family was affluent enough to send him to Robert College in Constantinople where he was ordained into the Congregationalist ministry in 1878. He studied for the Presbyterian ministry at Princeton Theological Seminary (Princeton University) but he became the minister of the Spring Garden Presbyterian Church in Philadelphia, Pennsylvania, in 1882 and remained there until 1885. During the period 1885-89 he was an 'independent preacher in Philadelphia' and the founder of and lecturer on 'Independent Religion' in New York City sometime during this period. Mr. Mangasarian, progressively skeptical, soon surrendered the words of Christ as his creed. In fact he came finally to understand that the Christ of Christianity was nothing but a myth. Consequently, in 1909, his congregation printed his first hardback book in the United States, *The Truth About Jesus — Is He a Myth?*" See http://www.atheists.org/Atheism/roots/mangasarian/.

54 See Mangasarian, *The Truth About Jesus*, chapter "Jesus of Paul," at http://www.infidels.org/library/historical/m_m_mangasarian/truth_about_jesus.html (emphasis added).

55 Ibid.

56 Fredriksen, *From Jesus to Christ*, p. 53.

57 Ibid., p. 52.

58 See Mangasarian, *The Truth About Jesus*, chapter "Jesus of Paul," at http://www.infidels.org/library/historical/m_m_mangasarian/truth_about_jesus.html (emphases added).

59 Fredriksen, *From Jesus to Christ*, p. 53.

60 "*Encyclopedia Biblica* was largely the idea and work of Prof. Robertson Smith who was a principal contributor of articles on Christianity to *Encyclopaedia Britannica* between 1875 and 1878. From this base, the *Encyclopedia Biblica* was created along with contributions from numerous other Christian scholars. The first edition was published around 1900." See http://www.cwru.edu/UL/preserve/Etana/encyl_biblica_a-d/preface.pdf.

61   Wheless, *Forgery in Christianity*, p. 231 (emphasis added).

62   See Graves, *The World's Sixteen Crucified Saviors*.

63   See Fredriksen, *From Jesus to Christ*.

64   See Graves, *The World's Sixteen Crucified Saviors*, p. 35.

65   Ibid., p. 36.

66   Ibid.

67   See *Encyclopædia Britannica,* under "Zoroaster," at http://www.britannica.com/eb/article?eu=80561.

68   Graves, *The World's Sixteen Crucified Saviors*, p. 37.

69   Ibid, Chapter XVI.

70   Ibid.

71   See *Encyclopædia Britannica*, under "Krishna," at http://www.britannica.com/eb/article?eu=47328.

72   See Graves, *The World's Sixteen Crucified Saviors*, chapter XVI.

73   Ibid.

74   See Acharya S., *The Christ Conspiracy*.

75   *Merriam-Webster Revised Unabridged Dictionary*, under "Euhemerism," at http://unabridged.merriam-webster.com/cgi-bin/unabridged?va=euhemerism&x=13&y=6.

76   See *The Urantia Book* (Chicago: Urantia Foundation, 1993). See also at http://www.urantia.org/papers/index.html.

Chapter 13 — The Spiritual and Scientific Foundations of Higher Consciousness

1   See Meredith Alexander, "Thirty Years Later, Stanford Prison Experiment Lives On," *Stanford Report*, August 22, 2001, at http://www.prisonexp.org/30years.htm.

2   Michael Talbot, *The Holographic Universe* (New York: Harper Collins, 1991), p. 1.

3   See David Bohm, *Wholeness and the Implicate Order* (London: Routledge, 2000).

4   See Karl Pribram, *Languages of the Brain: Experimental Paradoxes and Principles in Neuropsychology* (Monterey: Wadsworth Publishing, 1977).

5   Bohm, *Wholeness and the Implicate Order,* pp. 145-7, 177-8.

6   See Alain Aspect et al., *Levy Statistics & Laser Cooling* (Cambridge: Cambridge University Press, 2001). See also "Reality — the Holographic Universe" at http://www.keelynet.com/biology/reality.htm.

7   Bohm, *Wholeness and the Implicate Order*, pp. 208-212.

8   *Webster's Collegiate Dictionary* at http://unabridged.merriam-webster.com/cgi-bin/collegiate?va=paradigm (emphasis added).

9   An example of this "new genre" is an older book of Jane Roberts, *The Oversoul Seven Trilogy* (San Rafael: Amber-Allen, 1995).

10   In other dimensions of existence such as the astral plane, thought immediately produces outcomes that depend entirely on the individual generating them. Subjective belief and thought, while central to physical existence, occurs in a more certain way and at a more rapid rate in other dimensions or planes of existence.

11   See Ian Stevenson, *Twenty Cases Suggestive of Reincarnation* (Charlottesville: University Press of Virginia, 1999).

12   See Richard L. Thompson, *Alien Identities: Ancient Insights into Modern UFO Phenomena* (Alachua: Govardhan Hill, 1995); Whitley Strieber, *Confirmation: The Hard Evidence of Aliens Among Us* (New York: St. Martin's Press, 1998).

13   See Zecharia Sitchin, *The 12th Planet* (New York: Avon Books, 1978).

14   See http://www.scientificexploration.org/.

15   See http://www.newscientist.com/hottopics/quantum/quanum.jsp?id=22994400.

16   William A. Tiller, *Science and Human Transformation: Subtle Energies, Intentionality and Consciousness* (Walnut Creek: Pavior, 1997) p. 23.

17   See Jane Roberts, *Seth Material* (Cutchogue: Buccaneer Books, 1995).

18   God "is the One Who created for you all that is on the earth. Moreover He turned to the heaven and fashioned seven heavens with harmony. He is Full of Knowledge of all things" Holy Koran 2:29. "And We have created above you seven paths: We have never been unmindful of the Creation" Holy Koran 23:17. God "is the One Who created seven heavens one above another. You can see no faults in the creation of the Beneficent. Turn the vision again! Can you see any rifts?" Holy Koran 67:3. "Did you see how God created seven

heavens one above another and made the moon a light therein and made the sun a lamp?" Holy Koran 71:15-16.

19 See Charles Ponce, *Kabbalah: An Introduction and Illumination for the World Today* (San Francisco: Straight Arrow, 1986).

20 See Henry T. Laurency, *The Knowledge of Reality* (Stockholm: Henry T. Laurency, 1979).

21 "Hylozoics, Hylozoism: a doctrine that all matter is animated — used especially of the theories of early Greek philosophers — HYLOZOISM (Gr. iX,~, matter. ~ life), in philosophy, a term applied to any system which explains all life, whether physical or mental, as ultimately derived from matter ('cosmic matter,' Weldstoff). Such a view of existence has been common throughout the history of thought, and especially among physical scientists. Thus the Ionian school of philosophy, which began with Thales, sought for the beginning of all things in various material substances, water, air, fire (see Ionian School). These substances were regarded as being in some sense alive, and taking some active part in the development of being. This primitive hylozoism reappeared in modified forms in medieval and Renaissance thought, and in modern times the doctrine of materialistic monism is its representative. Between modern materialism and hylozoism proper there is, however, the distinction that the ancients, however vaguely, conceived the elemental matter as being in some sense animate if not actually conscious and conative." See http://3.1911encyclopedia.org/H/HY/HYLOZOISM.htm.

Chapter 14 — The Spiritual Practice of Higher Consciousness

1 See C. G. Jung and C. Kerenyi, *Essays on a Science of Mythology* (Princeton: Princeton University Press, 1993).

2 See Bill Moyers, *Joseph Campbell and the Power of the Myth* (New York: Doubleday, 1988).

3 Ibid., p.209.

4 Ibid.

5 Ibid., pp. 209-210.

6 See William A. Tiller, *Science and Human Transformation: Subtle Energies, Intentionality and Consciousness* (Walnut Creek: Pavior, 1997).

7 Paul acknowledges in his writings an awareness of theosophy especially as it relates to his structure of the inner worlds. There is an interesting parallel in the lives of Blavatsky (founder of theosophy) and Twitchell. It seems that both were inclined to invent themselves as needed. "In 1882, Madame Blavatsky turned over to an Anglo-

Indian newspaper editor and the Indian government a series of letters she claimed were from her teacher, one Koot Hoomi, although handwriting analysis later showed she had written them herself. In these letters, which contained a pastiche of Western occultism and inaccurate Indian mysticism, she revealed a seven-based cosmology in which there are seven planes of existence, seven races of man, and seven cycles of existence. These letters were later gathered into a book entitled *The Secret Doctrine* which, among other things large and small, included references to Atlantis and MU/Lemuria. According to *The Secret Doctrine*, Lemuria had been inhabited by hermaphroditic people who laid eggs — not very human-like by our standards. When these beings "discovered" sex, their downfall began. Blavatsky claimed, in her biography, to be a virgin, in spite of her age, and the facts that she had been married and had lived as mistress to a Slovenian singer, an English businessman, a Russian baron, and a Philadelphia merchant — though not at the same time." This is rather Twitchellian in character. In spite of this colorful history, Blavatsky made numerous contributions to the West's understanding of esotericism and created a society that has helped expand the paradigm of spiritual thought. See http://www.phoenixpages.com/ona/Origins/lemuria.htm.

8   See Rudolf Steiner, *Theosophy: An Introduction to the Supersensible Knowledge of the World and the Destination of Man* (New York: Kessinger, 1997.

9   See Annie W. Besant, *Popular Lectures on Theosophy* (New York: Kessinger, 1997.

10   See Charles W. Leadbeater, *A Textbook of Theosophy* (Wilmington: Anchor, 1998).

11   "Yuga — Sanskrit, yoke, pair, race of men, age of the world: one of the four ages of a Hindu world cycle each shorter and less righteous than the one preceding." See http://unabridged.merriam-webster.com/cgi-bin/unabridged?va=yuga&x=16&y=4.

12   See http://www.kheper.net/topics/Theosophy/root_races.html.

13   See Barbara A. Brennan, *Hands of Light: A Guide to Healing Through the Human Energy Field* (New York: Bantam Books, 1988).

14   Tiller, *Science and Human Transformation.*

15   Also called the *nuri sarup* (light body), *hsien* (through the "embryonic body"). In Taoism, it is called emotional body.

16   Spiritual Exercises — Another expression for the practice of meditation or contemplation. They also use mantras, recitations, or visualization. First popularized under this name by St. Ignatius

Loyola, though practiced in Yoga well before. Later adopted by this name in the religion of Eckankar and its progeny.

17   Joseph J. Weed, *Wisdom of the Mystic Masters* (West Nyack: Parker, 1988), p. 173.

18   Ibid.

Chapter 15 — Dreams: A Bridge to Higher Consciousness

1   See Barbara H. Fowler, *Love Lyrics of Ancient Egypt* (Chapel Hill: University of North Carolina Press, 1994); Joseph Kaster, *The Wisdom of Ancient Egyp* (London: Barnes and Noble, 1995); Dominic Montserrat, *Sex and Society in Graeco-Roman Egypt* (New York: Kegan Paul, 1996).

2   See "Dreams" at http://www.tryskelion.com/dreamhis.htm.

3   See "Dream" in *Encyclopædia Britannica* at http://www.britannica.com/eb/article?eu=117531&tocid=38748#38748.toc.

4   Sigmund Freud, *The Interpretation of Dreams* (New York: Avon, 1998), pp. 36-37.

5   See William Harris Stahl, *Commentary on the Dream of Scipio by MacRobus* (New York: Columbia University Press, 1990).

6   Freud, *The Interpretation of Dreams.*

7   See http://ourworld.compuserve.com/homepages/keithhearne/recentideas.htm.

8   Freud, *The Interpretation of Dreams,* p. 129.

9   Ibid., pp. 129-130.

10 See Carl Gustav Jung, *Dreams* (New York: MJF Books, 1974).

11 "Syzygy: a pair of correlatives, opposites, or otherwise related things; e.g., a pair of male and female Gnostic aeons [eternal beings that together form the fullness of the supreme being from whom they emanate and between whom and the world they are intermediaries]; the *syzygy* of Man and Church." See http://www.britannica.com/eb/article?eu=117398&tocid=28989&query=syzygy.

12 C. G. and Joan Chodorow, *Jung on Active Imagination* (London: Routledge, 1997), p. 3.

13 See http://www.mythsdreamssymbols.com/dreamsarchetypes.html.

14 See "Dream" in *Encyclopædia Britannica* at <http://www.britannica.com/eb/article?eu=117531>.

15   See "Hallucination" in *Encyclopædia Britannica* at <http://www.britannica.com/eb/article?eu=119400>.

16   See "Dream" in *Encyclopædia Britannica*. See also Rosalind D. Cartwright, Lynne Lamberg, *Crisis Dreaming: Using Your Dreams to Solve Your Problems* (New York: Harper Collins, 1992); Wilse B. Webb, *Sleep: An Active Process* (Duluth: Scott Foresman, 1973).

17   Jon Tolaas and Montague Ullman, "Extrasensory Communication and Dreams," in Benjamin B. Wolman, *Handbook of Dreams: Research, Theories, and Applications* (New York: Van Nostrand Reinhold, 1979), pp. 178-179.

18   See Ken Wilber, *The Collected Works of Ken Wilber* Volume Three: *A Sociable God; Eye to Eye* (Boston: Shambhala Publications, 1999).

19   See "Dream" in *Encyclopædia Britannica* at http://www.britannica.com/eb/article?eu=117531.

Chapter 16 — The Practical Side of Higher Consciousness

1   Delbert McClinton, *One of the Fortunate Few*. Lyrics at http://www.geocities.com/rimfirewa/tomuchstuf.gif.

2   Peggy Lee, *Is That All There Is*. Lyrics at http://www.leoslyrics.com/listlyrics.php?sid=%D1%03%84%C7%CC5%C0v.

3   See Deepak Chopra, *The Seven Spiritual Laws of Success: A Practical Guide to the Fulfillment of your Dreams* (San Rafael: Amber-Allen, 1994); Wayne Dwyer, *10 Secrets for Success and Inner Peace* (New York: Hay House, 2002).

4   See Ray Kurzweil, *The Age of Spiritual Machines: When Computers Exceed Human Intelligence* (New York: Penguin, 2000).

5   "The number seven represents 'spiritual perfection.' In Hebrew, the number seven (shevah) comes from the root word savah, which means 'to be full or satisfied, have enough of.' The number seven often venerates these ideas. On the seventh day, God rested from the work of creation since it was full, complete, good and perfect. In relation to time, seven marks the week of seven days used by all nations. Seven tells of eternal Sabbath-keeping for the people of God in all its everlasting perfection. In Daniel's 'time-oriented' prophecy, the number seven also points to spiritual perfection or completeness for the Jewish people." See Ethelbert W. Bullinger, *Number in Scripture: Its Supernatural Design and Spiritual Significance* (Grand Rapids: Kregel, 1980), pp. 158, 167-68. See also at http://www.harvardhouse.com/prophetictech/new/numerology/seven.htm.

BIBLIOGRAPHY

Bibliography

Alexander, Meredith. "Thirty Years Later, Stanford Prison Experment Lives On," *Stanford Report* (August 22, 2001).

Armstrong, Karen. *A History of God: The 4000-Year Quest of Judaism, Christianity and Islam.* New York: Ballantine, 1993.

Ashley-Farrand, Thomas. *Healing Mantras: Using Sound Affirmations for Personal Power, Creativity, and Healing.* New York: Ballantine Wellspring, 1999.

Aspect, Alain et al. *Levy Statistics & Laser Cooling.* Cambridge: Cambridge University Press, 2001.

Atwater, P. M. H. *Coming Back to Life: The After-Effects of the Near-Death Esperience.* New York: Ballantine, 1989.

Bach, Richard. *Illusions: The Adventures of a Reluctant Messiah.* New York: Dell,1989.

Bailey, Alice A. *The Externalisation of the Hierachy.* New York: Lucis, 1972.

Bailey, Alice A. and Djwjal Khul. *Ponder on This.* New York: Lucis, 1996.

Besant, Annie, W. *Popular Lectures on Theosophy.* New York: Kessinger, 1997.

Blackmore, Susan J. *Beyond the Body: An Investigation of Out-of-the-Body Experiences.* Chicago: Academy Chicago, 1992.

———. *Dying to Live: Near-Death Experiences.* Buffalo: Prometheus Books, 1993.

Blavatsky, H. P. *Isis Unveiled: A Master-key to the Mysteries of Ancient and Modern Science and Theology* vol 1 - *Science.* Pasadena: Theosophical University Press, 1998.

———. *Isis Unveiled: A Master-key to the Mysteries of Ancient and Modern Science and Theology* vol 2 - *Theology.* Pasadena: Theosophical University Press, 1998.

Blavatsky, H. P. *The Secret Doctrine: The Synthesis of Science, Religion, and Philosophy* vol 1 - *Cosmogenesis*. Pasadena: Theosophical University Press,1999.

———. *The Secret Doctrine: The Synthesis of Science, Religion, and Philosophy* vol 2 - *Anthropogenesis*. Pasadena: Theosophical University Press, 1999.

Bock, Janet. *The Jesus Mystery*. Los Angeles: Aura Books, 1980.

Bohm, David. *Wholeness and the Implicate Order.* London: Routledge, 2000.

———.*On Creativity*. Lee Nichol ed. New York: Routledge, 2002.

Bohm, David and Peat, David F. *Science, Order and Creativity*. New York: Routledge, 2000.

Bowman, Carol. *Children's Past Lives: How Past Life Memories Affect Your Child*. New York: Bantam, 1998.

Bradley, David. *An Introduction to the Urantia Revelation*. Arcata: White Egret, 1998.

Brennan, Barbara Ann. *Hands of Light: A Guide to Healing Through the Human Energy Field*. New York: Bantam Books, 1988.

Brennan, J. H. *The Astral Projection Workbook: How to Achieve Out-of-Body Experiences*. New York: Sterling, 1990.

Brown, Anita and Joanna Macy (trans.). *Rilke's Book of Hours: Love Poems to God*. New York: Riverhead, 1996.

Brown, Schuyler. *The Origins of Christianity: A Historical Introduction to the New Testament*. New York: Oxford University Press, 1993.

Browne, Sylvia (with Lindsay Harrison). *The Other Side: A Psychic's Guide to Our World and Beyond*. New York: Penguin, 1999.

Brunton, Paul Dr. *A Hermit in the Himalayas*. York Beach: Samuel Weiser, 1984.

Bullinger, Ethelbert W. *Number in Scripture: Its Supernatural Design and Spiritual Significance*. Grand Rapids: Kregel, 1980.

Byuyere, Rosalyn L. *Wheels of Light: A Study of the Chakras,* vol 1 Jeanne Farrens ed.Arcata: Bon Productions, 1989.

Capra, Fritjof. *The Tao of Physics: An Exploration of the Parallels Between Modern Physics and Eastern Mysticism*. Berkeley: Shambhala, 1975.

Carey, Ken. *The Starseed Transmissions*. San Francisco: Harper, 1991.

———. *Vision: A Personal Call to Create a New World*. San Francisco: Harper, 1995.

Cartwright, Rosalind D. and Lynne Lamberg, *Crisis Dreaming: Using Your Dreams to Solve Your Problems.* New York: Harper Collins, 1992.

Catholic Encyclopaedia, First edition, New York: McGraw-Hill, 1967. Second edition, Detroit: Thompson Gale, 2003.

Chodorow,   Joan C. G. *Jung on Active Imagination.* London: Routledge, 1997.

Choppra, Deepak. *The Seven Spiritual Laws of Success: A Practical Guide to the Fulfillment of Your Dreams.* New York: Amber-Allen, 1995.

Churchward, Col. James. *The Lost Continent of Mu.* Las Vegas: BE Books, 2001.

Clark, Glenn. *The Man Who Tapped the Secrets of the Universe.* Waynesboro: University of Science and Philosophy, 2000.

Clow, Barbara Hand. *Eye of the Centaur: A Visionary Guide into Past Lives.* Santa Fe: Bear and Company, 1989.

Concordex of the Urantia Book. Santa Barbara: Clyde Bedell Estate, 1991.

Cott, Jonathan. *Search for Omm Sety: A Story of Eternal Love.* New York: Warner, 1989.

Cramer, Todd and Doug Munson. *Eckankar: Ancient Wisdom for Today.* Minneapolis: Eckankar, 1993.

Davis, James. *The Rosetta Stone of God.* Minneapolis: Eckankar, 2000.

Davis, Roy Eugene. *A Master Guide to Meditation and Spiritual Growth with Techniques and Routines For All Levels of Practice.* Lakemont: CSA Press, 2002.

———. *An Easy Guide to Ayurveda: The Natural Way to Wholeness.* Lakemont: CSA Press, 1996.

———. *An Easy Guide to Meditation For Personal Benefits and Spiritual Growth.* Lakemont: CSA Press, 1995.

———. *How to Live Consciously in God: A Handbook of Spiritual Practice With 31 Inspirational Themes for Daily Reflection.* Lakemont: CSA Press, 2000.

———. *How to Use Your Creative Imagination.* Lakemont: CSA Press, 2002.

———. *Living in God: 366 Themes for Daily Meditative Contemplation and Spiritual Enrichment through the Year: With Life-Enhancing Affirmations and Inspirational Quotations.* Lakemont: CSA Press, 1997.

Davis, Roy Eugene. *The Science of God-Realization: Knowing Our True Nature and Our Relationship with the Infinite.* Lakemont: CSA Press, 2002.

———. *The Self-Revealed Knowledge that Liberates the Spirit: A Handbook of Essential Information for Experiencing a Conscious Relationship with the Infinite and Restoring Soul Awareness to Wholeness.* Lakemont: CSA Press,1997.

———.*The Spiritual Basis of Reap Prosperity: How to Always Be in the Flow of Resources and Supportive Events and Relationships for Your Highest Good.* Lakemont: CSA Press, 1999.

De Ropp, Robert S. *The Master Game: Pathways to Higher Consciousness beyond the Drug Experience.* New York: Dell, 1989.

Doane, T. W. *Bible Myths and Their Parallels in Other Religions.* Pomeroy: Health Research, 1948.

Doherty, Earl. *Challenging the Verdict: A Cross-Examinatiuon of Lee Strobel's "The Case for Christ."* Ottawa: Age of Reason, 2001.

———. *The Jesus Puzzle. Did Christianity Begin with a Mythical Christ?* Ottawa: Canadian Humanist, 2001.

Dragon Star and Panchadasi, S. *How to Travel to Other Dimensions: An 11-lesson course on what you will find there.* New Brunswick: Inner Light Publications, 2002.

Dwyer, Wayne. *10 Secrets for Success and Inner Peace.* New York: Hay House, 2002.

Eddy, Mary Baker. *Science and Health With Key to the Scriptures.* Boston: Writings of Mary Baker Eddy, 1994.

Edwards, Paul. *Reincarnation: A Critical Examination.* Amherst: Prometheus Books, 1996.

———. *Immortality.* Amherst: Prometheus Books, 1997.

Einstein, Albert. *Relativity: The Special and the General Theory.* New York: Bonanza Books, 1995.

Eliade, Mircea. *Patterns in Comparative Religion.* Lincoln: University of Nebraska Press, 1996.

Ellerbe, Helen. *The Dark Side of Christian History.* Orlando: Morningstar & Lark, 2001.

Ellwood, Robert S., and Harry Partin, *Religious and Spiritual Groups in Modern America.* Englewood Cliffs: Prentice-Hall, 1988.

Fast, Denise. *Book of Anami: For the Bold, the Adventuresome, the*

Visionary. Los Angeles: Brighter World, 1993.

Feuerstein, Georg. *The Yoga Tradition: Its History, Literature, Philosophy and Practice*. Prescott: Hohm Press, 2000.

Forsyth, Graham. *In the Many Hands of God*. Silver Spring: "ONE" Publishing, 2003.

Fowler, Barbara. H. *Love Lyrics of Ancient Egypt*. Chapel Hill: University of North Carolina Press, 1994.

Fredriksen, Paula. *From Jesus to Christ: The Origins of the New Testament Images of Jesus*. New Haven: Yale University Press, 1988.

Freud, Sigmund. *The Interpretation of Dreams*. New York: Avon Books, 1998.

Friedman, Richard Elliott. *Who Wrote the Bible*? San Francisco: Harper, 1997.

Fripp, Peter. *The Mystic Philosophy of Sant Mat*. New Delhi: Radha Soami Satsang Beas, 1995.

Frost, Gavin and Frost, Yvonne. *Astral Travel*. York Beach: Samuel Weiser, 1991.

Gawain, Shakti. *Creative Visualization: Use the Power of Your Imagination to Create What You Want in Your Life*. Novato: New World Library, 2002.

Geisler, Norman L. *Baker Encyclopedia of Christian Apologetics*. Grand Rapids: Baker Books, 1999.

———. *Christian Apologetics*. Grand Rapids: Baker Book House, 1988.

Govinda, Lama Anagarika. *The Way of the White Clouds: A Buddhist Pilgrim in Tibet*. Boston: Shambhala, 1972.

Graves, Kersey. *The World's Sixteen Crucified Saviors*. Escondido: Book Tree, 1999.

Gross, Darwin. *The Wisdom Notes*, Vol. II. Menlo Park: Eckankar, 1983.

Hafiz. *The Gift: Poems by Hafiz, the Great Sufi Master,* trans. by Daniel Ladinsky. New York: Penguin, 1999.

Harary, Keith and Weintraub, Pamela. *Have an Out-of-Body Experience in 30 Days:The Free Flight Program*. New York: St. Martin's Press, 1989.

———. *Lucid Dreams in 30 Days: The Creative Sleep Program*. New York: St.Martin's Press, 1989.

Hariharananda, Paramahansa. *The Original and Authenti Kriya Yoga of Babaji Maharaj and Lahiri Mahasaya: The Scientific Process of*

Soul-Culture and the Essence of All Religions. Canoga Park: Kriya Yoga Ashram, 1992.

Hassan, Steven. *Combatting Cult Mind Control.* Santa Fe: Park Street Press, 1999.

————.*Releasing the Bonds: Empowering People to Think for Themselves.* Somerville: Freedom of Mind Press, 2000.

Hawking, Stephen. *The Universe in a Nutshell.* New York: Bantam, 2001.

Healy,William and Healy, Mary Tenney. *Pathological Lying, Accusation and Swindling: A Study in Forensic Psychology.* Glenn Ridge: Patterson Smith, 1969.

Heinerman, John and Shupe, Andson. *The Mormon Corporate Empire.* Boston: Beacon Press, 1985.

Higgins, Gregory C. *Twelve Theological Dilemmas.* New York: Paulist Press, 1991.

Hill, Douglas and Williams, Pat. *The Supernatural.* London: Aldus Books, 1965.

Hubbard, L. Ron. *Dianetics.* Los Angeles: Bridge Publications, 1999.

James, William. *The Varieties of Religious Experience.* New York: Simon & Schuster Inc., 1997.

Jarvis, Jack. "Paul Twitchell, Man of Parts." *Seattle Post-Intelligencer,* July 9, 1963.

Johnson, Julian. *The Path of the Masters.* New Delhi: Radha Soami Satsang Beas,1985.

————. *With a Great Master in India.* New Delhi: Radha Soami Satsang Beas, 1994.

Juergensmeyer, Mark. *Radhasoami Reality: The Logic of a Modern Faith.* Princeton: Princeton University Press, 1991.

Jung, C. G. *Modern Man in Search of a Soul,* trans. by W. S. Dell and Cary F. Baynes. Orlando: Harcourt, 1933.

————. *Dreams,* trans. by R.F.C. Hull. Princeton: Princeton University Press, 1974.

————. *Critique of Psychoanalysis,* trans. by R.F.C. Hull. Princeton: Princeton University Press, 1975.

————. *Dream Analysis: Notes of the Seminar Given in 1928-1930,* William McGuire ed. Princeton: Princeton University Press, 1984.

————. *Jung on Active Imagination,* trans. by R.F.C. Hull. Princeton: Princeton University Press, 1997.

Jung, C. G. and C. Kerenyi. *Essays on a Science of Mythology: The*

Myth of the Divine Child and the Mysteries of Eleusis.
Princeton: Princeton University Press, 1978.

Kaster, Joseph. *The Wisdom of Ancient Egypt.* London: Barnes and
Noble, 1995.

Keyes, Jr, Ken. *Handbook to Higher Consciousness.* Arrojo Rande: Love
Line Books, 1997.

Khan, Hazrat Inayat. *The Mysticism of Sound and Music.* Boston:
Shambhala, 1991.

Klemp, Harold. *The Wind of Change.* Menlo Park: Illuminated Way
Press, 1980.

———. *The Book of ECK Wisdom.* Minneapolis: Eckankar, 1986.

———. *Soul Travelers of the Far Country.* Minneapolis: Eckankar, 1987.

———. *Journey of Soul: Mahanta Transcripts* - Book 1. Minneapolis:
Eckankar, 1988.

———. *How to Find God: Mahanta Transcripts* - Book 2.
Minneapolis: Eckankar, 1988.

———. *Child in the Wilderness.* Minneapolis: Eckankar, 1989.

———. *The Living Word.* Minneapolis: Eckankar, 1989.

———. *The Secret Teachings: Mahanta Transcripts* - Book 3.
Minneapolis: Eckankar, 1989.

———. *The Golden Heart.* Minneapolis: Eckankar, 1990.

———. *Cloak of Confusion: Mahanta Transcripts* - Book 5.
Minneapolis: Eckankar,1991.

———. *The Eternal Dreamer: Mahanta Transcripts* - Book 7.
Minneapolis:Eckankar, 1992.

———. *Wisdom of the Heart.* Minneapolis: Eckankar, 1992.

———. *Ask The Master,* Book 1. Minneapolis: Eckankar, 1993.

———. *The Dream Master: Mahanta Transcripts* - Book 8.
Minneapolis: Eckankar, 1993.

———. *Ask the Master,* Book 2. Minneapolis: Eckankar, 1994.

———. *We Come as Eagles: Mahanta Transcripts* - Book 9.
Minneapolis: Eckankar,1994.

———. *What is Spiritual Freedom? Mahanta Transcripts* -
Book 11. Minneapolis: Eckankar, 1995.

———. *How the Inner Master Works: Mahanta Transcripts* - Book 12.
Minneapolis: Eckankar, 1995.

———. *The Slow Burning Love of God.* Minneapolis: Eckankar, 1996.

———. *A Cosmic Sea of Words: The Eckankar Lexicon.* Minneapolis:
Eckankar, 1998.

Klemp, Harold. *The Art of Spiritual Dreaming*. Minneapolis: Eckankar, 1999.

————. *Wisdom of the Heart,* Book 2. Minneapolis: Eckankar, 1999.

————. *Autobiography of a Modern Prophet*. Minneapolis: Eckankar, 2000.

————. *Wisdom from the Master on Spiritual Leadership: Eck Reader's Guide*. Minneapolis: Eckankar, 2001.

————. "The Wisdom Notes," *The Mystic World of Eckankar* 34 (2002).

Krishna, Gopi. *Higher Consciousness and Kundalini*. Darien: Kundalini Research Foundation, 1993.

Kubler-Ross, Elisabeth. *On Life After Death*. Berkeley: Celestial Arts, 1991.

————. *On Death and Dying: What the Dying Have to Teach Doctors, Nurses, Clergy, and Their Own Families*. New York: Touchstone, 1997.

Kurzweil, Ray. *Age of Spiritual Machines: When Computers Exceed Human Intelligence*. New York: Penguin, 1999.

Lake, Gina. *Symbols of the Soul: Discovering Your Karma Through Astrology*. St. Paul: Llewellyn Publications, 2000.

————. *The Extraterrestrial Vision: Channeled Teachings from Theodore*. Livermore: Oughten House Publications, 1995.

Lane, David C. *The Radhasoami Tradition: A Critical History of Guru Successorship*. New York: Garland Publishers, 1992.

————. *The Making of a Spiritual Movement: The Untold Story of Paul Twitchell and Eckankar.* Del Mar: Del Mar Press, 1993.

————. *The Unknowing Sage: The Life and Work of Baba Faqir Chand*. Walnut: Mt. San Antonio College Press, 1993.

Laurency, Henry T. *The Knowledge of Reality.* Skovde (Sweden): Henry T. Laurency Foundation, 1979.

————. *The Philosophers Stone*. Skovde (Sweden): Henry T. Laurency Foundation, 1985.

Leadbeater, C. W. *The Astral Plane: Its Scenery, Inhabitants and Phenomena*. Kila: Kessinger Publishing, 1997.

————. *A Textbook of Theosophy.* Wilmington: Anchor, 1998.

————. *The Hidden Side of Things*. vol 2. Montana: Kessinger, 1998.

Leedom, Tim C., ed. *The Book Your Church Doesn't Want You to Read*. Dubuque: Kendall/Hunt, 2001.

Lewis, H. Spencer. *Self Mastery and Fate with the Cycles of Life.* San Jose: AMORC, 1982.

Lotz, Anne Graham. *Heaven: My Father's House.* Nashville: W Publishing, 2001.

MacGregor, Geddes. *Reincarnation in Christianity: A New Vision of the Role of Rebirth in Christian Thought.* San Francisco: Theosophical Publishing, 1989.

Mallon, Thomas. *Stolen Words: The Classic Book on Plagiarism.* Fort Washington: Harvest Book, 2001.

Mann, John and Lar Short. *The Body of Light: History and Practical Techniques for Awakening Your Subtle Body.* New York: Globe Press, 1990.

Mason, Mark. *In Search of the Loving God.* Eugene: Dwapara Press, 1997.

Mason, Paul T., and Randi Kreger. *Stop Walking on Eggshels.* Oakland: New Harbinger, 1998.

Massey, Gerald. *Ancient Egypt: The Light of the World,* 2 vols Kila: Kessinger, 2002.

———. *Book of Beginnings,* 2 vols Montana: Kessinger, 1992.

———. *Egyptian Book of the Dead and the Mysteries of Amenta* Kila: Kessinger,1997.

———. *Gerald Massey's Lectures.* Kila: Kessinger, 1997.

———. *The Historical Jesus and the Mythical Christ: Separating Fact From Fiction.* San Diego: Book Tree, 2000.

———. *The World's Great Year.* Edmonds: Sure Fire Press, 1988.

McClinton, Delbert. *One of the Fortunate Few.* 1997

McMakin, Dean. "The Life Of Paul Twitchell Modern-Day Founder of Eckankar." Documents from the McCracken County Public Library Special Collections, Paducah, Ky., 1992.

Meir, John P. *A Marginal Jew: Rethinking the Historical Jesus.* New York: Doubleday, 1991.

Mills, Harry. *Artful Persuasion: How to Command Attention, Change Minds, and Influence People.* New York: AMACOM, 2000.

Montserrat, Dominic. *Sex and Society in Graeco-Roman Egypt.* New York: Kegan Paul, 1996.

Moody, Raymond A., Jr. *Life after Life.* New York: Bantam, 1975.

Morimitsu, Phil. *In the Company of ECK Masters.* Minneapolis: Eckankar, 1987.

———. *The Seeker.* Minneapolis: Eckankar, 1992.

Moskovitz, Richard. *Lost in the Mirror: An Inside Look at Borderline Personality Disorder.* Lanham: Taylor, 2001.

Moyers, Bill. *Joseph Campbell: Power of Myth.* New York: Doubleday, 1988.

Murphy, Dr. Joseph. *The Power of your Subconscious Mind.* revised by Ian McMahan. New York: Bantam, 2001.

Myslobodsky, Michael S. *The Mythomanias: the Nature of Deception and Self-Deception.* Mahwah: Lawrence Erlbaum, 1997.

Myss, Caroline. *Anatomy of the Spirit: The Seven Stages of Power and Healing.* New York: Three Rivers Press, 1996.

———. *Sacred Contracts: Awakening Your Divine Potential.* New York: Harmony Books, 2001.

Ouspensky, P. D. *In Search of the Miraculous.* Orlando: Harcourt, Brace Jovanovich, 1977.

Pagels, Elaine. *The Gnostic Gospels.* New York: Vintage Books, 1989.

Peck, M. Scott. *People of the Lie: The Hope for Healing Human Evil.* New York: Touchstone, 1998.

Perkins, John. *PsychoNavigation: Techniques for Travel Beyond Time.* Rochester: Destiny Books, 1990.

Persinger, Michael A. *Neuropsychological Bases of God Beliefs.* New York: Praeger,1987.

———."Neuropsychologica Brevita: an application to traumatic (acquired) brain injury,"*Psychological Reports*, 1995, 77.

Ponce, Charles. *Kabbalah: An Inroduction and Illumination for the World Today.* San Francisco: Theosophical Publishing, 1984.

Porter, Bill. *Road to Heaven: Encounters with Chinese Hermits.* San Francisco: Mercury House, 1993.

Potter, Charles Francis. *The Lost Years of Jesus Revealed.* Greenwich: Fawcett, 1959.

Prabhupada, A. C. Bhaktivedanta Swami. *Bhagavad-Gita as It Is.* Australia:Bhakitvedanta Book Trust, 1993.

———. *The Science of Self-Realization.* Australia: Bhakitvedanta Book Trust, 1977.

———. *Sri Isopanisad: Discovering the Original Person.* Australia: Bhakitvedanta Book Trust, 1997.

Pribram, Karl H. *Languages of the Brain: Experimental Paradoxes and Principles in Neuropsychology.* Monterey: Wadsworth, 1977.

Prophet, Elizabeth Clare. *Reincarnation: The Missing Link in Christianity.* Corwin Springs: Summit University Press, 1997.

Puri, L.R. *Radha Soami Teachings*. New Delhi: Radha Soami Satsang Beas, 1995.

———. *Guru Nanak: His Mystic Teachings*. New Delhi: Radha Soami SatsangBeas, 2000.

Rampa, T. Lobsang. *Beyond the Truth*. London: Corgi Books, 1969.

———. *Living With the Lama*. London: Corgi Books, 1979.

Redfield, James. *The Celestine Prophecy*. New York: Warner Books, 1993.

Richards, Jay, and Gilder, George, et al. *Are We Spiritual Machines?: Ray Kurzweil vs. the Critics of Strong A.I.* Jay W. Richards ed. Seattle: Discovery Institute, 2002.

Ring, Kenneth. *Life at Death: A Scientific Investigation of the Near-Death Experience.*New York: Quills, 1980.

Roberts, Jane. *The Magical Approach*. New York: Amber-Allen, 1995.

———. *The Nature of Personal Reality: Specific Practical Techniques for Solving Everyday Problems and Enriching the Life You Know*. New York: Amber-Allen, 1994.

———. *The Oversoul Seven Trilogy: The Education of Oversoul Seven; The Further Education of Oversoul Seven; Oversoul Seven and the Museum of Time*. New York: Amber-Allen, 1995.

———. *The Seth Material*. Cutchogue: Buccaneer Books, 1970.

———. *Seth Speaks: The Eternal Validity of the Soul*. New York: Amber-Allen, 1994.

Rodgers, Suzanne. *Put a Little Tongue in Your Cheek (And More Awareness in Your Life!)*. North Newton: Alternative, 1985.

Rumi. *The Glance: Songs of Soul- Meeting*, trans. by Coleman Barks. New York: Penguin, 1999.

Russell, Walter. *The Message of the Divine Iliad*. Waynesboro: University of Science and Philosophy, 1971.

———. *A New Concept of the Universe*. Waynesboro: University of Science and Philosophy, 1989.

———. *The Secret of Light*. Waynesboro: University of Science and Philosophy, 1974.

———. *The Secret of Working Knowingly with God*. Waynesboro: University of Science and Philosophy, 1993.

———. *Your Day and Night*. Waynesboro: University of Science and Philosophy,1993.

S, Acharya. *The Christ Conspiracy: The Greatest Story Ever Sold*. Kempton: Adventures Unlimited Press, 1999.

Sanders, C. W. *The Inner Voice*. New Delhi: Radha Soami Satsang Beas, 1991.

Sargant, William. *Battle for the Mind: A Physiology of Conversion and Brain-Washing*. Los Altos: ISHK, 1997.

Sechrist, Elsie. *Dreams: Your Magic Mirror, with Interpretations of Edgar Cayce*. New York: Warner, 1974.

———. *Meditation: Gateway to Light*. Virginia Beach: A.R.E. Press, 1968.

Sethi, V.K. *Mira: The Divine Lover*. New Delhi: Radha Soami Satsang Beas, 1996.

Shah, Idries. *Tales of the Dervishes: Teaching-Stories of the Sufi Masters over the Past Thousand Years*. New York: E.P. Dutton, 1970.

Shroder, Tom. *Old Souls: The Scientific Evidence for Past Lives*. New York: Simon & Schuster, 1999.

Silva, Jose and Philip Miele. *The Silva Mind Control Method*. New York: Pocket Books, 1978.

Simpson, Patti. *Hello Friend: Reflections for the New Student*. Menlo Park: Illuminated Way Press, 1981.

———. *Paulji: A Memoir*. Menlo Park: Eckankar, 1985.

Singer, Margaret Thaler. *Cults in Our Midst: The Hidden Menace in Our Everyday Lives*. San Francisco: Jossey-Bass, 1996.

Singh, Kirpal. *The Crown of Life: A Study in Yoga*. Anaheim: Ruhani Satsang, 1983.

———. *Godman*. Anaheim: Ruhani Satsang, 1981.

Singh, Maharaj Charan. *Die to Live*. New Delhi: Radha Soami Satsang Beas, 1999.

———. *Spiritual Discourses* vol 1. New Delhi: Radha Soami Satsang Beas, 1997.

———. *Spiritual Discourses* vol 2. New Delhi: Radha Soami Satsang Beas, 1997.

Sitchin, Zeecharia. *The Twelfth Planet: Book One of the Earth Chronicles*. New York:Avon, 1978.

———. *The Stairway to Heaven: Book Two of the Earth Chronicles*. New York: Avon, 1980.

———. *The Wars of Gods and Men: Book Three of the Earth Chronicles*. New York: Avon, 1985.

———. *The Lost Realms: Book Four of the Earth Chronicles*. New York: Avon, 1990.

Sitchin, Zeecharia. *When Time Began: Book Five of the Earth Chronicles*. New York:Avon, 1993.

———. *The Lost Book of Enki: Memoirs and Prophecies of an Extraterrestrial God*. Santa Fe: Bear and Company, 2002

Smith, Huston. *The World's Religions: Our Great Wisdom Traditions*. New York: Harper Collins, 1991.

Stahl, William Harris. *Commentary on the Dream of Scipio by MacRobus*. New York: Columbia University Press, 1990.

Steiger, Brad. *In My Soul I Am Free*. Menlo Park: Illuminated Way Press, 1983.

Steiner, Rudolf. *Theosophy: An Introduction to the Supersensible Knowledge of the World and the Destination of Man*. New York: Kessinger, 1997.

Stevenson, Ian. *Twenty Cases Suggestive of Reincarnation*. Charlottesville: University Press of Virginia, 1974.

———. *Where Reincarnation and Biology Intersect*. Westport: Praeger, 1997.

Strength, Linda. *Soul Travel: An Experience*. Baltimore: America House, 2001.

Strieber, Whitley. *Confirmation: The Hard Evidence of Aliens Among Us*. New York: St. Martin's Press, 1998.

Strobel, Lee. *The Case for Christ*. Grand Rapids: Zondervan, 1998.

Stubbs, Tony. *An Ascension Handbook: Channeled Material from Serapis*. Lithia Springs: New Leaf, 1999.

Sullivan, Andrew. "Who Says the Church Can't Change," *Time Magazine* (June 17, 2002).

Talbot, Michael. *The Holographic Universe*. New York: Harper Collins, 1991.

Thompson, Richard L. *Alien Identites*. Alachua: Govardhan Hill, 1995.

———. *Mysteries of the Sacred Universe: The Cosmology of the Bhagavata Purana*. Alachua: Govardhan Hill, 2000.

Tiller, William A. *Science and Human Transformation: Subtle Energies, Intentionality and Consciousness*. Walnut Creek: Pavior, 1997.

Tillich, Paul. *Dynamics of Faith*. New York: Harper, 2001.

Tobias, Madeleine Landau, and Janja Lalich. *Captive Hearts, Captive Minds: Freedom and Recovery from Cults and Abusive Relationships*. Alameda: Hunter House, 1994.

Tolle, Eckhart. *The Power of Now: A Guide to Spiritual Enlightenment*. Novato: New World Library, 1999.

Twitchell, Paul. "The Bilocation Philosophy." *Orion Magazine* 10: (January 1964).

———. "The Flute of God." *Orion Magazine* 11 (1966).

———. *The Master Discourses*. Menlo Park: Eckankar, 1970.

———. *The ECK Satsang Discourses:* 3rd Series. Menlo Park: Eckankar, 1971.

———. *The Far Country*. Menlo Park: Illuminated Way Press, 1971.

———. *The Book of Spiritual Instructions for the ECK-Satsang Classes*. Menlo Park: Eckankar, 1972.

———. *The Wisdom of Eck*. Rosalind Dubin ed. San Diego: Illuminated Way Press, 1972.

———. *Eckankar Dictionary*. San Diego: Illuminated Way Press, 1973.

———. *Letters to Gail* vol 1. Menlo Park: Illuminated Way Press, 1973.

———. *ECKANKAR: Compiled Writings*. San Diego: Illuminated Way Press, 1975.

———. *ECKANKAR: Illuminated Way Letters 1966-1971*. San Diego: Illuminated Way Press, 1975.

———. *Letters to Gail* vol 2. Menlo Park: Illuminated Way Press, 1977.

———. *The Drums of ECK*. Menlo Park: Illuminated Way Press, 1978.

———. *The Tiger's Fang*. Menlo Park: Illuminated Way Press, 1979.

———. "New Concepts on the Ancient Teachings of Bilocation," *SCP Journal* 3 (1979): 51.

———. *Difficulties Of Becoming The Living ECK Master*. ed. by Eckankar. Menlo Park: Illuminated Way Press, 1980.

———. *The ECK Satsang Discourses:* 1st Series. Menlo Park: Eckankar, 1980.

———. *The ECK-Ynari: The Secret Knowledge of Dreams*. Menlo Park: Eckankar, 1980.

———. *The ECK Satsang Discourses:* 2nd Series. Menlo Park: Eckankar, 1980.

———. *Letters to a Chela*. Menlo Park: Eckankar, 1980.

———. *The Secret Way*. Menlo Park: Eckankar, 1980.

———. *Soul Travel: The Illuminated Way*. Menlo Park:Eckankar, 1980.

———. *The Wisdom Notes: Jan. 1968 - Oct. 1871*. Menlo Park: Eckankar, 1980.

———. *The Precepts of Eckankar*. Menlo Park: Eckankar, 1981.

———. *The ECK-Vidya: Ancient Science of Prophecy*. Menlo Park: Illuminated Way Press, 1982.

———. *Dialogues with the Master*. Menlo Park: Illuminated Way

Press, 1983.

Twitchell, Paul. *Eckankar: The Key to Secret Worlds*. Crystal: Illuminated
Way Publishing, 1987.

———. *The Flute of God*. Minneapolis: Eckankar, 1987.

———.*Shariyat-Ki-Sugmad*, Book One. Minneapolis: Eckankar, 1987.

———. *Stranger by the River,* 3rd ed. Minneapolis: Eckankar, 1987.

———. *Shariyat-Ki-Sugmad*, Book Two. Minneapolis: Eckankar, 1988.

———. *The Spiritual Notebook*. Minneapolis: Eckankar, 1990, 1992.

———. *The Key to Eckankar.* Minneapolis: Eckankar, 1995.

The Urantia Book: Part I-IV. Chicago: Urantia Foundation, 1993.

Van Auken, John. *Born Again and Again*. Virginia Beach: Inner Vision,
1989.

Van Dusen, Wilson. *The Presence of Other Worlds: The Findings of
Emanuel Swedenborg*. New York: Perennial Library, 1975.

Vieira, Waldo. *Projections of the Consciousness: A Diary of Out-of-
Body Experiences*. Rio de Janeiro: International Institute of
Projectiology and Conscientiology, 1997.

Walker, Benjamin. *Beyond the Body: The Human Double and the
Astral Planes*. Boston: Routledge and Kegan Paul, 1977.

Walsch, Neale Donald. *Conversations with God: An Uncommon
Dialogue*, Book 1. New York: Putnam, 1996.

———. *Friendship with God: An Uncommon Dialogue,* 3 vols. New
York: Putnam, 1999.

———. *Questions and Answers on Conversations with God*. Charlottesville: Hampton Roads, 1999.

———.*The New Revelations: A Conversation with God*. New York:
Atria, 2002.

Webb, Wilse. B. *Sleep: An Active Process*. Duluth: Scott Foresman, 1973.

Weed, Joseph J. *Wisdom of the Mystic Masters*. West Nyack: Parker,
1987.

Weiss, Brian L. *Many Lives, Many Masters*. New York: Simon &
Schuster, 1988.

———. *Messages from the Masters: Tapping into the Power of Love*.
New York: Warner, 2000.

Wells, G. A. *Did Jesus Exist?* London: Pemberton, 1986.

Wheless, Joseph. *Forgery in Christianity: A Documented Record of the
Foundations of the Christian Religion*. Kila: Kessinger, 1997.

———. *Is It God's Word*. Kila: Kessinger 1997.

White, Barron. *I Remember Paducah When....* Kuttawa: McClanahan, 2000.

White, J. Stanley. *Liberation of the Soul.* New Delhi: Radha Soami Satsang Beas,1994.

Wilber, Ken. *The Collected Works of Ken Wilber* vol III, *A Sociable God, Eye to Eye.* Boston: Shambhala Publications, 1999.

Winn, Denise. *The Manipulated Mind: Brainwashing, Conditioning and Indoctrination.* Cambridge: Malor Books, 2000.

Wolfe, Joan M. *The Stuff Dreams Are Made Of.* Lincoln: Writers Club Press, 2001.

Wolman, Benjamin B. *Handbook of Dreams: Research, Theories, and Applications* (New York: Van Nostrand Reinhold, 1979.

Wood, Flora E. *In Search of the Way.* New Delhi: Radha Soami Satsang Beas, 2000.

Yin, Amorah Quan. *The Pleiadian Workbook: Awakening Your Divine Ka.* Rochester: Bear and Company, 1996.

Yogananda, Paramahansa. *Autobiography of a Yogi.* Los Angeles: Self-RealizationFellowship, 1977.

GLOSSARY

Glossary

ALL THAT IS — Term for the omniscient, omnipresent, and omnipotent Being often called God.

Arahata — A teacher in Eckankar, Radhasoami, and related teachings.

Ashram — A Hindu word used by many paths to refer to a retreat for spiritual teaching.

Bourchakoum — Eckankar term for the "eagle eyed adepts," the Living Eck Master, members of the Vairagi Order.

Charged Words — Words (e.g., *Mahanta, Eck, Sugmad*) considered to carry great spiritual energy because of the idea forms and states of consciousness they represent.

Chela — a student studying spiritual subjects under a master.

Cosmogony — The study of the origin of the universe(s).

Cosmology — The study of the structure and nature of the universe(s).

Darshan — An Eckankar ceremony involving meeting the Master outwardly and being recognized by him; also a meeting with him on the inner and traveling with him. Each is thought to bring enlightenment.

DREAM, the — The act of creation of the universes by THE ONE.

Eck — Word used by Paul Twitchell to refer to many things, but mainly to spirit.

Eckankar — Organization created and founded by Paul Twitchell in 1965.

Focus unit — A controlled unit of time in which thoughts are centered on a particular idea or word.

God-soul — Term for the timeless spiritual aspect of each of us that exceeds and oversees that aspect known as "soul." Each is responsible for the eternal spiritual unfoldment of every sentient being.

Great Work — Term for the efforts of highly spiritually-developed persons who aid others in recognizing the innate spirituality within and the illusion of worshipping or depending on intermediaries for our return to the ONE.

High Initiate (HI) — Eckankar term for a member who has received the fifth initiation or higher.

Hylozoics — A doctrine that all matter is animated, used especially in the work of the ancient Greek philosopher Pythagoras. Also a term applied to a system of thought that explains all life, physical or mental, as derived from matter.

Law of Cause and Effect — The spiritual law that holds that we face the consequences of our actions, good and bad.

Law of Duality — The spiritual law that all things contain both positive and negative aspects simultaneously.

Law of Karma — (See Law of Cause and Effect.)

Law of Love — The spiritual law that holds that love is the energy that unites and guides the universe and is synonymous with sprit.

Law of Polarity — The spiritual law that holds that events, both positive and negative, good and bad, can evolve into apparent opposites, depending on the choices we make.

Law of Spirit — The spiritual law that holds that an intelligent and creative force is at work to guide and help us.

Law of Unity — The spiritual law that the universes were created by THE ONE. It is the basis for all other laws.

Living Eck Master — Eckankar term for the outer form of its spiritual leader.

Mahanta — Eckankar term for the inner form of its spiritual leader.

Mahdis — A Fifth Initiate in Eckankar

Mantra — An utterance, word, or phrase whose vibration helps to transcend the physical and have a range of experiences from soothing relaxation (as in TM) to travels in the inner worlds of God.

Master Principle — We are responsible for determining our state of consciousness, which shapes the outcomes, or effects, in our lives. "The greatest power that I possess is the power to decide what I will think next. From this decision my future is constructed."

Master Technique — The moment-by-moment monitoring of our consciousness, which helps us to shape outcomes in our lives. It is based on the control use of focus units that concentrate our thoughts on a particular idea.

Moloch — A pagan God of Middle-Eastern Antiquity; a dishonest practice of religion with the people, controlled by priestcraft.

Nine Silent Ones (Council of Nine, Spiritual Council) — Beings of the inner world mentioned by Paul Twitchell, encountered at length by Graham Forsyth. They are responsible for carrying out many tasks necessary for the operation of the inner and outer universes.

RESA — Regional Eck Spiritual Advisor.

Rod of ECK Power — The symbol of the power of the word of God. Eckankar claims it is given to that being chosen by the Sugmad (God) as It descends and enters into the new Living Eck Master.

Secret words (charged words) — Words used in inner travel to test the authenticity of beings encountered there as well as the validity of such travels and is unique to each person in Eckankar.

Soul — The spiritual component of each sentient being that operates a body in the physical and other inner bodies as part of the pattern of spiritual unfoldment.

Spirit — The force or energy that created and sustains the universe. It is the substance that guides, provides for, protects, and instructs each soul on its journey to higher consciousness.

Spiritual Exercises — Another expression for the practice of meditation or contemplation. They also use mantras, recitations, and visualiza-

tion. St. Ignatius Loyola popularized the term, though it was practiced in Yoga well before him. Eckankar later appropriated the term
as its own.

Sugmad (SUGMAD) — A word for God created by Paul Twitchell and
used in Eckankar.

THE ONE — A name for the creative source of the universe, God, ALL
THAT IS.

Upanishads — Writings from the last section of a collection of Hindu
scriptures called the Vedas.

Yuga — Sanskrit for yoke, pair, race of men, age of the world; one of the
four ages of a Hindu world cycle, each shorter and less righteous
than the predecessor.

INDEX

About the Author

Ford Johnson is an internationally recognized speaker on a wide range of spiritual and esoteric subjects. He has appeared before audiences throughout the United States, Canada, Europe, the Caribbean, and Africa. A teacher and student for more than thirty-five years, he has spoken on numerous television and radio programs both in the U.S. and abroad. He has taught the techniques of meditation and contemplation to thousands, enabling them to personally experience the inner realities of God.

Following two years of service in the first wave of Peace Corps Volunteers sent to West Africa in 1962, he earned a J.D. degree from the Harvard Law School. He is currently President of a Maryland based company that provides educational, residential and mental health services to youth and adolescents. Over the past twenty-five years, his various companies have also provided research, training and/or management support to the Office of the White House Press Secretary, the Drug Enforcement Administration, the National Institute of Allergy and Infectious Diseases, and the National Institute of Mental Health, among others.

He lives with his wife and three children in the Washington, D.C. suburbs where they have resided for over twenty years.